American Casino Guide

2004 Edition

Written and Edited By
Steve Bourie

Contributing Writers

Anthony Curtis
Bob Dancer
Larry Edell
John Grochowski
H. Scot Krause
Max Rubin
Jean Scott
Tom Ski
Henry Tamburin

This book is dedicated to my wife, Michelle.
Thank you for your love and support.

American Casino Guide - 2004 edition

Published By:
Casino Vacations
P.O. Box 703
Dania, Florida 33004
(954) 989-2766
Fax (954) 966-7048

e-mail: webmaster@americancasinoguide.com
website: americancasinoguide.com

ISBN: 1-883768-13-6
ISSN: 1086-9018

Table of Contents

About Your Guide

This guide has been written to help you plan your visit to casino gambling areas and also to help you save money once you are there. The first edition of this guide began 13 years ago as an eight-page newsletter and it has continued to grow each year as casino gambling has spread throughout the country. We have listed information on all of the states that offer any type of traditional casino table games or slot machines (including video lottery terminals). We have also included stories to help you understand how casinos operate; how video poker and slot machines work; how to make the best plays in blackjack, craps, roulette and baccarat; and how to take advantage of casino promotional programs. Additionally, we have included a casino coupon section that should save you many times the cost of this book.

Besides listing general information about each casino, this guide also notes those casinos that offer free fun books as well as those that have casino marketing departments. Knowing this information can be very helpful. As an example: almost every large casino has a "comp" program whereby you can get free rooms, food, shows, gifts or cash based upon your level of play at their table games or slot machines. Just call the casino and ask for their marketing department for details on their current programs. Another program many casinos offer is a free fun book. These are coupon books that contain free and discounted offers on various items such as: bets, food, drinks, shows, rooms, souvenirs and more. This guide lists all of the casinos that offer fun books, plus details on how to get them.

A good suggestion to save you money when visiting a casino is to join their slot club. It doesn't cost anything and you would be surprised at how quickly those points can add up to earn you gifts, cash, food or other complimentaries. Also, as a slot club member you will usually receive periodic mailings from the casino with money-saving offers that are generally not available to the public.

When using this guide please remember that all of the listed room rates reflect the lowest and highest prices charged during the year. During holidays and peak periods, however, higher rates may apply. Also, since the gambling games offered at casinos vary from state to state, a listing of available games is found at the start of each state heading. We hope you enjoy your guide and we wish you good luck on your casino vacation!

Your Best Casino Bets - Part I

by Henry Tamburin

The majority of casino players leave too much to chance when playing in a casino. To put it bluntly, they do not have a clue as to how to play. They are literally throwing their money away with little chance of winning. Luck most certainly has a lot to do with your success in a casino but what really separates the winners from the losers is the skill of the players. Granted, there is no guarantee that you will win, but on the other hand, there is no guarantee that you must lose. My objective in this article is to educate you on the casino games so that at the very least, you'll be able to enjoy yourself in the casino with a minimum risk to your bankroll.

Let's begin our understanding of casino gambling by learning how casinos win as much as they do. They don't charge admission, and they certainly don't depend on the luck of their dealers to generate the income they need to pay their overhead. In fact, they guarantee themselves a steady income by having a built in advantage, or house edge, on every bet. Think of it as a very efficient hidden tax that generates them a guaranteed daily profit.

Here's an example of how this works. Suppose we take a coin and play heads or tails. Every time you lose a flip of the coin you pay me $1. Every time you win a flip, I pay you 90¢. Would you play? I hope you said no. Here's why. In this simple game I would have an advantage over you and I created that advantage by not paying you at the true odds of one-to-one (or $1).

Casinos do this very same thing to create their advantage. They simply pay off winning bets at less than the true odds. For example, the true odds of winning a bet on number 7 on roulette are 37-to-1 (the latter means you have 37 chances to lose vs. one chance to win). If you get lucky and the roulette ball lands in the number seven slot, you'd expect the casino to pay you 37 chips as winnings for the one chip you bet on number 7 (37- to-1 payoff). If they did that, the casino's advantage would be zero. However, as I mentioned above, the casinos create their advantage by paying off winning bets at less than true odds. In the case of our bet on number 7, the winning payoff is 35 chips (instead of 37 chips). The two chips the casino quietly kept is what pays their bills. Mathematically, the casino advantage is 5.26% on this bet which simply means day in and day out, the casino expects to win (or keep) 5.26 % of all money wagered in roulette.

The casino games with the lowest casino advantage (less than 1.25%) and your best bets are blackjack, craps, baccarat, and video poker. Now don't sell the ranch and run over to your nearest casino just yet. These games, plus table poker, are your best bets but you must learn how to play these games properly to enhance your chances of winning. Here are some tips to get you started:

BLACKJACK - This is your best casino game, but you must learn how to play your hands (when to hit, stand, double-down, split, etc.). This is known as the basic strategy. Learn it and you can reduce the casino's advantage to virtually zero. And if you learn how to keep track of the cards as they are played (i.e. card counting) you can actually turn the tables on the casino and have the edge over them! Do not try to play blackjack if you haven't learned the correct basic strategy. If you do, your chances of winning are slim.

CRAPS - The game of craps intimidates most casino players because of the complicated playing layout and the multitude of bets. In fact craps is an easy game to play. And it also has some of the best bets in the casino (and also some of the worst). Your best bet is the pass line with odds and come with odds. Next best is a place bet on six or eight. Stay away from all other bets on the layout because the casino's advantage is too high.

ROULETTE - Every bet on the American roulette layout (with 0 and 00 on the wheel) has a high casino advantage. That goes for bets straight up on numbers that pay 35 to 1, as well as even money wagers on red or black. Atlantic City players get a break. If you bet on an even money payoff bet and 0 or 00 hits, you lose only half your wager. This cuts the casino's advantage in half. Also, some casinos offer a European layout with only one zero. This is a better bet than wheels with 0 and 00.

BACCARAT - Many casinos offer a low stakes version called mini-baccarat. Not a bad game to play. If you bet on the bank hand, the casino's edge is only 1.17%. And when you play baccarat, there are no playing decisions to make which makes the game very easy to play.

BIG SIX WHEEL - Stay away from spending a lot of time (and money) at this game. The casino's advantage is astronomical (11% to 26%). Its drawing card for the novice player is the low minimum bet ($1). Save your money for the better games.

CARIBBEAN STUD POKER - This popular cruise ship game has found its way to land and dockside casinos. Unlike regular table poker where players compete against each other, in this game the players play against the house. But the rules favor the casino and their advantage is about 5%. The part of this game that appeals to players is the progressive jackpot side bet. You should not make this side bet, however, unless the jackpot exceeds $280,000 for the $1 ante and the $1 jackpot bet.

PAI GOW POKER - Strange name for a casino game. The game is a cross between Pai Gow, a Chinese game of dominoes, and the American game of seven-card poker. Players are dealt seven cards and they must arrange (or set) their cards into a five-card poker hand and a two-card poker hand. Skill is involved in setting the two hands which can help reduce the casino's advantage.

SLOT MACHINES - Casinos earn more money from slot machines than all the table games combined. The casino's advantage varies from one machine to another. Typically the higher denomination machines ($1 and up) pay back more than the nickel, quarter and fifty cent machines. Slots are not your best bet in the casino, but here are a few tips: Always play the maximum number of coins the machine will accept or you won't be eligible for a bonus payoff for the jackpot. Don't waste hours looking for a machine that's "ready to hit." Join the slot clubs. They are free and you'll be rewarded with discounts and other freebies. Machines that have lower jackpots pay smaller amounts more frequently which means you normally get more playing time for your money. Some casinos now certify their machines to return 98% or more and these machines are your best bets.

VIDEO POKER - Your best bet if you enjoy playing slot machines. Skill is involved as well as learning to spot the better payoff machines. Check the full house, flush payoff schedule. On machines that pay on jacks or better the better paying machines pay nine coins for a full house and six coins for the flush for each coin played. These machines are known as 9/6 machines. They are readily available; seek them out.

KENO - This casino game has a very high casino advantage (usually 20% and up). Stay away if you are serious about winning.

RED DOG - This is the casino version of the old acey-deucey. The stakes are low, but the casino edge is a wee-bit steep (3.5%). If you play, only make the raise wager when the spread between the two cards is seven or more.

SIC BO - This is an oriental game in which players bet on the outcome of the roll of three dice. There are lots of bets on the layout, some that pay odds of 150-to-1. However, most have a very high casino advantage. Your best bet is a bet on the big or small wager.

LET IT RIDE - This casino table game is based on the all-American game of poker. Like Caribbean Stud Poker, players compete against the house rather than against each other. What makes this game so unique is that the players can remove up to two of their initial mandatory three bets if they don't think they can win. The objective is to end up with a five-card poker hand of at least 10's or higher. The higher the rank, the greater the payoff; up to 1,000-to-1 for the royal flush. The casino edge is about 3% and about 70% of the hands will be losing hands. If you are lucky enough to catch a high payoff hand, be smart, push your chair back, and take the money and run!

Henry Tamburin has more than 27 years experience as a casino player, author, columnist and instructor. He has written more than 500 articles on casino gambling for numerous national gaming publications. He is also the author of numerous books and instructional videos. You can visit his web site at http://www.smartgaming.com. Ordering information for his books and videos can be found on page 122 .

Your Best Casino Bets - Part II

by Steve Bourie

In the previous story Henry gave you his choices for your best casino bets based on which ones offer you the best mathematical odds. Now, Henry is a great mathematician who is truly an expert at crunching numbers to figure out what the theoretical odds are, but what about real life? By this I mean - at the end of the week, or the month, or the year, how much does a casino really make from blackjack, or craps, or roulette? Sure, you can do the math to calculate the casino advantage on a bank hand in mini-baccarat as 1.17%, but at the end of the day what percent of those bets on mini-baccarat actually wind up in the hands of the casino? Is it precisely 1.17%? or is it less? or is it more? And, if you knew how much the casino truly averaged on all of the games it offered, which one would turn out to be your best bet based on that information?

To find the answer to this question I began my search by looking at the annual gaming revenue report issued by Nevada's State Gaming Control Board. It lists the win percentages, based on the drop (an explanation of this term later), for all of the games offered by the casinos and you might be surprised at which game had the lowest win percentage. Go ahead and take a guess...nice try, but you're wrong! The answer is bingo, where casinos only won 1.30% of the money they handled! The first column below lists the actual win percentages based on the "drop" (an explanation of "drop" follows shortly) for Nevada's various games for the fiscal year from July 1, 2002 through June 30, 2003:

GAME	WIN %	ADJUSTED WIN %
Keno	27.67	27.67
Race Book	16.84	16.84
Sports Pool	6.65	6.65
Caribbean Stud Poker	29.95	5.99
Slot Machines	5.43	5.43
3-Card Poker	24.98	4.99
Roulette	23.56	4.71
Baccarat	22.94	4.58
Pai Gow Poker	22.44	4.58
Let It Ride	21.34	4.26
Pai Gow	20.09	4.01
Craps	14.64	2.92
Mini-Baccarat	13.63	2.72
Twenty-One	12.68	2.53
Bingo	1.30	1.30

Usually bingo would rank as one of the games with the worst odds, but not in Nevada where it's sometimes used as a "loss leader." Just like your local Kmart runs especially low prices on a couple of items to bring you into the store where they believe you'll buy some other items, Nevada casinos use bingo to bring people into their casinos, believing that while they're there they'll play other games and also develop a loyalty to that casino. Actually, some years the casinos offering bingo actually lose money on the game rather than make money. So, if you're a bingo player Nevada casinos are the best places you'll ever find to play your game.

Before we go on to the other games though you'll need a brief explanation of how the win percentages are calculated and we'll start off with a basic lesson in how casinos do their accounting.

Casinos measure their take in table games by the *drop* and the *win*. The *drop* is the count of all of the receipts (cash and credit markers) that go into the drop box located at the table. Later, an accounting is made to see how much more (or less) they have than they started with. This amount is known as the *win*.

What the first column in the table shows you is how much the casinos won as a percentage of the drop. For example, on the roulette table for every $100 that went into the drop box the casino won $23.56 or 23.56%. What it doesn't tell you, however, is how much the casinos won as a percentage of all the bets that were made. In other words, the drop tells you how many chips were bought at that table, but it doesn't tell you how many bets were made with those chips. For example, if you buy $100 worth of chips at a blackjack table and play $10 a hand you don't bet for exactly 10 hands and then leave the table, do you? Of course not. You win some hands and you lose some hands and if you counted all of the times you made a $10 bet before you left the table you would see that your original $100 in chips generated many times that amount in bets. In other words, there is a multiplier effect for the money that goes into the drop box. We know that for every dollar that goes into the drop box there is a corresponding number of bets made. To find out exactly what that number is I asked Henry for some help. He replied that there is no exact answer, but during a 1982 study of the roulette tables in Atlantic City it was discovered that the total amount bet was approximately five times the amount of the buy-in. This means that for every $100 worth of chips bought at the table it resulted in $500 worth of bets being made.

The multiplier effect for the money that goes into the drop box is also dependent on the skill of the player. A blackjack player that loses his money quickly because he doesn't know good playing strategy will have a much lower multiplier than a player who uses a correct playing strategy. For purposes of this story, however, we'll assume that they balance each other out and we'll also assume that all games have the same multiplier of five. We can now return to our win percentage tables and divide by five the percentages for those games that have a multiplier effect. These new adjusted numbers lets us know approximately how much the casinos actually won as a percentage of the amount bet on each of those games. Keep in mind, however, that besides bingo there are three other game categories that do not need to be adjusted: keno, race book and sports pool. They need no adjustment because there is no multiplier factor involved. On these particular games the casinos know the exact total of the bets they take in and the exact total of the bets they pay out.

After calculating our adjusted win numbers we can now go back and take another look at which games are your best casino bets. The worst game, by far, is keno with its 27.67% edge. Next comes the race book with 16.84%.

Sports betting has a casino win rate of 6.65% but that number actually deserves a closer look because there are really six different types of bets that make up that 6.65% figure: football - 6.21%; basketball - 6.77%; baseball - 3.28%; sports parlay cards - 34.70%; pari-mutuel sports - negative 4.69%; and other sports - 3.78%. As you can see, all sports bets carry a relatively low house edge, except for sports parlay cards which you may want to avoid.

Next on our list is Caribbean stud poker at 5.99%. That's followed by slot machines at 5.43%; three-card poker at 4.99%; roulette at 4.71%; baccarat at 4.58%; pai gow poker at 4.58%; let it ride at 4.26%; and pai gow at 4.01%.

Finally, we come to the three best casino bets that all have roughly the same edge of less than three percent: craps at 2.92%; minibaccarat at 2.72%; and twenty-one (blackjack) at 2.53%.

So there you have it. After discounting bingo, blackjack is your best casino bet! Henry said it was the a good game to play and he was right!

An important thing to keep in mind, however, is something else that Henry said about the game of blackjack: "you must learn how to play your hands." You should remember that of all the table games offered in a casino (other than poker), blackjack is the only one that is a game of skill. This means that the better you are at playing your cards, the better you will be able to beat the house average. The 2.53% figure shown is just an average and if you learn the proper basic strategies you should be able to cut it down even more. Good luck!

Ingredients Of A Successful Gambler

By Henry Tamburin

Casinos have several advantages over players when it comes to generating the income they need to stay in business. The most obvious and well publicized one is the mathematical advantage casinos generally have in all games. *Las Vegas Advisor* publisher, Anthony Curtis, gave one of the best definitions of the casino advantage when he stated, "Casino gambling is a form of entertainment, and the casino advantage is the price of admission."

Of course, players have control over how much "admission" they allow the casino to charge them. Certain games and bets have a higher casino advantage than others. It behooves players, therefore, to cut the cost of admission as much as possible by making only bets with the lowest casino advantage. Is that all that's required to become a successful gambler? Not really. The other not-so-obvious casino advantage is the one engineered by the casinos to "psyche" players into losing.

Since casinos have the mathematical edge over most players, they know as long as they can keep players making bets on their tables or putting coins in their slot machines, they will ultimately win money, and players will conversely lose money. The trick is to do this in a subtle way, so that players do not feel bad about losing and will return again to potentially lose more. Remember that casinos live or die on their ability to attract repeat customers!

The 24-hour, nonstop party atmosphere is designed to make it easy for customers to part with their money. Think about it. In a casino, the player is king and will be treated like royalty. The environment almost requires you to drop your inhibitions and have a ball. As Marvin Karlins aptly described in his classic book *Psyching Out Vegas,* "There is no room for party-poopers in the manufactured gaiety of the casinos. Winners are heralded by the ringing of bells and shouts of the dealers...this is a world where everything goes, it's fast, it's fun and it's loose, so visitors 'let it all hang out.' Unfortunately, what usually hangs out is 'the player's pants pockets,' the white flag of surrender."

The psyching effect continues as you make your first bet. We don't use real currency to make bets in a casino. Instead, we use casino chips. Why? It's easier for a dealer to collect losing bets and pay off winning bets with chips rather than currency--but casino managers also know that using chips encourages a player to bet more. Chips create the illusion that a player isn't really losing anything at all.

To further devalue the green chips, casinos refer to them as "quarter chips," just as red $5 chips are referred to as "nickels." The bottom line is that the simple act of converting currency to chips encourages a looser betting style in most players.

What happens when a gambler gets thirsty? No problem, drinks are on the house. In fact, all you can drink is yours for the asking. The fact that it might mar your playing judgment or you ability to act rationally is your problem, not the casino's. It's psychology at its best. After all, have you ever met a player who had a few too many, who's capable of making logical playing and betting decisions? Be wary of the "free" drinks. It's just another potential way of casinos psyching players into losing more.

Players get hungry, too, and casinos have a solution for that. It's called the comp. Sure, we'll let you eat it for free, but only if you play a little while longer. Comps tend to encourage gamblers to play longer, and many "free lunches" have cost players dearly. You should by all means get your fair share of comps for your level of betting. But don't get psyched into betting more or playing longer for the sake of the comp.

You can see the casino's psychological edge in action when you watch what happens to a high roller betting his last chip. A cocktail waitress is usually dispatched to bring him a drink "to make him feel better." His pal the pit boss will commiserate with the player telling him he's never seen such bad luck before. "Here," the pit boss says. "go take a break and have dinner and see the show on me. Your luck is bound to change."

After finishing a gourmet meal fit for a king at no cost, our friend enters the show theater (via the "comp line" of course) to a front row seat. Invariably, a comedian will make him laugh and he'll soon forget about the thousand dollar bankroll he just blew. After the show, the pit boss arranges a nice room for the evening for his tired and weary friend-- on the house, of course. As he dozes off to sleep, he contemplates what a good life this is. And when he awakes, he is refreshed and ready to "beat the tables" because "today will be my lucky day." In less than 24 hours, the casino has psychologically made the player forget his previous losses and they have what they want-- another repeat customer capable of more big losses.

Most players go to casinos with an attitude that makes it even easier to psyche them into losing. Most expect to lose, and therefore, aren't too surprised when they achieve their goal. They usually get carried away courtesy of the casino environment. Sure, they may be conservative back at home or at the office, but this is a place where anything goes. Taking all the free drinks offered by the casinos as a way to get even makes sense. And after players lose their bankroll, do they feel sorry for themselves? Heck no. It's easier to blame their losses on their rotten luck, that stupid player or the dumb dealer. And to put it into perspective, they conclude the loss was worth it because they had a good time. These are "happy losers," who have been psyched into accepting their losses in a positive way. (They're also in a state of denial.)

The casino environment also creates the "urge to splurge" in players. How? Well, if you are treated like royalty, you may spend your money like royalty. You see it all the time. Players like to be called by name by dealers and pit bosses, they enjoy the best food and service and they like being pampered. Couples who hesitate on spending a couple extra bucks on dinner or a movie back home think nothing of tossing $5 and $10 chips on a gaming table. Making players feel like kings and queens will encourage them to splurge. Not surprisingly, most do!

The bottom line is that to be a successful player, you must not only learn proper playing strategies and sound money management, you must also learn to control your emotions and prevent the casino's psychological edge from taking its toll. The real struggle is not between you and the casino, but as the high stakes player, author, and publisher, Lyle Stuart, so eloquently put it, "it's between you and yourself."

You will find plenty of temptations to keep you playing (and losing) in a casino, so you must develop a sense of awareness and self control to overcome the psychologically-engineered edge. Myron Stabisky summed it up when he wrote *Zen and the Art of Casino Gambling,* "When we can keep control over our emotions and stay aware of what is happening around us, we can enjoy a safe, highly enjoyable casino experience. However, when we become slaves to negative emotions and allow our egos to cloud our thinking, the luster of excitement quickly turns to something far less pleasant."

So what can you do to avoid being psyched into losing? First of all, remember that the casino is a place of business, run by shrewd executives who understand human emotions. Their goal is to separate you from your money as quickly and painlessly as possible, and do so in a way that will make you come back and do it again. Enter a casino expecting to win, not lose. There are no guarantees that you'll win, but neither is there a guarantee that you have to lose.

Make sure you are mentally alert when you play, go with a game plan and set realistic goals. Win or lose, don't let your emotions control you. If you must drink, stick with nonalcoholic beverages when you play. Remember that casino chips equal cash. It's your money you're throwing around, not theirs!

Be careful with credit, because the casinos would love to extend you some. If you can't handle it, don't use it. And be prepared for those inevitable losing sessions. Will you call it quits for the day, or be like most gamblers and dig in for more cash, hoping the tide will turn? Above all, develop the attitude that a small profit at the tables or machines is a lot better than no profit or no loss. After all, you can't be a winner unless you learn to quit a winner.

These attitudes require discipline. It may take time until you feel comfortable with them, but if you develop proper playing attitudes, you will have the mental edge you need to prevent the casino from psyching you into losing.

You can visit Henry's website at http://www.smartgaming.com.
Ordering information for his books and videos can be found on page 122 .

Casino Comps

by Steve Bourie

In the world of casino gambling a "comp" is short for complimentary and it refers to anything that the casino will give you for free in return for your play in their casino.

Naturally, the more you bet, the more the casino will be willing to give you back. For the truly "high roller" (those willing to bet thousands, tens of thousands or even hundreds of thousands on the turn of a card) there is no expense spared to cater to their every whim, including: private jet transportation, chauffeur-driven limousines, gourmet chef-prepared foods, the finest wines and champagnes, plus pampered butler and maid service in a $10 million penthouse suite. But what about the lower-limit bettor?

Well, it turns out that pretty much any gambler can qualify for comps no matter what their level of play and if you know you're going to be gambling anyway, you might as well ask to get rated to see what you can get on a comp basis.

When you sit down to play be sure to tell the dealer that you want to be rated and they'll call over the appropriate floorperson who will take down your name and put it on a card along with information on how long you play and how much you bet. The floorperson won't stand there and constantly watch you, instead they'll just glance over every once in awhile to see how much you're betting and note it on the card. If you change tables be sure to tell the floorperson so that they can continue to track your play at the new table.

Usually a casino will want you to play for at least three hours and virtually all casinos use the same formula to calculate your comp value. They simply take the size of your average bet and multiply it by: the casino's advantage on the game you're playing; the decisions per hour in your game; and the length of your play in hours. The end result is what the casino expects to win from you during your play and most casinos will return about 40% of that amount to you in the form of comps.

So, let's say you're a roulette player that averages $20 a spin and you play for four hours. What's that worth in comps? Well, just multiply your average bet ($20), by the casino's advantage in roulette (5.3%) to get $1.06, which is the average amount the casino expects to make on you on each spin of the wheel. You then multiply that by the number of decisions (or spins) per hour (40) to get $42.40, which is the average amount the casino expects to make on you after one hour. Then, multiply that by the total hours of play (4) to get $169.60, which is the average amount the casino expects to make on you during your

4 hours of play. Since the average casino will return about 40% of that amount in comps you should qualify for $67.84 in casino comps.

One thing to keep in mind about comps is that you don't have to lose in order to qualify. The casino only asks that you put in the time to play. So, in our example if, after 4 hours of gambling, our roulette player ended up winning $100, they would still be eligible for the same amount of $67.84 in comps.

The last thing to mention about comps is that some casino games require skill (blackjack and pai gow poker), or offer various bets that have different casino advantages (craps) so those factors are sometimes adjusted in the equation when determining the casino advantage in those games. Just take a look at the chart below to see how the average casino will adjust for skill in blackjack and pai gow poker as well as for the types of bets that are made in craps.

Game	Game Advantage	Decisions Per Hour
Blackjack	.0025 (Card Counter) .01 (Good Basic Strategy) .015 (Soft Player)	70
Roulette	.053	40
Craps	.005 (Pass Line/Full Odds) .01 (Knowledgeable) .04 (Soft)	144
Baccarat	.012	70
Mini-Baccarat	.012	110
Pai Gow Poker	.01 (Knowledgeable) .02 (Average)	25

Comp City U.S.A.

by Max Rubin

Casino Comps have always been synonymous with Las Vegas, high rolling, and living large. Certainly everyone who plays the high and fast game—and there aren't that many of them—has come to expect to be treated like a potentate at the casino's expense. But most gamblers still don't realize that the overwhelming majority of the billions of comp dollars dished out by casinos every year are spent on the average guy, and you don't have to risk a spare $10,000 to beat the system.

Fact is, the comp system is designed to reward gamblers at every level. Even if you play nickel slots or blackjack at $5 a hand, your action makes you eligible for something in the grand comp plan. The trick to getting your share is to understand what you're entitled to and then get more.

What Gets What - The first step is to size up your threshold for risk and to determine how much money you've got to play the game with. Casinos have one simple goal: take your money. That means that how much you wager—or how much they think you wager—is the prime determinant in how much in comps they're willing to give you. But you've gotta be careful. The strategy isn't to increase the amount that you gamble to get comps. On the contrary, it's to stay at your normal level, get the comps you qualify for, and use them to enhance your result (by either mitigating losses or augmenting wins). The following provides a good overview of what you can expect to get.

At the lowest levels, you'll have to be content with little comps, things like comped parking and funbook freebies. You get those just for showing up.

The next rung on the comp ladder is free drinks, which even the lowly single-nickel slot player (or someone who pretends to be) can get by flagging down a cocktail waitress. You only have to step up your play a little—quarter slots and $5-$10 table games—to graduate to the next level, which is where it starts getting good. These comps include free snack bar food, breakfasts in the coffee shops, and rounds of drinks at the bar. Double that action and you'll start getting the best buffets, dinner in the coffee shops, invitations to low-level events, and the little-known but highly valuable "casino rate" on a room (a discount that can knock up to 50% off the retail price). The two-fold secret to getting these comps is simple: If you play table games, ask for them. If you play machines, join the slot club.

It's no mystery that casinos give better comps to bigger players, and if you regularly bet $25-$100 a hand, or plug dollars into machine, you can look forward to gourmet meals and free seats in the showrooms in all but the most elegant Vegas megastores. Once you graduate to the $100-$350 bet level, it's essential to get "rated" if you're playing table games, which means the pit bosses have to log all of your action. If you're playing multi-coin dollar machines and use your VIP card, they're already tracking every coin you shove down the gullet of the no-armed bandits, so all you have to do is put in your hours to be put in a suite.

Beyond the $350-a-hand table game and $5-a-pull machine level, the sky's the limit for comps: private multi-room penthouse suites, limo rides, $500 rounds of golf, trips to the Super Bowl, shopping sprees at Neiman's, the works. Many of the high rollers who get this treatment have casino lines of credit in excess of $1 million, and at these levels, a strange symbiotic bond is forged between the casino and the gambler. The casino is happy because its winnings far exceed the expense of hosting the gambler. The gambler is happy because he considers the attention and status he receives a fair trade for the risk he's willing to take (and the losses he's willing to fade).

The biggest change in the evolution of the comp system over the past five years is that you can now get the comps you want where you want. There are now very few major cities in America that are more than 100 miles from a bona fide big-bet store, and earning comps has become easier—geographically at least—than ever before.

Some of the newer venues—especially in California, where they're still getting their feet wet and don't have sophisticated management or comp-tracking systems, and places like Illinois and Mississippi, which have brutal tax structures that don't leave much for the masses—make it fairly tricky to earn comps on the Vegas level. But that's not to say you can't get a comp-bang for your gambling buck outside Nevada. You can, and in some places with inadequately trained staffs and/or outdated comp systems, it actually gets easier. You just have to be more diligent in doing the research necessary to know which casinos are ripe for the taking.

Comp Wizardry - Now that you know that the prizes are out there—and everywhere—you might be wondering how well you can play the comp game. The bottom line is, anyone with a lick of sense can play it well. You can master perfect basic strategy blackjack, which is the skill-level you need to achieve, for about $2 (use one of the cards they sell in virtually every casino gift shop), and you can learn how to exploit the loopholes in every casino's comp system by reading my book, *Comp City, A Guide to Free Casino Vacations*. The book details the step-by-step techniques used by "comp wizards" to beat casinos at their own game by getting a dollar's worth of comps for every dime they lose. Short of taking this crash course in comp strategy, just asking for meals and tickets and line passes, and using your rating card every time you play is 90% of what you need to know in 95% of America's casinos, especially at the lower levels. They're giving away millions every day. Don't miss out on your share.

Max Rubin is a former casino idustry executive and author of the book "Comp City - A Guide to Free Casino Vacations." Ordering information for his book can be found on page 25.

Taking Advantage of Slot Clubs

by H. Scot Krause

Slot Clubs originated in Atlantic City over 20 years ago as a way to begin recognizing and rewarding the casino's good players. Today, slot clubs are the casino's most powerful marketing tool and the player's best benefit the casino has to offer. It's the best of both worlds for both the player and the casino.

To begin, perhaps the word "club" is a little misleading, since there are no dues to pay, meetings to attend or any of the usual aspects associated with joining a club. You do get a slot club membership card (also called a player's card) which is your key to unlocking the benefits and rewards of the casino you're playing in.

Typically, your slot club membership card is a plastic card, with your identifying number on it, that you will use while playing at any of the casino's slot or video poker machines or while playing table games. It resembles a credit card, but only in its appearance, and is in no way an actual credit card. I mention that because there are some people who actually, mistakenly believe they will be inserting a credit card into their slot machine and play on credit, and therefore they refuse to get their player's card and are basically denied any and all benefits they are entitled to!

So let's start at the beginning and walk through the slot card program, when and why to do it and discuss some benefits, rewards and perks.

When you enter any casino for the first time, ask someone immediately where you can find the slot club or players club booth before you put any money at play. At the booth, or club, you should find a rather friendly group of employees who will get you started, signed up and get your card for you pronto.

You'll probably need to fill out a short application form or at least give your identification card to the clerk. It's simply a way to register the card in your name. You usually don't need to give your social security number if you don't want to, but always give your birthday and anniversary dates when asked. They help identify you with the casino in case others have your same name and many times the birthday benefits are nothing short of fantastic.

Always ask the slot club personnel about how to use the card and any other current promotions or benefits in addition to using your card. There will usually be a brochure or literature available that you can take explaining all the club benefits. There may also be a sign-up bonus such as a free gift or free points when you register. Be sure to ask. Sometimes an easily obtainable coupon may be required, and the clerks can tell you where or how to get one. Finally, I like to request two cards when I join, and you might like to do the same. You'll find that you may lose one, or want to play two machines at one time. That's it! You're on your way.

When you're out on the casino floor, you'll notice a slot on the machines that your card fits into. When you decide which machine you want to play, put your card in the slot and leave it in the entire time you play that machine. (Note: Take a moment to look for the card reader slot and not the bill acceptor. If you accidentally put your card in the bill acceptor you'll probaly strip the magnetic reader off your card and it won't work).

Most machines will have some type of reader that will display your name, points earned or at least let you know your card has been accepted. It's not a swipe card, and you must leave it in the machine while you play. It's simply counting the coins, or credits, that go through the machine while you're playing and giving you credit in the form of points for the amount of money that cycles through the machine. (Some casinos consider time on the machine as well as money being cycled, but that is a little more rare than in years past). Now, while your playing, you'll be earning valuable points that become redeemable for anything from cashback to restaurant complimentaries (refered to as "comps") show tickets, gifts, reduced room rates or free rooms, to almost any amenity you may want or require.

Be sure to keep your card in the machine until you have completed your play and cashed all coins out of the machine. Some clubs base their points on a coin-out system, rather than coin-in. Of course, these rewards are based on total play and your rewards may vary according to point formulas created exclusively for the casino at which you're playing. I do caution you not to continue to play beyond your comfortable gambling range and budget just to earn a point level or comp. Let the comps fall in place as you play or when you return again in the future. Which brings me to another interesting thought. I've heard players refuse to get a card because they believe they won't return to the casino again. First of all, you never know what your future plans may hold. Second, you may earn enough points while you're on this trip to at least earn a small comp or some cash back before you leave.You'll at least get on the casino's mailing list for future specials and events. You may win a jackpot that will allow you to return sooner that you originally thought was possible. And finally, with as many consolidations and buy-outs as there are in the casino business today, the casino you're playing at today may be owned by someone else tomorrow, who may in turn, be closer to your home, and you'll be able to use your points with them. There's just no good excuse not to get a player's card at any casino you visit.

Here are a couple other tips when you plan to visit a casino and need to get a slot club card. Sometimes you can apply or sign-up in advance by mail registration or visiting the casino's website on the Internet. They will often mail you the card in advance or have it already prepared for you when you get to the casino. Call and ask ahead of time for this service and you'll save time and won't have to stand in long lines when you hit the casino floor. Sometimes, when you receive your card by mail or Internet sign-up, you'll get additional offers, coupons, gifts and funbook offers along with it.

Many casinos now employ slot club ambassadors, cash hosts, or enrollment representatives who will sign you up on the casino floor, making it even easier for you to enroll in the club. They often have additional incentives or perks they can give you when you sign up with them. You might also check to see if a card you have from another casino might work where you're playing now. Many casino corporations are beginning to combine their clubs to offer you benefits at any of their respective properties. We're sure to see more of this as consolidations and mergers continue to take place.

Now, let's take a little closer look at the benefits and reasons why you want to belong to these slot clubs. Obviously, the casinos want your business and will go to great lengths to have you return. In addition to the points you're earning while playing, which will entitle you to various comps as mentioned previously, your most valuable asset from joining the slot club will be your mailing list advantage. Offers to slot club members are mailed often and repeatedly for room specials, many times even free room offers, meal discounts (two for ones), and often other free offers. We've been mailed match play offers, double and triple point coupons, show and movie theater tickets, spa specials, gifts and gift certificates, drawing tickets, and a myriad of other offers.

The casino offers are based on levels of play, and better offers including lavish parties, Superbowl and New Year's Eve invitations, free participation to invited guest slot tournaments, limousine services, and even free round-trip airfare, are offerd to the casino's best players. Don't rule yourself out just because you don't think you'll reach those levels of play to be awarded those opportunities. Everyone is rewarded in some way for even the most nominal play. Just wait until your birthday rolls around and I can almost guarantee you'll get some fabulous offers from the casinos to spend your celebration with them!

Finally, we'll now take a look at some of the myths regarding slot clubs and player's cards and dispose of them accordingly. Here are some of the arguments I've heard against slot club cards, or excuses as to why players don't use them...

"I never win when I play with my card." The truth is your results would be the same regardless if you had a card in or not. There is no relation between the card counting coins through the machine and what comes up on the screen when you push the button. The card just records how much money is wagered. It has no memory of whether you have won or lost and it doesn't care.

"I don't want to be tracked," or "I don't want the casino to know how much I'm playing," or "I don't want the IRS to have my records." In fact, you do want the casino to track you so you can be rewarded for your play. They have no way of knowing you, or how they can help and reward you unless they know who you are, what you're playing and how much you're spending. The IRS does not have access to your gambling activities, but you, in fact, do. The slot club can provide you with a year end win-loss record of your play that may help you offset wins with losses for tax purposes.

"I don't need a card, I'm a local," or "I'm a tourist." Basically, you're one or the other, but either way you still should have a card. The casino's computers usually separate locals from tourists and tailor their offers accordingly. If you're going to play anyway, get a card!

"I always lose those cards." You can always have another card made. Get extras made. Why play without it? It's like losing your wallet. The card has so much value for you, yet you leave it in the machine. You don't forget your airline frequent flier card at the airport, or your grocery savings card when you go shopping, do you?

"I don't need a card, I'm leaving in an hour." It doesn't matter how long you will be staying or how soon you will be leaving. Remember that all-important mailing list, and that you just might return some time in the future or play at a sister property somewhere else. (Don't worry. Most casinos do not sell their mailing list names. They want you for themselves and are very selfish!)

All-in-all, I've never heard of one good reason not to join a slot club. In fact, I hope I've given you enough good reasons to always join every slot club at every casino you ever visit. Good luck and happy slot clubbing!

H. Scot Krause is employed in the casino business and has worked in entertainment and marketing. He has visited casinos from the Bahamas and Atlantic City, to Mississippi, and currently resides in Las Vegas, Nevada, with his wife, Donna. He writes promotional articles about Las Vegas and currently has a weekly column called "Vegas Values" which can be viewed at: www.americancasinoguide.com

Slot Clubs And Comps

by Steve Bourie

Before you start playing any kind of electronic gaming machine in a casino, whether it be a slot, video poker, video blackjack, or video keno machine, you should first join the casino's slot club to reap the rewards that your play will entitle you to. What is a slot club you ask? Well, it's very similar to a frequent flyer club, except that in these clubs you will earn cash or comps (free food, rooms, shows, etc.) based on how much money you put through the machines.

Virtually every major casino in the U.S. today has a slot club and joining is quite simple. Just go to the club's registration desk, present an ID, and you'll be issued a plastic card which is very similar to a credit card. When you walk up to a machine you'll see a small slot (usually at the top, or on the side) where you should insert your card before you start to play. The card will then record how much money you've played in that particular machine and then, based on the amount you put through, you will be eligible to receive cash (sometimes) and comps (always) back from the casino. Naturally, the more you gamble, the more they will give back to you.

Some casinos will give you a free gift, or some other kind of bonus (extra slot club points, free buffet, etc.) just for joining and since there's no cost involved, it certainly makes sense to join even if you don't plan on playing that much. As a club member you'll also be on the casino's mailing list and you'll probably be receiving some good money-saving offers in the mail. Additionally, some casinos offer discounts to their club members on hotel rooms, meals and gift shop purchases.

While almost no casino will give you cashback for playing their table games, virtually all casinos will give you cashback for playing their machines. The amount returned is calculated as a percentage of the money you put through the machines and it basically varies from as low as .05% to as high as 1%. This means that for every $100 you put into a machine you will earn a cash rebate of anywhere from five cents to $1. This may not seem like a great deal of money but it can add up very quickly. Additionally, some casinos (usually the casinos with the lower rates) will periodically offer double, triple or quadruple point days when your points will accumulate much more rapidly.

One other point to make about cashback is that the vast majority of casinos (about 90%) offer a lower cash rebate on their video poker machines than they do on their slot machines. Generally, the rate is about one-half of what the casino normally pays on its slot machines. As an example, on the Las Vegas Strip all of the following casinos offer their slot players a rebate of .67% but reduce that rate to .33% for video poker play: Treasure Island,

Mirage, New York New York, Excalibur, Luxor, Bellagio, Aladdin and Mandalay Bay. The reason for the reduced rate is that video poker is a game of skill and knowledgeable players can achieve a greater return on video poker games than they could on slots. Since the casino will make less money on video poker games they simply reduce their cash rebates accordingly. This is very important to keep in mind, especially if you're a bad video poker player, because you'll probably only be earning half the cash rebate you could be getting by just playing the slots.

Of course, the best situation is to be a smart video poker player and to find a casino that offers the same cash rebate to all of its player regardless of what kind of machine they play. This way you could be playing a good video poker game, combined with a good cash rebate, and this will allow you to be playing at a near 100% level! Quite a few of the "locals" casinos in Las Vegas that have low cash rebates (.05% to .15%) offer the same rate of return regardless of the type of machine. There are no casinos in Atlantic City that treat slot and video poker players equally for cash rebates.

One final point to make about cash rebates is that not all clubs will allow you to get your cashback immediately. In Atlantic City, for example, most of the casinos will send a voucher to your home address which you must bring back to the casino (usually within 90 days) to receive your cash. There are no casinos in Las Vegas that do this but you should make it a point to ask if your cashback from the slot club is available immediately. If not, you may find yourself being mailed a voucher that is worthless to you.

While not every casino's slot club will give you back cash it is standard for every slot club to allow you to earn "comps" for your machine play. "Comps" is short for complimentaries and it means various things that you can get for free from the casino: rooms, meals, shows, gifts, etc.

Once again, the comp you will earn is based on the amount of money you put through the machines but it is usually at a higher level than you would earn for cashback. After all, the real cost to a casino for a $15 meal is much less than giving you back $15 in cash so the casinos can afford to be more generous.

When it comes to casino slot club comp policies they basically fall into one of three categories. Some casinos have clubs that allow you to redeem your points for either cash at one rate, or comps at a reduced rate that will cost you fewer points. In these clubs, for example, you might have a choice of redeeming your 1,000 points for either $10 in cash or $20 in comps.

Another option (one that is commonly used by many "locals" casinos in Las Vegas) is for the casino to set a redemption schedule for each particular restaurant, or meal. For example: breakfast is 800 points, lunch is 1,200 points and dinner is 1,600 points. These are popular programs because players know exactly what is required to earn their comp.

At the other extreme is the practice of many casinos to base their comps on your total machine play but not to tell you exactly what's required to achieve it. At the Mirage, Caesars Palace and Treasure Island in Las Vegas, for example, you will earn cashback at a set schedule but you'll never quite know what you need to earn a food comp. You just have to go to the slot club booth, present your card, and ask if you can get a buffet or restaurant comp. The staff will then either give it to you or say you need some more play on your card before they can issue you a food comp.

And which casinos have the best slot clubs? Well, that would really be dependant on what's most important to you. If you're visiting from out of town you would probably want a slot club that's more generous with room comps so you could save money on your accomodations. However, if you're going to be playing at a casino near your home you would be more interested in which casino offers the best cashback rate and food comps. Whatever the situation, be sure to give most of your play to the casino that offers the best benefits for you and you'll soon be reaping the rewards of slot club membership!

Using Casino Coupons

by Jean Scott

Jean Scott is one of the country's most renowned and successful low rollers. She belongs to slot clubs. She participates in promotions and drawings. She uses funbooks. She befriends slot hosts. The Las Vegas Advisor pegged her the Queen of Ku Pon in 1994 and in 1995, the CBS news magazine ***48 Hours*** *aired an entire hour-long segment revolving around her, in which Dan Rather dubbed her the Queen of Comps. She has appeared in segments on* ***Hard Copy*** *and* ***Dateline*** *about how to beat the casinos, plus she frequently appears in* ***Discovery Channel*** *and* ***Travel Channel*** *programs about casino gambling.*

An overwhelming majority of gamblers in a casino are playing negative-expectation games, meaning the house has the mathematical edge, and they will usually lose money in short order. Remember, you can only win in the long run if you're not giving the casino that little "admission fee," its edge, on every bet. That's not to say it's not possible to win on a negative-expectation game one day, or one trip, or even for several trips in a row. But in the long run, if you play negative-expectation games, the house edge will see to it that you're a long-term loser.

Couponing affords you the opportunity to turn things around and have the edge in your favor. For example, if you're lucky enough to have a blackjack coupon that makes your first card an automatic ace, you're playing with a whopping 52% edge. No, you won't win on every coupon, no matter how big the edge, but you will get to the winning long-term much faster.

Therefore, because couponing takes the edge away from the casino and gives it to you, it is possible to gamble with a much smaller bankroll. Because you always have the edge, and sometimes quite a large one, you'll likely become an overall winner more quickly than playing a regular game without a coupon. Of course, you must make coupon bets that are compatible with your bankroll. If you have only a couple of hundred dollars, you better stick with $5-$10 and/or one-bet coupons. It takes a larger bankroll to play some large-bet or extended-time-play coupons, i.e. $25 matchplays or getting paid double for blackjack for the first hour of play. But if you make an effort to track down a lot of those smaller coupon plays, you'll be surprised how soon you can build up your bankroll for the bigger plays that yield even greater profits.

Couponing is an extremely important tool even for casino visitors who are playing positive-expectation games. For the skillful video poker player at the quarter level or the blackjack card counter who makes only low-level bets, couponing may be the first line of defense against the casino edge. My husband Brad and I played quarter video poker for many years, and all during that time our per-hour profit rate in couponing far exceeded what we had in video poker and became an important contributor to building our gambling bankroll so we could progress to higher denomination play.

Coupons for free or reduced-price food, drinks, hotel rooms, or shows are "found" money if you're not getting these amenities comped. I've known couples that paid full-price for a show when there was a 2-for-1 coupon in the unopened freebie magazine right in their hotel room. People are given a coupon book when they check into a casino hotel-and the maid finds it on the dresser after they check out, a coupon for $5 in free coin, with no playing requirement, still intact. (And guess who the maid sometimes knows that loves "leftover" coupons!)

Casinos used to be famous for their bargain-priced meals, rooms, and show tickets, but this is changing quickly; Las Vegas especially is going upscale. So if you're are on a limited budget, you'll find that the time and effort you spend looking for the non-gambling coupons will allow you to afford some of the higher-price splurges. Even though we play enough to get all the free drinks we usually want in a casino, I always carry a few drink coupons in my purse in case we want to meet friends in the lounge and not face a big bar bill. Now let's take a look at the different kinds of coupons offered to gamblers.

Matchplay - Whether it says "$5 matchplay" or "Bet $5 and We Will Pay You $10 If You Win," it means the same: The casino is giving you money. However, you can't take this money and stick it in your pocket. The "free" money must be used for a bet and comes with a condition: You must risk some of your own money at the same time.

Here's how it works: We'll use as an example the most common matchplay-a $5 coupon for blackjack. You go to a blackjack table and sit down at an empty space, placing your coupon on the betting circle for your seat, with a $5 bill on top of the coupon. Some casinos let that bill play; some exchange it for a $5 chip. In either case, you now have a $10 bet riding on this hand-your own $5 investment plus an extra bet of $5 that the casino has given you by "matching" your bet. If you win, the casino pays off at $10. If you lose, the casino merely takes away the coupon and the $5 of your own money that you put up.

This is how it works in general for all table games and all denominations of matchplay coupons. If you have a $25 matchplay, then the casino matches that amount and you have a $50 bet. You're paid off at $50 if you win, while giving up only your own $25 (and the coupon) if you lose. You will win about half the time on matchplay bets, depending on the game and the type of bets you make. A rule of thumb to figure out the value of a matchplay coupon is to cut the amount in half and subtract the house edge, which averages around 3%, depending on the game, the bet, and/or your skill level. I usually just subtract 10 cents on a $5 matchplay as a round figure. This renders a $5 matchplay worth about $2.40-plus. A $25 matchplay is worth about $12-plus ($25 divided by 2 minus 50 cents).

Non-Even-Money Matchplay Coupons - Almost all matchplays can be used only on even-money bets. However, if you get one that allows non-even money bets, the optimal use is to bet it on the longest longshot available-like straight-up on a number at roulette.

Example: If you're betting a $100 matchplay (use it once and lose it whether you win or lose) at single-zero roulette, taking a shot at straight-up on a number yields an expected value (EV) of $94.59 ($3,500 payoff/37 possible outcomes). If you bet on the banker at baccarat, your EV is about $49.47.

The problem is that you pay for your extra EV on this bet in roulette with *extreme* variance, but if you expect to get many more of these matchplays, it can make sense to maximize your EV in this way.

Lucky Bucks - This kind of coupon generally adds a dollar or two extra on an even-money bet. For example, with a 7-for-5 coupon, you put down the coupon with a $5 chip or bill and if you win, you're paid an extra $2. Like matchplays, you win on average about half the time, so the coupon is worth just a few cents less than half the bonus, about 97 cents.

There are also occasional 3-for-2 and 2-for-1 lucky bucks, but you often can't find a table with minimums that allow you to bet that small, and you're usually not permitted to use them with a larger bet even if you explain that you still only expect the same dollar bonus. I've given up trying to educate dealers (and even pit bosses) that this is actually to their advantage, since I'm putting more money at risk for the same measly bonus. (I guess I'm getting too old to argue over small change. Brad says it's about time!)

First Card Is An Ace - Put this coupon in the betting spot on a blackjack table with the bet listed on the coupon (usually $5) and it becomes your first card, a valuable ace. The dealer skips you on the first-card deal around, then gives you a second card. You play out the hand the same as if you were dealt a first-card ace, getting paid immediately if you're lucky to score a blackjack. Otherwise you hit, stand, split, or double as usual.

This coupon gives you an enormous 52% edge, although a bit more long term than other coupons, since you often have to split or double, which involves putting more money at risk. But it still doesn't take too many of these coupons to become an overall winner and to make this your favorite coupon, as it is mine.

Free Play - This is usually a coupon you get as a bonus reward for past play at a casino and an incentive to come back, sometimes referred to as bounce-back cash. If the coupon is for slot play, you usually have to go to the slot club to have credits activated on a slot or video poker machine and you have to play them through once before you can cash out your winnings.

If the coupon is for chips, you usually get special non-negotiable chips at the cage. These chips cannot be exchanged for cash, like regular chips, but must be played. These chips are usually *not* matchplay, but can be bet alone, with no money of your own at risk. When you win a bet with this kind of chip, you're paid in regular chips that you *can* cash in. You can usually continue to bet with these special non-negotiable chips until you lose them; therefore their worth is the face value of the chip.

Read the rules for all free-play coupons carefully and note any special instructions or restrictions. They're often date specific. The table-game chips might be "for one play only," and the ones for slot credits might specify or exclude certain machines

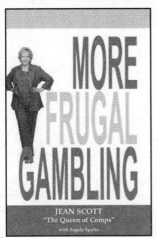

Taking Advantage Of Casino Promotions

by Jean Scott

All casinos are for-profit enterprises and they run promotions designed to add to their bottom line. If that's the case, however, you may be wondering how a promotion can ever be good for the customer.

The purpose of most casino advertising is not to persuade people to gamble. Rather, it's to persuade people to come through the advertiser's, rather than its competitor's doors. Promotions are an incentive for the gambler who's planning to play somewhere anyway. This gambler might have an opportunity to play the same games at several different casinos, so if he plays them at a casino where he can take advantage of a good promotion, this is an added value that can positively affect his bottom line.

So how do casinos benefit from promotions? Occasionally, they don't. Atlantic City for example, is famous for its bus wars. The casinos there get locked in battles for the business of the day-trippers who come in by bus from surrounding cities. Bus-fare rebates and other benefits escalate till the whole thing gets out of hand and all the casinos lose money. In fact, newspaper financial pages occasionally report that a bus war is responsible for a drop in quarterly revenues citywide. But no casino wants to be the first to cut back, afraid to lose a big share of its customer base.

Well-run promotions, however, are usually long-run moneymakers for casinos, which is why they're so prevalent. Good promotions bring in customers, new and old, who hope to benefit financially from the promotion itself, but will usually have a losing bottom line. Perhaps they don't fully understand the promotion or how to maximize its worth. Perhaps they're not knowledgeable about the games or haven't learned accurate strategies. Or maybe they're unaware of all the benefits of the slot club and comp systems. The purpose of this chapter is to help you avoid fattening up the casinos' profits by getting sucked into a promotion—then not knowing what to do with it.

How to Find Promotions - As I discussed in detail in *The Frugal Gambler,* I'm always on the lookout for a good promotion. When I fly to a casino destination, I look for promotional material at the airport-information and car-rental desks. I scour the racks of flyers in every tourist-information bureau I pass and check them in motel offices. I read billboards and casino marquees while driving to a casino.

When I walk into a casino, I look for banners, posters, and signs. I make a pass by the bell desk to look for freebie magazines that often tell about good current promotions. I read all the informational literature and magazines in my hotel room.

I always buy a daily local newspaper and pick up any newsweeklies in any casino town I'm in, to check for casino advertisements of promotions. In Las Vegas, in the "Neon" section of the Friday *Las Vegas Review-Journal*, Compton and Dancer write an excellent column called "Player's Edge," which focuses on promotions and lists the whens and wheres of current slot club point bonuses. Also in Vegas, *Gaming Today*, a sports-oriented weekly tabloid with a lot of casino promotional information, can be picked up free on Tuesdays in many casino race and sports books and on Wednesdays in some grocery stores.

And the slot club is a must-stop. I look for posters, or brochures and flyers I can pick up, to learn about promotions and events I might not have heard about elsewhere. And I always check with the slot club clerk, especially if I'm a new member or haven't received mailings from them, asking if there are any promotions going on.

I remember inquiring about promotions once at a riverboat casino that we hadn't visited before. I found out that it was double-points day for seniors. The clerk told me that the double-points schedule was always included on a monthly calendar sent to regular customers. However, since no sign about this bonus appeared anywhere in the casino, we never would've known to sign up for it if I hadn't asked.

Although all the above are good sources, if you're connected to the Internet, you have oceans of additional information on your computer. In fact, that's a good description—I sometimes feel like I'm drowning in it! But here are some Web sites that will get you to valuable promotional information quickly.

For information on Las Vegas, go to www.review journal.com/columnists/edge.html and read the " column I mentioned above. Click on www.americancasinoguide.com/Promotions/VEGAS-VALUES.shtml and you'll find promotional gold in Scot Krause's long Vegas Values list. And although I've always strongly recommended the Las Vegas Advisor newsletter (even before Huntington Press was my publisher), you can now enjoy their accurate and unbiased reporting online, with up-to-the-minute updates you can't get in weekly or monthly publications, at www.lasvegasadvisor.com. Check the "What's News" box for daily updates that often include promotion notices, and sign up for the free weekly e-letter, Las Vegas Advisor Lite. I help maintain a list of current bonus-point opportunities on this Web site—click on Bonus Slot Club Points—that will let you know where to play in Las Vegas to earn extra cashback and other benefits.

Many Web sites specialize in casino information; you can search for those that cover specific locations or limit themselves to particular casino games. Most casinos now have their own Web sites, which can be good places to find out about individual promotions, especially tournaments. For video poker

The Frugal Princess' Promotion Hints for the Casual Low Roller

Promotional tips from Jean Scott's daughter, and co-author, Angela Sparks

• Read the details of all promotions carefully, especially the fine print. If it's a drawing, do you have to be present to win? If you can't be there, you may want to give your tickets to someone who can. If it's a video poker promotion, what are the rules for multi-line machines? Sometimes they allow only one bonus per hand and sometimes only on the bottom line. If the promotion is a pool party, don't go out and buy a new swimsuit, as I almost did once. Luckily, I checked at the slot club desk and learned that these events are usually around, not in, the pool, are often dressy, even upscale.

• Check to make sure that a promotion you've heard about hasn't been discontinued or changed. You can avoid making a wasted trip, or worse, being disappointed after participating, by calling ahead and verifying details with the slot club.

• Choose promotions that fit into your schedule and accommodate your goals. If you have to start out a gambling vacation with a small bankroll or you're in the middle of a long losing streak, a time-stretching low-risk promotion can help maximize your gambling dollar. For example, entering tournaments with several rounds, looking for free spins, or using coupons for free souvenirs are good time-gobblers. On the other hand, if you're short on time, you might choose to skip all those that require a long wait in line or afford a low probability of winning anything of value, such as a scratch-card promotion with only one million-dollar prize.

• Be sure the promotion fits into your bankroll constraints. Try to avoid the temptation to play longer and lose more than you wanted just to get a promotional bonus. Even though earning double or triple points is great, your bankroll may dictate that you should quit playing before the bonus period ends.

• Remember that not all promotions are good values. I once saw an ad in a magazine that sounded great: Play four hours of blackjack and this casino would give you an airline voucher for a free companion ticket. I couldn't wait to call Mom about my frugal find! I was surprised—and disappointed—when she didn't sound very enthusiastic. I found out why after I took her suggestion to call the 800 number for further information. I learned, as Mom had already guessed, that you had to use a specific travel agency that sold you the first ticket at a price that was higher than two fares at a discount price elsewhere.

• Look to piggyback two or more promotions to make a play more valuable. On one occasion we found a casino that allowed Steve and me to use WinCard non-negotiable chips with funbook matchplay coupons for blackjack, roulette, and craps—something that's usually not allowed. We each played a $5 funny chip, backed by a $5 matchplay coupon. When we won, we were paid $10 in real chips and forfeited the coupon, but not the chip, which we could play again. Only when we lost did they take the coupon and the chip. For only the $20 buy-in for the chips in the two WinCard packages, we played a long time and cashed out a nice $50 profit when our funny money was finally gone.

players in all parts of the country, there is no better place to go than Skip Hughes' site (subscribe at www.vphomepage .com), where you get advance notice or current news about changes in schedules, machine placement, and the like, along with reviews of promotions, saving you miles of travel and hours of legwork to check out each promo yourself.

Internet bulletin boards are a rich source of information about promotions. I really don't know how I kept up before I bought a computer and jumped on the information highway in cyberspace.

Once Found, How to Participate - If you find out about a promotion from another player and you haven't received your own invitation, use the magic word and ask. I know many people who frequent Internet bulletin boards, find out about a promotion, and do this.

Say there's an invitational tournament in a casino where you play regularly. Talk to your host about how you love tournaments and you were wondering if he could check your play to see how close you are to getting invitations to them in the future. You'll be surprised, especially if you're fairly close to the playing requirements, how many times the host will put you into the current tournament right on the spot. Even if this doesn't happen, you haven't wasted your effort—you'll at least know how much more you need to play to score those valuable invites.

A word of caution here: The ways of casino marketing are strange indeed—often unfathomable, in fact. So don't be disappointed if this technique doesn't always work. You may hear of a good promotional offer sent out to customers who haven't been to the casino for a while—an offer that regular players can't get no matter whom they ask. Invitations for a promotion that includes cash coupons usually can't be snagged without an individual mailing to you directly—even if you ask nicely all over the casino—unless yours was lost in the mail. And many times, marketing offers come from a decision-making source that even hosts can't influence, so they can't help you.

Still Stalking the Wild Promotion - I covered many different kinds of promotions in *The Frugal Gambler* and most of that general information remains valid today. Bonus slot club points are still one of the strongest promotions for drawing us into a casino. Brad still loves promotions in which he can win casino logo jackets, and his closets are still jammed with them (although I did finally persuade him to get rid of the oldest ones during our huge garage sale in Indy before we moved permanently to Vegas).

However, many of the examples I gave of specific promotions no longer exist. Even some of the casinos I mentioned are no longer around. And in these last six years I've learned even more valuable lessons about many kinds of promotions; hopefully, they will be helpful to you in getting more bang for your buck. Following are two examples.

Senior-Citizen Promotions - In the first book, I stated that there weren't too many special deals for senior citizens, because casinos preferred promotions that targeted a broader range of customers. In addition, they thought that their prices, especially for food, were so low, seniors didn't need additional discounts. Well, casinos have recently awakened to Gray Power. It seems that they're now finding it's to their bottom-line advantage to cater to the older player, who's usually retired, has lots of free time, and, often, has a good amount of disposable income after a lifetime of frugality.

Las Vegas casinos, especially those off the Strip in the neighborhoods, are now setting up more special programs and promotions for seniors. The locals chain, Station Casinos, has an extensive "Salute to Seniors" program, including early-bird meal specials, morning exercise events, monthly entertainment with music and dancing, seminars on subjects that interest seniors (such as estate planning), and free bingo giveaways. This has also caught on in Mississippi, where there are numerous food specials and an occasional free seniors-only slot tournament or drawing. Midwestern riverboat casinos have offered special senior bonus-point days. Casinos on some Native American reservations have offered free health testing to seniors.

In Atlantic City, the Sands opened the luxurious Senior Class private lounge and Caesars redesigned a whole area called Temple Tower to cater to the special needs and wants of seniors, with additional handrails in guest bathrooms, brighter lighting in the halls, and shorter walks to the lobby and parking garage.

So, all you seniors, wherever you are, ask at the slot club desk if there are any promotions for you. They might even give you a special player's card that you'll be happy to carry, because it will put extra money in your pocket.

New-Customer Promotions - New-customer programs that promise to rebate some or all of your losses for your first play at a casino are among the strongest promotions around, but you need to take many things into consideration before you decide to take advantage of one.

First, read the details carefully. Determine when you can collect this rebate; most times you have to wait for the casino to mail you a time-sensitive voucher that can be redeemed only at the casino. Be sure you'll be able to return in the allotted time. Also be sure you can afford to do without the money you lose until you can get back to collect the rebate.

The specifics of each promotion vary, but a typical one might go something like this: The first hour you play after joining the slot club, the casino rebates up to $200 of losses. You must play the whole hour; you can't stop sooner, like as soon as you've lost the $200.

One good way to optimize the value of this promotion might be to take 75% of the rebate amount, in this example $150, and start playing on a $1 or even a $5 machine, hoping for some big hits before your $150 is gone. Set an amount, maybe $100 or $200, whereby if you're lucky and get ahead, you'll quit—happy that you made a nice profit and, like fire insurance, you didn't need the rebate. However, if you lose the $150, take the remaining $50 of your stake and play slowly at a much lower denomination, even one nickel at a time if necessary, to stretch it right to the end of the required hour. Multi-denomination machines are a great choice for a promo like this: You can adjust your level of play up or down, depending on the time.

A hint: Don't automatically assume that you won't qualify for a casino's new-member promotion because you joined the slot club several years before—even though you haven't played there for a while. Some casinos clear players from their computer systems if they haven't used their cards for a certain period of time. Check at the slot club to see whether or not you are indeed a member.

The Future of Promotions - In *The Frugal Gambler*, I posed the question, "Is the promotion train slowing down?" And I predicted that competition would keep it chugging away. Today, six years later, I see no reason to change my mind on this. Rapidly expanding Native American casinos in California will keep Las Vegas and Reno casinos hopping to find promotions that will lure the California drive-in visitor. New casino projects in Atlantic City will likely heat up the incentive bus wars. Riverboats will always try to come up with ways to increase the visits of local patrons.

Now that Brad and I live permanently in Las Vegas, we're inundated with at least 10 times more promotions than we have time to take advantage of. I think continued casino competition will ensure that the Golden Age of Promotions will last a long time.

Jean Scott and her husband, Brad, have been gambling for 19 years and have learned literally thousands of ways to make their money last longer in a casino. Jean shares these in the classic best-seller, "The Frugal Gambler," and the newly-released sequel, "More Frugal Gambling." She appears regularly on TV, especially on the Travel Channel, and writes for many gaming publications and online. You can visit her website at www.frugalgambler.biz

Slot Machines

by Steve Bourie

Virtually anyone who visits a casino, even for the first time, is familiar with a slot machine and how it operates: just put in your money, pull the handle and wait a few seconds to see if you win. It isn't intimidating like table games where you really need some knowledge of the rules before you play and it's this basic simplicity that accounts for much of the success of slot machines in the modern American casino.

As a matter of fact, the biggest money-maker for casinos is the slot machine with approximately 65 percent of the average casino's profits being generated by slot machine play. As an example, in Nevada's fiscal year ending June 30, 2003 the total win by all of the state's casinos was a little more than $9.5 billion. Of that amount, slightly more than $6.3 billion, or 66.3 percent, was from electronic machine winnings.

With this in mind, you must ask yourself, "can I really win money by playing slot machines?" The answer is a resounding yes...and no. First the "no" part: in simplest terms a slot machine makes money for the casino by paying out less money than it takes in. In some states, such as Nevada and New Jersey, the minimum amount to be returned is regulated. In Nevada the minimum is 75 percent and in New Jersey it's 83 percent. However, if you look at the slot payback percentages for those particular states in this book you will see that the actual average payback percentages are much higher. In New Jersey it's about 92 percent and in Nevada it's about 95 percent. Even though the actual paybacks are higher than the law requires, you can still see that on average for every $1 you play in an Atlantic City slot machine you will lose 8¢ and in a Las Vegas slot machine you will lose 5¢. Therefore, it doesn't take a rocket scientist to see that if you stand in front of a slot machine and continue to pump in your money, eventually, you will lose it all. On average, it will take you longer to lose it in Las Vegas rather than Atlantic City, but the result is still the same: you will go broke.

Gee, sounds kind of depressing, doesn't it? Well, cheer up because now we go on to the "yes" part. But, before we talk about that, let's first try to understand how slot machines work. All modern slot machines contain a random number generator (RNG) which is used to control the payback percentage for each machine. When a casino orders a slot machine the manufacturer will have a list of percentage paybacks for each machine and the casino must choose one from that list. For example, a manufacturer may have 10 chips available for one machine that range from a high of 98% to as low as 85%. All of these chips have been inspected and approved by a gaming commission and the casino is free to choose whichever chip it wants for that particular brand of machine.

In almost all instances, the casino will place a higher denomination chip in a higher denomination machine. In other words, the nickel machines will get the chips programmed to pay back around 87% and the $25 machines will get the chips programmed to pay back around 98%. A casino can always change the payback percentage, but in order to do that it must go back to the manufacturer to get a new RNG that is programmed with the new percentage. For this reason, most casinos rarely change their payback percentages unless there is a major revision in their marketing philosophy. And what exactly is a random number generator? Well, it's a little computer chip that is constantly working (as its name implies) to generate number combinations on a random basis. It does this extremely fast and is capable of producing hundreds of combinations each second. When you pull the handle, or push the spin button, the RNG stops and the combination it stops at is used to determine where the reels will stop in the pay window. Unlike video poker machines, you have no way of knowing what a slot machine is programmed to pay back just by looking at it. The only way to tell is by knowing what is programmed into the RNG.

As an example of the differences in RNG payout percentages I was able to get some statistics from International Game Technology (IGT), which is the world's largest manufacturer of slot machines, concerning the percentages that some of their slot machines are set to payback to players. The following list shows some of IGT's slot machines and the range of percentages that can be programmed into the random number generator on each machine:

Red White and Blue	85.03% - 97.45%
Texas Tea	87.00% - 97.00%
Addams Family	92.50% - 93.50%
I Dream of Jeannie	86.01% - 96.97%
Austin Powers	88.00% - 98.00%
Tabasco	85.00% - 98.03%
The Munsters	85.00% - 98.00%
Creature From The Black Lagoon	88.00% - 98.00%
Triple Lucky 7's	83.94% - 98.02%
Pink Panther	88.00% - 95.00%
Neon Nights	87.53% - 98.03%
Cleopatra	87.00% - 97.00%
Catch A Wave	85.02% - 98.03%
My Rich Uncle	85.00% - 98.00%

Once again, keep in mind that casinos generally set their slot paybacks based on each machine's denomination. Therefore, nickel machines will probably be set towards the lower number and $5-$25 machines will be set towards the higher number.

Okay, now let's get back to the "yes" part. Yes, you can win money on slot machines by using a little knowledge, practicing some money management and, mostly, having lots of luck. First, the knowledge part. You need to know what kind of player you are and how much risk you are willing to take. Do you want to go for the giant progressive jackpot that could make you a millionaire in an instant or would you be content walking away just a few dollars ahead?

An example of a wide-area progressive machine is Nevada's Megabucks where the jackpot starts at $7 million. These $1 machines are located at more than 125 Nevada casinos around the state and are linked together by a computer. It's fine if that's the kind of machine you want to play, but keep in mind that the odds are fairly astronomical of you hitting that big jackpot. Also, the payback percentage is lower on these machines than the average $1 machine. During Nevada's fiscal year ending June 30, 2003 Megabucks averaged around 88% payback while the typical $1 machine averaged a little more than 95%. So, be aware that if you play these machines you'll win fewer small payouts and it will be very difficult to leave as a winner. Unless, of course, you hit that big one! If you really like to play the wide-area progressive machines your best bet is probably to set aside a small percentage of your bankroll (maybe 10 to 15 percent) for chasing that big jackpot and saving the rest for the regular machines.

One other thing you should know about playing these wide-area progressives is that on most of them, including Megabucks, you will receive your jackpot in equal payments over a period of years (usually 25). You can avoid this, however, by playing at one of the casinos that link slot machines at their own properties and will pay you in one lump sum. The Circus Bucks slots at Circus Circus casinos in Nevada offer this as well as the Million Dollar Babies at Caesars Palace. There is also a wide-area progressive slot system called Cool Millions which will pay the first one million dollars immediately.

Knowledge also comes into play when deciding how many coins to bet. You should always look at the payback schedule posted on the machine to see if a bonus is payed for playing the maximum number of coins that the machine will accept. For example, if it's a two-coin machine and the jackpot payout is 500 coins when you bet one coin, but it pays you 1,200 coins when you bet two coins, then that machine is paying you a 200-coin bonus for playing the maximum number of coins and you should always bet the maximum two coins to take advantage of that bonus. However, if it's a two-coin machine that will pay you 500 coins for a one-coin bet and 1,000 coins for a two-coin bet, then there is no advantage to making the maximum bet on that machine and you should only bet the minimum amount.

Knowledge of which casinos offer the best payback percentages is also helpful. When available, we print that information in this book to help you decide where to go for the best return on your slot machine dollar. You may want to go to the Las Vegas Strip to see the free pirate show at Treasure Island, but take a look at the slot machine payback percentages for the Strip area casinos in the Las Vegas section and you'll see that you can get better returns for your slot machine dollar by playing at the off-Strip area casinos.

The final bit of knowledge you need concerns slot clubs. Every major casino has a slot club and you should make it a point to join the slot club before you insert your first coin. It doesn't cost anything to join and as a member you will be able to earn complimentaries from the casinos in the form of cash, food, shows, drinks, rooms or other "freebies." When you join the club you'll be issued a card (similar to a credit card) that you insert in the machine before you start to play and it will track how much you bet, as well as how long you play. Naturally, the more money you gamble, the more "freebies" you'll earn. Just make sure you don't get carried away and bet more than you're comfortable with just to earn some extra "comps." Ideally, you want to get "comps" for gambling that you were going to do anyway and not be pressured into betting more than you had planned.

Now let's talk about money management. The first thing you have to remember when playing slot machines is that there is no skill involved. Unlike blackjack or video poker, there are no decisions you can make that will affect whether you win or lose. It is strictly luck, or the lack of it, that will determine whether or not you win. However, when you are lucky enough to get ahead (even if it's just a little) that's where the money management factor comes in. As stated earlier, the longer you stand in front of a machine and put in your money, the more likely you are to go broke. Therefore, there is only one way you can walk away a winner and that's to make sure that when you do win, you don't put it all back in. You really need to set a "win goal" for yourself and to stop when you reach it. A realistic example would be a "win goal" of roughly 25 percent of your bankroll. If you started with $400, then you should stop if you win about $100. The "win goal" you decide on is up to you, but keep in mind that the higher your goal, the harder it will be to reach it, so be practical.

And what if you should happen to reach your goal? Take a break! Go have a meal, see a show, visit the lounge for a drink or even just take a walk around the casino. You may have the urge to keep playing, but if you can just take a break from the machines, even it's just for a short time, you'll have the satisfaction of leaving as a winner. If, later on, you get really bored and find that you just *have* to go back to the machines you can avoid a total loss by not risking more than half of your winnings and by playing on smaller denomination machines. If you made your winnings on $1 machines, move down to quarters. If you won on quarters, move down to nickels. The idea now is basically to kill some time and have a little fun knowing that no matter what happens you'll still leave as a winner.

And now, let's move on to luck. As stated previously, the ultimate decider in whether or not you win is how lucky you are. But, is there anything you can do to help you choose a "winning" machine? Not really, because there is no such thing. Remember, in the long run, no machine will pay out more than it takes in. There are, however, some things you could try to help you find the more generous machines and avoid the stingy ones. Keep in mind that all slot machine payback percentages shown in this book are averages. Some machines are programmed to pay back more and some machines are programmed to pay less. Also, like everything else in life, machines have good cycles where they pay out more than average and bad cycles where they pay out less than average. Ultimately, what you want to find is a high-paying machine in a good cycle. Of course if I knew how to find that machine I wouldn't be writing this story, instead I'd be standing in front of it with a $100 bill in my hand and looking for the change attendant. So, I guess you'll have to settle for my two recommendations as to how you *might* be able to find the better paying machines.

First, is the "accounting" method. With this method you start with a predetermined number of coins and after playing them you take an accounting of your results. If you have more than you started with you stay at that machine and start another cycle. Just keep doing this until the machine returns less than you started with. As an example, let's say you start with 20 coins. After playing those 20 coins you count how many you got back. If it's more than 20 you start over again with another 20 coins and then do another accounting. If, after any accounting, you get back less than the 20 you started with, stop playing and move on to a different machine. This is an especially good method because you have to slow down your play to take periodic accountings and you will always have an accurate idea of how well you are doing.

The other method is even simpler and requires no math. It's called the "baseball" method and is based on the principle of three strikes and you're out. Just play a machine until it loses three times in a row, then move on to another machine. Both of these methods will prevent you from losing a lot in a machine that is either set for a low payback or is going through a bad cycle; yet both can still allow you to take advantage of a high payback machine or one that is going through a good cycle. Good luck!

Play Slots on Your Computer!

Have hours of fun playing your favorite slots - the same actual slots that you'll find in casinos throughout the U.S.

IGT Slots and Multi-Play Video Poker - Play the most popular slots and video poker machines on your PC or Macintosh computer. Includes 50 of the best slot machines from IGT and over 50 of Action Gaming's famous "MultiPlay" video poker games. As a bonus, table games Blackjack and Spanish 21 are included. MultiPlay Video Poker, Blackjack and Spanish 21 have tutorial modes.

Slots include Wild Cherry, Double Diamond, Sizzling 7's, Ten Times Pay, Hot Peppers, Haywire, Balloon Bars and Red White & Blue.

Video Poker machines have the best machines in Triple, Five, Ten, Fifty and Spin Poker variety, including Jacks or Better, Deuces Wild, Double Bonus Joker Poker, Bonus Deluxe and more.

© 2001 King Features Syndicate, Inc./Fleischer Studios, Inc.

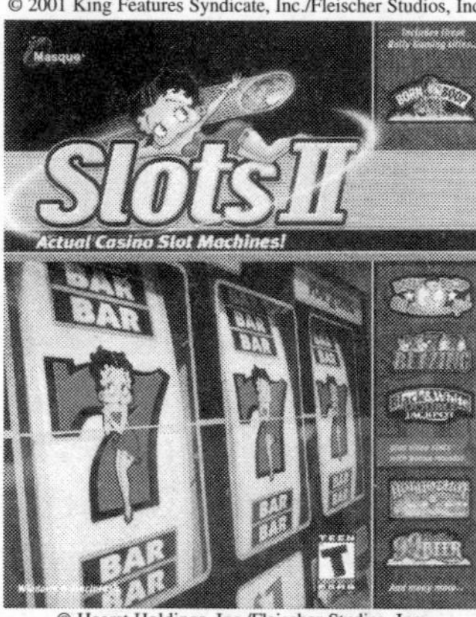

© Hearst Holdings, Inc./Fleischer Studios, Inc.

Slots II - Featuring Betty Boop! This CD lets you play the most popular slots from Bally. New features include Video Bonus machines with five reels.

The official Bally slot machines included are: Reel-Spinners, Betty Boop's Big Hit, Born To Boop, Betty Boop's Double Jackpot, Betty Boop All American Girl, Betty Boop's Re-Spin Roundup, Roaring 20s, In The Money, Krazy Kops, Swing Time, Blazing 7s, Joker Five Times Pay, Five Times Pay-7s, Diamond Line, Double Diamond Line, Diamonds & Devils, Ride To Riches, Bonus Times, Money Bars, Black & White 5 Times Pay, Black & White Double Jackpot, Ball of Fire, Fame & Fortune, French Quarters, Red Hot 7s, Silver & Gold, Stars & Bars, Triple Rose, Wild Rose, Double Trouble, Triple Gold , Diamonds & Roses, All American, Sevens 3-Line, Fire & Ice, Reel Gems, Black Velvet, California Dreaming and White Lightning. Video Slots with Bonus Payouts include: Hot Hot Hot, 99 Bottles of Beer, The Platypus Game, Boxcar Bonus, Money Poppers and Play The Market.

Windows: 95/98/NT/2000/ME, Pentium or better, 16 Mb RAM, 15 Mb Hard Disk Space
Macintosh: Power PC, System 7.5 or higher, 32 Mb RAM, 15 Mb Hard Disk

Regular retail price - $24.99 **Special discounted price only $19.99**
Shipping is $3.50 for first program and $1 for each additional program

Send check or money order to:

Casino Vacations
P.O. Box 703
Dania, FL 33004

Credit card orders call toll-free:
(800) 741-1596

order online at: **www.americancasinoguide.com**

The Slot Manager - 2004

by Steve Bourie

As stated in the previous story, the average U.S. casino makes about 65% of its profits from gaming machines but an interesting bit of information is that it didn't used to be that way. In fact, it used to be just the opposite! Table games were the big revenue producers for the casinos and it was usually the men who played those games while their wives were kept busy at the slot machines.

Back in the 40s and early 50s, the old mechanical slots were full of gears and springs and were actually powered by pulling the handle which started the reels spinning. One of the problems with these machines was that they were limited in the size of the jackpots they could offer because they could only accept one coin, plus the hoppers, still relying on those springs and gears, were limited in the number of coins they could pay out.

In the 60s the next generation of slots was introduced: the electromechanical. These machines still had a handle on the outside, but this time when you pulled it you activated an electric switch which started a motor to spin the reels. These machines increased the popularity of slots because they allowed multiple coin play and they also had electrically-powered hoppers that could pay out much larger jackpots.

In the 80s computer controlled slots were introduced. These new machines revolutionized the industry because everything was now controlled by a computer chip. These electronic marvels could offer progressive jackpots that were linked among different machines and it wasn't long before this new computer technology led to the introduction of a new game called video poker.

Today, the technology is so advanced that it allows slot machines that are hundreds of miles apart to be linked together by computer and offer jackpots that start at $10 million (Super Megabucks), or video poker to be played from five different decks at the same time (Five Deck Frenzy).

Although the technology constantly changes, one thing remains the same: the person generally responsible for the operation of the slot department is the slot manager. It is the slot manager who determines how the slot department will be laid out and how much the machines will be set to pay back.

As a slot player, you've probably had a few questions about how a slot department works: How do they decide where to put those slot machines out on the casino floor? Is winning purely luck? Are some machines really set to pay back more than others? And, if so, where do they put those better-paying machines? Well, the person with the answer to those questions would be the slot manager and each year I interview a different slot manager to get some perspective on how their particular slot department works and what goes into some of their business decisions.

For this year's book I spoke to Mark Seligman, slot manager at the Fiesta Casino in Henderson, Las Vegas. There are actually two Fiesta casinos (the other is on Ranch Drive in North Las Vegas) and both are very popular "locals" casinos that are widely-known for having an especially good assortment of high-paying video poker machines. Both Fiestas advertise themselves as "the official royal flush capital of the world" and statistics from the Nevada Gaming Control Board show that the gaming machines in both North Las Vegas and Henderson (shown as Boulder Strip on the annual report) have average payback percentages that are the highest in the U.S.

Mark began his career in 1991 in Black Hawk, Colorado as a slot technician and then moved to Las Vegas to work as the Slot Technical Manager to open up the Hard Rock Hotel Casino. He later held a slot manager position at the Silverton Hotel Casino, Senior Director of Property Operations with Harvey's in Council Bluffs, Iowa and then began his career with Station Casinos when he opened their Green Valley Ranch Station Casino before moving to the Fiesta Henderson.

Do you have a philosophy about laying out a slot floor as to where you place any particular machines?

We try to create excitement by having popular machines in every area of the casino and we do that in a lot of different ways: we put in popular machines; with signage; 99% or 100% payback machines; single and multi level progressives; Wheel of Fortune or Megabucks machines; etc. We strategically move our machines around to try and spread out the excitement evenly.

What are the most popular machines?

Obviously, we're a locals casino so we have a lot of educated video poker players and the 100% payback machines are some of the most popular. There's deuces wild, double bonus, loose deuces and joker's wild, etc. With the reel spinners quarter Wheel of Fortune is extremely popular and in the video reel category it's a lot of the newer IGT (International Game Technology) games: Enchanted Unicorn, Lucky Larry's Lobster Mania and Tabasco, plus the penny slots are extremely popular.

How do you decide which paytables to offer on your slot and video poker machines?

We're different than a Strip property, which has more reel slots where you can't tell the percentage payback. As a locals casino we have a lot more video poker games and an educated player knows which paytables are looser and which are tighter. So, we go out and research our competition and we try to provide the right amount of 100% games. When we're selecting which paytable(s) to use the industry kind of sets the norm and we vary it by what our competitors are doing. Generally, the higher the denomination, the higher the payback percentage.

Do you have set guidelines for the slots for your property?

Again there are industry norms. The payback percentages on our reel slots are set using the higher the denomination, the higher the payback method. But with the majority of our guests being an educated video poker player and the fact that the payback percentage of poker machines can be determined by the paytable selected, we can't do that. We have to have some nickel 100% payback games, then we have some nickel machines that are right at the industry norm. Within each denomination we go from 100% payback down to what the industry standard would be.

Do you believe your video poker players are better than the average Las Vegas visitor?

They know what they're looking for and they know how to play. We, meaning the two Fiesta casinos, probably have the highest percentage in the whole city as far as having the smartest and most educated gambler.

Let's talk about slot machines. When you order them I understand that you can decide what percentage you want them to pay back?

Yes. The manufacturer has a whole library of say "Red, White & Blue" paytables and when we order a machine, depending on what denomination we're ordering, we order the percentage that we want.

I assume that the higher the denomination the higher the machine is set to return?

Generally, yes!

Based on slot machine statistics from the Nevada Gaming Control Board I see that your casino consistently offers higher returns than the Strip casinos.

Yes, as a locals gaming operator our customers are sophisticated and they know a good deal when they see one. It's highly competitive and so our returns have to be higher.

Is that because you put higher percentage payback chips in your slot machines? Or, are your numbers skewed higher mainly because you have more high payback video poker games and players who know how to play them properly?

I would say that the answer to that is twofold. I believe that all of our reel spinning machines are set a notch or two looser than the Strip. But, compared to a Strip property, we have such a high concentration of video poker machines, which are going to be looser.

What percentage of your machines are slots?

At a local's property, 15 to 20 percent of the machines are reel-spinning machines and poker machines make up the remaining 80 to 85 percent. A Strip property is the exact opposite but I'm sure it varies a little bit.

Do you have a philosophy as to what percentage chip you would put in your slot?

We do have ranges set up by denomination. Again, we go back to the industry norm. That is a starting point, then we decide based on the area of the casino, player type, etc. which percentage to use. Remember, we are a locals casino we have to be looser then the strip.

From what you're saying, your nickel reel slots would have the lower payback percentages but how is that affected when that nickel slot is a nine-line machine where you could bet up to 45 coins at a time? Since someone could bet up to $2.25 per spin is that machine treated as an average nickel machine? Or, is it set to payback more?

They are treated differently and we increase the payback percentage because of the higher bets.

How much more is it set to payback?

It varies, but we definitely increase the payback percentage over what a single line machine would be.

Let's address some common questions that players have concerning slot machines. First, many people believe that some machines are always set to return more than others. You said that, yes, the machines are set to average different payback percentages based on their denomination? In other words, if your nickel machines average, let's say, a 94% payback does that mean that all of the machines are set around 94% or are half set higher and the other half set to lower so that they average around 94%?

When I put in a bank of slot machines on the floor, I put them all in at the same hold percentage. Obviously, it varies a little by the game type so if we say it's 94% one chip might be +.25% or it might be -.25% but that's only because different themes have slightly different payback percentages.

Would you do the same thing on a quarter or dollar machine?

Yes, as the denomination goes up we would give a higher payback, but again, all of the chips within that denomination would be relatively the same percentage chip.

Many players think that the slot machines on the end of aisles are set to pay back more than those within the aisle. Is there any truth to the rumor?

We don't practice that. I've heard that fallacy before and I've been at multiple casinos and I've never actually seen that practiced on the slot floor. I think that idea originated because there's a lot of traffic going by those machines at the ends of the aisles and people see the games in those high-traffic areas winning more often. But, as far as the percentage return is concerned, it's no higher than any other (within the same denomination). Just by nature, the busier the machine, the more it's going to pay.

What about the rumor that casinos can just flip a switch to "tighten" up their slot machines? Or, casinos "loosen" their machines during the week and then "tighten" them up on the weekends?

Well, it would take me two weeks to "tighten" my whole floor because I would have to get a new house number for each machine and then put it in our accounting system as a new machine. And, in order to do that, I have to take all of the money out of the old machine and have it all reconciled because the state audits all of my numbers every year to make sure every machine is properly accounted for. What I am saying is, "There's no magical switch."

And the Gaming Control Board inspects those chips?

Yes. They come out periodically, unannounced, and say, "we're here and we want to check those machines." They randomly check them and they will actually pull the EPROM (chip) out and put it in their own computer to check that the information in the chip is what they had approved.

Some video poker players think that you can change the odds of them getting certain hands anytime you want. Is there any truth to that?

No. All video poker programs use a 52-card deck (except for Jokers Wild whihc uses a 53 card deck), therefore the odds are always the same. The players mistakenly believe that we can change the odds so it won't hit as many four-of-a-kinds, or royal flushes, and that is just absolutely not true. We can't do that.

And why can't you do that?

Because the Gaming Control Board doesn't allow it and we would be shut down in a heartbeat if we did something like that. Not to mention that all of the chips are encrypted with a source code that's controlled by IGT (the gaming manufacturer) and the Gaming Control Board; they're the only ones that have the knowledge of the source code, which is a secret.

Just one last question for you: What advice would you give to the average slot video poker player who walks into your casino?

My advice is to just play and have fun! It doesn't matter whether the machine is 100% payback or 95% payback, you can win or lose. Those numbers are calculated over such a long period of time, on a reel machine it's 10 million pulls, so you would have to be there all that time to get that 100% payback. Your playtime in the life of the game is so small that anything could happen.

Since this interview Mark has moved to Texas Station Hotel and Casino in North Las Vegas. It is another locals casino owned by the same parent company (Station Casinos) and he says, "the same things apply at any Station Casinos property."

Slot Tournaments

by Steve Bourie

Slot tournaments are special contests arranged by casinos where participants who get the highest scores on slot machines within an allotted amount of time, or credits, are awarded cash or prizes. Some slot tournaments are offered free of charge but most require an entry fee.

Virtually every casino today offers slot tournaments and they're used by each casino's marketing department as a promotional tool to generate more business for the casino. An interesting thing about slot tournaments is that they aren't necessarily designed as money-making events for the casino.

Some casinos will give back all of the entry fees in the form of prizes and some won't. Those casinos that give back all of the money are happy to have the tournament's contestants in their hotel rooms and playing in their casino. The thinking at these casinos is that the tournament is generating extra business and they don't have to make money off the tournament itself. These are the best kinds of tournaments to play in but they aren't always easy to find. In other instances the casinos look at tournaments strictly as a money-making venture and they'll keep part of the entry fees for themselves. In either case, tournaments can sometimes provide extra value to you and they are occasionally worth looking into.

Each month *Las Vegas Advisor* gives information on upcoming tournaments in that city and many gaming magazines do the same for all of the major casinos throughout the country. These publications don't list much more than the required entry fee so you'll have to call each casino for more information on the specifics. You can probably get that information over the phone but it's best to ask for a brochure to be mailed to you. This way, you'll have an official written record of the tournament rules and regulations.

When looking at the prize structure of the tournament be sure to add up the total cash value of all the prizes and compare it to the total amount of money the casino will be getting in entry fees. For instance, if the entry fee is $200 and they're limiting the tournament to 200 entrants then the casino is generating $40,000 in entry fees. Are they offering that much in cash prizes? If so, then it's a good tournament. If they're only offering $25,000 in cash, then the casino is keeping $15,000 and you may want to shop around for a different tournament that offers you more "equity." By equity we mean the value you'll be receiving in relation to the cost to enter. Positive equity means the casino is giving back more in cash and benefits than it's charging to enter the tournament. Negative equity means just the opposite: the casino is charging more than it's giving back in cash and benefits. You should always try to find a positive equity tournament.

Another thing you'll need to add into the equation when considering your equity are the extra "freebies," or discounts, that the casino will add to the package. Most casinos will host a welcoming party for the contestants, plus a free lunch or dinner and an awards banquet at the end when the winners are announced. Generally, all casinos will also offer a discounted room rate to tournament participants and some will even throw in a surprise gift for everyone. If you don't need a room then that benefit won't add anything to the value you'll be receiving but for some players a discounted room rate could mean the difference between a positive and negative equity situation. Each tournament is different and you should be sure to add up the total of all the benefits you'll receive when deciding which tournament you want to enter.

One more thing to keep in mind when looking at a tournament's structure is how the prizes are distributed. If too much is given to the top finishers that leaves less to be distributed among the other contestants. The chances are pretty good that you're not going to win one of the top prizes so it will help if the lower-tier prizes are worthwhile.

One last thing to remember about tournaments is that in many of them it pays to enter early. Most tournaments offer an "early-bird" discount if you enter by a certain date and the entry fee rises after that date. The discount can be as high as 25 percent and, once again, the reduced rate could make the difference between a positive and a negative equity situation.

Once you've found the tournament that offers you the most equity you'll need a strategy for winning. What's the best strategy? Get lucky! Slot tournaments are pure luck and there really isn't anything you can do to help you win. So, just keep pushing that spin button and hope for a good score!

Personally, I only like to play games of skill (like blackjack and video poker) so I usually don't play in slot tournaments. There was, however, one instance where I played in a tournament because of the value it offered. A few years ago my friend Marvin and I were planning a trip to Las Vegas to attend the World Gaming Congress and Expo at the city's main convention center. This event is held each year and it's the world's largest trade show for the casino industry. The event took place during the middle of the week but we also wanted to stay over for the weekend. Unfortunately, the room rates are much higher on weekends and the hotels usually don't discount their rates very much on those days. After calling around to check rates we decided to look in the *Las Vegas Advisor* to find out about slot tournaments.

Boulder Station was having its *All Treats, No Trick*s slot tournament that same weekend. The entry fee was $199 but by entering before a certain date, the fee was reduced to $149 and there was a total of $40,000 in prize money up for grabs. The rules required 268 entrants, or else the total prize money could be reduced, but based on that required number the casino would be receiving $39,932 in prize money (assuming all early entrants) and awarding $40,000 in prize money which made this a slightly positive equity situation. Additionally, everyone received a t-shirt, a welcoming cocktail party, lunch at the *Pasta Palace,* an awards celebration and a reduced room rate of $25 for Friday and Saturday evening.

We had stayed at Boulder Station before and we both liked the property very much. We called the hotel's reservation department and they told us it would be $99 per night on Friday and Saturday. That was $198 for the two nights, plus 9% tax, for a total of $215.82 By entering the slot tournament our cost would be $149, plus $50 for the room for two nights, plus 9% tax (only on the room), for a total of $203.50 Hey, you want to talk about positive equity? This thing was great! Not only were they giving back all of the prize money, but in this case it was actually cheaper to enter the slot tournament than to get the room by itself!

The rules allowed us to enter as a team for the $149 fee and that also got us into the activities together. At the welcoming party we had an unlimited choice of alcoholic beverages or sodas, plus a large selection of finger sandwiches and other snacks. The *Pasta Palace* is a good restaurant and we had a great lunch there.

We weren't very lucky in the tournament and didn't finish high in the standings. Actually, we received the lowest cash prize which was $40. That brought our actual cost for the room and the tournament down to $163.50 which was still $52 cheaper than just getting the room by itself. Plus, we got the t-shirt, welcoming party and lunch as an added bonus.

As you can see, we saved some money by entering the slot tournament and we also had a lot of fun. You can do the same thing by checking out some of the tournaments that are available the next time you're planning a trip to a casino. Just use the toll-free numbers in this book to call the casino marketing departments, or pick up the latest issue of *Las Vegas Advisor,* or a general gaming magazine, for information on current tournaments.

Video Poker

by Steve Bourie

Okay, who knows the main difference between video poker and slot machines? C'mon now, raise your hands if you think you know it. If you said "a slot machine is a game of luck and video poker is a game of skill" then you are correct! When you play a slot machine there is no decision you can make which will affect the outcome of the game. You put in your money; pull the handle; and hope for the best. In video poker, however, it is your skill in playing the cards which definitely affects the outcome of the game.

Okay, who knows the other major difference between video poker and slot machines? Well, you're right again if you said "you never know what percentage a slot machine is set to pay back, but you can tell a video poker machine's payback percentage just by looking at it." Of course if you knew that answer then you also knew that video poker machines almost always offer you better returns than slot machines (provided you make the right playing decisions).

Now for those of you who didn't know the answers to those two questions, please read on. You others can skip the rest of this story as I am sure you're eager to get back to your favorite video poker machine.

First, let's cover the basics. Video poker has virtually the same rules as a game of five card draw poker. The only difference is that you have no opponent to beat and you can't lose more than your initial bet. First, you deposit from one to five coins in the machine to make your bet. You are then shown five cards on the video screen and your goal is to try to make the best poker hand possible from those cards. Since it is a draw game, you are given one opportunity to improve your hand. This is done by allowing you to discard from one, up to all five cards from your original hand. Of course, you don't have to discard any if you don't want to. After choosing which cards you want to keep (by pushing the button below each card), you then push the deal button and the machine will replace all of the other cards with new cards. Based on the resulting final hand the machine will then pay you according to the pay schedule posted on the machine. Naturally, the better your hand, the higher the amount the machine will pay you back.

That's pretty much how a video poker machine works from the outside, but what about the inside? Well, I had a few questions about that so I visited International Game Technology, which is the world's largest manufacturer of video poker machines (as well as slot machines), in January 2001 and spoke to their chief software engineer, James Vasquez. The full story story is in the slot machine section of this book, so I'll just refer here to some video poker questions which I asked.

Let's talk about the difference between video poker and slot machines. It's my understanding that with video poker you can't control the number of winning and losing combinations programmed into the computer chip, instead its based on a 52-card deck with a fixed number of combinations. Is that correct?

Vasquez: Yes, assuming there are no wild cards.

When the cards are dealt is it done on a serial basis where it's similar to cards coming off the top of a deck? Or, parallel where there are five cards dealt face up and one card is unseen underneath each of the initial five cards?

Vasquez: It's serial and the five later cards aren't determined until there is more player interaction at the time of the draw.

They aren't determined at the time of the deal?

Vasquez: No. They're determined at the time of the draw. That varies with the jurisdictional regulation actually. Some lottery jurisdictions tell you that you have to draw all 10 at once. Different jurisdictions write into their rules how they want it done, specifically on poker, because it's a simpler game and they understand it. They say they either want all 10 done at once, or however they want.

How is it done in Nevada? All ten at once, or five and five?

IGT: In Nevada it's five and five.

The talk with Jim Vasquez confirmed that in most regulated jurisdictions video poker machines use a Random Number Generator to shuffle a 52-card deck and then choose five cards to display to the player. (By the way, when played without wild cards, there are exactly 2,598,960 unique five-card poker hands possible.) Then, when the deal button is pushed, the next group of cards is chosen and dealt to the player.

One point must be made here regarding random outcomes in video poker machines. Please note that *gaming regulations* always require video poker machines to have random outcomes. You should be aware that there are casinos operating in places that *do not* have gaming regulations. Examples are cruise ships which operate in international waters, some Indian reservations that are not subject to state regulations, and virtually all Internet casinos. You should also be aware that the technology exists for machines to be set so they do not act randomly. These machines can be actually programmed to avoid giving the players better hands and they wind up giving the house a much bigger advantage. These machines are illegal in Nevada, New Jersey, Colorado and all other states that pattern their gaming regulations after those states. You may, however, come across them in unregulated casinos.

One final point you should keep in mind - IGT is not the only manufacturer of video poker machines. There are quite a few others and they may engineer their machines to work in a different manner. Their RNG may not stop in the same way and their draw cards may be dealt differently. IGT, however, is by far the largest and it is the type of machine you will most often encounter in a casino.

Now that you understand how a video poker machine works let's learn how to pick out the best paying ones. In the beginning of this story it was mentioned that "you can tell a video poker machine's payback percentage just by looking at it." That's true, but it takes a little bit of knowledge to know the difference among all the different types of machines. An example of some of the different machines available are: Jacks or Better, Bonus, Double Bonus, Double Double Bonus, Joker Poker and Deuces Wild. To make it even more confusing, not only are there different machines, but each of those machines can have a different pay schedule for the same hand.

Fortunately, every video poker machine's payback percentage can be mathematically calculated. Not only does this let you know which machines offer you the best return, but it also tells you the best playing decisions to make on that particular machine based on the odds of that combination occurring. The bad news, however, is that it's fairly impossible to do on your own so you'll have to either buy a book that lists all of the percentages and strategies or buy a computer program that does the work for you. Take a look at the tables on the next few pages and you'll see some different types of video poker games and their payback percentages (when played with maximum coin and perfect strategy). For those of you with a computer, *Bob Dancer Presents Win Poker* can determine the exact payback percentage for any video poker machine. It retails for $29.95 (see an ad for it in this book) and besides calculating percentages it will also allow you to play video poker on different types of machines and analyze hands to show you the expected return for each play. You can set the game to automatically show you the best decision each time or you can set it to just warn you if you make a wrong decision on your own. It's so simple that my 14-year-old son plays it and I'm confident he can play better than the average Las Vegas visitor. "I'm going for the flush, dad!"

If you have no desire to get quite that serious about learning video poker then I'll try to provide some general tips to help you out. First, you'll need to find the machines that offer you the highest returns. One of the best is the 9/6 Jacks or Better machine. Of course, you're probably wondering "what exactly is a 9/6 Jacks or Better machine?" Well, the Jacks or Better part refers to the fact that you won't win anything from the machine unless you have at least a pair of Jacks. The 9/6 part refers to the payback schedule on this kind of machine. As stated earlier, each machine can have a different payback schedule and there are at least 20 different kinds of payback schedules available on Jacks or Better machines. In Las Vegas the two most common Jacks or Better machines you will find are 8/5 and 9/6. Here's a comparison of their pay schedules (per coin, for five-coin play):

Hand	9/6	8/5
Royal Flush	800	800
Straight Flush	50	50
4-of-a-Kind	25	25
Full House	**9**	**8**
Flush	**6**	**5**
Straight	4	4
3-of-a-Kind	3	3
Two Pairs	2	2
One Pair J's	1	1

As you can see, the schedules are identical except for the better payoffs on the 9/6 machines for Flushes and Full Houses. The payback on a 9/6 machine is 99.5% with perfect play, while the 8/5 machines return 97.3% with perfect play. Of course, it doesn't make any sense to play an 8/5 machine if a 9/6 machine is available. Yet, in Las Vegas you'll see lots of people playing an 8/5 when a 9/6 can often be found in the same casino. The reason they do that is because they don't know any better; you do. Always look for the 9/6 machines. They can be found in every downtown Las Vegas casino and most, but not all, Strip casinos. In other states, including New Jersey, they won't be found as easily. On a trip to Mississippi I found a few, but it took some searching and not every casino had them.

One other common machine you will come across is an 8/5 Jacks or Better progressive. These feature the same 8/5 pay table as above except for the royal flush which pays a jackpot amount that is displayed on a meter above the machine. The jackpot will continue to build until someone hits a royal flush; then it will reset and start to build again. If the jackpot on a 25¢ machine is above $2,240 (for five coins) then you should play it. If it's below $2,240 then stick to the regular 9/6 machines.

Another good tip is to restrict your play to the same kind of machine all the time. Each video poker machine has its own particular strategy and what works best on a Jacks or Better machine is definitely much different from what works best on a Deuces Wild machine. I usually only play 9/6 Jacks or Better machines because that is what I practice on and I automatically know the best decision to make all the time. Keep in mind that when you calculate the payback percentage for a video poker machine the number you arrive at is based on perfect play. As an example, a 9/6 Jacks or Better video poker machine has a 99.5 percent payback with perfect play. This means that, theoretically, it will return $99.50 for every $100 played in the machine, but

Jacks or Better Pay Table Variations

(Per coin with maximum coin played and perfect strategy)

9/7 (at Stratosphere)

Royal Flush	800
Straight Flush	50
4-of-a-kind	25
Full House	***9***
Flush	***7***
Straight	4
3-of-a-kind	3
2 Pair	2
Jacks or Better	1
Payback	**100.8%**

9/6 with 4,700 coin jackpot

Royal Flush	940
Straight Flush	50
4-of-a-kind	25
Full House	***9***
Flush	***6***
Straight	4
3-of-a-kind	3
2 Pair	2
Jacks or Better	1
Payback	**99.90%**

9/6 with 4,000 coin jackpot

Royal Flush	800
Straight Flush	50
4-of-a-kind	25
Full House	***9***
Flush	***6***
Straight	4
3-of-a-kind	3
2 Pair	2
Jacks or Better	1
Payback	**99.54%**

8/5

Royal Flush	800
Straight Flush	50
4-of-a-kind	25
Full House	***8***
Flush	***5***
Straight	4
3-of-a-kind	3
2 Pair	2
Jacks or Better	1
Payback	**97.28%**

7/5

Royal Flush	800
Straight Flush	50
4-of-a-kind	25
Full House	***7***
Flush	***5***
Straight	4
3-of-a-kind	3
2 Pair	2
Jacks or Better	1
Payback	**96.15%**

6/5

Royal Flush	800
Straight Flush	50
4-of-a-kind	25
Full House	***6***
Flush	***5***
Straight	4
3-of-a-kind	3
2 Pair	2
Jacks or Better	1
Payback	**95.00%**

Bonus Poker Pay Table Variations

(Per coin with maximum coin played and perfect strategy)

7/5 Bonus

Royal Flush	800
Straight Flush	50
Four Aces	80
Four 2s 3s 4s	40
Four 5s-Ks	25
Full House	***7***
Flush	***5***
Straight	4
3-of-a-kind	3
2 Pair	2
Jacks or Better	1
Payback	**98.02%**

8/5 Bonus

Royal Flush	800
Straight Flush	50
Four Aces	80
Four 2s 3s 4s	40
Four 5s-Ks	25
Full House	***8***
Flush	***5***
Straight	4
3-of-a-kind	3
2 Pair	2
Jacks or Better	1
Payback	**99.17%**

9/6 Double Bonus

Royal Flush	800
Straight Flush	50
Four Aces	160
Four 2s 3s 4s	80
Four 5s-Ks	50
Full House	***9***
Flush	***6***
Straight	5
3-of-a-kind	3
2 Pair	1
Jacks or Better	1
Payback	**97.81%**

9/7 Double Bonus

Royal Flush	800
Straight Flush	50
Four Aces	160
Four 2s 3s 4s	80
Four 5s-Ks	50
Full House	***9***
Flush	***7***
Straight	5
3-of-a-kind	3
2 Pair	1
Jacks or Better	1
Payback	**99.11%**

10/7 Double Bonus

Royal Flush	800
Straight Flush	50
Four Aces	160
Four 2s 3s 4s	80
Four 5s-Ks	50
Full House	***10***
Flush	***7***
Straight	5
3-of-a-kind	3
2 Pair	1
Jacks or Better	1
Payback	**100.17%**

10/7 Triple Bonus

Royal Flush	800
Straight Flush	50
Four Aces	240
Four 5s-Ks	120
Four 2s 3s 4s	75
Full House	***10***
Flush	***7***
Straight	4
3-of-a-kind	3
2 Pair	1
Kings or Better	***1***
Payback	**98.52%**

Deuces Wild Pay Table Variations

(Per coin with maximum coin played and perfect strategy)

Short Pay

Natural Royal Flush	800
Four Deuces	200
Wild Royal Flush	25
5-of-a-kind	15
Straight Flush	9
4-of-a-kind	***4***
Full House	3
Flush	2
Straight	2
3-of-a-kind	1
Payback	**94.34%**

Full Pay

Natural Royal Flush	800
Four Deuces	200
Wild Royal Flush	25
5-of-a-kind	15
Straight Flush	9
4-of-a-kind	***5***
Full House	3
Flush	2
Straight	2
3-of-a-kind	1
Payback	**100.76%**

Not So Ugly (NSU) Deuces

Natural Royal Flush	800
Four Deuces	200
Wild Royal Flush	25
5-of-a-kind	***16***
Straight Flush	***10***
4-of-a-kind	***4***
Full House	***4***
Flush	***3***
Straight	2
3-of-a-kind	1
Payback	**99.73%**

Deuces Deluxe

Natural Royal Flush	800
Four Deuces	200
Natural Straight Flush	50
Wild Royal Flush	25
5-of-a-kind	15
Natural 4-of-a-kind	10
Wild Straight Flush	9
Wild 4-of-a-kind	4
Full House	4
Flush	3
Straight	2
3-of-a-kind	1
Payback	**100.34%**

only if the player makes the correct decision every time. If you make mistakes, and most players do, the return to the casino will be higher. If you play several different kinds of machines it becomes increasingly harder to remember the correct play to make and you will make mistakes. Therefore, it only makes sense to memorize the correct decisions for one kind of machine and to always play on that same kind of machine (of course, in order to learn those proper strategies, you may want to buy that book or software).

Now that you've decided which machines to play, you'll need some help with strategy. On the next two pages are charts that will give you an excellent simple strategy for both 9/6 and 8/5 video poker machines. These charts were derived from calculations using the *Bob Dancer Presents Win Poker* computer program and give you a near-perfect strategy. They aren't 100% perfect but they are close to it and will only be fractionally incorrect in some situations. The only difference between the two tables is shown in the poker hands that have been *italicized* in the 8/5 strategy tables.

Simple Strategy Table For 9/6 Jacks or Better

1. Royal Flush
2. Straight Flush
3. 4 of a kind
4. 4 card Royal Flush
5. Full House
6. Flush
7. 3 of a kind
8. Straight
9. 4 card Straight Flush
10. Two Pairs
11. 4 card inside Straight Flush
12. Pair of Jacks or higher
13. 3 card Royal Flush
14. 4 card Flush
15. 4 card straight with 3 high cards
16. Low Pair
17. 4 card Straight with 2 high cards
18. 4 card Straight with 1 high card
19. 3 card Inside Straight Flush with 2 high cards
20. 3 card Straight Flush with 1 high card
21. 4 card Straight with no high cards
22. 3 card Double Inside Straight Flush with 2 high cards
23. 3 card Inside Straight Flush with 1 high card
24. 3 card Straight Flush with no high cards
25. 4 card Inside Straight with 4 high cards
26. 2 card Royal Flush with no Ace or 10
27. 2 card Royal Flush with Ace and no 10
28. 3 card Double Inside Straight Flush with 1 high card
29. 3 card Inside Straight Flush with no high card
30. 4 card Inside Straight with 3 high cards
31. 3 high cards with no Ace
32. 2 high cards
33. 2 card Royal Flush with 10 and no Ace
34. 1 high card
35. 3 card Double Inside Straight Flush with no high card
36. All New Cards

Simple Strategy Table For 8/5 Jacks or Better

1. Royal Flush
2. Straight Flush
3. 4 of a kind
4. 4 card Royal Flush
5. Full House
6. Flush
7. 3 of a kind
8. Straight
9. 4 card Straight Flush
10. Two Pairs
11. 4 card inside Straight Flush
12. Pair of Jacks or higher
13. 3 card Royal Flush
14. 4 card Flush
15. 4 card straight with 3 high cards
16. Low Pair
17. 4 card Straight with 2 high cards
18. 4 card Straight with 1 high card
19. 3 card Inside Straight Flush with 2 high cards
20. 3 card Straight Flush with 1 high card
21. 4 card Straight with no high cards
22. 3 card Double Inside Straight Flush with 2 high cards
23. 3 card Inside Straight Flush with 1 high card
24. 3 card Straight Flush with no high cards
25. 4 card Inside Straight with 4 high cards
26. 2 card Royal Flush with no Ace or 10
27. 2 card Royal Flush with Ace and no 10
28. *3 high cards with no Ace*
29. *4 card Inside Straight with 3 high cards*
30. *3 card Double Inside Straight Flush with 1 high card*
31. *2 high cards*
32. *3 card Inside Straight Flush with no high card*
33. 2 card Royal Flush with 10 and no Ace
34. 1 high card
35. 3 card Double Inside Straight Flush with no high card
36. All New Cards

To use any chart just look up your hand and play it in the manner that is closest to the top of the chart. For example: you are dealt (6♣,6♦,7♥,8♠,9♣). You keep (6♣,6♦) rather than (6♦,7♥,8♠,9♣) because a low pair (#16) is higher on the chart than a four-card straight with no high cards (#21). Remember to always look for the highest possible choice on the chart when there are multiple ways to play your hand. As another example: you are dealt (8♣,8♦, J♥,Q♥,K♥). You keep (J♥,Q♥,K♥) rather than (8♣,8♦) because a three-card royal flush (#13) is higher on the chart than a low pair (#16). As a final, but radical, example of how to play your hand by the chart what would you do if you're dealt (6♥,10♥,J♥,Q♥,K♥)? Yes, you have to break up your flush by discarding the 6♥ and go for the royal flush because the four-card royal flush (#4) is higher on the chart than the pat flush (#6). When looking at the 9/6 chart there are a few things that should seem rather obvious:

1) A low pair is relatively good. Of the 36 possible hands, a low pair is #16 which means there are 20 hands worse than a low pair. If you look at the 15 hands that are better than a low pair eight of them are pat hands that require no draw. Of the other seven hands, six of them are four card hands and the remaining hand is a three-card royal flush.

2) Don't hold three cards trying to get a straight or flush. Nowhere on the chart do you see that you should hold three cards to try for a straight or flush. In some instances you should hold three cards to try for a straight flush, but *never* a straight or flush.

3) Rarely draw to an inside straight. Inside straights (6,7,_,9,10) appear only twice on the chart and only in rather bad positions: #30 (with three high cards) and #25 (with four high cards). It is much easier to draw to an outside straight (_7,8,9,10_) where you can complete your straight by getting the card you need on either end. Open end straights appear four times on the chart and in much higher positions than inside straights: #21 (with no high cards), #18 (with one high card), #17 (with two high cards) and #15 (with three high cards).

4) Don't hold a kicker. A kicker is an unpaired card held with a pair. For example (8,8,K) or (K,K,9) are examples of hands where an extra card (the kicker) is held. *Never* hold a kicker because they add no value to your hand!

If you would like to make your own video poker strategy charts there is a special software program that will allow you to do this. It's called *Tom Ski's Video Poker Strategy Master* and it allows you to generate your own video poker strategy charts on your home computer. You can make charts for full-pay Deuces Wild which can be found in many Nevada casinos (and the Copa Casino in Gulfport, Mississippi). It can also do Pick'Em which can be found in many different markets around the country, plus nine other common games.

For your information there are exactly 2,598,960 unique poker hands possible on a video poker machine (when played without a joker). On a 9/6 Jacks or Better machine a royal flush will occur about once every 40,000 hands; a

Other Video Poker Game Pay Tables

(Per coin with maximum coin played and perfect strategy)

Pick'Em Poker (five coin payout)

Royal Flush	6,000
Straight Flush	1,199
4-of-a-kind	600
Full House	90
Flush	75
Straight	55
3-of-a-kind	25
Two Pair	15
Pair 9's or Better	10
Payback	**99.95%**

All American Poker

Royal Flush	800
Straight Flush	200
4-of-a-kind	40
Full House	8
Flush	8
Straight	8
3-of-a-kind	3
Two Pair	1
Pair Jacks or Better	1
Payback	**100.72%**

Double Joker Full-Pay

Natural Royal Flush	800
Wild Royal Flush	100
5-of-a-kind	50
Straight Flush	25
4-of-a-kind	***9***
Full House	5
Flush	4
Straight	3
3-of-a-kind	2
2 Pair	1
Payback	**99.97%**

Double Joker Short-Pay

Natural Royal Flush	800
Wild Royal Flush	100
5-of-a-kind	50
Straight Flush	25
4-of-a-kind	***8***
Full House	5
Flush	4
Straight	3
3-of-a-kind	2
2 Pair	1
Payback	**98.10%**

straight flush about every 9,000 hands; four-of-a-kind about every 425 hands; a full house about every 87 hands; a flush about every 91 hands; a straight about every 89 hands; three-of-a-kind about every 14 hands; two pairs about every 8 hands; and a pair of Jacks or better about every 5 hands. The interesting thing to note here is that both a flush and a straight are harder to get than a full house, yet a full house always has a higher payback than either of them. The majority of the time, about 55% to be exact, you will wind up with a losing hand on a 9/6 machine.

The next bit of advice concerns how many coins you should bet. You should always bet the maximum amount (on machines returning 100% or more) because it will allow you to earn bonus coins when you hit the royal flush. Example: For a royal flush on a 9/6 machine with one coin played you receive 250 coins; for two coins you get 500; for three coins you get 750; for four coins you get 1,000 and for five (maximum) coins you get 4,000 coins. This translates into a bonus of 2,750 coins! A royal flush can be expected once every 40,400 hands on a 9/6 machine; once every 40,200 hands on an 8/5 machine; and once every 32,700 hands on an 8/5 progressive. The odds are high, but the added bonus makes it worthwhile. If you can't afford to play the maximum coins on a positive machine then move down to a lower denomination machine. And, if you absolutely insist on playing less than the maximum, be sure to play only one at a time. It doesn't make any sense to play two, three or four coins, because you still won't be eligible for the bonus.

One important thing to keep in mind when you look at the total payback on these video poker machines is that those numbers always include a royal flush and the royal flush plays a *very* big factor in the total return. As a matter of fact, the royal flush is such a big factor on video poker machines that you are actually expected to lose until you get that royal flush. Yes, even by restricting your play to video poker machines with a more than 100% payback you are *still* expected to lose money until you hit a royal flush. Once you hit that royal flush it will bring your cash back up to that 100% level but until it happens you should be fully aware that you are statistically expected to lose money.

According to video poker expert Bob Dancer, "on a 25¢ Jacks or Better 9/6 machine you will lose at a rate of 2.5% while you are waiting for the royal to happen. Another way to look at this is quarter players who play 600 hands per hour can expect to lose about $18.75 per hour, on average, on any hour they do not hit a royal." You really have to keep in mind that there are no guarantees when you play video poker. Yes, you are expected to get a royal flush about once every 40,000 hands but there are no guarantees that it will happen and if you don't get that royal flush it could cost you dearly.

A final tip about playing video poker concerns slot clubs. Every major casino has a slot club and you should make it a point to join the slot club before you insert your first coin. It doesn't cost anything to join and as a member you will have the opportunity to earn complimentaries from the casinos in the form of cash, food, shows, drinks, rooms or other "freebies." When you join the club you'll be issued a card (similar to a credit card) that you insert in the machine before you start to play and it will track how much you bet, as well as how long you play. Naturally, the more money you gamble, the more freebies you'll earn. Just make sure you don't get carried away and bet more than you're comfortable with just to earn some extra comps. Ideally, you want to get comps for gambling that you were going to do anyway and not be pressured into betting more than you had planned. Many clubs will also give you cash back for your play and that amount should be added into the payback percentage on the kind of machine you'll be playing. For example: at Treasure Island in Las Vegas, the slot club rebates .33% in cash for your video poker play (.67% for slots). By only playing 9/6 Jacks or Better machines with a return of 99.54% you can add the .33% rebate to get an adjusted figure of 99.87%. This means that you are, theoretically, playing an almost even game, *plus* you're still eligible for other room and food discounts on top of your cash rebate.

Choosing Video Poker Games

by John Grochowski

Way back in the early 1990s when the nationwide expansion of gambling was at its beginning and riverboat casinos were new, I asked a riverboat slot director why there was so little video poker on his floor.

``Our guests aren't ready for it,'' he told me. ``When we opened, we didn't know what everybody was going to play. We assumed it would be about normal for the Las Vegas Strip. We opened with about 17 percent video poker, and they sat there empty. All anyone wanted to play was the slots. So we dropped to 9 or 10 percent video poker.''

Things have changed. Slot directors move to other jobs at other casinos, and player tastes change. The current slot director at that same riverboat told me in 2000 that he now has 18 percent video poker, and players can't get enough of it. If he was starting from scratch, he'd turn 20, maybe even 25 percent of his floor over to video poker. What happened?

Video poker, it seems, is an acquired taste. You can see that clearly in casino gambling's capital city. Las Vegas visitors who stick to the Strip will see video poker taking up roughly 15 percent of the slot floors -- a little more in some casinos, a little less than others. But get off the Strip and check out the places that cater to the locals, places such as the Fiesta and Santa Fe in northwest Las Vegas, or Sunset Station and The Reserve to the southeast in Henderson. There you'll see row after row after row of video poker, 50 percent or more of the slot floor.

The difference is in the experience of the players. What the Las Vegas locals know, and what regular players in newer gaming markets are learning, is that they get a better run for their money on video poker than on the slots. Whereas slots on the Las Vegas Strip return an average of a little more than 95 percent of coins played to dollar players and a little less than 93 percent to quarter players, even the bad video poker games, the ones that experts warn to stay away from, return 95 percent with expert play. The good machines return 99 percent, even 100 percent or more in the long run -- although even on those machines there will be more losing sessions than winners, balanced out in the long run by the odd royal flush.

Video poker does it with a high hit frequency, too. On most Jacks or Better-based games, about 45 percent of all hands bring some return. That's a percentage slots were unable to approach until the advent of multiline, multicoin video slots, and on those games many "winners" bring returns of less than the wagers.

Not every player has access to those 100-percent machines. In new gaming markets, where demand for a place to play frequently outstrips available space, slot directors are able to use games that will maximize their profit margins. They know they can use a Jacks or Better game that pays 7-for-1 on full houses and 5-for-1 on flushes instead of a full-pay game that returns 9-for-1 and 6-for-1, and they'll still get plenty of play. There are good machines out there, too, but it's up to the player to learn to tell the difference.

JACKS OR BETTER: In video poker, when the casino wants to change the long-term payback percentage of a game, it changes the pay table. Given the same strategy, players get winning hands no more or less frequently, but some hands pay a little more or a little less.

In Jacks or Better, the base game around which many video poker variations are built, the payoffs that usually are changed are full houses and flushes. We look for games that pay 9-for-1 on full houses and 6-for-1 on flushes, with the full pay table being 250-for-1 on royal flushes (jumping to 4,000 coins with a five-coin wager), 50-for-1 on straight flushes, 25-for-1 on four of a kind, 9-for-1 on full houses, 6-for-1 on flushes 4-for-1 on straights, 3-for-1 on three of a kind, 2-for-1 on two pair and 1-for-1 on pairs of Jacks or better.

For each unit that the payoff on full houses or flushes drops, we lose about 1.1 percent of our long-term payback. On an 8-5 Jacks or Better game, with one-unit drops in both spots on the pay table, our average return drops to 97.3 percent. Drop the full house payback again to 7-for-1, and a 7-5 machine drops to 96.2 percent.

Given better options, a video poker player in the know would walk away from that 7-5 game. In Las Vegas, he might even leave the casino and look for a better deal next door or across the street. That's tough to do on a riverboat, or in a Native American casino that's miles away from the next option. So a player who finds the best video poker in a casino is 7-5 Jacks or Better has a decision to make. Does he take up table games? Does he just go home and skip his night's entertainment? Or does he sigh, decide that at least a 96-percent game is better than he'd get on the slots, and play anyway? Most take the third option.

BONUS POKER: The "bonuses" in Bonus Poker are on certain fours of a kind. Four 2s, 3s or 4s will bring you 40-for-1 and four Aces will bring 80-for-1 instead of the 25-for-1 that is standard on Jacks or Better and on the remaining quads in Bonus Poker.

Other than that, the pay table is the same as in Jacks or Better, with reduced paybacks on full houses and flushes. We look for games that pay 8-for-1 on full houses and 5-for-1 on flushes. That's a 99.2 percent game with expert play. Bonus Poker games often have 7-5 and 6-5 versions, with overall returns dropping about 1.1 percent for each unit the flush payoff drops.

There are no major strategy differences between Bonus Poker and the versions of Jacks or Better that pay 5-for-1 on the flush. Learn to play 8-5 Jacks, and you're ready for Bonus Poker.

DOUBLE BONUS POKER: If everyone could play this game perfectly and played only the best available version, the casinos would be supporting us instead of the other way around. Double Bonus Poker, which in its full-pay version pays 10-for-1 on full houses, 7-for-1 on flushes and 5-for-1 on straights, returns 100.17 percent in the long run with expert play.

The full pay table is as follows: 250-for-1 on royal flushes (jumping to 4,000 coins with a five-coin wager), 50-for-1 on straight flushes, 160-for-1 on four Aces, 80-for-1 on four 2s, 3s and 4s, 50-for-1 on four of a kind, 10-for-1 on full houses, 7-for-1 on flushes, 5-for-1 on straights, 3-for-1 on three of a kind, 1-for-1 on two pair and 1-for-1 on pairs of Jacks or better.

A few important things to note: Two pair pays only 1-for-1 instead of the 2-for-1 Jacks or Better players get. More of the overall payback is tied up in the higher end of the pay table. With five coins wagered, four Aces bring an 800-coin jackpot. I've had more than one former slot player tell me that Double Bonus is the game that pried them away from the reels, with a realistic secondary jackpot worth walking away with making the difference.

Few play at expert level, and the casinos are in no danger of losing money. There are some tricky little moves in this game that average players miss. For example, if we're dealt a full house that includes three Aces, our best play is to break up the full house and go for the fourth Ace. We'd never do that in Jacks or Better or Bonus Poker. Also, the 7-for-1 payback on flushes dictates that we hold three parts of a flush. Given 10 of diamonds, 8 of clubs, 6 of diamonds, 4 of hearts, 2 of diamonds, in 10-7 Double Bonus we'd hold the three diamonds, whereas in Jacks or Better we'd discard all five.

To change the payback percentage, the casino changes payoffs on full houses, flushes and sometimes straights. It's common to see Double Bonus games with 9-7 (99.1 percent) and 9-6 (97.8 percent pay tables), and I sometimes see pay tables as low as 8-5-4, paying 8-for-1 on full houses, 5-for-1 on flushes and 4-for-1 on straights. The 8-5-4 game pays only 94.2 percent with expert play, making it problematic as to whether a video poker player is really any better off on that game than on the reel slots.

DOUBLE DOUBLE BONUS POKER: The big change as compared to Double Bonus is that there are extra bonuses available on some fours of a kind provided the fifth card is a certain denomination. If four Aces are accompanied by a 2, 3 or 4, the usual 160-for-1 jackpot jumps to 400-for-1 -- a 2,000-coin bonanza with five wagered. If four 2, 3s or 4s are accompanied by an Ace, 2, 3 or 4, the 80-for-1 payoff jumps to 160-for-1.

Straights drop back to 4-for-1 on all versions of this game. The full-pay Double Double Bonus game pays 9-for-1 on full houses and 6-for-1 on flushes, and returns 98.9 percent with expert play.

It's not unusual to see Double Double Bonus in an 8-5 format, leaving a 96.8 percent game, and I've even seen 7-5, a 95.7 percent pay table in the long run with expert play.

One quick strategy tip: Do not hold fifth-card kickers without already having the four of a kind. If you're dealt three Aces, a 2 and a 9, discard both the 2 and the 9. Give yourself two chances to draw the fourth Ace instead of just one.

DEUCES WILD: Someday, I'm going to write a book with nothing but Deuces Wild pay tables and strategy variations. There are countless versions of Deuces Wild. Most video poker books focus on strategy for full-pay Deuces Wild, which is available only in Nevada. The 100.8 percent payback with expert play is too strong for regulators' tastes in most gaming markets and other than Nevada the only place you can find the game is at the Copa in Gulfport, Mississippi. It's a great game if you can find it. Most players can't.

Let's compare it to another game that video poker fans sometimes call ``Illinois Deuces.'' It doesn't say ``Illinois'' on the machine -- it just says Deuces Wild. Manufacturers and casino operators leave it to the player to tell the difference among pay tables, if they can.

The game isn't limited to Illinois. It's available nationwide. It just has that nickname because it rose to popularity in the early '90s at the Par-A-Dice casino in East Peoria, Illinois. Look at the following pay tables, and guess which one is the full-pay game, returning 100.8 percent, and which is Illinois Deuces, returning 98.9

Variation No. 1: Natural royal flush 250-for-1 (jumps to 4,000 coins for a five-coin bet); four 2s 200-for-1; royal flush with wild cards 25-for-1; five of a kind 15-for-1; straight flush 9-for-1; four of a kind 5-for-1; full house 3-for-1; flush 2-for-1; straight 2-for-1; three of a kind 1-for-1.

Variation No. 2: Natural royal flush 250-for-1 (jumps to 4,000 coins for a five-coin bet); four 2s 200-for-1; royal flush with wild cards 25-for-1; five of a kind 15-for-1; straight flush 9-for-1; four of a kind 4-for-1; full house 4-for-1; flush 3-for-1; straight 2-for-1; three of a kind 1-for-1.

The differences look minor, right? No. 1 pays 5-for-1 on four of a kind, while No. 2 pays only 4-for-1. But No. 2 pays 4-for-1 on full houses and 3-for-1 on flushes, but up a notch from the payouts on No. 1. So which is better? It's No. 1.

Some players fall into the trap of thinking that in poker, full houses and flushes are more common than four of a kind, so No. 2 must be the better game. That's exactly what the operators want you to think. In Deuces Wild, we get four of a kind more often than full houses and flushes combined. If you have two pair and one of the pair consists of 2s, you have four of a kind. If you have three 9s, an 8 and a 2, the wild deuces doesn't become an 8 to complete a full house, it takes the place of a 9 to give you four of a kind.

One major strategy difference comes when we're dealt two pairs. If we have two 9s and two 8s, strategy tables that focus on full-pay Deuces will tell you to keep only one pair. But in Illinois Deuces, where we get less for four of a kind and more for a full house, our best play is to keep both pairs and make a one-card draw for a full house. Let's try one more variation:

Variation No. 3: Natural royal flush 250-for-1 (jumps to 4,000 coins for a five-coin bet); four 2s 200-for-1; royal flush with wild cards 25-for-1; five of a kind 16-for-1; straight flush 13-for-1; four of a kind 4-for-1; full house 3-for-1; flush 2-for-1; straight 2-for-1; three of a kind 1-for-1.

Again, we have a Deuces variation that differs from full-pay in three places on the pay table. As in Illinois Deuces, four of a kind is reduced to 4-for-1, and we know that's important. Five of a kind goes up to 16-for-1 from the usual 15-for-1, and there's a big jump on straight flushes, to 13-for-1 from 9-for-1.

Those jumps aren't nearly enough to make up the difference. This game, nicknamed ``Colorado Deuces'' but available nationwide, returns only 96.8 percent with expert play.

There's no easy road map to all the variations of Deuces Wild. The key thing to remember is that changes on the low end of the pay table in Deuces Wild or any other video poker game have a greater effect than those higher on the pay table. With few exceptions such as four-of-a-kind in Deuces Wild, hands lower on the pay table occur more frequently than those higher up. An increase on full houses to 4-for-1 helps the player much more often than a bigger increase on straight flushes, and so makes a bigger difference in the long-term return.

So it goes with any video poker game. In Double Bonus, the four-of-a-kind bonuses, the enhanced payoffs on full houses, flushes and straights all are offset by one decrease low on the pay table -- the drop from 2-for-1 to 1-for-1 on two pair. When you next find an unfamiliar pay table, be aware. Any boost high on the pay table might look attractive, but check out what you're giving up to get it.

John Grochowski is the gaming columnist for the "Chicago Sun-Times" and a contributing writer to many gaming magazines. John is also the author of several books on casino gambling.

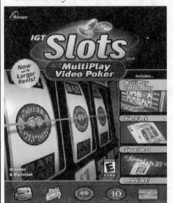

Are You A Chicken Or A Gambler?

by Bob Dancer

Congratulations! You've just been dealt one of the most interesting hands in video poker: K♥, Q♥, J♥, T♥, 9♥. A straight flush! Wonderful!

Your two best options are to be a "chicken" and keep the straight flush (i.e. hold all five cards) or to be a "gambler" and go for the royal (i.e. hold KQJT, pray, and draw). Whichever way you go, you'll have company. Many people will play it exactly the way you do.

Although many people aren't sure how to play this hand, in truth it isn't close at all. The correct play is correct by a mile. The wrong play is very wrong. However, which of the two plays is correct depends upon the game you are playing!

If you are playing a jacks or better type of game (including bonus poker, double bonus poker, double double bonus poker, plus a variety of others), being a checken is best. If you are playing deuces wild, being a gambler is far superior. How come there is such a difference?

First, let's look at the jacks or better games. Playing for dollars, the straight flush is worth $250. (You are playing five coins, aren't you?) This amount is constant. When you try for the royal, the amount of your win isn't constant, so we go with the average. You'll occasionally connect on the royal that pays you $4,000, but slightly more than half the time you'll end up with zero. The average amount ends up between $93 and $95, depending upon exactly how much flushes and straights are worth in the game you are playing. By any criteria, losing an average of at least $155 in one hand on a dollar game is a bundle.

In deuces wild games, the value of the 4-card royal remains in the $90 to $100 range, depending upon the schedule of the game. Although straights and flushes are worth a lot less in this game, if you draw one of the four deuces you'll end up with a wild royal that is worth $125 or so. The big difference comes in the value of keeping the straight flush. This is usually worth $45 or $50. Again, throwing away at least $40 because of misplaying one hand is huge.

There are two important lessons here. These lessons are basic in nature, but several players haven't mastered them.

First, the correct play for a given hand varies widely from game to game. I have seen players playing jacks or better with one hand, and deuces wild with the other, and making the same plays on both machines. This is a very expensive habit.

Second, each game has a variety of schedules. Jacks or better varieties, for example, can pay 30, 35, 40, 45, or even 50 for a full house. They can pay 25, 30, or 35 for a flush. The machines look alike, but they return very different amounts to the player. Although some casinos have signs "certifying" or "guaranteeing" a certain return on their best games, most casinos let you fend for yourself. If you can tell the difference between a good schedule and a bad one, you have a chance at this game. If you can't tell the difference, get prepared to lose, because bad schedules out-number good ones by a wide margin.

How do you find out which schedules are best? One way is to read. My columns in gaming magazines provide information, the book you're reading has good information on the subject, and several other authors have information in book form. No surprise, I think my stuff is excellent, but you'll find other writers in the bookstores too. By far the single-most useful tool to help you learn to play is a computer program that corrects you when you make a mistake. Though I may be biased, I highly recommend *Bob Dancer Presents WinPoker* software.

Surprisingly, one way that doesn't work real well is practice, practice, practice. While it is true that experienced players "miss" fewer hands than new players do, generally speaking the main thing that experience gives you in this game is the ability to make your mistakes faster.

Bob Dancer is a professional video poker player as well as a columnist for several gaming publications. Bob also markets a video poker software program that will allow you to practice numerous version of video poker at home on your computer. Ordering information for his software can be found on page 72.

Which One Is More Valuable?

by Bob Dancer

In each of the combinations below, decide which one, if either, is better. Sometimes one of the two combinations will be quite a bit better than the other. Sometimes they will be tied. But in no case will one be only slightly better than the other. In other words, there are no close calls here and good players need to understand these distinctions cold!

Usually I teach that pay schedules matter a lot. And they do! But in today's quiz they are not important. When considering Jacks or Better in today's quiz, how much you get for flushes and full houses is largely irrelevant. When considering Deuces Wild, you need to know that 3-of-a-kind returns even money (and that Two Pair and all single pairs return nothing), but the exact value you receive for flushes, 4-of-a-kinds, straight flushes, etc. is irrelevant, as long as these values are somewhat close to normal.

In each case, consider the value of the combinations "before the draw".

Q1: In Jacks or Better, which is more valuable J♥J♠ or A♥A♠?

Q2: In Jacks or Better, which is more valuable J♦ or A♦?

Q3: In Jacks or Better, which is more valuable Q♣J♣ or J♣T♣? (T stands for "ten")

Q4: In Jacks or Better, which is more valuable 2♥3♥4♥ or 3♥4♥5♥?

Q5: In Deuces Wild, which is more valuable Q♠T♠ or Q♠J♠?

Q6: In Deuces Wild, which is more valuable ***WW***5♦6♦ or ***WW***6♦7♦? (***W*** stands for wild card, in this case a deuce)

Q7: In Deuces Wild, which is more valuable ***WW***5♣6♣ or ***WW***5♣7♣?

ANSWERS

1: JJ is worth exactly the same as AA in Jacks or Better. They both give you your money back. Three jacks pays as much as three aces and four of one pays the same as four of the other. In various "Bonus" games, where four aces pay quite a bit more than four jacks, AA would be worth more than JJ. People who play bonus games, and are used to AA being worth more than JJ, sometimes forget to adjust their thinking when they are not playing the bonus game.

2: J is worth more than A. Either one is equally likely to pair up, become four of a kind or a royal. But in terms of straights and straight flushes, J is quite a bit better. Other than the royal, the A can only be part of an A2345 straight flush. The J can be part of a KQJT9, QJT98 or JT987 straight flush. The same goes for straights, although you can add the AKQJT straight to both.

A3: QJ is much better than JT in Jacks or Better. QJ has TWO high cards and JT only has ONE. This is by far the dominant fact. The fact that you can get more straights and straight flushes from JT than you can from QJ is not close to being strong enough to compensate for the extra high card.

A4: 345 is quite a bit stronger than 234. 345 is truly open-ended, and can be part of three different straight flushes: 7-high, 6-high and 5-high. 234 is too close to the bottom of the deck and can only be part of two different straight flushes: 6-high and 5-high.

A5: QJ is identical in value to QT in Deuces Wild. Any straight, straight flush or royal flush containing QJ also must contain the T, and any of these nice hands containing QT must also include the J. The distinguishing factor between this problem and Q3 above is that in Deuces Wild, there are no such things as "high cards". No pair of cards gives you your money back in Deuces Wild.

A6: ***WW***67 is more valuable than ***WW***56. The reason for this is how much room there is to move before the combination runs into the deuce. From WW67, there are 8 perfect cards giving you a straight flush. Specifically three cards on top (the 8,9,and T), three cards on the bottom (3,4, and 5) and the other two deuces. From WW56, there are only 7 perfect cards. There are still three perfect cards on top and two deuces, but now there are only two cards on the bottom (the 3 and the 4).

A7: ***WW***57 has exactly the same value as ***WW***56 in Deuces Wild. We showed in the last example that there were 7 perfect cards to complete the straight flush from ***WW***56. From ***WW***57, you'll notice two cards on top (the 8 and the 9), one in the middle (the 6), two on the bottom (the 3 and the 4) and the remaining two deuces. This also adds up to 7 perfect cards. In any game where holding ***WW***56 is correct (which would be games where the amount you receive for a flush and the amount you receive for a one-coin straight flush add up to 12 or higher), holding ***WW***57 would also be correct. In any game where holding ***WW***57 would not be correct (which would be games where the amounts you receive for a one-coin flush and straight flush add up to 11 or less), you would also not hold ***WW***56.

Bob Dancer is a professional video poker player as well as a columnist for several gaming publications. Bob also markets a video poker software program that will allow you to practice numerous version of video poker at home on your computer. Ordering information for his software can be found on page 72.

Million Dollar Video Poker

by Bob Dancer

Bob Dancer is the best known video poker player and writer in the world. In just six years, after coming to Las Vegas with a $6,000 bankroll, Dancer won more than $1 million playing beatable machines. His new book "Million Dollar Video Poker" recounts the events of those six years, with stories about his meteoric ups and downs, and lessons for players of all skill levels. Video poker is one of those rare casino games that can be beaten by a talented and informed player, and Dancer explains how it's done. Never before has a top video poker professional shared so many of his winning secrets. Below is an excerpt from Dancer's book.

Winning Is a Process, Not an Event - I'm frequently asked how much of the win was luck and how much was skill. I can't give you exact percentages on that. Every royal is lucky. Big royals are luckier. Discovering lucrative casino mistakes also requires a large amount of luck. If you look at the specific events of those six months, yes, a lot of luck was involved. But if you look at the pattern of winning year after year, there must have been a lot of skill there, too.

When people refer to "luck," they're usually citing specific events, such as, "Hitting three royals on the same day was very lucky." I don't believe that winning is a single event. I believe it's a process made up of zillions of events. Whatever those three royals paid will all be squandered back—unless you have a winning process to back them up. I'm so confident of this that I'm willing to bet a large amount of money that I'll be a gambling winner in at least four out of the next five years—starting from whenever the first bet is made. And I further believe that no sensible person would bet against me on this.

The reason I am so confident is that I understand the winning process—and always play within this understanding. In fact, anyone who understands the process and proceeds accordingly will also win at gambling. I'll go over that process here, which will also serve as a review and a summation of the book.

• Obtain a bankroll and keep it. This is critical. You have to be willing to do anything legal to get money, then hoard it once you have it. There will always be pressure on you to spend what you have. Many feel that since you can't take money with you when you die, you might as well spend it while you're living. I agree with this. However, since you don't know how long you will live, you must keep a sufficient bankroll for as long as you intend to play. I intend to play as long as I'm mentally capable, which probably means I'll die with my bankroll intact.

• Learn the games as if your life depended on it. Your bankroll is not as important as your life, but the player whose goal is to learn the game perfectly does a lot better than the player whose goal is to learn the game "well enough." A great resource for books, strategy cards and software can be found at www.greatstuff4gamblers.com (*and www.americancasinoguide.com*).

• Practice on a computer. This is actually a corollary of the previous paragraph, because you can't learn the games perfectly without using a computer. People who tell me that they're computer illiterate and too old to learn how to use one are simultaneously telling me that they are too old to learn how to win at video poker. Though I may be biased, I highly recommend *Bob Dancer Presents WinPoker* software.

• Learn to evaluate slot clubs and promotions. Do most of your playing during double points and other promotions. Many casinos have numerous promotions going on at once. Some (like half-price margaritas on Tuesday nights) will not fit in with winning, but many will.

• Know at least three or four different games well. Your primary games will be determined by what exists at the casinos you frequent. But when a good situation arises, you have to be ready to jump on it. If a particularly juicy promotion is good only for Double Bonus and you don't know that game, the promotion is useless to you.

• Never play any game where the house has the advantage, unless you recognize the play as strictly recreational and keep it in moderation. People pay to go bowling or to the movies, for example, so spending a few dollars to enjoy a few hours of nickel slots can be viewed in the same light. But playing slots or craps for significant stakes (however that's defined for you), or for extended periods of time, will destroy a bankroll.

• Understand the swings of the games. Know that you'll have more losing sessions than winning sessions. Either learn to deal with this or take on another hobby.

• Bet within your bankroll. My three-to-five-royals rule of thumb is crude, but serves well enough as an easy-to-remember guideline. If you're over-betting your bankroll, set a firm stop-loss restriction beforehand and stick to it.

• Never play while intoxicated, overly tired, angry, or otherwise not at your best. The machines are always playing their best game. It's a nip and tuck contest when you're at your best. When you're not, you'll take the worst of it.

• Review the strategies regularly. Even if you knew a strategy perfectly three months ago, the likelihood is that you've forgotten some of the obscure cases unless you've gone over them recently.

• Read. Most casino locations have a local publication with coupons and information of various sorts. Many locations have columnists with useful information. In Las Vegas as I write this, the best two sources are Jeffrey Compton and myself in the Friday "Neon" section of the Las Vegas Review-Journal (reprinted at www.reviewjournal.com) and Jean Scott in her weekly "Frugal Fridays" column at www.lasvegasadvisor.com. I write columns in Strictly Slots, Casino Player, Gambling Times, Jackpot!, San Diego Gaming Guide, and online at www.casino gaming.com. Skip Hughes has Video Poker Player and John Kelly presents good information in his monthly contributions to the Las Vegas Advisor. Other knowledgeable writers will arise.

• Participate in, or at least monitor occasionally, Internet video poker chat groups and mail lists. The oldest is vp-mail (the Skip Hughes Group), but it's only available to subscribers to Skip's www.vphomepage.com service. There are currently two quality free groups at winpoker@yahoogroups.com and vpfree@ yahoogroups.com. Others may arise.

• Set aside a few hours every trip to scout. Casinos change all the time. To find the really good opportunities, you have to go looking. If everyone on the Web is talking about a certain play, it might be good, but it's not great or probably won't last long. (When the word gets out, it's standing-room-only at the casino. Casinos will notice and address the situation, usually by diminishing the promotion.) The really great plays are kept quiet by those who discover them.

• Maintain your health. Playing long hours is grueling. Do what it takes in order to be able to survive it.

• Evaluate whether you're keeping your edge. There are people who could play a winning game a year ago, but can't today. Whether you're ahead or behind over the past six months is an important statistic. If you're behind, it might be that you've been unlucky, but it's more likely that you aren't playing a winning game. The edge you have playing video poker is, at best, very small. Since casinos keep making adjustments to increase their profits, you have to be making adjustments, too, or you'll be left behind.

• When you find a good situation, play it for as long as you can. There is always a chance of "killing the golden goose" by over-playing a good situation, but that risk is usually minimal unless you're playing for very large stakes.

• Enjoy yourself. Very few of us have managed to make a good living doing what we most enjoy. But it's possible to do and a worthy goal to pursue. If video poker ever becomes drudgery to you, I strongly advise you to find something else to do with the rest of your life.

Multi-Play Video Poker

by Tom Ski

Video poker has long been a favorite game of choice for many casino patrons. A great deal of work has been done analyzing payback percentages and bankroll requirements for traditional single line games. But then, a few years ago, a new variation of the game called Triple Play began to appear and it quickly spread like wildfire. Instead of playing just one hand at a time, this game would let you play the same starting hand three times. But how exactly does this variation affect the payback percentage and bankroll requirements?

To answer this question, I turned to Jazbo Burns who is one of the best video poker game theoreticians around. He wrote about this topic on his website at http://www.jazbo.com which also contains a lot of other very insightful information about video poker. Jazbo shows that the overall game percentage return is unchanged when playing triple play vs. single line play. The only difference is that you are now betting three times more money. So if you are playing a game that returns under 100%, you will lose three times more than usual, and if you are playing a game that returns over 100%, you will win three times more. But does the game require three times the bankroll?

Jazbo was able to address that question by first showing how the three hands are not independent of each other since they share the first five starting cards. And once a card is held, it is duplicated in all three hands. Thus there is a co-variance element involved in formulating bankroll considerations.

Jazbo went on to calculate the co-variance of many common video poker games. In the case of full pay 10-7 Double Bonus, Jazbo's formulas showed that while triple play allows the player to wager three times more money, the variance is only 1.24 times higher. This means that if you are faced with a choice of playing a multi-line machine at a lower denomination or a single-line game at a higher denomination, the multi-line game will require a smaller bankroll.

For example, let us suppose one could play five-line nickel 10-7 Double Bonus, or a single-line quarter version of the game. In the nickel game, you are betting five hands of five nickels each for a total of $1.25 in action. This is the same amount as the five quarters in the single line game. But the bankroll required for the five-line nickel game is less than 1/3 of the amount required for the single line quarter game.

If on the other hand, you are not concerned about a choice of denominations, but rather overall bankroll requirements within the same denomination, then single line play will always require a smaller bankroll than multi-line play. The bankroll required for triple play 10-7 Double Bonus would be 1.24 times greater than for single line offered at the same denomination, 1.48 times greater for five-play, 2.08 times greater for ten-play, and 6.88 times greater for fifty-play. The percentage increase in bankroll required for all other types of video poker games will be very nearly the same as the increase shown in this 10-7 Double Bonus example. As one other example, the increase for single line 9/6 to triple line 9/6 is around 1.22 times greater and other games will all vary around 1.21 times to 1.28 times.

So is multi-line video poker a better game to play vs. single-line play? The answer will vary depending upon different circumstances. Single-line play is always better if you are playing a game that returns less than 100% simply because you are betting less, and thus will lose less. If you are playing a positive expectation game, and you want to minimize bankroll fluctuations, you can play single-line games, or, better yet, if available, move down in denomination and play multi-line games. If you want to maximize your hourly win rate, and you have an adequate bankroll for the higher variance of multi-line games, then you should play the multi-line games. For example, if you have three times the bankroll required for a single-line quarter game, then you have enough to play a ten-line version of the same game since the ten-line version only requires a 2.08 times greater bankroll.

While 10/7 Double Bonus is usually the only positive game that can be found on multi-line games, there are times when a special casino promotion can make other games worthwhile. Such promotions might include double or triple cashback points, or a special four-of-a-kind that pays double. Limiting your play to such opportunities will help increase your chances of winning and thus making your casino visit a more enjoyable experience.

Tom Ski is an expert video poker theoretician and has written about video poker for several gaming magazines. His software program "Video Poker Strategy Master" can generate extremely accurate strategies for almost any conventional VP game or paytable. Ordering information for his software can be found on the next page.

Blackjack

by Steve Bourie

Blackjack is the most popular casino game in America and one of the biggest reasons for that is its relatively simple rules that are familiar to most casino visitors. Blackjack also has a reputation as being "beatable" and although that is true in some cases, the vast majority of players will always be playing the game with the house having a slight edge over them.

At most blackjack tables there are 7 boxes, or betting areas, on the table. This means that up to 7 people can play at that table and each player has their own box in front of them in which they'll place their bet. Now, before you take a seat at any blackjack table the first thing you should do is to take a look at the sign that's sitting on each table because it will tell you the minimum amount that you must bet on each hand. If you're a $5 player you certainly wouldn't want to sit at a table that has a $25 minimum so, once again, be sure to look before you sit down.

Once you're at the table you'll need chips to play with and you get them by giving your cash to the dealer who will exchange it for an equal amount of chips. Be careful, however, that you don't put your cash down into one of the betting boxes because the dealer might think you're playing it all on the next hand!

After everyone has placed their bets in their respective boxes the dealer will deal out 2 cards to each player. He will also deal 2 cards to himself; one of those cards will be face up and the other face down. Now, if you've ever read any brochures in a casino they'll tell you that the object of the game of blackjack is to get a total of cards as close to 21 as possible, without going over 21. However, that really isn't the object of the game. The true object is to beat the dealer and you do that by getting a total closer to 21 than the dealer, or by having the dealer bust by drawing cards that total more than 21.

The one thing that's strange about blackjack is that the rules can be slightly different at each casino and this is the only game where this happens. If you play baccarat, roulette or craps you'll find that the rules are virtually the same at every casino in the U.S. but that isn't the case with blackjack. For example, in Atlantic City all of the casinos use 6 or 8 decks of cards that are always dealt from a little rectangular box called a shoe and the cards are always dealt face up. In Las Vegas, some casinos will offer that same kind of game while others will offer games that use only 1 or 2 decks that are dealt directly from the dealer's hand and all of the cards will be dealt face down. To make it even stranger, some casinos in Las Vegas will offer both kinds of games in their

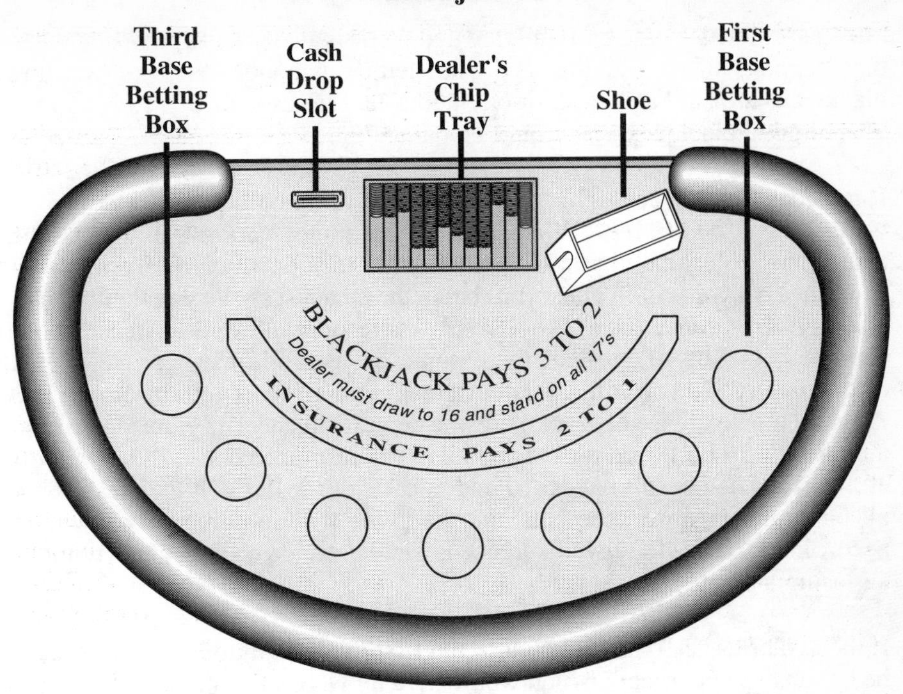

Typical Blackjack Table Layout

casinos and the rules will probably change when you move from one table to another. There can also be other rules variations concerning doubling down and splitting of pairs but we'll talk about those later. For now, just be aware that different casinos can have different blackjack rules and some of those rules will be good for you while others will be bad for you. Hopefully, after reading this story you'll know the good rules from the bad ones and which tables are the best ones to play at.

For our purposes, we'll assume we're playing in a casino that uses 6 decks of cards that are dealt out of a shoe and all of the player's cards are dealt face up. By the way, whenever you play blackjack in a casino where the cards are dealt face up don't touch the cards. In that kind of game the dealer is the only who is allowed to touch the cards and if you do happen to touch them they'll give you a warning not to do it again - so, don't touch the cards!

After the cards are dealt the players must determine the total of their hand by adding the value of their two cards together. All of the cards are counted at their face value except for the picture cards - jack, queen and king which all have a value of 10 - and the aces which can be counted as either 1 or 11. If you have an ace and any 10-value card you have a blackjack which is also called a natural and your hand is an automatic winner, unless the dealer also has a blackjack in which case the hands are tied. A tie is also called a ***push*** and when that happens it's a standoff and you neither win nor lose. All winning blackjacks are paid at 3-to-2, or one-and-a-half times your bet, so if you bet $5 and got a blackjack you would be paid $7.50

If the dealer has an ace as his up card the first thing he'll do is ask if anyone wants to buy ***insurance***. When you buy insurance you're betting that the dealer has a blackjack by having a 10 as his face down card. To make an insurance bet you would place your bet in the area just above your betting box that says "insurance pays 2-to-1" and you're only allowed to make an insurance bet of up to one-half the amount of your original bet. So, if you originally bet $10 you could only bet a maximum of $5 as your insurance bet. After all the insurance bets are made the dealer will check his face down card and if it's a 10 he'll turn it over and all of the insurance bets will be paid off at 2-to-1. If he doesn't have a 10 underneath, the dealer will then take away all of the losing insurance bets and the game will continue. By the way, according to basic strategy, insurance is a bad bet and you should never make an insurance bet.

If the dealer has a 10 as his up card the first thing he'll do is check to see if he has an ace underneath which would give him a blackjack. If he does have an ace he'll turn it face up and start collecting the losing bets that are out on the table. If he doesn't have an ace underneath the game will continue. In some casinos, however, the dealer won't check his hole card until after all of the hands are played out.

If the dealer doesn't have an ace or a 10 as his up card the game continues and the dealer will start with the player to his immediate left to see if they want another card. If a player wants another card they indicate that with a hand signal by tapping or scratching the table with their finger to show they want another card. Taking a card is also known as ***hitting*** or taking a hit. If a player doesn't want another card they would just wave their hand palm down over their cards. Not taking another card is known as ***standing***. The reason hand signals are used is because it eliminates any confusion on the part of the dealer as to exactly what the player wants and it also allows the security people to follow the game on the closed-circuit cameras that are hung from the ceiling throughout the casino.

Keep in mind that the hand signals will be slightly different if you're playing in a casino where the cards are dealt face down and you're allowed to pick them up. In that situation a player would signal that they wanted another card by scratching the table with the edges of the two cards they're holding. If they didn't want another card, they would simply place their two cards under the bet in their box.

In either case, if a player draws another card the value of that card is added to the total of the other cards and the player can continue to draw cards unless he gets a total of more than 21 in which case he busts and loses his bet.

When a player doesn't want any more cards, or stands, the dealer then moves on to the next player and after all of the players are finished then it's the dealer's turn to play. While each player can decide whether or not they want another card the dealer doesn't have that option and he must play by a fixed set of rules that require him to draw a card whenever his total is 16 or less and to stop when his total is 17 or more. If the dealer goes over 21 then he has busted and all of the players remaining in the game will be paid 1-to-1, or even money, on their bet.

If the dealer doesn't bust then each player's hand is compared to the dealer's. If the player's total is higher than the dealer's then they win and are paid even money. If the player's hand has a total that is lower than the dealer's hand then the player loses his bet. If the player and the dealer have the same total then it's a tie, or a push and neither hand wins. After all of the bets have been paid off, or taken by the dealer, a new round begins and new hands are dealt to all of the players.

When deciding how to play your hand there are also three other options available to you besides standing or hitting. The first is called ***doubling down*** and most casinos will allow a player to double their bet on their first two cards and draw only one more card. To do this you would place an amount equal to your original bet right next to it and then the dealer would give you one more card, sideways, to indicate that your bet was a double down. To double down in a game where the cards are dealt face down you would turn up your original two cards and tell the dealer you wanted to double down. Then, after you double your bet, the dealer would give you one more card face down. Some casinos may have restrictions on this bet and may only allow you to double down if the total of your 2 cards is 10 or 11, but it's always to your advantage if they allow you to double down on any two cards.

Another thing you can do is ***split*** your cards if you have a pair and then play each card as a separate hand. For example, if you had a pair of 8's you would place a bet equal to your original bet right next to it and tell the dealer you wanted to split your pair. The dealer would then separate your two 8's and give you one card on your first 8. Unlike doubling down, however, you are not limited to only getting one card and you can play your hand out normally. When you were finished with your first hand the dealer would then give you a card on your other 8 and you would play that hand out. Although I said that you weren't limited to just one card on your splits there is one instance where that will happen and that's when you split aces. Virtually all casinos will only give you one card on each ace when you split them. Also, if you get a 10-value card with your ace it will only count as 21 and not as a blackjack so you'll only get even money on that bet if you win. Besides splitting pairs you can also split all 10-value cards such as jack-king or 10-queen but it would be a very bad idea to do that because you would be breaking up a 20 which is a very strong hand and you should never split 10's. By the way, if you wanted to split a pair in a casino where the cards are dealt face down you would simply turn your original 2 cards face-up and then tell the dealer that you wanted to split them.

The last option you have is not available in most casinos but you may come across it in a few Las Vegas Strip casinos and it's called ***surrender***. With the surrender option you're allowed to lose half of your bet if you decide you don't want to play out your hand after looking at your first 2 cards. Let's say you're dealt a 10-6 for a total of 16 and the dealer has a 10 as his face-up card. A 16 is not a very strong hand, especially against a dealer's 10, so in this case it would be a good idea to surrender your hand and when the dealer came to your cards you would say "surrender." The dealer would then take half of your bet and remove your cards. Surrender is good for the player because in the long run you will lose less on the bad hands you're dealt and you should always try to play in a casino that offers the surrender option.

All right, we've covered the basics of how to play the game of blackjack and all of the possible options a player has, so the next question is how do you win? Well, the best way to win is to become a card counter, but for the average person that isn't always possible so let's start off by taking a look at basic blackjack strategy.

Computer studies have been done on the game of blackjack and millions of hands have been analyzed to come up with a basic formula for how to play your hand in any given situation. The main principle that these decisions are based on is the dealer's up card because, remember that the dealer has no say in whether or not he takes a card - he must play by the rules that require him to draw a card until he has a total of 17 or more. Now, according to these computer calculations the dealer will bust more often when his up card is a 2,3,4,5 or 6 and he will complete more hands when his up card is a 7,8,9,10-value card or an ace. Take a look at the following chart that shows how each up-card affects the dealer's chance of busting:

Chance The Dealer's Up Card Will Bust

2	35%
3	38%
4	40%
5	43%
6	42%
7	26%
8	24%
9	23%
10	21%
Ace	11%

As you can see, the dealer will bust most often when he has a 5 or 6 as his upcard and he will bust the least amount, approximately 11% of the time, when his upcard is an ace. This means it's to your advantage to stand more often when the dealer's upcard is a 2 through 6 and hope that the dealer will draw cards that make him bust. It also means that when the dealer's upcard is a 7 through ace he will complete more of his hands and in that situation you should draw cards until you have a total of 17 or more.

Now let's show you how to play your hands by using the basic strategy and we'll start off with the ***hard hand*** strategy and by hard hand I mean a 2-card total without an ace. A hand with an ace is known as a soft hand because the ace can be counted as either a 1 or an 11. So, if you had an ace-6 you would have a soft 17 hand and if you had a 10-6 you would have a hard 16 hand. Later on we'll take a look at how to play soft hands, but for now we'll concentrate on the hard hand totals. Oh yes, one more thing, the basic strategy I'm going to give you applies to casinos where they deal more than one deck at a time and the dealer stands on soft 17 which is the situation you'll find in the majority of casinos today. So, keep in mind that the strategy would be slightly different if you were playing against a single deck and it would also be slightly different if the dealer hit a soft 17.

Whenever your first 2 cards total 17 through 21, you should stand, no matter what the dealer's up card is.

If your cards total 16, you should stand if the dealer has a 2 through 6 as his upcard otherwise, draw a card. By the way, 16 is the worst hand you can have because you will bust more often with 16 than with any other hand. So, if that's the case then why would you want to ever hit a 16? Well, once again, those computer studies have shown that you should hit a 16 when the dealer has 7 through ace as his upcard because in the long run you will lose less often. This means that yes, 16 is a terrible hand, but you should hit it because if you don't you will lose even more often than when you do take a card.

If your cards total 15, you should also stand if the dealer has a 2 through 6 as his upcard otherwise, draw cards until your total is 17 or more.

The same rules from 15 and 16 also apply if your cards total 14. Stand if the dealer has a 2 through 6, otherwise draw cards until your total is 17 or more. The same rules also apply if your cards total 13. Stand if the dealer has a 2 through 6, otherwise draw cards until your total is 17 or more.

When your cards total 12 you should only stand when the dealer has a 4,5 or 6 as his upcard, remember - those are his 3 weakest cards and he will bust more often with those cards, so you don't want to take a chance on busting yourself. If the dealer's upcard is a 2 or a 3, then you should take just one card and stop on your total of 13 or more. Finally, if the dealer has a 7 through ace as his upcard then you should draw cards until your total is 17 or more.

When your cards total 11 you would always want to hit it because you can't bust, but before you ask for a card you should consider making a double down bet. If the casino allows you to double down then you should do that if the dealer has anything but an ace as his upcard. After you double down the dealer would give you just one additional card on that hand. If the dealer's upcard is an ace then you shouldn't double down. Instead, you should hit the hand and continue to draw until your total is 17 or more. If the casino doesn't allow you to double down then you should just hit your hand and then, depending on your total, play it by the rules I gave you for the hands that totaled 12 through 21. So, if you had an 11 and the dealer had a 5 as his upcard, you should take a card. Then let's say you draw an ace which gives you a total of 12. Well, as I said before, if you have a 12 against a dealer's 5 you should stand and that's how you should play that hand.

If your total is 10 you would, once again, want to double down unless the dealer showed an ace or a 10. If the dealer had an ace or a 10 as his upcard you should hit your hand and then use the standard rules for a hand valued at 12 through 21. So, if you had a 10 and the dealer had an 8 as his up card you would want to double down and take one more card. If you weren't allowed to double, then you would take a hit and let's say you got a 4 for a total of 14. You should then continue to hit your hand until your total is 17 or more.

If your total is 9 you would want to double down whenever the dealer was showing a 3,4,5 or 6 as his upcard. If the dealer had a 2 as his upcard, or if he had a 7 through ace as his upcard, you should hit your hand and then use the standard playing rules as discussed before. So, let's say you had a 9 and the dealer had a 4 as his upcard you would want to double down and take one more card. If you weren't allowed to double then you should take a hit and let's say you got a 2 for a total of 11, you would then take another hit and let's say you got an ace. That would give you a total of 12 and, as I showed you previously, you should stand on 12 against a dealer's 4.

Finally, if your total is 8 or less you should always take a card and then use the standard playing rules that we already discussed.

Now, let's take a look at splitting pairs, but keep in mind that the rules for splitting will change slightly depending on whether or not the casino will allow you to double down after you split your cards. Most multiple deck games allow you to double down after splitting so that's the situation we'll cover first and then I'll tell you about the changes if you're not allowed to double down after splitting.

Basic Strategy - Single Deck

Dealer stands on soft 17 • Double on any 2 cards • Double allowed after split

Your	Dealer's Upcard									
Hand	**2**	**3**	**4**	**5**	**6**	**7**	**8**	**9**	**10**	**A**
17	ALWAYS STAND ON HARD 17 (OR MORE)									
16	-	-	-	-	-	H	H	H	H*	H
15	-	-	-	-	-	H	H	H	H*	H
14	-	-	-	-	-	H	H	H	H	H
13	-	-	-	-	-	H	H	H	H	H
12	H	H	-	-	-	H	H	H	H	H
11	ALWAYS DOUBLE									
10	D	D	D	D	D	D	D	D	H	H
9	D	D	D	D	D	H	H	H	H	H
8	H	H	H	D	D	H	H	H	H	H
A,8	-	-	-	-	D	-	-	-	-	-
A,7	-	D	D	D	D	-	-	H	H	-
A,6	D	D	D	D	D	H	H	H	H	H
A,5	H	H	D	D	D	H	H	H	H	H
A,4	H	H	D	D	D	H	H	H	H	H
A,3	H	H	D	D	D	H	H	H	H	H
A,2	H	H	D	D	D	H	H	H	H	H
A,A	ALWAYS SPLIT									
10,10	ALWAYS STAND (NEVER SPLIT)									
9,9	Sp	Sp	Sp	Sp	Sp	-	Sp	Sp	-	-
8,8	ALWAYS SPLIT									
7,7	Sp	Sp	Sp	Sp	Sp	Sp	**Sp**	H	-*	H
6,6	Sp	Sp	Sp	Sp	Sp	**Sp**	H	H	H	H
5,5	NEVER SPLIT (PLAY AS 10 HAND)									
4,4	H	H	**Sp**	**Sp**	**Sp**	H	H	H	H	H
3,3	**Sp**	**Sp**	Sp	Sp	Sp	Sp	Sp	H	H	H
2,2	**Sp**	H	Sp	Sp	Sp	Sp	H	H	H	H

- =Stand H=Hit D=Double Sp=Split *= Surrender if allowed

shaded boxes show strategy changes from chart on next page

Basic Strategy - Single Deck

Dealer stands on soft 17 • Double on any 2 cards • Double NOT allowed after split

Your Hand	Dealer's Upcard									
	2	**3**	**4**	**5**	**6**	**7**	**8**	**9**	**10**	**A**
17	ALWAYS STAND ON HARD 17 (OR MORE)									
16	-	-	-	-	-	H	H	H	H*	H*
15	-	-	-	-	-	H	H	H	H*	H
14	-	-	-	-	-	H	H	H	H	H
13	-	-	-	-	-	H	H	H	H	H
12	H	H	-	-	-	H	H	H	H	H
11	ALWAYS DOUBLE									
10	D	D	D	D	D	D	D	D	H	H
9	D	D	D	D	D	H	H	H	H	H
8	H	H	H	D	D	H	H	H	H	H
A,8	-	-	-	-	D	-	-	-	-	-
A,7	-	D	D	D	D	-	-	H	H	-
A,6	D	D	D	D	D	H	H	H	H	H
A,5	H	H	D	D	D	H	H	H	H	H
A,4	H	H	D	D	D	H	H	H	H	H
A,3	H	H	D	D	D	H	H	H	H	H
A,2	H	H	D	D	D	H	H	H	H	H
A,A	ALWAYS SPLIT									
10,10	NEVER SPLIT (ALWAYS STAND)									
9,9	Sp	Sp	Sp	Sp	Sp	-	Sp	Sp	-	-
8,8	ALWAYS SPLIT									
7,7	Sp	Sp	Sp	Sp	Sp	Sp	H	H	-*	H
6,6	Sp	Sp	Sp	Sp	Sp	H	H	H	H	H
5,5	NEVER SPLIT (PLAY AS 10 HAND)									
4,4	NEVER SPLIT (PLAY AS 8 HAND)									
3,3	H	H	Sp	Sp	Sp	Sp	H	H	H	H
2,2	H	Sp	Sp	Sp	Sp	Sp	H	H	H	H

- =Stand H=Hit D=Double Sp=Split *= Surrender if allowed

Basic Strategy - Multiple Decks

Dealer stands on soft 17 • Double on any 2 cards • Double allowed after split

Your Hand	Dealer's Upcard									
	2	3	4	5	6	7	8	9	10	A
17	ALWAYS STAND ON 17 (OR MORE)									
16	-	-	-	-	-	H	H	H*	H*	H*
15	-	-	-	-	-	H	H	H	H*	H
14	-	-	-	-	-	H	H	H	H	H
13	-	-	-	-	-	H	H	H	H	H
12	H	H	-	-	-	H	H	H	H	H
11	D	D	D	D	D	D	D	D	D	H
10	D	D	D	D	D	D	D	D	H	H
9	H	D	D	D	D	H	H	H	H	H
8	ALWAYS HIT 8 (OR LESS)									
A,8	ALWAYS STAND ON SOFT 19 (OR MORE)									
A,7	-	D	D	D	D	-	-	H	H	H
A,6	H	D	D	D	D	H	H	H	H	H
A,5	H	H	D	D	D	H	H	H	H	H
A,4	H	H	D	D	D	H	H	H	H	H
A,3	H	H	H	D	D	H	H	H	H	H
A,2	H	H	H	D	D	H	H	H	H	H
A,A	ALWAYS SPLIT									
10,10	ALWAYS STAND (NEVER SPLIT)									
9,9	Sp	Sp	Sp	Sp	Sp	-	Sp	Sp	-	-
8,8	ALWAYS SPLIT									
7,7	Sp	Sp	Sp	Sp	Sp	Sp	H	H	H	H
6,6	Sp	Sp	Sp	Sp	Sp	H	H	H	H	H
5,5	D	D	D	D	D	D	D	D	H	H
4,4	H	H	H	Sp	Sp	H	H	H	H	H
3,3	Sp	Sp	Sp	Sp	Sp	Sp	H	H	H	H
2,2	Sp	Sp	Sp	Sp	Sp	Sp	H	H	H	H

- =Stand H=Hit D=Double Sp=Split *= Surrender if allowed

Basic Strategy - Multiple Decks

Dealer stands on soft 17 • Double on any 2 cards • Double NOT allowed after split

Your Hand	Dealer's Upcard									
	2	3	4	5	6	7	8	9	10	A
17	ALWAYS STAND ON HARD 17 (OR MORE)									
16	-	-	-	-	-	H	H	H*	H*	H*
15	-	-	-	-	-	H	H	H	H*	H
14	-	-	-	-	-	H	H	H	H	H
13	-	-	-	-	-	H	H	H	H	H
12	H	H	-	-	-	H	H	H	H	H
11	D	D	D	D	D	D	D	D	D	H
10	D	D	D	D	D	D	D	D	H	H
9	H	D	D	D	D	H	H	H	H	H
8	ALWAYS HIT 8 (OR LESS)									
A,8	ALWAYS STAND ON SOFT 19 (OR MORE)									
A,7	-	D	D	D	D	-	-	H	H	H
A,6	H	D	D	D	D	H	H	H	H	H
A,5	H	H	D	D	D	H	H	H	H	H
A,4	H	H	D	D	D	H	H	H	H	H
A,3	H	H	H	D	D	H	H	H	H	H
A,2	H	H	H	D	D	H	H	H	H	H
A,A	ALWAYS SPLIT									
10,10	ALWAYS STAND (NEVER SPLIT)									
9,9	Sp	Sp	Sp	Sp	Sp	-	Sp	Sp	-	-
8,8	ALWAYS SPLIT									
7,7	Sp	Sp	Sp	Sp	Sp	Sp	H	H	H	H
6,6	**H**	Sp	Sp	Sp	Sp	H	H	H	H	H
5,5	NEVER SPLIT (PLAY AS 10 HAND)									
4,4	H	H	H	**H**	**H**	H	H	H	H	H
3,3	**H**	**H**	Sp	Sp	Sp	Sp	H	H	H	H
2,2	**H**	**H**	Sp	Sp	Sp	Sp	H	H	H	H

- =Stand H=Hit D=Double Sp=Split *= Surrender if allowed

shaded boxes show strategy changes from chart on previous page

As I said earlier, when your first two cards are the same most casinos will allow you to split them and play them as two separate hands so let's go over the basic strategy rules on when you should do this.

The first thing you should remember is that you always split aces and 8's. The reason you split aces is obvious because if you get a 10 on either hand you'll have a perfect 21, but remember that you won't get paid for a blackjack at 3-to-2, instead it'll be counted as a regular 21 and you'll be paid at even money. If you have a pair of 8's you have 16 which is a terrible hand and you can always improve it by splitting your 8's and playing them as separate hands.

The next thing to remember about splitting pairs is that you never split 5's or 10's. Once again, the reasons should be rather obvious, you don't want to split 10's because 20 is a great hand and you don't want to split 5's because 10 is a great hand to draw to. Instead, you would want to double down on that 10, unless the dealer was showing a 10 or an ace as his upcard.

2's, 3's and 7's should only be split when the dealer is showing a 2 through 7 as his upcard. Split 4's only when the dealer has a 5 or 6 as his upcard (remember 5 and 6 are his weakest cards!), 6's should be split whenever the dealer is showing a 2 through 6 and finally, you should always split 9's unless the dealer is showing a 7, 10 or ace. The reason you don't want to split 9's against a 10 or an ace should be rather obvious, but the reason you don't want to split them against a 7 is in case the dealer has a 10 as his hole card because in that case your 18 would beat out his 17.

If the casino will not allow you to double down after splitting then you should make the following three changes: For 2's and 3's only split them against a 4,5,6 or 7; never split 4's; and for a pair of 6's only split them against a 3,4,5 or 6. Everything else should be played the same.

Now, let's take a look at how to play ***soft hands*** and remember a soft hand is any hand that contains an ace that can be counted as 1 or 11. For a soft hand of 19 or more you should always stand.

For soft 18 against a 2,7 or 8 you should always stand. If the dealer shows a 9, 10 or an ace you should always take a hit and for a soft 18 against a 3,4,5 or 6 you should double down, but if the casino won't allow you to double then you should just stand.

For soft 17 you should always take a hit, but if the casino allows you to double down, then you should double against a dealer's 3,4,5 or 6.

For soft 16 or a soft 15 you should always take a hit, but if the casino allows you to double down then you should double against a dealer's 4,5 or 6.

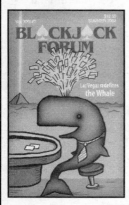

For soft 14 you should always take a hit, but if the casino allows you to double down then you should double against a dealer's 5 or 6.

Finally, for a soft 13 you should always take a hit, but if the casino allows you to double down then you should double against a dealer's 5 or 6.

The last thing we need to cover is surrender which, as noted before, isn't offered in many casinos but it is an option that does work in your favor and if available, you should play in a casino that offers it. The surrender rules are very simple to remember and only apply to hard totals of 15 or 16. If you have a hard 16 you should surrender it whenever the dealer has a 9, 10 or ace as his upcard and if you have a hard 15 you should surrender it whenever the dealer has a 10 as his upcard. That's all there is to surrender.

Now that you know how to play the game and you have an understanding of the basic strategy let's take a quick look at how the rules variations can affect the game of blackjack. As noted before, various computer studies have been made on blackjack and these studies have shown that each rule change can either hurt or help the player by a certain amount. For example, a single-deck game where you can double on any first 2 cards (but not after splitting pairs), the dealer stands on soft 17 and no surrender is allowed has no advantage for the casino when using the basic strategy. That's right, in a game with those rules in effect the game is dead even and neither the casino nor the player has an edge!

Take a look at the following chart and you'll see how some rules changes can hurt you or help you as a player. Minus signs in front mean that the casino gains the edge by that particular amount while plus signs mean that you gain the edge by that amount.

RULES THAT HURT YOU		RULES THAT HELP YOU	
Two decks	-0.32%	Double after split	+0.13%
Four decks	-0.49%	Late surrender	+0.06%
Six decks	-0.54%	Resplit Aces	+0.14%
Eight decks	-0.57%	Double anytime	+0.20%
Dealer hits soft 17	-0.20%		
No soft doubling	-0.14%		

As you can see, it's always to your advantage to play against as few decks as possible. The house edge goes up substantially as you go from 1 deck to 2, but the change is less dramatic when you go from 2 to 4, or from 4 to 6, and it's barely noticeable when you go from 6 to 8. You can also see that you would prefer not to play in a casino where the dealer hits a soft 17 because that gives the dealer a slight edge. You would also want to play in a casino where you're allowed to double down on your soft hands or else you would be giving another added edge to the casino.

You can also see from these charts that you would want to play in a casino where you were allowed to double down after splitting cards and you would also want to play in a casino that offered surrender. The other two rules variations that help the player are somewhat rare but they were put in to show you how these rules changes can affect your odds in the game. Some casinos will allow you to resplit aces again if you draw an ace to one of your original aces and this works to your advantage. Also, some casinos will allow you to double down on any number of cards rather than just the first two. In other words, if you got a 2- 4-3-2 as your first four cards you would then be allowed to double down on your total of 11 before receiving your 5th card. If they allow you to do this then, once again, you have a rule that works in your favor.

The point of showing you these charts is to help you understand that when you have a choice of places to play you should always choose the casino that offers the best rules. So, if you find a single-deck game with good rules you could be playing an even game by using the basic strategy, or at worst be giving the casino an edge of less than one-half of 1%.

Now, there is one way that you can actually have the edge working in your favor when you play blackjack and that's by becoming a card counter. As I said before, card counting is not for the average person but I do think it's important that you understand the concept of card counting and if you think you'd like to learn more about counting cards then it's something you can follow up on later.

Many people think that to be a card counter you have to have a photographic memory and remember every single card that's been played. Fortunately, it's not quite that difficult. Actually, the main concept behind card counting is the assumption that the dealer will bust more often when there are a lot of 10's in the deck and that he will complete more hands when there are a lot of smaller cards in the deck. Now, if you stop to think about it, it makes sense doesn't it? After all, the dealer has to play by set rules that make him take a card until he has a total of 17 or more. If there are a lot of 2's, 3's and 4's in the deck the dealer won't bust very often when he draws cards, but if there are a lot of 10's in the deck then chances are he will bust more often when he is forced to draw cards.

The card counter tries to take advantage of this fact by keeping a running total of the cards that have been played to give him an idea of what kind of cards remain in the deck. If there are a lot of 10 cards remaining in the deck then the counter will bet more money because the odds are slightly in his favor. Of course, if there are a lot of small cards remaining then the counter would only make a small bet because the odds would be slightly in favor of the dealer. Another thing that the card counter can do is to change his basic strategy to take advantage of the differences in the deck.

There are at least a dozen different card counting systems but let's take a quick look at a relatively simple one (it's also the most popular) and it's called the high-low count. With this system you assign a value of +1 to all 2's, 3's, 4's, 5's and 6's, while all 10's, Jacks, Queens, Kings and Aces are assigned a value of -1. The remaining cards: 7, 8 and 9 have no value and are not counted.

+1 = 2, 3, 4, 5, 6
-1 = 10, J, Q, K, A

When you look at these numbers you'll see that there are an equal number of cards in each group: there are five cards valued at +1 and five cards valued at -1. This means that they balance each other out and if you go through the deck and add them all together the end result will always be a total of exactly zero.

What a card counter does is to keep a running total of all the cards as they're played out and whenever the total has a plus value he knows that a lot of small cards have appeared and the remaining deck is rich in 10's which is good for the player. But, if the total is a minus value then the counter knows that a lot of 10-value cards have appeared and the remaining deck must be rich in low cards which is bad for the player. To give you an example of how to count let's say the following cards have been dealt on the first hand from a single deck:

2, 3, 3, 4, 5, 5, 5, 6, = +8
J, K, Q, A, = -4
Total = +4

As you can see, there were eight plus-value cards and four minus-value cards which resulted in a total count of +4. This means that there are now four more 10-value cards than low cards remaining in the deck and the advantage is with the player. Naturally, the higher the plus count, the more advantageous it is for the player and counters would be proportionally increasing their bets as the count got higher. The card counter would also be using the same basic strategy we spoke about previously, except for certain instances where a slight change would be called for.

On the other hand, if the count is negative, a card counter will always bet the minimum amount. Of course, they would prefer not to bet at all, but the casinos don't like you to sit at their tables and not bet so the counter has to bet something and the minimum is the least they can get by with.

There is one more important thing to explain about card counting and it's called the ***true count***. The true count is a measure of the count per deck rather than a ***running count*** of all the cards that have been played and to get the true count you simply divide the running count by the number of decks remaining to be played. As an illustration, let's say you're playing in a 6-deck game and the count is +9. You look at the shoe and estimate that 3 decks remain to be played. You then divide the count of +9 by 3 to get +3 which is the true count. As another example, let's say you're in an 8-deck game with a count of +12 and there are 6 decks left to be played. You divide +12 by 6 to get +2 which is the true count. To put it another way, a +2 count in a double-deck game with 1 deck left to be played is the same as a +4 count in a 4-deck game with 2 decks left to be played, which is the same as a +6 count is a 6-deck game with 3 decks left to be played, which is the same as a +12 count in an 8-deck game with 6 decks left to be played.

For the card counter it is crucial to always take the running count and then divide it by the number of decks remaining in order to get the true count because all betting and playing decisions are based on the true count rather than the running count.

Of course, if you're playing in a single-deck game the running count and the true count are initially the same. The more you get into the deck, however, the more weight is given to the running count because there is less than one deck remaining. So, if the running count was +3 and only a 1/2-deck remained you would calculate the true count by dividing +3 by 1/2 (which is the same as multiplying by 2/1, or 2) to get a true count of +6. As another example, if the running count was +2 and about 2/3 of the deck remained you would divide +2 by 2/3 (the same as multi-plying by 3/2 or, 1 and 1/2) to get +3.

As you can see, the count becomes much more meaningful as you get closer to the last cards in the deck and that's why casinos never deal down to the end. Instead, the dealer will insert a plastic card about 2/3 or 3/4 of the way in the deck and when that card is reached the dealer will finish that particular round and then shuffle the cards. How far into the deck(s) that plastic card is inserted is known as the ***penetration point*** and card counters always look for a dealer that offers good penetration. The card counter knows that the further into the deck(s) the plastic card is placed the more meaningful the true count will be and the more advantageous it will be for the card counter.

So, now that you know how those card counters keep track of the cards, what kind of advantage do you think they have over the casino? Well, not too much. Depending on the number of decks used, the rules in force, and the skill of the counter, it could be as much as 2% but that would be at the high end. Probably 1% would be closer to the actual truth. This means that for every $1,000 in bets that are made the card counter will win $10. Not exactly a huge amount but there are people out there who do make a living playing the game.

If you would like to learn more about blackjack, as well as more about card counting, be sure to take a look at the some of the ads in this book for ordering information on some very helpful books, newsletters, videos and computer software.

When Good Games Go Bad

by John Grochowski

Table pits are full of games that are basically good - easy to learn, fun to play and with house edges that are low enough to give you a decent run for your money. But good games can go bad. Some casino operators aren't satisfied with the steady flow of chips from your side of the table to theirs. They toughen the rules, shorten the payouts and turn these friendly seeming games into bankroll muggers. What then? What do you do when your good game has transformed into an evil twin? Well, first you have to recognize what has gone wrong. Then you have to stay away. Let's take a look at the rap sheets of some good games gone bad.

Three Card Poker: In its original version, this stud poker-based game seems mild-mannered enough. On play against the dealer, the house edge is 3.37% of the ante or 2.01% of total action, taking into consideration the bet equal to the ante made by players who like their cards. In the Pair Plus bet, which pays off whenever the player has a pair or better, the house edge is 2.32%. That's pretty good by standards of new games. The house edge is higher than those on baccarat, the best bets in craps and blackjack against a basic strategy player. But then again, house edges on some craps bets are as high as 16.67%, and an average blackjack player faces a house edge of 2% to 2.5% that's right in the ballpark with the edge on Three Card Poker.

It's a friendly little game, one just about anyone can pick up in a hand or three. Pair Plus takes no strategy, and strategy on play against the dealer is about as easy as it gets - follow your ante with a bet any time you have Queen-6-4 or better, and fold lesser hands.

So what can turn this easy-going test of luck and skill into a money-grubbing monster? It starts with the bonus payoffs on play vs. the dealer. In the original version of Three Card Poker, not only do you win even money on your ante-bet combination if your hand beat a dealer's qualifying hand, or on the ante if the dealer failed to qualify with a queen or better, but there is bonus payoff of five times your ante if you're dealt a straight flush, four times your ante for three of a kind and equal to your ante on a straight. Casinos that want your money a little bit quicker reduce payoffs to 4-1 on straight flushes and 3-1 on three of a kind, increasing their edge to 2.28% of the ante and 3.83% of total action.

Others take it down another notch, paying only 3-1 on straight flushes and 2-1 on three of a kind, raising their edge to 2.56% of the ante and 4.28% of total action.

That's really small potatoes, kind of a misdemeanor bankroll assault. The full scale attack comes in Pair Plus. The original pay table designed by Englishman Derek Webb pays 40-1 on a straight flush, 30-1 on three of a kind, 6-1 on a straight, 4-1 on a flush and even money on a pair. Since Shufflemaster has taken over the game from Webb, several new pay tables have popped up. One drops three of a kind payoffs to 25-1, raising the house edge to 3.49%. Another drops straight flushes to 35-1 to go with the reduced pay on three of a kind. That ups the house edge to 4.58%.

But the real bad boy of Three Card Poker is a Pair Plus pay table that leaves the straight flush and three of a kind pays at their maximum level, but reduces flushes to 3-1. Three-card flushes occur about once per 20 hands, compared with once per 460 hands for straight flushes and once per 425 hands for three of a kind. A reduced payoff on flushes affects far more hands than reduced payoffs on straight flushes and three of a kinds combined. And that magnifies the effect on the house edge, sending it soaring to a whopping 7.28%.

Instead of the house taking an average of $2.32 per $100 wagered, it takes $7.28. Instead of average losses for a $5 bettor playing 50 hands an hour being $5.80, they're $18.18. That's no misdemeanor assault. That's full-scale bankroll battery.

Let It Ride: Many new table games were designed to entice players with the promise of a big jackpot, a promise that works so well in attacting players to slot machines. But the thought of actually paying a big jackpot makes some operators twitchy. The result is Let It Ride is called an "aggregate limit," which seems to closely resemble a bait-and-switch. What happens is that the table felt will show a 1,000-1 payoff on a royal flush, the same as at almost any other Let It Ride table. But if you bet too much, you'll not get the full payoff.

Let's say the casino places a $15,000 aggregate limit on payoffs - a situation I've seen. If you bet $5 on each of the three spots and wind up with a royal flush, you get paid your $15,000. But what if you bet $10 on each spot? You should get $30,000, but you don't. You just get $15,000.

To compound the problem, not every casino that uses an aggregate limit advertises the fact. It's not always on the sign with betting limits and house rules. If you ask if there's an aggregate limit, they have to tell you, but if you don't you'll never know - unless you hit the big one and find yourself the bait-and-switch victim.

Your best defense: Ask if there's an aggregate limit before you play. If there is, keep your bets small enough that you'll get the full payoff should you be lucky enough to hit a royal.

The aggregate limit isn't the only tool of mayhem toward your bankroll in Let It Ride. There's also the side bet in the Bonus version of the game. Players make a $1 side bet in addition to their bets on the regular game, then get paid a bonus if their hands are good enough.

Bonus Let It Ride comes with a confusing array of pay tables. Some pay $20,000 on a royal flush, some only $10,000. Some pay $6 on two pair, some pay $4, some pay $3 and some don't pay anything at all. Two pair is where most versions start payoffs, but a few start with a high pair, and a few start at three of a kind.

Straights are stable with $25 payoffs, and flushes are stable at $50, but otherwise there is confusion, with differing payoffs on every possible winning hand.

When all the confusion clears, one fact is left standing. There's not just one pickpocket here. Every single version stands ready to lighten your wallet. In the best version of the bonus bet, payoffs are $20,000 for a royal flush, $2,000 for a straight flush, $100 for four of a kind, $75 for a full house, $50 for a flush, $25 for a straight, $9 for three of a kind and $6 for two pair. The house edge: 13.77%. Got that? The house keeps $13.77 out of every $100 you bet, and that's the good version.

How bad can it get? One pay table starts with $20,000 for a royal, then goes to $1,000 for a straight flush, $300 for four of a kind, $150 for a full house, $50 for a flush, $25 for a straight, just $5 for three of a kind and nothing - not a dime - for two pair. The house edge: 36.52%. You might as well write the casino a check and make better use of your time. Compare that to the house edges of 3.5% of one bet or 2.8% of the ante on the basic Let It Ride game. Your best strategy to avoid a bankroll mugging? Skip the bonus bets, and play the basic game - after you've determined there is no aggregate limit.

Blackjack: Any experienced blackjack player knows about the main weapons the casino has in its arsenal. Anytime the casino hits soft 17, limits the hands on which the player can double down or prohibits doubling down after splitting pairs, it siphons off the cash a little faster.

The give-and-take of good/bad house rules has been with us for decades. But in recent years, table games managers have become edgy over their blackjack profits. There are enough customers who play reasonably well that casinos don't make their money as fast off blackjack as they do off Caribbean Stud, Let It Ride, Three Card Poker and other games in which player strategy can't take as big a bite off the house edge. With table games space ever-shrinking as slot machines continue to gain in popularity, casino operators look to put more bite in their most popular table game.

Take continuous shufflers. Please. These don't change the odds of the game. A player won't lose any more money per $100 wagered with continuous shufflers than with hand-shuffles or automatic shufflers that are not continuous. Continuous shufflers are a more insidious attack on your wallet. They speed up the game. With no breaks for shuffles, you play more hands per hour, bet more money per hour and give the house edge extra time to work against you. Casinos take a more direct approach with a recent wrinkle. Some houses are now paying only 6-5 on blackjacks instead of the traditional 3-2. If you wager $5 and are are dealt a blackjack, your payoff would be only $6 instead of the traditional $7.50.

That makes a bigger difference than you might think. Blackjacks occur about once per 21 hands, meaning the rule comes into play about two to three times per hour for each player at a full table, and up to 10 times an hour for a customer playing head-to-head with the dealer.

That adds about 1.4% to the house edge, and in blackjack, that's huge. With the 6-5 rule, the average player faces a house edge of 3.4% to 3.9%, instead of the usual 2 to 2.5. This single rule quadruples or more the house edge against a basic strategy player, who can cut the house edge to .2% or so on many single-deck or double-deck games and .5% - plus or minus a tenth or two - on six-deck games.

If you think that's a holdup, well, beware of games bearing gifts. A blackjack variation called Super Fun 21 looks like a dream game at first glance:

* Cards are dealt from a single deck.
* Players may double down on any number of cards, including after splitting pairs.

* After the dealer has checked for blackjack, player may surrender half the bet instead of finishing the hand, even after hitting, splitting or doubling down.
* Any hand totaling 20 or less with six cards pays even money instantly, unless the player has doubled down.
* Any hand totaling 21 with five or more cards pays 2-1 instantly, unless the player has doubled down.
* Player blackjacks always win, even if the dealer also has a blackjack.
* Player blackjacks in diamonds pay 2-1.

Those are extras that'll make a player's eyes light up, even though the dealer hits soft 17. If all else was normal there would be a big player edge at Super Fun. But while holding out the carton of candy in one hand, this game holds a sledgehammer in the other.

** Player blackjacks, except those with two diamonds, pay even money instead of the usual 3-2.

The positive rules limit the carnage, but even so, Super Fun has a house edge of .77% that's roughly quadruple that on most single-deck games, and 1.5 to twice as high as that on most six-deck games.

If that's not enough to entice you away from regular blackjack games, there's always the array of side bets casinos sometimes use to distract you while taking a little extra cash from you:

21 Madness: The player makes a $1 wager in addition to the regular blackjack bet. Then, if the player is dealt a two-card 21, he or she gets to push a button to start a lighted display, which stops to reveal a bonus payoff from $5 to $1,000. This would be a break-even bet if the average payoff was $21. We don't know for sure what the average is - the lighted display is governed by a slot machine-like random number generator. But observation by a team in Australia suggests the average is $16, which would leave a house edge of 23.8%. That's not necessarily the case here. The average payoff could be higher or lower. Still, this looks like a bet to leave alone.

Progressive Blackjack: Mikohn Gaming, which distributes Caribbean Stud, Caribbean Draw and other table games with progressive jackpots, developed this side bet that pays off according to the number of aces in the player's hand. It involves a $1 bet in addition to a regular blackjack wager. The player is paid $3 if the hand includes one ace, $15 for two aces of different suits, $50 for two suited aces, $200 for three unsuited aces, $1,000 for three suited aces, $2,000 for four unsuited aces and the progressive jackpot, which starts at $25,000 for four red or four black aces. At the beginning jackpot of $25,000, the house edge is a lofty 53%. Ouch.

Royal Match: The side bet pays off if the player's first two cards are of the same suit, with a larger payoff for King-Queen of the same suit - a "Royal Match." The most common version pays 2.5-1 on most matches, and 25-1 on a royal match. Suited hands are more common with more decks in play, so the house edge at Royal Match actually decreases as the number of decks increase. With six decks, the edge is 6.7%. In a single-deck game, the house edge is 10.9%.

There are other side bets, but you get the idea. They exist to take your focus off the better game - regular blackjack - and switch it onto the fool's gold of promised riches. To your self-defense kit in protecting yourself from the casino aresnal, add "Skip the side bets." Watch the Three Card Poker pay tables. Ask about aggregate limits in Let It Ride. Stick to regular blackjack. Skip the side bets. Don't fall victim to good games gone bad.

John Grochowski is the gaming columnist for the "Chicago Sun-Times" and a contributing writer to many gaming magazines. John is also the author of several books on casino gambling.

Meet The "King" Of Card Counters

by Steve Bourie

Blackjack is the most popular table game in any U.S. casino and one of the reasons for its enduring popularity is the fact that the game has a reputation of being "beatable." Naturally, the thought of being able to beat casinos at their own game has driven many players to spend countless hours studying basic strategy charts in the hope that they'll learn how to play their hands properly and be able to win consistently.

Unfortunately, even when playing perfect basic strategy, the average player will still be playing at a disadvantage. Yes, those players will have some sessions where they get lucky and win, but in the long run the odds will catch up with them and they will lose money.

The reality of the situation is that only an experienced card counter can be a long-term winner and, even though the counter should eventually come out with a profit, there are likely to be many losing sessions along the way.

To help lessen the inherent risks in the game, many card counters have found it advantageous to play on teams. By pooling their money they have a bigger bankroll to work with and they can also reduce the volatility of the game by playing at more than one table at a time. Additionally, by having a team they can get in many more hours of play than they would be able to do if they were playing alone.

One of the most successful card counting teams in the world is run by Tommy Hyland. I first saw Hyland about four years ago on the CBS TV show "48 Hours." They did a segment on card counters and, through the use of a hidden camera, Hyland was shown being ejected from a major Las Vegas Strip casino by a pit boss who recognized him as a counter.

I must admit that I was intrigued by the video footage and through the years I continued to hear from various sources about Hyland's success with his card counting teams. I thought an interview with Hyland would be interesting and, through some mutual friends, I eventually got to meet him. He agreed to the interview and the following conversation took place in Las Vegas in early 2003.

When did you first get involved in blackjack ?

It was 1979. I was going to school in Ohio and my roommate and I were both interested in gambling. We happened to be in a mall one day and we saw Revere's book "Playing Blackjack as a Business." We got it and read it and then we started practicing. We started going to Atlantic City once in a while and it kind of went from there. I basically started playing full-time in April 1979.

Did you make money right away when you first started?

Pretty much. I didn't have very much money to start with. I think I had $1,000 or $2,000 but the casinos were offering early surrender, which was a rule that gave you an advantage off the top. After about four or five months I built up my bankroll to $4,000. What really got me going though, was after I taught a friend of mine to play also.

He had a few thousand dollars and we were playing separately, but then we met these other two card counters who were playing small stakes also in Atlantic City and that's how we really got rolling. We each put up $4,000, so now we were playing off of a $16,000 bankroll and we started winning immediately. Way better than we should have and I guess after about a month or so of play, we built the $16,000 up to $60,000. We got really lucky. Then in December 1979 we won a fair amount of money during the famous card counting experiment where the casinos let known card counters play for about two weeks. We won quite a lot during that period.

Was Ken Uston playing at that time?

Yes. At that time there were two casinos open – Resorts and Caesars. We decided to play at Resorts and his group was playing at Caesars so we didn't see that much of him but we would see him occasionally.

Was he a well known card counter at the time?

Yes. When I saw him playing by then, he was in the newspapers, on TV, and the radio all the time. He was the most famous card counter.

Did he know you guys?

Not really, we were playing real small compared to how he was playing, but eventually I got to know him. I probably had lunch or dinner with him five times and talked with him on the phone a few times, stuff like that.

There are some stories about Uston saying that he really wasn't as successful as he professed to be. Do you have any comment on that?

I don't have any firsthand knowledge whether he was a good player. I do know he was a heavy drinker and had some drug problems also.

He died of a drug overdose?

Supposedly. He died in France, you know possible complications from drugs, but I also heard it was a heart attack.

He was certainly a likeable guy, very charismatic. You know a lot of card counters were down on him, saying the games would be a lot better if it wasn't for him. I have the opposite view. I liked the fact that he would sue the casinos, he would go before these gaming commissions and try to win the right for counters to play. I kind of liked that. He wasn't letting the casinos push him around. I think if it wasn't for him, the casinos would have been more abusive than they have been toward counters.

After your initial success there with your four-man team, then what did you do?

Well, two of our guys – Doug and Dave – bought Wong's "Blackjack in Asia" book which talked about some games in Asia that had great rules and no heat (scrutiny from the pit personnel), so they decided to go off to Asia.

I think by this time I had between $50,000 and $100,000 and I thought I was the richest guy in the world even though I was only a 23-year-old kid. I decided to train some more of my friends at the golf course to play. I would put up the money and they would get a percentage of what they won. I trained one or two and we did really well. Luckily, I picked some good guys and they worked out well. Then, things just snowballed unbelievably. Eventually, the team got a little bit out of control.

I would have somebody calling me or asking me to teach them how to play at least once a week. I had a hard time saying no and ultimately, things got a little disorganized. We probably had some slippage (skimming, sloppy play) as a result of that. At this time we had about 30 or 40 people on the team.

You were bankrolling 30 or 40 people?

I was the main investor, but these people would win and they would invest some of their winnings back in the bankroll, and I think we also got some outside people to invest – parents or relatives. It was an evolving thing.

When you say these other people would "invest" does that mean you needed more money for your bankroll? Your initial bankroll wasn't big enough?

Well, we wanted to bet high. There were two main teams around back then: Ken Uston's and the Czech team, a bunch of guys from Czechoslovakia and we were kind of in awe at how high they were betting. We were trying to win money and also get a bankroll to bet as high as they were.

How high would they bet?

They were betting the table maximum at a very small advantage (1/2 of one percent). We wanted to be able to do that too because we had read the books which said that the more you bet the higher your hourly win rate would be.

And the table max was $1,000?

During the experiment it was $1,000 but then they lowered it to $500.

Okay, so you had some success, you expanded, and then it wound up being like 30 or 40 people on your team. What happened next?

What happened was it got a little unwieldy with all these people. Then Atlantic City took out early surrender and that's when the game became a lot harder to beat. You had to be more skilled and more disciplined. I think what happened was that we had our first losing bankroll. We took a little break and some people quit or went off to play on their own. Four or five of us joined up with three other guys that were playing mostly in Vegas.

One of these guys was from Princeton and another guy was from Michigan University. They were real smart guys and we started playing using these advanced techniques, mainly shuffle tracking. There were a lot of real juicy shuffles here in Las Vegas and also in Atlantic City.

What year was this?

This would have been about 1982.

So you formed another team. Did you ever play by yourself?

Not really. Maybe a few months here and there, but I've always pretty much been with a group or a team.

Why do you like teams as opposed to doing it on your own?

There are a lot of reasons that teams are good. Obviously, there are some negatives but I think the positives far outweigh the negatives. The main advantage of having a team is that it really smooths out the fluctuations. I mean, if you play by yourself, it's hard to get enough hours to assure a win. You could play for a year or so, play perfectly, and still be behind. If you have a six or seven man team that's virtually impossible. The other thing is that you can bet a lot higher by pooling your money. If five people have $100,000 you can bet as if you all had $500,000 and that's a huge advantage. There's also a sense of camaraderie and team spirit. I've been fortunate to play with some really creative people. You sit around and bounce different ideas around and you come up with some really good ideas that you wouldn't have come up with on your own.

So when you came out here and joined up with the other guys to form a new team how did you do?

We did really well. Like I said, we were mostly playing shuffles. We were playing a lot in Vegas and a little bit in Atlantic City. We were also traveling around to the Caribbean and in general it went really well. We made quite a bit of money.

How long did that last?

I'm really bad at chronology, but this was 1982 to probably 1990. I still play with some of those same guys today.

It was basically the same team for eight years?

No. It was a bit of a mix because what happened is we would have these little projects where we would have big players come in, so it wasn't like a stagnant thing. There were people constantly in and out and we would actually have 30 or 40 people but a lot of them were part-time.

Some casinos would be offering a really good game and we would look for different ways to exploit it. A lot of these guys had friends and we had this big pool of people that we would have to teach how to do everything. We might have one particular game that we could exploit and we would teach some new guy everything he had to do to beat it. Or, maybe some guy had a good look and a good act, so we would just teach him basic strategy and we could give signals to do all the rest of the stuff. We had a whole host of projects and different schemes to exploit some weakness in a particular casino. We had people coming in and out; somebody would play for us for one year and we would never see them again. We had guys from Australia, China, everywhere. It was an exciting time with a lot of adventure.

What happened to the team in 1990?

Well, what happened was, as we made some pretty good money these other guys lost a lot of their interest in blackjack and they wanted to do other things. One guy went off to do horse racing in Hong Kong. He's famous for that in the gambling circles. Another guy got into the stock market. Some of the guys dabbled in poker for a year or two.

It's really been kind of an ongoing thing, but basically we're still doing the same stuff today. Blackjack is a little tougher right now but some of those original people are still invested in blackjack even though they are doing other things. I have some people who have played for 15 to 20 years and still play pretty much full-time and then I have some others that play part-time. I guess since 1982, it's never like one team has ended and a new one started, it's kind of been an evolving thing with people leaving and coming back.

So, since you first started back in 1979, you've always continued to have teams in one form or another?

Right.

Where are your teams now? Do you play throughout the United States? Is everyone together? Or, do they spread out all over the place?

We don't play as much in Vegas and Atlantic City as we used to. Those games are not as good as elsewhere in the country, so we're spread out all over the country. You know, a lot of people when they hear "blackjack team," they think you all go to the same casino together and you sit on the same table together and play, but that's not what we do. I mean we do have some games with big players and call people in, but we mainly just pool our money and we all go our various ways and we keep track of the results. Then, at a certain agreed upon date, we split the profits. We split the proceeds about every six months.

So each player plays for six months?

Well, the bankroll lasts for six months and then we split it up and start another one. We've done it that way for several years. We used to play to a "money target which meant that we played until we won a certain amount of money. There are advantages and disadvantages of doing it both ways.

If you hit your "money target" before the six months was up, would you stop playing?

That's what I'm saying, we did it two different ways. We used to have a money target and not have a time limit. We would just play until we won that amount of money and that has its advantages too. Everybody's striving for a goal, everybody's trying to hit the target, but it has a lot of disadvantages too. You never know how much money you are going to have and when you'll have it. So, lately we've been doing it by the time target. Play for six months and then investors get a share, players get a share, stuff like that.

Do you always make money?

No. We've had some devastating bankrolls where you lose for quite a while. Basically, we've been pretty successful, but we've had some rough times where you have a nice chunk of money and you thought you'd never have to worry again and then, suddenly, you're almost broke.

How rare is it to lose money after a six month period?

It's pretty rare...but it does happen. The whole key is getting in a lot of hours. If you get in a lot of hours and the people are honest, you basically cannot lose. A lot of players now are part-time and we aren't getting in that many hours and I think out of the last three years we only lost money in one of the six-month periods

How many people are on your team?

About 15. A lot of these are part-time and there are about five or six people that play full-time. I also make some temporary arrangements with people that I know are good players. I have a couple guys coming out for the Super Bowl and they may not play again until the next Super Bowl. We just have a certain arrangement for that weekend.

But mostly your team is spread out all over the country?

Right.

Do you play yourself?

Yeah, I still play. I play a fair amount. I'm basically addicted to golf, so if it wasn't for golf I would play a lot more, but I try and make myself play at least once a week.

Here in Vegas?

Whenever I'm in a location where I can play.

Do they let you play in Vegas?

I can still play some places in Vegas. I don't play very long and I don't bet super high, but I play a few hours a week.

What's your maximum bet?

A lot of times when I go into a casino I'll say to myself "I think I'll bet small today. I'll only go up to $500 or $600 and try not to get any attention. "But, what invariably happens is the count gets real high and I just blast it out there. I usually don't bet more than $2,000 on a hand.

Doesn't that draw a lot of attention?

Yeah, it does and I usually can't stay for the next shoe but most times I'll finish that one shoe.

You use the high/low method?

Yes, I've always used the high/low. I've never used any other count.

What would you say has been the biggest change in blackjack since your early years?

There's been a lot of change. I guess the biggest change would be the proliferation of the casinos. Instead of having two states with blackjack, at least half the states have blackjack now. But that's been countered by the fact that the casinos are getting smarter. The spread of information is a huge change. That's been bad for us. We haven't benefitted as much from technology as the casinos have. It used to be if you got barred in a casino in Vegas, maybe a week later all the casinos in Vegas would have your picture or something like that. Now, if you get barred somewhere, numerous casinos throughout the world may have your picture within minutes. So that's been a big change. The games are also definitely worse, but there are more games so it's still possible to make a nice living from blackjack.

Do you have any funny stories about your blackjack exploits?

One that comes to mind is that I trained a lot of people to play and one summer I had a son of my parents' longtime friends. He was in college and had heard about blackjack and the success we had and decided he would like to play for the summer.

He came to Atlantic City and he picked it up real fast. He was a smart guy. He played in Atlantic City and he did well. Then he had a break during the college year and decided he'd like to make a trip to Vegas. He was all excited about the trip but it was a little scary to him because he had heard all these stories about how they might do something to you if you won a lot of money and they thought you were a card counter. So, naturally, he was a little apprehensive.

What year was this?

This would have been in the early 80s. He went to Vegas and he was playing at the old Sands Casino and he couldn't lose a hand. He had all these chips on the table and was getting real excited about how much he was winning. Then he noticed he was getting some attention from the pit, so he figured this would be a good time to take all his chips and take a break to go count them. So, he goes into the bathroom, he has all these chips in his pockets and he's pulling them out and counting them when, all of a sudden, there's a loud knock on the stall door. He opens the door and looks out and sees a big security guard there staring at him while he has his chips and money all over the place and the guard goes, "What are you doing?" And he says, "...sorry, I was winning a lot of money and I was just counting it to just see how I was doing." And the guy says, "In the ladies room?"

Was he playing by himself or he was on the team?

He was out there playing on the team. Like I say, what we do basically is give somebody money to go play and we just let them loose, they go play wherever they want to, or they may have a particular casino in mind to go play.

Isn't it a problem if you go back to a casino all the time and you're winning? Because they always track you and eventually they will know that you are counting cards.

Right. The more you win, the less welcome you are going to be at casinos. So, that does happen. Today, there are so many casinos, you can use different names. You may play a casino, have a big win, not go back there for a year or so and then play as a different guy the next time. We do that all the time. We used to use disguises a lot.

Didn't you once disguise yourself as Santa Claus?

Yeah. Back in Atlantic City before Ken Uston won his case, they used to have this three-step process for barring counters. The first time they caught you, or if they just thought you were a card counter, they read you a card. We used to call this step one and basically the card would just say that you are no longer allowed to play blackjack, but you were allowed to play any other casino game.

Now, if they caught that same person a second time, they would tell them you are no longer allowed on the premises. Then, if that same person came back again and they discovered them, they would then arrest them for trespassing.

What happened was that, as you played more and more, you would get the step one card read to you at every casino but, then you would just sneak back in, or try and look different or play a different shift.

We thought it was outrageous that you could get kicked out of a casino just for knowing how to play. We felt we were on the right side of this and we decided we were just going to play. We didn't care what card they read to us and a lot of times we would get arrested for trespassing.

It was Christmas Eve and I decided I would dress up as Santa Claus even though I had already been read step two in this particular casino but they wouldn't know who it was, so they wouldn't be able to arrest me for trespassing. I was just playing and everybody was coming up to me..."Hey Santa Claus, how're you doing?"

Everybody thought it was funny, but then all of a sudden the count went up and I was betting real big. At that time we used to do these things we called "raids" where we would send everybody in there. We would have 10 or 15 people go in the same casino at the same time, figuring if they're reading the card to one guy, somebody else would be able to get some bets out there. So, we had a whole bunch of people in there and one of us heard the pit guy on the phone..."Yeah I got a guy down here on one table betting double thousands, I think I remember him, and then there's this guy over here betting purple chips, and over here is Santa Claus going crazy." It was kind of funny but they were good sports about it. They told me no more blackjack and they didn't try to do anything else. They saw the humor in it.

What do you see in the future for blackjack? Obviously, it's a cat and mouse game between you and the casinos. Do you think you'll always be able to do this? Or, do you think the casinos will come up with things to thwart you, such as continuous shuffling machines?

Luckily for us, the continuous shuffling machines don't seem to be too popular with the general public. A lot of the attraction of blackjack is that pretty much everybody who gambles in a casino has heard that blackjack is the only game you can beat. So, the casinos would be taking a risk by putting in a totally unbeatable game with all continuous shufflers. They just don't seem too popular.

What I have noticed is that a lot casinos will put them in on their smaller-limit tables but they won't put them on their higher-limit tables because most high rollers don't want to play them. Also, it seems to me they are now taking as many out as they are putting in. I don't think they are a major threat and I don't think that they are going to spread to where almost everybody is going to have them.

People like the idea of having a hot shoe and going on a streak. To have a never ending shoe doesn't seem to be that popular with the general public. Even though, if you're not counting, it shouldn't really matter, but the public's perception is that it does matter and I don't think the public will accept them.

I think for the next decade or so there is certainly money to be made in blackjack. If you move around and you are disciplined, it is still possible to make a good living playing blackjack. Although it is still shocking to me that casinos are able to treat skilled players the way they do.

I remember saying to a guy back in the early 80s, when I was being forced into a back room, "you won't be able to do this in a few years. The courts will stop this." It's obviously a violation of civil rights and it just amazes me – well it doesn't really amaze me – but it's sad that the casinos are so powerful and they can get away with the things they do. After Ken Uston won his court case in New Jersey, I figured all the states eventually would stop treating skilled players as criminals, but that hasn't been the case. We have to fight for every inch. The casinos still take a lot of liberties with what they do and they treat us terribly. It just never seemed fair that they can offer a game to the public, say what the rules are, and then abuse people that just play by those rules.

It's a shame that the casinos don't have the same attitude towards professional blackjack players as they do towards professional sports bettors. I bet some sports and the sports books are incredibly gracious and nice whether I win or lose. Most of the personnel are really friendly and seem to enjoy matching wits with all of their customers, no matter what their skill level.

Right now Missouri and Atlantic City are the only two states with laws preventing casinos from barring card counters?

Right but it's a little fuzzy elsewhere. I'm not sure exactly what the law is in Illinois or Indiana, but it's likely they aren't allowed to do it there either. Plus, there are lots of jurisdictions all over the world that aren't allowed to bar a card counter. Like some of the provinces in Canada and Australia which have a lot of laws to protect counters.

Well, from the casino's perspective, they are in business to make money. Do you think they should really let you play if you can beat them?

Absolutely. They have the choice as to whether or not they want to offer the game. Or, they could offer only continuous shuffle blackjack, or they could change the rules to make naturals (two-card 21s) pay even money, or pay six-to-five, like they're doing now in some places. These measures would virtually prevent anyone from getting an edge at blackjack.

They should be able to put up whatever game they want, but they should have to smile and deal; and that should be the end of it. They shouldn't be able to only deal to drunks or people that aren't too sharp. Every other game is like that – it's only blackjack where they take people in the back room, attempt to intimidate them and even arrest them.

They're still doing that nowadays?

Oh yeah. I don't mean to say that it happens all the time. Most places are pretty nice but it still happens. There are lawsuits all the time for people getting roughed up. It just kind of depends on the place and the particular person in the casino that takes a dislike to you, or how much you win.

I haven't heard many stories about backrooming people but I know I've heard stories where counters were rousted from their room in the middle of the night and kicked out.

Absolutely. That happened to me this year. It happens all the time. The other thing they do now, with these plastic card keys, is they change the code on the computer, so when you go up to your room after a long night of playing you find that you're locked out. You go down to the front desk and the clerk will say, "oh, just a minute sir, there seems to be a problem" and all of a sudden security will be there to escort you up to your room to kick you out. Surely that's not legal, but you don't really have much recourse. None of the lawyers want to take these cases because as long you don't get beat up or something, you don't have any real damages.

The casinos do a lot of things that are either in a gray area or they are definitely not allowed to do, but you don't have much recourse it seems to me. The casinos are very powerful in Nevada. Most of the horror stories are heard from Nevada, but there are some from other places. That's the one thing I have to give Ken Uston credit for. You never hear any of those stories in Atlantic City. That's the one nice thing. Whenever you're in Atlantic City, playing by the rules, you don't have to worry about some sort of nonsense going on.

And that's because they're not allowed to bar counters in Atlantic City?

Right.

Some players believe that Uston ruined blackjack in Atlantic City with his lawsuits. They say you can't get a decent game because of him but you actually have the opposite opinion?

Yeah, I'm a firm believer that what he did was good. I'd rather play a little worse game and not be worried about having some problem in the middle of the night.

When it happened to you, were you in the room?

Yes, it was in Mississippi and I was in the room. Actually, when I made my last play at the blackjack table I saw some guy kind looking at me funny, but I thought I was just getting a little paranoid, so I left the casino and went to a movie.

When I came back to my room, I was sitting there reading, it was around 11 at night, and the phone rang. I picked it up and the person on the other end hung up. I wondered what that was about and then about 15 minutes later there were five security guards at my door telling me that I was being asked to leave immediately. They marched me through the casino with my suitcase and they were surrounding me. I had to go cash out all my chips. It was embarrassing

Were you there as a guest of the casino?

Yeah.

I would imagine if you were paying for the room they couldn't do that?

You would think so, but I'm sure they would. I would have been happy to pay but I never tried that. I'm sure they would say no, you're getting kicked out. I don't think that would have worked. A lot of times they will renege when you're there as a guest of the casino. They will come to your room, march you down to the front desk and make you pay some exorbitant rate before they will let you leave. That happens fairly often.

Do you have any advice for the average blackjack player?

I think probably the best advice I could give them, is that it's not as hard to learn to play blackjack as most people think. The most common misconception is that you have to be some sort of math whiz or memory expert in order to do it.

You mean to count cards?

Well, the only way to play blackjack successfully is to count cards. With the stakes I play, I see other people playing high stakes and it boggles my mind that they can be so successful in business and work so hard to make all this money and they are willing to just gamble it away so easily. It's absolutely ridiculous not to at least learn basic strategy.

It takes a reasonably intelligent person maybe 10 hours to memorize it totally. If they're too lazy to do that, they can even put the strategy card on the table. Almost every casino will let you put the basic strategy card on the table and it's just crazy to be playing at a big disadvantage when you can be playing at a very small disadvantage

Learning to keep track of the cards only takes 15 to 20 hours. You just get a deck of cards, you flip them and you practice. Even if you don't learn anything else, that's enough to give you a slight edge over the house. If you just keep the running count and play basic strategy you can get an advantage. So, it's not a daunting mission to learn how to do it; it's not that difficult. Now, doing it full-time, or trying to make money full-time is difficult, but there's no reason the average person can't at least play a break-even game of blackjack.

Disturbing Trends In Blackjack

By Henry Tamburin

Over the past year changes have been made to the game of blackjack which have not been good for the player. Most of these changes occurred in Las Vegas. Let's hope they don't show up elsewhere.

The first change occurred when the majority of strip casinos decided to install continuous shuffling machines (CSM's) on their blackjack tables. These devices allowed the dealers to reshuffle after every hand, which makes card counting futile.

But CSM's not only hurt card counters; they have a negative effect on the average player. The reason is because the casinos get 20% more hands played on average per hour with these devices because there is no downtime for manual shuffles. Unless a player slows down when he plays, he will be playing more hands per hour and his potential hourly loss will increase (remember the casinos have the edge over the average player). My advice is to stay away from any CSM dealt game.

The next change occurred when the majority of strip casinos converted their rules to "dealer hit soft 17" from dealer stand on soft 17. That tiny rule change costs the player about 0.2% of his total betting action. And that assumes the player knows the changes to the basic playing strategy, which many do not.

Then came the introduction of the "new" single deck game called Super Fun 21. The game uses a single deck of cards (which most players know has better odds) and a whole bunch of player favorable rules (like doubling on any number of cards and being able to surrender even after doubling). But player blackjacks (except in diamonds) only pay even money. The latter negates all the player favorable rules resulting in a game with an 85% increase in casino's edge (up to 0.95%).

Next came the single deck game to end all single deck games. Las Vegas strips casinos were even advertising it on their marquees. It doesn't have a name but you'll know it because player blackjacks in this single deck game are paid at only 6 to 5 (or 2.4 to 2) odds instead of the usual 3 to 2 odds. That one rule change boosts the casino's edge to about 1.5%. Every player takes a hit with this game so stay away.

And finally, there's the six-deck game disguised as a double deck game. The dealer shuffles six decks but only deals two decks by hands. When you approach the table it appears to be a two-deck game but it's not. This is a deadly game for unsuspecting card counters.There is one way to stop this negative trend in blackjack. Don't play these games.

Henry Tamburin is the author of six best-selling books including Blackjack: Take The Money & Run. For a free copy of his Blackjack Insider newsletter visit his web site at www.smartgaming.com.

Continuous Shuffling Machines in Blackjack

by Henry Tamburin

Ever since Edward Thorp published his ground breaking card counting system in 1962, skillful blackjack players have been able to get the edge over the casino by keeping track of specific cards as they are dealt by the dealer. Now a new innovation, touted as "a card counter's worst nightmare" claims to once and for all eliminate the advantage that card counters possess. The product is a new continuous multi-deck shuffler dubbed "The King" by its developer Shuffle Master Inc. of Las Vegas.

So what does this device do that threatens to make card counting obsolete? And does it have any effect on the casual blackjack player who is not card counting? Read on for the answers.

What makes this shuffler different from other automatic shufflers is that it completely randomizes the cards from a round of play with the other cards in the shuffler and then completely randomizes the delivery of the shuffled cards to the shoe. Here's how this "double randomization" process works.

After a round is over, the dealer inserts the cards into the shuffler. The cards are then randomized using an elevator system. The discards are placed on the elevator and then randomly placed into one of 19 elevator stops or shelves. The shuffler then randomly selects a shelf of cards and delivers those cards to the dealing shoe. These cards become the next group of cards dealt. The result, according to the folks at Shuffle Master, is "complete and total unpredictability."

How do these new shufflers wipe out the card counter's advantage? Card counters keep track of high and low value cards from one round to the next. They know when the remaining decks of cards in the playing shoe contain an excess of high value cards over low value cards. When this occurs the edge shifts in their favor and they increase their bets. Typically a skilled counter can gain a 1.0 to 1.5% advantage over the casino with this technique.

Essentially this new shuffler "immediately" recycles and deals cards from a 4-deck shoe on every round. More importantly, because any card can be delivered to a shelf and any shelf of cards can be delivered to the shoe, every discard re-inserted immediately following a hand has a chance to appear in the next round. The net result of this technology is that a card counter's advantage is eliminated.

How confident is Shuffle Master of the integrity of their new shuffler? A few summers ago they were offering $100,000 to anyone who could show through mathematical analysis and/or computer simulation how a player can gain the advantage using the new shuffler. Nobody claimed the 100 grand.

There is no question that this new shuffler is going to be hard to beat. Not only does it thwart card counters but also a system used by players called "shuffle tracking" where skilled players have been able to track a group of cards through the dealer's shuffling routine and know when these cards will be dispensed from the shoe. This knowledge obviously gives the shuffle tracker a big advantage over the casino. However, the "random in, random out" process of shuffling from a totally enclosed continuous shuffler makes shuffle tracking obsolete.

The continuous shuffler will not alter the odds of the game for the casual blackjack player who does not count cards. But because more hands are dealt per hour with the shuffler, a casual player's bankroll won't last as long. That's another reason why casinos like the shuffler. The game is faster and as long as they have the edge over the average blackjack player, the casino's stand to win more money per hour. In other words, if you are a casual blackjack player, the more hands you play, the more money you will lose.

Dealers who have used the new shuffler have given it mixed reviews. Some of the negatives are that it doesn't give them a break from the physically tiresome monotonous task of dealing. One dealer mentioned to me that she often likes to carry on a casual conversation with players while she shuffles the cards but with the new shuffler "it's all business all the time."

It would seem that the continuous shuffler has lots of benefits for the casinos but none for the player. It eliminates card counting and shuffle tracking for the skilled player and results in higher hourly loss rates for the casual player. Maybe that's why Shuffle Master named the new continuous shuffler "The King."

Henry Tamburin is one of America's most popular casino gaming writers and best-selling authors. For more of his winning advice visit his web site for casino players at www.smartgaming.com. Ordering information for his books and videos can be found on page 122.

Craps

by Steve Bourie

At first glance the game of craps looks a little intimidating because of all the various bets you can make but actually the game itself is very simple, so first let me explain the game without any reference to the betting.

Everyone at the craps table gets a turn to roll the dice, but you don't have to roll if you don't want to. The dice are passed around the table clockwise and if it's your turn to roll you simply take two dice and roll them to the opposite end of the table. This is your first roll of the dice which is also called the "come-out" roll. If you roll a 7 or 11 that's called a "natural" and you win, plus you get to roll again. If you roll a 2,3 or 12 those are all called "craps" and you lose, but you still get to roll again. The only other possible numbers you can roll are 4,5,6,8,9 or 10 and if one of those numbers shows up, then that number becomes your "point" and the object of the game is to roll that number again before you roll a 7.

If a 7 shows up before your "point" number does then you lose and the dice move on to the next shooter. If your "point" number shows up before a 7 does, then you have made a "pass." You then win your bet and you get to roll again. That's all there is to the game of craps.

Now that you know how to play the game, let's find out about the different kinds of bets you can make. Two of the best bets you'll find on the craps table are in the areas marked "pass" and "don't pass". When you bet on the "pass" line you're betting that the shooter will win. To make a pass line bet you put your bet right in front of you on the pass line. Pass line bets are paid even-money and the house edge on a pass line bet is 1.41% You can also bet on the "don't pass" line in which case you're betting that the shooter will lose. To make a don't pass bet you put your bet in front of you in the don't pass area. Don't pass bets are also paid even-money and the house edge on them is 1.40%

In reality, the odds are always 1.41% against the shooter and in favor of the "don't pass" bettor by that same amount. Of course, if you're a "don't pass" bettor the casinos don't want to give you a bet where you have an edge so they have a rule in effect on "don't pass" bets where on the come out roll if the shooter throws a 12, you don't win. You don't lose either, the bet is just considered a "push," or tie, and nothing happens. In some casinos they may make 2 instead of 12 the number that's a push. Just look on the don't pass line and you'll you see the word "bar" and then the number that the casino considers a push. In our illustration it says bar 12, so in this casino your bet on the don't pass line will be a push if the come-out roll is a 12. This rule is what gives the casino its advantage on don't pass bets and it doesn't matter whether the casino bars the 2 or 12 the result is the same 1.40% advantage for the house.

All right, let's say you put $10 on the pass line and you roll the dice. If you roll 7 or 11 you win $10 and if you roll 2,3 or 12 you lose $10. So, what happens if you roll any of the other numbers? Well, as I said before, that number becomes your point and you have to roll that number again before you roll a 7 in order to win your pass line bet.

Once your point is established the dealer at each end of the table will move a marker into the box that corresponds to your point number to let everyone at the table know what your point is. The marker that's used has two different sides. One side is black with the word "off" and the other side is white with the word "on." Before any point is established the marker is kept in the Don't Come box with the black side facing up until you roll a point number and then the dealer turns it over to the white side and moves it inside the box that contains your point number.

For example let's say your come-out roll is a 4. The dealer simply turns the marker over to the white side that says "on" and places it in the 4 box. This let's everyone know that 4 is your point and that you will continue to roll the dice, no matter how long it takes, until you roll a 4, which will make you a winner, or a 7, which will make you a loser.

Now, keep in mind that once your point is established you can't remove your pass line bet until you either win, by throwing your point, or lose, by rolling a 7. The reason for this is that on the come out roll the pass line bettor has the advantage because there are 8 ways to win (by rolling a 7 or 11) and only 4 ways to lose (by rolling a 2, 3 or 12). If a point number is rolled, no matter what number it is, there are then more ways to lose than to win and that's why the bet can't be removed. If you were allowed to remove your bet everyone would just wait for the come-out roll and if they didn't win they would take their bet back which would give them a big advantage over the house and, as you know, casinos don't like that, so that's why you can't remove your bet.

As previously noted, the pass line is one of the best bets you'll find, but there is a way to make it even better because once your point number is established the casino will allow you to make another bet that will be paid off at the true odds. This is a very good bet to make because the casino has no advantage on this bet.

In this instance, since your point was 4, the true odds are 2-to-1 and that's what your bet will be paid off at: $2 for every $1 you bet. This is called an "odds bet," "taking the free odds" or "betting behind the line" and to make this bet you simply put your chips directly behind your pass line bet. There is a limit to how much you're allowed to bet and for many years most casinos allowed a maximum of 2 times the amount of your pass line bet. Nowadays, however, many casinos offer 5 times odds and some casinos are even allowing up to 100 times odds. In Las Vegas, Casino Royale is one casino that offers 100 times odds.

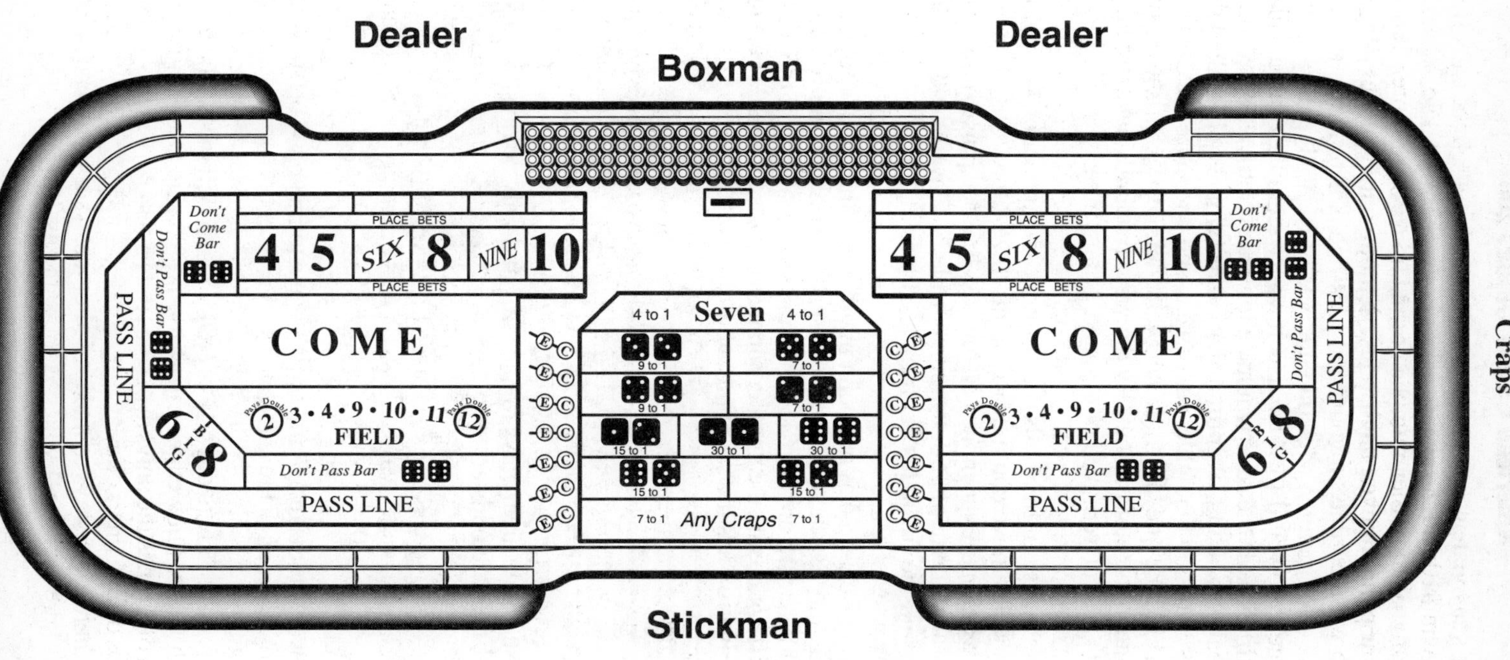

Typical craps table layout

Because the casino has no advantage on these bets you are effectively lowering the house edge on your total pass line bet by taking advantage of these free odds bets. For example, the normal house edge on a pass line bet is 1.41% but if you also make a single odds bet along with your pass line bet you will lower the house edge on your total pass line bets to .85%. If the casino offers double odds then the edge on your bets is lowered to .61% With triple odds the edge is lowered to .47% and if you were to play in a casino that allowed 10 times odds the edge would be lowered to only .18% which means that, statistically speaking, over time, that casino would only make 18¢ out of every $100 you bet on that table. As you can see, the more the casino allows you to bet behind the line, the more it lowers their edge, so it's always a good idea to take advantage of this bet. By the way, free odds bets, unlike regular pass line bets, can be removed or reduced, at any time.

All right, let's make our free odds bet on our point number of 4 by putting $20 behind the line. Then we continue to roll until we either roll a 4 or a 7. If a 4 came up we would get even money on the pass line bet, plus 2-to-1 on the free odds bet, for a total win of $50. But, if we rolled a 7, we would lose both the pass line bet and the free odds bet for a total loss of $30.

In this example we used 4 as our point number, but there are 5 other numbers that could appear and here are the true odds for all of the possible point numbers: the 4 and 10 are 2-to-1; the 5 and 9 are 3-to-2; and the 6 and 8 are 6-to-5. You'll notice that the numbers appear in pairs and that's because each paired combination has the same probability of occurring.

7 = 6 ways 1+6,6+1,2+5,5+2,3+4,4+3
6 = 5 ways 1+5,5+1,2+4,4+2,3+3
8 = 5 ways 2+6,6+2,3+5,5+3,4+4

As you can see there are 6 ways to make a 7 and only 5 ways to make a 6 or 8. Therefore, the true odds are 6-to-5.

7 = 6 ways 1+6,6+1,2+5,5+2,3+4,4+3
4 = 3 ways 1+3,3+1,2+2
10 = 3 ways 4+6,6+4,5+5

There are 6 ways to make a 7 and only 3 ways to make a 4 or 10, so the true odds are 6-to-3, which is the same as 2-to-1;

7 = 6 ways 1+6,6+1,2+5,5+2,3+4,4+3
5 = 4 ways 1+4,4+1,2+3,3+2
9 = 4 ways 3+6,6+3,4+5,5+4

and finally, there are 6 ways to make a 7, but just 4 ways to make a 5 or 9, so the true odds here are 6-to-4 which is the same as 3-to-2.

It's important that you remember these numbers, because 1.- you want to make sure that you're paid the right amount when you do win and 2.- you want to make sure that when you make your odds bets you make them in amounts that are paid off evenly.

As an example, if your point is 5 and you have $5 on the pass line, you wouldn't want to bet $5 behind the line because at 3-to-2 odds the casino would have to pay you $7.50 and they don't deal in change. When making the odds bet on the 5 or 9 you should always bet in even amounts and in the situation just mentioned most casinos would allow you to add an extra $1 so you would have $6 out and they could pay you $9, if you won. The only other situation where this occurs is on the 6 and 8 where the payoff is 6-to-5. So, in that instance you want to make your bets in multiples of $5. Also, if your pass line bet is $15, most casinos will allow you to bet $25 behind the line because, if you win, it's quicker for them to pay you $30, rather than dealing in $1 chips to give you $18 for $15. When situations like this exist, it's good to take advantage of them and bet the full amount you're allowed because that helps to lower the casino edge even more.

We've spent all this time talking about pass line betting, so what about don't pass betting? Well, everything applied to pass line betting works pretty much just the opposite for don't pass betting. If you put $10 on don't pass you would win on the come out roll if the shooter rolled a 2 or 3, you would tie if the shooter rolled a 12, and you would lose if the shooter rolled a 7 or 11. If any other number comes up then that becomes the shooter's point number and if he rolls a 7 before he rolls that same point number, you will win. If he rolls his point number before he rolls a 7, you will lose.

Don't pass bettors are also allowed to make free odds bets to back up their original bets, however, because the odds are in their favor they must lay odds rather than take odds. This means that if the point is 4 or 10, the don't pass bettor must lay 2-to-1, or bet $10 to win $5; on 5 or 9 he must lay 3-to-2, or bet $6 to win $4; and on 6 or 8 he must lay 6-to-5, or bet $6 to win $5. By taking advantage of these free odds bets the casino advantage is slightly lowered on the total don't pass bets to .68% with single odds; .46% with double odds; .34% with triple odds and .12% with 10 times odds. If you want to you can remove, or reduce the amount of your free odds, bet at any time. To make a free odds bet on don't pass you should place your odds bet right next to your original bet and then put a chip on top to connect the two bets. Keep in mind that when you make a free odds bet on don't pass the casino will allow you to make your bet based on the payoff, rather than the original amount of your don't pass bet. In other words, if the casino offered double odds, the point was 4 and you had $10 on don't pass, you would be allowed to bet $40 because you would only win $20 which was double the amount of your original $10 bet. Since you have to put out more money than you'll be getting back, laying odds is not very popular at the craps table and you'll find that the vast majority of craps players would rather bet with the shooter and take the odds. Statistically speaking, it makes no difference whether you are laying or taking the odds because they both have a zero advantage for the house.

One last point about don't pass betting is that once the point is established, the casino will allow you to remove your don't pass bet if you want to - but don't do it! As noted before, on the come out roll the pass line bettor has the advantage because there are 8 rolls that can win and only 4 that can lose, but once the point is established, there are more ways the shooter can lose than win, so at that point the don't pass bettor has the advantage and it would be foolish to remove your bet.

Now, let's take a look at the area marked come and don't come. Since you already know how to bet pass and don't pass, you should easily understand come and don't come because they're the exact same bets as pass and don't pass, except for the fact that you bet them after the point has already been established.

Let's say that the shooter's point is 6 and you make a come bet by putting a $5 chip anywhere in the come box. Well, that's just like making a pass line bet, except that the shooter's next roll becomes the come-out roll for your bet. If the shooter rolls a 7 or 11, you win. If a 2,3, or 12 is rolled you lose, and if anything else comes up then that becomes your point and the shooter must roll that number again before rolling a 7 in order for you to win. In this example if the shooter rolled a 4 the dealer would move your $5 come bet up into the center of the 4 box and it would stay there until either a 4 was rolled, which would make you a winner, or a 7 was rolled which would make you a loser. The house edge on a come bet is the same 1.41% as on a pass line bet. You are allowed free odds on your come bet and you make that bet by giving your chips to the dealer and telling him you want to take the odds. The dealer will then place those chips slightly off center on top of your come bet to show that it's a free odds bet. By the way, if you win, the dealer will put your winnings back in the come bet area so be sure to pick them up off the table or else it will be considered a new come bet.

One other point to note here is that when you make a come bet your bet is always working on every roll, even a come-out roll. However, when you take the odds on your come bets they are never working on the come-out roll. That may sound a little confusing, but here's what it means. In our example the shooter's initial point was 6 and then we made a $5 come bet. The shooter then rolled a 4 which became the point for our come bet. The dealer then moved our $5 come bet to the middle of the 4 box at the top of the table. We then gave $10 to the dealer and said we wanted to take the odds on the 4. On the next roll the shooter rolls a 6 which means he made a pass by rolling his original point number. The next roll will then become the shooter's come-out roll and the odds bet on our 4 will not be working. If the shooter rolls a 7 the pass line bettors will win and we will lose our $5 come bet because he rolled a 7 before rolling a 4. The dealer will then return our $10 odds bet because it wasn't working on the come-out roll. Now, if you want to, you can request that your odds bet be working on the come-out roll by telling the dealer. Then he'll put a marker on top of your bet to show that your odds bet is in effect on the come-out roll.

Naturally, don't come betting is the same as don't pass betting, except again for the fact that the bet isn't made until after the point is established. In this case let's say the point is 5 and you make a don't come bet by placing a $5 chip in the don't come box. Well, once again, that's just like making a don't pass bet except that the shooter's next roll becomes the come-out roll for your bet. If the shooter rolls a 2 or 3, you win. If a 7 or 11 is rolled, you lose. If a 12 is rolled it's a standoff and if anything else comes up then that becomes your point and the shooter must seven-out, or roll a 7, before rolling that point number again in order for you to win. In this example if the shooter rolled a 10 the dealer would move your $5 don't come bet into the upper part of the 10 box and it would stay there until either a 7 was rolled, which would make you a winner, or a 10 was rolled which would make you a loser. The house edge on a don't come bet is the same 1.40% as on a don't pass bet and you can make a free odds bet on your don't come bet by giving your chips to the dealer and telling him you want to lay the odds. The dealer will then place those chips next to and on top of your don't come bet to show that it's a free odds bet. The final point to note here is that don't come bets, as well as the free odds bets on them, are always working - even on the come-out roll.

Now let's talk about place betting and that refers to the 6 numbers you see in the area at the top of the table: 4,5,6,8,9 and 10. Anytime during a roll you can make a bet that one of those numbers will appear before a 7 and if it does you will receive a payoff that is slightly less than the true odds. For example: the true odds are 2-to-1 that a 4 or 10 will appear before a 7. However, if you make a place bet on the 4 or 10 you will only be paid off at 9-to-5 and that works out to a casino advantage of 6.67%

The true odds of a 5 or 9 appearing before a 7 are 3-to-2, but on a place bet you would only receive a payoff of 7-to-5 which works out to a casino edge of 4.0%. Finally, on the 6 and 8 the true odds are 6-to-5 that one of those numbers will appear before a 7, but on a place bet you would only be paid off at 7-to-6 which means the casino would have an edge of 1.52% on this bet.

As you can see, making a place bet on the 6 or 8 gives the casino its lowest edge and this means that a place bet on the 6 or 8 is one of the best bets you will find on the craps table.

When you want to make a place bet you aren't allowed to put the bet down yourself, you have to let the dealer do it for you. To do this you would just drop your chips down onto the table and tell the dealer what bet you wanted to make. For example you could put three $5 chips down and say "Place the 4,5 and 9." The dealer would then put $5 on the edge of the 4 box, $5 on the edge of the 5 box and $5 on the edge of the 9 box. You'll notice that when the dealer puts your bets on the edge of the boxes they will always be placed in an area that corresponds to where you're standing at the table and this helps the dealer to remember who placed that bet.

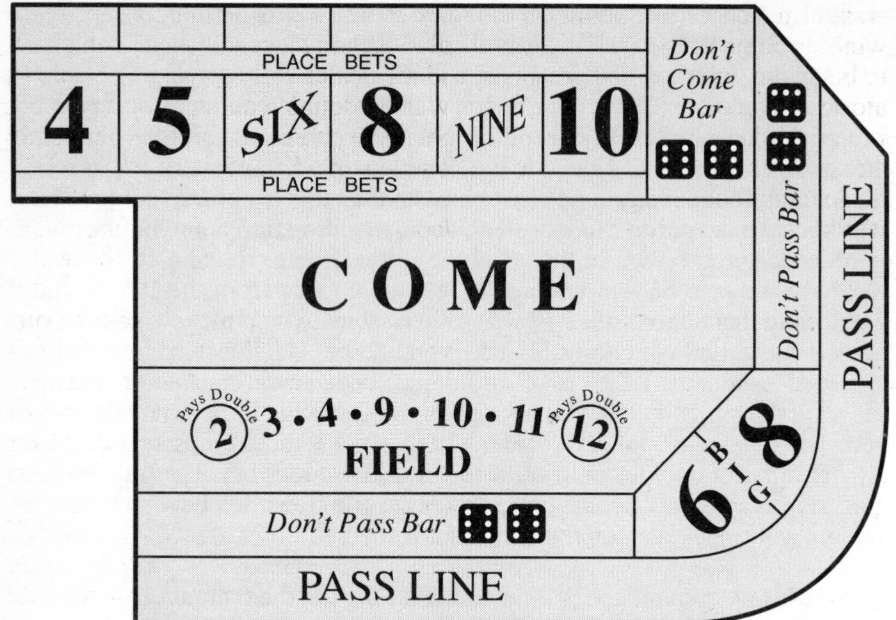

Enlargement of right side of craps layout

When making a place bet you don't have to bet more than one number and you don't have to bet the same amount on each number. You should, however, make sure that you always bet in multiples of $5 whenever you bet on the 4,5,9 or 10 and in multiples of $6 whenever you bet the 6 and 8. This will allow you to always get the full payoff on your bet. If, for example, you bet $3 on the 6 and you won you would only get back even-money, or $3, rather than the $3.50 which your bet should have paid and this results in an even bigger advantage for the casino. Another thing about place bets is that, unlike pass line bets, you can remove your place bets at any time and you do that by telling the dealer you want your bet down and he will take your chips off the table and return them to you. You could also tell the dealer that you didn't want your bet to be working on any particular roll or rolls and you do this by saying for example "off on the 5." The dealer would then put a little button on top of your bet that said "off" and he would remove it when you told him you wanted that number working again.

When we spoke about come bets before I mentioned that come bets are always working on every roll, but that's not the case with place bets because place bets are never working on the come-out roll. If you wanted to, however, you could ask for your place bet to be working on the come out roll by telling the dealer you wanted it working and he would place a button on top of your bet that said "on" to show that your bet was working on the come-out roll.

One last point about place bets is that when you win the dealer will want to know what you want to do for your next bet and you have three choices: if you want to make the same bet just say "same bet" and the dealer will give you your winning chips and leave your original place bet on the table. If you don't want to bet again, just say "take it down" and the dealer will return your place bet along with your winnings. And if you want to double your bet just say "press it" and the dealer will add your winning chips to your other place bet and return any extra chips to you. For example, if you won a $10 place bet on the 5 the dealer would have to give you back $14 in winning chips. If you said "press it" the dealer would add $10 to your place bet and return the remaining $4 in chips to you.

Besides, place betting there is also another way to bet that one of the point numbers will show up before a 7 does and that's called buying a number. A buy bet is basically the same as a place bet except you have to pay a commission of 5% of the amount of your bet and then if you win, the casino will pay you at the true odds. When making a buy bet you should always remember to bet at least $20 because 5% of $20 is $1 and that's the minimum amount the casino will charge you. The reason for the $1 minimum is because that's the smallest denomination chip they have at the craps table and they won't make change for anything under $1. The casino edge on any buy bet for $20 works out to 4.76% so let's take a look at a chart that shows the difference between buying and placing the point numbers.

Point Number	Casino Edge Buy Bet	Casino Edge Place Bet
4 or 10	4.76%	6.67%
5 or 9	4.76%	4.00%
6 or 8	4.76%	1.52%

As you can see the only numbers that you would want to buy rather than place are the 4 and 10 because the 4.76% edge on a buy bet is lower than the 6.67% edge on a place bet. For 5 and 9 the 4.76% edge on a buy bet is slightly worse than the 4.00% edge on a place bet and for the 6 and 8 the 4.76% is a hefty three times higher than the 1.52% edge on the place bet.

To buy the 4 or 10 you would just put your chips down on the layout and tell the dealer what bet you wanted to make. For example, if you put down $21 and said "buy the 10." The dealer will then keep the $1 chip for the house and put your $20 in the same area as the place bets but he'll put a button on top that says "buy" to let him know that you bought the number rather than placed it. Buy bets, just like place bets, can be removed at any time and are always off on the come-out roll. Also, if you do remove your buy bet you will get your 5% commission back.

Besides buy bets where you're betting with the shooter and hoping that a point number will appear before a 7 does, there are also lay bets where you're doing just the opposite - you're betting against the shooter and hoping that a 7 will appear before a point number does.

Lay bets are also paid at the true odds and you have to pay a 5% a commission of the amount you will win rather than the amount you're betting. Once again, when making a lay bet you should always remember to make them based on a minimum payoff of $20 because 5% of $20 is $1 and that's the minimum amount the casino will charge you.

Lay Number	Payoff	Casino Edge
4 or 10	$40 for $20	2.44%
5 or 9	$30 for $20	3.23%
6 or 8	$24 for $20	4.00%

For 4 and 10 you'll have to lay $40 to win $20 and the casino edge is 2.44%; for the 5 and 9 you'll have to lay $30 to win $20 and the casino edge is 3.23%; and for the 6 and 8 you'll have to lay $24 to win $20. The casino edge on that bet is 4.00%.

To make a lay bet you would just put your chips down on the layout and tell the dealer what you wanted to bet. For example, if you put down $41 and said "lay the 10." The dealer would then keep the $1 chip for the house and put your $40 in the same area as the don't come bets but he'll put a button on top that says "buy" to let him know that it's a lay bet. Lay bets, unlike buy bets, are always working on come-out rolls. Lay bets are, however, similar to buy bets in that they can be removed at any time and if you do remove your lay bet you will also receive your 5% commission back.

There are only a few other bets left located on the ends of the table to discuss and two of them are the big 6 and the big 8 which are both very bad bets. To bet the big 6 you place a chip in the big 6 box and then if the shooter rolls a 6 before rolling a 7 you win even money, or $1 for every $1 you bet. To bet the big 8 the same rules would apply: you put your bet in the box and then hope that the shooter rolls an 8 before rolling a 7 so you could win even money on your bet. The big 6 and big 8 can both be bet at any time and both are always working, even on the come-out roll. The casino edge on both the big 6 and the big 8 is 9.1%, which is the biggest edge we've seen so far. But, if you think back about some of the other bets we discussed doesn't this bet sound familiar? It should. This bet is the exact same as a place bet on the 6 or 8, but instead of getting paid off at 7-to-6 we're only getting paid off at even-money! Why would you want to bet the big 6 or big 8 at a house edge of more than 9% instead of making a place bet on the 6 or 8 at a house edge of only 1.5%? The answer is you wouldn't - so don't ever make this bet because it's a sucker bet that's only for people who don't know what they're doing.

The last bet we have to discuss on the player's side of the table is the field bet which is a one-roll bet that will pay even money if a 3,4,9,10 or 11 is rolled and 2-to-1 if a 2 or 12 is rolled. To make a field bet you would just place your chip anywhere in the field box and at first glance it doesn't seem like a bad bet.

After all, there are 7 numbers you can win on and only 4 numbers you can lose on! The only problem is that there are 20 ways to roll the 4 losing numbers and only 16 ways to roll the 7 winning numbers and even after factoring in the double payoff for the 2 and 12 the casino winds up with a hefty 5.6% advantage. In some casinos they pay 3-to-1 on the 2 (or the 12) which cuts the casino edge in half to a more manageable 2.8%, but as you've seen there are still much better bets you can make. By the way, if you win on a field bet the dealer will put your winning chips right next to your bet so it's your responsibility to pick them up, or else they'll be considered a new bet!

Now, let's take a look at some of the long-shots, or proposition bets in the center of the table. When you look at these bets one of the first things you'll notice is that, unlike the bets on the other side of the table, the winning payoffs are clearly labeled. The reason they do that is so you can see those big payoffs and want to bet them, but as you'll see, although the payoffs are high, so are the casino advantages.

All of the proposition bets are controlled by the stickman and he is the person who must make those bets for you. So, if you wanted to make a $1 bet on "any craps" you would throw a $1 chip to the center of the table and say "$1 any craps" and the stickmen would place that bet in the proper area for you. Then if you won, the stickman would tell the dealer at your end of the table to pay you. You should also be aware that they will only pay you your winnings and keep your original bet in place. If you don't want to make the same bet again, you should tell the stickman that you want your bet down and it will be returned to you.

There are only four proposition bets that are not one-roll bets and they are known as the "hardways." They are the hard 4, hard 6, hard 8 and hard 10. To roll a number the hardway means that the number must be rolled as doubles. For example 3 and 3 is a hard 6, but a roll of 4-2, or 5-1 are both called an easy 6, because they are easier to roll than double 3's.

To win a bet on hard 10 the shooter has to roll two 5's before rolling a 7 or an easy 10 such as 6-4 or 4-6. To win a bet on hard 4 the shooter has to roll two 2's before rolling a 7 or an easy 4 such as 3-1 or 1-3. The true odds of rolling a hard 4 or hard 10 are 8-to-1, but the casino will only pay you 7-to-1 which works out to a casino advantage of 11.1% on both of these bets.

To win a bet on hard 6 the shooter must roll two 3's before rolling a 7 or an easy 6 such as 5-1, 1-5; or 4-2, 2-4. To win a bet on hard 8 the shooter must roll two 4's before rolling a 7 or an easy 8 such as 6-2, 2-6 or 5-3, 3-5. The true odds of rolling a hard 6 or hard 8 are 10-to-1, but the casino will only pay you 9-to-1 which works out to a casino advantage of 9.1% on both of these bets.

As noted before, all of the other proposition bets are one-roll bets which means that the next roll of the dice will decide whether you win or lose. As you'll see, the house edge on all of these bets is very high and they should all be avoided.

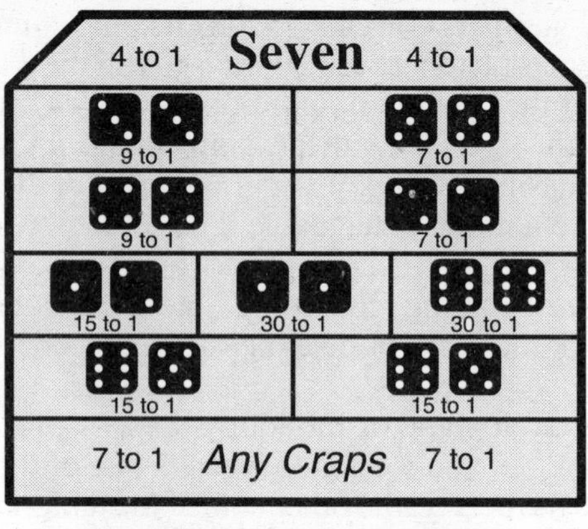

Two different types of proposition bets layouts

For the any craps bet you will win if a 2,3,or 12 is thrown on the next roll and lose if any other number comes up. The true odds are 8-to-1 but the casino will only pay you at 7-to-1 which gives them an edge of 11.1% on this bet and you'll notice that the stickman can put your bet either in the any craps box or, more likely, he'll put it on the circled marked "C" which stands for craps. The reason your bet will be placed in the "C" circle is that it's put in the circle that corresponds to where you're standing at the table and it makes it easier for the stickman to know who that bet belongs to.

For a craps 2 bet you win if the next roll is a 2 and lose if any other number shows up. The true odds are 35-to-1 but the casino will only pay you 30-to-1 which means that the edge on this bet is 13.9% In some casinos the odds for this bet will be shown as 30-for-1 which is actually the same as 29-to-1 and this results in an even bigger edge of 16.7% for the casino

A craps 12 bet works the same as a craps 2 bet, except that now you will only win if a 12 is thrown. Again, the true odds are 35-to-1 but you will only be paid at 30-to-1 which means the casino edge on this bet is the same 13.9% as in the last craps 2 bet. Also if the bet is shown on the layout as 30-for-1 the casino edge is raised to 16.7%

For a craps 3 bet you will only win if the next throw is a 3. The true odds are 17-to-1, but the casino will only pay you 15-to-1 which results in a casino advantage of 11.1% Once again, in some casinos the payoff will be shown as 15-for-1 which is the same as 14-to-1 and the house edge in that casino is an even higher 16.7%

The 11 bet is similar to the craps 3 bet, except that now the only number you can win on is 11. The true odds of rolling an 11 are 17-to-1, but the casino will only pay you 15-to-1 which gives them an 11.1% advantage. Additionally, if the payoff is shown on the layout as 15-for-1 rather than 15-to-1 the casino edge will be even higher at 16.7% By the way, because 11 sounds so much like 7 you will always hear 11 referred to at the table as "yo" or "yo-leven" to eliminate any confusion as to what number you are referring to. So, if you wanted to bet $5 on 11 you would throw a $5 chip to the stickman and say "$5 yo" and then he will either place it in the 11 box or place it on top of the "E" circle that corresponds to where you're standing at the table.

With a horn bet you are betting on the 2,3,11 and 12 all at once. A horn bet has to be made in multiples of $4 because you're making 4 bets at one time and you'll win if any one of those 4 numbers shows up on the next roll. You'll be paid off at the odds for the number that came in and you'll lose the rest of your chips. For example, if you make an $8 horn bet, this is the same as betting $2 on the 2, $2 on the 3, $2 on the 11 and $2 on the 12. If the number 2 came in you would get paid off at 30-to-1 so you would get back $60 in winnings and the casino would keep the $6 that you lost for the three $2 bets on the 3,11 and 12. The only advantage of a horn bet is that it allows you to make 4 bad bets at once rather than one at a time.

The last proposition bet we have to look at is also the worst bet on the craps table and it's the any 7 bet. With this bet you win if a 7 is rolled and lose if any other number comes up. The true odds are 5-to-1, but the casino will only pay you at 4-to-1 which gives them an edge of 16.7%

So there you have it! We've gone over all the possible bets you can make and now it's time to tell you how to win at the game of craps. Unfortunately, as you've seen, craps is a negative expectation game which means that every bet you make has a built-in advantage for the house. Actually, there is one bet that the casino has no advantage on and do you remember the name of that one? That's right it's the free odds bet and it's great that the casino has no advantage on that bet but the only way you're allowed to make that bet is to first make a negative expectation bet on pass/don't pass or come/don't come, so in essence, there are no bets you can make where you have an advantage over the house and in the long run the game of craps is unbeatable.

So, if that's the case then how do you win? Well, in reality there is only one way to win in craps and that way is to get lucky! Of course, this is easier said than done, but you will find it much easier to come out a winner if you only stick to the bets that offer the casino its lowest edge and those are the only bets you should ever make.

If you want to bet with the shooter I suggest you make a pass line bet, back it up with the free odds and then make a maximum of two come bets that are also both backed up with free odds. For example if double odds are allowed, you could start with a $5 pass line bet and say a 4 is rolled. You would then put $10 behind the line on your 4 and make a $5 come bet. If the shooter then rolled an 8 you would take $10 in odds on your come bet on the 8 and make another $5 come bet. If the shooter then rolled a 5 you would take $10 in odds on your come bet on the 5 and then stop betting. The idea here is that you always want to have a maximum of three numbers working and once you do, you shouldn't make anymore bets until one of your come numbers hits, in which case you would make another come bet, or if your pass line bet wins and then you would follow that up with another pass line bet. The important thing to remember is not to make more than two come bets because you don't want to have too much out on the table if the shooter rolls a 7. By using this betting system you'll only be giving the casino an edge of around .60% on all of your bets and with just a little bit of luck you can easily walk away a winner.

If you wanted to be a little more aggressive with this betting system there are some modifications you could make such as making a maximum of three come bets rather than two, or you could add place bets on the 6 and 8. Remember that a place bet on either the 6 or 8 only gives the casino a 1.52% advantage and that makes them both the next best bets after pass/don't pass and come/don't come. To add the place bets you would start off the same as before, but after you've made your second come bet you would look at the 6 and 8 and if they weren't covered you would then make a $6 place bet on whichever one was open or on both. By adding the place bets on the 6 and 8 you would always have at least three numbers in action and you could have as many as five covered at one time.

One final option with this system is to gradually increase the amount of your pass line and come bets by 50%, or by doubling them, and then backing them up with full odds, but I would only suggest you do this if you've been winning for awhile because it could get very expensive if the table was cold and no one was rolling many numbers. Of course, if the table got real cold you could always change your strategy by betting against the shooter and the strategy for that is basically just the opposite of the one I just told you about.

To bet against the shooter you would start with a $5 don't pass bet which you would back up with single free odds and then bet a maximum of two don't come bets that are both backed up with single odds. The reason you don't want to back up your bets with double odds is because when you're betting against the shooter you have to lay the odds which means you're putting up more money than you'll be getting back and, once again, it could get very expensive if a shooter got on a hot roll and made quite a few passes.

For an example of this system let's say you start with a $5 don't pass bet and a 4 is rolled. You would then lay the odds by putting $10 next to your $5 don't pass bet and then make a $5 don't come bet. If the shooter then rolled an 8 you would lay $6 in odds on your don't come bet on the 8 and make another $5 don't come bet. If the shooter then rolled a 5 you would lay $9 in odds on your come bet on the 5 and then stop betting. The idea here is that you always want to have a maximum of three numbers working and once you do, you shouldn't make anymore bets until one of your don't come numbers wins, in which case you would make another don't come bet, or if your don't pass bet wins and then you would follow that up with another don't pass bet. Once again, the important thing to remember is not to make more than two don't come bets because you don't want to have too much out on the table if the shooter gets hot and starts to roll a lot of numbers. With this system you'll always have a maximum of three numbers in action and you'll only be giving the casino an edge of about .80% on all of your bets. Some options to bet more aggressively with this system are to increase your free odds bets to double odds rather than single odds and also to make three don't come bets, rather than stopping at two. The choice is up to you but remember that because you must lay the odds and put out more money than you'll be getting back you could lose a substantial amount rather quickly if the roller got hot and made a lot of point numbers.

Now, one last point I want to make about betting craps is that the bankroll you'll need is going to be much bigger than the bankroll you'll need for playing any other casino game. If you're betting with the shooter you'll have one $5 pass line bet with double odds and two come bets with double odds which means that you could have as much as $45 on the table that could be wiped out with the roll of a 7. If you're betting against the shooter you'll have $5 on don't pass with single odds and two don't come bets with single odds which means you could have as much as $44 on the table that could be wiped out if the shooter got on a "hot" roll and made a lot of numbers. As I said before, you need to have an adequate bankroll to be able to ride out the losing streaks that can happen and you need to be able to hold on until things turn around and you start to win.

So how much of a bankroll is enough? Well, I would say about 7 times the maximum amount of money you'll have out on the table is adequate and 10 times would be even better. In both of our examples then you should have a bankroll of at least $300. If you don't have that much money to put out on the table then you might want to consider having less money out on the table by making only one come or don't come bet rather than two or maybe even just limiting your bets to pass and don't pass along with the free odds.

Just remember that it doesn't matter whether you want to bet with the shooter or against the shooter - both of these systems will give you the best chance of winning because they allow the casino only the slightest edge and with a little bit of luck you can easily come out a winner. Good luck!

Maximizing Comps In Craps

by Larry Edell

If you play in casino, you probably know about comps. If you play craps, you probably know that your game affords the casino a very small advantage - only about 1% on some bets. And if you take full advantage of the comps the casino offers, you can make more money in comps than in winnings! Sometimes, you can even triple your comps in relationship to the initial money wagered! In order to maximize your comps you need to choose the proper casino, have good money management, and develop a systematic business plan to execute it all.

Choosing A Casino - A casino that will maximize both your profits and your entertainment expectations is extremely important. A lot of people end up at casinos due to the proliferation of "fun books" that are mailed or given out at tourist bureaus. These coupons will give you free hot dogs, drinks or coffee cups. But is this really the best method to choose a casino?

If you play craps for profit, you need to carefully choose a resort that will maximize your comps while offering favorable playing conditions. For example, some casinos offer 100X odds while others offer only 2X odds. And, some casinos offer comp credit for your spread rather than for individual bets. Both of these are terrific advantages for the craps player.

However, after you have finished playing for the required amount of time and get your "free" meal or show, you might find that this is not exactly what you wanted. For example, say you visit a particular casino that offers 100X odds but they have standard rooms, no major show, and there is only one mediocre restaurant. Even though this casino offered superior playing conditions, you're bound to get tired of going there several times a year.

Another casino offers only 2X odds, however, they offer a superior show, five different restaurants, and a Jacuzzi suite. Although this casino's craps policies are less favorable than the first one, you might end up getting more value for your money in the long run.

Before you gamble, you should call a casino on their 800 number and ask to speak to a casino host. Tell him (or her) that you would like to try their casino out. Ask about the different restaurants, shows, and rooms they offer. Ask if they base comps on individual bet or spread. Ask about the minimum bets and time required to get a free room. Write down the answers and call the other casinos you're interested in, so you can make an accurate comparison. The "ideal" casino is different for every crapshooter.

A friend of mine smokes cigars and chooses his casino by the brands of cigars that are offered as comps. Someone else might only want to stay in a hotel that offers a jacuzzi, or an adjustable bed. Perhaps you would like a casino that has several different room floor plans, or one that has two shows instead of just one. One resort might have a terrific Chinese restaurant, while another might have a good Italian one. So, be sure to choose your casino on what YOU want - not what they want you to have!

Money Management - Many people will walk up to a craps table and then just keep on playing until they lose all of their money. It doesn't matter if they are $100 ahead or even $500 ahead - they just keep on playing. These people have no win goal.

The reason you need a win goal is because tables fluctuate. You can be $100 up one moment and $100 down the next. How do you know when to stop and still leave with a profit?

Your win goal should be based on your individual session money, and should be 30% of your buy in. For example, if you buy in with $100 and are $30 ahead you should quit. Leave the table and go to your room, or have lunch. Then an hour or so later, buy in with your $130 and quit when you've won $39. Be precise. Be disciplined. Follow the plan! Set a win goal and stick to it!

If you keep on playing until you lose all of your money you will do exactly that. When you play craps you need a definite, unchangeable win goal - something you can (excuse the pun) shoot for. You can't just play haphazardly and hope to win thousands from a $5 bet on a monster roll.

The opposite of a win goal is a loss limit, and its also 30% - very easy to remember! If you buy in for $100, you leave when you win or lose $30. If you buy in for $500 you leave when you win or lose $150.

You need a loss limit because if you play thinking that you brought $100 so the most you can lose is $100, then you certainly will lose it all. A lot of people bring $500 to a casino expecting to lose. It doesn't bother them because it was "extra" money that they could afford to spend on entertainment. So they break it up into five sessions of $100 each and just keep on playing until it's all gone. Wouldn't it be better to come home with $350 rather than nothing?
One of the cardinal rules of craps is to increase your bets while winning but decrease them while losing. But when many people start losing, they keep on playing as if nothing was different, or worse, they keep increasing their bets. Don't do it! You need a loss limit, and you need to stick to it. It is not a disgrace to come home after a weekend and only win $150. Or even $50. You can always lie to your friends about it. But when it comes to your own hard earned cash, you've got to protect it.

Go into a session expecting to win "only" $30 on a $100 buy in. Stop when you reach it. If you're losing, quit when you lose $30. In five $100 sessions the most you can lose is $150. You can, however, win more than $150, because your win limit increases on each win, even though you have the same win limit! So, stick to your guns. Set a win goal and a loss limit. Over the long run, you'll win more and lose less.

Business Plan - First of all, you should be a rated player and get a comp card. If your favorite casino has a separate card for slot play, get one of those, too. This way, whenever your favorite casino has any promotions of any kind, you will get mailings from them for free offers! Sometimes it is even possible to combine the promotions of the slot and table games offers.

You should also apply for casino credit. You can call the cage and ask how to do this. Your potential credit is based on your checking account balance, so the higher your balance, the higher your credit. Not only is casino credit more convenient, but in many cases you can withdraw your credit and use it free for 30 days. You'll also have a higher comp rating and be an established player in the eyes of the casino.

When you begin playing, just give the dealer your comp card and ask for your buy in. He will check your rating and give it to you in a minute or two. For example you might say "a thousand please" and he might say "in blacks or greens." He will then count out your chips on the table and set them aside while they check their computer.

Once you have the chips, you can play with the full amount, or not. For example, you can play with $500 worth and put the other $500 in your pocket and use it later or cash it in and use it in another casino if you like. When you leave the table, you may be asked if you want to pay off your marker. Don't be intimidated by this request, and just say no. Most casinos require that you pay back your markers in 30 days or it will adversely affect your credit with them in the future.

It is to your benefit to buy in with a larger amount than you will play with. Your comps are calculated by three criteria - (1) your buy in, (2) your first bet and (3) your average bet. So, if your buy in and first bet are larger than normal, your comps will be bumped up a little.

Something else you can do to increase your comps is to tip the dealers. Tipping will also get the dealers on your side so you can set the dice easier. The dealers will also notice your playing patterns and help you however they can - including bumping up your comps. The dealers would rather have you, a good tipper back in their casino, than an inexperienced player who doesn't tip.

Finally, you should notice the dealer's name tags and call them by name. Be friendly with them. If they remember your first name and use it when you leave the table, you've done a good job - and they'll be doing everything they can to get you back!

Savings - Now, let's get to specific savings. If you play four hours each day for three days the casino will usually give you two free nights lodging, 18 meals (3 meals a day for three days for two people) and two shows! Let's take a closer look at these free, extra added benefits that you receive just by playing the way you normally would.

Let's say you are a $50 player and play for 4 hours a day. You could receive $300 in hotel benefits, $180 in restaurant benefits, and $100 in shows. This is a total of $580 you didn't have before! This means that even if you break even playing, you are really $580 ahead!

Two weekend nights at a nice hotel can cost $150 per night or a total of $300. But if you play a little more you can request a Jacuzzi room or a two bedroom suite worth $200 per night.

Eighteen meals at $10 each (buffet or coffee shop only) is $180. This includes three meals per day for two people. But if you play a little more you can eat in one of the casino's gourmet restaurants, which is worth triple what the buffet or coffee shop costs.

Finally you get two show tickets worth $50 each or a total of $100. If you play a little more, you can get four, better show tickets in a different casino. These four tickets could be worth $400 which is $300 more than your original tickets.

To get the extra goodies you need to play 6-8 hours instead of four hours every day. Or you could just play with a partner or spouse. Achieving that higher level of comps is not difficult if you and your partner (who occupy the same hotel room) both play. In this case you would both only have to be $50 players to make $1,300 extra in three days. Just ask the boxman to combine your play. The pit might even bump you both up a little, as they really want good players to return to their casinos. They know that by giving you more comps, you'll be encouraged to return - and bring your friends with you!

Now, let's say you are both $50 players and play for the same four hours. You could receive $400 in hotel benefits (Jacuzzi suite), $500 in restaurant benefits (gourmet meals) and $400 in shows (in a different casino) - a grand total of $1,300! This means that if you just broke even while playing, you really made a profit of $1,300!

Conclusion - So if you want to minimize your losses by maximizing your comps you should -

1. Call a casino host and discuss your needs with him!
2. Choose a casino based on benefits, not features!
3. Have a realistic win goal and loss limit!
4. Increase your bets when winning, decrease them when losing!
5. Get a comp card and play only with casino credit!
6. Maximize your first bet and your buy in.
7. Tip the dealers and call them by name.
8. Find out which comps you want and what levels they require.
9. Adjust your bankroll, comp wants, or play with a partner.
10. Get up to $1,300 in FREE comps that you didn't have before!

And, as always, good luck at the casinos!

Larry Edell is the publisher of "The Crapshooter," the only newsletter devoted to the game of craps. For a free copy of Larry's newsletter see the coupon section in the back of this book. You can also visit his website at www.thecrapshooter.com

Roulette

by Steve Bourie

Virtually all American casinos use a double-zero roulette wheel which has pockets numbered from 1 to 36, plus 0 and 00 for a total of 38 pockets. This is in contrast to Europe where a single-zero wheel is used and the game has always been the most popular in the casino.

There are usually six seats at the roulette table and to help the dealer differentiate what each player is betting every player is assigned a different color chip which they purchase right at the table. Each table has its own minimum chip values and that information is usually posted on a sign at the table. As an example let's say a table has a $1 minimum chip value. This means that when you give the dealer your money the colored chips he gives you in return must have a minimum value of $1 each. So, if you gave the dealer $50 he would ask what value you wanted on the chips and if you said $1 he would give you 50 colored chips.

If you prefer, you could say you wanted the chips valued at $2 each and he would just give you 25 chips rather than 50. You can make the value of your colored chips anything you want and you'll notice that when the dealer gives you your chips he'll put one of your chips on the railing near the wheel with a marker on top to let him know the value of your chips. Later on when you're done playing at that table you must exchange your colored chips for regular chips before leaving. The colored chips have no value anywhere else in the casino so don't leave the table with them.

Besides the minimum chip value, there is also a minimum amount that must be bet on each spin of the wheel. Once again, the minimums are probably posted on a sign at the table and if it says $2 minimum inside and $5 minimum outside this means that if you are betting on any of the 38 numbers that pay 35-to-1 the total of all your bets must be $2. You could make two different $1 bets or one $2 bet, it doesn't matter except that the total of all your bets on the numbers must be at least $2. The $5 minimum outside means that any of the outside bets that pay 2-to-1, or even money, require that you bet $5 each time. On the outside bets you can't make a $3 bet and a $2 bet to meet the minimums - you have to bet at least $5 every time. After you've exchanged your cash for colored chips you're ready to place your first bet so, let's see what your options are:

You can make a ***straight*** bet where you only bet on one number and if it comes in you'll be paid 35-to-1. The casino advantage on this bet is 5.26% and by the time you're done with this roulette section I'm sure you'll be very familiar with that number.

Another choice you have is to do a ***split***. This is where you put a chip on the line that separates two numbers. If either number comes up you'll be paid at 17-to-1. The casino advantage on this bet is 5.26%.

If you put a chip in an area that splits 4 numbers this is called a ***corner*** bet and if any one of those 4 numbers comes in you will be paid off at 8-to-1. The casino advantage on this bet is 5.26%.

If you put a chip at the beginning of a row of 3 numbers, this is called a ***street*** bet and if any one of those 3 numbers shows up you will be paid off at 11-to-1. The casino advantage on this bet is 5.26%.

You can also put a chip on the line between two streets so that you have a ***double street*** covered and if any one of those 6 numbers come in you'll be paid off at 5-to-1. The casino advantage on this bet is?... you guessed it...5.26%.

The only other bet you can make on the inside numbers is the ***5- number*** bet where you place one chip in the upper left corner of the number 1 box. If any one of those 5 numbers comes in you'll be paid off at 6-to-1 and what do you think the casino advantage is on this bet? Nope, I gotcha... it's 7.89%. Actually, this is the worst possible bet on the roulette table and the only bet you'll come across that doesn't have a 5.26% house edge on the double-zero roulette wheel. You should never make this bet.

One quick word here about "to" and "for" when discussing odds. Whenever the odds are stated as "to" this means that in addition to the stated payoff you also receive your original bet back. In other words, if you won your single number bet in roulette you would receive 35-to-1, which is a 35-chip payoff, plus you'd still keep your original one-chip bet, so you end up with 36 chips. Now if the odds are stated as "for" that means you do not receive back your original bet. If the odds in your single number bet were 35-*for*-1 you would still receive a 35-chip payoff but the casino would keep your original one-chip bet so you would only end up with 35 chips. The only place in a casino where the odds are always stated as "for" is in video poker. You might also come across it on a couple of craps bets where the odds are stated as "for-one" rather than "to-one" in order to give the casino a slightly better edge.

Now, getting back to our roulette examples, let's look at all of the outside bets that you can make and keep in mind that the house edge on all of these outside bets is...do you remember the number?...that's right...5.26%.

There are three bets you can make that will pay you even money, or 1-to-1, which means that if you win, you will get back one dollar for every dollar you bet:

Red or black - If you put a chip on red then a red number must come up in order for you to win. If the ball lands on a black number, 0 or 00 - you lose. The same thing goes for black - you lose if it comes in red, 0 or 00 and you win if the ball lands on a black number.

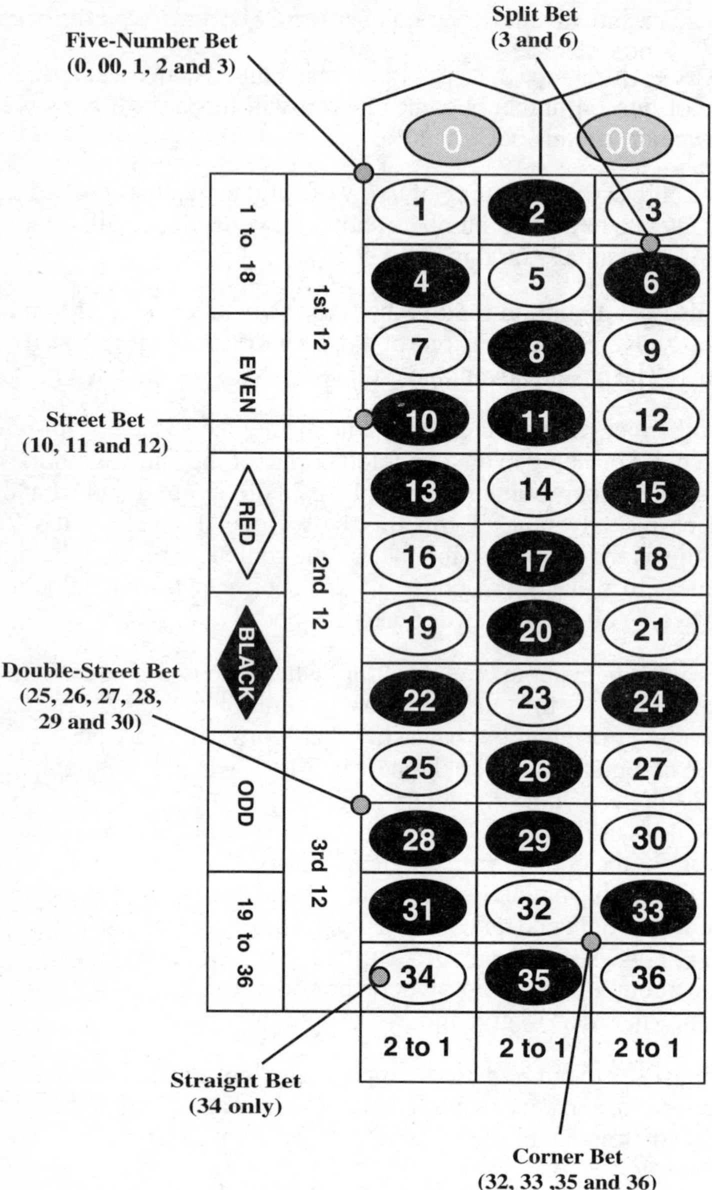

Typical felt layout for placing bets on American double-zero roulette wheel

Odd or even **-** If you put a chip on odd then the ball must land on an odd number in order for you to win. If it lands on 0, 00, or an even number - you lose. If you bet on even, you win if an even number shows up and lose if the ball lands on 0, 00 or an odd number.

1 through 18 and 19 through 36 **-** If you bet on 1 through 18, then you win if a number from 1 through 18 comes in and you lose if the ball lands on 0, 00 or a number higher than 18. Similarly, if you bet on 19 through 36, you win if one of those numbers comes in and you lose on 0, 00 or any number lower than 19.

The only other bets left are the ***dozens*** and columns bets. If you look at the roulette betting layout you can see three areas that each correspond to 12-number sections on the table. The one marked 1st 12 covers the numbers from 1 to 12, the one marked 2nd 12 covers the numbers from 13 to 24 and the other one that's marked 3rd 12 covers the last section of numbers from 25 to 36. If you bet on the 1st 12 you would win if a number from 1 to 12 came in and you would lose if anything else came in, including 0 or 00. The same principle holds true for each of the other dozen bets where you would win if a number in that section came in and you would lose if anything else showed up. All dozens bets pay 2-to-1.

The last bet to look at is the ***column*** bet and that is also a bet that pays 2-to-1. There are three possible column bets you can make and you'll notice that each area corresponds to the numbers in the column directly above it. So, if you put a chip under the first column you will win if any of the numbers in that column come in and you will lose if any other number, including 0 or 00 shows up. Once again, the same rule is in effect for each of the other columns where you would win if the number appears in the column above your bet and you would lose if it doesn't.

All right, now you know all the possible bets and you know how to make them at the table. So, the next question is "How do you win?" and the answer to that is very simple - You have to get lucky! And that's the ONLY way you can win at roulette. As you found out earlier, every bet, except for the 5-number bet, which I'm sure you'll never make, has a house edge of?...that's right...5.26%. So, feel free to put your chips all over the table and then just hope that you're lucky enough to have one of your numbers come up. You see, it just doesn't matter what you do because you'll always have that same house edge of 5.26% working against you on every bet you make.

Now, you may have heard of a system for roulette where you should place your bets only on the numbers that are evenly spaced out around the wheel. For example, if you wanted to play only four numbers, you could bet on 1,2,31 and 32 because when you looked at a roulette wheel, you would notice that if you divided it into four equal parts, you would have a number that appears in each of the four sections. So, is this a good system? Well, actually it's no better and no worse than any other roulette system. The fact is that it's purely a matter of chance where the ball happens to land and it makes no difference whether the numbers you choose are right next to each other or evenly spaced out on the wheel. Each number has an equal chance to occur on every spin of the wheel and the house edge always remains at 5.26%.

You can probably tell that I wouldn't recommend roulette as a good game to play because there are other games that offer much better odds, but if you really insist on playing the game I have three good suggestions for you. #1 - Go to Atlantic City! In Atlantic City if you make an even-money outside bet, like red or black, odd or even, 1 through 18 or 19 through 36 and if 0 or 00 come up, the state gaming regulations allow the casino to take only half of your bet. Because you only lose half of your bet this also lowers the casino edge on these outside bets in half to 2.63%. This rule is only in effect for even-money bets so keep in mind that on all other bets the house edge still remains at that very high 5.26%.

The second suggestion I have for you also involves some travel and here it is: Go to Europe! The game of roulette began in Europe and many casinos over there use a single-zero wheel which makes it a much better game because the house edge on a single-zero roulette wheel is only 2.70%. To make it even better, they have a rule called "en prison" which is similar to the Atlantic City casino rule. If you make an even-money outside bet and the ball lands on 0 you don't lose right away. Instead, your bet is "imprisoned" and you have to let it ride on the next spin. Then, if your bet wins, you can remove it from the table. Because of this rule, the casino edge on this bet is cut in half to 1.35% which makes it one of the best bets in the casino and almost four times better than the same bet when it's made on a standard double-zero roulette wheel in the United States.

Now, if you're not into traveling and you don't think you can make it to Atlantic City or Europe, then you'll just have to settle for suggestion #3 which is: Win quickly! Naturally, this is easier said than done, but in reality, if you want to win at roulette the best suggestion I can give you is that you try to win quickly and then walk away from the table because the longer you continue to bet the longer that big 5.26% house edge will keep eating away at your bankroll. One major principle of gambling is that in order to win you must only play the games that have the lowest casino edge and, unfortunately, roulette is not one of them.

Before closing out this look at roulette, let's take a minute to examine one of the most famous betting systems of all time and the one that many people frequently like to use on roulette. It's called the Martingale system and it is basically a simple system of doubling your bet whenever you lose. The theory behind it is that sooner or later you'll have to win and thus, you will always come out ahead. As an example, let's say you're playing roulette and you bet $1 on red, if you lose you double your next bet to $2 and if you lose that then you double your next bet to $4 and if you lose that you double your next bet to $8 and so forth until you eventually win. Now, when you finally do win you will end up with a profit equal to your original bet, which in this case is $1. If you started the same system with a $5 bet, you would have to bet $10 after your first loss, $20 after your second loss and so forth, but whenever you won you would end up with a $5 profit.

In theory, this sounds like a good idea but in reality it's a terrible system because eventually you will be forced to risk a great amount of money for a very small profit. Let's face it, even if you only wanted to make a $1 profit on each spin of the wheel, sooner or later you will hit a major losing streak where you will have to bet an awful lot of money just to make that $1 profit. For example, if you go eight spins without a winner, you would have to bet $256 on the next spin and if that lost then you'd have to bet $512. Would you really want to risk that kind of money just to make $1? I don't think so. You may think that the odds are highly unlikely that you would lose that many bets in a row, but eventually it will happen and when it does you will suffer some astronomical losses. One other problem with this system is that eventually you won't be able to double your bet because you will have reached the casino maximum, which in most casinos is $500 on roulette. Just keep in mind that the Martingale system works best when it's played for fun on paper and not for real money in a casino. If it was truly a winning system it would have bankrupted the world's casinos years ago.

Baccarat

by Steve Bourie

When you think of Baccarat you probably think of a game that's played by the casino's wealthiest players who sit at a private table and can afford to bet tens of thousands of dollars on the flip of a card and you know what? You're right! The game of Baccarat has always had a reputation as being for the richest gamblers and that usually scared off the average player, but nowadays more and more people are discovering that Baccarat is really a good game for the small stakes player because 1.-it has a relatively small advantage for the casino and 2.-it's very simple to play.

The mini-Baccarat table is the kind of Baccarat table you're most likely to find in the standard American casino and the game is played pretty much the same as regular Baccarat except that in the mini version all of the hands are dealt out by the dealer and the players never touch the cards. Other than that, the rules are virtually the same. Oh yes, one other difference you'll find is that the betting minimums will always be lower on mini-Baccarat and it's usually pretty easy to find a table with a $5 minimum.

Now, as I said before the game of Baccarat is very simple to play and that's because the only decision you have to make is what bet you want to make from the three that are available: player, banker or tie. After the players make their bets the game begins and two 2-card hands are dealt from a shoe that contains 8 decks of cards. One hand is dealt for the banker and another hand is dealt for the player. The values of the two cards in each hand are added together and the object of the game is to have a total as close to 9 as possible. After the values of the first two cards in each hand are totaled, a third card can be drawn by either the player, the banker or both. But, the decision as to whether or not a third card should be drawn is not decided by the dealer or the players - it is only decided by the rules of the game.

Actually the name Baccarat comes from the Italian word for zero and as you'll see there are lots of zeros in this game because when you add the cards together all of the 10's and all of the face cards are counted as zeros, while all of the other cards from ace though 9 are counted at their face value. So, a hand of Jack, 6 has a total of 6; 10,4 has a total of 4; king, 7 has a total of 7; and ace, queen which would be a great hand in blackjack, only has a total of 1. The other thing about adding the cards together is that no total can be higher than 9. So, if a total is 10 or higher you have to subtract 10 to determine its value. For example, 8,8 totals 16 but you subtract 10 and your total is 6; 9,5 has a total of 4; 8,3 has a total of 1; and 5,5 has a total of 0.

Once again, the object of the game of Baccarat is to have a total as close to 9 as possible, so after the first two cards are dealt if either the player or banker hand has a total of 9 then that's called a "natural" and that hand is the winner. If neither hand has a total of 9 then the next best possible hand is a total of 8 (which is also called a "natural") and that hand would be the winner. If both the player and the banker end up with the same total then it's a tie and neither hand wins.

Now, if neither hand has an 8 or a 9 then the rules of the game have to be consulted to decide whether or not a third card is drawn. Once that's done, the values of the cards are added together again and whichever hand is closest to a total of 9 is the winner. If both hands end up with the same total then it's a tie and neither hand wins.

If you want to bet on the player hand just put your money in the area marked "player" and if you win you'll be paid off at even-money, or $1 for every $1 you bet. The casino advantage on the player bet is 1.36%. If you want to bet on the banker hand you would place your bet in the area marked "banker" and if you win, you'll also be paid off at even-money, but you'll have to pay a 5% commission on the amount you win. So, if you won $10 on your bet, you would owe a 50¢ commission to the house. The 5% commission is only required if you win and not if you lose. The dealer will keep track of the amount you owe by putting an equal amount in a small area on the table that corresponds to your seat number at the table. So, if you're sitting at seat #3 and won $10 on the bank hand the dealer would pay you $10 and then put 50¢ in the #3 box. This lets him know how much you owe the casino in commissions and when you get up to leave the table you'll have to pay the dealer whatever amount is in that box. After adjusting for that 5% commission the casino advantage on the banker bet is 1.17%

Finally, if you want to bet on a tie you would place your bet in the area marked "tie" and if you win you'll be paid off at 8-to-1, or $8 for every $1 you bet. The big payoff sounds nice but actually this is a terrible bet because the casino advantage is a very high 14.1% and this bet should never be made.

As you've seen, the casino advantage in Baccarat is very low (except for the tie bet) and the rules are set in advance so no decisions are made by either the players or the dealer about how to play the cards. This means that, unlike blackjack where you have to decide whether or not you want another card, you have no decisions to make and no skill is involved. This also means that Baccarat is purely a guessing game, so even if you've never played the game before you can sit at a table and play just as well as anyone who's played the game for 20 years! This is the only game in the casino where this can happen and that's why I tell people that Baccarat is an especially good game for the beginning player because you need no special knowledge to take advantage of those low casino edge bets.

The only part of Baccarat that gets a little confusing is trying to understand the rules concerning the draw of a third card, but remember, the rules are always the same at every table and they'll usually have a printed copy of the rules at

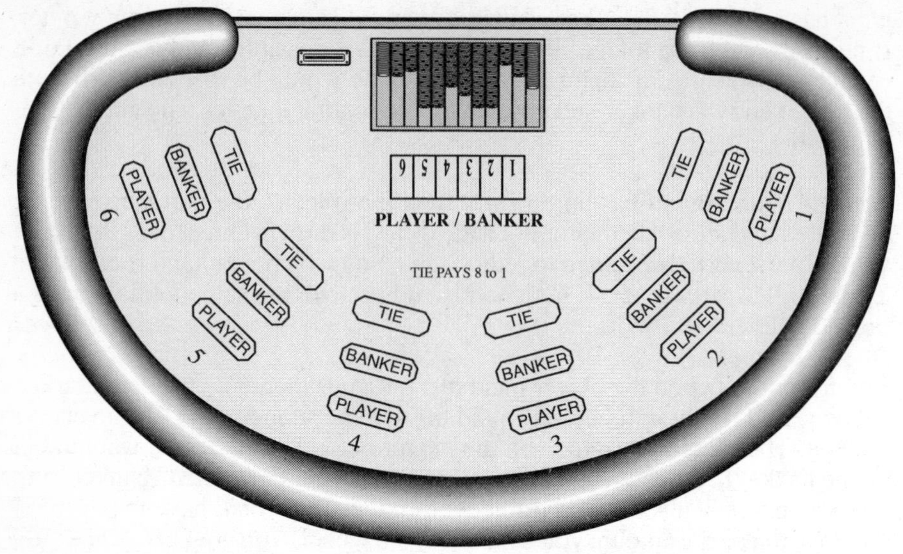

A Sample Mini-Baccarat Table Layout

the table and will give you a copy if you ask for it. After playing the game for awhile you'll start to remember the rules on your own, but until then here's a rundown on how it works:

As noted before, if the first two cards in either hand total 8 or 9, then the game is over and the highest total wins. If the totals are both 8 or both 9 then it's a tie and neither hand wins. For any other total the rules have to be consulted and it's always the player hand that goes first. If the player hand has a total of 6 or 7, it must stand. The only other totals it can possibly have are 0,1,2,3,4 or 5 and for all of those totals it must draw a card.

PLAYER HAND RULES

8,9	STANDS (Natural)
6,7	STANDS
0,1,2,3,4,5	DRAWS

There, that wasn't too hard to understand was it? If the player hand has a total of 6 or 7 it stands and for anything else it has to draw a card. Well, that was the easy part because now it gets a little complicated.

After the player hand is finished the banker hand must take its turn and if its first 2 cards total 0,1 or 2 it must draw a card. If its two cards total 7 it must stand and if the total is 6 it will stand, but only if the player hand did not take a card.

BANK HAND RULES

8,9	STANDS (Natural)
0,1,2	DRAWS
6	STANDS (If player took no card)
7	STANDS

The only other possible totals the bank can have are 3,4,5 or 6 and the decision as to whether or not a 3rd card is drawn depends on the 3rd card that was drawn by the player hand.

When the banker hand has a total of 3 it must stand if the player's 3rd card was an 8 and it must draw if the player's 3rd card was any other card.

IF BANK HAS 3 and

Player's third card is 8 - BANK STANDS
Player's third card is 1,2,3,4,5,6,7,9,10 - BANK DRAWS

When the banker hand has a total of 4 it must stand if the player's 3rd card was a 1,8,9, or 10 and it must draw if the player's 3rd card was any other card.

IF BANK HAS 4 and

Player's third card is 1,8,9,10 - BANK STANDS
Player's third card is 2,3,4,5,6,7 - BANK DRAWS

When the banker hand has a total of 5 it must draw if the player's 3rd card was a 4,5,6 or 7 and it must stand if the player's 3rd card was any other card.

IF BANK HAS 5 and

Player's third card is 1,2,3,8,9,10 - BANK STANDS
Player's third card is 4,5,6,7 - BANK DRAWS

When the banker hand has a total of 6 it must draw if the player's 3rd card was a 6 or 7 and it must stand if the player's 3rd card was any other card.

IF BANK HAS 6 and

Player's third card is 1,2,3,4,5,8,9,10 - BANK STANDS
Player's third card is 6 or 7 - BANK DRAWS

There you have it - those are the rules of Baccarat concerning the draw of a third card. As you saw they were a little complicated, but remember that you don't have to memorize the rules yourself because the dealer will know them and play each hand by those rules, but you can always ask for a copy of the rules at the table to follow along.

Now let's try some sample hands: The player hand has queen,9 for a total of 9 and the banker hand has 4,4 for a total of 8. Which hand wins? Both hands are naturals, but the player hand total of 9 is higher than the banker hand total of 8, so the player hand is the winner.

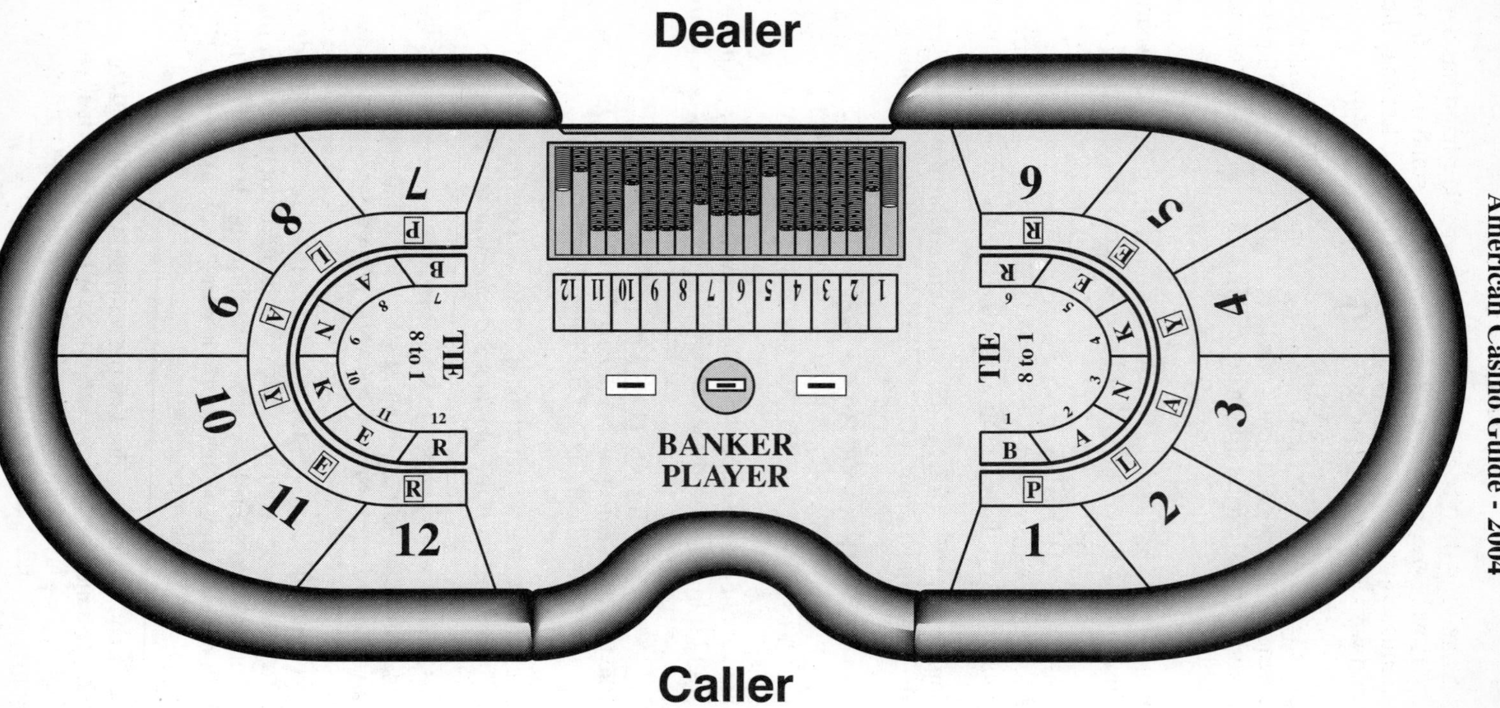

A 12-Seat Baccarat Table Layout

If the player hand has 4,2 for a total of 6 and the banker hand has ace, jack which totals 1, what happens? The player hand must stand on its 6 and the banker hand must always draw when it has a total of 0,1 or 2. Let's say the bank draws a 7 and wins 7 to 6.

What happens when the player hand has king, 5 and the bank hand has 2,4? The player hand must draw and let's say it gets a 7 for a total of 2. The banker hand has a total of 6 and if it could stand on that total it would win because its 6 is higher than the 2 held by the player. Of course, if you were betting on banker that's exactly what you would want to happen but, unfortunately for you, the rules require the bank hand to draw another card whenever its first two cards total 6 and the third card drawn by the player is a 7. So now, instead of having a winning hand you have to hope that the card you draw isn't a 5, which would give you a total of 1 making you a loser. You also wouldn't want to draw a 6 because that would give you a total of 2 which would give you a tie. In this case let's say that the bank hand goes on to draw an 8 which gives it a total of 3 and it wins 3 to 2.

Baccarat Rules Summary

Player Hand

When the first two cards total	
0-1-2-3-4-5	Draws
6-7	Stands
8-9	Natural (Banker cannot draw)

Banker Hand

When the first player's two cards total	DRAWS when player's third card is	STANDS when third card is
0-1-2	Always Draws	
3	1-2-3-4-5-6-7-9-0	8
4	2-3-4-5-6-7	1-8-9-0
5	4-5-6-7	1-2-3-8-9-0
6	6-7	1-2-3-4-5-8-9-0
7		Stands
8-9		Stands (Natural)

If the Player's hand does not draw a third card, then the Banker's hand stands on a total of 6 or more.

If the player hand has 3,ace for a total of 4 and the banker hand has 8,7 for a total of 5, what happens? The player hand must draw and say it gets a 9 for a total of 3. Once again, the banker hand would like to stand on its total because it would win, but the rules have to be consulted first and in this case when the banker's first 2 cards total 5 and the player's third card drawn is a 9 the banker hand must stand, so the banker hand wins 5 to 3.

Finally, let's say the player hand has 4,3 for a total of 7 and the banker hand has 6,10 for a total of 6. The player hand must always stand on totals of 6 or 7 and the banker hand must also stand on its total of 6 because the player hand didn't take a third card. The player hand wins this one 7 to 6.

All right, now that you know how to play Baccarat we come to the important question which is - how do you win? Well, as I said before, if you bet on player you'll only be giving the casino a 1.36% edge and if you bet on banker you'll be giving the casino an even more modest edge of just 1.17%. While both of these are pretty low edges to give the casino you're still stuck with the fact that the casino will always have an edge over you and in the long run the game of Baccarat is unbeatable. So, if that's the case then how do you win? Well, the answer to that is very simple - You have to get lucky! And that's the ONLY way you can win at Baccarat. Of course, this is easier said than done, but fortunately, in the game of Baccarat, you have the option of making two bets that require no skill and both offer the casino a very low edge especially when you compare them to roulette where the house has a 5.26% advantage on a double-zero wheel and slot machines where the edge is about 8% to 10% I always stress the point that when you gamble in a casino you have to play the games that have the lowest casino edge in order to have the best chance of winning and with that in mind you can see that Baccarat is not that bad a game to play for the recreational gambler.

Now let's take a quick look at one of the most common systems for betting on Baccarat. One thing that many Baccarat players seem to have in common is a belief in streaks and the casinos accommodate these players by providing scorecards at the table that can be used to track the results of each hand. Many players like to bet on whatever won the last hand in the belief that it will continue to come in and they hope for a long streak.

The thinking for these players is that since Baccarat is purely a guessing game it's just like guessing the outcome of a coin toss and chances are that a coin won't alternately come up heads, tails, heads, tails, heads, tails but rather that there will be streaks where the same result will come in for awhile. So, is this a good system? Well, actually, it's no better and no worse than any other system because no matter what you do you'll still have the same casino edge going against you on every bet you make: 1.36% on the player and 1.17% on the banker. The one good thing about a system like this though is that you don't have to sit there and guess what you want to play each time. Instead, you go into the game knowing how you're going to play and you don't have to blame yourself if your guess is wrong, instead you get to blame it on your system!

A Few Last Words

by Steve Bourie

When I sit down to put this book together each year I try to make sure that everything in here will help to make you a better and more knowledgeable gambler when you go to a casino.

I try to include stories that will help you understand how casinos operate, how to choose the best casino games and also how to play those games in the best way possible.

My philosophy with this book is that gambling in a casino is fun and for about 99% of the people who visit casinos that statement is true. The vast majority of people who gamble in casinos are recreational players who enjoy the fun and excitement of gambling. They know that they won't always win and they also realize that over the long term they will most likely have more losing sessions than winning ones. They also understand that any losses they incur will be the price they pay for their fun and they only gamble with money they can afford to lose. In other words, they realize that casino gambling is a form of entertainment, just like going to a movie or an amusement park, and they are willing to pay a price for that entertainment. Unfortunately, there are also some people who go to casinos and become problem gamblers.

According to Gamblers Anonymous you may be a problem gambler if you answer yes to at least seven of the following 20 questions:

1. Do you lose time from work due to gambling?
2. Does gambling make your home life unhappy?
3. Does gambling affect your reputation?
4. Do you ever feel remorse after gambling?
5. Do you ever gamble to get money with which to pay debts or to otherwise solve financial difficulties?
6. Does gambling cause a decrease in your ambition or efficiency?
7. After losing, do you feel you must return as soon as possible and win back your losses?
8. After a win, do you have a strong urge to return and win more?
9. Do you often gamble until your last dollar is gone?
10. Do you ever borrow to finance your gambling?
11. Do you ever sell anything to finance your gambling?

12. Are you reluctant to use your "gambling money" for other expenses?
13. Does gambling make you careless about the welfare of your family?
14. Do you ever gamble longer than you planned?
15. Do you ever gamble to escape worry or trouble?
16. Do you ever commit, or consider committing, an illegal act to finance your gambling?
17. Does gambling cause you to have difficulty sleeping?
18. Do arguments, disappointments, or frustrations create within you an urge to gamble?
19. Do you have an urge to celebrate good fortune by a few hours of gambling?
20. Do you ever consider self-destruction as a result of your gambling?

If you believe you might have a gambling problem you should be aware that help is available from The National Council on Problem Gambling, Inc. It is the foremost advocacy organization in the country for problem gamblers and is headquartered in Washington, D.C. It was formed in 1972 as a non-profit agency to promote public education and awareness about gambling problems and operates a 24-hour nationwide help line at 1-800-522-4700, plus a website at www.ncpgambling.org Anyone contacting that organization will be provided with the appropriate referral resources for help with their gambling problem.

Another good source for anyone seeking help with a gambling problem is Gambler's Anonymous. They have chapters in many cities throughout the U.S. as well as in most major cities throughout the world. You can see a list of all those cities on their website at www.gamblersanonymous.org or contact them by telephone at (213) 386-8789.

A third program, Gam-Anon, specializes in helping the spouse, family and close friends of compulsive gamblers rather than the gamblers themselves.If you are adversely affected by a loved one who is a compulsive gambler, then Gam-Anon is an organization that may benefit you. They have a website at www.gam-anon.org that lists the cities which host meetings. They can also be contacted by telephone at (718) 352-1671.

I sincerely hope that none of you reading this book will ever have a need to contact any of these worthwhile organizations, but it was an issue that I felt should be addressed.

ARIZONA

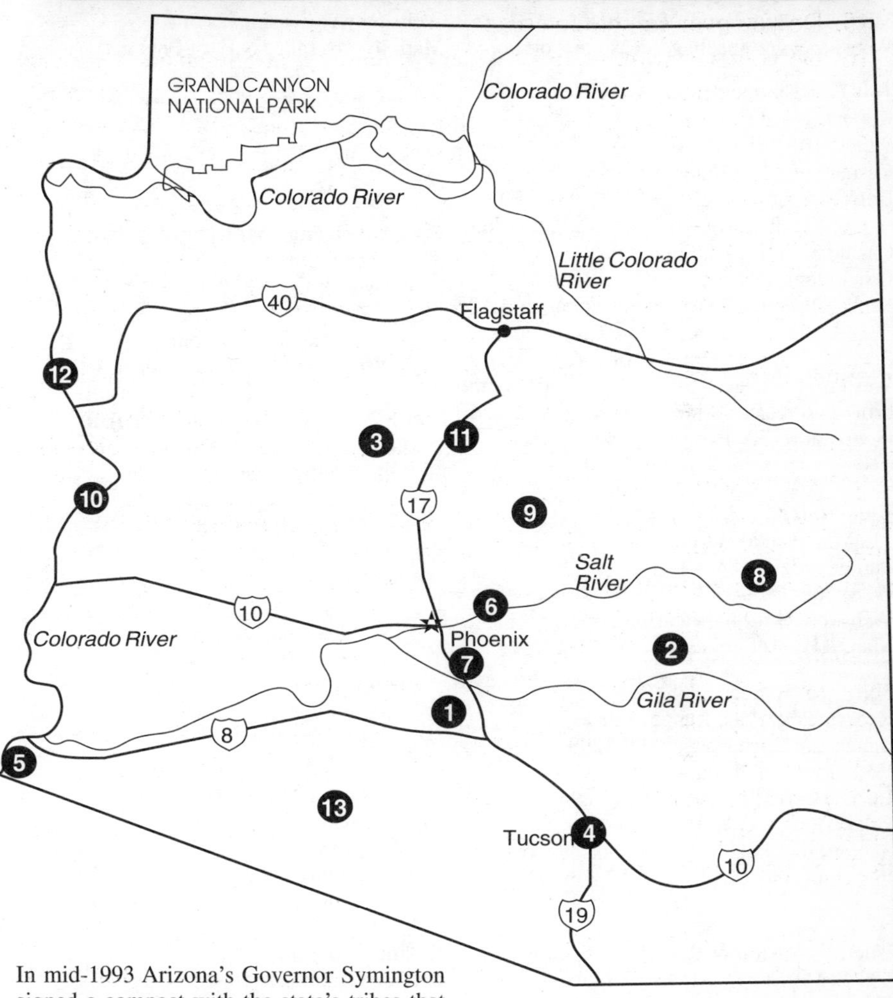

In mid-1993 Arizona's Governor Symington signed a compact with the state's tribes that allowed them to offer slot machines on their reservations.

The compact originally didn't allow for any table games but in early 2003 blackjack was added as a permissible table game. The casinos are also permitted to offer video versions of craps and roulette.

Arizona tribes aren't required to release information on their slot machine percentage paybacks, however, according to the Arizona Department of Gaming, the terms of the compact require each tribes' machines to return the following minimum and maximum paybacks: video poker and video blackjack - 83% to 100%, slot machines - 80% to 100%, keno - 75% to 100%. Each tribe is free to set its machines to pay back anywhere within those limits.

All Arizona casinos have slots, video poker and video keno. Optional games include: blackjack (BJ), video craps (VC), video roulette (VR), poker (P), live keno (K), bingo (BG) and simulcasting (S). The minimum gambling age is 21 and all casinos are open 24 hours. For more information on Arizona call the state's Office of Tourism at (602) 364-3700.

Apache Gold Casino Resort
P.O. Box 1210
San Carlos, Arizona 85550
(928) 475-7800
Map: **#2** (90 miles E. of Phoenix)
Website: www.apachegoldcasinoresort.com

Toll-Free Number: (800) APACHE-8
Rooms: 147 Price Range: $55-$95
Suites: 10 Price Range: $75-$150
Restaurants: 1 Liquor: Yes
Buffets: B-$6.95 (Sat/Sun) L-$7.95 D-$9.95/ $15.95 (Fri)/$10.45 (Sat)/$10.95 (Sun)
Casino Size: 10,000 Square Feet
Other Games: BJ, P, K, BG, S, VR
Senior Discount: 10% room discount for AAA AARP members. 15% for Club members.
Special Features: Hotel is off-property Best Western. Packages (Sun-Thu) include room, drink and meal. 18-hole golf course. Convenience store. RV Park w/full hookups.

Blue Water Casino
119 W. Riverside Drive
Parker, Arizona 85344
(928) 669-7777
Website: www.bluewaterfun.com
Map: **#10** (160 miles W. of Phoenix)

Toll-Free Number: (888) 243-3366
Rooms: 200 Price Range: $39-$125
Suites: 25 Price Range: $99-$299
Restaurants: 5 Liquor: Yes
Buffet: B- $6.95 L-$7.95 D-$8.95
Other Games: P, K, BG
Senior Discount: 10% room discount (except in summer) for AAA and AARP members.

Bucky's Casino & Resort
530 E. Merritt
Prescott, Arizona 86301
(928) 776-1666
Website: www.buckyscasino.com
Map: **#3** (91 miles S.W. of Flagstaff, Junction of Hwy. 69 & Hwy. 89)

Toll-Free Number: (800) SLOTS-44
Room Reservations: (800) 967-4637
Rooms: 81 Price Range: $99-$149
Suites: 80 Price Range: $129-$199
Restaurants: 2 Liquor: Yes
Other Games: BJ, P, BG
Special Features: Located in Prescott Resort Hotel. Free on-site shuttle service. Gas station and mini-mart. AAA/AARP room discount

Casino Arizona - Indian Bend
9700 E. Indian Bend
Scottsdale, Arizona 85256
(480) 850-7777
Website: www.casinoaz.com
Map: **#6** (15 miles N.E. of Phoenix)

Toll-Free Number: (877) 7-24-HOUR
Restaurants: 1 Liquor: Yes
Other Games: BJ, P

Casino Arizona - McKellips
524 N. 92nd Street
Scottsdale, Arizona 85256
(480) 850-7777
Website: www.casinoaz.com
Map: **#6** (15 miles N.E. of Phoenix)

Toll-Free Number: (877) 7-24-HOUR
Restaurants: 5 Liquor: Yes
Buffets: B-$13.95 (Sun) L-$7.95 D-$10.95/$15.95 (Fri/Sat)
Other Games: BJ, P, K, BG, S

Casino Del Sol
5655 W. Valencia
Tucson, Arizona 85746
(520) 883-1700
Website: www.casinodelsol.com
Map: **#4**

Toll-Free Number: (800) 344-9435
Restaurants: 1 Liquor: Yes
Other Games: BJ, P
Special Features: 4,400-seat amphitheater.

Casino of the Sun
7406 S. Camino De Oeste
Tucson, Arizona 85746
(520) 883-1700
Website: www.casinosun.com
Map: **#4**

Toll-Free Number: (800) 344-9435
Restaurants: 2 Liquor: No
Buffets: L-$7.25 D-$8.25
Other Games: BJ, P, BG
Special Features: Smoke shop. Gift shop. 50% food discount on Tuesdays and Wednesdays.

Cliff Castle Casino & Hotel Lodge
555 Middle Verde Road
Camp Verde, Arizona 86322
(928) 567-9031
Website: www.cliffcastle.com
Map: **#11** (50 miles S. of Flagstaff)

Toll-Free Number: (800) 381-SLOT
Room Reservation Number: (800) 524-6343
Rooms: 82 Price Range: $74-$79
Suites: 2 Price Range: $89
Restaurants: 5 Liquor: Yes
Other Games: BJ, VC, VR, K, P, BG
Casino Size: 114,000 Square Feet
Special Features: Casino is in Cliff Castle Lodge. Bowling alley. Kid's Quest childcare facility. Arcade. $10 off room rates to AAA or AARP members Sunday-Thursday.

Cocopah Casino & Bingo
15136 S. Avenue B
Somerton, Arizona 85350
(928) 726-8066
Map: **#5** (13 miles S.W. of Yuma)
Website: www.wincocopahcasino.com

Toll-Free Number: (800) 23-SLOTS
Restaurants: 1 Snack Bar Liquor: No
Other Games: BJ, BG
Special Features: RV park (800-537-7901). 18-hole golf course. New expanded casino expected to open in early 2004.

Desert Diamond Casino - I-19
1100 West Pima Mine Road
Sahuarita, Arizona 85629
(520) 294-7777
Website: www.desertdiamondcasino.net
Map: **#4**

Toll-Free Number: (866) 332-9467
Restaurants: 2 Liquor: Yes
Casino Size: 35,000 Square Feet
Other Games: BJ, VR, P, K, BG

Desert Diamond Casino - Nogales
7350 S. Nogales Highway
Tucson, Arizona 85706
(520) 294-7777
Website: www.desertdiamondcasino.net
Map: **#4**

Toll-Free Number: (866) 332-9467
Restaurants: 2 Liquor: Yes
Casino Size: 15,000 Square Feet
Other Games: BJ, VR, BG

Fort McDowell Casino
P.O. Box 18359
Fountain Hills, Arizona 85269
(602) 837-1424
Website: www.fortmcdowellcasino.com
Map: **#6** (25 miles N.E. of Phoenix)

Toll-Free Number: (800) THE-FORT
Restaurants: 3 (1 open 24 hours) Liquor: Yes
Buffets: B-$4.95/$7.95 (Sat-Sun)
D-$14.95
Other Games: BJ, P, K, BG, S,
Special Features: Free valley-wide transportation (reservations required). Gift shop.

Gila River Casino - Lone Butte
1200 S. 56th Street
Chandler, Arizona 85226
(520) 796-7777
Website: www.wingilariver.com
Map: **#7** (10 miles S.W. of Phoenix)

Toll-Free Number: (800) WIN-GILA
Restaurants: 1 Liquor: No
Casino Size: 30,000 Square Feet
Other Games: P

Gila River Casino - Vee Quiva
6443 N. Komatke Lane
Laveen, Arizona 85339
(520) 796-7777
Website: www.wingilariver.com
Map: **#7** (10 miles S.W. of Phoenix)

Toll-Free Number: (800) WIN-GILA
Restaurants: 2 Liquor: No
Casino Size: 30,000 Square Feet
Other Games: P, BG

Gila River Casino - Wild Horse
5512 W. Wild Horse Pass
Chandler, Arizona 85226
(520) 796-7727
Website: www.wingilariver.com
Map: **#7** (25 miles S.E. of Phoenix)

Toll-Free Number: (800) WIN-GILA
Restaurants: 1 Liquor: No
Casino Size: 60,000 Square Feet
Other Games: VC, VR, P, K, BG

Golden Hasan Casino
PO Box 10
Ajo, Arizona 85321
(520) 362-2746
Website: www.desertdiamondcasino.net
Map: **#13** (125 miles S.W. of Phoenix)

Restaurants: 1 Snack Bar
Hours: 10am-12am/10am-1am (Fri-Sat)

Harrah's Ak Chin Casino Resort
15406 Maricopa Road
Maricopa, Arizona 85239
(480) 802-5000
Website: www.harrahs.com
Map: **#1** (25 miles S. of Phoenix)

Toll-Free Number: (800) HARRAHS
Rooms: 142 Price Range: $55-$150
Suites: 4 Price Range: $300
Restaurants: 4 (1 open 24 hours) Liquor: Yes
Buffets: L-$8.99
D-$12.99/$14.99 (Fri-Sun)
Casino Size: 43,000 Square Feet
Other Games: BJ, VC, VR, P, K, BG
Senior Discount: Various, if 50, or older
Special Features: Two bars. Live entertainment. Native-American crafts store and smoke shop. Fitness center. Pool with swim-up bar. Large buffet discount with slot card.

Hon-Dah Resort Casino
777 Highway 260
Pinetop, Arizona 85935
(928) 369-0299
Website: www.hon-dah.com
Map: **#8** (190 miles N.E. of Phoenix)

Toll-Free Number: (800) 929-8744
Rooms: 126 Price Range: $89-$109
Suites: 2 Price Range: $150-$180
Restaurants: 1 Liquor: Yes
Buffets: B- $3.95/$13.95(Sun)
D-$13.95 (Fri-Sat)
Casino Size: 20,000 Square Feet
Other Games: BJ, P, BG (Sun/Mon)
Special Features: 200-space RV park. Waterfall wildlife attraction in hotel lobby. Convenience store. Gas station. Cigar bar. Gift shop.

Mazatzal Casino
P.O. Box 1820
Hwy. 87, Milemarker 251
Payson, Arizona 85547
(928) 474-6044
Website: www.777play.com
Map: **#9** (90 miles N.E. of Phoenix)

Toll-Free Number: (800) 777-7529
Restaurants: 2 Liquor: Yes
Casino Size: 35,000 Square Feet
Other Games: BJ, K, BG
Senior Discount: 10% off food, if 55, or older
Special Features: Packages (Sun-Thu) with local motels include: discounted room, Fun Books, breakfast for two, plus free shuttle. Sports bar. Video arcade. Gift shop.

Paradise Casino
450 Quechan Drive
Yuma, Arizona 85364
(760) 572-7777
Website: www.paradise-casinos.com
Map: **#5** (244 miles W. of Tucson)

Toll-Free Number: (888) 777-4946
Restaurants: 1 Liquor: Yes
Buffets: L/D-$4.25
Casino Marketing: (760) 572-2463
Other Games: P, K, BG
Senior Discount: 20% off food, if 65, or older
Special Features: $8.88 prime rib and lobster specials on Friday. Part of casino is located across the state border in California.

Spirit Mountain Casino
8555 South Highway 95
Mohave Valley, Arizona 86440
(928) 346-2000
Map: **#12** (15 miles S. of Bullhead City)

Restaurants: 1 Snack Bar Liquor: Yes
Casino Size: 12,000 Square Feet
Special Features: Adjacent to 120-space RV park. Convenience store. Gas station.

Yavapai Casino
1501 E. Highway 69
Prescott, Arizona 86301
(928) 445-5767
Website: www.buckyscasino.com
Map: **#3** (91 miles S.W. of Flagstaff)

Toll-Free Number: (800) SLOTS-44
Restaurants: 1 Snack Bar Liquor: No
Other Games: BG (Wed-Sun)
Special Features: Located across the street from Bucky's Casino. Free shuttle bus service.

CALIFORNIA

On March 7,2000 California voters approved a statewide referendum that legally allowed the state's Indian tribes to begin offering electronic gaming machines, blackjack, and other house-banked card games. The games of craps and roulette are not permitted. However, some casinos offer modified versions of those games that are played with cards rather than dice or roulette wheels.

Most California card rooms also offer some form of player-banked blackjack but, because they are prohibited by law from playing blackjack, the game is usually played to 22 rather than 21. Additionally, players must pay a commission to the house on every hand they play. The amount will vary depending on the rules of the house but, generally, it's about two to five percent of the total amount bet. There are slightly more than 100 card rooms in California and you can see a listing of all of them on the *americancasinoguide.com* website.

California's tribes aren't required to release information on their slot machine percentage paybacks and as of July, 2003 the state of California did not require any minimum returns on gaming machines.

Unless otherwise noted, all California casinos are open 24 hours and offer: slots, video poker, and video keno. Optional games offered include: blackjack (BJ), Spanish 21 (S21), mini-baccarat (MB), poker (P), pai gow poker (PGP), Caribbean stud poker (CSP), let it ride (LIR), three card poker (TCP), bingo (BG), casino war (CW) and simulcasting (S). The minimum gambling age is 18 (21 if alcohol is served).

Although most of the casinos have toll-free numbers be aware that many of those numbers will only work for calls made within California. Also, many of the casinos are in out-of-the-way locations, so it is advisable to call ahead for directions, especially if you will be driving at night.

For more information on visiting California call the state's department of tourism at (800) 862-2543.

Agua Caliente Casino
32-250 Bob Hope Drive
Rancho Mirage, California 92270
(760) 321-2000
Website: www.hotwatercasino.com
Map: **#3** (115 miles E. of L. A.)

Toll-Free Number: (866) 858-3600
Restaurants: 3 Liquor: Yes
Buffets: B-$6.95 L-$9.95
D-$15.95/$20.95 (Fri-Sat)
Other Games: BJ, MB, CSP, TCP,
P, PGP, BG (Sun-Thu)
Special Features: $1 off buffets and 2-for-1 breakfast buffet (Mon-Fri) for slot club members. Associated with Spa Casino. 1,000-seat showroom.

Alturas Casino
901 County Road 56
Alturas, California 96101
(530) 233-3141
Map: **#27** (250 miles N.E. of Sacramento)

Restaurants: 1 Snack Bar Liquor: No
Hours: 9am-Midnight/1am (Fri-Sat)
Other Games: Slots Only,
BG (Sun/Mon/Wed-Fri)
Senior Discount: Mondays specials if 55 or older

Augustine Casino
84001 Avenue 54
Coachella, California 92236
(760)391-9500
Website: www.augustinecasino.com
Map: **#8** (125 miles E. of L. A.)

Toll-Free Number: (888) 752-9294
Restaurants: 2 Liquor: Yes
Buffets: L-$5.95/$8.95 (Sun)
D-$7.95/$12.95 (Fri-Sat)/$8.95 (Sun)
Other Games: BJ, TCP, S21

Barona Valley Ranch Resort and Casino
1932 Wildcat Canyon Road
Lakeside, California 92040
(619) 443-2300
Website: www.barona.com
Map: **#1** (15 miles N.E. of San Diego)

Toll-Free Number: (888) 7-BARONA
Room Reservations: (877) 287-2624
Rooms: 387 Price Range: $79-$149
Suites: 10 Price Range: $250-$450
Restaurants: 4 Liquor: No
Buffets: B/L-$9.99/$12.99 (Sat-Sun)
D-$14.99/$16.99 (Fri-Sat)
Other Games: BJ, BG, B, MB, P, CSP, PGP,
TCP, LIR, CW, S
Special Features: Food court. Wedding chapel. 18-hole golf course. Buffet discounts for slot club members.

Black Bart Casino
P.O. Box 1177
Willits, California 95490
(707) 459-7330
Map: **#11** (160 miles N.W. of Sacramento)

Restaurants: 1 Deli Liquor: No
Hours: 8am-2am/24 hours (Fri/Sat)
Casino Size: 3,000 Square Feet
Other Games: Slots Only

Black Oak Casino
19400 Tuolumne Road North
Tuolumne, California 95379
(209) 928-9300
Website: www.blackoakcasino.com
Map: **#5** (100 miles S.E. of Sacramento)

Toll-Free Number: (877) 747-8777
Restaurants: 1 Liquor: Yes
Casino Size: 22,000 Square Feet
Other Games: BJ, TCP

Blue Lake Casino
777 Casino Way
Blue Lake, California 95525
(707)668 -9770
Website: www.bluelakecasino.com
Map: **#34** (10 miles N. of Eureka)

Restaurants: 3 Liquor: No
Buffet: B/L- $4.95/$5.95(Sat)/$6.95(Sun)
D-$7.95/$9.95(Wed/Fri)
Other Games: BJ, S21, TCP, LIR, BG

Cache Creek Indian Bingo & Casino
14455 Highway 16
Brooks, California 95606
(530) 796-3118
Website: www.cachecreek.com
Map: **#2** (35 miles N.W. of Sacramento)

Toll-Free Number: (800) 452-8181
Restaurants: 4 Liquor: No
Buffets: L-$8/$10 (Sat-Sun)
D-$12/$16 (Fri-Sun)
Casino Size: 18,000 Square Feet
Other Games: BJ, P, CSP, PGP, BG (Sun-Thu)

Cahuilla Creek Casino
PO Box 390845
Anza, California 92539
(909) 763-1200
Website: www.cahuillacreek.com
Map: **#19** (30 miles S. of Palm Springs)

Restaurants: 1 Liquor: Yes
Buffets: Brunch-$8.95 (Thu/Sun)
Other Games: BJ, P
Special Features: Free supervised children's play area.

Casino Morongo
49750 Seminole Drive
Cabazon, California 92230
(909) 849-3080
Website: www.casinomorongo.com
Map: **#3** (90 miles E. of L. A.)

Toll-Free Number: (800) 252-4499
Restaurants: 2 Liquor: Yes
Casino Size: 100,000 Square Feet
Other Games: BJ, P, CSP, TCP, LIR, MB PGP, BG (Wed-Sun)
Special Features: Charges players a commission on their blackjack games. Slot club members get food and gas discounts.

Casino Pauma
777 Pauma Reservation Road
Pauma Valley, California 92061
(760) 742-2177
Website: www.casinopauma.com
Map: **#20** (35 miles N.E. of San Diego)

Toll-Free Number: (877) 687-2862
Restaurants: 1 Liquor: Yes
Buffets: L-$5.95 D-$7.95
Casino Size: 35,000 Square Feet
Other Games: P, TCP, PGP
Senior Discount: 2-for-1 lunch buffet, if 55+
Special Features: Offers card versions of craps and roulette. 95-cent breakfast special. 2-for-1 prime rib (Sun-Thu).

Cherae Heights Casino
P.O. Box 635
Trinidad, California 95570
(707) 677-3611
Website: www.cheraeheightscasino.com
Map: **#4** (25 miles N. of Eureka)

Toll-Free Number: (800) 684-BINGO
Restaurants: 1 Snack Bar Liquor: No
Buffets: B/L-$18 (Sun)
Other Games: BJ, P, BG (Wed-Sun)

Chicken Ranch Bingo
16929 Chicken Ranch Road
Jamestown, California 95327
(209) 984-3000
Map: **#5** (100 miles S.E. of Sacramento)

Toll-Free Number: (800) 752-4646
Restaurants: 1 Snack Bar Liquor: No
Hours: 9am-1am Daily
Casino Size: 35,000 Square Feet
Other Games: Slots only, BG (Thu-Sun)

Chuk Chansi Gold Resort & Casino
711 Lucky Lane
Coarsegold, California 93614
(559) 692-5200
Website: www.chukchansigold.com
Map: **#25** (35 miles N. of Fresno)

Toll-Free Number: (866) 794-6946
Rooms: 192 Prices: $59-$139
Restaurants: 5 Liquor: Yes
Buffets: B-$6.99 L-$8.99 D-$11.99
Other Games: BJ, S21, MB, TCP, PGP, LIR

Chumash Casino
3400 East Highway 246
Santa Ynez, California 93460
(805) 686-0855
Website: www.chumashcasino.com
Map: **#13** (40 miles N.W. of Santa Barbara)

Toll-Free Number: (800) 728-9997
Restaurants: 1 Liquor: No
Buffets: B-$6.95, L-$7.50
Senior Discount: Free breakfast Wed, from 6-10 am if 55 or older
Other Games: BJ, P, PGP, BG, LIR, TCP

Colusa Casino & Bingo
P.O. Box 1267
Colusa, California 95932
(530) 458-8844
Website: www.colusacasino.com
Map: **#6** (75 miles N. of Sacramento)

Toll-Free Number: (800) 655-U-WIN
Restaurants: 1 Liquor: Yes
Buffets: L-$7.99 D-$9.99
Senior Discount: Tue/Sun 8:00am-3:30pm seniors receive free $5 slot play, coffee, pastries, slot tournament, if 55 or older.
Other Games: BJ, P, CSP, TCP, PGP, BG (Fri-Tue)

Coyote Valley Shodakai Casino
7751 N. State Street
Redwood Valley, California 95470
(707) 485-0700
Website: www.coyotevalley.com
Map: **#23** (115 miles N. of San Francisco)

Toll-Free Number: (800) 332-9683
Restaurants: 1 Snack Bar Liquor: No
Other Games: BJ, PGP, BG (Fri-Tue)

Diamond Mountain Casino
900 Skyline Drive
Susanville, California 96130
(530) 252-1100
Website: www.susanvillecasino.com
Map: **#31** (160 Miles N.E. of Sacramento)

Restaurants: 1 Liquor: Yes
Other Games: BJ, P
Senior Discount: 25% off in deli, if 55, or older

Eagle Mountain Casino
P.O. Box 1659
Porterville, California 93258
(559) 788-6220
Website: www.eaglemtncasino.com
Map: **#21** (60 miles S.E. of Fresno)

Toll-Free Number: (800) 903-3353
Restaurants: 2 Liquor: No
Buffets: B-$3.99 L/D-$4.99
Casino Size: 9,600 Square Feet
Other Games: BJ, LIR, BG (Thu-Sun)

Elk Valley Casino
2500 Howland Hill Road
Crescent City, California 95531
(707) 464-1020
Website: www.elkvalleycasino.com
Map: **#7** (84 miles N. of Eureka)

Toll-Free Number: (888) 574-2744
Restaurants: 1 Liquor: No
Casino Size: 23,000 Square Feet
Other Games: BJ, P, BG (Fri-Mon)
Senior Discount: Lunch discount Tue, if 55+

Fantasy Springs Casino
82-245 Indio Springs Drive
Indio, California 92203
(760) 342-5000
Website: www.fantasyspringsresort.com
Map: **#8** (125 miles E. of Los Angeles)

Toll-Free Number: (800) 827-2WIN
Restaurants: 4 (1 open 24 hours) Liquor: Yes
Buffets: Brunch-$14.95 (Sun)
Casino Size: 95,000 Square Feet
Other Games: BJ, S21, MB, P, CSP, TCP, BG, S
Fun Book: Go to Fan Club desk
Senior Discount: Bingo discount, if 55+
Special Features: Bowling alley. Card version of craps. $5 off brunch for slot club members.

Feather Falls Casino
3 Alverda Drive
Oroville, California 95966
(530) 533-3885
Website: www.featherfallscasino.com
Map: **#22** (100 miles N. of Sacramento)

Toll-Free Number: (877) OK-BINGO
Restaurants: 1 Liquor: Yes
Buffets: B-$6.99 (Sun)
D-$9.99 /$13.99 (Sat)/$15.99(Fri)
Casino Size: 38,000 Square Feet
Other Games: BJ, P, TCP
Senior Discount: Drawings Wed if 55 or older.
Special Features: Charges players a commission on their blackjack games.

Gold Country Casino
4020 Olive Highway
Oroville, California 95966
(530) 538-4560
Website: www.gold-country-casino.com
Map: **#22** (100 miles N. of Sacramento)

Toll-Free Number: (800) 334-9400
Restaurants: 1 Snack Bar Liquor: No
Other Games: BJ, BG (Sat-Wed)

Golden Acorn Casino and Travel Center
1800 Golden Acorn Way
Campo, CA 91906
(619)938-6000
Website: www.goldenacorncasino.com
Map: **#33** (40 miles S.E. of San Diego)

Toll-Free Number: (866) 794-6244
Restaurants: 2 (Open 24 hours) Liquor: Yes
Other Games: BJ, PGP, TCP, LIR
Fun Book: Given with slot club sign-up
Senior Discounts: Tue/Thu 6am-6pm
free fun book if, 55 or older
Special Features: 33-acre travel center with auto and truck stop and convenience store.

Harrah's Rincon Casino & Resort
33750 Valley Center Road
Valley Center, California 92082
(760) 760-751-3100
Website: www.harrahs.com
Map: **#20** (35 miles N.E. of San Diego)

Toll-Free Number: (877) 777-2457
Rooms: 201 Prices: $79-$300
Suites: 17 Prices: Casino Use Only
Restaurants: 5 Liquor: Yes
Buffets: B-$13.99 (Sat-Sun) L-$9.99
D-$16.99 (Wed)/$19.99 (Sat)/
$18.99 (Sun/Thu)/$25.99 (Fri)
Casino Size: 45,000 Square Feet
Other Games: BJ, PGP, MB, TCP, LIR

Havasu Landing Resort & Casino
5 Main Street
Havasu Lake, California 92363
(760) 858-4593
Website: www.havasulanding.com
Map: **#18** (200 miles E. of L. A.)

Toll Free Number: (800) 307-3610
Restaurants: 1 Liquor: Yes
Hours: 9:30am-12:30am/2:30am (Fri/Sat)
Other Games: BJ, TCP (Wed-Sun)
Casino Size: 6,000 Square Feet
Special Features: Marina, RV park and campground rentals. Mobile homes on lake available for daily rental, call (760) 858-5410.

Hopland Sho-Ka-Wah Casino
13101 Nakomis Road
Hopland, California 95449
(707) 744-1395
Website: www.shokawah.com
Map: **#23** (100 miles N. of San Francisco)

Toll Free Number: (888) 746-5292
Restaurants: 2 Liquor: Yes
Other Games: BJ, S21, P, PGP, BG

Jackson Rancheria Casino & Hotel
12222 New York Ranch Road
Jackson, California 95642
(209) 223-1677
Website: www.jacksoncasino.com
Map: **#9** (60 miles S.E. of Sacramento)

Toll-Free Number: (800) 822-WINN
Rooms: 99 Price Range: $89-$124
Suites: 4 Price Range: $169-$259
Restaurants: 2 Liquor: No
Buffets: B-$12.95 (Sat/Sun)/L-$8.95/
$10.95(Sat/Sun)/D-$12.95/$15.95 (Fri)
Other Games: BJ, PGP, LIR, TCP,
BG (Mon-Wed)
Senior Discount: 10% off buffet, if 55, or older

Konocti Vista Casino
2755 Mission Rancheria Road
Lakeport, California 95453
(707) 262-1900
Website: www.kvcasino.com
Map: **#23** (120 miles N. of San Francisco)

Toll-Free Number: (800) FUN-1950
Restaurants: 1 Liquor: No
Other Games: BJ, LIR, TCP
Senior Discount: $10 in matchplay on Sun/Fri if 55, or older

La Jolla Slot Arcade
2200 Hwy 76
Pauma Valley, California 92061
(760) 742-3066
Website:www.lajollaindians.com
Map: **#29** (190 miles N. of Sacramento)

Restaurants: No Liquor: No
Hours: 8am-11pm/2am (Fri/Sat)
Other Games: Slots only
Special Features: Campground, waterpark, and trading post.

Lucky Bear Casino
P.O. Box 729
Hoopa, California 95546
(530) 625-5198
Map: **#24** (30 miles N.E. of Eureka)

Restaurants: 1 Snack Bar Liquor: No
Hours: 10am-Mid/1am (Fri/Sat)
Other Games: Slots only

Lucky 7 Casino
350 N. Indian Road
Smith River, California 95567
(707) 487-7777
Website: www.lucky7casino.com
Map: **#7** (100 miles N. of Eureka)

Toll-Free Number: (866) 777-7170
Restaurants: 1 Liquor: Yes
Other Games: BJ, BG (Sun/Tue/Wed)
Casino Size: 24,000 Square Feet

Mono Wind Casino
37302 Rancheria Lane
Auberry, California 93602
(559) 855-4350
Map: **#25** (30 miles N.E. of Fresno)

Restaurants: 1 Liquor: Yes
Buffets: L-$5.95 (Tue-Sun)
Other Games: BJ, PGP, BG
Senior Discount: 10% off in restaurant, if 55+

Paiute Palace Casino
PO Box 1325
Bishop, California 93514
(760) 873-4150
Website: www.paiutepalace.com
Map: **#26** (130 miles N.E. of Fresno)

Toll-Free Number: (888) 3-PAIUTE
Restaurants: 1 Liquor: No
Buffets: Brunch-$5.99 (Sun)
Other Games: BJ, P
Fun Book: Ask at cashier cage
Senior Discount: 10% off in restaurant, if 55+

Pala Casino
11154 Highway 76
Pala, California 92054
(760) 510-5100
Website: www.palacasino.com
Map: **#20** (35 miles N.E. of San Diego)

Toll-Free Number: (877) 946-7252
Rooms: 425 Prices: $109-$149
Suites: 82 Prices: $159-$299
Restaurants: 6 Liquor: Yes
Buffets: L-$8.99/$11.99(Sat/Sun)
D-$12.99/$18.99 (Fri)
Other Games: BJ, MB, TCP, PGP,
CSP, LIR, CW, B
Special Features: Fitness center and spa.

Palace Indian Gaming Center
17225 Jersey Avenue
Lemoore, California 93245
(559) 924-7751
Website: www.thepalace.net
Map: **#10** (50 miles S. of Fresno)

Toll-Free Number: (800) 942-6886
Restaurants: 4 Liquor: Yes
Buffets: L-$6.99 D-$10.99/$4.99(Thu)
Casino Size: 105,000 Square Feet
Other Games: BJ, P, PGP, LIR, BG

Paradise Casino
450 Quechan Drive
Ft Yuma, California 92283
(760) 572-7777
Website: www.paradise-casinos.com
Map: **#37** (170 miles E. of San Diego)

Toll-Free Number: (888) 777-4946
Restaurants: 1 Liquor: Yes
Buffets: L/D-$4.25
Casino Marketing: (760) 572-2463
Other Games: P, K, BG
Senior Discount: 20% off food, if 65, or older
Special Features: $8.88 prime rib and lobster specials on Friday. Part of casino is located across state border in Arizona.

Pechanga Resort and Casino
45000 Pala Road
Temecula, California 92592
(909) 693-1819
Website: www.pechanga.com
Map: **#28** (50 miles N. of San Diego)

Toll-Free Number: (888) PECHANGA
Rooms: 489 Price Range: $99-$200
Suites: 33 Price Range: $179-$359
Restaurants: 6 Liquor: No
Buffets: L-$8.99/$7.99
D- $11.49/$16.50(Sat/Sun)
Other Games: BJ, P, PGP, TCP, BG
Special Features: 170-space RV park with full hook-ups. Live entertainment and headliner acts. 2am-5am buffet for $3.95.

Pit River Casino
20265 Tamarack Avenue
Burney, California 96013
(530) 335-2334
Map: **#29** (190 miles N. of Sacramento)

Toll-Free Number: (888) 245-2992
Restaurants: 1 Snack Bar Liquor: No
Hours: 10am-Midnight Daily
Other Games: BJ, BG, TCP
Senior Discount: $5 match play given on Sundays and Mondays, if 55, or older.

Red Fox Casino & Bingo
300 Cahto Drive
Laytonville, California 95454
(707) 984-6800
Map: **#30** (150 miles N.W. of Sacramento)

Toll-Free Number: (888) 4-RED-FOX
Restaurants: 1 Snack Bar Liquor: No
Hours: 10am-Mid/2am (Fri/Sat)
Other Games: BJ, BG

River Rock Casino
3250 Hwy 128 East
Geyserville, California 95441
(707) 857-2777
Website: www.river-rock-casino.com
Map: **#32** (75 miles N. of San Fran.)

Restaurants: 2 Liquor: No
Buffets: B- $6.50 (Sat/Sun) L-$8.50
D-$10.50/$14.50 (Sat/Sun)
Other Games: BJ, PGP, TCP

Robinson Rancheria Bingo & Casino
1545 E. Highway 20
Nice, California 95464
(707)275-9000
Website: www.robinsonrancheria.biz
Map: **#11** (100 miles N.W. of Sacramento)

Toll-Free Number: (800) 809-3636
Restaurants: 2 Liquor: No
Buffets: L-$5.95 D-$9.99/$12.99 (Fri/Sat)
Casino Size: 37,500 Square Feet
Other Games: BJ, P, PGP, BG
Fun Book: Ask at cage on birthday
Senior Discount: Free lunch buffet and $10 matchplay on Mondays 9am-Noon, if 55, or older. Free bingo on Thursday.

Rolling Hills Casino
655 Barham Avenue
Corning, California 96021
(532) 528-3500
Website: www.rollinghillscasino.com
Map: **#36** (115 miles N. of Sacramento)

Toll-Free Number: (888) 331-6400
Restaurants: 3 Liquor: No
Buffet: B-$6.45 L-$8.45
D-$10.95/$14.95(Wed)
Other Games: BJ, PGP, TCP

San Manuel Indian Bingo & Casino
5797 North Victoria Avenue
Highland, California 92346
(909) 864-5050
Website: www.sanmanuel.com
Map: **#12** (65 miles E. of L. A.)

Toll-Free Number: (800) 359-2464
Restaurants: 2 Snack Bars Liquor: Yes
Casino Size: 75,000 Square Feet
Other Games: BJ, P, BG, PGP
Senior Discount: $10 bingo buy-in Fri, if 55+
Special Features: Charges players a commission on their blackjack games. Live entertainment weekly. Nonsmoking areas.

Soboba Casino
23333 Soboba Road
San Jacinto, California 92583
(909) 654-2883
Website: www.soboba.net
Map: **#3** (90 miles E. of L. A.)

Toll-Free Number: (888) 772-SOBOBA
Restaurants: 3 Liquor: Yes
Buffets: L-$8.95/$13.95(Sun)D-$10.95(Wed)/
$12.95(Thu)/$15.95(Fri)
Casino Size: 52,000 Square Feet
Other Games: BJ, MB, PGP, LIR, TCP

Spa Casino
140 N. Indian Canyon Drive
Palm Springs, California 92262
(760) 323-5865
Website: www.sparesortcasino.com
Map: **#3** (115 miles E. of L. A.)

Toll-Free Number: (800) 258-2WIN
Room Reservations: (800) 854-1279
Rooms: 215 Price Range: $89-$239

Suites: 15 Price Range: $189-$279
Restaurants: 2 (1 open 24 hours) Liquor: Yes
Casino Size: 15,000 Square Feet
Other Games: BJ, P, PGP, LIR
Senior Discount: Various on Wed., if 55+
Special Features: Hotel offers hot mineral spa with massages and facials. 10% room discount for seniors (55+) and AAA members.

Sycuan Casino
5469 Dehesa Road
El Cajon, California 92019
(619) 445-6002
Website: www.sycuancasino.com
Map: **#14** (10 miles E. of San Diego)

Toll-Free Number: (800) 279-2826
Restaurants: 6 Liquor: No
Buffets: L-$8.95 D-$12.95
Casino Size: 73,000 Square Feet
Other Games: BJ, MB, P, PGP, BG, LIR, CSP, S
Senior Discount: Senior day Wed, $5 matchplay, free breakfast, and 50% off buffet.

Table Mountain Casino & Bingo
8184 Table Mountain Road
Friant, California 93626
(559) 822-2485
Website: www.tmcasino.com
Map: **#15** (15 miles N. of Fresno)

Toll-Free Number: (800) 541-3637
Restaurants: 4 Liquor: No
Buffets: L-$7.99/$9.99(Sat/Sun) D-$9.99
Other Games: BJ, S21, P, PGP, LIR, TCP BG (Wed-Sun)

Thunder Valley Casino
1200 Athens Ave
Lincoln, California 95648
(916) 408-7777
Website: www.thundervalleyresort.com
Map: **#35** (35 miles N.E. of Sacramento)

Toll-Free Number: (866) 871-7771
Restaurants: Liquor: Yes
Buffets: B- $7.99/ L-$11.99/D-$16.99
Other Games: BJ, PGP
Special Features: Affiliated with Station Casinos of Las Vegas.

Trump 29 Casino
46200 Harrison Place
Coachella, California 92236
(760) 775-5566
Website: www.trump29.com
Map: **#8** (130 miles E. of L. A.)

Toll-Free Number: (800) 841-6666
Restaurants: 2 Liquor: Yes
Other Games: BJ, MB, P, PGP, CSP, LIR
Special Features: Fast-food court.

Twin Pine Casino
22223 Highway 29 at Rancheria Road
Middletown, California 95461
(707) 987-0197
Website: www.twinpine.com
Map: **#32** (70 miles W. of Sacramento)

Toll-Free Number: (800) 564-4872
Restaurants: 1 Liquor: No
Other Games: BJ, PGP, BG
Special Features: Daycare facility.

Valley View Casino
16300 Nyemii Pass Road
Valley Center, California 92082
(760) 291-5500
Website: www.valleyviewcasino.com
Map: **#20** (35 miles N.E. of San Diego)

Toll-Free Number: (866) 726-7277
Restaurants: 2 Liquor: Yes
Buffets: B- $5.99 (Mon-Fri)/$8.99(Sat/Sun)
L-$7.99/$8.99 (Sat/Sun)
D-$11.99(Mon/Wed)/$15.99(Thu-Sun)
Other Games: BJ, TCP
Special Features: Slot club members receive $2 off buffet and 2-for-1 buffet on Wed.

Viejas Casino
5000 Willows Road
Alpine, California 91901
(619) 445-5400
Website: www.viejas.com
Map: **#16** (25 miles E. of San Diego)

Toll-Free Number: (800) 84-POKER
Restaurants: 5 Liquor: Yes
Buffets: L-$8.99/$15.99(Sun)
D-$11.99/$13.99 (Fri)
Other Games: BJ, MB, P, CSP, LIR, PGP, BG, S
Special Features: Charges players a commission on some of their blackjack games. Factory outlet shopping center.

Win-River Casino
2100 Redding Rancheria Road
Redding, California 96001
(530) 243-3377
Website: www.win-river.com
Map: **#17** (163 miles N. of Sacramento)

Toll-Free Number: (800) 280-8946
Restaurants: 1 Snack Bar Liquor: Yes
Casino Size: 37,000 Square Feet
Other Games: BJ,TCP, LIR, BG (Sun-Thu)
Special Features: Comedy club, entertainment center.

COLORADO

Colorado casinos can be found in the mountain towns of Black Hawk, Central City and Cripple Creek. There are also two Indian casinos (which abide by Colorado's limited gaming rules) in Ignacio and Towaoc.

Gambling is limited in two aspects: one, only electronic games (including slots, video poker, video blackjack and video keno) and the table games of poker, blackjack, let it ride and three-card poker are allowed. Two, a single wager cannot exceed $5.

The rules for poker are such that a raise is considered a separate bet. Three raises per round are allowed. On the last round, two players may go "head-to-head" with an unlimited number of raises. Nine varieties of poker are approved for casino play. Texas Hold 'Em, 7-Card Stud and Omaha are the most popular choices.

Blackjack wagers are limited to a $5 maximum, with most casinos allowing a $2 or $3 minimum bet. However, doubles and splits are considered separate bets. Colorado casinos employ Vegas Strip rules and most allow doubling after splits. Since pairs may be split three times (to make up to four hands) it is theoretically possible to bet $40 on what began as a single $5 wager.

Multiple action blackjack is also available in Colorado. Multiple action allows a player to place up to three bets (of up to $5 each) on a single blackjack hand. This hand is then played for three rounds against the same dealer upcard. Several Colorado casinos offer multiple action blackjack.

Here's information, as supplied by Colorado's Division of Gaming, showing the slot machine payback percentages for each city's casinos for the one-year period from July 1, 2002 through June 30, 2003:

	Black Hawk	Central City	Cripple Creek
5¢ Slots	92.81%	92.13%	**93.46%**
25¢ Slots	94.78%	**94.79%**	94.68%
$1 Slots	95.19%	**95.54%**	95.41%
$5 Slots	**96.48%**	94.09%	95.30%
All	94.44%	94.12%	**94.50%**

These numbers reflect the percentage of money returned on each denomination of machine and encompass all electronic machines including video poker and video keno. The best returns for each category are highlighted in bold print.

The maximum hours Colorado casinos can operate are from 8am until 2am and the minimum gambling age is 21.

The two major gaming-oriented magazines n Colorado are *The Gambler* and the *Rocky Mountain News Gaming Guide*. Both are free, and available in most casinos. Look in them for ads for casino coupons or fun books. The *Denver Post* Weekend section (published every Friday) also contains coupons and fun book offers for the casinos in Black Hawk and Central City.

For more information on visiting Black Hawk call (303) 582-5221, for Central City information call (800) 542-2999 and for Cripple Creek information call (877) 858-GOLD. For general information on Colorado call the state's tourism board at (800) 433-2656.

Black Hawk

Map Location: **#1** (35 miles west of Denver. Take U.S. 6 through Golden to Hwy 119. Take Hwy 119 to Black Hawk. Another route is I-70 West to exit 244. Turn right onto Hwy. 6. Take Hwy 6 to 119 and into Black Hawk.)

The Lodge at Black Hawk and the Isle of Capri are the only two casinos with hotel rooms in that city. The next closest lodging is at Harvey's Casino, 3/4-mile up Gregory St. in Central City (see Central City listings for particulars). Another alternative is the Gold Dust Lodge, located on Hwy. 119 about 1.5 miles from the Black Hawk casinos. The Gold Dust features 23 remodeled rooms with private baths, TV and telephones.

The casinos in Black Hawk and Central City are located one mile apart. The Black Hawk Shuttle Service provides free transportation around Black Hawk and Harvey's runs a free shuttle service from Black Hawk to Central City.

There are a few bus tour programs operating between the metropolitan Denver area and Black Hawk/Central City. These programs are bargain priced ($10 or less) and usually affiliated with one or two casinos that will reimburse a portion of the tour charge and also provide coupons or fun books. Check the "Weekend" section of the Friday *Denver Post* and *Rocky Mountain News* for bus tour ads and for casino ads that feature coupons.

All casinos offer electronic games (slots, video poker, video blackjack and video keno). Some casinos also offer: blackjack (BJ), poker (P), let it ride (LIR) and three card poker (TCP).

Black Hawk Station
141 Gregory Street
(303) 582-5582

Restaurants: 1 (snack bar)
Casino Size: 2,055 Square Feet
Other Games: BJ

Bull Durham Saloon & Casino
110 Main Street
(303) 582-0810
Website: www.bulldurhamcasino.com

Restaurants: 1 (snack bar)
Casino Size: 2,547 Square Feet
Other Games: BJ
Fun Book: Ask at cage
Senior Discount: Special Fun Book if 55+

Bullwhackers Casino
101 Gregory Street
(303) 271-2500
Website: www.bullwhackers.com

Toll-Free Number: (800) GAM-BULL
Restaurants: 1
Casino Size: 16,019 Square Feet
Senior Discount: Specials on Tue/Wed if 55+
Special Features: Includes **Bullpen Sports Casino.**

Canyon Casino
131 Main Street
(303) 777-1111
Website: www.canyoncasino.net

Restaurants: 1
Casino Size: 14,030 Square Feet
Special Features: Connected to **Grand Plateau Casino**.

Colorado Central Station Casino
340 Main Street
(303) 582-3000
Website: www.coloradocentralstation.com

Restaurants: 2
Buffet: B-$4.95 L-$7.95 D-$9.95
Casino Size: 16,410 Square Feet
Other Games: BJ
Special Features: 50% buffet discount with slot club card.

Eureka! Casino
211 Gregory Street
(303) 582-1040
Website: www.eureka-casino.com

Restaurants: 1
Casino Size: 1,902 Square Feet
Special Features: 50¢ strawberry margarita.

Fitzgeralds Casino
101 Main Street
(303) 582-6162
Website: www.fitzgeralds.com/blackhawk

Toll-Free Number: (800) 538-5825
Restaurants: 1
Casino Size: 9,874 Square Feet
Other Games: BJ, TCP

Gilpin Hotel Casino
111 Main Street
(303) 582-1133
Website: www.thegilpincasino.com

Restaurants: 2
Casino Size: 10,597 Square Feet

Golden Gates Casino
261 Main Street
(303) 582-1650
Website: www.goldengatescasino.com

Toll-Free Number (866) 343-1994
Casino Size: 8,063 Square Feet
Other Games: BJ, TCP
Special Features: Free sandwich and chips for players 11am-1:30pm and 5:00pm-7:30pm Connected to **Golden Gulch Casino**.

Isle of Capri Casino - Black Hawk
401 Main Street
(303) 998-7777
Website: www.isleofcapricasino.com

Toll-Free Number (800) 843-4753
Rooms: 107 Price Range: $95-$179
Suites: 130 Price Range: $115-$208
Restaurants: 3 (1 open 24 hours)
Buffets: B-$7.99 L-$8.99 D-$14.99
Casino Size: 20,808 Square Feet
Other Games: BJ, LIR, TCP
Senior Discount: Specials Mon-Thu if 50+
Special Features: Parking garage.

The Lodge Casino at Black Hawk
240 Main Street
(303) 582-1771
Website: www.thelodgecasino.com

Toll-Free Number: (877) 711-1177
Rooms: 47 Price Range: $85-$140
Suites: 3 Price Range: $220-$270
Restaurants: 3
Buffets: B-$5.49 L-$8.59 D-$11.99
Casino Size: 22,357 Square Feet
Other Games: BJ, P, LIR, TCP
Special Features: $10 off room for slot club and AAA/AARP members (Sun-Thu). Parking garage. Skybridge to Mardi Gras Casino.

Mardi Gras Casino
333 Main Street
(303) 582-5600
Website: www.mardigrasbh.com

Restaurants: 1
Casino Size: 14,196 Square Feet
Other Games: BJ, P, TCP
Special Features: Skybridge to Lodge Casino.

Mountain High Casino
111 Richman Street
Black Hawk, Colorado 80422
(303) 567-1234
Website: www.mtnhighcasino.com

Restaurants: 4 Buffets: L-$8.99 D-$12.99
Casino Size: 28,381 Square Feet
Other Games: BJ, P, TCP
Senior Discount: Various Mon-Fri if 55+
Special Features: 25% off food (Mon-Fri) for slot club members.

Red Dolly Casino
530 Gregory Street
(303) 582-1100

Restaurants: 1
Casino Size: 2,265 Square Feet
Special Features: 10-ounce steak dinner for $4.95. 20-ounce steak dinner for $6.95.

Richman Casino
100 Richman Street
(303) 582-0400

Restaurants: 1
Casino Size: 2,328 Square Feet
Other Games: BJ

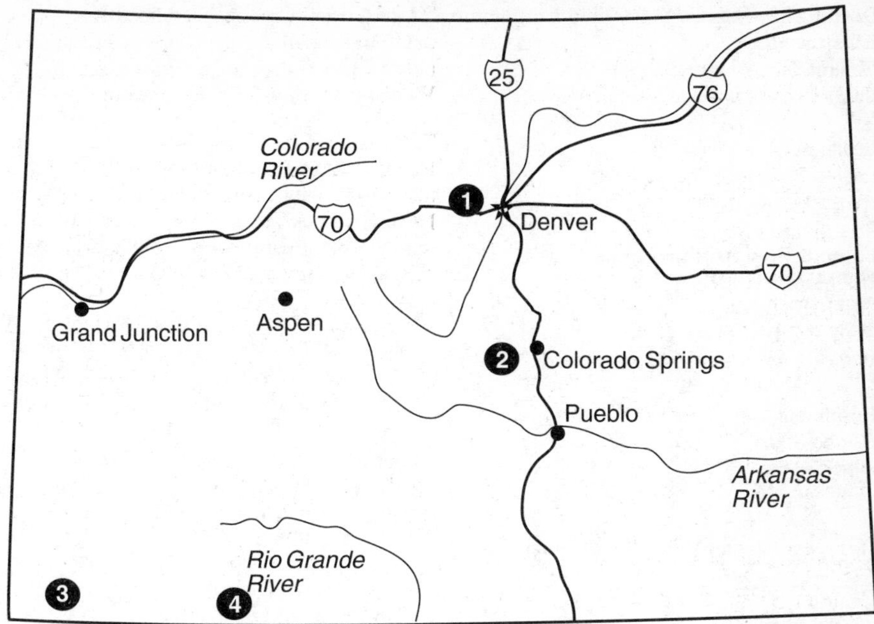

Riviera Black Hawk Casino
444 Main Street
(303) 582-1000
Website: www.rivierablackhawk.com

Buffet: L-$7.99 D-$12.99
Casino Size: 26,053 Square Feet
Other Games: BJ, P
Special Features: Parking garage. Pizza Hut.

Silver Hawk
100 Chase Street
(303) 271-2500
Website: www.bullwhackers.com

Toll-Free Number: (800) GAM-BULL
Restaurants: 1
Casino Size: 3,696 Square Feet
Senior Discount: Specials on Tue/Wed if 55+

Wild Card Saloon & Casino
112 Main Street
(303) 582-3412

Restaurants: 1 (snack bar)
Casino Size: 3,129 Square Feet

Central City

Map location: **#1** (same as Black Hawk). Central City is located one mile from Black Hawk. Turn left at the third stoplight on Hwy. 119 and proceed up Gregory Street.

Harvey's is the only casino hotel in Central City but there are also a few bed & breakfasts: the Gregory Inn (7 rooms, $55 to $155, 303-582-5561), Chateau L'acadienne (3 rooms, $60 to $94, 303-582-5209) and the High Street Inn (3 rooms, $75 to $85, 303-582-0622).

For Central City tourism information call (800) 542-2999.

Doc Holliday Casino
101 Main Street
Central City, CO 80427
(303) 582-1400

Restaurants: 1
Casino Size: 3,098 Square Feet

Dostal Alley Saloon & Gaming Emporium
1 Dostal Alley
Central City, CO 80427
(303) 582-1610

Restaurants: 1 Snack Bar
Casino Size: 741 Square Feet

Famous Bonanza/Easy Street
107 Main Street
(303) 582-5914
Central City, CO 80427
Website: www.famousbonanza.com

Restaurants: 1
Casino Size: 7,324 Square Feet
Other Games: BJ, TCP

Harvey's Wagon Wheel Hotel/Casino
321 Gregory Street
Central City, CO 80427
(303) 582-0800
Website: www.centralcitycasino.com

Toll-Free Number: (800) 924-6646
Rooms: 118 Price Range $79-$139
Suites: 6 Price Range $140-$175
Restaurants: 2
Casino Size: 33,207 Square Feet
Other Games: BJ, P, TCP
Special Features: Tony Roma's restaurant. Covered parking garage.

Cripple Creek

Map Location: **#2** (47 miles west of Colorado Springs. Take exit 141 at Colorado Springs off I-25. Go west on Hwy. 24 to the town of Divide. Turn left onto Hwy. 67 and go 18 miles to Cripple Creek.)

Cripple Creek has several hotel/casinos the largest of which is the Double Eagle Hotel & Casino. There is also a 67-room motel, Gold King Mountain Inn, located 1/8-mile from the casinos, which offers rates of $49 (Winter) to $99 (Summer) per night. Free shuttle service is provided to and from the casinos. For hotel reservations, call 1-800-445-3607.

Many Cripple Creek casinos hand out coupons and Fun Books at their doors. Also check the ads in the *Colorado Springs Gazette*, the *Pueblo Chieftain* and the free tourist magazines.

Some Cripple Creek parking lots charge a fee of $3 to $5 which is usually reimbursed by the casino. Check at the lot for each particular casino's parking rules. For Cripple Creek tourism information call (877) 858-GOLD.

All casinos offer electronic games (slots, video poker, video blackjack and video keno). Some casinos also offer: blackjack (BJ), poker (P), let it ride (LIR) and three card poker (TCP).

Black Diamond Casino
425 E. Bennett Avenue
Cripple Creek, Co 80813
(719) 689-2898

Restaurants: 1 (snack bar)
Casino Size: 1,417 Square Feet
Special Features: Free drink coupon handed out at door. Real gold vein in wall (upstairs). Free soup for players. Video arcade.

Brass Ass Casino
264 E. Bennett Avenue
Cripple Creek, Co 80813
(719) 689-2104
www.midnightrose.com/htmls/brassass.htm

Restaurants: 1 (snack bar)
Casino Size: 2,627 Square Feet
Special Features: Free hot dogs and popcorn. Connected to **Midnight Rose** and **J.P McGill's**.

Bronco Billy's Sports Bar & Casino
233 E. Bennett Avenue
Cripple Creek, Co 80813
(719) 689-2142
Website: www.broncobillyscasino.com

Toll Free Number: (877) 989-2142
Restaurants: 2
Other Games: BJ, TCP
Casino Size: 8,223 Square Feet
Fun Book: Ask at cashier's cage
Special Features: Includes **Buffalo Billy's** casino. 49¢ breakfast. $6.95 t-bone steak special. Double jackpots at top two minutes of every hour and 12am-1:30am every night.

Colorado Grande Gaming Parlor
300 E. Bennett Avenue
Cripple Creek, Co 80813
(719) 689-3517
Website: www.cripple-creek.co.us/grand.html

Restaurants: 1
Casino Size: 2,942 Square Feet
Senior Discount: Free lunch Tuesdays with AARP card and slot club card
Special Features: 50% off dining for slot club members.

Creeker's Casino
274 E. Bennett Avenue
Cripple Creek, Co 80813
(719) 689-3239
Website: www.creekerscasino.com

Restaurants: 1
Buffets: L/D-$7.95/$19.95 (Sat)
Senior Discount: 50% off Tue-Thu buffet if 50 or older
Casino Size: 3,999 Square Feet
Special Features: Wedding chapel. $1 buffet discount with slot club card. Video arcade.

Double Eagle Hotel & Casino
442 E. Bennett Avenue
Cripple Creek, Co 80813
(719) 689-5000
Website: www.decasino.com

Toll-Free Reservations: (800) 711-7234
Rooms: 146 Price Range: $60-$100
Suites: 12 Price Range: $120-$240
Restaurants: 2
Buffets: B-$6.95
D-$8.95/$16.95 (Fri)/$14.95 (Sat)
Casino Size: 15,889 Square Feet
Other Games: BJ, P, TCP
Fun Book: Show bus receipt at slot club
Special Features: Free self-parking. Video arcade. AAA, AARP and slot club members get 10% room discount.

Gold Rush Hotel & Casino/Gold Digger's Casino
209 E. Bennett Avenue
Cripple Creek, Co 80813
(719) 689-2646
Website: www.grushcasino.com

Toll-Free Number: (800) 235-8239
Rooms: 14 Price Range: $59-$89
Restaurants: 2
Casino Size: 6,104 Square Feet
Other Games: BJ, LIR
Special Features: **Gold Digger's** and **Gold Rush** are interconnected. $3.99 steak special. 49-cent breakfast. 10% room discount to military and AARP.

Imperial Hotel & Casino
123 N. Third Street
Cripple Creek, Co 80813
(719) 689-2922
Website: www.imperialcasinohotel.com

Toll-Free Number: (800) 235-2922
Rooms: 29 Price Range: $45-$85
Suites: 2 Price Range: $100-$145
Restaurants: 2
Casino Size: 4,599 Square Feet

Johnny Nolon's Casino
301 E. Bennett Avenue
Cripple Creek, Co 80813
(719) 689-2080
Website: www.johnnynolons.com

Restaurants: 2
Casino Size: 5,815 Square Feet
Special Features: 50% off meals for slot club members.

J.P. McGill's Hotel & Casino
232 E. Bennett Avenue
Cripple Creek, Co 80813
(719) 689-2497
www.midnightrose.com/htmls/jpmcgills.htm

Toll-Free Number: (888) 461-7529
Rooms: 36 Price Range: $40-$100
Suites: 5 Price Range: $155-$210
Restaurants: 1
Casino Size: 7,532 Square Feet
Special Features: Connected to **Midnight Rose** and **Brass Ass**. 10% room discount for slot club members. Free popcorn and hot dogs for players. Free parking.

Midnight Rose Hotel & Casino
256 E. Bennett Avenue
Cripple Creek, Co 80813
(719) 689-2865
Website: www.midnightrose.com

Toll-Free Number: (800) 635-5825
Rooms: 19 Price Range: $40-$95
Restaurants: 3
Casino Size: 9,201 Square Feet
Other Games: P
Special Features: Connected to **Brass Ass** and **J.P McGill's**. 10% room discount for slot club members.

Uncle Sam's Casino
251 E. Bennett Avenue
Cripple Creek, Co 80813
(719) 689-2222
Website: www.grushcasino.com

Casino Size: 1,208 Square Feet
Special Features: Free hot dogs for players.

Virgin Mule
259 E. Bennett Avenue
Cripple Creek, Co 80813
(719) 689-2734

Restaurants: 1 snack bar
Casino Size: 547 Square Feet

Womacks/Legends Hotel & Casino
200-220 E. Bennett Avenue
Cripple Creek, Co 80813
(719) 689-0333
Website: www.womackscasino.com

Toll-Free Number: (888) 966-2257
Rooms: 21 Price Range: Casino Use Only
Suites: 3 Price Range: Casino Use Only
Restaurants: 1
Casino Size: 9,559 Square Feet
Other Games: BJ, TCP
Special Features: **Womacks** and **Legends** are interconnected. Rooms for club members only. Free parking.

Indian Casinos

Sky Ute Casino and Lodge
14826 Highway 172 N.
Ignacio, Colorado 81137
(970) 563-3000
Website: www.skyutecasino.com
Map Location: **#4** (345 miles S.W. of Denver, 20 miles S.E. of Durango)

Toll-Free Number: (888) 842-4180
Room Reservations: (800) 876-7017
Rooms: 36 Price Range: $45-$79
Restaurants: 2 Liquor: No
Buffets: B-$4.99 (Sat-Sun) L-$6.99
D-$8.99/$13.99 (Fri-Sat)
Hours: 24 Hours Daily
Other Games: BJ, TCP, Bingo (Wed/Thu/Sun)
Senior Discount: 10% room and restaurant discount, if 50, or older
Special Features: Southern Ute Cultural Center and Museum is located next to casino.

Ute Mountain Casino & RV Park
3 Weeminuche Drive/P.O. Drawer V
Towaoc, Colorado 81334
(970) 565-8800
Website: www.utemountaincasino.com
Map Location: **#3** (425 miles S.W. of Denver, 11 miles S. of Cortez on Hwys. 160/166)

Toll-Free Number: (800) 258-8007
Restaurants: 1 Liquor: No
Buffets: B-$4.50 (Sat-Sun) L-$5.95
D-$7.75/$12.95 (Fri)
Casino Size: 32,000 Square Feet
Hours: 8am-4am Daily
Other Games: BJ, P, LIR, TCP,
Keno, Bingo (Fri-Tue)
Fun Book: Given at local motels/RV parks
Senior Discount: 15% off food if 55, or older.
Special Features: 84-space RV Park. Ute Tribal Park tours available.

CONNECTICUT

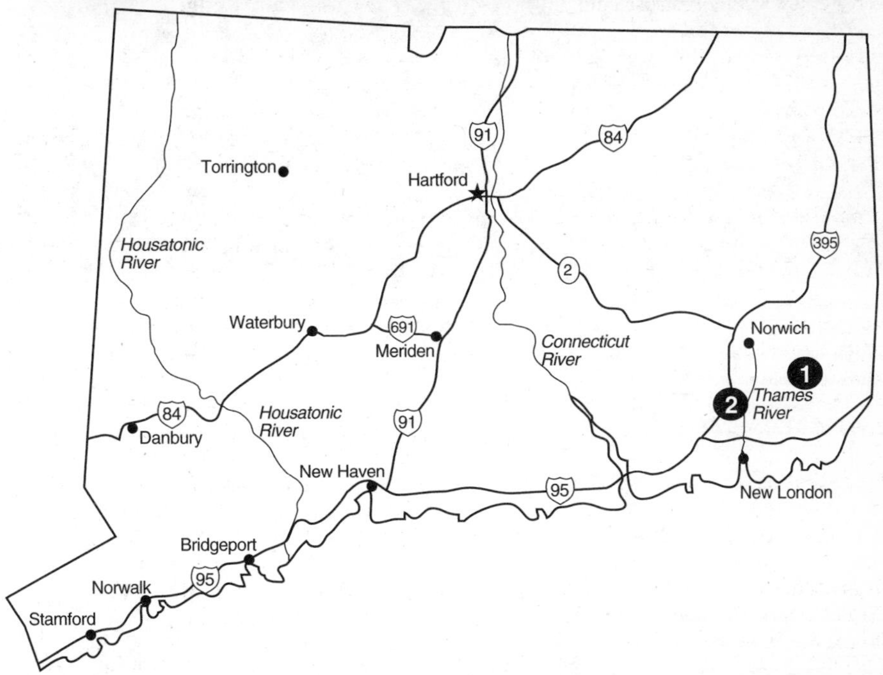

Foxwoods was New England's first casino. It is also the largest casino in the world and the world's most profitable casino.

The Mashantucket Pequot Tribe which operates Foxwoods had to sue the state to allow the casino to open. They argued that since the state legally permitted "Las Vegas Nights," where low-stakes casino games were operated to benefit charities, then the tribe should be entitled to do the same. Eventually, they won their case before the U.S. Supreme Court and began construction of their casino which was financed by a Malaysian conglomerate (after 22 U.S. lenders turned down their loan requests).

When the casino first opened in February 1992, slot machines were not permitted. In January 1993 a deal was made between Governor Weicker and the Pequots which gave the tribe the exclusive right to offer slot machines in return for a yearly payment of 25% of the gross slot revenue.

In early 1994 the Mohegan tribe signed a compact with the state that allows them to offer casino gambling at their reservation in Uncasville (map location #2). The same 25% of the gross slot revenue payment schedule also applies to the Mohegans. The payment schedules at both casinos are subject to cancellation, however, if the state legalizes any other form of casino gambling. The Mohegan casino opened in October 1996.

The minimum gambling age at both properties is 18 for bingo and 21 for the casino. Both casinos are also open 24 hours. For information on visiting Connecticut call the state's Vacation Center at (800) 282-6863.

The games offered at Foxwoods are: blackjack, craps, roulette, baccarat, mini-baccarat, big six wheel, bingo, poker, pai gow poker, Caribbean stud poker, let it ride, keno, pull tabs, red dog, casino war and chuck-a-luck. There is also a simulcast facility with parimutuel betting.

Foxwoods is the world's largest casino with over 300,000 square feet of gaming space. The property features three hotels, 24 food outlets, three regular casinos, a smoke-free casino, a slots-only casino, a high-limts casino, a race book, a 3,200-seat bingo room and a total of more than 6,500 electronic gaming machines.

Foxwoods Resort Casino
Route 2
Mashantucket, Connecticut 06338
(860) 312-3000
Website: www.foxwoods.com
Map Location: **#1** (45 miles S.E. of Hartford; 12 miles N. of I-95 at Mystic). From I-95 take exit 92 to Rt. 2-West, casino is 7 miles ahead. From I-395 take exit 79A to Rt. 2A follow to Rt. 2-East, casino is 2 miles ahead.

Toll-Free Number: (800) FOXWOODS
Hotel Reservations: (800) FOXWOODS
Rooms: 1,416 Price Range: $140-$325
Suites: 198 Price Range: $175-$1,500
Restaurants: 24 (3 open 24 hours)
Buffets: B-$7.95 L-$13.95 D-$13.95
Casino Size: 314,492 Square Feet
Casino Marketing: (800) 99-SLOTS
Special Features: Three hotels with pool, spa, beauty salon and golf. Headline entertainment. Five nightclubs including a BB King Nite Club and Club BB. Gift shops. *Wampum Card* members earn complimentaries at table games, slots, poker and race book. 10% room discount for AAA and AARP members.

Foxwoods is continually undergoing expansions and by the summer of 2004 it will add a Hard Rock Cafe, a Wampum Trading Post Super Store, an expanded Pequot Trader Outlet, 850 additional slot machines and 2,100 additional parking spaces adjacent to the Rainmaker Casino. In 2005 it will also open two Rees Jones designed golf courses.

The following information is from Connecticut's Division of Special Revenue regarding Foxwoods' slot payback percentages:

Denomination	Payback %
5¢	89.19
25¢	90.97
50¢	90.81
$1.00	92.32
$5.00	94.80
$10.00	94.79
$25.00	95.26
$100.00	96.80
Average	**91.80**

These figures reflect the total percentages returned by each denomination of slot machine from July 1, 2002 through June 30, 2003. Foxwoods' total win on its slot machines during that year was slightly more than $785 million and of that amount 25%, or slightly more than $196 million, was paid to the state.

Keep in mind that the casino doesn't pay any tax on its table games and therefore it isn't required to report the profits on that part of its operation.

The games offered at Connecticut's other casino, Mohegan Sun, are: blackjack, craps, roulette, baccarat, mini-baccarat, pai gow, wheel of fortune, bingo, pai gow poker, Caribbean stud poker, let it ride, Spanish 21, casino war, sic bo and keno. There is also a simulcast facility with pari-mutuel betting.

Mohegan Sun Casino
1 Mohegan Sun Boulevard
Uncasville, Connecticut 06382
(860) 862-8000
Website: www.mohegansun.com
Map Location: **#2** (Take I-95 Exit 76/I-395 North. Take Exit 79A (Route 2A) East. Less than 1 mile to Mohegan Sun Boulevard)

Toll-Free Number: (888) 226-7711
Room Reservations: (888) 777-7922
Rooms: 1,020 Price Range: $175-$400
Suites: 180 Price Range: $300-$1,000
Restaurants: 29 (3 open 24 hours)
Buffets: B-$7.95 L-$13.95 D-$13.95
Casino Size: 295,000 Square Feet
Special Features: Food court with specialty food outlets. 6,000-square-foot Kid's Quest - supervised children's activity center. On-site gas station. Free nightly entertainment in the Wolf Den Showroom.

Here's information from Connecticut's Division of Special Revenue regarding Mohegan Sun's slot payback percentages:

Denomination	Payback %
5¢	86.58
25¢	90.89
50¢	90.61
$1.00	92.06
$5.00	94.61
$10.00	96.34
$25.00	96.01
$100.00	96.33
$500.00	98.56
Average	**92.02**

These figures reflect the total percentages returned by each denomination of slot machine from July 1, 2002 through June 30, 2003.

The total win on all of their slot machines during that period was slightly less than $764 million and of that amount 25%, or almost $191 million, was paid to the state.

DELAWARE

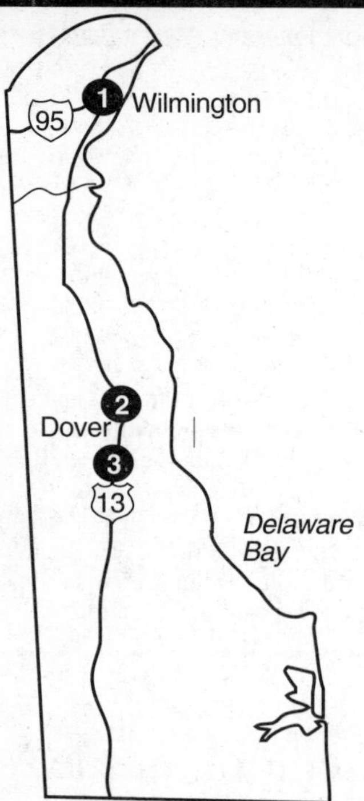

Delaware's three pari-mutuel facilities all feature slot machines. Technically, the machines are video lottery terminals (VLT's) because they are operated in conjunction with the Delaware Lottery. Unlike VLT's in other states, however, Delaware's machines pay out in cash. The VLT's also play other games including: video poker, video keno and video blackjack.

By law, all video lottery games must return between 87% and 95% of all wagers on an annual basis. Games can return above 95% but only with the Lottery Director's approval. According to figures from the Delaware Lottery for the six-month period from January 1, 2003 through June 30, 2003 the average VLT return at Delaware Park was 92.33%, at Dover Downs it was 91.60% and at Midway Slots & Simulcast it was 91.41%.

The minimum gambling age is 21 for slots and 18 for horse racing. For more information on visiting Delaware call the state's tourism office at (800) 441-8846.

For more information on visiting Delaware call the state's tourism office at (800) 441-8846.

Delaware Park Racetrack & Slots
777 Delaware Park Boulevard
Wilmington, Delaware 19804
(302) 994-2521
Website: www.delpark.com
Map Location: **#1**

Toll-Free Number: (800) 41-SLOTS
Restaurants: 8
Hours: 8am-4am (Mon-Sat)/Noon-2am (Sun)
Valet Parking: $3
Special Features: Live thoroughbred racing late April through mid-November. Daily simulcasting of horse racing.

Dover Downs Slots
1131 N. DuPont Highway
Dover, Delaware 19901
(302) 674-4600
Website: www.doverdowns.com
Map Location: **#2**

Toll-Free Number: (800) 711-5882
Rooms: 220 Price Range: $125-$195
Suites: 12 Price Range: $225-$745
Restaurants: 3 Buffets: B/L/D-$12.95
Hours: 8am-4am (Mon-Sat)/Noon-2am (Sun)
Valet Parking: $2
Casino Size: 80,000 Square Feet
Special Features: Live harness racing November through April. Daily simulcasting of horse racing.

Midway Slots & Simulcast
Delaware State Fairgrounds
U.S. 13 South
Harrington, Delaware 19952
(302) 398-4920
Website: www.midwayslots.com
Map Location: **#3** (20 miles S. of Dover)

Toll-Free Number: (888) 88-SLOTS
Restaurants: 2 Buffets: L/D-$10.99
Hours: 8am-2am (Mon-Thu)/4am (Fri-Sat)
Noon-2am (Sunday)
Valet Parking: $2
Senior Discount: Various, if 50, or older
Special Features: Live harness racing April-June and August-October. Daily simulcasting of horse racing.

FLORIDA

Florida does not have legalized casino gambling. It does, however, have a thriving day-cruise industry which offers gamblers the opportunity to board ships that cruise offshore where casino gambling is legal. From the east coast the boats sail three miles out into the Atlantic Ocean and from the west coast the boats travel nine miles out into the Gulf of Mexico.

There are a variety of boats in operation ranging from Port Canaveral's 1,800-passenger Ambassador II cruise ship all the way down to the yacht-sized SunCruz Casino boat in Key Largo which carries 149 passengers.

Generally, you will find that the larger ships have more of a variety of things to do besides the gambling, but the cost will be a little higher because of added port/service charges. Most of the ships that sail from the major ports, such as Port Everglades and the Port of Palm Beach, will add port/service charges to the quoted cruise price. Usually, there is also a charge to park your car at those locations. Since late 1994 many smaller ships have begun operations and because they don't dock at the large ports they usually don't have port/service charges added to their cruise prices. Also, most of them offer free parking. You will find that almost all of the ships (especially in the Miami/Ft. Lauderdale area) are constantly running price specials so don't be surprised if you call and are quoted a price lower than the regular brochure rates listed here.

The nearest Caribbean casinos are in the Bahamas with one on Grand Bahama Island: The Royal Oasis Casino Resort (800) 223-1818.

The Royal Oasis Casino operates a 727 jet charter service which has two flights daily from the Fort Lauderdale airport. One flight leaves at 9am and returns at 5:15pm. The other flight leaves at 6:30pm and returns at 12:45am. Grand Bahama Island is 90 miles from Fort Lauderdale and the flight takes 30 minutes. Look in the coupon section in the back of this book for a special free trip offer to the Royal Oasis Casino.

The other two casinos are in the Bahamian capital of Nassau which is on New Providence Island: Crystal Palace Casino (800) 222-7466 and Atlantis, Paradise Island (800) 321-3000. Technically, Atlantis is on Paradise Island and not Nassau because you have to cross a bridge in downtown Nassau to get to the property.

There is daily scheduled jet service on several airlines to the Nassau airport from both Miami and Fort Lauderdale. Nassau is 150 miles from Miami and the flying time is approximately 45 minutes.

Unless otherwise noted, all Florida casino boats offer: blackjack, craps, roulette, slots and video poker. Some casinos also offer: mini-baccarat (MB), poker (P), pai gow poker (PGP), three-card poker (TCP), Caribbean stud poker (CSP), let it ride (LIR), big 6 wheel (B6) and bingo (BG). Each boat sets its own minimum gambling age: on some boats it's 21 and on others it's 18. The minimum drinking age on all boats is 21.

For Florida visitor information call (888) 735-2872. For information on the Florida Keys or Key West call (800) 352-5397.

Daytona Beach

Map Location: **#12**

SunCruz Casino - Daytona
4880 Front Street
Ponce Inlet, Florida 32127
(386) 322-9600
Website: www.suncruzcasino.com

Reservation Number: (800) 474-DICE
Gambling Age: 18 Ship's Registry: U.S.A.
Food Service: A la Carte Menu
Schedule:
11:00am - 4:00pm (Mon-Fri)
12:00pm - 5:00pm (Sat/Sun)
7:00pm - 12:00am/12:30am (Fri/Sat)
Price: $10 Port Charges: Included
Parking: Free
Casino Size: 18,000 Square Feet
Other Games: MB, P, LIR, CSP, TCP
Senior Discount: Sail free Wed if 55 or older
Special Features: 560-passenger *SunCruz III* departs from Ponce Inlet near Down the Hatch restaurant. Must be 18, or older, to board.

Fort Lauderdale

Map Location: **#2**

SeaEscape
3045 N. Federal Highway
Fort Lauderdale, Florida 33306
(954) 453-2200
Website: www.seaescape.com

Reservation Number: (877) SEA-ESCAPE
Gambling Age: 18
Ship's Registry: Bahamas
Food Service: Buffet Included
Schedule:
11:00am - 4:30pm (Tue-Sun)
7:30pm - 12:30am (Mon-Thu)
7:30pm - 1:30am (Fri/Sat)
6:30pm- 11:30pm (Sun)
Prices: Day- $24.95/$34.95 (Sun)
Eve- $24.95 (Sun-Thu)/$29.95 (Fri/Sat)
Port Charges: $3 Security Charge: $3
Parking: $7
Other Games: MB, P, CSP, TCP, LIR, BG
Senior Discount: $5 off regular fare on any cruise, if 55, or older
Special Features: 1,050-passenger *MV Island Adventure* sails from Port Everglades in Fort Lauderdale. All prices are for advance purchase tickets only - $10 surcharge on tickets purchased at pier. Showroom with live entertainment. Full-service dinner upgrade available. Private cabin rentals. Children's prices offered on day cruises. Call for reservation to poker room. Must be 21 or older on evening cruises unless accompanied by parent or legal guardian.

St. Tropez Casino Cruises
2170 S.E. 17th Street Suite-306
Ft Lauderdale, Florida 33316
(954) 463-6433
Website: www.sttropezcasinocruises.com
Reservation Number: (800) 575-5520
Gambling Age: 18 Ship's Registry: U.S.A.
Buffets: L-$10.99 D-$15.99
Schedule:
11:30am - 5:00pm (Daily)
7:45pm - 12:45am/1:45am (Fri-Sat)
6:45pm - 11:45pm (Sun)
Price: Free Port Charges: Included
Parking: $7
Other Games: B, P, CSP, PGP, CSP
Special Features: 800-passenger *St. Tropez* departs from Pier 22 at Port Everglades. Must be 18, or older, to board and show photo ID.

SunCruz Casino - Hollywood
647 E. Dania Beach Boulevard
Dania, Florida 33004
(954) 929-3800
Website: www.suncruzcasino.com

Reservation Number: (800) 474-DICE
Gambling Age: 18 Ship's Registry: U.S.A.
Food Service: L-$5 D-$7
Schedule:
11:00am - 4:15pm (Mon-Fri)
12:00pm - 5:30pm (Sat-Sun)
7:30pm - 12:30am (Sun-Thu)
7:30pm - 1:15am (Fri/Sat/holidays)
Price: $10
Port Charges: Included Parking: Free
Other Games: MB, P, LIR, CSP, TCP
Special Features: 600-passenger, twin-hulled, *SunCruz VI* departs from Martha's Restaurant on A1A in Hollywood. Must be 18, or older, to board. Slot club offers cashback. A la carte menu also available. 10x odds on craps.

Fort Myers Beach

Map Location: **#5** (40 miles N. of Naples)

Big "M" Casino
450 Harbor Court
Fort Myers Beach, Florida 33931
(239) 765-7529
Website: www.bigmcasino.com

Toll-Free Number: (888) 373-3521
Gambling Age: 21 Ship's Registry: U.S.A.
Buffets: Brunch-$5.95 D-$12.95
Schedule:
10:30am - 4:30pm (Daily)
6:00pm -11:30pm (Daily)
Prices: $15 Day/$10 Eve/$20 (Fri/Sat Eve)
Port Charges: Included
Parking: Free (Valet also free)
Other Games: LIR, No Craps
Special Features: 400-passenger *Big M* sails from Moss Marina next to Snug Harbor on Fort Myers Beach. Must be 21, or older, to board. Cashback for slot play.

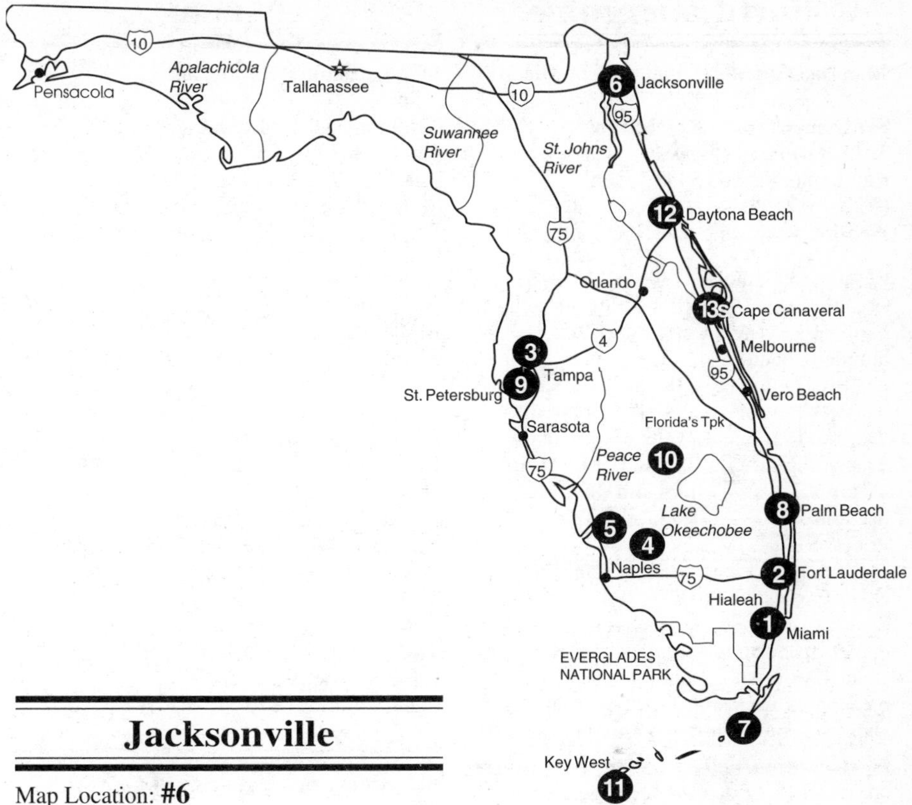

Jacksonville

Map Location: **#6**

La Cruise Casino
4738 Ocean Street
Atlantic Beach, Florida 32233
(904) 241-7200
Website: www.lacruise.com

Reservation Number: (800) 752-1778
Gambling Age: 18 Ship's Registry: Panama
Food Service: A la Carte
Schedule:
10:00am - 3:00pm (Tue-Thu)
11:00am - 4:00pm (Sat)
1:00pm - 6:00pm (Sun)
7:00pm -12:00am (Mon-Sat)
Price: Free
Port Charges: Included Parking: Free
Other Games: P, CSP, B6, BG
Special Features: 450-passenger *La Cruise* sails from Mayport Village. Must be 18, or older, to board. Free drink with boarding.

SunCruz Casino - Jacksonville
4378 Ocean Street
Atlantic Beach, Florida 32233
(904) 249-9300
Website: www.suncruzcasino.com

Toll-Free Number: (800) 474-DICE
Gambling Age: 18 Ship's Registry: U.S.A.
Buffets: $8 (Fri-Sat eves/Sun afternoon)
Food Service: A la carte menu
Schedule
11:00am - 4:00pm (Mon-Fri)
11:00am - 4:30pm (Sat-Sun)
7:00pm - 12:00am (Sun-Thu)
7:00pm - 12:30am (Fri/Sat/Holidays)
Price: Free
Port Charges: Included Parking: Free
Other Games: MB, P, CSP, LIR
Special Features: 495-passenger, *SunCruz X* departs from Mayport Village. Must be 18 or older to board.

Key Largo

Map Location: **#7** (50 miles S. of Miami)

SunCruz Casino - Key Largo
99701 Overseas Highway
Key Largo, Florida 33037
(305) 451-0000
Website: www.suncruzcasino.com

Reservation Number: (800) 474-DICE
Gambling Age: 18 Ship's Registry: U.S.A.
Food Service: A la Carte Snack Bar
Shuttle Schedule:
Departs/Returns 2:00pm (Wed/Sat/Sun)
Departs/Returns 5:00pm/5:30 (daily)
Departs/Returns 7:30pm/8:00 (daily)
Departs/Returns 9:45pm/10:15 (Fri/Sat)
Returns 12:45am (Sun-Thu)
Returns 1:15am (Fri/Sat)
Prices: $10
Port Charges: Included Parking: Free
Other Games: CSP, TCP
Special Features: 149-passenger *SunCruz I* departs from Holiday Inn docks in Key Largo. Boat stays offshore and a water taxi shuttles passengers back and forth according to the above schedule. Must be 18, or older, to board.

Key West

Map Location: **#11**

Key West Casino Cruises
237 Front Street
Key West, Florida 33040
(305) 295-7775
Website: www.kwcasinocruises.com

Toll-Free Number: (866) 874-PLAY
Gambling Age: 18 Ship's Registry: U.S.
Food Service: Buffet included
Schedule:
1:00pm - 5:00pm (Thu/Sun)
7:00pm - 11:30pm (Sun-Thu)
7:00pm -12:00am (Fri/Sat)
Price: $11.95
Port Charges: Included Parking: See below
Other Games: P, CSP
Special Features: 160-passenger *Rendezvous* sails from marina at the Hilton Hotel. Must be 18, or older, to board. Self-parking is $3 per hour at Hilton but you can park at city garage for $1 per hour and take a shuttle to the hotel.

Miami

Map Location: **#1**

Atlantic Casino Cruises
1280 Fifth Street
Miami Beach, Florida 33139
(305) 532-2111
Web Site: www.atlanticcasinomiami.com

Reservation Number: (305) 532-2111
Gambling Age: 18 Ship's Registry: U.S.A.
Buffet: $9.95
Schedule: 12:30 - 5:00pm (Daily)
7:30pm - 12:00am (Daily)
1:15am - 5:30am (Fri-Sun)
Price: $14.95/$4.95 (Local Residents)
Port Charges: Included Parking: Free
Other Games: MB, LIR
Special Features: 650-passenger, *Atlantic* departs from Miami Beach Marina. Must be 18, or older, to board. Free valet parking.

The Card Room Casino
300 Biscayne Boulevard
Miami, Florida 33139
(305) 350-2273

Reservation Number: (866) LUCKY-21
Gambling Age: 18 Ship's Registry: U.S.A.
Schedule: 7:45pm - 12:30am (Daily)
Price: Free Parking: $4
Special Features: 400-passenger boat departs from behind Dupont Plaza. Free buffet.

Casino Princesa
100 S. Biscayne Boulevard
Miami, Florida 33131
(305) 379-LUCK
Website: www.casinoprincesa.com

Reservation Number: (305) 379-LUCK
Gambling Age: 21 Ship's Registry: U.S.A.
12:30pm - 5:00pm (Daily)
7:30pm -12:30am (Daily)
1:00am - 6:00am (Sat)
Prices: $9.95 Port Charges: Included
Parking: $8 Valet Parking: $9/$12 (Fri-Sun)
Other Games: MB, P, LIR
Special Features: 600-passenger *Casino Princesa* sails from Bayside Marketplace in downtown Miami. Must be 21, or older, to board. A la carte food menu.

The IGT Casino Chip Program

Because of the intense competition among South Florida's casino boats some of them are involved in a special promotional program that can provide some great savings to casino-goers. The program involves the *In Good Taste* (IGT) credit card which offers a 25% discount on gambling chips purchased with the card.

The IGT card has been around for more than 30 years and originally started as a discount credit card for use only at restaurants. You can still use the card for a 25% discount at restaurants but it now offers that same discount in other areas including: airline travel, hotel lodging, cruises, vacations, florists, dry cleaners, magazine subscriptions and more.

Whenever you make a purchase with the IGT card you receive a 25% discount when you are billed. They do not, however, give a discount on the tax or tip. As an example, let's say you charge a $100 dinner on the card, plus $6 tax and a $15 tip for a total of $121. When you get your bill from IGT you will be charged $75 for the dinner ($100 less 25%), plus $6 tax and the $15 tip for a total of $96. Upon receipt of the bill you also have the option of paying it by check or charging it to your Visa, MasterCard or Discover card.

As of August 2003 there were six casino boats in South Florida participating in the IGT program. On the Princesa or Card Room, you can purchase up to $125 in special chips with the IGT card. You will only be billed $93.75 by IGT which means you are starting off $31.25 ahead. You can receive all $125 worth of chips in $5 or $25 denominations. These special chips can only be played on table games and cannot be cashed - they must be played. If you win your bet you will be paid with regular chips and the special IGT chips will continue to remain in play until your bet loses. You are allowed to participate in the IGT program once per week on the Princesa and twice per week on the Card Room.

The SeaEscape and both SunCruz boats in Hollywood and Key Largo also participate in the IGT program and they will all permit you to buy up to $250 in chips. On SeaEscape you can get all $5 chips but on the SunCruz boats you must choose to receive either $100 in $5 chips, or $250 in $25 chips. If you opt for $5 chips you will be required to bet a minimum of $10 each time. The rest of the program is pretty much the same with IGT billing you $75 for the $100 in chips, or $187.50 for the $250 in chips, meaning you are starting off either $25 or $62.50 ahead. You are limited to one buy-in per month at both on SunCruz boats and once per week on SeaEscape.

The St. Tropez in Ft. Lauderdale also participates in the IGT program with a slight difference. You may make a purchase of up to $500 on your IGT card and you will receive double that amount in matchplay chips. You can receive the matchplay chips in $5 or $25 denominations and each time you bet a matchplay chip it must be matched with a regular chip. If you win your bet both your regular chip and matchplay chip will be paid off with regular chips. Regardless of whether you win or lose, however, the matchplay chip will be taken by the casino. Once again, when you are billed by IGT you will receive a 25% discount. You are limited to $1,500 per week for chip purchases on the St. Tropez.

The IGT program is truly a powerful program because you are starting off with a major mathematical advantage over the house. Lest you forget, it is supposed to be the other way around! On rare occasions some Las Vegas casinos have special chip programs similar to this where you can get maybe a 5% edge at best - $1,050 in special chips for $1,000 - but never as high as 25% like this program offers; it's very advantageous for the players. How come it works in South Florida? Three probable reasons:

1 - Competition. There are quite a few boats to choose from so the boats have to offer something extra to get people in their casinos.

2 - Bad players. The average South Florida casino-goer is a recreational gambler and not very knowledgeable. The casino edge against these players is much higher than knowledgable gamblers who know the proper playing strategies.

3 - Time. You're stuck on a boat for 3-1/2 hours with nowhere to go. It probably takes no more than 30 minutes to go through the IGT chips and end up with all regular chips. If you were in a land-based casino you could simply walk out and take your money home but on a casino boat you still have another three hours to go before it heads back to shore. With all that time on your hands you have nothing left to do but gamble and all of those bad blackjack players usually give it all back to the casinos.

Keep in mind that if you're a perfect basic strategy blackjack player the highest mathematical casino edge on any of these boats' blackjack games is about one-half of one percent, so you should have an excellent chance of coming out a long-term winner with the IGT program.

The usual cost for a one year IGT membership is $48 but they will give you a free 6-month membership if you live in certain metropolitan areas. Call them at 800-4-IGT-USA or visit their website at www.igtcard.com for more details.

Scouting Report - South Florida Casino Boats

SeaEscape - All six-deck blackjack: dealer stands soft 17, double down on any first two cards, resplit any pair (except aces), double after split allowed and late surrender offered. The casino edge against a perfect basic strategy player is .34%. The craps game offers a maximum of 2X odds.

Only 25¢ video poker machines. Jacks or Better with 6/5 (95% return) and 7/5 (96.15% return) pay tables. Surprisingly good 10/7 Double Bonus (100.17% return), plus some 7/5 Double Bonus (98.02% return) machines.

SunCruz, Hollywood - Six-deck ($25 minimum) and eight-deck ($5 minimum) games: dealer stands on soft 17, double down on any first two cards, resplit any pair (except aces), double after split allowed and late surrender offered. The casino edge in this game against a perfect basic strategy player is .34% against six decks and .36% with eight decks in play.

Craps game offers 5X odds. For video poker players there are some 25¢ Jacks or Better machines with 6/5 (95% return), 7/5 (96.15% return) and 8/5 (97.28% return) paytables. At the $1 level there are 8/5 Jacks or Better (97.28% return) and also some 7/5 Bonus (98.02% return) games. The only casino boat with a cashback slot club (0.50%) and double cashback on Tuesday during the day cruise only.

Palm Beach Princess - Six-deck ($25 minimum) and eight-deck ($5 minimum) games: dealer stands on soft 17, double down on any first two cards, resplit any pair (except aces) and double after split allowed. No surrender. The casino edge against a perfect basic strategy player is .41% against six decks and .43% with eight decks in play. Anyone can buy in at the cage for $1,000 and receive $100 in $25 matchplay chips.

Craps game has 2X odds. Dollar and 25¢ video poker with 7/5 Jacks or Better (96.15% return) or 7/5 Bonus (98.01% return).

St. Tropez - All six-deck blackjack: dealer stands soft 17, double down on any first two cards, resplit any pair (except aces), double after split allowed and late surrender offered. The casino edge against a perfect basic strategy player is .34%.

The craps game offers a maximum of 5X odds. Only 25¢ video poker machines. Jacks or Better with 6/5 paytable (95% return).

Palm Beach

Map Location: **#8**

Palm Beach Princess
One E. 11th Street
Riviera Beach, Florida 33404
(561) 845-2101
Website: www.pbcasino.com

Reservation Number: (800) 841-7447
Gambling Age: 21 Ship's Registry: Panama
Food Service: Buffet Included
Schedule & Prices:
11:00am - 4:30pm (Mon-Fri) $30
11:00am- 4:30pm (Sat/Sun) $35
6:30pm - 11:45pm (Sun-Thu) $30
6:30pm - 12:30am (Fri/Sat) $35
Port Charges: Included Parking: $5
Casino Size: 15,000 Square Feet
Other Games: SB, LIR, P, BG
Senior Discount: $5 or $10 discount, if 55+
Special Features: 850-passenger *Palm Beach Princess* sails from Port of Palm Beach. Rates subject to seasonal variations. Private cabin rentals. Swimming pool. Lounge with live entertainment, cabaret shows, games, dancing. Children only allowed on day cruises. Must be 21, or older, to board on evening cruises.

Port Canaveral

Map Location: **#13** (60 miles S. of Daytona Beach)

Sterling Casino Lines
Terminal B
Cape Canaveral, Florida 32920
(407) 783-2212
Website: www.sterlingcasinolines.com

Reservation Number: (800) ROLL-7-11
Gambling Age: 21 Ship's Registry: Bahamas
Buffets: Included
Schedule:
11:00am - 4:00pm (Daily)
7:00pm - 12:00am (Daily)
Port Charges: Included Parking: Free
Casino Size: 75,000 Square Feet
Other Games: B, MB, LIR
Special Features: 1,800-passenger, *Ambassador II* departs from terminal 2 at Port Canaveral. Free live entertainment in the lounge. Must be 21, or older, to board.

SunCruz Casino - Port Canaveral
610 Glen Cheek Drive
Cape Canaveral, Florida 32920
(321) 799-3511
Website: www.suncruzcasino.com

Toll-Free Number: (800) 474-DICE
Gambling Age: 18 Ship's Registry: U.S.A.
Buffets: L-$5.00 D-$7.00
Schedule
11:00pm - 4:00pm (Mon-Sat)
1:00pm - 6:00pm (Sun)
7:00pm - 12:00am (Sun-Thu)
7:00pm - 12:30am (Fri/Sat/Holidays)
Price: Free
Port Charges: Included Parking: Free
Other Games: MB, P, CSP, LIR, TCP
Special Features: 1,000-passenger, *SunCruz VIII* departs from Port Canaveral. Must be 18 or older to board. A la carte food menu also available.

St. Petersburg

Map Location: **#9**

SunCruz Casino - John's Pass
12788 Kingfish Drive
Treasure Island, Florida 33706
(727) 895-3325
Website: www.suncruzcasino.com

Reservation Number: (800) 474-DICE
Gambling Age: 18 Ship's Registry: U.S.A.
Buffets: L-$5 D-$7
Schedule:
11:30am - 5:00pm (Daily)
7:00pm -12:30am (Daily)
Prices: $10
Port Charges: Included Parking: Free
Other Games: MB, P, CSP, LIR
Senior Discount: $5 Mon/Fri morning if 50+
Special Features: 590-passenger *SunCruz V* sails from Kingfish Wharf at John's Pass on Treasure Island (next to Gator's). Must be 18 or older to sail. A la carte food menu also available.

Indian Casinos

Florida has six Indian gaming locations. The Seminole Tribe has five and the sixth is on the Miccosukee's reservation.

There is no state-tribal compact in effect in Florida and as of August, 2003 the only games offered are: high-stakes bingo, video pull tabs and low-limit poker games (maximum $2 bet, 3 raises per round, no limit to number of rounds). All are open 24 hours (except Brighton) and the minimum gambling age is 18.

Brighton Seminole Bingo and Casino
Route 6, Box 611
Okeechobee, Florida 34974
(863) 763-9268
Website: www.seminoletribe.com/enterprises/brighton/casino.shtml
Map Location: **#10** (75 miles N.W. of West Palm Beach)

Toll-Free Number: (800) 360-9875
Hours: 10am-1am (Tue-Sun)
Restaurants: 1 Liquor: No
Casino Size: 27,000 Square Feet
Special Features: Poker starts at 3pm. No poker on Sunday.

Coconut Creek Casino
5550 NW 40th Street
Coconut Creek, Florida 33073
(954) 977-6700
Website: www.seminoletribe.com/enterprises/hollywood/coco.shtml
Map Location: **#2**

Toll-Free Number: (866) 2-CASINO
Restaurants: 1 snack bar (open 24 hours)
Liquor: No

Hollywood Seminole Gaming
4150 N. State Road 7
Hollywood, Florida 33021
(954) 961-3220
Website: www.seminoletribe.com/enterprises/hollywood/casino.shtml
Map Location: **#2** (5 miles S. of Fort Lauderdale)

Toll-Free Number: (800) 323-5452
Restaurants: 2 Snack Bars Liquor: Yes
Casino Size: 73,500 Square Feet
Special Features: 750-room Hard Rock Hotel expected to open by spring of 2004.

Miccosukee Indian Gaming
500 S.W. 177 Avenue
Miami, Florida 33194
(305) 222-4600
Website: www.miccosukee.com
Map Location: **#1**

Toll-Free Number: (800) 741-4600
Room Reservations: (877) 242-6464
Rooms: 256 Price Range: $69-$109
Suites: 46 Price Range: $125-$189
Restaurants: 2 (1 open 24 hours) Liquor: Yes
Buffets: B-$7.95 L/D-$10.95

Seminole Gaming Palace and Casino
5223 N. Orient Road
Tampa, Florida 33610
(813) 621-1302
Website: www.seminoletribe.com/enterprises/tampa/gaming.shtml
Map Location: **#3**

Toll-Free Number: (800) 282-7016
Restaurants: 1 Cafeteria Liquor: Yes
Special Features: 250-room Hard Rock Hotel expected to open by spring of 2004.

Seminole Gaming Palace and Casino
506 South 1st Street
Immokalee, Florida 33934
(941) 658-1313
Map Location: **#4** (35 miles N.E. of Naples)

Toll-Free Number: (800) 218-0007
Restaurants: 2 (1 open 24 hours) Liquor: Yes
Casino Size: 43,000 Square Feet

GEORGIA

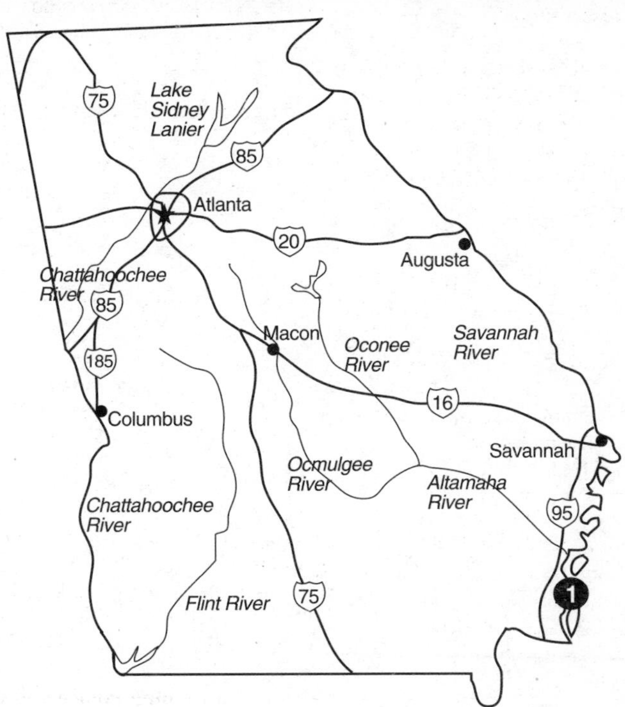

There is one casino boat in Georgia which sails three miles out into international waters where casino gambling is permitted.

For information on visiting Georgia call the state's tourism department at (800) 847-4842.

Emerald Princess Dinner Cruise & Casino
One St. Andrews Court
Brunswick, Georgia 31520
(912) 265-3558
Website: www.emeraldprincesscasino.com
Map Location: **#1** (75 miles S. of Savannah)

Reservation Number: (800) 842-0115
Gambling Age: 18
Ship's Registry: Panama
Buffets: Included
Schedule
11:00am - 4:00pm (Sat)
1:00pm - 6:00pm (Sun)
7:00pm - 12:00am (Mon-Thu)
7:00pm - 1:00am (Fri-Sat)
Prices: Range from $10-$25
Port Charges: Included
Parking: Free
Games Offered: Blackjack, Craps, Roulette, Caribbean Stud Poker
Special Features: 400-passenger *Emerald Princess* sails from Brunswick Landing Marina in downtown Brunswick. Reservations are required for all cruises. Packages with hotel accommodations are available. No one under 18 permitted to board.

IDAHO

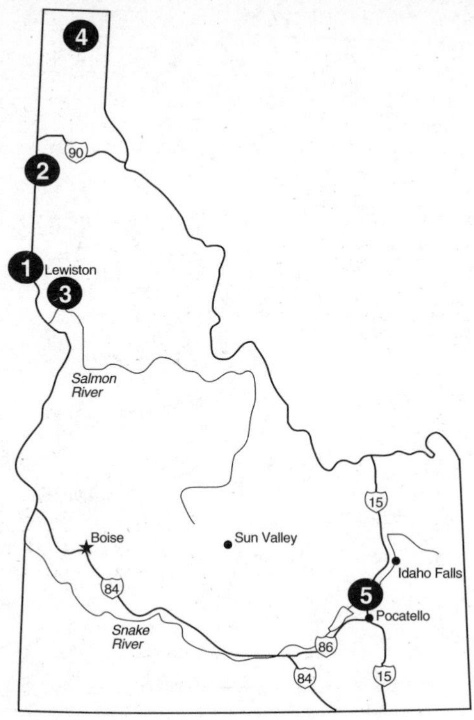

Idaho has five Indian casinos that offer electronic pull-tab machines and other video games. The machines don't pay out in cash. Instead they print out a receipt which must be cashed by a floor attendant or taken to the cashier's cage. Some casinos also offer bingo.

According to David High in the attorney general's office the terms of the compact between the tribes and the state do not require any minimum payback percentage that the gaming machines must return to the public.

The minimum gambling age at all casinos is 18 and they are all open 24 hours. For Idaho tourism information call (800) 635-7820

Bannock Peak Casino
1707 W. Country Road
Fort Hall, Idaho 83204
(208) 235-1308
Map Location: **#5** (5 miles N. of Pocatello)

Casino Size: 5,000 Square Feet
Other Games: Only gaming machines.

Clearwater River Casino
17500 Nez Perce Road
Lewiston, Idaho 83501
(208) 746-5733
Website: www.crcasino.com
Map Location: **#1** (250 miles N. of Boise)

Toll-Free Number: (877) 678-7423
Restaurants: 1 Snack Bar Liquor: No
Casino Size: 30,000 Square Feet
Other Games: Bingo (Thu-Sun)
Special Features: 33-space RV park.

Coeur D'Alene Casino Resort Hotel
U.S. Highway 95/P.O. Box 236
Worley, Idaho 83876
(208) 686-5106
Website: www.cdacasino.com
Map Location: **#2** (350 miles N. of Boise)

Toll-Free Number: (800) 523-2464
Rooms: 93 Price Range: $75-$90
Suites: 3 Price Range $175-$350
Restaurants: 2 Liquor: Yes
Buffet: B-$4.99/$6.99 (Sat-Sun)
L-$6.99/$11.99 (Sun) D-$11.99/
$13.99 (Sat)/$9.99(Wed)/$15.99(Fri)
Casino Size: 30,000 Square Feet
Other Games: Bingo (Fri-Sun), Simulcasting
Senior Discount: 10% off Fri bingo, if 55+

Coyote Casino
404 Main Street
Kamiah, Idaho 83536
(208) 935-7860
Website: www.crcasino.com
Map Location: **#3** (225 miles N. of Boise)

Toll-Free Number: (877) 678-7423
Restaurants: 1 Liquor: No
Hours: 24 Hours Daily
Casino Size: 2,300 Square Feet

Kootenai River Inn & Casino
Kootenai River Plaza
Bonners Ferry, Idaho 83805
(208 267 8511
Website: www.kootenairiverinn.com
Map Location: **#4** (450 miles N. of Boise)

Toll-Free Number: (800) 346-5668
Rooms: 47 Price Range: $75-$111
Suites: 4 Price Range $119-$124
Restaurants: 1 Liquor: Yes
Buffets: B-$9.95 (Sun)
Casino Size: 30,000 Square Feet
Other Games: Bingo (Wed/Fri/Sun)
Special Features: Hotel affiliated with Best Western. 10% AAA/AARP room discount.

Shoshone-Bannock Gaming
P.O. Box 868
Fort Hall, Idaho 83203
(208) 237-8778
Website: www.sho-ban.com
Map Location: **#5** (5 miles N. of Pocatello)

Toll-Free Number: (800) 497-4231
Restaurants: 1 Snack Bar Liquor: No
Casino Size: 15,000 Square Feet
Other Games: Bingo (Wed-Sun)

ILLINOIS

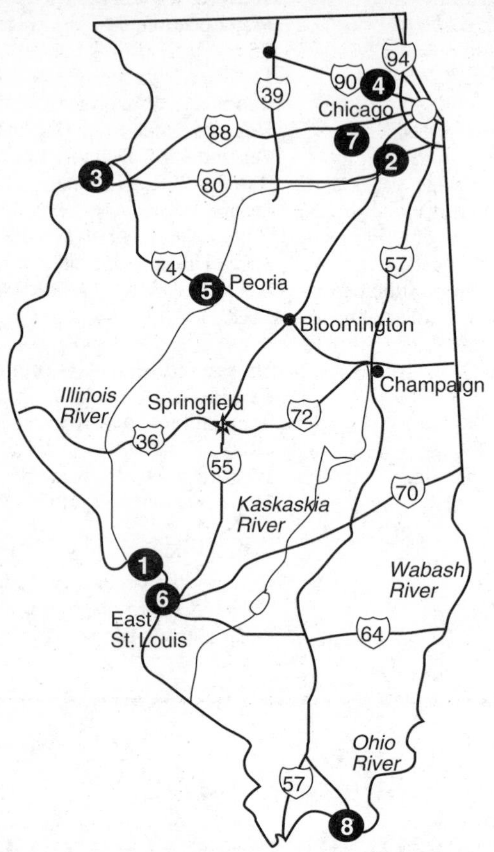

Illinois was the second state to legalize riverboat casinos. Riverboat casinos began operating there in September 1991 with the launching of the first boat: the Alton Belle.

All Illinois riverboats remain dockside and do not cruise. Unlike Mississippi, however, the casinos are not open 24 hours and state law limits the number of gaming licenses to 10. As of August 2003, there were nine casinos in operation and the 10th license was being pursued by several different gaming companies.

Here's information from the Illinois Gaming Board showing each casino's average slot payback percentage for the one-year period from June 1, 2002 through May 30, 2003:

CASINO	PAYBACK %
Casino Queen	94.78
Alton Belle	94.54
Grand Victoria	94.27
Rock Island	93.81
Empress	93.48
Hollywood	93.26
Par-A-Dice	93.10
Harrah's Joliet	92.60
Harrah's Metropolis	91.87

These figures reflect the total percentages returned by each casino for all of their electronic machines. As you can see, the Casino Queen returned the most to its slot machine players, while Harrah's in Metropolis returned the least.

Admission is free to all Illinois casinos (see NOTE below) and, unless otherwise noted, all casinos offer: slots, video poker, blackjack, craps, roulette and Caribbean stud poker. Some casinos also offer: let it ride (LIR), baccarat (B), mini-baccarat (MB), poker (P), pai gow poker (PGP) and three-card poker (TCP). The minimum gambling age is 21.

NOTE: In mid-2003 the state legislature raised the taxes on Illinois casinos to the highest in the nation (up to 70%). In mid-August 2003, in response to the increased taxes, four casinos cut their hours of operation. Additionally, Harrah's Joliet started charging admission. Other casinos may institute the same changes, so if you are planning a visit to an Illinois casino you may want to contact them first to see if their hours of operation or admission policies have changed.

For more information on visiting Illinois contact the state's Bureau of Tourism at (800) 226-6632.

Alton Belle Riverboat Casino
219 Piasa Street
Alton, Illinois 62002
(618) 474-7500
Website: www.argosycasinos.com
Map Location: **#1** (260 miles S.W. of Chicago. 25 miles N. of St. Louis, MO)

Reservation Number: (800) 336-SLOT
Restaurants: 3
Buffets: L-$8.45 D-$12.45
Valet Parking: $5 (Free for club members)
Casino Hours: 10am-4am Daily
Casino Size: 23,000 Square Feet
Other Games: LIR, TCP
Casino Marketing: (800) 711-GAME
Senior Discount: 10% off buffets, if 50, or older and member of senior slot club
Special Features: Casino feature both a 1,200-passenger modern yacht and also a barge docked on the Mississippi River.

Casino Queen
200 S. Front Street
E. St. Louis, Illinois 62201
(618) 874-5000
Website: www.casinoqueen.com
Map Location: **#6** (290 miles S.W. of Chicago)

Reservation Number: (800) 777-0777
Rooms: 150 Price Range: $89-$149
Suites: 7 Price Range: $300
Buffets: B-$5.95 L-$8.99/$10.99 (Sun)
D-$12.99
Valet Parking: $4
Casino Hours: 9am-7am
Casino Size: 27,500 Square Feet
Other Games: MB, LIR, PGP
Senior Discount: Wed. 9am-Mid. if 50 or older receive 2-for-1 buffet, 35% off in gift shop and free valet parking.
Special Features: 2,500-passenger, old-fashioned, paddlewheeler docked on the Mississippi river. 140-space RV park. Sports Bar with 27 tv's and live entertainment on weekends. MetroLink light-rail station at doorstep. 10% room discount to AAA members. $1 off buffets for slot club members.

Empress Casino Hotel Joliet
2300 Empress Drive
Joliet, Illinois 60436
(815) 744-9400
Website: www.empresscasino.com
Map Location: **#2** (43 miles S.W. of Chicago)

Reservation Number: (888) 4-EMPRESS
Rooms: 85 Price Range: $59-$120
Suites: 17 Price Range: Only through casino
Restaurants: 3
Buffets: B- $6.99 (Sat) L-$9.99/$13.99 (Sun)
D-$14.99 (Tue-Thu)/$15.99/$16.99 (Mon)
$21.99 (Fri)
Valet Parking: Free
Casino Hours: 10am-4am Daily
Casino Size: 36,266 square feet
Other Games: LIR, B, TCP
Special Features: 2,500-passenger barge docked on the Des Plaines River. Rooms are at on-property Empress Hotel. 80-space RV park.

Grand Victoria Casino
250 S. Grove Avenue
Elgin, Illinois 60120
(847) 888-1000
Website: www.grandvictoria-elgin.com
Map Location: **#4** (41 miles N.W. of Chicago)

Reservation Number: (847) 888-1000
Restaurants: 3
Buffets: L-$7.50/$16.10 (Sat-Sun)
D-$10.70 (Mon-Thu)/$16.10 (Fri-Sun)
Valet Parking: $5
Casino Hours: 8:30am-6:30am
Casino Size: 29,850 Square Feet
Other Games: B
Senior Discount: 10% off buffet, if 65, or older
Special Features: 1,200-passenger paddle wheeler-replica docked on the Fox River. Free valet parking Mon-Thu for slot club members.

Harrah's Joliet
150 N. Scott Street
Joliet, Illinois 60431
(815) 740-7800
Website: www.harrahs.com
Map Location: **#2** (43 miles S.W. of Chicago)

Admission: $2 (Platinum members)
$5 (Gold members)
Free (Diamond members and one guest)
Reservation Number: (800) HARRAHS
Rooms: 200 Price Range: $59-$159
Suites: 4 Price Range: Casino Use Only
Restaurants: 2
Buffets: B- $4.99/$8.99 (Sat-Sun)
L-$11.99/$15.99 (Sat-Sun)
D-$14.99/$15.99 (Mon)/$18.99 (Fri-Sun)
Valet Parking: $5
Casino Hours: 10am-4am Daily
Casino Size: 39,000
Other Games: MB, P, LIR
Special Features: Casino is on a barge docked on the Des Plaines River. Room discount with slot club card.

The Best Places To Play In The Chicago Area

by John Grochowski

The Chicago casino market is in a tax-induced state of flux, with the return of fees for admission, parking and soft drinks and the decline of promotions making this a much less player-friendly market than it has been since casinos stopped charging admission in 1994.

The state of Illinois, facing a budget crunch and wanting to realize more revenue from the casinos, had two options before the state legislature in the spring of 2003: either increase the state gaming tax from a 50-percent top rate that was already the highest in the nation to a staggering maximum of 70 percent, or increase the number of legal gaming positions per license from the current 1,200.

Pushed by the governor, the legislature chose the tax hike. Coupled with a $5 head tax, that's made low-limit play a losing proposition for the casinos. Casinos lose money on a senior citizen or other player on a budget who milks a little entertainment out of a $20 bill. Even if the player loses the full $20 at a casino paying the top tax rate, the state gets $14 in the gaming tax and takes another $5 in the head tax—$19 out of the $20.
If the player has a couple of soft drinks, that takes care of that, and there's nothing left to pay for the lights, not to mention salaries, maintenance, purchase of equipment and any other expenses of operation.

That has brought on not only the new fees and decrease in promotions, but also has caused the casinos to eliminate licensed slots such as Wheel of Fortune and Monopoly as well as copyrighted table games such as Let It Ride and Three Card Poker.

Across the state border in Indiana, the picture for players is much brighter. Having gone dockside and ended cruise requirements in 2002, in 2003 Indiana approved 24-hour gaming. There is no limit on gaming positions, so Indiana casinos are much larger than their Illinois competitors. And there are no admission fees or soft drink charges.

So the pendulum, which had swung toward Illinois casinos, has swung back toward Indiana. In the Chicago area, with four Illinois casinos and four Indiana casinos within about a 45-minute drive of the city, Indiana is where players — especially low-limit players, will now find many of the best deals:

Roulette: All Chicago-area casinos have standard American double-zero roulette. If there's a strongest play here, it's at Majestic Star and Trump casinos in Gary, Ind., which have the lowest table limits, usually requiring a total bet of $5, either inside or outside.

Craps: Binion's Horseshoe in Hammond, Ind., raised the bar for the entire area when it went to 100x odds in 1999. Now you'll find 10x odds or 20x odds almost everywhere — all the odds an average player can afford, and more. Horseshoe caters to table players, though, and continues to be the casino of choice for craps shooters.

Blackjack: All blackjack in the Chicago area is either the six-deck or eight-deck variety. Part of the reason is an Illinois regulation that requires all blackjack games to be dealt from a shoe. Empress in Joliet, Illinois, briefly experimented with a two-deck shoe game with good rules, and found itself inundated with card counters.

Hollywood Casino in Aurora, Illinois, tried a two-deck game with terrible rules, and that failed, too. The difference in the games is in the rules that shave a tenth of a percent here and add a tenth there. The best set is at Empress, with six-deck games that have the dealer stand on all 17s and permit the player to double down on any first two cards, including after splitting pairs, and permit the player to resplit Aces.

From time to time, Empress' leadership has been challenged by Trump and Majestic Star in Gary, which match Empress rule-for-rule except for the Ace resplits. They've sometimes made up the difference by off-and-on experiments offering late surrender.

Video Poker: Majestic Star is now clearly the best video poker casino in the Chicago area, especially for low-limit players. It has 9-6 Jacks or Better (99.5 percent return with expert play) and 9-7 Double Bonus Poker (99.1 percent) on large banks of IGT Game King machines, both at the quarter and dollar level. The Game Kings include many more 99-percent-plus games, especially at the dollar level. There is some variation in pay tables from machine-to-machine, but some include Not So Ugly Deuces Wild (99.7), 9-6 Bonus Poker Deluxe (99.6), 8-5 Bonus Poker (99.2), 8-5 Triple Bonus Poker (99.8) and 10-6-5 Joker's Wild, two pair or better (99.9). Even nickel players can get in on the act. Majestic Star's 50 Play Poker machines have 9-6 Jacks or Better. Slot club benefits have been cut in the last year. The combination of cash back and bonus cash vouchers once exceeded a full percent. Now the total is less than half a percent, but that still leaves Majestic Star as close as it gets to heaven for a video poker player in the Chicago market.

The long-time video poker leader, Empress Casino in Joliet, Ill., lost a big attraction when it moved from its boats onto a two-story barge in the spring of 2003. For eight years, Empress had offered the single best video poker game in the Chicago area — dollar 10-7 Double Bonus Poker, with a progressive jackpot on the royal flush. With expert play, 10-7 Double Bonus is a 100.17 percent game with expert play with the royal at the rollover value of $4,000 for five coins played.

Problem is, Illinois law states that no electronic gaming device may have a theoretical payback percentage above 100 percent. Testing in 1995 didn't pick up on just how good 10-7 Double Bonus is, but when Empress tried to have the game recertified for the new machines it was buying for the barge, it failed to meet the state standard. The Illinois Gaming Board denied permission to continue the game. Still, Empress remains a pretty good video poker casino, especially for the dollar player. Dollar Game Kings include several 99-percent or better games, including Not So Ugly Deuces (99.7), Bonus Poker (99.2) and ACES Bonus Poker (99.3). On multi-hand machines, including Triple Play/Five Play and Ten Play, Empress has 9-6 Jacks or Better and Not So Ugly Deuces. Empress also has the best deal in the area on the the Multi Strike Poker games. Its machines are multidenomination, with play for quarters, halves or dollars.

At the 25-cent and 50-cent level, the games are 98-percenters such as 9-5 Jacks or Better (98.4), but at the dollar level, the player gets 9-6 Jacks or Better and other 99-plus-percent games.

Game variety: Blackjack, craps, roulette and Caribbean Stud, and to a lesser extent mini-baccarat, are common games in the Chicago area. If you're looking for anything more exotic, the place to look is Indiana. In Illinois, the combination of the limit on gaming positions and the reluctance by operators to pay licensing fees means copyrighted games are a dying breed.

Across the border, Let It Ride, Three Card Poker, Caribbean Draw and pai-gow poker are easy to find, and you'll find a few rarities like Bonus 6 Stud at Trump, Boston Five at Majestic Star and Play Four at Horseshoe. For Illinois to match all that, laws are going to have to change.

John Grochowski is the gaming columnist for the "Chicago Sun-Times" and a contributing writer to many gaming magzines. John is also the author of several books on casino gambling. For ordering information on John's books: be sure to look for his ads in the front part of this book.

Harrahs Metropolis
203 S. Ferry Street
Metropolis, Illinois 62960
(618) 524-2628
Website: www.harrahs.com
Map Location: **#8** (Across from Paducah, KY. Take exit 37 on I-24)

Toll-Free Number: (800) 935-7700
Restaurants: 2
Buffets: B-$11.99 (Sat-Sun) L-$9.99
D-$13.99/$15.99 (Fri-Sun)
Hours: 9am-7am
Valet Parking: $5
Other Games: MB, LIR
Casino Size: 29,760 Square Feet
Casino Marketing: (800) 929-5905
Special Features: 1,300-passenger sidewheeler replica docked on the Ohio River. 120-room Amerihost Inn across street from casino (800-434-5800).

Hollywood Casino - Aurora
1 New York Street Bridge
Aurora, Illinois 60506
(630) 801-7000
Website: www.hollywoodcasinoaurora.com
Map Location: **#7** (41 miles W. of Chicago)

Toll Free Number: (800) 888-7777
Restaurants: 5
Buffets: L-$11.99 D-$15.99/$15.99 (Fri)
Valet Parking: $5
Casino Hours: 10am-4am Daily
Casino Size: 41,384 Square Feet
Other Games: MB, LIR, TCP
Senior Discount: 2-for-1 lunch buffet Wed/Thu if 55 or older and slot club member
Special Features: Casino is on a barge docked on the Fox River. Marquee Club members get $3 buffet discount.

Jumer's Casino Rock Island
1735 First Avenue
Rock Island, Illinois 61201
(309) 793-4200
Website: www.jumerscri.com
Map Location: **#3** (170 miles W. of Chicago)

Reservation Number: (800) 477-7747
Restaurants: 1 on boat adjacent to casino
Buffets: L-$6.95 D-$9.95
Valet Parking: Free
Casino Hours: 8am-3am Daily
Casino Size: 17,200 Square Feet
Senior Discount: Free buffet (Mon-Thu) if you earn a minimum of 200 points on slots or buy in for at least $50 and play for a minimum of50 minutes on tables, if 50, or older.
Special Features: 1,200-passenger old-fashioned paddlewheel boat on the Mississippi River. Restaurant is on the *Effie Afton* which is another boat docked next to the casino.

Par-A-Dice Hotel Casino
21 Blackjack Boulevard
East Peoria, Illinois 61611
(309) 698-7711
Website: www.par-a-dice.com
Map Location: **#5** (170 miles S.W. of Chicago)

Toll-Free Number: (800) 332-5634
Room reservations: (800) 547-0711
Rooms: 208 Price Range: $87-$107
Suites 12 Price Range: $98-$250
Restaurants: 4
Buffets: B-$6.95 L-$8.95
D-$11.95/ $15.95 (Fri/Sat)
Valet Parking: $5
Casino Hours: 8:30am-4:30am
Casino Size: 26,116 Square Feet
Other Games: LIR, TCP
Special Features: 1,600-passenger modern boat docked on the Illinois River. Rooms can only be booked through casino on weekends.

INDIANA

In June 1993 Indiana became the sixth state to legalize riverboat gambling. All riverboats offer dockside gambling and, unless otherwise noted, are open 24 hours.

Admission is free to all casinos except for two: Argosy and Aztar. However, if you're a rated player from another casino you may get free admission to these casinos. Call ahead to ask them about their requirements.

Following is information from the Indiana Gaming Commission regarding average slot payout percentages for the one-year period from January 1 through December 31, 2002:

CASINO	PAYBACK %
Argosy	94.12
Belterra	93.15
Caesars Indiana	93.13
Blue Chip	92.99
Horseshoe Casino	92.82
Grand Victoria	92.61
Majestic Star	92.36
Trump Casino	92.30
Casino Aztar	91.99
Harrah's	91.80

These figures reflect the total percentages returned by each casino for all of their electronic machines including slot machines, video poker, video keno, etc.

Unless otherwise noted, all casinos offer: blackjack, craps, roulette, slots, video poker, video keno and Caribbean stud poker. Optional games include: baccarat (B), mini-baccarat (MB), poker (P), pai gow poker (PGP), three card poker (TCP), Spanish 21 (S21), big 6 wheel (B6) and let it ride (LIR). The minimum gambling age is 21. For more information on visiting Indiana call (800) 289-6646.

Argosy Casino & Hotel - Lawrenceburg
777 Argosy Parkway
Lawrenceburg, Indiana 47025
(812) 539-8000
Website: www.argosycasinos.com
Map Location: **#3** (95 miles S.E. of Indianapolis)

Toll-Free Number: (888) ARGOSY-7
Rooms: 300 Price Range: $79-$175
Suites: 6 Price Range: $160-$310
Restaurants: 4
Buffets: B-$6.95 L-$9.95
D-$13.95/$17.95 (Fri/Sat)
Valet Parking: $3
Admission: $3/ $5 (Fri/Sat)
Casino Size: 74,300 Square Feet
Other Games: MB, B6, LIR, SP21, TCP
Casino Marketing: (888) ARGOSY-7
Senior Discount: $1 off admission Sun-Thu and Fri/Sat 9am-5pm, if 55, or older
Special Features: 4,000-passenger modern yacht docked on the Ohio River. Closest casino to Cincinnati. Reservations are recommended, especially for weekends and holidays.

Belterra Casino and Resort
777 Belterra Drive
Belterra, IN 47020
(812) 427-4008
Website: www.belterracasino.com
Map Location: **#1** (35 miles S.W. of Cincinnati, Ohio)

Toll-Free Number: (888) 235-8377
Rooms: 308 Price Range: $79-$149
Suites: Casino use only
Restaurants: 5
Buffets: B-$7.95/$14.95 (Sun) L-$9.95 D-$14.95
Valet Parking: Free
Casino Size: 38,000 Square Feet
Other Games: S21, PGP, TCP, LIR
Special Features: 2,600-passenger sidewheeler docked on the Ohio River. Health club and spa. 18-hole golf course.

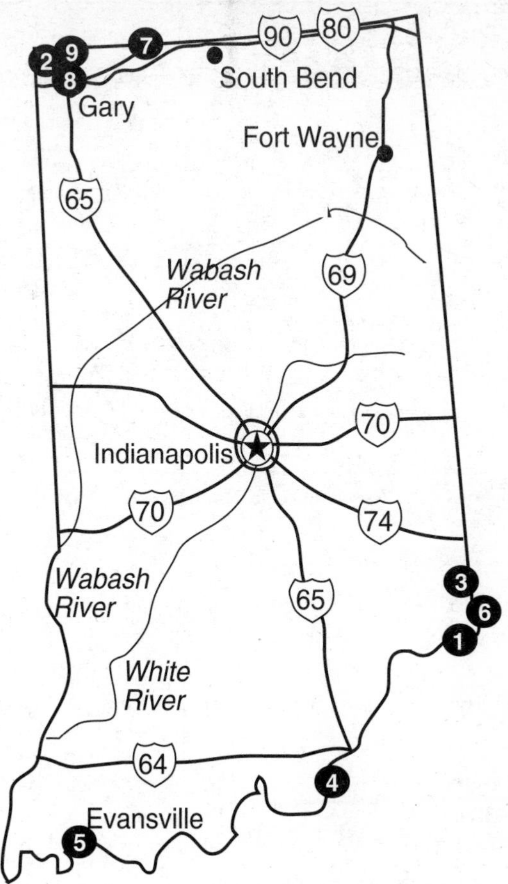

Blue Chip Casino
2 Easy Street
Michigan City, Indiana 46360
(219) 879-7711
Website: www.bluechip-casino.com
Map Location: **#7** (40 miles E. of Chicago)

Reservation Number: (888) 879-7711
Rooms: 180 Price Range: $79-$109
Suites: Casino use only
Restaurants: 3
Buffets: B-$7.95 L-$9.95
D-$14.95/$17.95 (Sat)
Valet Parking: Free
Hours: 8am-3am/24 Hours (Thu-Sat)
Casino Size: 25,000 Square Feet
Other Games: MB, P, LIR, TCP
Senior Discount: 2-for-1 lunch buffet Tue if 55+
Special Features: 2,000-passenger modern yacht docked in a man-made body canal.

Caesars Indiana
11999 Avenue of the Emperors
Elizabeth, Indiana 47117
(812) 969-6000
Website: www.caesarsindiana.com
Map Location: **#4** (20 miles S. of New Albany)

Rooms: 503 Prices: Price Range: $74-$169
Toll-Free Number: (888) 766-2648
Buffets: B-$7.95/$11.95 (Sat-Sun) L-$8.95
D-$13.95/15.95 (Fri)
Valet Parking: Free
Casino Size: 90,000 Square Feet
Other Games: S21, B, MB, P, PGP, LIR, B6
Senior Discount: Various on Wed if 55 or older
Special Features: 5,000-passenger sidewheeler docked on the Ohio River.

The 5,000-passenger *Glory of Rome* at Caesars Indiana is the world's largest riverboat casino.

Casino Aztar
421 N.W. Riverside Drive
Evansville, Indiana 47708
(812) 433-4000
Website: www.casinoaztar.com
Map Location: **#5** (168 miles S.W. of Indianapolis)

Toll-Free Number: (800) DIAL-FUN
Rooms: 240 Price Range: $74-$115
Suites: 10 Price Range: $139-$205
Restaurants: 5
Buffets: B-$6.95 L-$7.95
Valet Parking: Free
Hours: 8am-5am/24 Hours (Fri-Sat)
Admission: $3
Casino Size: 47,863 Square Feet
Other Games: MB, LIR, B6, P
Senior Discount: Coffee, donuts and 25% off all restaurants and gift shops on Mondays 8am-9am. 10% off rooms and food all other days if 55 or older
Special Features: 2,700-passenger old fashioned paddlewheeler docked on the Ohio River. 10% room discount for AAA members. Aztar slot club members get free admission.

Grand Victoria Casino & Resort
600 Grand Victoria Drive
Rising Sun, Indiana 47040
(812) 438-1234
Website: www.hyatt.com
Map Location: **#6** (40 miles S.W. of Cincinatti)

Reservation Number: (800) GRAND-11
Rooms: 201 Price Range: $69-$139
Restaurants: 4
Buffets: B-$6.95 L-$8.95/$12.95 (Sun)
D-$12.95/$15.95 (Fri)
Valet Parking: Free
Hours: 8am-5am/24 Hours (Fri-Sat)
Casino Size: 40,000 Square Feet
Other Games: S21, LIR, P, TCP
Senior Discount: Various 10% discounts if 55+
Special Features: 3,000-passenger paddle wheeler docked on Ohio River. Hotel is Hyatt. Golf course. Single-zero roulette

Harrah's East Chicago
One Showboat Place
East Chicago, Indiana 46312
(219) 378-3000
Website: www.harrahs.com
Map Location: **#9** (12 miles E. of Chicago)

Reservation Number: (877) 496-1777
Rooms: 286 Prices: $75-$200
Suites: 7 Prices: Casino Use Only
Restaurants: 5
Buffets: B-$9.99/$20.99 (Sat-Sun) L-$13.99
D-$17.99/$24.99 (Fri-Sat)
Valet Parking: $5 but discounted for Total Rewards Card members
Casino Size: 53,000 Square Feet
Other Games: S21, MB, P, PGP, LIR, TCP
Special Features: 3,750-passenger modern yacht docked on Lake Michigan.

Horseshoe Casino Hammond
777 Casino Center Drive
Hammond, Indiana 46320
(219) 473-7000
Website: www.horseshoe.com
Map Location: **#2** (10 miles E. of Chicago)

Reservation Number: (866) 711-7463
Restaurants: 3
Buffets: B-$9.99/$24.99 (Sun) L-$13.99
D-$17.99/$24.99 (Fri-Sat)
Valet parking: $5/$3 with slot club card.
Casino Size: 43,000 Square Feet
Other Games: B, MB, P, TCP, LIR
Senior Discount: Free valet Mondays, if 55+
Special Features: 3,000-passenger modern yacht docked on Lake Michigan. Slot club members get 15% off food and in gift shop.

Majestic Star Casino
1 Buffington Harbor Drive
Gary, Indiana 46406
(219) 977-7777
Website: www.majesticstar.com
Map Location: **#8** (15 miles E. of Chicago)

Reservation Number: (888) 2B-LUCKY
Restaurants: 6
Valet Parking: Free
Casino Size: 25,000 Square Feet
Other Games: S21, MB, B, PGP, TCP, LIR, B6
Special Features: 1,300-passenger modern yacht docked on Lake Michigan. Slot club members get 25% discount at deli.

Trump Hotel Casino
1 Buffington Harbor Drive
Gary, Indiana 46406
(219) 977-8980
Website: www.trumpindiana.com
Map Location: **#8** (15 miles E. of Chicago)

Reservation Number: (888) 218-7867
Rooms: 300 Price Range: $65-$99
Restaurants: 3 (1 Deli on boat)
Valet Parking: Free
Casino Size: 37,000 Square Feet
Other Games: B, MB, PGP, B6
Senior Discount: Various on Mon, if 50+
Special Features: 2,300-passenger modern yacht docked on Lake Michigan.

IOWA

Iowa was the first state to legalize riverboat gambling. The boats began operating on April Fools Day in 1991 and passengers were originally limited to $5 per bet with a maximum loss of $200 per person, per cruise. Because of these restrictions several boats later moved to Mississippi which offered 24-hour, no-limit, dockside gambling.

In September 1991 the first riverboats began operating in the bordering state of Illinois and these boats didn't have Iowa's restrictive bet or loss limits. The increased competition from these boats cut deeply into the profitability of the Iowa boats and in early 1994 the Iowa legislature voted to eliminate the gambling restrictions. Additionally, a provision was added to allow slot machines (no video poker) to be placed at the state's four pari-mutuel facilities, subject to voter approval. The slot machine measure passed in referendums in three of the four affected counties.

Here's information, as supplied by the Iowa Racing and Gaming Commission, showing the electronic gaming machine payback percentages for all non-Indian locations for the 2003 fiscal year from July 1, 2002 through June 30, 2003:

LOCATION	PAYBACK %
Prairie Meadows	94.12
Rhythm City	93.48
Isle of Capri - Bettendorf	93.47
Dubuque Diamond Jo	93.40
Isle of Capri - Marquette	93.30
Dubuque Greyhound	93.29
Bluffs Run	93.24
Ameristar	93.16
Belle of Sioux City	93.15
Lakeside	93.12
Mississippi Belle II	93.02
Harrah's	92.96
Catfish Bend	92.78

These figures reflect the total percentages returned by each riverboat casino or pari-mutuel facility for all of its electronic machines including: slots, video poker, video keno, etc. As you can see, Prairie Meadows returned the most to their players, while Catfish Bend returned the least.

Admission to all Iowa riverboat casinos is free. Most boats cruise from June through October and remain dockside from November through May although there might be slight differences in those schedules among the various boats.

Iowa is also home to three Indian casinos. Unless otherwise noted, all riverboats and Indian casinos offer: blackjack, roulette, craps, slots and video poker. Some casinos also offer: mini-baccarat (MB), poker (P), pai gow poker (PGP), Caribbean stud poker (CSP), let it ride (LIR), big 6 (B6), bingo (BG), keno (K), three card poker (TCP) and Spanish 21 (S21). The minimum gambling age is 21.

For more information on visiting Iowa call the state's tourism department at (800) 345-4692.

Ameristar Casino Council Bluffs
2200 River Road
Council Bluffs, Iowa 51501
(712) 328-8888
Website: www.ameristarcasinos.com
Map Location: **#8**

Toll-Free Number: (877) 462-7827
Rooms: 152 Price Range: $89-$189
Suites: 8 Price Range: $225-$275
Restaurants: 4 (1 open 24 hours)
Buffets: L-$7.99
D-$12.99/$9.99 (Tue/Sun)/$14.99 (Wed)
Casino Size: 38,040 Square Feet
Schedule: Cruises 7:30am-9:30am weekdays (Apr-Oct), then remains dockside 24 hours
Other Games: S21, PGP, CSP, LIR, TCP
Senior Discount: 15% off food and hotel gift shop, if 55, or older
Special Features: 2,700-passenger sidewheeler replica that cruises the Missouri River. Sports bar. Video arcade. Kids Quest supervised children's entertainment center.

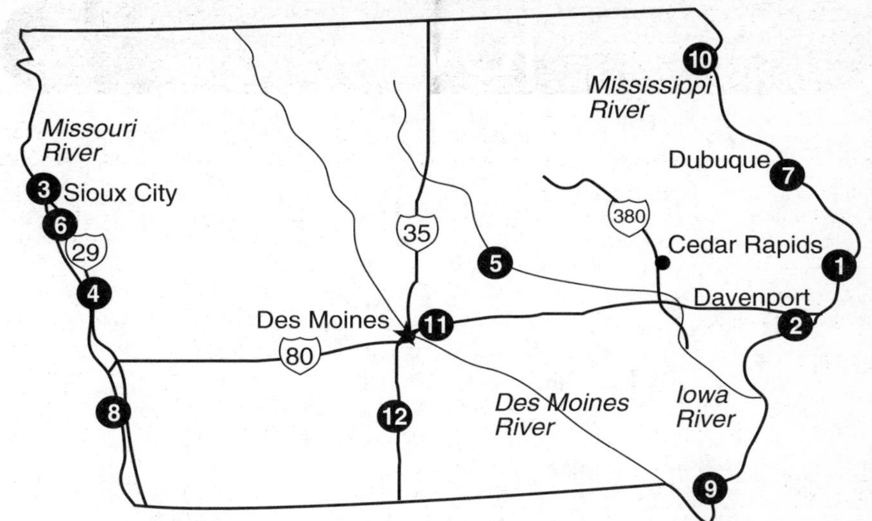

Argosy's Belle of Sioux City Casino
100 Larsen Park Road
Sioux City, Iowa 51101
(712) 294-5600
Website: www.argosycasinos.com
Map Location: **#3**

Toll-Free Number: (800) 424-0080
Restaurants: 2 (1 open 24 hours)
Buffets: B-$3.99
Casino Size: 8,430 Square Feet
Schedule: Cruises 7:30am-9:30am weekdays (Apr-Oct), then remains dockside 24 hours
Other Games: S21, PGP, CSP, TCP
Fun Book: Given at Iowa welcome centers
Special Features: 1,200-passenger old-fashioned stern wheeler that cruises the Missouri River. Slot club members get 10% discount at gift shop.

Catfish Bend Casino
902 Riverview Drive
Fort Madison, Iowa 52627
(319) 372-2946
Website: www.catfishbendcasino.com
Map Location: **#9** (180 miles S.E. of Des Moines)

Toll Free Number: (800) 372-2946
Restaurants: 2
Buffets: L-$6.95 D-Varies from $7 to $13
Schedule: Opens 8:00am, cruises May-Aug from 8am-10am (Mon-Sat), then remains dockside and stays open until 2am/24 hours (Wed-Sun)
Casino Size: 14,572 Square Feet
Other Games: S21, P, CSP, LIR
Senior Discount: Various on Thursday, if 50+
Special Features: 1,500-passenger paddle wheeler that cruises the Mississippi River. Charge for cruise is $10 (adults), $5 for children. Docks in Burlington from November through April.

Dubuque Diamond Jo Casino
3rd Street Ice Harbor
Dubuque, IA 52004
(319) 583-7005
Website: www.diamondjo.com
Map Location: **#7**

Toll-Free Number: (800) LUCKY-JO
Restaurants: 2
Buffets: B-$5.50 (Sun) L-$6.95/$8.50 (Sun) D-$13.95 (Fri-Sat Only)
Valet Parking: $2
Schedule: Cruises 7:30am-9:30am (Mon-Fri), then remains dockside and stays open until 3am/24 hours (Fri/Sat)
Casino Size: 17,813 Square Feet
Other Games: P, CSP, LIR
Senior Discount: Players club members, 55 or older, freevalet parking 9am-4pm daily and freebreakfast 7:30-9:30am Monday-Friday
Special Features: 1,600-passenger old-fashioned steamboat replica that cruises the Mississippi River. Players club members get 20% buffet discount and 25% discount in gift shop.

Harrah's Casino - Council Bluffs
One Harrah's Boulevard
Council Bluffs, Iowa 51501
(712) 329-6000
Website: www.harrahs.com
Map Location: **#8**

Toll Free Number: (800) HARRAHS
Rooms: 240 Price Range: $59-$179
Suites: 11 Price Range $199
Restaurants: 3 (1 open 24 hours)
Buffets: B-$6.99 L-$8.99/$12.99 (Sun)
D-$12.99/$11.99 (Mon/Sat/Sun)
Schedule: Cruises 7:30 am to 9:30 am, then remains dockside and stays open 24 hours
Casino Size: 28,006 Square Feet
Other Games: P, PGP, CSP, LIR, B6, S21
Special Features: 2,365-passenger paddle wheel-replica that cruises the Missouri River.

Isle of Capri Casino - Bettendorf
1821 State Street
Bettendorf, Iowa 52722
(563) 359-7280
Website: www.isleofcapricasino.com
Map Location: **#2**

Toll-Free Number: (800) 724-5825
Rooms: 256 Price Range: $74-$95
Restaurants: 3
Buffets: B-$4.95 L-$7.95 D-$12.95
Schedule: Cruises 7am-9am (Mon-Fri), then remains dockside and stays open 24 hours
Other Games: P, PGP, CSP, TCP, LIR
Casino Size: 26,744 Square Feet
Senior Discount: Various on Tue/Thu if 50+
Special Features: 2,500-passenger old-fashioned paddle wheeler that cruises the Mississippi River.

Isle of Capri Casino - Marquette
P.O. Box 460
Marquette, Iowa 52158
(563) 873-3531
Website: www.isleofcapricasino.com
Map Location: **#10** (60 miles N. of Dubuque)

Toll-Free Number: (800) 4-YOU-BET
Rooms: 22 Price Range: $85
Suites: 3 Price Range: $125
Restaurants: 1
Buffets: B-$5.99/$8.99 (Sun) L-$6.99
D-$9.99/$11.99 (Fri/Sat)
Schedule: Open 9am, cruises 10:00am to noon (Mon-Fri), then remains dockside and stays open until 3am/24 hours (Fri-Sat)
Casino Size: 18,747 Square Feet
Other Games: CSP, LIR, TCP
Fun Book: Distributed by local hotels
Senior Discount: Various on Tue/Thu if 50+
Special Features: 1,200-passenger paddle wheeler that cruises the Mississippi River.

Lakeside Casino Resort
777 Casino Drive
Osceola, Iowa 50213
(641) 342-9511
Website: www.lakesidecasino.net
Map Location: **#12**

Toll-Free Number: (877) 477-5253
Rooms: 60 Price: $69-$125
Suites: 3 Prices $145
Restaurants: 2
Buffets: B-$5.25 L-$6.25
D-$9.50/$11.50(Fri-Sat)
Schedule: Cruises 7:30am-9:30am (Mon-Fri) and 7:00 am-9:00 am (Sat-Sun) then remains dockside stays open 24 hours
Casino Size: 25,000 Square Feet
Other Games: S21, LIR, TCP
Senior Discount: Various on Mon if 50+
Special Features: 1,500-passenger old-fashioned paddle wheeler that cruises on West Lake. 47-space RV park. Fishing/boating dock. Free coffee, juice and muffins during cruises.

Mississippi Belle II
Showboat Landing
Clinton, Iowa 52733
(563) 243-9000
Map Location: **#1** (83 miles E. of Cedar Rapids)

Toll-Free Number: (800) 457-9975
Restaurants: 1
Buffets: B-$6.95 (Sat-Sun) L-$6.95
D-$8.99 (Tue)/$9.99 (Sun/Wed/Thu)$10.99
Schedule: Opens 9am, cruises 1pm-3pm (Mon-Fri,May-Oct), then remains dockside and stays open until 2am/4am (Fri/Sat)
Casino Size: 9,952 Square Feet
Other Games: S21, P, CSP, LIR , TCP
Special Features: 1,000-passenger old-fashioned paddle wheeler that cruises the Mississippi River.

Rhythm City Casino
130 West River Drive
Davenport, Iowa 52801
(319) 328-8000
Website: www.rhythmcitycasino.com
Map Location: **#2** (80 miles S.E. of Cedar Rapids)

Toll-Free Number: (800) BOAT-711
Rooms: 98 Price Range: $59-$95
Suites: 23 Price Range: $125
Restaurants: 2 (1 open 24 hours)
Buffets: B-$3.95 L-$6.95/$10.95 (Sun)
D-$9.95/$11.95 (Fri-Sat)
Schedule: Cruises 7:00-9:00am (Apr-Sept, Mon-Fri), then remains dockside and stays open 24 hours
Casino Size: 30,044 Square Feet
Other Games: S21, PGP, CSP, LIR
Senior Discount: Various on Tue/Wed if 50+
Special Features: 2,200-passenger riverboat cruises the Mississippi River.

Indian Casinos

Casino Omaha
1 Blackbird Bend, Box 89
Onawa, Iowa 51040
(712) 423-3700
Map Location: **#4** (30 miles S. of Sioux City, 60 miles N. of Omaha, 4 miles W. of I-29 at exit 112)

Toll-Free Number: (800) 858-U-BET
Restaurants: 1 Liquor: Yes
Buffets: L-$6.00
D-$8.00/$9.50 (Sat)/$11.50 (Fri)
Hours: 8am-2am/24 Hours (Fri/Sat)
Other Games: P
Casino Size: 30,000 Square Feet
Fun Book: Coupons available at the slot club booth on some weekdays.

Meskwaki Bingo & Casino
1504 305th Street
Tama, Iowa 52339
(641) 484-2108
Website: www.meskwaki.com
Map Location: **#5** (40 miles W. of Cedar Rapids)

Toll-Free Number: (800) 728-4263
Rooms: 204 Price Range: $69-$99
Suites: 4 Price Range: $175
Restaurants: 4 Liquor: No
Buffets: B-$5.25 L-$7.25 D-$8.25
Hours: 24 Hours Daily
Other Games: S21,P, CSP, LIR, MB, TCP
K, BG, Simulcasting
Senior Discount: $1 off buffet if 55+
Special Features: 70-space RV park
NOTE: Due to a Tribal dispute this casino may be closed. Before going to this casino you should call first to make sure it is open.

Winnavegas
1500 330th Street
Sloan, Iowa 51055
(712) 428-9466
Website: www.winnavegas-casino.com
Map Location: **#6** (20 miles S. of Sioux City)

Toll-Free Number: (800) 468-9466
Restaurants: 1 Liquor: Yes
Buffets: L-$4.95 D-$6.95
Hours: 24 Hours Daily
Other Games: MB, P, CSP, LIR, BG

Pari-Mutuels

Bluffs Run Casino
2701 23rd Avenue
Council Bluffs, Iowa 51501
(712) 323-2500
Website: www.harrahs.com
Map Location: **#8** (102 miles S. of Sioux City)

Toll-Free Number: (800) BET-2-WIN
Restaurants: 4 (1 open 24 hours)
Buffets: B-$4.99 L-$5.99/$8.99 (Sun)
D-$8.99/$11.99 (Mon)
Hours: 24 Hours Daily
Casino Size: 35,200 Square Feet
Other Games: Only slots
Special Features: Owned by Harrah's. Live dog racing (Tue-Sun). Horse and dog race simulcasting. 120-space RV park. Free shuttle service from local hotels.

Dubuque Greyhound Park & Casino
1855 Greyhound Park Drive
Dubuque, Iowa 52001
(563) 582-3647
Website: www.dgpc.com
Map Location: **#7**

Toll-Free Number: (800) 373-3647
Restaurants: 1
Buffets: L-$7.95 D-$10.95
Hours: 9am-3am/24 hours (Fri/Sat)
Casino Size: 11,675 Square Feet
Other Games: Only slots
Senior Discount: $2 off buffet, if 55, or older
Special Features: Live dog racing (Wed-Sun) during season which runs from May through October. Greyhound and thoroughbred simulcasting all year. Free valet parking.

Prairie Meadows Racetrack & Casino
1 Prairie Meadows Drive
Altoona, Iowa 50009
(515) 967-1000
Website: www.prairiemeadows.com
Map Location: **#11** (5 miles E. of Des Moines)

Toll-Free Number: (800) 325-9015
Restaurants: 1
Buffets: B-$4.50 L-$5.50 D-$10.95
Hours: 24 Hours Daily
Casino Size: 39,324 Square Feet
Other Games: Only slots
Senior Discount: 15% restaurant and gift shop discount, if 55, or older
Special Features: Live thoroughbred and quarter-horse racing during season which runs from April through November. Simulcasting of dog and horse racing all year.

KANSAS

There are four Indian tribes in Kansas with casinos. According to officials at the Kansas State Gaming Agency the terms of the state's compacts with the tribes regarding the minimum payback amounts on their machines are not a matter of public record and no information can be released.

Unless otherwise noted, all Kansas casinos are open 24 hours and offer the following games: blackjack, craps, roulette, slots and video poker. Other games include: poker (P), Caribbean stud poker (CSP), let it ride (LIR), three card poker (TCP) and bingo (BG). The minimum gambling age is 21.

For more information on visiting Kansas call (800) 2-KANSAS.

Casino White Cloud
777 Jackpot Drive
White Cloud, Kansas 66094
(785) 595-3430
Map Location: **#2**

Toll-Free Number: (877) 652-6115
Restaurants: 1 Liquor: Only Beer and Wine
Buffets: L-$5.75 D-$8.00
Casino Size: 21,000 Square Feet
Casino Hours: 9am-1am/3am (Fri/Sat)
Other Games: TCP, P, BG, K, No Roulette
Special Features: No alcohol served on Sunays.

Golden Eagle Casino
1121 Goldfinch Road
Horton, Kansas 66439
(785) 486-6601
Map Location: **#3** (45 miles N. of Topeka)
Website: www.goldeneaglecasino.com

Toll-Free Number: (888) 464-5825
Restaurants: 2 Liquor: No
Buffets: B-$3.95 L-$5.95
D-$7.95/$8.95(Thu-Sat)/$10.95 (Tue)
Other Games: P, LIR
Senior Discount: Free breakfast Fri-Sun if 55+

Harrah's Prairie Band Casino and Hotel
12305 150th Road
Mayetta, Kansas 66509
(785) 966-7777
Website: www.harrahs.com
Map Location: **#4** (17 miles N. of Topeka)

Toll-Free Number: (800) HARRAHS
Rooms: 100 Price Range: $99-$139
Restaurants: 2 Liquor: Only Beer and Wine
Buffets: B-$6.99 L-$7.99/$9.99 (Sun)
D-$11.99 (Sun-Th)/$13.99 (Fri/Tu)/$15.99 (Mon)
Casino Size: 63,000 Square Feet
Other Games: P, CSP, LIR, TCP
Special Features: No alcohol served on Sundays.

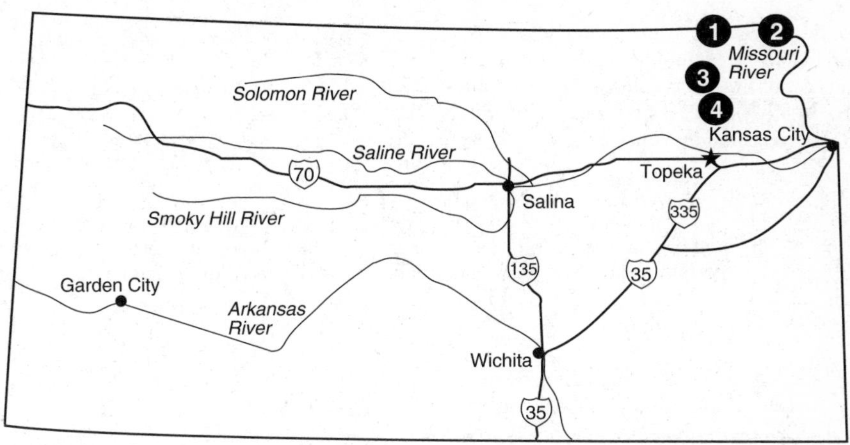

Sac & Fox Casino
1322 U.S. Highway 75
Powhattan, Kansas 66527
(785)-467-8000
Map Location: **#1** (60 miles N. of Topeka)
Website: www.sacandfoxcasino.com

Toll-Free Number: (800) 990-2946
Restaurant: 3 Liquor: Yes
Buffets: B-$3.95 L-$6.95 D-$8.95
Casino Size: 40,000 Square Feet
Other Games: CSP, LIR, TCP
Senior Discount: $1 off meals if 55 or older
Special Features: 24-hour truck stop. Golf driving range. RV hook-ups. No alcohol served on Sundays.

LOUISIANA

Louisiana was the fourth state to approve riverboat casino gambling and its 1991 gambling law allows a maximum of 15 boats statewide. In 1992 a provision was added for one land-based casino in New Orleans.

The state also has three land-based Indian casinos and two gaming machines-only casinos located at pari-mutuel facilities. Additionally, video poker is permitted at Louisiana truck stops, OTB's and bars/taverns in 31 of the state's 64 parishes (counties).

As of August 2003 there were 14 riverboat casinos in operation in 12 different locations (the two Lake Charles locations each have two boats) and a 15th casino was being built by Pinnacle Gaming (Boomtown/Casino Magic) in Lake Charles. The new casino is expected to open sometime in mid-2004. All riverboat casinos in Louisiana are required to remain dockside and all are open 24 hours.

Gaming regulations require that gaming machines in casinos be programmed to pay back no less than 80% and no more than 99.9%. For video gaming machines at locations other than casinos the law requires a minimum return of 80% and a maximum return of 94%.

Louisiana gaming statistics are not broken down by individual properties. Rather, they are classified by region: Baton Rouge (BR) , Lake Charles (LC), New Orleans (NO) and Shreveport/Bossier City (SB).

The Baton Rouge casinos consist of the Argosy and Casino Rouge. The Lake Charles casinos include Harrah's and Isle of Capri. New Orleans area casinos are: Bally's, Boomtown, Harrah's (landbased) and Treasure Chest. The Shreveport/Bossier city casinos include: Casino Magic, Hollywood, Isle of Capri, Harrah's and Horseshoe.

Here's information, as supplied by the Louisiana State Police-Riverboat Gaming Section, showing the average electronic machine payback percentages for each area's casinos for the eight-month period from October, 2002 through May, 2003:

	BR	LC	NO	SB
5¢	**91.65%**	89.65%	90.59%	89.78%
25¢	**93.75%**	91.42%	92.27%	92.12%
$1	**94.52%**	92.97%	93.61%	93.94%
$5	94.54%	94.76%	**95.16%**	95.12%
All	**93.14%**	92.14%	92.39%	92.99%

These numbers reflect the percentage of money returned on each denomination of machine and encompass all electronic machines including video poker and video keno. The best returns for each category are highlighted in bold print and you can see that the Baton Rouge area casinos offered the best returns in almost every category.

The casino games offered are: blackjack, craps, roulette, slots and video poker. Optional games include: Spanish 21 (S21), baccarat (B), mini-baccarat (MB), poker (P), Caribbean stud poker (CSP), pai gow poker (PGP), let it ride (LIR), casino war (CW), three-card poker (TCP), big 6 wheel (B6), keno (K) and bingo (BG). The minimum gambling age is 21 for casino gaming and 18 for pari-mutuel betting.

For more information on visiting Louisiana call the state's tourism department at (800) 633-6970.

Bally's Casino Lakeshore Resort
1 Stars & Stripes Boulevard
New Orleans, Louisiana 70126
(504) 248-3200
Website: www.ballysno.com
Map Location: **#4**

Toll-Free Number: (800) 57-BALLY
Restaurants: 1 (Snack bar on boat)
Buffets: B-$5.95/ $12.95 (Sun)
L-$8.95/$15.95 (Fri) D-$12.95/$15.95 (Fri-Sat)
Casino Size: 30,000 Square Feet
Other Games: P, CSP, PGP, LIR, TCP
Senior Discount: 15% discount on buffets & logo shop on Mon/Thu if 55 or older
Special Features: 1,200-passenger paddle wheeler that remains dockside on Lake Pontchartrain. Buffets, restaurant and sports bar are located in landbased terminal.

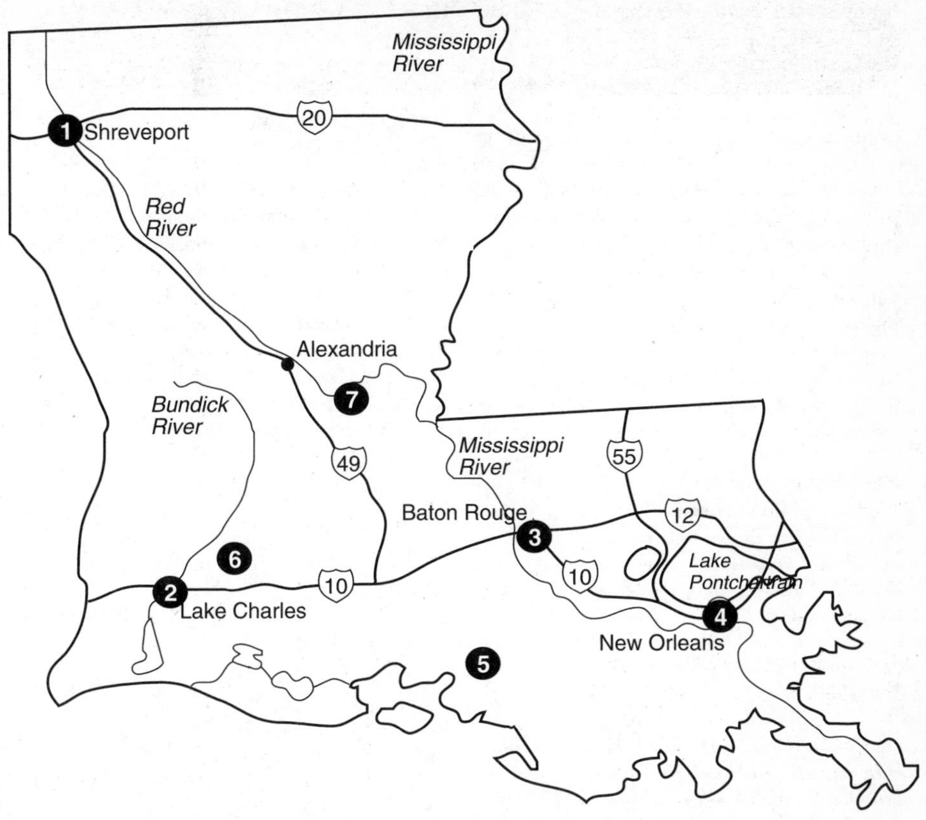

Belle of Baton Rouge
103 France Street
Baton Rouge, Louisiana 70802
(225) 378-6000
Website: www.argosycasinos.com
Map Location: **#3**

Toll-Free Number: (800) 676-4847
Restaurants: 4 (1 on boat)
Buffets: D-$19.95 (Fri) Brunch-$19.95 (Sun)
Casino Size: 29,000 Square Feet
Other Games: MB, CSP, LIR
Senior Discount: If 50, or older, join Belles and Beaus Senior Club for monthly offers
Special Features: 1,500-passenger paddle wheeler on the Mississippi River. 300-room Sheraton Hotel is adjacent to casino (call 800-325-3535). 10% off food/drink for slot club members.

Boomtown Casino - Bossier City
300 Riverside Drive
Bossier City, Louisiana 71171
(318) 746-0711
Website: www.boomtowncasinos.com
Map Location: **#1** (across the Red River From Shreveport)

Toll-Free Number: (866) 462-8696
Rooms: 100 Price Range: $85-$125
Suites: 88 Price Range: $105-$145
Restaurants: 4
Buffets: B-$5.99 L-$9.99
D-$12.99/$14.99 (Fri-Sat)
Casino Size: 28,000 Square Feet
Other Games: S21, MB, CSP, LIR, TCP
Special Features: 1,925-passenger paddle wheeler on the Red River.

Boomtown Casino - Westbank
4132 Peters Road
Harvey, Louisiana 70058
(504) 366-7711
Website: www.boomtowncasinos.com
Map Location: **#4** (a suburb of New Orleans)

Toll-Free Number: (800) 366-7711
Restaurants: 4 (1 snack bar on boat)
Buffets: B/L-$8.95 D-$14.95/$16.95 (Fri)
Casino Size: 30,000 Square Feet
Other Games: MB, P, PGP, CSP, LIR, TCP
Fun Book: Need coupon from local hotels
Senior Discount: $2 off buffets, if 55, or older
Special Features: 1,600-passenger paddle wheeler on the Harvey Canal.

Casino Rouge
1717 River Road North
Baton Rouge, Louisiana 70802
(225) 381-7777
Website: www.casinorouge.com
Map Location: **#3**

Toll-Free Number: (800) 44-ROUGE
Restaurants: 4 (1 snack bar on boat)
Buffets: L-$8.95/$16.95 (Sun)
D-$11.95/$15.95 (Fri)/$13.95 (Sat)
Casino Size: 28,146 Square Feet
Other Games: MB, P, CSP, LIR, TCP, B6
Special Features: 1,500-passenger paddle wheeler on the Mississippi River. Slot club members get 10% off in buffet (Tue-Thu) and gift shop.

Harrah's Lake Charles
800 Bilbo Street
Lake Charles, Louisiana 70601
(337) 437-1500
Website: www.harrahs.com
Map Location: **#2** (220 miles W. of New Orleans)

Toll-Free Number: (800) 977-PLAY
Restaurants: 5 (1 open 24 Hours)
Rooms: 132 Price Range: $79-$149
Buffets: L-$9.99 D-$15.99
Other Games: MB, P, PGP, CSP, LIR, TCP
Casino Marketing: (800) 625-BOAT
Special Features: Includes two paddlewheel boats: 1,700-passenger Pride of Lake Charles, and the 1,460-passenger Star Casino. Rooms also available at nearby Holiday Inn (800-367-1814).

Harrah's New Orleans
4 Canal Street
New Orleans, Louisiana 70130
(504) 533-6000
Website: www.harrahs.com
Map Location: **#4**

Toll-Free Number: (800) HARRAHS
Restaurants: 2 (1 open 24 hours)
Buffet: B-$7.99 L-$11.99/$18.99 (Sun)
D-$18.99/$21.99 (Fri-Sat)
Casino Size: 100,000 Square Feet
Other Games: B, MB, CSP, LIR, P, PGP
Valet Parking: $5 every two hours
(Free to Diamond and Platinum members)
Special Features: Land-based casino. Five themed gaming areas. Food court. Daily live jazz music. $11.99 late-night buffet.

Harrah's Shreveport
315 Clyde Fant Parkway
Shreveport, Louisiana 71101
(318) 424-7777
Website: www.harrahs.com
Map Location: **#1**

Toll-Free Number: (800) HARRAHS
Rooms: 514 Price Range: $79-$200
Restaurants: 3 (1 open 24 hours)
Buffet: B-$14.99 (Sun) L-$10.99/$12.99 (Sat)
D-$12.99-$18.99 (Varies)
Valet Parking: $3/$5 (Fri-Sun)
Casino Size: 30,000 Square Feet
Other Games: MB, CSP, LIR, TCP
Special Features: 1,650-passenger paddle wheeler on the Red River.

Hollywood Casino Shreveport
451 Clyde Fant Parkway
Shreveport, Louisiana 71101
(318) 220-0711
Website: www.hollywoodcasinoshreveport.com
Map Location: **#1**

Hotel Reservations: (877) 602-0711
Suites: 403 Price Range: $110-$230
Restaurants: 4
Buffet: B-$6.99 (Sun) L-$10.99
D-$13.99/$18.99 (Fri)
Casino Size: 29,607 Square Feet
Other Games: MB, CW, P, PGP,
CSP, LIR, TCP
Special Features: 1,500-passenger paddle wheeler on the Red River. Large display of movie memorabilia.

Horseshoe Casino Hotel - Bossier City
711 Horseshoe Boulevard
Bossier City, Louisiana 71111
(318) 742-0711
Website: www.horseshoe.com
Map Location: **#1** (across the Red River from Shreveport)

Toll-Free Number: (800) 895-0711
Suites: 606 Price Range: $110-$200
Restaurants: 5 (1 open 24 hours)
Buffets: B-$8.95 (Fri-Mon) L-$10.95
D-$12.95/$13.95 (Mon-Tue)/$16.95 (Fri)
Other Games: MB, CSP, LIR, TCP
Casino Size: 29,500 Square Feet
Senior Discount: 10% buffet discount if 50+
Special Features: 2,930-passenger paddle wheeler on the Red River. 100x odds on craps. AARP room discount.

Isle of Capri - Bossier City
711 Isle of Capri Boulevard
Bossier City, Louisiana 71111
(318) 678-7777
Website: www.isleofcapricasino.com
Map Location: **#1** (across the Red River from Shreveport)

Toll-Free Number: (800) 475-3847
Suites: 304 Price Range: $85-$125
Inn Rooms: 225 Price Range: $39-$69
Restaurants: 3 (1 open 24 Hours)
Buffets: B-$6.99 L-$8.99 D-$14.99
Casino Size: 30,000 Square Feet
Other Games: MB, PGP, CSP, TCP, LIR
Senior Discount: Weekly specials, if 50, or older
Special Features: 1,650-passenger paddle wheeler on the Red River. Slot club members get room and buffet discounts.

Isle of Capri - Lake Charles
100 Westlake Avenue
Westlake, Louisiana 70669
(337) 430-0711
Website: www.isleofcapricasino.com
Map Location: **#2** (220 miles W. of New Orleans)

Toll-Free Number: (800) THE-ISLE
Rooms: 493 Price Range: $59-$139
Restaurants: 5
Buffets: B-$5.99 L-$7.99/$13.99 (Sat-Sun)
D-$13.99
Casino Size: 48,900 Square Feet
Other Games: B, MB, P, PGP, CSP,
TCP, LIR, B6
Senior Discount: If 50, or older, go to
promotions booth for special coupons
Special Features: Two 1,200-passenger paddle wheelers, *Crown* and *Grand Palais*, on Lake Charles.

Treasure Chest Casino
5050 Williams Boulevard
Kenner, Louisiana 70065
(504) 443-8000
Website: www.treasurechest.com
Map Location: **#4** (a suburb of New Orleans)

Toll-Free Number: (800) 298-0711
Restaurants: 2 (1 open 24 hours)
Buffets: B-$3.99/$10.99 (Sun) L-$8.99
D-$8.99
Casino Size: 25,767 Square Feet
Other Games: MB, CSP, LIR, TCP
Senior Discount: If 50, or older, join Treasured
Friends for different monthly specials
Special Features: 1,900-passenger paddle wheeler on Lake Pontchartrain.

Indian Casinos

Cypress Bayou Casino
P.O. Box 519
Charenton, Louisiana 70523
(318) 923-7284
Website: www.cypressbayou.com
Map Location: **#5** (75 miles S. of Baton Rouge)

Toll-Free Number: (800) 284-4386
Restaurants: 3 Liquor: Yes
Casino Hours: 12pm-2am/4am (Fri-Sat)
Casino Size: 125,000 Square Feet
Other Games: B6, CSP, LIR, TCP
Casino Marketing: (800) 284-4386
Special Features: Land-based casino. Gift shop. Cigar bar. Oyster bar.

Grand Casino Coushatta
777 Coushatta Drive
Kinder Louisiana 70648
(318) 738-7300
Website: www.gccoushatta.com
Map Location: **#6** (35 miles N.E. of Lake Charles)

Toll-Free Number: (800) 584-7263
Rooms: 373 Price Range: $89-$129
Suites: 90 Price Range: Casino Guests Only
Restaurants: 6 (1 open 24 hours) Liquor: Yes
Buffets: L-$8.50/$12.99 (Sun)
D-$10.99/$14.99 (Fri/Sat)
Casino Size: 71,000 Square Feet
Other Games: MB, P, PGP, CSP, LIR, B6
Special Features: Land-based casino. 156-space RV park. Kids Quest childcare center. Video arcade. 18-hole golf course.

Paragon Casino Resort
711 Paragon Place
Marksville, Louisiana 71351
(318) 253-1946
Website: www.paragoncasinoresort.com
Map Location: **#7** (30 miles S.E. of Alexandria)

Toll-Free Number: (800) 946-1946
Rooms: 335 Price Range: $59-$119
Suites: 57 Price Range: $90-$325
Restaurants: 5 (1 open 24 hours) Liquor: Yes
Buffets: B-$7.50 L-$7.99
D-$10.99/$15.99 (Fri)
Casino Size: 100,000 Square Feet
Other Games: B6, MB, P, PGP,
CSP, LIR, TCP,
Special Features: Land-based casino. 166-space RV Park. Kids Quest childcare center. Video arcade. $10 room discount for AAA and AARP members. 18-hole golf course.

Pari-Mutuels

Delta Downs Racetrack & Casino
2717 Highway 3063
Vinton, Louisiana 70668
(337) 589-7441
Website: www.deltadowns.com
Map Location: **#5** (75 miles S. of Baton Rouge)

Toll-Free Number: (800) 589-7441
Restaurants: 2 and 1 snack bar
Buffets: L-$7.99/$12.99 (Sat)/(12.99 (Sun)
D-$9.99/$12.99 (Fri-Sat)
Other Games: Only machines
Special Features: Live thoroughbred and quarter-horse racing (Thu-Sun) early November through late June. Simulcasting offered all year.

Evangeline Downs Racetrack & Casino
Opelousas, Louisiana 70570
(337) 896-7223
Website: www.evangelinedowns.com
Map Location: **#8** (30 milesW. of Baton Rouge)

EXPECTED TO OPEN BY MARCH 2004
Restaurants: 2
Other Games: Only machines
Special Features: Cuurent racetrack is located in Lafayette. New casino and racetrack is expected to open by March 2004 in Opelousas. Horse racing at new facility will start in 2005. Live thoroughbred and quarter-horse racing (Mon/Thu-Sat) early April through late August. Simulcasting offered all year.

Harrah's Louisiana Downs
8000 E. Texas Street
Bossier City, Louisiana 71111
(318) 742-5555
Website: www.deltadowns.com
Map Location: **#1**

Restaurants: 5
Other Games: Only machines
Special Features: Live thoroughbred and quarter-horse racing (Thu-Sun) late June through early November. Simulcasting offered all year.

MASSACHUSETTS

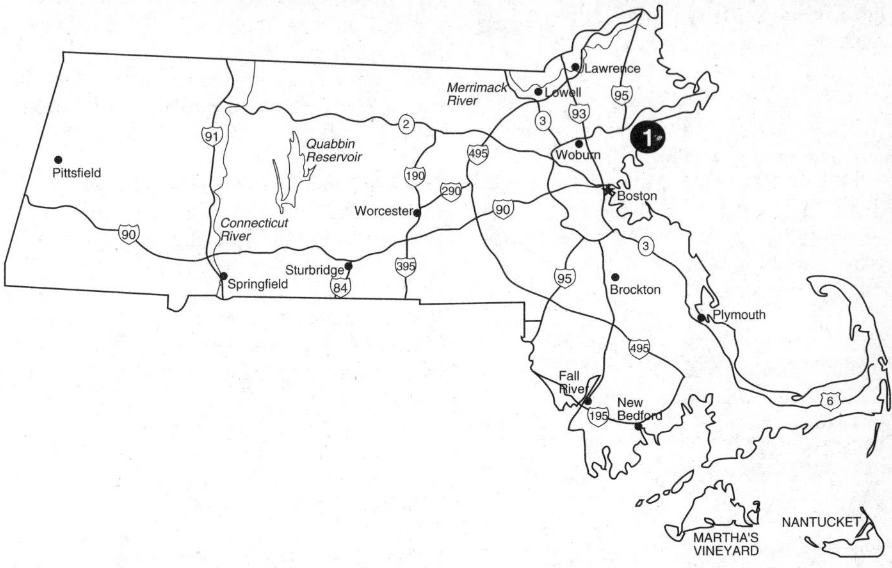

There is one gambling cruise ship in Massachusetts which sails three miles out into international waters where casino gambling is permitted.

The games offered include: blackjack, craps, roulette, baccarat, Caribbean stud poker, three-card poker, let it ride, slots, video poker and bingo.

For information on visiting Massachusetts call (800) 447-MASS.

Horizon's Edge Casino Cruises
76 Marine Boulevard
Lynn, MA 01905
Website: www.horizonsedge.com
Map Location: **#1** (8 miles N.E. of Boston)
(781) 581-7733

Toll-Free Reservations: (800) 582-5932
Gambling Age: 21
Ship's Registry: U.S.
Buffets: Included
Schedule:
11:00am - 5:00pm
6:30pm - 11:30pm
7:00pm -12:30am (Fri)
7:00pm -1:00am (Sat)
Prices: $25 (Mon-Fri Day/Sun-Thu Eve)
$35 (Sat-Sun Day/Fri-Sat Eve)
Port Charges: Included
Parking: Free
Senior Discount: 2-for-1 Saturday morn if 55+
Special Features: 490-passenger *Horizon's Edge* sails from Marina off of Lynnway in Lynn. Sails seasonally from May through November. No one under 21 permitted to board.

MICHIGAN

One of Michigan's most popular casinos is actually in Canada. It's Casino Windsor in Ontario which is just across the river from downtown Detroit.

All winnings are paid in Canadian currency and the minimum gambling age is 19. The casino is open 24 hours and offers the following games: blackjack, craps, single-zero roulette, baccarat, mini-baccarat, big six wheel, pai-gow poker, Caribbean stud poker, three-card poker and let it ride.

Casino Windsor
377 Riverside Drive East
Windsor, Ontario N9A 7H7
(519) 258-7878
Website: www.casinowindsor.com
Map Location: **#12**

PRICES ARE IN CANADIAN DOLLARS
Toll-Free Number: (800) 991-7777
Room Reservations: (800) 991-8888
Rooms: 349 Price Range: $99-$300
Suites: 40 Price Range: $250-$1,000
Restaurants: 5 (1 open 24 hours)
Buffets: L-$15.65/$19.95 (Sat-Sun)
D-$17.95/$22.95 (Fri-Sun)
Casino Size: 100,000 Square Feet
Special Features: Nautical theme with 60-foot waterfall, babbling brook, periodic water and light show. AARP/AAA 10% room discount (Sunday through Thursday only).

In November 1996 Detroit voters approved, by a 51% to 49% margin, a referendum to allow three casinos in the downtown area.

All three casinos are open 24 hours and offer the following games: blackjack, craps, roulette, baccarat, mini-baccarat, Caribbean stud poker, three-card poker, pai gow poker, let it ride, big 6 wheel and casino war. The minimum gambling age at all Detroit casinos is 21 and all three casinos offer free valet parking.

Greektown Casino
555 E. Lafayette Blvd.
Detroit, Michigan 48226
(313) 223-2999
Website: www.greektowncasino.com
Map Location: **#12**

Toll free Number: (888) 771-4386
Restaurants: 5 (1 open 24 hours)
Casino Size: 75,000 Square Feet

MGM Grand Detroit Casino
1300 John C. Lodge
Detroit Michigan 48226
(313) 393-7777
Website: http://detroit.mgmgrand.com
Map Location: **#12**

Toll-Free Number: (877) 888-2121
Restaurants: 4
Buffets: L- $14.95/$12.95 (Sun) D-$17.95
Casino Size: 75,000 Square Feet.
Other Games: Spanish 21
Special Features: Packages offered by local hotels include: room, two buffets and free gift.

MotorCity Casino
2901 Grand River Avenue
Detroit, MI 48201
(313) 237-7711
Website: www.motorcitycasino.com
Map Location: **#12**

Toll-Free Number: (877) 777-0711
Restaurants: 4
Buffets: B-$10.95 L-$15.95 D-$19.95/$28.95 (Fri)
Casino Size: 75,000 Square Feet
Other Games: Spanish 21

There are 16 Indian casinos in Michigan and the tribes are not required to release information on their slot machine payback percentages. However, according to officials at the Michigan Gaming Control Board, which is responsible for overseeing the tribal-state compacts, "the machines must meet the minimum

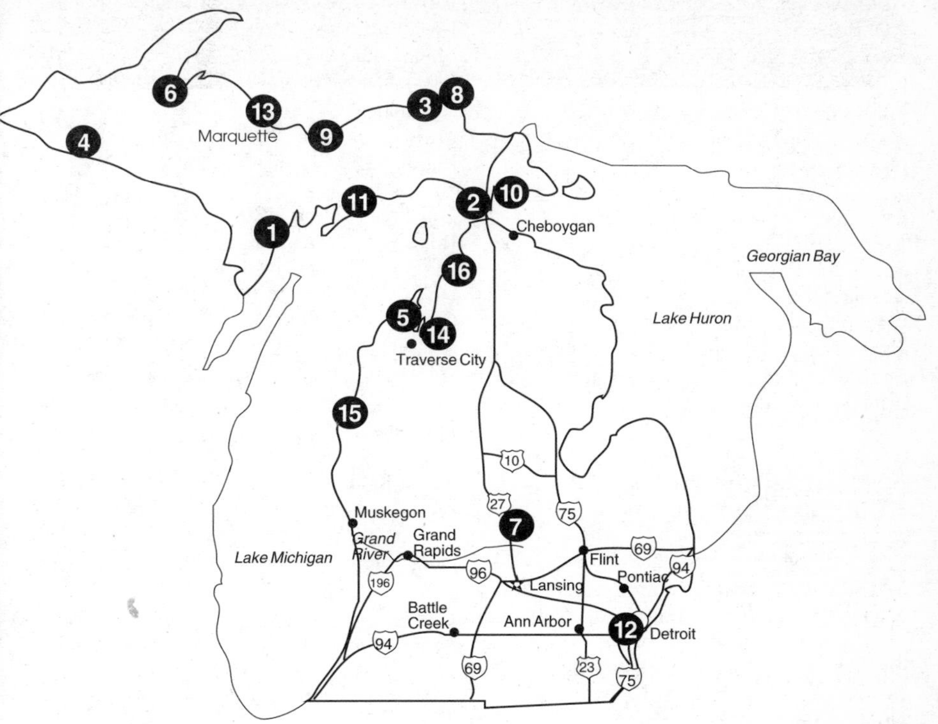

standards for machines in Nevada or New Jersey." In Nevada the minimum return is 75% and in New Jersey it's 83%. Therefore, Michigan's Indian casinos must return at least 75% in order to comply with the law.

Unless otherwise noted, all Indian casinos in Michigan are open 24 hours and offer the following games: blackjack, slots and video poker. Other games offered include: craps (C), roulette (R), baccarat (B), mini-baccarat (MB), poker (P), Caribbean stud poker (CSP), let it ride (LIR), three-card poker (TCP), keno (K) and bingo (BG).

The minimum gambling age is 21 at all Indian casinos except for the following seven where it's 18: Leelanau Sands, Turtle Creek, Chip-In's, Ojibwa, Ojibwa II, Lac Vieux and Soaring Eagle.

For more information on visiting Michigan call the state's department of tourism at (800) 543-2937.

Bay Mills Resort & Casino
11386 Lakeshore Drive
Brimley, Michigan 49715
(906) 248-3715
Website: www.4baymills.com
Map Location: **#3** (12 miles S.W. of Sault Ste. Marie)

Toll-Free Number: (888) 4-BAY-MILLS
Rooms: 142 Price Range: $59-$89
Suites: 4 Price Range: $140-$230
Restaurants: 2 (1 open 24 hrs) Liquor: Yes
Buffets: B-$5.95 L-$6.95
D-$9.95/$11.95 (Fri-Sat)
Casino Size: 15,000 Square Feet
Other Games: C, R, CSP, LIR, K
Fun Book: Given with slot club membership
Senior Discount: 10% room discount (Sun-Thu). Wednesday is Senior's Day from 8am-2pm with buffet discounts and cash drawings, if 60, or older
Special Features: Free shuttle to King's Club and Kewadin casinos. 18-hole golf course.

Chip-In's Island Resort & Casino
P.O. Box 351
Harris, Michigan 49845
(906) 466-2941
Website: www.chipincasino.com
Map Location: **#1** (13 miles W. of Escanaba on Hwy. 41)

Toll-Free Number: (800) 682-6040
Rooms: 102 Price Range: $80
Suites: 11 Price Range: $90-$153
Restaurants: 2 Liquor: Yes
Casino Size: 135,000 Square Feet
Other Games: C, R, P, CSP, TCP, LIR, K, BG
Special Features: 53-space RV park. Indoor heated pool. Fitness center.

Kewadin Casino - Christmas
N7761 Candy Cane Lane
Munising, Michigan 49862
(906) 387-5475
Website: www.kewadin.com
Map Location: **#9** (40 miles E. of Marquette)

Toll-Free Number: (800) KEWADIN
Restaurants: 1 Liquor: Yes
Hours: 8am-3am
Casino Size: 3,060 Square Feet
Other Games: LIR, TCP
Senior Discount: Various specials Wednesdays from 8am to 7pm, if 50, or older
Special Features: Free local-area shuttle service. Coupon book distributed by local motels.

Kewadin Casino - Hessel
3 Mile Road, Box 789
Hessel, Michigan 49745
(906) 484-2903
Website: www.kewadin.com
Map Location: **#10** (20 miles N.E. of St. Ignace)

Toll-Free Number: (800) KEWADIN
Restaurants: 1 Deli Liquor: Yes
Hours: 9am-12am/1am (Fri/Sat)
Casino Size: 6,500 Square Feet
Senior Discount: Various specials Thursdays from 9am to 7pm, if 50, or older
Special Features: Free local-area shuttle service. BJ only open Thu-Sun from 2pm.

Kewadin Casino - Manistique
US 2 East, Rte 1, Box 1533D
Manistique, Michigan 49854
(906) 341-5510
Website: www.kewadin.com
Map Location: **#10** (95 miles S.E. of Marquette)

Toll-Free Number: (800) KEWADIN
Rooms: 40 Price Range: $45-$65
Restaurants: 1 Deli Liquor: Yes
Hours: 8am-3am/24 Hours (Fr-Sat)
Casino Size: 25,000 Square Feet
Other Games: C, R, LIR, TCP
Senior Discount: Various specials Wednesdays from 8am to 7pm, if 50, or older
Special Features: Rooms are at Kewadin Inn about one mile from casino. Room discounts for AARP and AAA members. Sports bar. Gift shop. Free shuttle service from local motels. Coupon book distributed by local motels. Table games are only open 10am-2am daily.

Kewadin Casino Hotel - Sault Ste. Marie
2186 Shunk Road
Sault Ste. Marie, Michigan 49783
(906) 632-0530
Website: www.kewadin.com
Map Location: **#8**

Toll-Free Number: (800) KEWADIN
Rooms: 300 Price Range: $79-$95
Suites: 20 Price Range: $109-$131
Restaurants: 2 Liquor: Yes
Buffets: B-$5.95/$8.95 (Sun) L-$8.50
D-$11.95/$14.50 (Fri/Sat)
Casino Size: 85,123 Square Feet
Other Games: C, R, P, CSP, LIR, K, TCP
Senior Discount: Various on Thu if 50 or older
Special Features: Free shuttle service to local motels and airport. 75-space RV park. 20% room discount (Sun-Thu) for AARP and AAA members.

Kewadin Casino - St. Ignace
3039 Mackinaw Trail
St. Ignace, Michigan 49781
(906) 643-7071
Website: www.kewadin.com
Map Location: **#2** (50 miles S. of Sault Ste. Marie)

Toll-Free Number: (800) KEWADIN
Restaurants: 1 Deli Liquor: Yes
Buffets: B-$3.95 L-$7.95
D-$10.95/$13.95 (Fri)/$14.50 (Sat)
Casino Size: 56,168 Square Feet
Other Games: C, R, P, PGP, CSP, LIR, K, TCP
Senior Discount: $5 in tokens on Thu from 7am-7pm, if 50 or older
Special Features: Local motels/hotels offer packages with free shuttle service. Sports bar.

Kings Club Casino
12140 W. Lakeshore Drive
Brimley, Michigan 49715
(906) 248-3700
Website: www.4baymills.com
Map Location: **#3** (12 miles S.W. of Sault Ste. Marie)

Toll-Free Number: (888) 422-9645
Restaurants: 1 Deli Liquor: Yes
Casino Size: 7,400 Square Feet
Hours: 8am-2am/4am (Fri-Sat)
Seniors Discount: Various on Tue if 50 or older
Special Features: Four miles from and affiliated with Bay Mills Resort & Casino.

Lac Vieux Desert Casino
N 5384 US 45 North
Watersmeet, Michigan 49969
(906) 358-4226
Website: www.lacvieuxdesert.com
Map Location: **#4** (49 miles S.E. of Ironwood)

Toll-Free Number: (800) 583-3599
Room Reservations: (800) 895-2505
Rooms: 61 Price Range: $60-$75
Suites: 15 Price Range: $75-$140
Restaurants: 1 Liquor: Yes
Buffets: L-$7.95 D-$9.95/$16.95 (Fri-Sat)
Table Game Hours: 10am-4am Daily
Slot Hours: 24 Hours Daily
Other Games: C, R, LIR, BG
Senior Discount: Various on Tuesdays if 55+
Special Features: 9-hole golf course. 10% hotel discount for AAA and AARP members.

Leelanau Sands Casino
2521 N.W. Bayshore Drive
Sutton's Bay, Michigan 49682
(231) 271-4104
Website: www.casino2win.com
Map Location: **#5** (4 miles N. of Sutton's Bay)

Toll-Free Number: (800) 922-2946
Room Reservations: (800) 930-3008
Rooms: 51 Price Range: $89-$123
Restaurants: 1 Liquor: Yes
Buffets: D-$8.95 (Fri-Sat)
Casino Size: 72,000 Square Feet
Hours: 10am-2am/24 Hours (Fri/Sat)
Other Games: C, R, LIR, TCP
Senior Discount: Specials on Tuesdays if 55+
Special Features: Rooms are at nearby GTB Motel.

Little River Casino
2700 Orchard Drive
Manistee, Michigan 49660
(231) 723-1535
Website: www.littlerivercasinos.com
Map Location: **#15** (60 miles S.W of Traverse City)

Toll-Free Number: (888) 568-2244
Rooms: 88 Price Range: $79-$129
Suites: 12 Price Range: $109-$199
Restaurants: 1 Liquor: Yes
Buffets: D-$17.95 (Fri-Sat)
Casino Size: 75,000 Square Feet
Other Games: C, R, P, LIR, CSP, TCP
Senior Discount: Wednesday specials if 55+
Special Features: 46-space RV park open April-November. 10% room discount for AAA/AARP members.

Ojibwa Casino Resort
797 Michigan Avenue
Baraga, Michigan 49908
(906) 353-6333
Website: www.ojibwacasino.com
Map Location: **#6** (30 miles S. of Houghton)

Toll-Free Number: (800) 323-8045
Rooms: 38 Price Range: $54-$60
Suites: 2 Price Range: $75
Restaurants: 1 Liquor: Yes
Buffets: B-$7.95 (Sun) L-$5.95
D-$8.95/$10.95 (Fri)
Casino Size: 17,000 Square Feet
Table Game Hours: 11am-2am/4am (Fri-Sat)
Slot Hours: 24 Hours Daily
Other Games: C, R, P, LIR, BG (Mon-Thu)
Special Features: 8-lane bowling alley. Room discounts for AAA/AARP and club members.

Ojibwa Casino - Marquette
105 Acre Trail
Marquette, Michigan 49855
(906) 249-4200
Website: www.ojibwacasino.com
Map Location: **#13**

Toll-Free Number: (888) 560-9905
Restaurants: 1 Snack Bar Liquor: Yes
Table Hours: 12pm-4am/24 Hours (Fri/Sat)
Slot Hours: 24 Hours Daily
Other Games: C, R, P, LIR, TCP
Senior Discount: Monday specials if 55+

Soaring Eagle Casino & Resort
6800 E Soaring Eagle Boulevard
Mount Pleasant, Michigan 48858
(517) 775-5777
Website: www.soaringeaglecasino.com
Map Location: **#7** (65 miles N. of Lansing)

Toll-Free Number: (888) 7-EAGLE-7
Rooms: 491 Price Range: $129-$189
Suites: 21 Price Range: $269-$369
Restaurants: 3 (2 open 24 hrs) Liquor: Yes
Buffets: B:$8.75 L- $12.75/$13.75 (Mon-Tue)
D-$12.75/$13.75 (Mon-Tue)
Casino Size: 150,000 Square Feet
Other Games: C, R, P, CSP, LIR, TCP, BG
Senior Discount: 50% off breakfast buffet on Wednesdays, if 55, or older
Special Features: Casino is in two separate buildings. Kid's Quest childcare center. Video arcade. Gift shop. Art gallery. 10% room discount for AAA/AARP members.

Turtle Creek Casino
7741 M-72 East
Williamsburg, Michigan 49690
(231) 267-9574
Website: www.casino2win.com
Map Location: **#14** (8 miles E. of Traverse City)

Toll-Free Number: (888) 777-8946
Restaurants: 2 (1 is Deli) Liquor: Yes
Casino Size: 29,000 Square Feet
Other Games: C, R, TCP, LIR

Victories Casino & Hotel
1966 U.S. 131 South
Petoskey, Michigan 49770
(231) 439-9100
Website: www.victories-casino.com
Map Location: **#16** (50 miles S.W of Cheboygan)

Toll-Free Number: 877-4-G42-6464
Rooms: 136 Price Range: $39-$59
Suites: 8 Price Range- $139-$159
Restaurants: 1 Liquor: Yes
Buffets: B-$5.50 L-$7.50 D-$8 to $16.50
Casino Size: 33,000 Square Feet
Hours: 8am-4am Daily
Other Games: R, P, CSP, LIR, TCP
Senior Discount: Wed/Sun specials if 55+
Fun Book: Given to hotel guests and groups
Special Features: Hotel is 1/4-mile from casino and rooms offer views of Little Traverse Bay. Free shuttle service to/from local hotels.

MINNESOTA

All Minnesota casinos are located on Indian reservations and under a compact reached with the state the only type of table game permitted is blackjack. Additionally, the only kind of slot machines allowed are the electronic video variety. Therefore, you will not find any mechanical slots that have traditional reels - only video screens.

The tribes are not required to release information on their slot machine percentage paybacks. According to the terms of the compact between the state and the tribes, however, the minimum and maximum payouts are regulated as follows: video poker and video blackjack - 83% to 98%, slot machines - 80% to 95%, keno - 75% to 95%. Each tribe is free to set its machines to pay back anywhere within those limits.

The hours of operation are listed for those casinos that are not open on a 24-hour basis. Unless otherwise noted, all casinos offer: video slots, video poker, video keno and blackjack. The minimum gambling age is 18 (21 if liquor is served).

For more information on visiting Minnesota call the state's office of tourism at (800) 657-3700.

Black Bear Casino & Hotel
1785 Highway 210
Carlton, Minnesota 55718
(218) 878-2327
Website: www.blackbearcasinohotel.com
Map Location: **#1** (130 miles N. of Twin Cities)

Toll-Free Number: (888) 771-0777
Reservation Number: (800) 553-0022
Rooms: 158 Price Range: $39-$109
Suites: 60 Price Range: $59-$129
Restaurants: 2 (open 24 hours) Liquor: Yes
Buffets: L-$7.95 D-$8.95/$15.95 (Thu)
Casino Size: 65,000 Square Feet
Other Games: Bingo, Video Craps
Senior Discount: Specials Mon/Tue if 55+
Special Features: Hotel is connected to casino by a skywalk. 10% room discount for AAA and AARP members.

Fond-du-Luth Casino
129 E. Superior Street
Duluth, Minnesota 55802
(218) 722-0280
Website: www.fondduluthcasino.com
Map Location: **#3** (150 miles N.E. of Twin Cities)

Toll-Free Number: (800) 873-0280
Restaurants: 2 Snack Bars Liquor: Yes
Casino Size: 20,000 Square Feet
Casino Hours: 10am-2am/24 hours (Fri/Sat)
Other Games: Bingo
Senior Discount: Fun book Mon-Wed if 55+
Special Features: One hour free parking in lot adjacent to casino (must be validated in casino). Free shuttle to/from Black Bear Casino.

Fortune Bay Resort/Casino
1430 Bois Forte Road
Tower, Minnesota 55790
(218) 753-6400
Website: www.fortunebay.com
Map Location: **#4** (150 miles N.E. of Twin Cities. 24 miles N.E. of Virginia, MN on the S. shore of Lake Vermilion)

Toll-Free Number: (800) 992-7529
Hotel Reservations: (800) 555-1714
Rooms: 83 Price Range: $57-$101
Suites: 33 Price Range: $81-$151
Restaurants: 2 Liquor: Yes
Buffets: B-$4.95 L-$4.95/$8.95 (Mon/Thu)
D-$11.95/$13.95 (Mon/Fri)/$14.95 (Sat)
Casino Size: 17,000 Square Feet
Other Games: Bingo (Wed-Sun), Keno
Senior Discount: Specials Mon & Thu if 55+
Special Features: Located on S.E. shore of Lake Vermilion. 34-space RV Park. Snowmobile and hiking trails. 18-hole golf course.

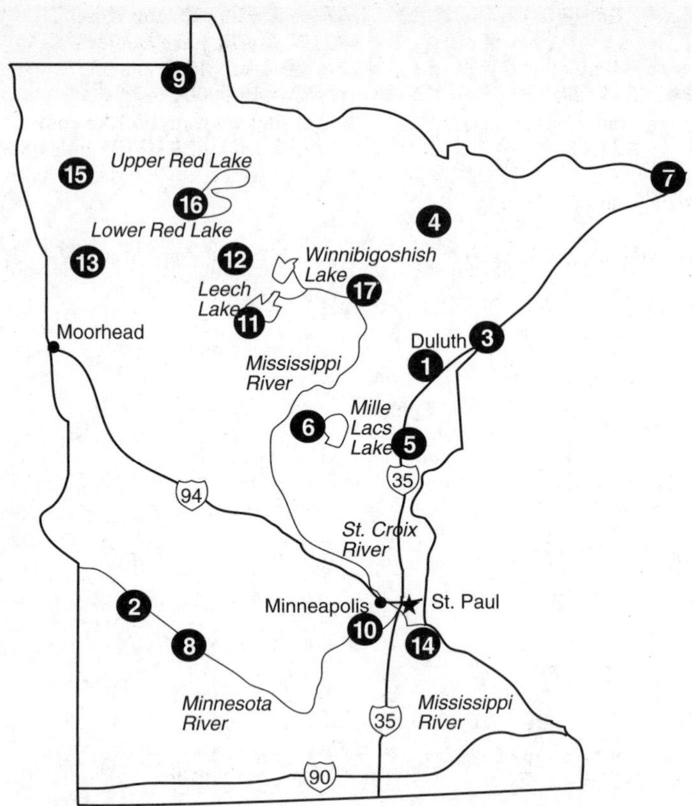

Grand Casino Hinckley
777 Lady Luck Drive
Hinckley, Minnesota 55037
(320) 384-7777
Website: www.grandcasinosmn.com
Map Location: **#5** (75 miles N. of Twin Cities. One mile E. of I-35's Hinckley exit on Hwy. 48)

Toll-Free Number: (800) 472-6321
RV/Chalet Reservations: (800) 995-4726
Hotel Reservations: (800) 468-3517
Rooms: 485 Price Range: $55-$85 (Hotel)
Price Range: $30-$80 (Inn)
Price Range: $40-$95 (Chalet)
Suites: 46 Price Range: $75-$190
Restaurants: 5 Liquor: Yes
Buffets: L-$6.99 D-$9.99 (Sun-Mon)/ $11.99 (Wed-Sat)/$16.99 (Tue)
Casino Size: 54,800 Square Feet
Other Games: Electronic Bingo (Thu-Mon)
Casino Marketing: (800) GRAND-76
Special Features: 222-space RV park. Kid's Quest childcare center. 18-hole golf course. Free pet kennel. 10% AAA room discount.

Grand Casino Mille Lacs
777 Grand Avenue
Onamia, Minnesota 56359
(320) 532-7777
Website: www.grandcasinosmn.com
Map Location: **#6** (90 miles N. of Twin Cities. On Highway 169 on the W. shore of Lake Mille Lacs)

Toll-Free Number: (800) 626-5825
Room Reservations: (800) HOTEL-17
Rooms: 284 Price Range: $38-$139
Suites: 14 Price Range: $90-$250
Restaurants: 4 Liquor: No
Buffets: L-$7.50 D-$9.99 to $15.99
Casino Size: 42,000 Square Feet
Other Games: Electronic Bingo (Sun-Fri)
Casino Marketing: (800) GRAND-76
Special Features: Resort has two hotels and one is off-property. Kid's Quest childcare center. Video arcade. Free pet kennel. AAA members receive 10% room discount.

Grand Portage Lodge & Casino
P.O. Box 233
Grand Portage, Minnesota 55605
(218) 475-2401
Website: www.grandportagemn.com
Map Location: **#7** (N.E. tip of Minnesota. 300 miles N. of Twin Cities. On Highway 61, five miles from the Canadian border)

Reservation Number: (800) 543-1384
Rooms: 100 Price Range: $66-$85
Restaurants: 2 Liquor: Yes
Other Games: Bingo
Special Features: On shore of Lake Superior. Hiking, skiing and snowmobile trails. Gift shop. Marina. 10-space RV park and 10-tent campground. Free shuttle service to and from Thunder Bay, Ontario.

Jackpot Junction Casino Hotel
P.O. Box 420
Morton, Minnesota 56270
(507) 644-3000
Website: www.jackpotjunction.com
Map Location: **#8** (110 miles S.W. of Twin Cities)

Toll-Free Number: (800) WIN-CASH
Rooms: 253 Price Range: $55-$85
Suites: 23 Price Range: $100-$200
Restaurants: 3 (1 open 24 hours) Liquor: Yes
Buffets: B-$5.99 L-$6.99 D-$8.99
Other Games: Bingo (Thu-Tue)
Senior Discount: 25% off Wed lunch or dinner buffets if 55+
Special Features: 40-unit campground with full RV hookup. Kids Quest childcare center. 18-hole golf course. Gift shop.

Little Six Casino
2354 Sioux Trail N.W.
Prior Lake, Minnesota 55372
(952) 445-9000 (Mystic Lake)
Map Location: **#10** (25 miles S.W. of Twin Cities. On County Road 83, 3 miles S. of Canterbury Downs)

Toll-Free: (800) 262-7799 (Mystic Lake)
Restaurants: 1 Liquor: No
Hours: 10am-4am Daily/24 hours (Fri-Sat)
Special Features: 1/2-mile north of Mystic Lake Casino.

Mystic Lake Casino Hotel
2400 Mystic Lake Boulevard
Prior Lake, Minnesota 55372
(952) 445-9000
Website: www.mysticlake.com
Map Location: **#10** (25 miles S.W. of Twin Cities. On County Road 83, 3 miles S. of Hwy 169)

Toll-Free Number: (800) 262-7799
Reservation Number: (800) 813-7349
Rooms: 400 Price Range: $69-$109
Suites: 16 Price Range: $119-$359
Restaurants: 4 (3 open 24 hours) Liquor: No
Buffets: B-$12.95 (Sat-Sun) L-$8.95 D-$14.95/$19.95 (Wed)
Casino Size: 102,000 Square Feet
Other Games: Bingo, Video Roulette and Craps, Let it Ride
Senior Discount: Free breakfast on Tues if 55+
Fun Book: Given to new slot club members
Special Features: Free shuttle bus service from Twin Cities area. Also has a second casino - Dakota Country with 45,000-square-feet of gaming space. 122-space RV park. Health club. Childcare facility.

Northern Lights Casino
6800 Y Frontage Rd NW
Walker, Minnesota 56484
(218) 547-2744
Website: www.northernlightscasino.com
Map Location: **#11** (175 miles N. of the Twin Cities. Near the S. shore of Lake Leech four miles S. of Walker, MN at the junction of Highways 371 & 200)

Toll-Free Number: (800) 252-7529
Toll-Free Number: (877) 544-4879
Room reservations: (866) 652-4683
Rooms: 105 Price Range: $100-$120
Suites: 4 Price Range: $165-$190
Restaurants: 2 Liquor: Yes
Buffets: B-$8.95 (Sat-Sun) L-$6.50 D-$8.95/$14.95 (Thu)/$12.95(Fri-Sat)
Casino Size: 40,000 Square Feet
Other Games: Bingo
Special Features: 90-foot dome simulates star constellations.

Palace Casino Hotel
6280 Upper Cass Frontage Rd NW
Cass Lake, Minnesota 56633
(218) 335-7000
Website: www.palacecasinohotel.com
Map Location: **#12** (220 miles N.W. of Twin Cities)

Toll-Free Number: (800) 228-6676
Room Reservations: (800) 442-3910
Rooms: 54 Price Range: $40-$65
Suites: 16 Price Range $50-$80
Restaurants: 2 (1 open 24 hours) Liquor: No
Casino Size: 30,000 Square Feet
Other Games: Bingo
Special Features: Limited space RV park.

Prairie's Edge Casino Resort
5616 Prairie's Edge Lane
Granite Falls, Minnesota 56241
(320) 564-2121
Website: www.priariesedgecasino.com
Map Location: **#2** (110 miles W. of Twin Cities. Five minutes S.E. of Granite Falls on Highway 67 E.)

Toll-Free Number: (866) 293-2121
Rooms: 79 Price Range: $59-$69
Suites: 10 Price Range: $129-$159
Restaurants: 2 Liquor: Yes
Buffets: D-$8.95
Casino Size: 36,000 Square Feet
Senior Discount: Specials on Mondays if 55+
Special Features: Children's arcade. Convenience store.

Seven Clans Casino Red Lake
Highway 1 East
Red Lake, MN 56671
(218) 679-2500
www.sevenclanscasino.com/redlake.htm
Map Location: **#16** (31 miles N. of Bemidji)

Toll-Free Number: (888) 679-2501
Restaurants: 1 Liquor: No
Casino Size: 19,800 Square Feet
Casino Hours: 10am-1am/9am-2am (Thu-Sat)
Other Games: Bingo (Fri-Sun)
Senior Discount: Specials on Mondays if 55+

Seven Clans Casino Thief River Falls
Rt 3, Box 168A
Thief River Falls, Minnesota 56701
(218) 681-4062
Website: www.sevenclanscasino.com
Map Location: **#15** (275 miles N.W. of Minneapolis)

Toll-Free Number: (800) 881-0712
Suites: 151 Price Range: $55-$109
Restaurants: 1 (open 24 hours) Liquor: No
Buffets: B-$5.99 L-$6.95
D-$6.95/$11.95 (Fri)
Casino Size: 16,000 Square Feet
Senior Discount: Specials on Tuesdays and 10% off buffets at all times, if 55+
Special features: Indoor water park.

Seven Clans Casino Warroad
1012 E. Lake Street
Warroad, MN 56763
(218) 386-3381
www.sevenclanscasino.com/warroad.htm
Map Location: **#9** (400 miles N.W. of Twin Cities)

Toll-Free Number: (800) 815-8293
Rooms: 34 Price Range: $39-$66
Suites: 7 Price Range: $48-$94
Restaurants: 1 Liquor: No
Casino Size: 19,875 Square Feet
Other Games: Bingo (Wed-Sun)
Senior Discount: Specials on Thursdays if 55+
Special Features: Hotel is not attached to casino. Free shuttle service is provided.

Shooting Star Casino Hotel
777 Casino Boulevard
Mahnomen, Minnesota 56557
(218) 935-2701
Website: www.starcasino.com
Map Location: **#13** (250 miles N.W. of Twin Cities)

Room Reservations: (800) 453-STAR
Rooms: 360 Price Range: $47-$55
Suites: 30 Price Range: $65-$85
Restaurants: 3 Liquor: Yes
Buffets: B-$4.99 L-$6.99
D-$8.99/$12.99 (Fri)/$10.99 (Sat)
Other Games: Bingo, Poker
Senior Discount: $5 off room, if 50, or older
Special Features: 47-space RV park. Childcare facility.

Treasure Island Resort Casino
5734 Sturgeon Lake Road
Red Wing, Minnesota 55066
(651) 388-6300
Website: www.treasureislandcasino.com
Map Location: **#14** (40 miles S.E. of Twin Cities. Halfway between Hastings and Red Wing, off Highway 61 on County Road 18)

Toll-Free Number: (800) 222-7077
Room Reservations: (888) 867-7829
Restaurants: 3 Liquor: Yes
Rooms: 250 Price Range: $59-$99
Suites: 28 Price Range: $125-$195
Buffets: B-$10.75 (Sat-Sun) L-$8.25
D-$11.25/$14.95 (Thu)/$13.25 (Fri-Sat)
Casino Size: 110,000 Square Feet
Other Games: Bingo, Video Craps and Roulette
Senior Discount: First Wednesday of each month 10am-2pm get coupon book if 55+
Special Features: 95-space RV park. 136-space marina. Dinner and sight-seeing cruises.

White Oak Casino
45830 US Hwy 2
Deer River, MN 56636
(218) 246-9600
Website: www.whiteoakcasino.com
Map Location: **#17** (5 miles N.W. of Grand Rapids)

Toll-Free Number: (800) 653-2412
Restaurants: 1 Snack Bar Liquor: Yes
Casino Size: 11,000 Square Feet
Senior Discount: Free fun book Tue, if 50+
Fun Book: Given Thursdays, if 50 or under

Pari-Mutuels

Canterbury Park
1100 Canterbury Road
Shakopee, Minnesota 55379
(952) 445-7223
Website: www.canterburypark.com
Map Location: **#10** (22 miles S.W. of Twin Cities.)

Toll-Free Number: (800) 340-6361
Admission: $4
Self-Parking: Free Valet Parking: $6
Restaurants: 2
Buffets: D-$9.95 (Thu-Fri)/$7.95 (Sat-Sun)
Other Games: Blackjack, Poker, Pai Gow Poker, Let It Ride, Caribbean Stud Poker, 3-Card Poker
Special Features: Free admission to 24-hour card room where players must pay a commission on each hand for all games except regular poker. Live horse racing May-September. Daily simulcasting.

MISSISSIPPI

Mississippi was the third state to legalize riverboat gambling when it was approved by that state's legislature in 1990. The law restricts casinos to coast waters (including the Bay of St. Louis and the Back Bay of Biloxi) along the Mississippi River and in navigable waters of counties that border the river.

Mississippi law also requires that riverboats be permanently moored at the dock and they are not permitted to cruise. This allows the riverboats to offer 24-hour dockside gambling. The Isle of Capri in Biloxi was the first casino to open on August 1, 1992 followed one month later by The President.

Since the law does not require that the floating vessel actually resemble a boat, almost all of the casinos are built on barges. This gives them the appearance of a land-based building, rather than a riverboat.

The Mississippi Gaming Commission does not break down its slot statistics by individual properties. Rather, they are classified by region. The **Coastal** region includes Biloxi, Gulfport and Bay Saint Louis. The **North** region includes Tunica, Greenville and Lula. The **Central** region includes Vicksburg and Natchez.

With that in mind here's information, as supplied by the Mississippi Gaming Commission, showing the machine payback percentages for each area's casinos for the one-year period from June 1, 2002 through May 30, 2003:

	Coastal	North	Central
5¢ Slots	91.61%	90.86%	**91.84%**
5¢ Prog.	90.26%	89.43%	**91.64%**
25¢ Slots	**93.24%**	92.66%	93.17%
25¢ Prog.	90.02%	90.64%	**91.12%**
$1 Slots	95.19%	**95.46%**	95.38%
$1 Prog.	91.87%	92.59%	**94.09%**
$5 Slots	95.78%	**96.27%**	94.76%
All	93.71%	**93.88%**	93.47%

These numbers reflect the percentage of money returned on each denomination of machine and encompass all electronic machines including video poker and video keno. The best returns for each category are highlighted in bold print and you can see that all of the gaming areas offer rather similar returns on their machines.

Mississippi is one of the few states that breaks down its progressive machine statistics separately and you can see that the return is always less on machines with progressive jackpots.

Unless otherwise noted, all casinos are open 24 hours and offer: slots, video poker, blackjack, craps, roulette and Caribbean stud poker.

Other game listings include: Spanish 21 (S21), baccarat (B), mini-baccarat (MB), poker (P), pai gow poker (PGP), let it ride (LIR), three card poker (TCP), big six wheel (B6), casino war (CW) and keno (K). The minimum gambling age is 21.

For more information on visiting Mississippi call the state's tourism department at (866) SEE-MISS. For Biloxi tourism information call (800) 237-9493 and for tourism information on Robinsonville call (888) 4-TUNICA.

Bay St. Louis

Map Location: **#2** (on St. Louis Bay, 40 miles E. of New Orleans)

Casino Magic - Bay St. Louis
711 Casino Magic Drive
Bay St. Louis, Mississippi 39520
(228) 467-9257
Website: www.casinomagic.com

Toll-Free Number: (800) 5-MAGIC-5
Rooms: 498 Price Range: $59-$159
Suites: 78 Price Range: $225
Restaurants: 5 (1 open 24 hours)
Buffets: B-$7.99 L-$8.99/$13.49 (Sun) D-$13.45
Casino Size: 39,500 Square Feet
Other Games: MB, PGP, LIR, TCP
Special Features: 100 hook-up RV Park. 25-slip marina. 18-hole golf course.

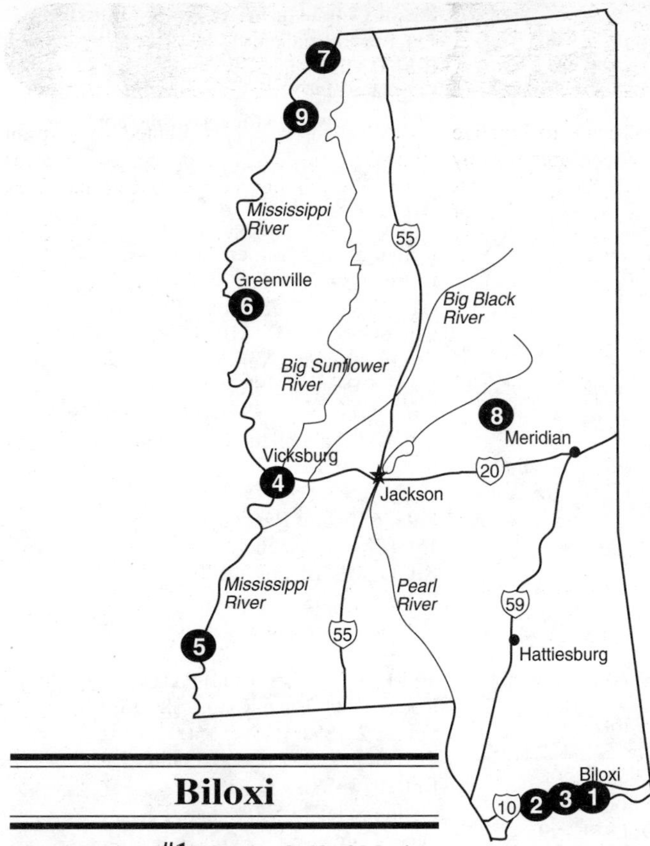

Biloxi

Map Location: **#1** (On the Gulf of Mexico, 80 miles E. of New Orleans)

Beau Rivage
875 Beach Boulevard
Biloxi, Mississippi 39530
(228) 386-7111
Website: www.beaurivageresort.com

Toll-Free Number: (888) 750-7111
Room Reservations: (888) 56-ROOMS
Rooms: 1,740 Price Range: $69-$249
Suites: 95 Price Range: $275-$350
Restaurants: 12 (1 open 24 hours)
Buffets: B-$8.99/$14.99 (Sat/Sun)
L-$10.99 D-$14.99/$19.99 (Fri)
Casino Size: 71,669 Square Feet
Other Games: B, MB, PGP, LIR, TCP, CW
Casino Marketing: (888) 567-2328
Senior Discount: 50% off Friday breakfast or lunch buffets, if 55 or older and club member
Special Features: Microbrewery. Health spa and salon. 31-slip marina. Master coffee roaster. Retail shopping promenade.

Boomtown Casino - Biloxi
676 Bayview Avenue
Biloxi, Mississippi 39530
(228) 435-7000
Website: www.boomtownbiloxi.com

Toll-Free Number: (800) 627-0777
Restaurants: 2 (1 open 24 hours)
Buffets: B-$5.99 L-$7.99 D-$12.99
Casino Size: 33,632 Square Feet
Other Games: PGP, TCP, No CSP
Senior Discount: If 50, or older, join Wild Bunch Seniors Club for various discounts
Fun Book: Look for rack card in local hotels or at Welcome Center on Hwy 90
Special Features: Family video arcade. Western gift and clothing shop. 24-hour bakery.

Casino Magic - Biloxi
195 E. Beach Boulevard
Biloxi, Mississippi 39530
(228) 386-4600
Website: www.casinomagic.com

Toll-Free Number: (800) 5-MAGIC-5
Rooms: 292 Price Range: $65-$249
Suites: 86 Price Range: $220-$349
Restaurants: 4 (1 open 24 hours)
Buffets: B-$7.99 L-$8.99/$13.49 (Sun)
D-$13.49
Casino Size: 48,860 Square Feet
Other Games: PGP, LIR, TCP
Fun Book: Available through local hotels/motels
Senior Discount: 1/2 off Wed breakfast
buffet if 50+
Special Features: Free comedy club show on Monday nights. All suites have jacuzzis.

Grand Casino Biloxi
265 Beach Boulevard
Biloxi, Mississippi 39530
(228) 436-2946
Website: www.grandbiloxi.com

Toll-Free Number: (800) 946-2946
Rooms: 1,000 Price Range: $49-$229
Suites: 64 Price Range: $159-$299
Restaurants: 6 (1 open 24 hours)
Buffets: B-$7.99 L-$8.99 D-$12.99
Casino Size: 106,300 Square Feet
Other Games: MB, PGP, LIR, TCP, P, B6
Special Features: Kid's Quest childcare center. Spa. Specialty retail shops. Golf packages.

Imperial Palace Hotel & Casino
850 Bayview Avenue
Biloxi, Mississippi 39530
(228) 436-3000
Website: www.ipbiloxi.com

Toll-Free Number: (800) 436-3000
Toll-Free Number: (888) WIN-AT-IP
Room Reservations: (800) 634-6441
Rooms: 1,000 Price Range: $49-$129
Suites: 14 Price Range: $139-$189
Restaurants: 10 (1 open 24 hours)
Buffets: B-$5.95/$19.95 (Sun) L-$7.95
D-$11.95/$12.95 (Fri/Sat)
Casino Size: 70,000 Square Feet
Other Games: MB, PGP, LIR, TCP, B6
Special Features: Six-screen movie theater. Comedy Club. Health spa. Video arcade.

Isle of Capri Casino & Hotel - Biloxi
151 Beach Boulevard
Biloxi, Mississippi 39530
(228) 436-4753
Website: www.isleofcapricasino.com

Toll-Free Number: (800) 843-4753
Rooms: 367 Price Range: $79-$139
Suites: 4 Price Range: $219
Restaurants: 3 (1 open 24 hours)
Buffets: B-$7.25 L-$7.95 D-$13.95
Casino Size: 32,500 Square Feet
Other Games: S21, MB, PGP, LIR, TCP
Senior Discount: Various on Tue/Thu if 50+
Special Features: Slot club members receive room discounts. 10% room discount for AAA and AARP members. Health club.

Palace Casino Resort
158 Howard Avenue
Biloxi, Mississippi 39530
(228) 432-8888
Website: www.palacecasinoresort.com

Toll-Free Number: (800) PALACE-9
Rooms: 234 Price Range: $89-$159
Suites: 2 Price Range: $500
Restaurants: 3 (1 open 24 hours)
Buffets: L-$8.99 D-$13.99
Casino Size: 43,500 Square Feet
Other Games: S21, PGP, TCP
Special Features: Health spa. 20-slip marina. Players club members receive discount on dinner buffet.

President Casino Broadwater Resort
2110 Beach Boulevard
Biloxi, Mississippi 39531
(228) 385-3500
Website: www.broadwater.com

Toll-Free Number: (800) THE-PRES
Rooms: 500 Price Range: $59-$125
Suites: 12 Price Range: $120-$330
Restaurants: 3 (1 open 24 hours)
Buffets: B-$5.49 L-$8.49/$12.49 (Fri-Sat)
D-$13.99
Casino Size: 38,000 Square Feet
Other Games: P, TCP, No CSP
Fun Book: Need coupon from local card racks
Senior Discount: $3.49 breakfast and $5.99
lunch Mon-Thu, if 50, or older
Special Features: Marina. Golf packages.

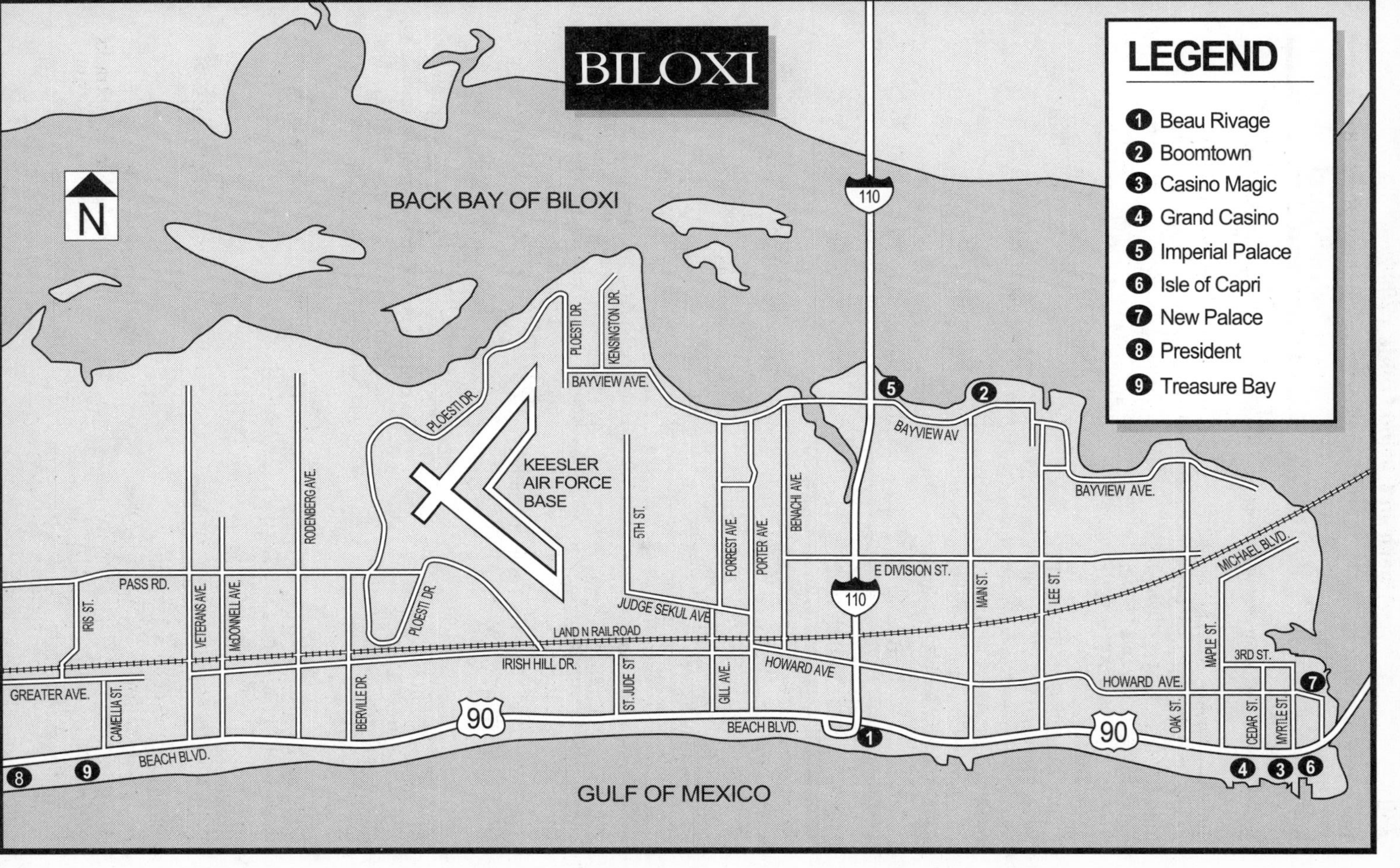
BILOXI
LEGEND
1 Beau Rivage
2 Boomtown
3 Casino Magic
4 Grand Casino
5 Imperial Palace
6 Isle of Capri
7 New Palace
8 President
9 Treasure Bay
N
BACK BAY OF BILOXI
GULF OF MEXICO
KEESLER AIR FORCE BASE
110
90
BAYVIEW AVE.
BAYVIEW AV
PLOESTI DR.
KENSINGTON DR.
RODENBERG AVE.
5TH ST.
FORREST AVE.
PORTER AVE.
BENACHI AVE.
E DIVISION ST.
MAIN ST.
LEE ST.
MICHAEL BLVD.
MAPLE ST.
3RD ST.
HOWARD AVE.
HOWARD AVE
OAK ST.
CEDAR ST.
MYRTLE ST.
PASS RD.
IRIS ST.
VETERANS AVE.
McDONNELL AVE.
JUDGE SEKUL AVE
LAND N RAILROAD
IRISH HILL DR.
ST. JUDE ST
GILL AVE.
GREATER AVE.
CAMELLIA ST.
IBERVILLE DR.
BEACH BLVD.

Treasure Bay Casino Resort
1980 Beach Boulevard
Biloxi, Mississippi 39531
(228) 385-6000
Website: www.treasurebay.com

Toll-Free Number: (800) PIRATE-9
Rooms: 262 Price Range: $59-$119
Suites: 8 Price Range: $189-$338
Restaurants: 3 (1 open 24 hours)
Buffets: B-$5.95 L-$7.95 D-$13.95
Size: 40,000 Square Feet
Other Games: S21, PGP, LIR, TCP
Senior Discount: Various for club members 55+
Special Features: Casino is 400-foot replica of 18th century pirate ship and fort that is built on a barge. On-site brewery. 10% room discount to AARP members.

Greenville

Map Location: **#6** (On the Mississippi River, 121 miles N.W. of Jackson)

Bayou Caddy's Jubilee Casino
242 S. Walnut Street
Greenville, Mississippi 38701
(662) 335-1111

Restaurants: 3 (1 open 24 hours)
Casino Size: 28,500 Square Feet
Other Games: TCP
Senior Discount: Join Wild Bunch Seniors Club for free Hot Seat Wednesdays entry.

Lighthouse Point Casino
199 N. Lakefront Road
Greenville, Mississippi 38701
(662) 334-7711

Toll-Free Number: (800) 878-1777
Rooms: 148 Price Range: $65-$79
Suites: 19 Price Range: $75-$81
Restaurants: 1
Buffets: B-$11.95 (Sun) L-$6.95 (Mon-Fri)
D-$11.95 (Wed-Sat)
Casino Size: 22,000 Square Feet
Other Games: PGP, No Roulette, No CSP
Special Features: Hotel is Fairfield Marriott which is across the street. Casino is on an actual paddlewheel boat.

Gulfport

Map Location: **#3** (On the Gulf of Mexico, 70 miles E. of New Orleans)

Copa Casino
777 Copa Boulevard
Gulfport, Mississippi 39501
(228) 863-3330
Website: www.thecopacasino.com

Toll-Free Number: (800) 946-6272
Restaurants: 3
Buffets: B-$2.99 L-$7.99
D-$12.99/$14.99 (Fri/Sat)
Casino Size: 43,025 Square Feet
Other Games: S21, TCP, P, PGP, No CSP
Senior Discount: Various for club members 50+
Special Features: Casino is on a barge.

Grand Casino Gulfport
3215 W. Beach Boulevard
Gulfport, Mississippi 39501
(228) 870-7777
Website: www.grandgulfport.com

Toll-Free Number: (800) WIN-7777
Room Reservations: (800) 354-2450
Rooms: 1000 Price Range: $59-$199
Suites: 74 Price Range: $149 and up
Restaurants: 7 (1 open 24 hours)
Buffets: B-$7.99 L-$8.99/$12.99 (Sat/Sun)
D-$12.99
Casino Size: 105,000 Square Feet
Other Games: MB, P, PGP, LIR, TCP, K
Special Features: Kids Quest childcare. Video arcade. Three-acre pool area and lazy river ride. Unisex spa and salon. Golf packages.

The Best Places To Play On The Gulf Coast

Roulette - There are no casinos on the Gulf Coast that offer single-zero roulette.

Craps - Almost all casinos on the Gulf Coast (including Casino Magic in Bay St. Louis) offer 10x odds. The two exceptions are Boomtown and Beau Rivage which both limit players to 5x odds.

Blackjack - Gulf Coast casinos offer some of the best blackjack outside of Nevada and, unlike downtown Las Vegas, there are no casinos that hit soft 17. This rule is advantageous for the player by .20%. All of the recommendations in this section apply to players using perfect basic strategy for each particular game.

Only four casinos offer single-deck games. The Copa in Gulfport's rules are: double down on any two card total of 10 or more, splitting allowed, late surrender and no doubling after splitting. The casino edge in this game is .23%. A slightly better single-deck game can be found at Casino Magic in Bay St. Louis which doesn't allow surrender but does allow resplitting of aces. The casino advantage here is .22%. The two Grand Casinos offer a single-deck game that pays even-money on blackjack but you should definitely avoid this game because the casino edge is more than 2%.

Seven casinos are tied for best double-deck and they all have the following rules: double down on any first two cards, re-split any pair (including aces) and doubling allowed after splitting. This works out to a casino edge of just .14% and it's offered at: Casino Magic in Bay St. Louis and Biloxi, both Grand Casinos, Imperial Palace, Treasure Bay and The Palace. The Copa in Gulfport offers a similar game except late surrender is allowed in place of resplitting aces. The casino edge here is also .14%.

Next best are four casinos that offer the same rules as the Copa's, with the exception of late surrender: Beau Rivage, Boomtown, President and Isle of Capri. The casino edge in these games is .19%.

For six-deck shoe games the best place to play is Beau Rivage which allows doubling down on any first two cards, doubling after splitting, late surrender and resplitting of aces. The casino advantage in this game is .26%. That same game, without resplitting of aces, is offered at the Copa and the edge there works out to .33%. Next best are both Casino Magic properties, both Grand Casinos, Imperial Palace, The Palace and Treasure Bay which all offer the same rules as Beau Rivage with the exception of late surrender. The edge in these games is .34%.

Boomtown, Isle of Capri and the President all offer standard six-deck shoe games that allow doubling down on any first two cards and doubling after splitting. The edge on these games is .41%.

Casino Magic casinos in Biloxi and Bay St. Louis, and the Grand Casino in Gulfport, offer eight-deck shoe games with doubling on any two cards, double after split and resplitting aces allowed which works out to a .36% casino advantage. Isle of Capri offers the same eight-deck shoe game with no resplitting of aces and this works out to a .43% casino advantage.

Video Poker - Good video poker players know that five of the best varieties of machines to look for are: 9/6 Jacks or Better, 10/7 Double Bonus, full pay Deuces Wild, full pay Jokers Wild, and All American. By playing one of these five kinds of machines, playing the maximum coin and using perfect strategy, you can achieve the following payback percentages: 99.5% on 9/6 Jacks or Better, 100.17% on 10/7 Double Bonus, 100.65% on full pay Jokers Wild, 100.7% on All American and 100.7% on full pay Deuces Wild. Fortunately, Mississippi's Gulf Coast's choice of machines is nearly as good as in Nevada, which is quickly depleting it inventory of best paying machines. As a matter of fact, the widest variety of positive pay schedules is concentrated at Copa Casino in Gulfport and the Copa is the only casino outside Nevada that offers full pay Deuces Wild. The Copa also has 9/6 Jacks or Better in quarter and dollar progressives and 50-cent non-progressives, 10/7 Double Bonus in quarter progressives and 50-cent non-progressives and full pay Kings or Better Joker's Wild in 50 cents and dollars, both non-progressives.

Besides the Copa, 9/6 Jacks is offered at every casino on the Coast except at Grand Casino Biloxi and at Boomtown. Beau Rivage has it in quarter, 50-cent, dollar and $25 Triple Play/Five Play. Palace Casino has it only in dollars, but Casino Magic Biloxi offers it in quarters, 50 cents and dollars, all progressives. Isle of Capri has the game in quarter and $5 machines, while Imperial Palace has it in nickel, quarter and 50-cent machines. President Casino offers nickels, quarters and dollars, and some, those at the quarter and dollar VP bars, are progressives. Treasure Bay has the game in quarter, dollar and $5 progressives. Grand Casino Gulfport has three Triple Play/Five Play machines that have 50-cent and dollar 9/6 Jacks. Casino Magic Bay St. Louis has several Triple Play/Five Play machines in quarter, 50-cent and dollar denominations.

The Copa is getting some competition in the 10/7 Double Bonus and Jokers Wild area. Casino Magic Bay St. Louis has recently imported some quarter IGT MultiPokers with those positive games. Quarter All Americans can be found at the Isle of Capri, Grand Gulfport (which also boasts nickel games) and Casino Magic Bay St. Louis. Both Grand Casinos offer quarter, 50-cent and dollar Aces & Faces, which, when played with perfect strategy and max coins, return 99.3%.

One especially popular game on the Gulf Coast is 16/10 Not-So-Ugly Deuces with a payback of 99.73%. Beau Rivage, the President and Casino Magic Biloxi all have the game in Triple Play/Five Play and/or 50 Play, but the Beau has it in it multi-denominational machines (which also house Super Aces Bonus, 99.8%) while the other two casinos have it in only in nickels. Another Deuces variation is Double Deuces with a payback of 99.6%, now playing at the Copa's Showbar.

Lula

Map Location **#9** (On the Mississippi River, 70 miles S. of Memphis, TN)

Isle of Capri Casino & Hotel - Lula
777 Isle of Capri Parkway
Lula, Mississippi 38644
(662) 363-4600
Website: www.isleofcapricasino.com

Toll-Free Number: (800) 789-5825
Toll-Free Number: (800) THE-ISLE
Rooms: 173 Price Range: $40-$99
Suites: 4 Price Range: $55-$120
Restaurants: 4 (1 open 24 hours)
Buffets: B-$5.95 L-$8.95 D-$12.95
Casino Size: 55,000 Square Feet
Other Games: S21, MB, LIR, TCP
Senior Discount: Various Tue-Thu, if 50+
Special Features: Two movie theaters. 10% hotel discount for AAA and AARP members.

Natchez

Map Location: **#5** (on the Mississippi River, 102 miles S.W. of Jackson)

Isle of Capri Casino & Hotel - Natchez
53 Silver Street
Natchez, Mississippi 39120
(601) 445-0605
Website: www.isleofcapricasino.com

Toll-Free Number: (800) 722-LUCK
Toll-Free Number: (800) THE-ISLE
Rooms: 147 Price Range: $49-$99
Suites: 5 Price Range: $135-$165
Restaurants: 2
Buffets: L-$6.95 D-$10.95/$12.95 (Fri-Sun)
Size: 14,300 Square Feet
Other Games: TCP, No CSP
Special Features: Casino is built on barge that resembles 1860's paddlewheeler.

Tunica

Map Location: **#7** (on the Mississippi River, 28 miles S. of Memphis, TN)

Bally's Casino Tunica
1450 Bally's Boulevard
Tunica Resorts, Mississippi 38664
(662) 357-1500
Website: www.ballysms.com

Toll-Free Number: (800) 382-2559
Rooms: 235 Price Range: $35-$105
Suites: 8 Price Range: $250-$425
Restaurants: 2 (1 open 24 hours)
Buffets: B-$6.95 L-$8.75 D-$13.00
Casino Size: 40,000 Square Feet
Other Games: TCP
Senior Discount: If 55, or older, receive 50% off daily buffets, if players club member
Special Features: Refrigerators in every room. Free buffet on Thursdays for ladies who are slot club members.

Fitzgerald's Casino/Hotel
711 Lucky Lane
Tunica Resorts, Mississippi 38664
(662) 363-5825
Website: www.fitzgeraldstunica.com

Toll-Free Number: (800) 766-LUCK
Room Reservations: (888) 766-LUCK
Rooms: 507 Price Range: $29-$99
Suites: 70 Price Range: $69-$199
Buffets: B-$5.95 Sun Brunch-$8.25
L-$7.75 D-$9.95
Restaurants: 3 (1 open 24 hours)
Casino Size: 33,000 Square Feet
Other Games: LIR, TCP
Senior Discount: 10% AARP room discount
Special Features: Indoor pool and spa. Sports pub.

Gold Strike Casino
100 Casino Center Drive
Tunica Resorts, Mississippi 38664
(662) 357-1111
Website: www.goldstrikemississippi.com

Toll-Free Number: (888) 24K-PLAY
Room Reservations: (888) 245-7829
Rooms: 1,130 Price Range: $49-$99
Suites: 70 Price Range: $169-$239
Restaurants: 3
Buffets: B-$7.75 L-$8.75
D-$14.50/$18.95 (Fri)
Casino Size: 50,486 Square Feet
Other Games: MB, PGP, LIR, P, TCP
Casino Marketing: (800) 871-CLUB
Special Features: Food court with three fast-food restaurants. Health spa. Starbucks.

Grand Casino Tunica
13615 Old Highway 61 N.
Tunica Resorts, Mississippi 38664
(662) 363-2788
Website: www.grandtunica.com

Toll-Free Number: (800) 946-4946
Rooms: 1,356 Price Range: $39-$139
Suites: 117 Price Range: $149-$220
Restaurants: 8 (1 open 24 hours)
Buffets: B-$7.99 L-$8.99
D-$14.99/$16.99 (Fri)
Casino Size: 140,000 Square Feet
Other Games: MB, P, PGP, LIR, TCP, B6
Special Features: World's largest dockside casino. 18-hole golf course. Kid's Quest childcare. 200-space RV park. Spa and salon.

Harrah's Tunica
1100 Casino Strip Boulevard
Tunica Resorts, Mississippi 38664
(662) 363-7777
Website: www.harrahs.com

Reservation Number: (800) HARRAHS
Rooms: 180 Price Range: $59-$129
Suites: 20 Price Range: $149 and up
Restaurants: 3 (open 24 hours)
Buffets: L-$8.75 D-$12.99/$15.99 (Sat)
Casino Size: 50,000 Square Feet
Other Games: LIR, TCP
Senior Discount: 10% room discount for
AARP members (Sun-Thu)
Special Features: River Bend Links golf course.

Hollywood Casino Tunica
1150 Casino Strip Resorts Boulevard
Tunica Resorts, Mississippi 38664
(662) 357-7700
Website: www.hollywoodtunica.com

Toll-Free Number: (800) 871-0711
Rooms: 437 Price Range: $59-$149
Suites: 57 Price Range: $129-$350
Restaurants: 3 (1 open 24 hours)
Buffets: B-$6.99/$10.99 (Sun) L-$7.99
D-$10.99/$16.99 (Fri)
Size: 54,000 Square Feet
Other Games: LIR, TCP
Special Features: Collection of Hollywood memorabilia. 123-space RV park. Slot club members get 10-15% discount in hotel, restaurants and gift shop. Indoor pool and jacuzzi. 18-hole golf course.

Horseshoe Casino & Hotel
1021 Casino Center Drive
Tunica Resorts, Mississippi 38664
(662) 357-5500
Website: www.horseshoe.com

Toll-Free Number: (800) 303-7463
Rooms: 200 Price Range: $59-$89
Suites: 311 Price Range: $99-$129
Restaurants: 2 (1 open 24 hours)
Buffets: B-$7.75/$13.25 (Sun) L-$8.75
D-$14.75/$22.15 (Fri)
Casino Size: 63,000 Square Feet
Other Games: MB, LIR, P, PGP, TCP
Special Features: Blues & Legends Hall of Fame Museum. Bluesville Nightclub.

Sam's Town Hotel & Gambling Hall
1477 Casino Strip Boulevard
Tunica Resorts, Mississippi 38664
(662) 363-0711
Website: www.samstowntunica.com

Toll-Free Number: (800) 456-0711
Rooms: 850 Price Range: $39-$109
Suites: 44 Price Range: $59-$199
Restaurants: 4 (1 open 24 hours)
Buffets: B-$7.95 L-$8.95/$9.95 (Fri/Sat)
D-$12.95/$17.95 (Fri-Sat)
Corky's Barbecue Buffet: D-$8.95
Size: 96,000 Square Feet
Other Games: P, PGP, LIR, TCP, K
Casino Marketing: (800) 946-0711
Senior Discount: 20% off discounts if 50+

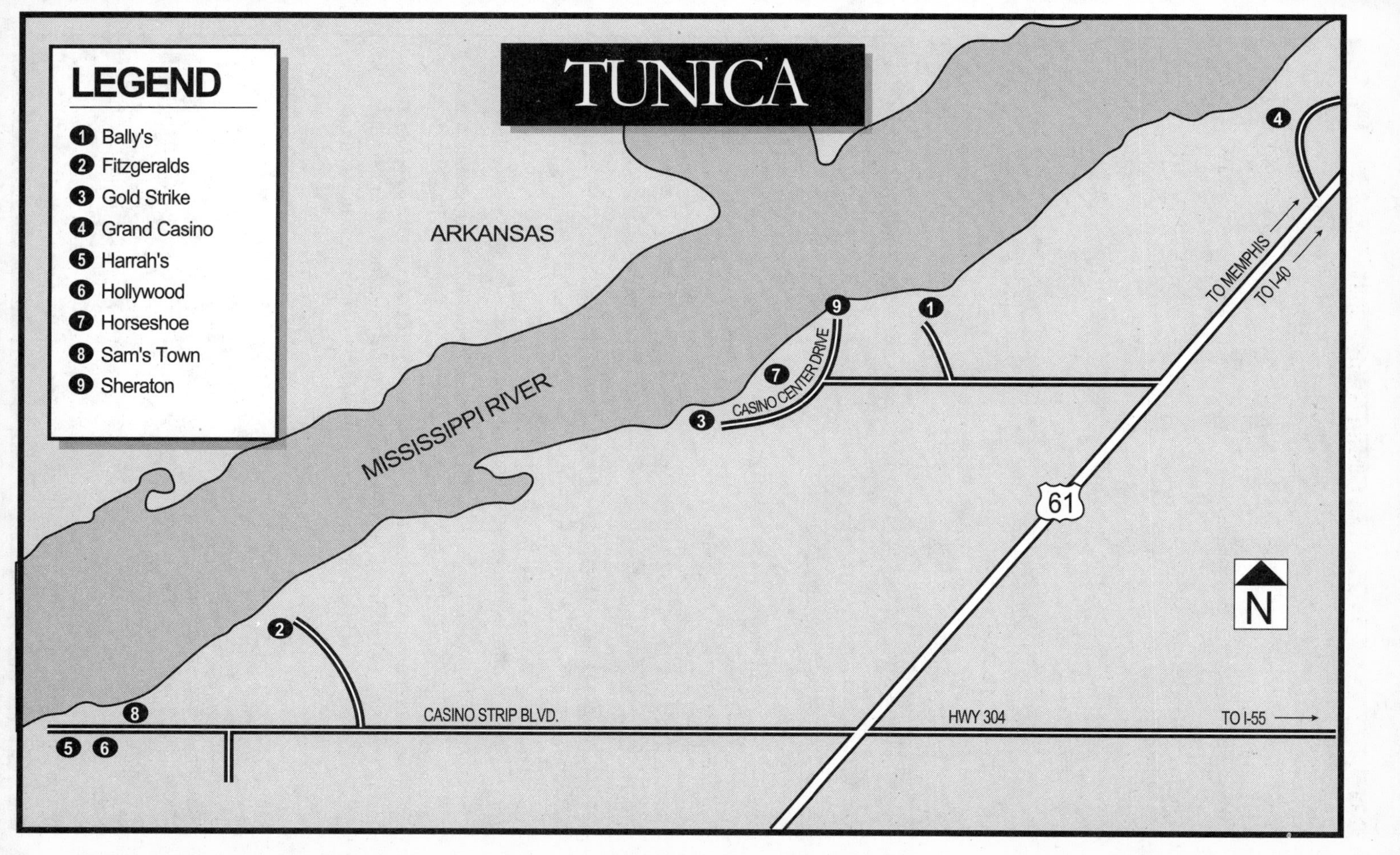

TUNICA
LEGEND
1 Bally's
2 Fitzgeralds
3 Gold Strike
4 Grand Casino
5 Harrah's
6 Hollywood
7 Horseshoe
8 Sam's Town
9 Sheraton
ARKANSAS
MISSISSIPPI RIVER
CASINO CENTER DRIVE
TO MEMPHIS
TO I-40
61
N
CASINO STRIP BLVD.
HWY 304
TO I-55

TUNICA

THE SOUTH'S CASINO CAPITAL℠

BIG-NAME, WORLD-CLASS CASINO HOTEL RESORTS and plenty of our warm Southern hospitality await you in Tunica, Mississippi, located just south of Memphis. These land-based casino resorts offer world-class action 24 hours a day, with no gaming limits.

What to do between games? Many of the world's top-name entertainers are familiar faces in the showrooms of Tunica. And we have championship golf courses, sporting clays, pools, luxurious spas and factory outlet shopping. All this plus world-class food at unbeatable prices and a friendly, inviting and exciting atmosphere make Tunica America's fastest-growing resort destination. For more information visit us on the web.

CALL NOW FOR YOUR FREE VALUE-PACKED WINNER'S GUIDE

TUNICAMISS.COM

TUNICA
MISSISSIPPI

1-888-4TUNICA TOLL FREE 1-888-488-6422

The Best Places To Play In Tunica

Roulette -The only single-zero roulette wheel can be found at the Grand Casino. The house edge in this game is cut from 5.26% down to a more reasonable 2.70%. Be aware, however, that the Grand only has one table in the casino that offers this single-zero game while there are five other tables with the more common double-zero wheel.

Craps - All Tunica casinos offer 20x odds. Some casinos also pay triple (rather than double) on 12 in the field which cuts the house edge on this bet in half from 5.6% to 2.8%. The four casinos offering this slightly better field bet are: Hollywood, Horseshoe, Gold Strike and Sam's Town.

Blackjack - The blackjack games in Tunica are most similar to those offered in downtown Las Vegas. Every casino offers both single and double-deck games, as well as six-deck shoe games. That's good. The bad part, however, is that dealers hit soft 17 at all blackjack games, except for the six-deck game at the Grand Casino. This results in an extra advantage for the house of .20%. All of the following recommendations apply to players using perfect basic strategy for each particular game.

For single-deck players, Tunica has some of the best games in the country because all allow doubling down on any first two cards (but no doubling after splitting). The best one-deck games can be found at the Horseshoe, Gold Strike, Grand and Sheraton which all allow resplitting of pairs, including aces. The casino edge in this game is .15%.

At Bally's, Hollywood and Sam's Town they offer a game identical to the above except they won't allow you to resplit aces and this results in a slightly higher house edge of .18%.

The Grand, Bally's, Gold Strike, Hollywood, Sheraton and Horseshoe are the best places to play double-deck because their games have the following rules: double down on any first two cards, resplit any pair (including aces), and double down after split. This works out to a casino edge of .35%.

Tunica's remaining three casinos: Sam's Town, Harrah's and Fitzgeralds, all offer the next best game. The only rule change from the previous casinos is that you aren't allowed to resplit aces and the casino edge in this game is .40%.

The best six-deck blackjack game in Tunica can be found at the Grand which has rules identical to those offered in the best two-deck games, plus they allow you to double after splitting and it's the only game in town where the dealer stands on soft 17. The casino advantage in this game is .34%.

Bally's, Gold Strike, Hollywood, Horseshoe and Sheraton have games identical to the Grand game except they hit soft 17 and that results in a slightly higer casino advantage of .56%. The remaining six-deck games are those offered at Fitzgeralds and Sam's Town. Both offer a game with a slightly higher casino edge of .63% because they hit soft 17 and won't allow you to resplit aces. Harrah's is the only casino to offer eight-deck games. The rules are similar to the .63% game except they allow late surrender which lowers the casino edge down to .56%.

Video Poker - Good video poker players know that five of the best varieties of machines to look for are: 9/6 Jacks or Better, 10/7 Double Bonus, full pay Deuces Wild, full pay Jokers Wild, and All American. By playing one of these five kinds of machines, playing the maximum coin and using perfect strategy, you can achieve the following payback percentages: 99.5% on 9/6 Jacks or Better, 100.17% on 10/7 Double Bonus, 100.65% on full pay Jokers Wild, 100.7% on All American and 100.7% on full pay Deuces Wild. Unfortunately, Tunica's choice of machines is not nearly as good as on the Gulf Coast or in Nevada, which is quickly depleting its inventory of best paying machines.

9/6 Jacks or Better can be found in most of Tunica's casinos, with the exceptions being: Bally's, the Grand and the Horseshoe. Gold Strike and Fitzgerald's have it in quarters and Sam's Town dollars. Harrah's, Hollywood and the Sheraton have it in quarters, 50 cents and dollars, while Gold Strike and Hollywood also have it in $5; Hollywood even has a $25 machine.

Oddly enough, Not-So-Ugly Deuces with a payback of 99.73% can be found at four Tunica area casinos: Gold Strike, Fitzgerald's and Hollywood all have it in quarter machines, but Harrah's has a lone $5 Five Play. That's an incredible $125 per hand. But NSUD has about the same volatility as full pay Deuces Wild and is a good game for quarter players.

Quarter 9/7 Double Bonus machines (99.11% payback) can be found at the Grand Casino, Sam's Town and Gold Strike (Fitzgerald's has them in nickels). $1 9/7 games can be found at Horseshoe and Harrah's. Most of the other Tunica casinos have 9/6 Double Bonus games in both quarter and dollar machines, but with an expected return of just 97.81%, you would be better off seeking out the higher paying 9/7 machines.

The Grand Casino and Sheraton offer Jacks or Better machines with the following pay table (per coin with maximum coins played): Royal Flush, 800; Straight Flush, 50; 4 aces, 80; 4 jacks/queens/kings, 40; 4 2s - 10s, 25; full house, 8; flush, 5; straight, 4; 3-of-a-Kind, 3; two pair, 2; pair of jacks or better, 1. This same kind of machine is known in the Las Vegas area as 8/5 Bonus Poker Aces and Faces. With perfect strategy and max coins played, it returns 99.3%.

Sheraton Casino & Hotel
1107 Casino Center Drive
Tunica Resorts, Mississippi 38664
(662) 363-4900

Toll-Free Number: (800) 391-3777
Suites: 140 Price Range: $89-$169
Restaurants: 4 (1 open 24 hours)
Buffets: B-$6.95 L-$7.95
D-$12.95/$16.95 (Fri)
Casino Size: 32,800 Square Feet
Other Games: S21, PGP, LIR, TCP

Vicksburg

Map Location: **#4** (on the Mississippi River, 44 miles W. of Jackson)

Vicksburg is one of the most historic cities in the South and is most famous for its National Military Park where 17,000 Union soldiers are buried. The Park is America's best-preserved Civil War battlefield and you can take a 16-mile drive through the 1,858-acre Park on a self-guided tour. In the Park you can also see the U.S.S. Cairo, the only salvaged Union Ironclad. Admission to the Park is $4 per car and allows unlimited returns for seven days.

Downtown Vicksburg is also home to several museums: The Old Court House ($3 admission), Gray and Blue Naval ($2.50 admission), Antique Doll and Toy ($2 admission); and Coca-Cola ($2.95 admission).

There are also about 12 historic homes in Vicksburg that are open to the public for narrated tours. Admission prices are $5 for adults and $2 to $3 for children 12 and under. Some of the homes also function as Bed and Breakfasts and rooms can be rented for overnight stays.

For more information on visiting Vicksburg call the city's Convention and Visitors Bureau at (800) 221-3536.

Ameristar Casino Hotel - Vicksburg
4146 Washington Street
Vicksburg, Mississippi 39180
(601) 638-1000
Website: www.ameristarcasinos.com

Reservation Number: (800) 700-7770
Rooms: 146 Price Range: $69-$99
Suites: 4 Price Range: $99-$129
Restaurants: 3 (1 open 24 hours)
Buffets: B-$4.99 L-$5.99/$11.99 (Sun)
D-$9.99/$15.99 (Fri/Sat)
Casino Size: 42,500 Square Feet
Other Games: S21, LIR, TCP
Special Features: AAA 10% room discount.

Harrah's Vicksburg
1310 Mulberry Street
Vicksburg, Mississippi 39180
(601) 636-DICE
Website: www.harrahs.com
NOTE: This property is being sold and is expected to have new ownership by early 2004.

Toll-Free Number: (800) 843-2343
Rooms: 101 Price Range: $69-$169
Suites: 16 Price Range: $210 and up
Restaurants: 3 (1 open 24 hours)
Buffets: B-$4.99/$6.99 (Sat-Sun)
L-$6.99/$11.99 (Sun)
D-$10.99/$12.99 (Fri-Sun)
Casino Size: 20,909 Square Feet
Other Games: S21, TCP, No CSP
Special Features: Casino is on 1,200-passenger paddlewheel riverboat. Planet 4 Kids childcare. 10% AAA/AArp room discount.

Isle of Capri Casino & Hotel - Vicksburg
3990 Washington Street
Vicksburg, Mississippi 39180
(601) 636-5700
Website: www.isleofcapricasino.com

Toll-Free Number: (800) THE-ISLE
Rooms: 61 Price Range: $59-$99
Suites: 61 Price Range: $99-$149
Restaurants: 2 (1 open 24 hours)
Buffets: B-$5.95/$9.95(Sun) L-$6.95
D-$10.50/$13.99 (Fri-Sun)
Casino Size: 24,000 Square Feet
Other Games: S21, TCP
Senior Discount: Various discounts if 50+
Special Features: 67-space RV park. Room discount for slot club members.

Rainbow Casino
1380 Warrenton Road
Vicksburg, Mississippi 39182
(601) 636-7575
Website: www.rainbowcasino.com

Toll-Free Number: (800) 503-3777
Rooms: 85 Price Range: $40-$75
Restaurants: 1
Buffets: B-$3.99 L-$5.99/$6.99 (Sat/Sun)
D-$8.99/$13.99 (Fri/Sat)
Casino Size: 25,000 Square Feet
Other Games: S21, TCP
Senior Discount: Various discounts if 50+
Special Features: Hotel is Amerihost Inn which offers complimentary continental breakfast and morning newspaper. Players club members receive $1 discount on buffet.

Indian Casino

Pearl River Resort & Casino
Highway 16 West
Philadelphia, Mississippi 39350
(601) 650-1234
Website: www.pearlriverresort.com
Map Location: **#8** (81 miles N.E. of Jackson)

Toll-Free Number: (800) 557-0711
Silver Star Rooms: 450 Prices: $59-$124
Silver Star Suites: 50 Prices: $180-$780
Golden Moon Rooms: 572 Prices: $99-$144
Golden Moon Suites: 144 Prices: $180-
Restaurants: 12 (1 open 24 hours)
Silver Star Buffet: L-$5.99/$10.99 (Sat/Sun)
D-$7.99/$10.95 (Fri)
Golden Moon Buffet: B-$8.99 L-$9.99
D-$13.99
Silver Star Casino Size: 90,000 Square Feet
Golden Moon Casino Size: 90,000 Square Feet
Other Games: B, MB, LIR, P, TCP, B6
Special Features: Resort consists of two separate hotel/casinos across the street from each other. 18-hole golf course. 15-acre water theme park. Health spa. Beauty salon. Gift shop. Specialty retail shops. 10% room discount for AAA/AARP members (Sun-Thu).

MISSOURI

In November, 1992 Missouri voters approved a state-wide referendum to allow riverboat gambling. That made Missouri the fifth state to approve this form of gambling. There is no limit to the number of licenses that may be issued by the state's gaming commission and all boats remain dockside.

Missouri's riverboat casinos initially conducted two-hour gaming sessions with a $500 loss-limit on each session. In early 2000 the law was changed to allow offer continuous boardings. However, the state's loss limit provision is still in force and you are not allowed to lose more than $500 within a two-hour period. All casinos base that two-hour period beginning on even hour times: 12-2, 2-4, 4-6, 6-8, 8-10, 10-12.

When you first enter a casino you must present an ID to receive a slot club card which will be used to track your chip and/or slot token purchases. Once you have purchased $500 worth of chips or tokens you will not be able to buy anymore until the beginning of the next even hour. There is no limit on winnings.

Admission is free to all Missouri casinos except for the President and Aztar. However, if you're a rated player from another casino you may get free admission to those casinos. Call ahead to ask them about their requirements.

Unlike dockside gaming in Mississippi, most Missouri casinos are not open 24 hours and the hours of operation are listed for each casino.

Here's information from the Missouri Gaming Commission regarding the payback percentages for each casino's electronic machines for the eight-month period from October 1, 2002 through May 31, 2003:

CASINO	PAYBACK %
Argosy	94.05
President	93.42
Ameristar-K.C.	93.17
Isle of Capri K.C.	93.09
Harrah's M.H.	93.00
Ameristar-St. Charles	92.90
Harrah's K.C.	92.76
St. Jo Frontier	92.61
Isle of Capri-Boonville	92.59
Mark Twain	92.24
Aztar	90.09

These figures reflect the total percentages returned by each casino for all of their electronic machines including slot machines, video poker, video keno, etc. As you can see, Argosy Casino returned the most to its slot machine players, while Casino Aztar returned the least. Although these numbers are only for an eight-month period they pretty much remain constant with the same casinos at the top and bottom of the list.

Unless otherwise noted, all casinos offer: slots, video poker, craps, blackjack, roulette and Caribbean stud poker. Optional games include: baccarat (B), mini-baccarat (MB), poker (P), pai gow poker (PGP), let it ride (LIR), Spanish 21 (S21) and three-card poker (TCP). The minimum gambling age is 21.

For more information on visiting Missouri call the state's Travel Center at (800) 877-1234.

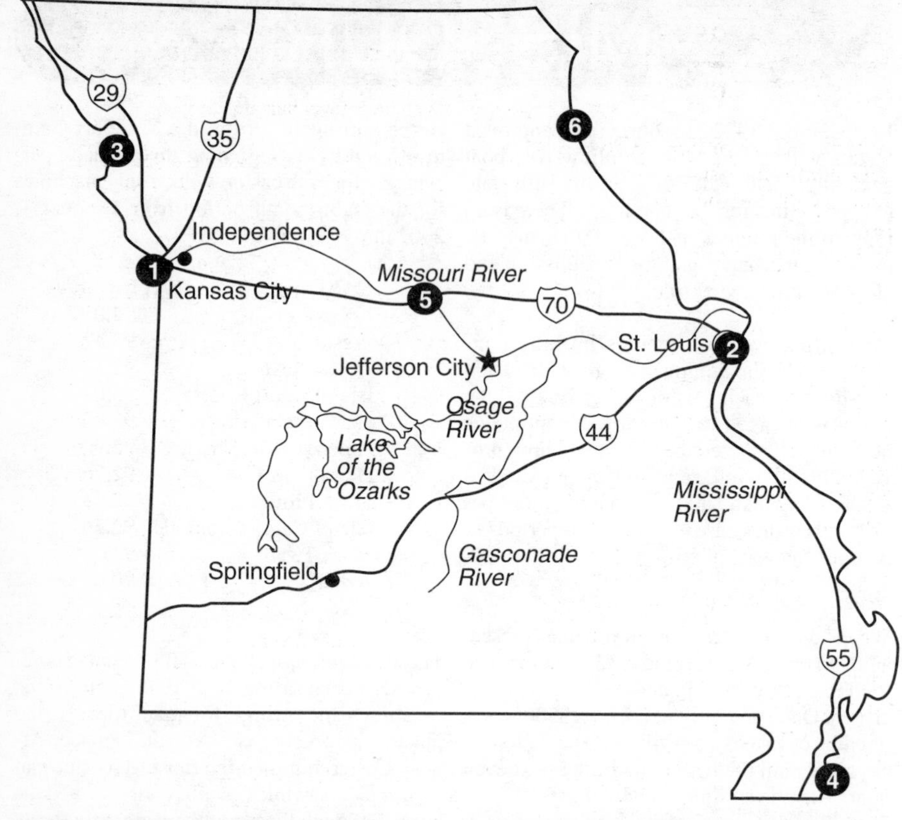

Boonville

Map Location: **#5** (100 miles E. of Kansas City)

Isle of Capri Casino - Boonville
100 Isle of Capri Boulevard
Boonville, Missouri 65233
(660) 882-1200
Website: www.isleofcapricasino.com

Toll-Free Number: THE-ISLE
Restaurants: 3
Buffets: B-$10.99 (Sun) L-$8.99
D-$11.99 to $14.99
Hours: 8am-5am/24 hours (Fri-Sat)
Valet Parking: Free
Casino Size: 28,000 Square Feet
Other Games: S21, LIR, TCP, No CSP
Senior Discount: Free buffet on Tue/Thu with qualified slot play and if 50 or older
Special Features: 600-passenger barge that remains dockside on the Missouri River.

Caruthersville

Map Location: **#4** (200 miles S. of St. Louis)

Casino Aztar
777 East Third Street
Caruthersville, Missouri 63830
(573) 333-6000

Toll-Free Number (800) 679-4945
Restaurants: 1
Buffets: D-$9.99 (Fri-Sat)
Hours: 10am-2am/4am (Fri/Sat)
Admission: $3 Valet Parking: $2
Senior Discount: Free admission and valet parking, if 55 or older
Casino Size: 12,000 Square Feet
Other Games: LIR, TCP
Special Features: 875-passenger sternwheeler that remains dockside on the Mississippi River. Restaurant and sports bar. Gift shop.

Kansas City

Map Location: **#1**

Ameristar Casino Hotel Kansas City
3200 North Ameristar Drive
Kansas City, Missouri 64161
(816) 414-7000
Website: www.ameristarcasinos.com

Toll-Free Number: (800) 499-4961
Rooms: 176 Price Range: $79-$169
Suites: 12 Price Range: $349
Restaurants: 14
Buffets: L-$8.99 D-$12.99 to $19.99
Hours: 8am-5am/24hrs (Fri/Sat)
Valet Parking: $5
Other Games: MB, P, PGP, LIR, TCP
Special Features: One 4,000-passenger barge that remain dockside on the Missouri River. Nine fast food outlets. Bavarian brew pub. 18 theater movie complex. $2 buffet discount for slot club members.

Argosy Casino
777 N.W. Argosy Parkway
Riverside, Missouri 64150
(816) 746-3100
Website: www.argosycasinos.com

Toll-Free Number: (800) 900-3423
Restaurants: 4 (Deli on boat)
Buffets: B-$6.49 L-$8.49
D-$10.49/$13.99 (Thu)/$17.99 (Fri-Sat)
Hours: 8am-5am/24 hours (Fri/Sat)
Valet Parking: $4
Casino Size: 30,000 Square Feet
Other Games: S21, PGP, LIR, TCP
Senior Discount: SVP club members receive discounts on select days, if 55, or older
Special Features: 1,800-passenger old-fashioned paddle wheeler that remains dockside on the Missouri River.

Harrah's North Kansas City
One Riverboat Drive
Kansas City, Missouri 64116
(816) 472-7777
Website: www.harrahs.com

Toll-Free Number: (800) HARRAHS
Rooms: 200 Price Range: $89-$150
Suites: 15 Price Range: $139-$190
Restaurants: 4 (Deli on both boats)
Buffets: B-$6.99 L-$8.99/$12.99 (Sat/Sun)
D-$12.99/$15.99 (Thu/Sat)
D-$17.99 (Wed/Fri)
Hours: 8am-5am/24 Hrs (Fri/Sat)
Casino Size: 60,000 Square Feet
Valet Parking: $5
Other Games: MB, LIR, PGP, TCP
Special Features: 1,700-passenger paddlewheeler that remain dockside on the Missouri River. Sports bar. Video arcade. Room discount and $1 buffet discount with Harrah's card.

Isle of Capri Casino - Kansas City
1800 E. Front Street
Kansas City, Missouri 64120
(816) 855-7777
Website: www.isleofcapricasino.com

Toll-Free Number: (800) 946-8711
Restaurants: 3
Buffets: B-$4.95 L-$8.95/$10.95 (Sun)
D-$14.95/$17.95 (Fri/Sat)/$12.95 (Sun)
Hours: 8am-5am/24 hours (Fri/Sat)
Valet Parking: Free
Casino Size: 30,000 Square Feet
Other Games: LIR, PGP, TCP
Senior Discount: Food discounts on Thursdays if slot club member and 50+
Special Features: 2,000-passenger Caribbean-themed barge that remains dockside in a man-made lake fed by the Missouri River.

La Grange

Map Location: **#6** (150 miles N.W. of St. Louis)

Mark Twain Casino
104 Pierce Street
La Grange, Missouri 63348
(573) 655-4770
Website: www.casinomarktwain.com

Toll-Free Number: (866) 454-5825
Restaurants: 2
Buffets: B-$2.99 (Mon-Tue)
D-$8.95 (Mon)/$12.95 (Wed)
Hours: 8am-2am/4am (Fri/Sat)
Casino Size: 8,000 Square Feet
Other Games: S21, TCP, No CSP
Senior Discount: 10% off food Mon-Wed if 55+
Special Features: 600-passenger barge that remains dockside on the Mississippi River. 8-space RV park.

St. Joseph

Map Location: **#3** (55 miles N. of Kansas City)

St. Jo Frontier Casino
77 Francis Street
St. Joseph, Missouri 64501
(816) 279-5514
Website: www.stjocasino.com

Toll-Free Number: (800) 888-2946
Restaurants: 4
Buffets: B-$4.49 L-$5.99 D-$8.10
Hours: 8am-2am/4am (Fri/Sat)
Valet Parking: Not Offered
Casino Size: 9,260 Square Feet
Other Games: S21, LIR, TCP, No CSP
Casino Marketing: (800) WIN-STJO
Senior Discount: 2-for-1 breakfast buffet on Wed, if 55, or older
Special Features: 1,146-passenger paddlewheel boat that remains dockside on the Missouri River. Entertainment barge next to the casino has a bar and gift shop. Conference center.

St. Louis

Map Location: **#2**

In addition to the three St. Louis-area casinos shown below, the Casino Queen in E. St. Louis, Illinois is also a nearby casino. It is located on the other side of the Mississippi river from downtown St. Louis. Additionally, the Alton Belle in Alton, Illinois is about 25 miles north of St. Louis. Both Illinois casinos are not restricted by the $500 loss limit (per two-hours) that is in effect in Missouri casinos.

Ameristar Casino St. Charles
P.O. Box 720
St. Charles, Missouri 63302
(314) 949-4300
Website: www.ameristarcasinos.com

Toll-Free Number: (800) 325-7777
Restaurants: 3
Buffets: B-$4.99 L-$8.99/$12.99 (Sat/Sun)
D-$13.99 (Wed/Thu/Sun)/$18.99 (Mon)
D-$16.99 (Tue/Fri/Sat)
Hours: 8am-5am/24hrs (Fri-Sat)
Valet Parking: $5
Casino Size: 115,000 Square Feet
Other Games: MB, LIR, P, PGP, TCP
Senior Discount: Sun-Thu from 8am-6pm receive double points, gift shop discounts, $1 lunch and free valet, by joining *Golden Opportunities*, if 55, or older
Special Features: 2,000-passenger barge that remains dockside on the Missouri River.

Harrah's St. Louis
777 Casino Center Drive
Maryland Heights, Missouri 63043
(314) 770-8100
Website: www.harrahs.com

Toll-Free Number: (800) HARRAHS
Rooms: 277 Price Range: $79-$199
Suites: 14 Price Range: $169-$299
Restaurants: 6
Buffets: B-$6.99 L-$8.99/$12.99 (Sat/Sun)
D-$13.99/$16.99 (Tue/Thu-Sat)
Hours: **Island**: 11am-5am/24 hours (Fri/Sat)
Mardi Gras: 8am-5am/24 hours (Fri/Sat)
Valet Parking: $5
Senior Discount: 99-cent deli special, if 50+
Casino Size: 120,000 Square Feet Total
Other Games: S21, MB, LIR, PGP, TCP
Senior Discount: $1.50 off lunch buffet, 10% gift shop discount, cash drawings Tue/Fri, if 50, or older with Player's Club Card
Special Features: Two 3,200-passenger barges that remain dockside on the Missouri River.

President Casino - St. Louis
800 North First Street
St. Louis, Missouri 63102
(314) 622-3000
Website: www.presidentcasino.com

Toll-Free Number: (800) 772-3647
Restaurants: 2
Buffets: L/D-$9.50
Hours: 8am-4am/24hrs (Fri/Sat)
Admission: $2 (First-time only)
Parking: Free with casino validation
Valet Parking: $5
Other Games: S21, MB, LIR, P, PGP, TCP
Senior Discount: 2-for-1 lunch buffet and other discounts on Thursdays, if 55, or older
Special Features: 2,500-passenger, art deco riverboat that remains dockside on the Mississippi River near the Gateway Arch. Free shuttle service to and from all downtown hotels. One block from Laclede's Landing Metro Link Light Rail Station.

MONTANA

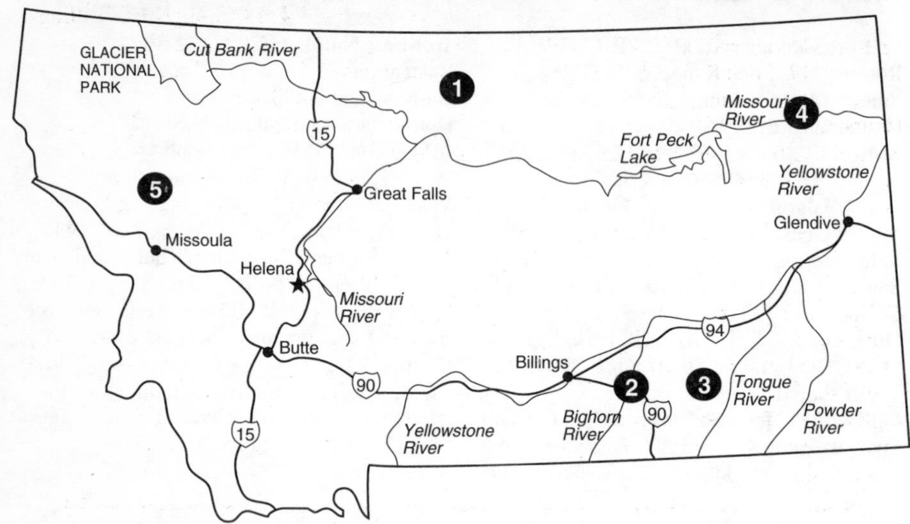

Montana law permits bars and taverns to have up to 20 video gaming devices that play video poker, video keno, or video bingo. These machines are operated in partnership with the state and are not permitted to pay out in cash; instead, they print out a receipt which must be taken to a cashier. The maximum bet on these machines is $2 and the maximum payout is limited to $800. Montana gaming regulations require these machines to return a minimum of 80%.

There are five Indian Tribes offering video gaming machines that also print out a receipt. The maximum bet on these machines is $2 and the maximum payout is capped at $1,000. According to Wilbur Raymond of Montana's Gambling Control Division, there are no minimum payback amounts required for gaming machines on Indian reservations. The minimum gambling age in Montana is 18.

For Montana tourism information call (800) VISIT-MT.

Charging Horse Casino
P.O. Box 128
Lame Deer, Montana 59043
(406) 477-6677
Map Location: **#3** (90 miles S.E. of Billings on Hwy. 212)

Restaurants: 1 Snack Bar Liquor: No
Hours: 7am-2am Daily

4 C's Cafe & Casino
Rocky Boy Route, Box 544
Box Elder, Montana 59521
(406) 395-4863
Map Location: **#1** (75 miles N.E. of Great Falls)

Restaurants: 1 Liquor: No
Hours: 9am-2:30am Daily

KwaTaqNuk Casino Resort
303 Highway 93
E. Polson, Montana 59860
(406) 883-3636
Map Location: **#5** (65 miles N. Of Missoula)

Room Reservations: (800) 882-6363
Rooms: 112 Price Range: $79-$129
Restaurants: 1 Liquor: Yes
Hours: 24 Hours Daily
Special Features: Hotel is Best Western. 10% AAA room discount. Indoor pool and hot tub.

Little Big Horn Casino
P.O. Box 580
Crow Agency, Montana 59022
(406) 638-4000
Map Location: **#2** (65 miles S.E. of Billings)

Restaurants: 1 Liquor: No
Hours: 8am-2am/3am (Fri/Sat)

Silver Wolf Casino
Highway 25 East
P.O. Box 726
Wolf Point, Montana 59201
(406) 653-3476
Map Location: **#4** (180 miles N.E of Billings)

Restaurants: 1 Snack Bar Liquor: No
Hours: 11am-Mid Daily
Other Games: Bingo

NEVADA

All Nevada casinos are open 24 hours and, unless otherwise noted, offer: slots, video poker, craps, blackjack, and roulette. The minimum gambling age is 21. For Nevada tourism information call (800) 237-0774.

Other games in the casino listings include: sports book (SB), race book (RB), Spanish 21 (S21), baccarat (B), mini-baccarat (MB), pai gow (PG), poker (P), pai gow poker (PGP), Caribbean stud poker (CSP), let it ride (LIR), three-card poker (TCP), sic bo (SIC), keno (K), big 6 wheel (B6) and bingo (BG).

Amargosa Valley

Map Location: **#8** (91 miles N.W. of Las Vegas on Hwy. 95)

Longstreet Inn and Casino
Route 373, HCR 70
Amargosa Valley, Nevada 89020
(775) 372-1777
Website: www.longstreetinn.com

Toll-Free Number: (800) 508-9493
Rooms: 46 Price Range: $59-$69
Suites: 14 Price Range: $89
Restaurants: 2
Other Games: No Craps or Roulette
Senior Discount: 20% off meals, if 65 or older
Special Features: 50-space RV Park. 9-hole par-3 golf course. 24-hour convenience store.

Stateline Saloon
Route 15, Box 566R
Amargosa Valley, Nevada 89020
(775) 372-5238
Website: www.statelinesaloon.com

Restaurants: 1
Other Games: No Craps or Roulette

Battle Mountain

Map Location: **#9** (215 mile N.E. of Reno on I-80)

Nevada Hotel & Casino
8 E. Front Street
Battle Mountain, Nevada 89820
(775) 635-2453

Restaurants: 1
Casino Size: 840 Square Feet
Other Games: No Craps or Roulette

Beatty

Map Location: **#10** (120 miles N.W. of Las Vegas on Hwy. 95)

Burro Inn Motel & Casino
Highway 95 South
Beatty, Nevada 89003
(775) 553-2225
Website: www.burroinn.com

Reservation Number: (800) 843-2078
Rooms: 61 Price Range: $35-$45
Suites: 1 Price Range: $65
Restaurants: 1
Other Games: No Craps or Roulette
Fun Book: Given to hotel guests.
Special Features: 43-space RV park. Four miles from Rhyolite ghost town.

Exchange Club Casino & Motel
119 N. Main Street
Beatty, Nevada 89003
(775) 553-2368
Website: www.exchangeclubcasino.com

Room Reservations: (888) 561-2333
Rooms: 44 Price Range: $38-$48
Suites: 1 Price Range: $68
Restaurants: 1 (open 24 hours)
Casino Size: 7,620 Square Feet
Other Games: P, No Craps or Roulette
Fun Book: Ask at motel office

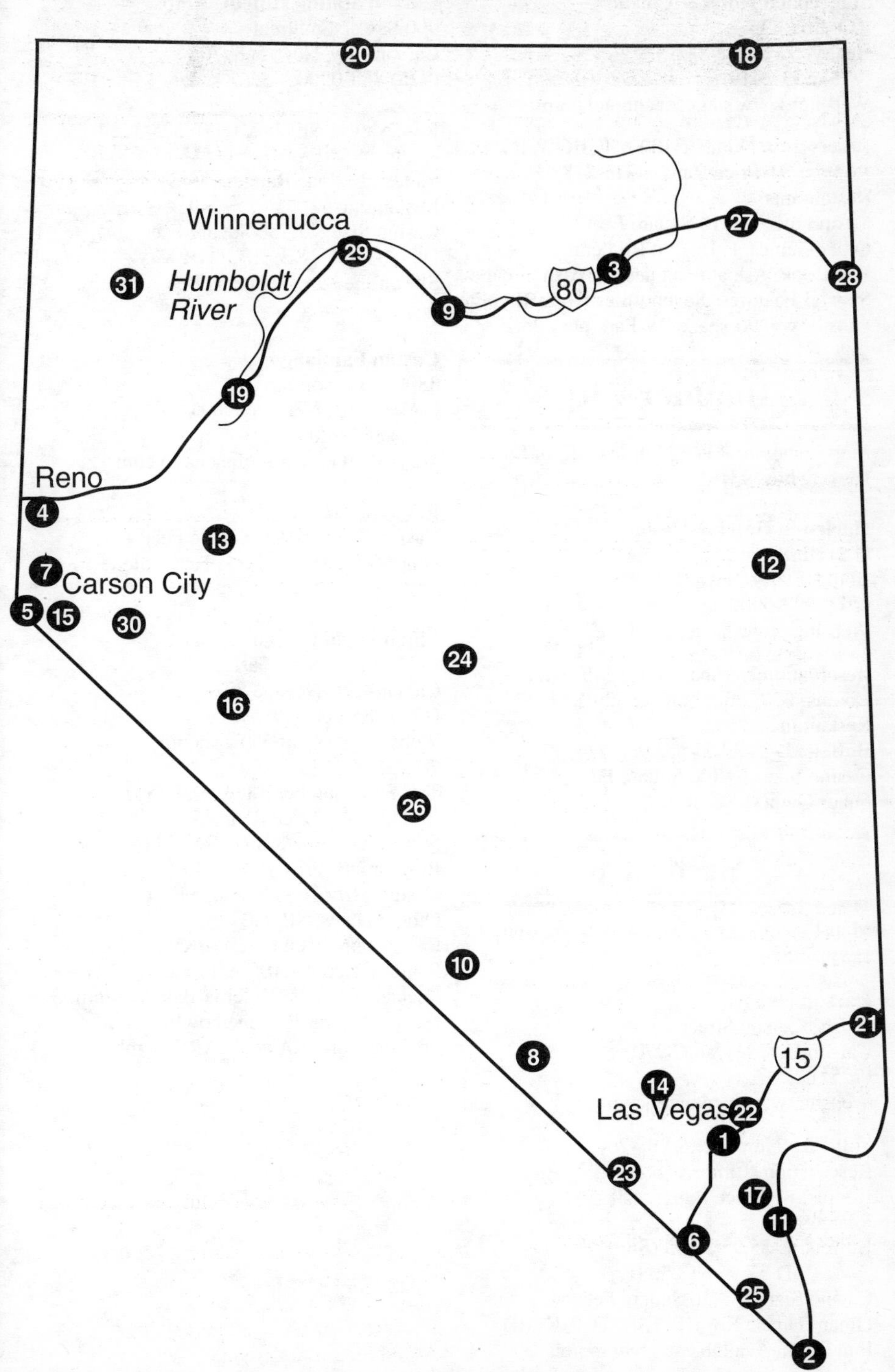
20
18
Winnemucca
29
27
3
28
31
Humboldt
River
80
9
19
Reno
4
13
7
Carson City
12
5
15
30
24
16
26
10
21
15
8
14
Las Vegas
22
1
23
17
11
6
25
2

Stagecoach Hotel & Casino
P.O. Box 836
Beatty, Nevada 89003
(775) 553-2419
Website: www.stagecoachhotel.com

Reservation Number: (800) 4-BIG-WIN
Rooms: 50 Price Range: $35-$48
Restaurants: 2
Casino Size: 8,810 Square Feet
Other Games: P, B6, No Roulette
Fun Book: Ask at front desk or cashier cage
Special Features: Seven miles from Rhyolite ghost town. 90-space RV Park next door.

Boulder City

Map Location: **#11** (22 miles S.E. of Las Vegas on Hwy. 93)

Hacienda Hotel & Casino
U.S. Highway 93
Boulder City, Nevada 89005
(702) 293-5000
Website: www.haciendaonline.com

Reservation Number: (800) 245-6380
Rooms: 378 Price Range: $29-$79
Restaurants: 3
Buffets: L-$4.99 D-$6.99
Casino Size: 19,300 Square Feet
Other Games: SB, RB

Carson City

Map Location: **#7** (32 miles S. of Reno on Hwy. 395)

Carson Nugget
507 N. Carson Street
Carson City, Nevada 89701
(775) 882-1626
Website: www.ccnugget.com

Toll-Free Number: (800) 426-5239
Reservation Number: (800) 338-7760
Rooms: 82 Price Range: $38-$61
Restaurants: 5
Buffets: L-$5.95/$7.95 (Sun)
D-$7.95/$13.50 (Fri)
Casino Size: 24,320 Square Feet
Other Games: SB, RB, LIR, TCP, K, BG
Fun Book: Available at local motels
Senior Discount: 10% off room/food, if 50+
Special Features: Rare gold display.

Carson Station Hotel/Casino
900 S. Carson Street
Carson City, Nevada 89702
(775) 883-0900

Reservation Number: (800) 528-1234
Rooms: 92 Price Range: $55-$85
Suites: 3 Price Range: $80-$105
Restaurants: 2
Casino Size: 12,750 Square Feet
Other Games: SB, RB, PGP, K
Special Features: Hotel is Best Western.

Casino Fandango
3800 S. Carson Street
Carson City, Nevada 89005
(775) 885-7000
Website: www.casinofandango.com

Restaurants: 1
Casino Size: 10,000 Square Feet
Other Games: No Craps, No Roulette

Piñon Plaza Casino Resort
2171 Highway 50 East
Carson City, Nevada 89701
(775) 885-9000
Website: www.pinonplaza.com

Toll-Free Number: (877) 519-5567
Rooms: 148 Price Range: $50-$90
Suites: 22 Price Range: $90-$125
Restaurants: 2
Casino Size: 16,926 Square Feet
Other Games: SB, RB
Fun Book: Given to resort/RV guests
Senior Discount: 10% off food, if 55 or older
Special Features: Hotel is Best Western. 30-space RV park. 32-lane bowling center. 10% off room for AAA and AARP members.

Elko

Map Location: **#3** (289 miles N.E. of Reno on I-80)

Commercial Casino
345 4th Street
Elko, Nevada 89801
(775) 738-3181
Website: www.fh-inc.com

Toll-Free Number: (800) 648-2345
Restaurants: 2
Casino Size: 6,440 Square Feet
Other Games: No Craps or Roulette
Fun Book: Show out-of-Elko ID at cashier cage
Special Features: Oldest continually operating casino in Nevada. 10-foot-tall stuffed polar bear in casino. Large gunfighter art collection.

Gold Country Motor Inn
2050 Idaho Street
Elko, Nevada 89801
(775) 738-8421

Room Reservations: (800) 621-1332
Rooms: 140 Price Range: $65-$109
Rooms: 11 Price Range: $99-$119
Restaurants: 1
Casino Size: 2,359 Square Feet
Other Games: No Craps or Roulette
Special Features: Motor Inn is Best Western.

Red Lion Inn & Casino
2065 Idaho Street
Elko, Nevada 89801
(775) 738-2111
Website: www.redlioncasino.com

Reservation Number: (800) 545-0044
Rooms: 223 Price Range: $76-$119
Suites: 2 Price Range: $259
Restaurants: 2 (1 open 24 hours)
Buffets: B-$7.25 L-$7.75
D-$9.50/$12.50 (Sat)/$15.95 (Fri)
Casino Size: 20,350 Square Feet
Other Games: SB, RB, P, LIR, TCP, K, BG
Fun Book: Ask at Player's Club Booth
Special Features: Air junkets offered from 90 U.S. cities-call (800) 258-8800. Sports bar. AAA room discount and AARP room and food discount.

Stockmen's Hotel & Casino
340 Commercial Street
Elko, Nevada 89801
(775) 738-5141
Website: www.fh-inc.com

Reservation Number: (800) 648-2345
Rooms: 141 Price Range: $31-$60
Restaurants: 2
Casino Size: 7,030 Square Feet
Other Games: SB, TCP, No Roulette
Fun Book: Show out-of-Elko ID at cashier cage
Special Features: 24-hour shuttle service.

Ely

Map Location: **#12** (317 miles E. of Reno on Hwy. 50)

Hotel Nevada & Gambling Hall
501 Aultman Street
Ely, Nevada 89301
(775) 289-6665
Website: www.hotelnevada.com

Reservation Number: (888) 406-3055
Rooms: 45 Price Range: $19-$48
Restaurants: 1
Casino Size: 2,980 Square Feet
Other Games: P, No Craps or Roulette
Fun Book: Ask at front desk
Special Features: Built in 1929. Historical display of mining, ranching and railroad artifacts. 10% room discount to AARP members

Fallon

Map Location: **#13** (61 miles E. of Reno on Hwy. 50)

Bird Farm
128 E. Williams Avenue
Fallon, Nevada 89406
(775) 423-7877

Other Games: P, No Blackjack or Roulette
Special Features: Craps played after 7pm.

Bonanza Inn & Casino
855 W. Williams Avenue
Fallon, Nevada 89406
(775) 423-6031

Rooms: 74 Price Range: $39-$50
Suites: 2 Price Range: $50-$68
Restaurants: 1
Casino Size: 5,830 Square Feet
Other Games: K, No Craps or Roulette
Fun Book: Only given to hotel guests
Senior Discount: AARP discount.

Depot Casino & Restaurant
875 W. Williams Avenue
Fallon, Nevada 89406
(775) 423-2411

Restaurants: 1
Casino Size: 6,855 Square Feet
Other Games: BG, No Craps or Roulette
Special Features: Blackjack only played Wed-Sat after 6pm.

Stockman's Casino
1560 W. Williams Avenue
Fallon, Nevada 89406
(775) 423-2117

Toll-Free Number: (800) HOLIDAY
Rooms: 98 Price Range: $59-$79
Suites: 8 Price Range: $89-$139
Restaurants: 2
Casino Size: 7,587 Square Feet
Other Games: K, No Roulette or Craps
Senior Discount: Various, if 60 or older
Special Features: Hotel is Holiday Inn Express. 10% AAA room discount.

Gardnerville

Map Location: **#15** (45 miles S. of Reno on Hwy. 395)

Sharkey's Nugget
P.O. Box 625
Gardnerville, Nevada 89410
(775) 782-3133

Restaurants: 1
Casino Size: 694 Square Feet
Other Games: No Craps or Roulette. BJ opens at 4pm/12pm (Fri-Sat)

Topaz Lodge & Casino
1979 Highway 395 South
Gardnerville, Nevada 89410
(775) 266-3338
Website: www.enterit.com/topaz3338

Reservation Number: (800) 962-0732
Rooms: 59 Price Range: $55-$68
Restaurants: 1
Buffets: B-$8.95 (Sun)
D-$13.95(Fri)/$9.95(Sat)
Casino Size: 12,800 Square Feet
Other Games: BG, No Roulette

Gerlach

Map Location: **#31** (107 miles N.E. of Reno)

Bruno's Country Club
445 Main Street
Gerlach, Nevada
(775) 557-2220

Rooms: 40 Price Range: $45-$55
Restaurants: 1
Other Games: No Craps or Roulette

Hawthorne

Map Location: **#16** (138 miles S.E. of Reno on Hwy. 95)

El Capitan Resort Casino
540 F Street
Hawthorne, Nevada 89415
(775) 945-3321
Website: www.elcapitanresortcasino.com

Toll Free: (800) 922-2311
Rooms: 103 Price Range: $50-$55
Restaurants: 1
Casino Size: 10,000 Square Feet
Other Games: No Craps or Roulette
Fun Book: Ask at front desk

Henderson

Map Location: **#17** (15 miles S.E. of Las Vegas on Hwy. 93)

Barley's Casino & Brewing Co.
4500 E. Sunset Road #30
Henderson, Nevada 89014
(702) 458-2739

Restaurants: 1
Casino Size: 10,000 Square Feet
Other Games: SB
Special Features: Located in a strip mall. Four varieties of beer micro-brewed on premises.

Casino MonteLago
8 Strata di Villaggio
Henderson, NV 89011
(702) 939-8888
Website: www.casinomontelago.com

Toll Free Number: (877) 553-3555
Restaurants: 2 (1 open 24 hours)
Casino Size: 30,000 Square Feet
Other Games: SB, MB, PGP, LIR
Special Features: Large assormentof full-pay video poker.

Eldorado Casino
140 Water Street
Henderson, Nevada 89015
(702) 564-1811
Website: www.boydgaming.com

Restaurants: 2
Casino Size: 17,756 Square Feet
Other Games: SB, K, BG

Fiesta Henderson Casino Hotel
777 West Lake Mead Drive
Henderson, Nevada 89015
(702) 558-7000

Toll-Free Number: (866) 469-7666
Rooms: 224 Price Range: $19-$129
Suites: 8 Price Range: $99-$299
Restaurants: 4 (1 open 24 hours)
Buffets: B-$9.99 (Sat/Sun) L-$6.99
D-$9.99/$14.99
Casino Size: 65,560 Square Feet
Other Games: SB, RB, PGP, LIR, TCP, K, BG
Senior Discount: Join Fun Club, if 50 or older
Special Features: Beer garden. Video arcade.

Green Valley Ranch Resort
2300 Paseo Verde Drive
Henderson, Nevada 89012
(702) 617-7777
Website: www.greenvalleyranchresort.com

Reservation Number: (866) 782-9487
Rooms: 200 Price Range: $99-$239
Suites: 45 Price Range: $204-$354
Restaurants: (1 open 24 hours)
Buffets: B-$6.99 L-$8.99
D-$14.99/$16.99 (Fri-Sun)
Casino Size: 91,861 Square Feet
Other Games: SB, RB, B, MB, PG,
PGP, LIR, TCP

Hyatt Regency Lake Las Vegas Resort
101 Montelago Boulevard
Las Vegas, Nevada 89011
(702) 567-1234
Web site: www.lakelasvegas.hyatt.com

Reservation Number: (800) 55-HYATT
Rooms: 449 Price Range: $115-$525
Suite: 47 Price Range: $750-$900
Restaurants: 4
Casino Size: 6,500 Square Feet
Other Games: MB
Special Features: Located by large private lake. 18-hole Jack Nicklaus designed golf course.

Jokers Wild
920 N. Boulder Highway
Henderson, Nevada 89015
(702) 564-8100
Website: www.boydgaming.com

Restaurants: 1
Buffets: D-$5.99(Sun/Wed/Thu)/$9.99 (Fri)
Casino Size: 23,698 Square Feet
Other Games: SB, K
Senior Discount: $1 off dinner, if 55 or older

Klondike Sunset Casino
444 West Sunset
Henderson, Nevada 89015
(702) 568-7575

Restaurants: 1
Casino Size: 7,700 Square Feet
Other Games: No Craps

Railroad Pass Hotel & Casino
2800 S. Boulder Highway
Henderson, Nevada 89015
(702) 294-5000
Website: www.railroadpass.com

Toll-Free Number: (800) 654-0877
Rooms: 100 Price Range: $37-$65
Suites: 20 Price Range: $47-$85
Restaurants: 3 (1 open 24 hours)
Buffets: B-$5.99 (Sat-Sun) L-$4.99
D-$6.99/$7.99 (Fri-Sat)
Casino Size: 12,803 Square Feet
Other Games: SB, RB
Fun Book: Show out-of-state ID at front desk
Senior Discount: Food discount Mon, if 55+
Special Features: Video arcade. Gift shop.

Skyline Restaurant & Casino
1741 N. Boulder Highway
Henderson, Nevada 89015
(702) 565-9116

Restaurants: 1
Buffets: L-$4.45
Casino Size: 8,500 Square Feet
Other Games: SB, RB, No Craps or Roulette
Fun Book: Available at local hotels/motels

Sunset Station Hotel and Casino
1301 W. Sunset Road
Henderson, Nevada 89014
(702) 547-7777
Website: www.sunsetstation.com

Toll free: (888) 319-4655
Reservation Number: (888) 786-7389
Rooms: 448 Price Range: $45-$105
Suites: 18 Price Range: $99-$139
Restaurants: 12 (1 open 24 hours)
Buffets: B-$4.99/$8.99 (Sat-Sun)
L-$6.99 D-$9.99
Casino Size: 133,409 Square Feet
Other Games: SB, RB, S21, MB, P, PGP,
LIR, TCP, K, BG
Special Features: 13-screen movie theater. Kid's Quest childcare center. Video arcade.

Indian Springs

Map Location: **#14** (35 miles N.W. of Las Vegas on Hwy. 95)

Indian Springs Casino
372 Tonopah Highway
Indian Springs, Nevada 89018
(702) 879-3456
Website: www.indianspringscasino.com

Reservation Number: (877) 977-7746
Restaurants: 1
Rooms: 45 Price Range: $35-$49
Other Games: No Craps or Roulette
Fun Book: Ask at cashier cage
Special Features: Room discount for AAA and AARP members. RV park. Convenience store.

Jackpot

Map Location: **#18** (Just S. of the Idaho border on Hwy. 93)

Barton's Club 93
Highway 93
Jackpot, Nevada 89825
(775) 755-2341

Toll-Free Number: (800) 258-2937
Rooms: 98 Price Range: $43-$70
Suites: 4 Price Range: $90-$135
Restaurants: 2
Buffets: B-$5.93 (Sat-Sun) D-$9.93 (Wed/
Thu/Sat/Sun)/$10.93 (Fri)
Casino Size: 9,550 Square Feet
Other Games: K, LIR
Fun Book: Ask at registration desk

Cactus Pete's Resort Casino
1385 Highway 93
Jackpot, Nevada 89825
(775) 755-2321
Website: www.ameristarcasinos.com

Reservation Number: (800) 821-1103
Rooms: 272 Price Range: $57-$89
Suites: 28 Price Range: $150-$185
Restaurants: 5
Buffets: B-$9.99 (Sat)/$12.99 (Sun)
L-$5.99 D-$9.99/$14.99 (Fri-Sat)
Casino Size: 25,351 Square Feet
Other Games: SB, P, PGP, LIR, K
Senior Discount: 15% off room/restaurants, 20% off gift shop if 60, or older.
Special Features: Every Wed 5pm-11pm all restaurants are half-price. 18-hole golf course. Free dinner on birthday and anniversary.

Horseshu Hotel & Casino
Highway 93
Jackpot, Nevada 89825
(702) 755-7777
Website: www.ameristars.com

Reservation Number: (800) 432-0051
Rooms: 110 Price Range: $27-$85
Suites: 10 Price Range: $125-$185
Restaurants: 1 Casino Size: 3,520 Square Feet
Other Games: No Roulette

Jean

Map Location: **#6** (22 miles S.W. of Las Vegas on I-15; 12 miles from the California border)

Gold Strike Hotel & Gambling Hall
1 Main Street/P.O. Box 19278
Jean, Nevada 89019
(702) 477-5000
Website: www.goldstrike-jean.com

Reservation Number: (800) 634-1359
Rooms: 800 Price Range: $19-$49
Suites: 13 Price Range: $50-$110
Restaurants: 5
Buffets: B-$7.50 (Sat/Sun) L-$6.96
D-$8.03/$9.64 (Fri)/$9.11 (Sat)
Casino Size: 37,006 Square Feet
Other Games: CSP
Fun Book: Ask at hotel registration desk
Special Features: Free shuttle to Nevada Landing. $1.99 breakfast special. Burger King.

Nevada Landing Hotel & Casino
2 Goodsprings Road/P.O. Box 19278
Jean, Nevada 89019
(702) 387-5000
Website: www.nevadalanding.com

Reservation Number: (800) 628-6682
Rooms: 287 Price Range: $19-$54
Suites: 16 Price Range: $70-$125
Restaurants: 4
Buffets: B-$7.50 (Sat/Sun) L-$6.96
D-$8.03/$9.64 (Fri)/$9.11 (Sat)
Casino Size: 35,700 Square Feet
Other Games: SB, PGP, CSP
Fun Book: Ask at hotel registration desk
Special Features: Free shuttle to Gold Strike. $1.99 breakfast special.

Lake Tahoe

Map Location: **#5** (directly on the Nevada/California border; 98 miles northeast of Sacramento and 58 miles southwest of Reno).

The Lake Tahoe area is best known for its many recreational activities with skiing in the winter and water sports in the summer. Lake Tahoe Airport is located at the south end of the basin. The next closest airport is in Reno with regularly scheduled shuttle service by bus.

Incline Village and Crystal Bay are on the north shore of Lake Tahoe, while Stateline is located on the south shore. For South Lake Tahoe information call the Lake Tahoe Visitors Authority at (800) AT-TAHOE and for North Lake Tahoe information call the Incline Village/Crystal Bay Convention & Visitors Authority at (800) GO-TAHOE.

Here's information, as supplied by Nevada's State Gaming Control Board, showing the slot machine payback percentages for all of the south shore casinos for the fiscal year beginning July 1, 2002 and ending June 30, 2003:

Denomination	Payback %
5¢ Slots	90.59
25¢ Slots	93.54
$1 Slots	95.17
$1 Megabucks	88.70
$5 Slots	95.54
All Slots	94.20

And here's that same information for the north shore casinos:

Denomination	Payback %
5¢ Slots	92.63
25¢ Slots	94.91
$1 Slots	95.43
$1 Megabucks	90.28
$5 Slots	96.03
All Slots	94.88

These numbers reflect the percentage of money returned to the players on each denomination of machine. All electronic machines including slots, video poker and video keno are included in these numbers.

Optional games in the casino listings include: sports book (SB), race book (RB), Spanish 21 (S21), baccarat (B), mini-baccarat (MB), poker (P), pai gow poker (PGP), Caribbean stud poker (CSP), let it ride (LIR), three-card poker (TCP), keno (K) and bingo (BG).

Bill's Casino
U.S. Highway 50/P.O. Box 8
Stateline, Nevada 89449
(775) 588-2455
Website: www.harrahs.com

Restaurants: 1 (open 24 hours)
Casino Size: 18,000 Square Feet
Special Features: Separate casino that is owned by Harrah's Lake Tahoe.

Caesars Tahoe
55 Highway 50
Stateline, Nevada 89449
(775) 588-3515
Website: www.caesars.com

Reservation Number: (800) 648-3353
Rooms: 403 Price Range: $69-$160
Suites: 37 Price Range: $379-$750
Restaurants: 5 (1 open 24 hours)
Buffets: B/L-$9.99/$10.99 (Sat)/$14.99 (Sun)
D-$12.99/$19.99 (Fri-Sat)/$13.99 (Sun)
Casino Size: 40,000 Square Feet
Other Games: SB, RB, B, MB, PG, PGP
LIR, TCP, B6, K
Special Features: On south shore of Lake Tahoe. Health spa. Planet Hollywood restaurant.

Cal-Neva Lodge Resort
Hotel, Spa & Casino
P.O. Box 368
Crystal Bay, Nevada 89402
(775) 832-4000
Website: www.calnevaresort.com

Reservation Number: (800) CAL-NEVA
Rooms: 180 Price Range: $79-$139
Suites: 27 Price Range: $169-$209
Restaurants: 1
Casino Size: 9,700 Square Feet
Other games: P
Special Features: Straddles California/Nevada state line on north shore of Lake Tahoe. Lake view rooms. European Spa. Three wedding chapels. Florist. Photo studio. Bridal boutique. Gift shop. Airport shuttle. Internet cafe.

Crystal Bay Club
14 Highway 28
Crystal Bay, Nevada 89402
(775) 831-0512

Restaurants 2 (1 open 24 hours)
Casino Size: 10,300 Square Feet
Special features: Children's arcade.

Harrah's Lake Tahoe
Highway 50/P.O. Box 8
Stateline, Nevada 89449
(775) 588-6611
Website: www.harrahs.com

Reservation Number: (800) HARRAHS
Rooms: 451 Price Range: $129-$259
Suites: 62 Price Range: $199-$800
Restaurants: 7 (1 open 24 hours)
Buffets: B-$10.99/$13.99 (Sat)/$17.99 (Sun)
L-$11.99 D-$17.99/$24.99 (Fri-Sat)
Casino Size: 56,600 Square Feet
Casino Marketing: (800) 346-6569
Other Games: SB, B, MB, PG, PGP
CSP, LIR, TCP, K
Special Features: On south shore of Lake Tahoe. Health club. Pet kennel.

Harveys Resort Hotel/Casino - Lake Tahoe
P.O. Box 128 - Highway 50
Stateline, Nevada 89449
(775) 588-2411
Website: www.harrahs.com

Toll-Free Number: (800) 553-1022
Reservation Number: (800) HARVEYS
Rooms: 740 Price Range: $39-$279
Suites: 36 Price Range: $250-$679
Restaurants: 8 (1 open 24 hours)
Buffets: B-$10.99/$13.99 (Sat)/$17.99 (Sun)
L-$11.95 D-$17.99/$24.99 (Fri-Sat)
Casino Size: 80,780 Square Feet
Other Games: SB, RB, S21, MB, P, PGP, CSP, LIR, TCP, B6, K
Special Features: On south shore of Lake Tahoe. AAA room discount. Health Club. Arcade.

Hyatt Regency Lake Tahoe Resort & Casino
P.O. Box 3239
Incline Village, Nevada 89450
(775) 832-1234
Website: www.laketahoehyatt.com

Toll-Free Number: (800) 553-3288
Reservation Number: (800) 233-1234
Rooms: 412 Price Range: $99-$350
Suites: 48 Price Range: $425-$1100
Restaurants: 2 (1 open 24 hours)
Buffets: B-$29.95 (Sun)
D-$22.00 (Fri)/$20.00 (Sat)
Casino Size: 9,550 Square Feet
Other Games: SB, PG, LIR, TCP
Senior Discount: Up to 50% off room, if 62+
Special Features: On north shore of Lake Tahoe. Two Robert Trent Jones golf courses.

Lake Tahoe Horizon
50 Highway 50/P.O. Box C
Lake Tahoe, Nevada 89449
(775) 588-6211
Website: www.horizoncasino.com

Toll-Free Number: (800) 322-7723
Reservation Number: (800) 648-3322
Rooms: 519 Price Range: $99-$169
Suites: 20 Price Range: $300-$500
Restaurants: 5 (1 open 24 hours)
Buffets: D-$9.95/$11.95 (Fri-Sat)
Casino Size: 30,999 Square Feet
Other Games: SB, RB, S21, P, PGP, TCP, K
Senior Discount: 10% to 25% off room, if 50+
Special Features: On south shore of Lake Tahoe. Outdoor heated pool with 3 hot tubs. Wedding chapel. Video arcade. Baskin-Robbins store.

Lakeside Inn & Casino
Highway 50 & Kingsbury Grade
Stateline, Nevada 89449
(775) 588-7777
Website: www.lakesideinn.com

Toll-Free Number: (800) 523-1291
Room Reservations: (800) 624-7980
Rooms: 123 Price Range: $79-$119
Suites: 2 Price Range: $110-$280
Restaurants: 2 (open 24 hours)
Casino Size: 18,175 Square Feet
Other Games: SB, RB, K
Special Features: On south shore of Lake Tahoe. Gift shop. Video arcade.

Tahoe Biltmore Lodge & Casino
#5 Highway 28/P.O. Box 115
Crystal Bay, Nevada 89402
(775) 831-0660
Website: www.tahoebiltmore.com

Reservation Number: (800) BILTMOR
Rooms: 92 Price Range: $59-$119
Suites: 7 Price Range: $129-$169
Restaurants: 2 (1 open 24 hours)
Casino Size: 10,480 Square Feet
Other Games: SB, RB, K
Fun Book: Show out-of-state ID at casino cage
Special Features: On north shore of Lake Tahoe. All rooms include free breakfast. Video arcade.

Las Vegas

Map Location: **#1**

Las Vegas is truly the casino capital of the world! While many years ago the city may have had a reputation as an "adult playground" run by "shady characters," today's Las Vegas features many family-oriented facilities run by some of America's most familiar corporate names.

Las Vegas has more hotel rooms - 130,000 - than any other city in the U.S. and it attracts more than 31 million visitors each year. The abundance of casinos in Las Vegas forces them to compete for customers in a variety of ways and thus, there are always great bargains to be had, but only if you know where to look.

Las Vegas Advisor newsletter publisher, Anthony Curtis is the city's resident expert on where to find the best deals. His monthly 12-page publication is always chock full of powerful, money-saving, profit-making, and vacation enhancing tips for the Las Vegas visitor and here are some of his thoughts on the Best of Las Vegas:

Best Las Vegas Bargain
Shrimp Cocktail, 99¢, Golden Gate

The Golden Gate's 99¢ shrimp cocktail is not only the current best bargain in town, it's been one of the best for more than 40 years. The six-ounce sundae glass full of shrimp was introduced back in 1957 for 50¢ and remained at that price until it was raised to 99¢ in 1991. All shrimp. No filler. Served 24 hours a day.

Best Room Rate
Free, Las Vegas Hotel-Casinos

The only other vacation scenario that includes this possibility involves a tent, sleeping bag, and a lot of wilderness. Why would casinos give rooms away? Competition. Hotels with 3,000, 4,000, and 5,000 rooms open, and the owners of hotels with only 1,000 or 2,000 rooms get nervous. Lulls, city-wide occupancy levels sometimes plummet below 90%, especially in December. Gasp! But mostly, it's the gambling. Gambling winnings subsidize the room department (and the food department, and the alcohol department, and the entertainment department, and ...). The best way to get in on the free-room bonanza is to join slot clubs.

Best Loss Leader
5¢ Coffee, Westward Ho

Coffee is cheap, but it's not this cheap. For a super nostalgia blast from the past, grab a cuppa Joe at the Ho for just a nickel at Nickel Nick's snack bar. Another five red cents and two thin dimes get you a fresh donut. Throw in an eight-bit newspaper and you've got the All-American breakfast for less than one smacker.

Best Breakfast
Fantasy Market Buffet, Palms, $5.99

Breakfast buffets rank among the best bargains in Las Vegas, and the best in town is at the Palms. In addition to the usual breakfast fare, the Palms' Fantasy Market Buffet features cooked-to-order omelets, eggs Benedict, knishes, fresh potato pancakes, and a complete Hawaiian breakfast of Portuguese sausage, eggs, and rice—all for $5.95.

Best Buffet
Feast Around the World, Texas Station, $4.99-$10.99

The Texas Station Feast now takes top honors among Las Vegas' 50 or so buffet offerings. It's another multi-station superbuffet, offering Italian, Mexican, Chinese, seafood, barbecue, a big dessert selection, and even a chili bar. Already a fantastic buffet for the price, last year the price was lowered during the summer to an unbelievable $6.99 for dinner.

Best Sunday Brunch
Bally's, $53

A vacation-topping Sunday brunch is the perfect Las Vegas splurge, and the epic Sterling Brunch at Bally's is as good as it gets. Despite being the highest-priced spread in town, the Sterling Brunch still qualifies as a bargain, offering sushi, oysters and clams, lobster tail, prime meats, and fantastic desserts, including goblets of fresh berries. The brand of champagne changes, but it's always a step or two above that served at the other brunches.

Best Meal
Steak Dinner, $4.95, Ellis Island

Carrying on the tradition of the legendary Las Vegas steak dinners is the Ellis Island "filet-cut" sirloin. This complete dinner comes with choice of soup or salad, baked potato, and garlic toast for just $4.95. The 10-ounce steak is thick, so it can be cooked perfectly to specifications. Though available 24 hours a day seven days a week in the cafe, this great dinner is listed nowhere on the menu; you have to ask for it.

Best Snack Bar
Binion's Horseshoe

The two 24-hour snack bars at Binion's Horseshoe are still tops in town. The soup of the day is $2, the greasy-but-tasty chili is $3, and the turkey sandwiches—still made from real turkey—are $3.50. The best deal remains the daily chef's special of ham and beans (a different bean every day), served with cornbread, for $3.

Best Prime Rib
California, $5.99

As the prices of prime rib specials rises around town, the long-running special in the downtown California's coffee shop is still just $5.99. The meal comes with an all-you-can-eat salad bar, vegetable, rolls, and cherries jubilee for dessert. If the lines are long, look for a seat at the big counter. Hours sometimes change, but this one's usually available 5-10 p.m. daily.

Best Freebie
Pirate Show, TI

The famous pirate show in front of TI (formerly Treasure Island) has been revamped to convey a sexier theme. Who cares—it's still one of Las Vegas' great free shows with lots of swashbuckling action and a ship that actually sinks. It plays six times a night, weather cooperating, every 90 minutes starting at 4:30 p.m. The best viewing area, at the north end of the veranda at the Battle Bar, should be staked out as early as 45 minutes prior to show times. Another good viewing locale is the plank bridge between the ships, as close to the frigate-side rope railing as possible. It is necessary to arrive at least 30 minutes prior to show time to secure a good spot. It's a good show for young children, unless they are bothered by crowds, in which case you should watch from the sidewalk across the street.

Best Funbook
Casino Royale,
Free (for new slot club sign-ups)

You have to be a new slot-club member to get it, but the best funbook in town is at the center-Strip Casino Royale. The offers change, but almost always include several powerful gambling coupons. Recent versions have had values exceeding $100.

Unlike New Jersey, the Nevada Gaming Control Board does not break down its slot statistics by individual properties. Rather, they are classified by area.

The annual gaming revenue report breaks the Las Vegas market down into two major areas: the Strip and downtown. There is also a very big locals market in Las Vegas and those casinos are shown in the gaming revenue report as the Boulder Strip and North Las Vegas areas.

When choosing where to do your slot gambling, you may to keep in mind the following slot payback percentages for Nevada's fiscal year beginning July 1, 2002 and ending June 30, 2003:

5¢ Slot Machines
The Strip - 90.32%
Downtown - 91.50%
Boulder Strip - **93.03%**
N. Las Vegas - 92.97%

25¢ Slot Machines
The Strip - 92.59%
Downtown - 94.83%
Boulder Strip - 96.47%
N. Las Vegas - **96.63%**

$1 Slot Machines
The Strip - 94.67%
Downtown - 95.35%
Boulder Strip - 96.48%
N. Las Vegas - **97.21%**

$1 Megabucks Machines
The Strip - 89.12%
Downtown - 88.55%
Boulder Strip - 87.76%
N. Las Vegas - **89.41%**

$5 Slot Machines
The Strip - 95.33%
Downtown - 95.61%
Boulder Strip - **96.53%**
N. Las Vegas - 96.50%

All Slot Machines
The Strip - 93.85%
Downtown - 94.32%
Boulder Strip - **95.34%**
N. Las Vegas - 95.32%

These numbers reflect the percentage of money returned to the players on each denomination of machine. All electronic machines including slots, video poker and video keno are included in these numbers and the highest-paying returns are shown in bold print.

As you can see, the machines in downtown Las Vegas pay out 1% to 2% more than those located on the Las Vegas Strip for the lower denomination 5¢ and 25¢ machines. When you get to the $1 and $5 machines the difference is less noticeable but you can clearly see that the downtown casinos almost always return more than the Strip area casinos. This information is pretty well known by the locals and that's why many of them do their slot gambling away from the Strip unless they are drawn by a special slot club benefit or promotion.

Returns even better than the downtown casinos can be found at some of the other locals casinos along Boulder Highway such as Boulder Station and Sam's Town and also in the North Las Vegas area which would include the Fiesta, Santa Fe and Texas Station casinos. Not only are those numbers among the best returns in the Las Vegas area, they are also among the best payback percentages for anywhere in the United States.

One area where the Strip casinos do offer an advantage over the locals casinos is in the game of blackjack. You will find that all downtown and North Las Vegas casinos will "hit" a soft 17 (a total of 17 with an ace counted as 11 rather than one). This is a slight disadvantage (-0.20%) for the player and the Strip casinos do not hit a soft 17.

As mentioned before, one of the best sources for finding out about the best "deals" on a current basis in the Las Vegas area is the *Las Vegas Advisor*. It is a 12-page monthly newsletter published by gaming expert Anthony Curtis. *Las Vegas Advisor* accepts no advertising and each issue objectively analyzes the best values in lodging, dining, entertainment and gambling to help you get the most for your money when visiting Las Vegas. The newsletter is especially well known for its "Top Ten Values" column which is often quoted by major travel publications. Each subscription also comes with a benefit package valued at more than $600. Ordering information for *Las Vegas Advisor* can be found later in this section.

There are many free tourist magazines that run coupon offers for casino fun books or special deals. Some sample titles are: *Tour Guide, Showbiz, What's On In Las Vegas, Best Read Guide* and *Today in Las Vegas.* All of these magazines are usually available in the hotel/motel lobbies or in the rooms themselves. If a fun book listing in this section says to look for an ad in a magazine, then it can probably be found in one of these publications.

For Nevada tourism information call (800) NEVADA-8. For Las Vegas information call the city's Convention & Visitors Authority at (702) 892-0711, or visit their Website at: www.lasvegas24hours.com.

Other games in the casino listings include: sports book (SB), race book (RB), Spanish 21 (S21), baccarat (B), mini-baccarat (MB), pai gow (PG), poker (P), pai gow poker (PGP), Caribbean stud poker (CSP), let it ride (LIR), three-card poker (TCP), red dog (RD), big 6 wheel (B6), sic bo (SIC), keno (K) and bingo (BG).

Aladdin Hotel & Casino
3667 Las Vegas Boulevard S.
Las Vegas, Nevada 89109
(702) 785-5555
Website: www.aladdincasino.com

Reservation Number: (877) 333-9474
Rooms: 1,878 Price Range: $99-$299
Parlor Rooms: 466 Price Range: $279-$349
Suites: 223 Price Range: $299-$1,199
Restaurants: 21
Buffets: B-$11.99/$17.99 (Sat-Sun)
L-$13.99 D-$19.99
Casino Size: 102,916 Square Feet
Other Games: SB, RB, B, MB, PG, PGP,
CSP, LIR, TCP
Special Features: 130-store retail mall. 7,000-seat Theater of the Performing Arts. Health spa and salon.

Arizona Charlie's - Boulder
4575 Boulder Highway
Las Vegas, Nevada 89121
(702) 951-9000
Website: www.azcharlies.com

Reservation Number: (888) 236-9066
Rooms: 300 Price Range: $35-$65
Restaurants: 3 (1 open 24 hours)
Buffets: B-$4.29 L-$5.75 D-$7.75
Casino Size: 35,500 Square Feet
Other Games: SB, RB, PGP, BG
Senior Discount: 10% off buffet, if 55 or older
Special Features: 239-space RV park. $2.49 steak & eggs special.

Arizona Charlie's - Decatur
740 S. Decatur Boulevard
Las Vegas, Nevada 89107
(702) 258-5200
Website: www.azcharlies.com

Reservation Number: (800) 342-2695
Rooms: 245 Price Range: $34-$89
Suites: 10 Price Range: $75-$195
Restaurants: 5 (1 open 24 hours)
Buffets: B-$4.29 L-$5.75 D-$7.75
Casino Size: 63,933 Square Feet
Other Games: SB, RB, P, PGP, LIR, K, BG
Senior Discount: 10% off buffet, if 55 or older
Special Features: 24-hour 50-lane bowling center. Video arcade. $2.49 steak/eggs special.

Bally's Las Vegas
3645 Las Vegas Blvd. South
Las Vegas, Nevada 89109
(702) 739-4111
Website: www.ballyslv.com

Toll-Free Number: (800) 7-BALLYS
Reservation Number: (888) 215-1078
Rooms: 2,814 Price Range: $59-$220
Suites: 265 Price Range: $160-$499
Restaurants: 6 (1 open 24 hours)
Buffets: B-$10.95 L-$12.95 D-$17.95
Casino Size: 68,278 Square Feet
Other Games: SB, RB, S21, B, MB, PG, PGP
CSP, LIR, TCP, SIC, B6, K
Senior Discount: 15% off rooms, if 50 or older
Fun Book: Given to hotel guests at check-in
Special Features: 20 retail stores. Free monorail to MGM Grand. "Jubilee" stage show.

Barbary Coast Hotel & Casino
3595 Las Vegas Blvd. South
Las Vegas, Nevada 89109
(702) 737-7111
Website: www.barbarycoastcasino.com

Reservation Number: (888) 227-2279
Rooms: 200 Price Range: $59-$109
Suites: 12 Price Range: Casino Use Only
Restaurants: 3 (1 open 24 hours)
Casino Size: 32,000 Square Feet
Other Games: SB, RB, MB, LIR, TCP, PGP
Fun Book: Given to hotel guests at check-in
and to new slot club sign-ups
Special Features: Located in the heart of the Strip.

Barcelona Hotel & Casino
5011 E. Craig Road
Las Vegas, Nevada 89115
(702) 644-6300
Website: www.barcelonalasvegas.com

Toll-Free Number: (800) 223-6330
Rooms: 178 Price Range: $25-$60
Restaurants: 1 (open 24 hours)
Casino Size: 2,220 Square Feet
Other Games: SB, RB, No Craps
Senior Discount: $5 off room, if 62, or older,
Special Features: Special weekly and monthly room rates. $5 AAA room discount.

Bellagio
3600 Las Vegas Blvd. South
Las Vegas, Nevada 89109
(702) 693-7111
Website: www.bellagioresort.com

Reservation Number: (888) 987-6667
Rooms: 2,688 Price Range: $129-$469
Suites: 308 Price Range: $325-$5,500
Restaurants: 12 (2 open 24 hours)
Buffets: B-$12.95/$21.95 (Sat-Sun)
L-$15.95 D-$24.55/$31.95 (Fri-Sat)
Casino Size: 156,257 Square Feet
Other Games: SB, RB, B, MB, P, PG, SIC
PGP, CSP, LIR, TCP, B6, K
Special Features: Lake with nightly light and water show. Shopping mall. Two wedding chapels. Beauty salon and spa. Cirque du Soleil's "O" stage show.

Binion's Horseshoe Casino and Hotel
128 E. Fremont Street
Las Vegas, Nevada 89101
(702) 382-1600
Website: www.binions.com

Toll-Free Number: (800) 937-6537
Reservation Number: (800) 622-6468
Rooms: 300 Price Range: $29-$189
Suites: 34 Price Range: $55-$500
Restaurants: 3 (1 open 24 hours)
Casino Size: 48,429 Square Feet
Other Games: SB, RB, MB, P, LIR,
TCP, B6, K
Special Features: Home of World Series of Poker. Steak House on 23rd floor offers panoramic views of Las Vegas.

Boardwalk Hotel and Casino
3750 Las Vegas Blvd. South
Las Vegas, Nevada 89109
(702) 735-2400
Website: www.hiboardwalk.com

Reservation Number: (800) 635-4581
Rooms: 645 Price Range: $59-$129
Suites: 11 Price Range: $125-$750
Restaurants: 5 (2 open 24 hours)
Buffets: B-$6.99 L-$7.99 D-$9.99
Casino Size: 23,000 Square Feet
Other Games: SB, RB, LIR, TCP
Special Features: 24-hour buffet.

Boulder Station Hotel & Casino
4111 Boulder Highway
Las Vegas, Nevada 89121
(702) 432-7777
Website: www.stationcasinos.com

Toll-Free Number: (800) 981-5577
Reservation Number: (800) 683-7777
Rooms: 300 Price Range: $29-$109
Restaurants: 13 (1 open 24 hours)
Buffets: B-$4.99 L-$6.99 D-$9.99
Casino Size: 89,433 Square Feet
Other Games: SB, RB, MB, P, PGP,
LIR, TCP, K, BG
Special Features: $1.49 Sauza margaritas. 11-screen movie complex. Kid Quest childcare center.

Caesars Palace
3570 Las Vegas Blvd. South
Las Vegas, Nevada 89109
(702) 731-7110
Website: www.caesars.com

Toll-Free Number: (800) 634-6001
Reservation Number: (800) 634-6661
Rooms: 2,469 Price Range: $99-$500
Suites: 250 Price Range: $450-$5,000
Restaurants: 9 (1 open 24 hours)
Buffets: B-$13.99 L-$15.99/$19.99 (Sat-Sun)
D-$21.99
Casino Size: 149,200 Square Feet
Other Games: SB, RB, S21, B, MB, PG,
PGP, CSP, LIR, TCP, B6, K
Special Features: Health spa. Beauty salon. Shopping mall with 125 stores and interactive attractions. "Celine Dion" stage show.

The Best Places To Play In Las Vegas

Roulette - The best roulette game in Las Vegas can be found in the London Club at the Aladdin which has single-zero wheel with a surrender rule in effect. Single-zero roulette has only a 2.70% edge as compared to the usual 5.26% edge on a double-zero roulette wheel. Additionally, the surrender rule means that if you make an even-money bet (odd-even, red-black, or high-low) and zero comes in, then you only lose half of your bet. This lowers the house edge to just 1.35% on those particular bets. The minimum demonination chip is $5 and the minimum bet is $5 inside/$25 outside.

Single-zero wheels, without a surrender rule, can be found at Monte Carlo (only open Friday and Saturday evenings), Stratosphere, MGM Grand, Caesars Palace, Bellagio, Mandalay Bay, Paris and Venetian. The house edge in this game is 2.70%. Be aware, however, that all of these casinos offer single-zero wheels at just some of their roulette games and not all of them. Only the Stratosphere offers $5 minimum bets, the minimum is $25 at all others (sometimes $10 during the day), except for Bellagio and Mandalay Bay ($100 minimums).

Craps - Only one casino allows up to 100x odds on their crap tables: Casino Royale (minimum bet is $3).

Blackjack - All recommendations in this section apply to basic strategy players. For single-deck games players should always look for casinos that pay the standard 7.5-to-5 for blackjacks. A recent trend is for many casinos (mostly on the Strip) to only pay 6-to-5 for blackjack and this increases the casino edge in this game tremendously (from .06% to 1.45%).

The best single-deck game is at Fiesta Rancho which offers a game with a casino edge of .06%. The rules are: dealer hits soft 17, double down on any first two cards, split any pair, re-split any pair (except aces), and double after splitting. Next best is a similar game offered at the Horseshoe where they won't let you double after splitting but you are allowed to re-split aces. The casino advantage in this game is .15%

Next best are seven casinos that offer single-deck with the same rules as the Fiesta, except they don't allow doubling after splitting: El Cortez, Four Queens, Golden Gate, Gold Spike, Hacienda, Lady Luck, Las Vegas Club, Silverton and the Western. The casino edge here is .18%.

The best double-deck game in Las Vegas is offered at Caesars Palace with the following rules: dealer stands on soft 17, double down on any first two cards, re-split any pair (except aces), double down after split and late surrender. This works out to a casino edge of just .14% but there is a minimum bet requirement of $100.

Next best are 10 casinos that offer those same rules, except for late surrender: Venetian, Bellagio, Mirage, Palms, Luxor, New York New York, Riviera, San Remo, Stardust and Treasure Island. The casino edge in these games is .19%. Keep in mind that these games aren't offered at every table, just some of them, so you'll have to look around each casino to find these better game. Also, many of these casinos will require higher minimum bets (usually $50 and up). The lowest minimums can be found at the Riviera, Stardust and San Remo which all have $5 or $10 minimums.

For six-deck shoe games the best casinos have these rules: dealer stands on soft 17, double after split allowed, late surrender offered and resplitting of aces allowed. The casino edge in this game works out to .26% and you can find it at many of the major casino properties: Bellagio, Caesars Palace, Golden Nugget, Luxor, Palms, Monte Carlo, Aladdin, Mandalay Bay, MGM Grand, Mirage, New York New York, Hard Rock, Treasure Island and the Venetian. The minimum bet at some of these casinos can be as high as $50 but a few are as low as $10 (MGM Grand). Many of these casinos also offer this same game with identical rules except that they will hit soft 17. The limits in the game are lower ($5 to $10) but the casino's mathematical edge in this game is raised to .46% Casinos offering this version of the game are: Treasure Island, Palms, Golden Nugget and New York New York. Two casinos, Monte Carlo and Venetian, also offer an eight-deck game with the same rules as the .26% six-deck game. This raises the casino advantage to .49%.

Video Poker - Video Poker - Las Vegas is the best place in the world for video poker. The three best varieties to look for are: 9/6 Jacks or Better, 10/7 Double Bonus and full-pay Deuces Wild. By only playing these three kinds of machines, playing the maximum coin and using perfect strategy you can achieve, theoretically, the following payback percentages: 99.54% on 9/6 Jacks or Better, 100.17% on 10/7 Double Bonus and 100.76% on full-pay Deuces Wild. All three kinds can be found in 25-cent denominations in the following casinos: Arizona Charlie's (Boulder and Decatur), California, Casino Montelago, El Cortez, both Fiestas, Palms, Plaza, Sam's Town, San Remo, Santa Fe, Texas Station, Palace Station, and Silverton. By restricting your play to just these machines and taking advantage of the slot club benefits offered at these casinos you should be able to play at a 100%+ level.

$1 full-pay Deuces Wild machines are extremely rare (if not extinct) but 9/6 games can be found at the $1 level in many casinos ($1 10/7 games are rarer).

On the Strip generally the best machines you will find are 9/6 Jacks or Better which can be found in nearly every casino. Generally, 9/6 for dollars is most prevalent at Strip casinos, while at off-Strip casinos quarter games are easier to find. The only Strip locations to offer 10/7 Double Bonus are Circus Circus, Riviera, San Remo and Stratosphere. Only the Boardwalk and San Remo offer full pay Deuces Wild on the Strip.

Another good game, Pick 'Em is less common, but at 99.9%, it is often the best game that can be found on the Strip. PE can be found in Bally's Gamemakers at New York New York, LV Hilton, Bally's, Paris, Flamingo, Fremont, Gold Coast, and Casino Montelago.

Equally important to visitors are slot clubs that will readily provide free rooms and food. The Las Vegas Hilton sends out good free room offers and has the strongest cashback in town (1.1% for slots and .55% for video poker). New York New York, Bellagio, Venetian and Treasure Island are notable for decent video poker, luxurious accommodations and great room offers.

Slots - For slot players it pays to play where the machines are set to return the most. According to the Nevada Gaming Control Board, for the fiscal year ending June 30, 2003, the average Las Vegas Strip slot machine returned 93.85% while the average downtown casino's slots returned 94.32%. Higher returns, however, could be found in north Las Vegas which is home to the "locals" casinos: Fiesta, Jerry's Nugget, Texas Station and Santa Fe Station. The average return on these machines was 95.32%. Even marginally better returns could be found among the Boulder Highway and Henderson casinos such as Sam's Town, Boulder Station and Fiesta where the average return was 95.34%.

California Hotel & Casino
12 Ogden Avenue
Las Vegas, Nevada 89101
(702) 385-1222
Website: www.thecal.com

Reservation Number: (800) 634-6505
Rooms: 781 Price Range: $39-$110
Suites: 74 Price Range: Casino Use Only
Restaurants: 4 (1 open 24 hours)
Casino Size: 35,848 Square Feet
Other Games: SB, PGP, LIR, TCP, K
Special Features: 93-space RV park. Offers many charter packages from Hawaii.

Casino Royale & Hotel
3411 Las Vegas Blvd. South
Las Vegas, Nevada 89109
(702) 737-3500
Website: www.casinoroyalehotel.com

Toll-Free Number: (800) 854-7666
Rooms: 151 Price Range: $39-$99
Suites: 3 Price Range: $150-$299
Restaurants: 3 (1 open 24 hours)
Casino Size: 15,000 Square Feet
Other Games: S21, CSP
Fun Book: Given with slot initial club sign-up
Special Features: TCBY, Denny's and Subway. Refrigerator in every room. Low-limit games.

Castaways Hotel Casino & Bowling Center
2800 Fremont Street
Las Vegas, Nevada 89104
(702) 385-9123
Website: www.castaways-lv.com

Reservation Number: (800) 826-2800
Rooms: 416 Price Range: $29-$89
Suites: 4 Price Range: $99-$199
Restaurants: 3 (1 open 24 hours)
Casino Size: 74,300 Square Feet
Other Games: SB, RB, PGP, TCP, K, BG
Special Features: 106-lane bowling center.

Circus Circus Hotel & Casino
2880 Las Vegas Blvd. South
Las Vegas, Nevada 89109
(702) 734-0410
Website: www.circuscircus.com

Reservation Number: (800) 634-3450
Rooms: 3,770 Price Range: $34-$139
Suites: 122 Price Range: $99-$278
Restaurants: 9 (2 open 24 hours)
Buffets: B-$7.99 L-$7.99 D-$8.99
Casino Size: 107,195 Square Feet
Other Games: SB, RB, MB, P, PGP, CSP, LIR, TCP, B6, K
Special Features: Free circus acts 11 a.m. to midnight. 370-space RV park. Wedding chapel. Midway and arcade games. Indoor theme park.

El Cortez Hotel & Casino
600 E. Fremont Street
Las Vegas, Nevada 89101
(702) 385-5200
Website: www.elcortezhotelcasino.com

Reservation Number: (800) 634-6703
Rooms: 299 Price Range: $25-$45
Suites: 10 Price Range: $40-$47
Restaurants: 2 (1 open 24 hours)
Casino Size: 45,300 Square Feet
Other Games: SB, RB, MB, P, PGP, K
Special Features: Video arcade. Gift shop and ice cream parlor. Barber shop. Beauty salon.

Ellis Island Casino
4178 Koval Lane
Las Vegas, Nevada 89109
(702) 734-8638
Website: www.ellisislandcasino.com

Restaurants: 2
Casino Size: 12,466 Square Feet
Other Games: SB
Special Features: Super 8 Motel next door. Microbrewery. $4.95 steak dinner. Single-deck blackjack.

Free Things To See In Las Vegas!

Masquerade Village

The Masquerade Show in the Sky is a $25-million extravaganza in the sky and on the stage at the Rio Hotel & Casino. Five floats travel on an overhead track above the casino, while numerous dancers, musicians, aerialists and stiltwalkers perform on stage, or from attractions that drop from the ceiling or from two circular lifts that rise from the floor.

There are four differently themed shows on a rotating schedule daily at 3:30, 4:30, 5:30, 7, 8, 9 and 10 p.m.

Excalibur Hotel/Casino
3850 Las Vegas Blvd. South
Las Vegas, Nevada 89109
(702) 597-7777
Website: www.excaliburcasino.com

Reservation Number: (800) 937-7777
Rooms: 4,008 Price Range: $49-$209
Suites: 46 Price Range: $275-$375
Restaurants: 5 (1 open 24 hours)
Buffets: B-$8.99 L-$9.99 D-$11.49
Casino Size: 121,544 Square Feet
Other Games: SB, RB, S21, MB, P, PGP, CSP, LIR, TCP, B6, K
Special Features: Canterbury wedding chapel. Fun Book: Given to hotel guests at check-in Strolling Renaissance entertainers. Video arcade and midway games. Nightly "Tournament of Kings" dinner show.

Fiesta Casino Hotel
See North Las Vegas section

Fitzgeralds Las Vegas
301 Fremont Street
Las Vegas, Nevada 89101
(702) 388-2400
Website: www.fitzgeralds.com

Reservation Number: (800) 274-5825
Rooms: 634 Price Range: $28-$80
Suites: 14 Price Range: $100-$250
Restaurants: 4 (1 open 24 hours)
Buffets: B-$6.49/$7.99 L-$5.99 D-$9.99/$12.99 (Wed)
Casino Size: 42,301 Square Feet
Other Games: S21, LIR, TCP, K
Fun Book: Coupons given at promotions kiosk
Senior Discount: 10% off room, if 55 or older

Flamingo Las Vegas
3555 Las Vegas Blvd. South
Las Vegas, Nevada 89109
(702) 733-3111
Website: www.flamingolasvegas.com

Reservation Number: (800) 732-2111
Rooms: 3,565 Price Range: $60-$250
Suites: 215 Price Range: $350-$750
Restaurants: 8 (1 open 24 hours)
Buffets: B-$8.75 L-$10.95 D-$15.95
Casino Size: 76,763 Square Feet
Casino Marketing: (800) 225-4882
Other Games: SB, RB, S21, B, MB, P, PGP, CSP, LIR, TCP, SIC, B6, K
Special Features: Health Spa. Shopping arcade. Afternoon "Bottoms Up" stage show.

Four Queens Hotel/Casino
202 Fremont Street
Las Vegas, Nevada 89101
(702) 385-4011
Website: www.fourqueens.com

Reservation Number: (800) 634-6045
Rooms: 690 Price Range: $35-$89
Suites: 48 Price Range: $74-$240
Restaurants: 4 (1 open 24 hours)
Casino Size: 27,389 Square Feet
Other Games: SB, RB, PGP, CSP, LIR, TCP, K
Special Features: 99¢ shrimp cocktail.

Fremont Hotel & Casino
200 E. Fremont Street
Las Vegas, Nevada 89101
(702) 385-3232
Website: www.fremontcasino.com

Reservation Number: (800) 634-6460
Rooms: 428 Price Range: $35-$99
Suites: 24 Price Range: Casino Use Only
Restaurants: 4 (1 open 24 hours)
Buffets: B-$5.79 L-$6.49 D-$9.99/ $11.99 (Wed/Sat)/$14.99 (Sun/Tue/Fri)
Casino Size: 30,244 Square Feet
Other Games: SB, RB, PGP, CSP, LIR, TCP, K
Special Features: 99¢ shrimp cocktail.

Gold Coast Hotel & Casino
4000 W. Flamingo Road
Las Vegas, Nevada 89103
(702) 367-7111
Website: www.goldcoastcasino.com

Toll-Free Number: (888) 402-6278
Rooms: 750 Price Range: $32-$139
Suites: 27 Price Range: $150-$225
Restaurants: 5 (1 open 24 hours)
Buffets: B-$4.95/$9.95 (Sun) L-$6.95 D-$9.95/$10.95 (Sun)
Casino Size: 71,000 Square Feet
Other Games: SB, RB, MB, PGP, TCP, K, BG
Special Features: 70-lane bowling center. Showroom. Free childcare. $8.95 Texas T-bone steak special in coffee shop.

Gold Spike Hotel & Casino
400 E. Ogden Avenue
Las Vegas, Nevada 89101
(702) 384-8444
Website: www.goldspikehotelcasino.com

Reservation Number: (800) 634-6703
Rooms: 100 Price Range: $25-$30
Suites: 7 Price Range: $35-$40
Restaurants: 1 (open 24 hours)
Casino Size: 5,820 Square Feet
Other Games: BG, No Craps or Roulette

Golden Gate Hotel & Casino
One Fremont Street
Las Vegas, Nevada 89101
(702) 385-1906
Website: www.goldengatecasino.net/index.cfm

Reservation Number: (800) 426-1906
Rooms: 106 Price Range: $32-$55
Restaurants: 2 (2 open 24 hours)
Casino Size: 9,090 Square Feet
Other Games: SB, RB, CSP, LIR
Special Features: 99¢ shrimp cocktail. Oldest hotel in Vegas (opened 1906).

The Golden Nugget
129 E. Fremont Street
Las Vegas, Nevada 89101
(702) 385-7111
Website: www.goldennugget.com

Toll-Free Number: (800) 634-3403
Reservation Number: (800) 634-3454
Rooms: 1,805 Price Range: $54-$139
Suites: 102 Price Range: $175-$3,750
Restaurants: 5 (1 open 24 hours)
Buffets: B-$6.75 L-$7.75 D-$11.75 Sunday-$12.75 All Buffets
Casino Size: 34,680 Square Feet
Other Games: SB, RB, MB, PGP, CSP, LIR, TCP, B6, K
Special Features: World's largest gold nugget (61 pounds) on display.

The Best Vegas Values

By H. Scot Krause

Welcome to "Vegas Values!" For those of you who may be unfamiliar with the title, it's an exclusive weekly column found only at: www.americancasinoguide.com, the companion website to this book. The column is updated weekly with what we consider to be some of the best, current entertainment, gambling and dining values, and promotions located throughout Las Vegas. Tune in and click on every week beginning Sunday for the latest news and information for the upcoming week, along with a steady, growing list of ongoing promotions. Listed below are examples and excerpts from the "Vegas Values" column. We hope at least some of the listings are enlightening for you and will help you enjoy your Las Vegas vacation a little more by taking advantage of these promotions and specials.

Barbary Coast: Offering a 24-hour Prime Rib or 16 oz. T-Bone Special in The Victorian Room for $11.95. Dinners include soup or salad and choice of potato. (Note: This is a small Coffee Shop-type restaurant and is often crowded and on a waiting list. Try off-peak times for faster service or arrive early to put your name on the waiting list before you play there).

Binion's Horseshoe: Tuesday Night Slot Tournaments. Players get an entry into the tournaments by earning a minimum of 5,000 points each week prior to the tournaments. A total of $1,750 is awarded in cash prizes. The slot tournament prize money breakdown is as follows: 1st $750; 2nd $500; 3rd $250; 4th $150; 5th $100; plus session money of $25 for the highest score from each round. A maximum of 100 people are accepted to play in the tournament which begins at 7:00 p.m. so it's best to qualify early and reserve your spot. They also offer similar style Video Poker Tournaments held on Thursday nights. (Tip: Use the coupons from this year's edition of the American Casino Guide for FREE tournament entries!)

Boulder Station: Purchase an entree at Guadalajara (Mexican Restaurant) on your birthday and receive a FREE Dessert.

Caesars Palace: Earn your first 10 points and receive a FREE Medallion; earn 75 and get a FREE Connection Cap; earn 125 points and receive a FREE T-shirt. The gifts are all free so you can keep your points for additional cash back and comps.

California: The Market Street Cafe offers a daily Prime Rib Special that includes salad bar, entree, potato, vegetable, and cherries jubilee over ice cream for dessert for $5.99. Ask for it if you don't see it on the menu.

Cannery: Offering an ongoing promotion of a 100-coin bonus on the four-of-a-kind card-of the-day. See complete details posted in the casino.

Casino MonteLago: Opened at Lake Las Vegas in May, 2003. Advertising the most 100%+ Video Poker machines in Las Vegas. Club Uno pays .25% in comps or "Free Play." Over 600 multi-denomination Video Poker games paying back 100% or more with optimal play.

Ellis Island: New members signing up for the Passport Player's Club currently receive 5,000 FREE slot club points (a $5.00 value, although you cannot redeem them until you reach at least 10,000 points in the club,) plus a Deck of Cards.

Four Queens: New members signing up for the Reel Winner's slot club receive a FREE t-shirt with 40 points earned in first 24 hours of play.

Gold Coast: They have long offered one of the best steak specials in all of Las Vegas. It's a huge Texas T-Bone that includes potato, onion rings, Texas toast, baked beans and a 16 oz. draft beer, all for $8.95. It's available 24 hours a day, seven days a week.

Las Vegas Hilton: Ongoing dining specials: Steak & Pasta Dinner 5 -11 pm. and Steak & Eggs Breakfast 11 p.m. to 5 a.m., each $4.95 in the Paradise Café.

Main Street Station: An often overlooked promotion called "Score with Four," continues at MSS. Hit any 4-of-a-kind, straight flush, royal flush or 300-coin slot win and receive a scratch card for additional cash. Most of the scratch cards are of the $1.00 to $5.00 variety, but they claim to offer cards valued at $20, $50 and $100, as well as rare $5,000 cards.

Orleans: Play the Big Easy Sunday Night Free Entry Keno Contest. No minimum buy-in. Just register at the Keno Department for the contest before you play, with a chance to win the first prize of $500. Second place is $200 and prizes are awarded through fifth place, for cash and dinners. Contest starts at 5:30 p.m. every Sunday night.

Orleans and Suncoast: Late-night Breakfast Specials served in the coffee shop including Steak and Eggs with potatoes and toast for $1.95 and three additional breakfast specials for 99 cents each. Served from midnight to 9:00 a.m. at Suncoast, and midnight to 7:00 a.m. at Orleans, to guests over 21 years of age.

Palms: Earn 600 points in any one day and receive a $3.00 off coupon for the Fantasy Market Buffet. Ongoing promotion. After earning the 600 points, visit the Club Palms slot club booth for your voucher.

Sam's Town: Willy & Jose's birthday special is a FREE T-Shirt, FREE Margarita and a FREE Desert with a minimum of $10 entrée purchase on your birthday.

Tropicana: Has a "FREE PULL" Slot Machine located on the strip right in front of the hotel entrance. Prizes range from cash, to show tickets, to meal comps. Minimum prize is usually a coupon book, drink coupon, or a deck of cards.

Wild Wild West: Serves an eight-ounce burger platter complete with fries and all the trimmings for $1.99. Available 24 hours in the coffee shop.

Wildfire Casino: Sign up as a new member for the Rewards Club and receive FREE Slot Play! Visit the slot club booth to pick up a player's card and set your PIN. You will automatically receive free cash slot play (minimum $3) for an amount up to $100 on your new card. Insert your card and enter your PIN in any slot or video poker machine to activate your free play cash. Promotion is for new slot club members only. That's it for this edition...

Luck, royals, good food and jackpots to all...

As a reminder: please remember that all casino promotions are subject to change and may be cancelled at any time by management's discretion. It's always best to call ahead or visit the promotions/slot club booth prior to playing.

H. Scot Krause is a freelance writer and researcher, originally from Cleveland, Ohio. He is an eight year resident of Las Vegas who reports, researches, and writes about casino games, events and promotions for The American Casino Guide as well as other publications and marketing/consulting firms. Questions or comments for Scot may be addressed to The Discussion Board at: www.americancasinoguide.com

Hard Rock Hotel & Casino
4455 Paradise Road
Las Vegas, Nevada 89109
(702) 693-5000
Website: www.hardrockhotel.com

Toll-Free Number: (800) HRD-ROCK
Rooms: 340 Price Range: $59-$299
Suites: 28 Price Range: $350-$500
Restaurants: 2 (1 open 24 hours)
Casino Size: 30,000 Square Feet
Other Games: SB, RB, B, MB, PGP, CSP, LIR, TCP, B6
Special Features: Rock and Roll memorabilia display. Beach Club with cabanas and sandy beaches. Lagoon with underwater music.

Harrah's Las Vegas
3475 Las Vegas Blvd. South
Las Vegas, Nevada 89109
(702) 369-5000
Website: www.harrahs.com

Toll-Free Number: (800) 392-9002
Reservation Number: (800) HARRAHS
Rooms: 2,672 Price Range: $49-$195
Suites: 94 Price Range: $250-$350
Restaurants: 8 (1 open 24 hours)
Buffets: B-$9.99/$15.99 (Sat-Sun) L-$10.99 D-$14.99
Casino Size: 87,700 Square Feet
Other Games: SB, RB, B, MB, PGP, CSP, LIR, TCP, B6, K
Special Features: Mardi Gras-themed casino. "Clint Holmes" stage show. Improv Comedy Club.

Horseshoe Casino and Hotel
See Binion's Horseshoe in this section

Hotel San Remo Casino & Resort
115 East Tropicana Avenue
Las Vegas, Nevada 89109
(702) 739-9000
Website: www.sanremolasvegas.com

Reservation Number: (800) 522-7366
Rooms: 694 Price Range: $29-$149
Suites: 17 Price Range: $109-$209
Restaurants: 4 (1 open 24 hours)
Other Games: SB, LIR, TCP, K
Casino Size: 27,000 Square Feet
Special Features: "Showgirls of Magic" stage show. Comedy Club.

Imperial Palace Hotel & Casino
3535 Las Vegas Blvd. South
Las Vegas, Nevada 89109
(702) 731-3311
Website: www.imperialpalace.com

Reservation Number: (800) 634-6441
Rooms: 2,700 Price Range: $52-$102
Suites: 225 Price Range: $92-$282
Restaurants: 9 (1 open 24 hours)
Buffets: B-$6.25 L-$7.50 D-$8.50
Casino Size: 47,780 Square Feet
Other Games: SB, RB, MB, PGP, CSP, LIR, TCP, B6, K
Casino Marketing: (800) 351-7400
Special Features: Auto museum (admission charge). Video arcade. Wedding chapel. Independent medical facility.

Jerry's Nugget
See North Las Vegas section

Key Largo Casino & Quality Inn
377 East Flamingo Road
Las Vegas, Nevada 89109
(702) 733-7777

Reservation Number: (800) 634-6617
Rooms: 314 Price Range: $40-$129
Restaurants: 1
Casino Size: 9,172 Square Feet
Other Games: SB, RB No Craps
Fun Book: Given to hotel guests at check-in
Senior Discount: 10% off room, if 50 or older
Special Features: All rooms are mini-suites with wet bars/refrigerators. Coin laundry. Gift shop. Free airport/Strip shuttle 8am-11:30pm daily.

Klondike Hotel & Casino
5191 Las Vegas Boulevard S.
Las Vegas, Nevada 89119
(702) 739-9351

Rooms: 150 Price Range: $29-$99
Restaurants: 1
Casino Size: 7,700 Square Feet
Other Games: No Craps

Lady Luck Casino Hotel
206 N. Third Street
Las Vegas, Nevada 89101
(702) 477-3000
Website: www.ladylucklv.com

Toll-Free Number: (800) 634-6580
Room Reservations: (800) LADY-LUCK
Rooms: 792 Price Range: $29-$150
Suites: 134 Price Range: $45-$500
Restaurants: 4 (2 open 24 hours)
Buffets: B-$6.95 D-$10.95/$14.95 (Sat)
Casino Size: 17,150 Square Feet
Other Games: SB, RB, PGP, LIR, TCP
Fun Book: Ask at Mad Money booth

Las Vegas Auto/Truck Plaza
8050 S. Industrial Road
Las Vegas, Nevada 89118
(702) 361-1176

Restaurants: 1 (Open 24 hours)
Casino Size: 1,700 Square Feet
Other Games: TCP, No Craps or Roulette
Special Features: Players Club gives table players comps/discounts in stores and restaurants.

Las Vegas Club Hotel & Casino
18 E. Fremont Street
Las Vegas, Nevada 89101
(702) 385-1664
Website: www.playatlvc.com

Reservation Number: (800) 634-6532
Rooms: 410 Price Range: $29-$89
Suites: 7 Price Range: $129-$200
Restaurants: 4 (1 open 24 hours)
Casino Size: 48,500 Square Feet
Other Games: SB, RB, MB, PGP, K
Special Features: Sports themed-casino with large collection of sports memorabilia.

Las Vegas Hilton
3000 Paradise Road
Las Vegas, Nevada 89109
(702) 732-5111
Website: www.lvhilton.com

Reservation Number: (800) 732-7117
Rooms: 2,956 Price Range: $45-$159
Suites: 305 Price Range: $150-$17,500
Restaurants: 14 (1 open 24 hours)
Buffets: B-$8.99/$12.99 (Sat/Sun)
L-$9.99 D-$13.99
Casino Size: 74,287 Square Feet
Other Games: SB, RB, S21, B, MB, PG, PGP,
CSP, LIR, TCP, B6, K
Casino Marketing: (800) 457-3307
Coupon Book: Given to hotel guests
Special Features: *Star Trek: The Experience* - an interactive adventure. World's largest race and sports book. Health club. Jogging track.

Longhorn Casino
5288 Boulder Highway
Las Vegas, Nevada 89122
(702) 435-9170

Restaurants: 1 (open 24 hours)
Casino Size: 1,675 Square Feet
Other Games: No Craps or Roulette
Special Features: $1 blackjack games.

Luxor Las Vegas
3900 Las Vegas Blvd. South
Las Vegas, Nevada 89119
(702) 262-4000
Website: www.luxor.com

Reservation Number (800) 288-1000
Rooms: 3,962 Price Range: $69-$209
Suites 464 Price Range: $169-$500
Restaurants: 9 (1 open 24 hours)
Buffets: B-$9.99 L-$10.49 D-$16.49
Casino Size: 100,000 Square Feet
Other Games: SB, RB, B, MB, PG, P, PGP,
CSP, LIR, TCP, B6, K
Casino Marketing: (800) 956-0289
Special Features: 30-story pyramid-shaped hotel with Egyptian theme. "Blue Man Group" and "Midnight Fantasy" stage shows.

Free Things To See In Las Vegas!

Buccaneer Bay Battle

To mark the 10th anniversary of Treasure Island (TI). A new show features the Sirens of TI, sexy females who battle it out with a band of renegade male pirates in a modern interpretation of the Battle of Buccaneer Bay.

Live action shows daily at 5:30, 7, 8:30, 10 and 11:30p.m (Fri-Sat only). Lines start forming in front about 45 minutes before showtime. To avoid the huge crowds get there early and then go into the resort and head to the Battle Bar. Grab a table near the railing, order a soda or a domestic draft beer, and for just a few dollars you'll have a front row seat for the show!

Main Street Station Hotel & Casino
200 N. Main Street
Las Vegas, Nevada 89101
(702) 387-1896
Website: www.mainstreetcasino.com

Toll-Free Number: (800) 713-8933
Reservation Number: (800) 465-0711
Rooms: 406 Price Range: $35-$125
Suites: 14 Price Range: Casino Use Only
Restaurants: 4 (1 open 24 hours)
Buffets: B-$5.29/$8.99 (Sat-Sun) L-$7.49
D-$10.29/$14.99 (Fri)/$11.99 (Tue/Thu)
Casino Size: 26,918 Square Feet
Other Games: PGP, LIR, TCP

Mandalay Bay
3950 Las Vegas Blvd. South
Las Vegas, Nevada 89109
(702) 632-7777
Web Sit: www.mandalaybay.com

Reservation Number: (877) 632-7000
Rooms: 3,220 Price Range: $119-$449
Suites: 424 Price Range: $149-$899
Restaurants: 16 (1 open 24 hours)
Buffets: B-$11.75/$21.75 (Sun)
L-$13.75 D-$21.75
Casino Size: 137,540 Square Feet
Other Games: SB, RB, B, MB, P, PG,
PGP, CSP, LIR, TCP, B6
Special Features: 424-room Four Seasons Hotel on 35th-39th floors. *House of Blues* restaurant. Sand and surf beach with lazy river ride. Shark Reef exhibit (admission charge). Spa.

MGM Grand Hotel Casino
3799 Las Vegas Blvd. South
Las Vegas, Nevada 89109
(702) 891-1111
Web-Site: www.mgmgrand.com

Toll-Free Number: (800) 929-1111
Reservation Number: (800) 646-7787
Rooms: 5,005 Price Range: $99-$349
Suites: 752 Price Range: $199-$15,000
Restaurants: 8 (1 open 24 hours)
Buffets: B-$10.99/$14.99 (Sat-Sun)
L-$13.99 D-$19.99
Casino Size: 171,300 Square Feet
Other Games: SB, RB, S21, B, MB, PG,
PGP, CSP, LIR, TCP, B6, K
Special Features: World's largest hotel. Comedy Club. Rainforest Cafe. Midway games and arcade. Free lion habitat exhibit. "Zumanity" and "La Femme" stage shows.

The Mirage
3400 Las Vegas Blvd. South
Las Vegas, Nevada 89109
(702) 791-7111
Website: www.themirage.com

Reservation Number: (800) 627-6667
Rooms: 3,044 Price Range: $99-$399
Suites: 281 Price Range: $275-$2,500
Restaurants: 11 (1 open 24 hours)
Buffets: B-$11.00/$17.50 (Sat-Sun) L-$13.50 D-$17.50
Casino Size: 93,300 Square Feet
Other Games: SB, RB, S21, B, MB, PG, P, PGP, CSP, LIR, TCP, B6, K
Special Features: Siegfried & Roy's Secret Garden and Dolphin Habitat (admission charge). Aquarium display at check-in desk. Royal white tiger habitat viewing area (free). Simulated volcano with periodic "eruptions." "Siegfried & Roy" and "Danny Gans" shows.

Monte Carlo Resort & Casino
3770 Las Vegas Blvd. South
Las Vegas, Nevada 89109
(702) 730-7777
Website: www.montecarlo.com

Reservation Number: (800) 311-8999
Rooms: 3,002 Price Range: $69-$299
Suites: 259 Price Range: $139-$169
Restaurants: 7 (1 open 24 hours)
Buffets: B-$9.99/$15.45 (Sun) L-$10.49 D-$14.49
Casino Size: 102,197 Square Feet
Other Games: SB, RB, B, MB, PG, P, PGP, CSP, LIR, TCP, B6, K
Special Features: Food court with McDonald's, Nathan's, Sbarro's, Haagen Daz and bagel shop. Microbrewery. Pool with lazy river ride. Health spa. 12 retail shops. "Lance Burton, Master Magician" stage show.

Nevada Palace Hotel & Casino
5255 Boulder Highway
Las Vegas, Nevada 89122
(702) 458-8810
Website: www.nvpalace.com

Reservation Number: (800) 634-6283
Rooms: 210 Price Range: $40-$75
Restaurants: 2 (1 open 24 hours)
Buffets: B-$4.99 (Sat-Sun) D-$5.99/$9.99 (Fri)
Casino Size: 15,000 Square Feet
Other Games: SB, K

New Frontier Hotel & Casino
3120 Las Vegas Blvd. South
Las Vegas, Nevada 89109
(702) 794-8200
Website: www.frontierhotelcasino.com

Toll-Free Number: (800) 421-7806
Reservation Number: (800) 634-6966
Rooms: 550 Price Range: $39-$129
Suites: 434 Price Range: $59-$199
Restaurants: 4 (1 open 24 hours)
Buffets: B-$8.95/$12.95 (Sat-Sun) D-$12.95/$15.95 (Fri)
Casino Size: 42,609 Square Feet
Other Games: SB, RB, S21, PGP, CSP, LIR, TCP, B6, K, BG

New York-New York Hotel & Casino
3790 Las Vegas Blvd. South
Las Vegas, Nevada 89109
(702) 740-6969
Website: www.nynyhotelcasino.com

Reservation Number: (800) 693-6763
Rooms: 2,024 Price Range: $75-$189
Suites: 12 Price Range: Casino Use Only
Restaurants: 7 (1 open 24 hours)
Casino Size: 86,754 Square Feet
Other Games: SB, RB, MB, PGP, SIC CSP, LIR, TCP, B6, K
Special Features: Replica Statue of Liberty and Empire State Building. *Manhattan Express* roller coaster. *ESPN Zone* restaurant.

The Orleans Hotel & Casino
4500 W. Tropicana Avenue
Las Vegas, Nevada 89103
(702) 365-7111
Website: www.orleanscasino.com

Reservation Number: (800) ORLEANS
Rooms: 1,368 Price Range: $39-$159
Suites: 58 Price Range: $199-$1,499
Restaurants: 9 (1 open 24 hours)
Buffets: B-$5.95/$11.95 (Sun) L-$6.95 D-$11.95/$15.95 (Mon)/$12.95 (Wed)
Casino Size: 145,000 Square Feet
Other Games: SB, RB, MB, P, PGP, LIR, TCP, K
Special Features: 70-lane bowling center. 18-screen movie theater. Kids Tyme childcare. Seattle's Best Coffee. Free shuttle to the Strip and other Coast properties.

Free Things To See In Las Vegas!

Fremont Street Experience

This $70 million computer-generated sound and light show takes place 90 feet in the sky over a pedestrian mall stretching four city blocks in downtown Las Vegas. It has more than 2.1 million lights, 208 speakers and needs 121 computers to make it all run like clockwork.

There are more than eight different shows with themes that include Country Western, Las Vegas Legends, a special Christmas Show, and more. Showtimes are 7:30 p.m. and then on the hour from 8 p.m. through midnight. (During winter months the 7:30 p.m. show is moved to 7 p.m.)

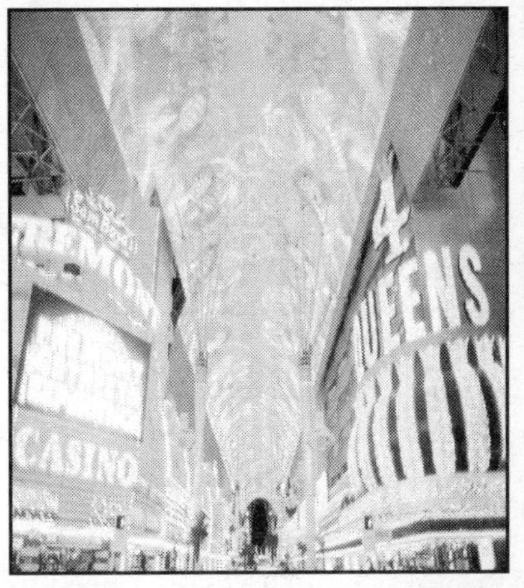

O'Shea's Casino
3555 Las Vegas Blvd. South
Las Vegas, Nevada 89109
(702) 697-2767

Toll-Free: (800) 329-3232 ask for O'Shea's
Other Games: S21, LIR
Special Features: Property is part of the Flamingo. Burger King.

Palace Station Hotel & Casino
2411 West Sahara Avenue
Las Vegas, Nevada 89102
(702) 367-2411
Website: www.palacestation.com

Reservation Number: (800) 544-2411
Rooms: 949 Price Range: $29-$99
Suites: 82 Price Range: $89-$139
Restaurants: 5 (1 open 24 hours)
Buffets: B-$4.99/$8.99 (Sat/Sun) L-$6.99 D-$9.99
Casino Size: 84,000 Square Feet
Other Games: SB, RB, MB, P, PG, PGP, LIR, TCP, K, BG
Special Features: Nonsmoking slot area.

The Palms
4321 Flamingo Road
Las Vegas, Nevada 89103
(702) 942-7777
Website: www.thepalmslasvegas.com

Toll Free Number: (866) 942-7777
Reservation Number: (866) 942-7770
Rooms: 447 Price Range: $59-$149
Suites: 60 Price Range: $109-$600
Restaurants: 7 (1 open 24 hours)
Buffets: B-$5.99/$12.99 (Sat-Sun) L-$6.99 D-$11.99/$15.99 (Fri)
Casino Size: 64,576 Square Feet
Other Games: SB, RB, MB, P, PGP, CSP, LIR, TCP, K, BG
Special Features: 14-theater cineplex.

Paris Casino Resort
3655 Las Vegas Blvd. South
Las Vegas, Nevada 89109
(702) 946-7000
Website: www.paris-lv.com

Reservation Number: (888) BON-JOUR
Rooms: 2,916 Price Range: $65-$300
Suites: 300 Price Range: $350-$5,000
Restaurants: 7 (1 open 24 hours)
Buffets: B-$12.95 L-$17.95 D-$24.95
Casino Size: 66,451 Square Feet
Other Games: SB, RB, S21, MB, PGP, CSP, LIR
Special Features: Replicas of Paris landmarks. 50-story Eiffel Tower with restaurant/observation deck.

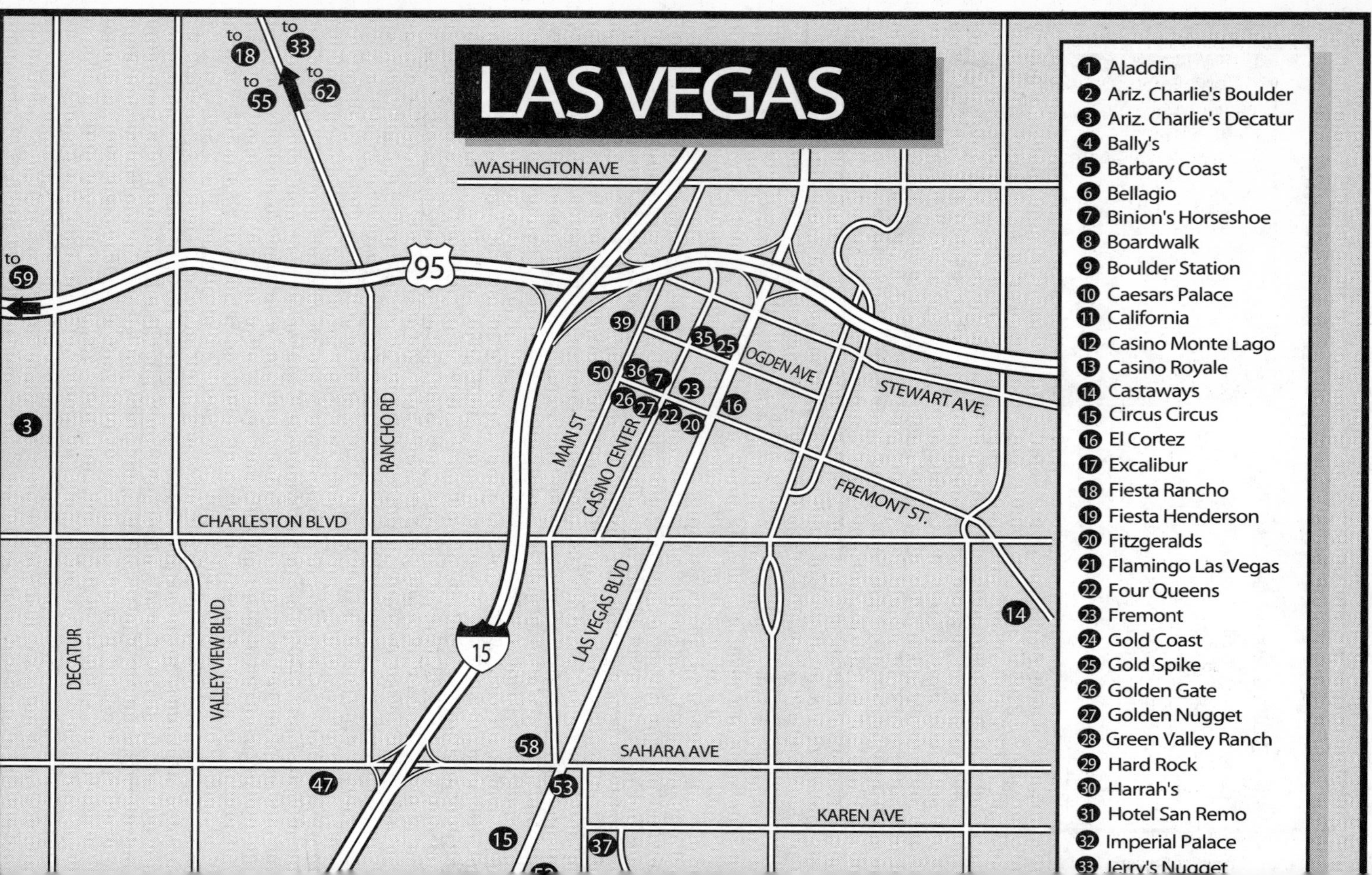
LAS VEGAS
WASHINGTON AVE
CHARLESTON BLVD
SAHARA AVE
KAREN AVE
RANCHO RD
DECATUR
VALLEY VIEW BLVD
MAIN ST
CASINO CENTER
LAS VEGAS BLVD
OGDEN AVE
STEWART AVE.
FREMONT ST.
95
15
to 18
to 33
to 55
to 62
to 59
1 Aladdin
2 Ariz. Charlie's Boulder
3 Ariz. Charlie's Decatur
4 Bally's
5 Barbary Coast
6 Bellagio
7 Binion's Horseshoe
8 Boardwalk
9 Boulder Station
10 Caesars Palace
11 California
12 Casino Monte Lago
13 Casino Royale
14 Castaways
15 Circus Circus
16 El Cortez
17 Excalibur
18 Fiesta Rancho
19 Fiesta Henderson
20 Fitzgeralds
21 Flamingo Las Vegas
22 Four Queens
23 Fremont
24 Gold Coast
25 Gold Spike
26 Golden Gate
27 Golden Nugget
28 Green Valley Ranch
29 Hard Rock
30 Harrah's
31 Hotel San Remo
32 Imperial Palace

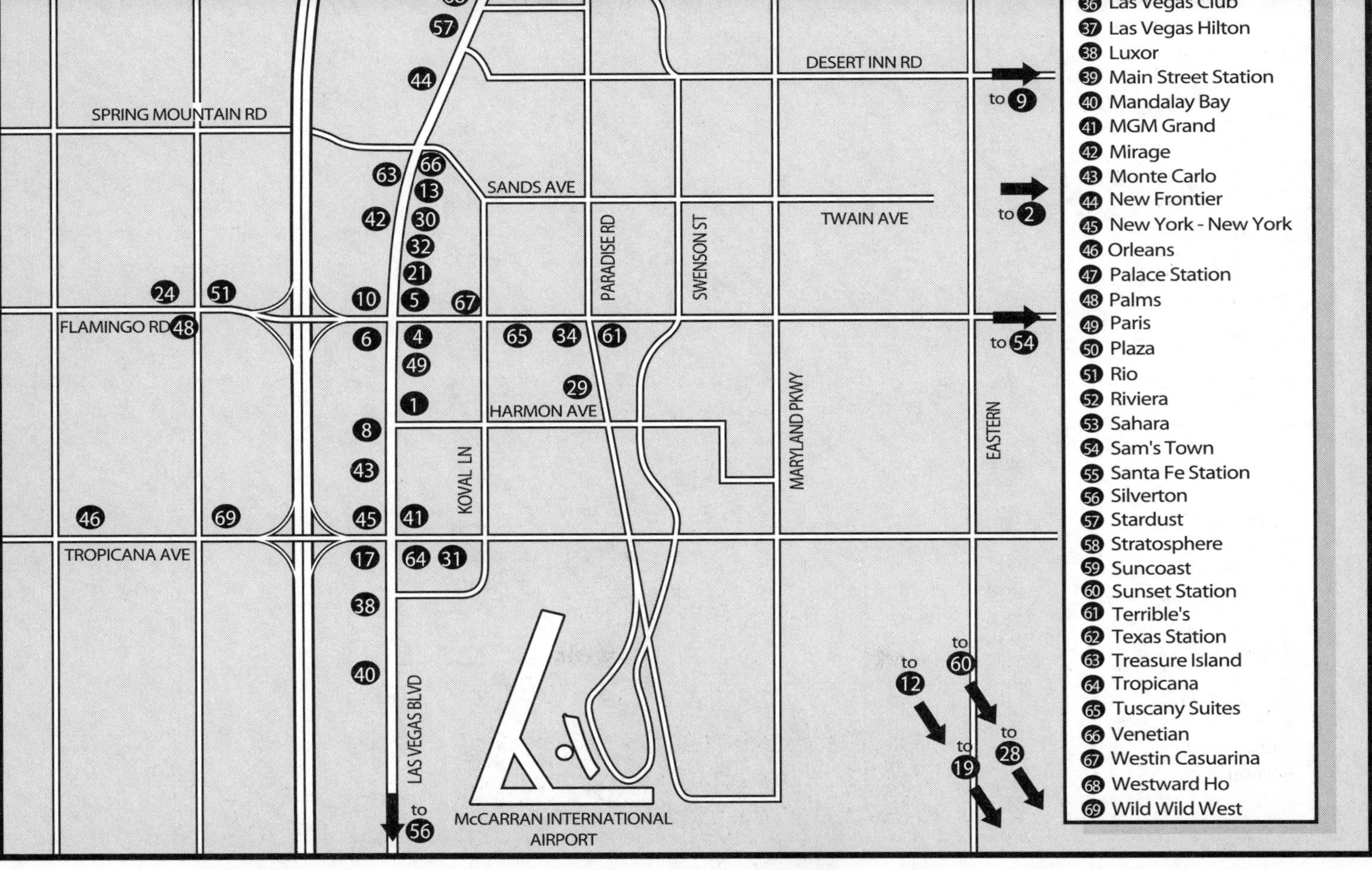

DESERT INN RD
SPRING MOUNTAIN RD
SANDS AVE
TWAIN AVE
PARADISE RD
SWENSON ST
FLAMINGO RD
HARMON AVE
MARYLAND PKWY
EASTERN
KOVAL LN
TROPICANA AVE
LAS VEGAS BLVD
McCARRAN INTERNATIONAL AIRPORT
to 9
to 2
to 54
to 12
to 60
to 19
to 28
to 56
36 Las Vegas Club
37 Las Vegas Hilton
38 Luxor
39 Main Street Station
40 Mandalay Bay
41 MGM Grand
42 Mirage
43 Monte Carlo
44 New Frontier
45 New York - New York
46 Orleans
47 Palace Station
48 Palms
49 Paris
50 Plaza
51 Rio
52 Riviera
53 Sahara
54 Sam's Town
55 Santa Fe Station
56 Silverton
57 Stardust
58 Stratosphere
59 Suncoast
60 Sunset Station
61 Terrible's
62 Texas Station
63 Treasure Island
64 Tropicana
65 Tuscany Suites
66 Venetian
67 Westin Casuarina
68 Westward Ho
69 Wild Wild West

Plaza Hotel & Casino
1 Main Street
Las Vegas, Nevada 89101
(702) 386-2110
Website: www.plazahotelcasino.com

Reservation Number: (800) 634-6575
Rooms: 1,037 Price Range: $35-$80
Suites: 60 Price Range: $70-$300
Restaurants: 3 (1 open 24 hours)
Casino Size: 55,660 Square Feet
Other Games: SB, RB, MB, P, PGP, LIR, TCP, K, BG
Special Features: Domed center-stage restaurant offers full view of Fremont Street Experience.

Rampart Casino
see North Las Vegas section

Rio Suites Hotel & Casino
3700 W. Flamingo Road
Las Vegas, Nevada 89103
(702) 252-7777
Website: www.playrio.com

Reservation Number: (800) PLAY RIO
Suites: 2,563 Price Range: $69-$425
Restaurants: 16 (1 open 24 hours)
Buffets: B-$9.99/$17.99 (Sat/Sun) L-$11.99 D-$16.99
Seafood Buffets: D-$29.99 (opens 4pm)
Casino Size: 111,468 Square Feet
Other Games: SB, RB, B, MB, PG, PGP, CSP, LIR, TCP, B6, K
Special Features: Masquerade Village area offers free "Masquerade Show in the Sky" daily at 3:30, 4:30, 5:30, 7, 8, 9 and 10pm. 25 retail shops. Three wedding chapels. "Scintas" stage show.

Riviera Hotel & Casino
2901 Las Vegas Blvd. South
Las Vegas, Nevada 89109
(702) 734-5110
Website: www.rivierahotel.com

Toll-Free Number: (800) 634-3420
Reservation Number: (800) 634-6753
Rooms: 2,100 Price Range: $29-$159
Suites: 154 Price Range: $125-$650
Restaurants: 5 (1 open 24 hours)
Buffets: B-$8.50/$15.99 (Sat-Sun) L-$9.50 D-$12.99
Casino Size: 109,800 Square Feet
Other Games: SB, RB, S21, MB, PGP, CSP, LIR, TCP, SIC, B6, K
Fun Book: Look for coupon in magazines
Special Features: Burger King, Pizza Hut, Panda Express and Quizno's Subs. Three stage shows: "Splash," "An Evening at La Cage" and "Crazy Girls." Comedy Club.

Sahara Hotel & Casino
2535 Las Vegas Blvd. South
Las Vegas, Nevada 89109
(702) 737-2111
Website: www.saharahotelandcasino.com

Toll-Free Number: (800) 634-6645
Reservation Number: (800) 634-6666
Rooms: 1,949 Price Range: $29-$119
Suites: 100 Price Range: $105-$375
Restaurants: 5 (1 open 24 hours)
Buffets: B/L-$6.99/$9.99 (Sat-Sun) D-$7.99/$9.99 (Sat)
Casino Size: 46,480 Square Feet
Other Games: SB, RB, S21, PG, P, PGP, LIR, B6, K
Fun Book: Show out-of-state ID at cashier cage
Special Features: *NASCAR* Cafe. *Sahara Speedworld* with roller coaster, race car simulator and other attractions.

Sam's Town Hotel & Gambling Hall
5111 Boulder Highway
Las Vegas, Nevada 89122
(702) 456-7777
Website: www.samstown.com

Toll-Free Number: (800) 897-8696
Reservation Number: (800) 634-6371
Rooms: 620 Price Range: $39-$125
Suites: 30 Price Range: $99-$275
Restaurants: 6 (1 open 24 hours)

Free Things To See In Las Vegas!

MGM Grand Lion Habitat

MGM Grand's $9 million Lion Habitat is located inside the property near the entertainment dome and it showcases up to five lions daily.

The Habitat is open from 11 a.m. to 10 p.m. daily and features four separate waterfalls, overhangs, a pond and Acacia trees. There are numerous viewing areas that will allow you to get an upclose view of the lions, including overhead and beneath you as you follow the walkway.

The Habitat has a retail souvenir shop and, for a $20 fee, you can have your photo taken with a lion club. For more information on the Lion Habitat you can call the MGM Grand at (800) 929-1111, or visit their web site at www.mgmgrand.com

Buffets: B-$8.99 (Sat-Sun) L-$6.99
D-$9.99/$12.99 (Wed)/$16.99 (Fri)
Casino Size: 118,000 Square Feet
Other Games: SB, RB, S21, P, PGP, LIR, TCP, K, BG
Special Features: Indoor promenade with free laser-light show 4 times daily. 24-hour 56-lane bowling center. Two RV parks with 500 spaces. 18-theater movie complex. Childcare center.

San Remo
See Hotel San Remo in this section

Santa Fe Hotel & Casino
See North Las Vegas section

Silver Saddle Saloon
2501 E.Charleston Boulevard
Las Vegas, Nevada 89104
(702) 474-2900

Restaurants: 1
Other Games: No Craps or roulette. Blackjack only played 5pm-4am (Fri)/5pm-4am (Sat)

Silverton Hotel Casino & RV Resort
3333 Blue Diamond Road
Las Vegas, Nevada 89139
(702) 263-7777
Website: www.silvertoncasino.com

Toll-Free Number: (800) 588-7711
Rooms: 292 Price Range: $35-$79
Suites: 8 Price Range: $59-$175
Restaurants: 5 (1 open 24 hours)
Buffets: B-$4.99/$5.99 (Sat)/$8.99 (Sun)
L-$6.99 D-$8.99/$10.99 (Tue/Wed/Thu/Sat)/ $9.99 (Sun)/$13.99 (Fri)
Casino Size: 32,134 Square Feet
Other Games: SB, RB, PGP, LIR, TCP, K
Fun Book: Given to slot club members
Senior Discount: Join Silver Seekers Club, if 55+
Special Features: 460-space RV park. 3 pools with Jacuzzi and water slides. 24-hour grocery store. Free shuttle to Strip.

Slots-A-Fun
2890 Las Vegas Blvd. South
Las Vegas, Nevada 89109
(702) 794-3814

Toll-Free Number: (800) 354-1232
Restaurants: 1 Subway Sandwich Shop
Casino Size: 16,733 Square Feet
Other Games: CSP, LIR
Fun Book: Ask at cashier cage
Special Features: 99-cent 1/4-pound hot dog. $1 blackjack and craps. 25-cent roulette.

Stardust Resort & Casino
3000 Las Vegas Blvd. South
Las Vegas, Nevada 89109
(702) 732-6111
Website: www.stardustlv.com

Toll-Free Number: (800) 824-6033
Reservation Number: (800) 634-6757
Rooms: 1,552 Price Range: $49-$135
Suites: 195 Price Range: $95-$350
Restaurants: 6 (1 open 24 hours)
Buffets: B-$6.99 L-$7.99 D-$10.99
Casino Size: 53,538 Square Feet
Other Games: SB, RB, B, MB, P, PGP, CSP, LIR, TCP, B6, K
Fun Book: Ask at Logo shop
Special Features: "Wayne Newton" stage show.

Stratosphere Hotel & Casino
2000 Las Vegas Blvd. South
Las Vegas, Nevada 89117
(702) 380-7777
Website: www.stratospherehotel.com

Reservation Number: (800) 99-TOWER
Rooms: 2,444 Price Range: $39-$129
Suites: 250 Price Range: $114-$229
Restaurants: 5 (1 open 24 hours)
Buffets: B-$6.49 L-$7.49/$10.99 (Sun) D-$10.99/$14.99 (Fri/Sun)
Casino Size: 56,500 Square Feet
Other Games: SB, RB, MB, PGP, CSP, LIR, TCP, B6, K
Senior Discount: tower admission discount if 55, or older
Fun Book: Given to hotel guests at check-in
Special Features: 135-story observation tower (admission charge). Two thrill rides. Revolving restaurant. 50 retail stores. Kid's Quest childcare center. Video arcade. "American Superstars" evening stage show. "Viva Las Vegas" afternoon stage show. AAA/AARP room discount.

Sunset Station
See Henderson section

Terribles's Hotel and Casino
4100 Paradise Road
Las Vegas, Nevada 89156
(702) 733-7000
Website:www.terribleherbst.com

Reservation Number: (800) 640-9777
Rooms: 370 Price Range: $29-$49
Restaurants: 2 (one open 24 hours)
Buffets: B: $4.99/$8.99 (Sun) L-$6.99 D-$9.99/$12.99 (Thu)
Casino Size: 23,123 Square Feet
Other Games: SB, RB, K, BG
Special Features: McDonald's restaurant.

Texas Station
See North Las Vegas section

Treasure Island (TI)
3300 Las Vegas Blvd. South
Las Vegas, Nevada 89109
(702) 894-7111
Website: www.treasureislandlasvegas.com

Reservation Number: (800) 944-7444
Rooms: 2,665 Price Range: $69-$329
Suites: 220 Price Range: $129-$999
Restaurants: 8 (1 open 24 hours)
Buffets: B-$7.99/$12.99 (Sat-Sun) L-$8.99/$12.99 (Sat-Sun) D-$12.99
Casino Size: 71,129 Square Feet
Other Games: SB, RB, S21, B, MB, PG, PGP, CSP, LIR, TCP, B6, K
Special Features: Lagoon with live-action sea battle every 90 minutes from 5:30pm until 10pm/11:30 (Fri-Sat). Health spa/salon. Two wedding chapels. Ben &Jerry's. Starbucks. Krispy Kreme. Cirque du Soleil's "Mystere" stage show.

Free Things To See In Las Vegas

The Forum Shops

This isn't your everyday shopping mall. It's more like Beverly Hills' Rodeo Drive located at Caesars Palace with more than 70 specialty retail shops including: Gucci, Louis Vuitton, Gianni Versace, FAO Schwartz, Guess, Fendi and a Spago restaurant.

As you walk through the mall be sure to stop at the Festival Fountain or Atlantis and see the seven-minute animatronic shows where statues come to life. The mall opens at 10am daily and closes at 11pm (12am Fri-Sat). Showtimes at the Festival Fountains are every hour, on the hour. Atlantis shows begin on the hour, starting at 11 a.m. and continue every other hour (Mon-Thu), or every hour on weekends.

Tropicana Resort & Casino
3801 Las Vegas Blvd. South
Las Vegas, Nevada 89109
(702) 739-2222
Website: www.tropicanalv.com

Reservation Number: (888) 826-8767
Rooms: 1,877 Price Range: $39-$159
Suites: 115 Price Range: $160-$240
Restaurants: 5 (1 open 24 hours)
Buffets: B/L-$8.95/$12.95 (Sat-Sun)
D-$12.95/$14.95 (Wed)
Casino Size: 60,700 Square Feet
Other Games: SB, RB, PGP, CSP, LIR, TCP
Senior Discount: Various, if 65 or older
Special Features: Wedding chapel. Swim-up blackjack table. Free wildlife walk and bird show Fri-Wed at 11am, 12:30pm and 2pm. "The Best of the Folies Bergere" evening stage show. "The Illusionary Magic of Rick Thomas" afternoon stage show. Comedy club.

Tuscany Suites & Casino
255 East Flamingo Road
Las Vegas, Nevada 89109
(702) 893-8933
Website:www.tuscanylasvegas.com

Reservation Number: (877) 887-2261
Suites: 760 Price Range: $49-$179
Restaurants: 2 (1 open 24 hours)
Casino Size: 35,000 Square Feet
Other Games: TCP
Special Features: All suite hotel.

The Venetian Resort Hotel Casino
3355 Las Vegas Blvd. South
Las Vegas, Nevada 89109
(702) 414-1000
Website: www.venetian.com

Reservation Number: (888) 283-6423
Suites: 4,046 Price Range: $149-$10,000
Restaurants: 17 (1 open 24 hours)
Casino Size: 105,344 Square Feet
Other Games: SB, RB, S21, B, MB, PG, PGP, CSP, LIR, TCP, B6
Special Features: Recreates city of Venice with canals, gondoliers and replica Campanile Tower, St. Mark's Square, Doge's Palace and Rialto Bridge. 90 retail stores. Madame Tussaud's Wax Museum. Guggenheim/Hermitage Museum. Canyon Ranch Spa.

Western Hotel & Casino
899 East Fremont Street
Las Vegas, Nevada 89101
(702) 384-4620

Reservation Number: (800) 634-6703
Rooms: 116 Price Range: $17-$22
Restaurants: 1 (open 24 hours)
Casino Size: 15,125
Other Games: BG, No Craps

Westin Casuarina Hotel & Casino
160 East Flamingo Road
Las Vegas, Nevada 89109
(702) 836-9775
Website: www.starwood.com

Reservation Number: (800) 228-3000
Rooms: 815 Price Range: $149-$219
Suites: 10 Price Range: Not Set at Press Time
Restaurants: 1 (open 24 hours)
Casino Size: 15,000 Square Feet

Westward Ho Hotel & Casino
2900 Las Vegas Blvd. South
Las Vegas, Nevada 89109
(702) 731-2900
Website: www.westwardho.com

Reservation Number: (800) 634-6803
Rooms: 750 Price Range: $27-$51
Suites: 48 Price Range: $61-$300
Restaurants: 2 (1 open 24 hours)
Buffets: B/L-$6.95
Casino Size: 34,275 Square Feet
Other Games: LIR
Special Features: Room-front parking. Some 3-bedroom apartments available.

Wild Wild West Casino
3330 West Tropicana Avenue
Las Vegas, Nevada 89103
(702) 736-8988

Reservation Number: (800) 634-3488
Rooms: 305 Price Range: $35-$55
Restaurants: 1 (open 24 hours)
Casino Size: 6,314 Square Feet
Other Games: SB
Special Features: Part of Station Casinos group.

Laughlin

Map location: **#2** (on the Colorado River, 100 miles south of Las Vegas and directly across the river from Bullhead City, Arizona)

Laughlin is named after Don Laughlin, who owns the Riverside Hotel & Casino and originally settled there in 1966. The area offers many water sport activities on the Colorado River as well as at nearby Lake Mojave.

For Laughlin tourism information call: (800) 4-LAUGHLIN. You can also visit their Website at: www.visitlaughlin.com.

Here's information, as supplied by Nevada's State Gaming Control Board, showing the slot machine payback percentages for all of Laughlin's casinos for the fiscal year beginning July 1, 2002 and ending June 30, 2003:

Denomination	Payback %
5¢ Slots	90.37
25¢ Slots	94.66
$1 Slots	95.39
$1 Megabucks	88.18
$5 Slots	96.21
All Slots	94.07

These numbers reflect the percentage of money returned to the players on each denomination of machine. All electronic machines including slots, video poker and video keno are included in these numbers.

Optional games in the casino listings include: sports book (SB), race book (RB), Spanish 21 (S21), baccarat (B), mini-baccarat (MB), poker (P), pai gow poker (PGP), Caribbean stud poker (CSP), let it ride (LIR), three-card poker (TCP), keno (K), big 6 wheel (B6) and bingo (BG).

Colorado Belle Hotel Casino & Microbrewery
2100 S. Casino Drive
Laughlin, Nevada 89029
(702) 298-4000
Website: www.coloradobelle.com

Reservation Number: (800) 477-4837
Rooms: 1,176 Price Range: $19-$95
Suites: 48 Price Range: $125-$175
Restaurants: 6

Buffets: B-$5.99 L-$6.99
D-$7.99/$14.99 (Fri)
Casino Size: 48,135 Square Feet
Other Games: SB, S21, P, PGP, CSP, LIR, K
Special Features: Children's arcade. Sand beach. Microbrewery. Krispy Kreme doughnut shop.

Don Laughlin's
Riverside Resort Hotel & Casino
1650 S. Casino Drive PMB 500
Laughlin, Nevada 89029
(702) 298-2535
Website: www.riversideresort.com

Reservation Number: (800) 227-3849
Rooms: 1,404 Price Range: $22-$49
Executive Rooms: 93 Price Range: $69-$99
Restaurants: 7
Buffets: B-$5.99 L-$6.99/$7.99 (Sun)
D-$6.99/$8.99 (Fri-Sat)
Casino Size: 80,763 Square Feet
Other Games: SB, RB, P, CSP, LIR, TCP, K, BG
Senior Discount: 10% AARP room discount
Fun Book: Given to anyone 55 or older
Special Features: 840-space RV park. Six-plex cinema. Classic car exhibit. 34-lane bowling center. Childcare center. Food court.

Edgewater Hotel Casino
2020 S. Casino Drive
Laughlin, Nevada 89029
(702) 298-2453
Website: www.edgewater-casino.com

Reservation Number: (800) 677-4837
Rooms: 1,420 Price Range: $20-$65
Suites: 23 Price Range: $75-$220
Restaurants: 4
Buffets: B-$5.99 L-$6.99
D-$8.99/$16.99 (Fri)
Casino Size: 53,953 Square Feet
Other Games: SB, RB, S21, B6, TCP
PGP, CSP, LIR, K, BG
Casino Marketing: (800) 289-8777
Senior Discount: Room discount, if 55, or older
Fun Book: Look in brochure racks for coupon
Special Features: Video arcade. 99¢ shrimp cocktail. 99¢ hot dog. Free airport shuttle. Krispy Kreme donut shop.

Flamingo Laughlin
1900 S. Casino Drive
Laughlin, Nevada 89029
(702) 298-5111
Website: www.flamingolaughlin.com

Reservation Number: (888) 662-5825
Rooms: 1,900 Price Range: $19-$100
Suites: 90 Price Range: $85-$350
Restaurants: 6 (1 open 24 hours)
Buffets: B-$5.99 L-$6.99 D-$8.99
Casino Size: 57,155 Square Feet
Other Games: SB, RB, S21, MB, P, PGP,
CSP, LIR, TCP, B6, K
Fun Book: Ask at Magic Club booth
Special Features: Burger King. Colorado River tour cruises. $1 off buffet for slot club members.

Golden Nugget Laughlin
2300 S. Casino Drive
Laughlin, Nevada 89029
(702) 298-7111
Website: www.gnlaughlin.com

Reservation Number: (800) 237-1739
Rooms: 300 Price Range: $29-$85
Suites: 4 Price Range: $150-$300
Restaurants: 5 (1 open 24 hours)
Casino Size: 32,600 Square Feet
Other Games: SB, RB, TCP, K
Casino Marketing: (800) 955-7568
Special Features: 10% room discount for AAA and AARP members. Suites must be booked through the casino. Gift shop.

Harrah's Laughlin Casino & Hotel
2900 S. Casino Drive
Laughlin, Nevada 89029
(702) 298-4600
Website: www.harrahs.com

Reservation Number: (800) HARRAHS
Rooms: 1,571 Price Range: $25-$95
Suites: 100 Price Range: Casino Use Only
Restaurants: 5
Buffets: B/L-$7.99 D-$10.99
Casino Size: 47,000 Square Feet
Other Games: SB, RB, PGP, CSP, LIR, TCP, K
Special Features: Beach and health club with massage services. McDonalds. Baskin-Robbins. Cinnabon.

Pioneer Hotel & Gambling Hall
2200 S. Casino Drive
Laughlin, Nevada 89029
(702) 298-2442
Website: www.pioneerlaughlin.com

Reservation Number: (800) 634-3469
Rooms: 395 Price Range: $25-$80
Suites: 20 Price Range: $48-$100
Restaurants: 2 (1 open 24 hours)
Buffets: B-$5.95 L/D-$7.95/$12.95 (Fri)
Casino Size: 19,500 Square Feet
Other Games: LIR, TCP, K

Ramada Express Hotel & Casino
2121 S. Casino Drive
Laughlin, Nevada 89029
(702) 298-4200
Website: www.ramadaexpress.com

Toll-Free Number: (800) 243-6846
Rooms: 1,501 Price Range: $25-$69
Suites: 55 Price Range: $89-$119
Restaurants: 5 (1 open 24 hours)
Buffets: B-$5.99 D-$8.99
Casino Size: 44,7020 Square Feet
Other Games: SB, RB, TCP, LIR, K
Casino Marketing: (800) 343-4533
Fun Book: Given at slot club booth
Special Features: $1 million display of railroad antiques and memorabilia. Free ride on steam train. Train-shaped swimming pool. Arcade. $1 off buffet for slot club members.

River Palms Resort Casino
2700 S. Casino Drive
Laughlin, Nevada 89029
(702) 298-2242
Website: www.rvrpalm.com

Reservation Number: (800) 835-7903
Rooms: 995 Price Range: $25-$60
Suites: 8 Price Range: $70-$350
Restaurants: 7 (1 open 24 hours)
Buffets: B-$5.99/$7.99 (Sun) L-$6.99 D-$7.99
Casino Size: 71,300 Square Feet
Other Games: SB, RB, P, CSP, TCP, LIR, K, BG
Casino Marketing: (800) 835-7904
Senior Discount: Various specials Fri, if 50+

Lovelock

Map Location: **#19** (92 miles N.E. of Reno on I-80)

Sturgeon's Casino
1420 Cornell Avenue
Lovelock, Nevada 89419
(775) 273-2971
Website: www.ramada.com

Toll-Free Number: (888) 234-6835
Rooms: 74 Price Range: $40-$69
Spa Rooms: 2 Price Range: $75-$100
Restaurants: 1
Buffets: $6.95 (Sun)
Casino Size: 5,625 Square Feet
Other Games: No Craps or Roulette
Special Features: Hotel is Ramada Inn. Room discount for AAA and AARP members.

McDermitt

Map Location: **#20** (Just S. of the Oregon border on Hwy. 95)

Say When
P.O. Box 375
McDermitt, Nevada 89421
(775) 532-8515

Restaurants: 1
Casino Size: 5,940 Square Feet
Other Games: No Craps or Roulette

Mesquite

Map Location: **#21** (77 miles N.E. of Las Vegas on I-15 at the Arizona border)

Here's information, as supplied by Nevada's State Gaming Control Board, showing the slot machine payback percentages for all of the Mesquite area casinos for the fiscal year beginning July 1, 2002 and ending June 30, 2003:

Denomination	Payback %
5¢ Slots	93.22
25¢ Slots	95.51
$1 Slots	95.62
$1 Megabucks	89.74
$5 Slots	96.27
All Slots	94.79

These numbers reflect the percentage of money returned on each denomination of machine and encompass all electronic machines including slots, video poker and video keno.

CasaBlanca Hotel-Casino-Golf-Spa
950 W. Mesquite Boulevard
Mesquite, Nevada 89027
(702) 346-7259
Website: www.casablancaresort.com

Reservation Number: (800) 459-7529
Rooms: 500 Price Range: $39-$89
Suites: 18 Price Range: $99-$249
Restaurants: 3 (1 open 24 hours)
Buffets: B-$5.49 L-$6.49/$9.99 (Sun)
D-$8.49/$12.99 (Fri-Sat)
Casino Size: 25,975 Square Feet
Other Games: SB, RB, PGP, LIR, TCP, K
Special Features: 45-space RV park. 18-hole golf course. Health spa.

Eureka Casino & Hotel
275 Mesa Boulevard
Mesquite, Nevada 89027
(702) 346-4600
Website: www.eurekamesquite.com

Reservation Number: (800) 346-4611
Rooms: 192 Price Range: $29-$89
Suites: 18 Price Range: $59-$139
Restaurants: 2 (1 open 24 hours)
Buffets: B-$4.95 L-$8.95 D-$10.95
Casino Size: 31,100 Square Feet
Other Games: SB, RB, P, PGP, BG
Fun Book: Given to new slot club members.

Oasis Resort•Casino•Golf•Spa
P.O. Box 360
Mesquite, Nevada 89024
(702) 346-5232
Website: www.oasisresort.com

Reservation Number: (800) 21-OASIS
Rooms: 1,000 Price Range: $28-$69
Suites: 100 Price Range: $69-$139
Restaurants: 3 (1 open 24 hours)
Buffets: B-$5.45/$7.49 (Sun)
L-$6.45 D-$7.77
Casino Size: 34,700 Square Feet
Other Games: SB, RB, P, PGP, TCP, LIR, K
Special Features: 50-space RV park. 18-hole golf course. Wagon trail rides. Shotgun sports club. Health club and spa. 2-for-1 breakfast and lunch buffets Sun-Thu.

Virgin River Hotel/Casino/Bingo
100 Pioneer Boulevard
Mesquite, Nevada 89027
(702) 346-7777
Website: www.virginriver.com

Reservation Number: (800) 346-7721
Rooms: 720 Price Range: $25-$45
Suites: 2 Price Range: $250
Restaurants: 2 (1 open 24 hours)
Buffets: B-$4.49/$5.49 (Sat-Sun)
L-$5.49/$6.49 (Sat-Sun)
D-$8.49/$10.49 (Tue/Fri/Sat)
Casino Size: 36,000 Square Feet
Other Games: SB, RB, P, K, BG
Special Features: 24-lane bowling center. Four movie theaters. Lagoon pool with waterfall and slide. Video arcade.

Minden

Map Location: **#15** (42 miles S. of Reno on Hwy. 395)

Carson Valley Inn
1627 Highway 395 N.
Minden, Nevada 89423
(775) 782-9711
Website: www.cvinn.com

Reservation Number: (800) 321-6983
Rooms: 220 Price Range: $59-$109
Suites: 9 Price Range: $119-$169
Restaurants: 3 (1 open 24 hours)
Casino Size: 20,300 Square Feet
Other Games: SB, RB, TCP, K
Senior Discount: Get Senior Inn Club card if 50 or older for various discounts
Fun Book: Given to lodge/hotel/RV park guests
Special Features: 60-space RV park. 24-hour convenience store. Wedding chapel. Golf, hunting and ski packages offered. Childcare center.

N. Las Vegas

Map Location: **#22** (5 miles N.E. of the Las Vegas Strip on Las Vegas Blvd. N.)

Bighorn Casino
3016 E. Lake Mead Boulevard
N. Las Vegas, Nevada 89030
(702) 642-1940

Restaurants: 1
Casino Size: 3,740 Square Feet
Other Games: No Craps or Roulette

Cannery Hotel & Casino
2121 E Craig Road
N. Las Vegas, Nevada 89030
(702)507-5700
Website: www.cannerycasinos.com

Toll-Free Number: (866) 999-4899
Rooms: 201 Price Range: $59-$119
Restaurants: 4 (1 open 24 hours)
Buffets: L-$7.95/$10.95 (Sun)
D-$10.95/$11.95 (Tue)/$15.95(Thu)
Casino Size: 50,000 Square Feet
Other Games: SB, PGP, TCP

Fiesta Casino Hotel
2400 N. Rancho Drive
Las Vegas, Nevada 89130
(702) 631-7000
Website: www.stationcasinos.com

Reservation Number: (800) 731-7333
Rooms: 100 Price Range: $39-$139
Restaurants: 7
Buffets: B-$3.99/$7.99 (Sat-Sun) L-$5.99
D-$8.99/$10.99 (Sat-Sun)/$14.99 (Wed)/
$13.99 (Fri)
Casino Size: 59,951 Square Feet
Other Games: SB, PGP, LIR, TCP, K, BG
Special Features: Drive-through sports book. Coffee bar.

Jerry's Nugget
1821 Las Vegas Blvd. North
N. Las Vegas, Nevada 89030
(702) 399-3000
Website: www.jerrysnugget.com

Restaurants: 2
Casino Size: 33,101 Square Feet
Other Games: SB, RB, K, BG
Special Features: European Bakery.

Mahoney's Silver Nugget
2140 Las Vegas Blvd. North
N. Las Vegas, Nevada 89030
(702) 399-1111
Website: www.mahoneyscasino.com

Restaurants: 1
Casino Size: 18,100 Square Feet
Other Games: SB, BG, No Roulette
Special Features: 24-lane bowling center.

Opera House Saloon & Casino
2542 Las Vegas Blvd. North
N. Las Vegas, Nevada 89030
(702) 649-8801

Restaurants: 1
Casino Size: 4,420 Square Feet
Other Games: BG, No Craps or Roulette

The Poker Palace
2757 Las Vegas Blvd. North
N. Las Vegas, Nevada 89030
(702) 649-3799

Restaurants: 1
Casino Size: 25,000 Square Feet
Other Games: SB, RB, P, BG,
No Craps or Roulette

Ramada Inn Speedway Casino
3227 Civic Center Drive
N. Las Vegas, Nevada 89030
(702) 399-3297
Website: www.ramada.com

Reservation Number: (877) 333-9291
Rooms: 92 Price Range: $39-$79
Suites: 3 Price Range: $119
Restaurants: 1
Casino Size: 15,540 Square Feet
Other Games: RB, SB
Special Features: Closest hotel/casino to Las Vegas Motor Speedway.

Rampart Casino
221 N. Rampart Boulevard
Las Vegas, Nevada 89128
(702) 507-5900
Website: www.rampartcasino.com

Toll-Free Number: (866) 999-4899
Reservation Number: (877) 869-8777
Rooms: 216 Price Range: $119-$149
Suites: 70 Price Range: $209-$299
Restaurants: 3
Buffets: L-$7.95/$10.95 (Sun)
D-$15.95 (Thu)
Casino Size: 73,472 Square Feet
Other Games: SB, RB, MB, PGP, TCP, K
Special Features: Hotel is JW Marriott. Golf course. Spa. Mall.

Santa Fe Station Hotel & Casino
4949 North Rancho Drive
Las Vegas, Nevada 89130
(702) 658-4900
Website: www.stationcasinos.com

Toll Free Number: (866) 767-7770
Reservation Number: (800) 678-2846
Rooms: 200 Price Range: $39-$99
Restaurants: 3 (1 open 24 hours)
Casino Size: 87,279 Square Feet
Other Games: SB, RB, PGP, LIR, K, BG
Special Features: Ice skating arena. 24-hour 60-lane bowling center. Iguana Bar and Sports Bar.

Suncoast Hotel and Casino
9090 Alta Drive
Las Vegas, Nevada 89145
(702) 636-7111
Website: www.suncoastcasino.com

Toll-Free Number: (866) 636-7111
Rooms: 432 Price Range: $59-$119
Suites: 40 Price Range: $250-$400
Restaurants: 6 (1 open 24 hours)
Buffets: B-$4.95/ $10.95 (Sun) L-$7.95
D-$10.95/ $11.95 (Tue)/ $15.95 (Fri)
Casino Size: 92,000 Square Feet
Other Games: SB, RB, MB, PGP, LIR, TCP, BG
Fun Book: Given to hotel guests at check-in
Special Features: 64-lane bowling center. 16-screen movie theater. Kids Tyme childcare. Seattle's Best Coffee. Free airport and Strip shuttle. Free shuttle to other Coast properties.

Texas Station
2101 Texas Star Lane
N. Las Vegas, Nevada 89102
(702) 631-1000
Website: www.texasstation.com

Reservation Number: (800) 654-8888
Rooms: 200 Price Range: $39-$109
Restaurants: 5 (1 open 24 hours)
Buffets: B-$4.99/$8.99 (Sat-Sun)
L-$6.99 D-$9.99/$10.99 (Fri-Sun)
Casino Size: 123,045 Square Feet
Other Games: SB, RB, P, PGP, LIR,
TCP, K, BG
Special Features: 18-screen movie theater. 60-lane bowling center. Kids Quest childcare.

Pahrump

Map Location: **#23** (59 miles W. of Las Vegas on Hwy. 160)

Mountain View Recreation Center
1750 S. Pahrump Valley Boulevard
Pahrump, Nevada 89048
(775) 727-7777

TEMPORARILY CLOSED DUE TO FIRE
Restaurants: 1
Buffets: B-$2.95 L-$3.95 D-$5.95
Casino Size: 18,000 Square Feet
Other Games: No Craps or Roulette
Senior Discount: 10% off Sat-Thu dinner buffets, if 55 or older.

Pahrump Nugget Hotel & Gambling Hall
681 S. Highway 160
Pahrump, Nevada 89048
(775) 751-6500
Website: www.pahrumpnugget.com

Toll Free Number: (866) 751-6500
Rooms: 75 Price Range: $49-$89
Restaurants: 3 (1 open 24 hours)
Buffets: B/L-$3.99 D-$5.99/$6.99 (Fri)
Casino Size: 20,471 Square Feet
Other Games: SB, P, K, BG
Senior Discount: 2-for-1 dinner buffet
Mon-Thu if 55 or older
Special Features: Video arcade. Supervised children's play area. Food court with McDonalds, Dairy Queen and sub shop. 10% room discount if 55 or older.

Saddle West Hotel/Casino & RV Park
1220 S. Highway 160
Pahrump, Nevada 89048
(775) 727-1111
Website: www.saddlewest.com

Reservation Number: (800) 433-3987
Rooms: 148 Price Range: $42-$115
Suites: 10 Price Range: $60-$140
Restaurants: 2 (1 open 24 hours)
Buffets: B-$4.99/$6.99 (Sat-Sun) L-$5.99
D-$6.99/$8.99 (Fri)/$7.99 (Sat)
Casino Size: 18,457 Square Feet
Other Games: SB, RB, K, BG, No Roulette
Senior Discount: 10% discount on buffets and room rates if 55, or older
Special Features: 80-space RV park. Room discount for AARP and AAA members. Closest casino to Death Valley National Park. Fun Book given to hotel guests.

Terrible's Lakeside Casino & RV Park
5870 S. Homestead Road
Pahrump, Nevada 89048
(775) 751-7770
Website: www.terribleherbst.com

Toll Free Number: (888) 558-LAKE
Restaurants: 1
Buffets: B-$3.99 L-$4.99 D-$5.99
Casino Size: 8,300 Square Feet
Other Games: SB, K, BG, No Craps or Roulette
Senior Discount: 10% off buffets, if 55 or older
Special Features: 160-space RV park. Terrible's general store and Chevron gas station.

Terrible's Town
771 Frontage Road
Pahrump, Nevada 89048
(775) 751-7777
Website: www.terribleherbst.com

Toll Free Number: (888) 837-7425
Restaurants: 1
Casino Size: 10,100 Square Feet
Other Games: SB, RB, K, BG
Fun Book: Ask in casino
Special Features: Blimpie's, Pizza Hut and Baskin-Robbins food outlets. General store and Chevron gas station.

Primm

Map Location: **#6** (25 miles S.W. of Las Vegas on I-15; 9 miles from the California border)

Buffalo Bill's Resort & Casino
31700 Las Vegas Blvd S.
Primm, Nevada 89019
(702) 382-1212
Website: www.primadonna.com

Toll-Free Number: (800) FUN-STOP
Rooms: 1,242 Price Range: $25-$60
Suites: 15 Price Range: $205
Restaurants: 5 (1 open 24 hours)
Buffets: B-$6.25 L-$6.95 D-$7.95
Casino Size: 62,130 Square Feet
Other Games: SB, RB, S21, P, PGP, CSP
LIR, TCP, B6, K, BG
Fun Book: Look for coupon in brochure racks
Special Features: Roller coaster. Flume ride. Two water slides. Movie theater. Train shuttle connects to Whiskey Pete's and Primm Valley.

Primm Valley Resort & Casino
31900 Las Vegas Blvd S.
Primm, Nevada 89019
(702) 382-1212
Website: www.primadonna.com

Reservation Number: (800) FUN-STOP
Rooms: 661 Price Range: $32-$70
Suites: 4 Price Range: $205
Restaurants: 3 (1 open 24 hours)
Buffets: B-$6.25/$9.95 (Sat-Sun) L-$6.95
D-$7.95/$13.95 (Fri)
Casino Size: 38,049 Square Feet
Other Games: SB, RB, S21, MB, PGP,
CSP, LIR, TCP, K, BG
Fun Book: Look for coupon in brochure racks
Special Features: 199-space RV park. Free monorail to Whiskey Pete's.

Whiskey Pete's Hotel & Casino
100 W. Primm Boulevard
Primm, Nevada 89019
(702) 382-1212
Website: www.primadonna.com

Reservation Number: (800) FUN-STOP
Rooms: 777 Price Range: $20-$50
Suites: 4 Price Range: $205
Restaurants: 4 (1 open 24 hours)
Buffets: B-$5.95 L-$6.25 D-$6.95
Casino Size: 36,400 Square Feet
Other Games: SB, RB, S21, PGP, CSP, LIR, TCP, K
Fun Book: Look for coupon in brochure racks
Special Features: Al Capone's car and Bonnie & Clyde's "death" car on display. Free monorail service to Primm Valley.

Reno

Map Location: **#4** (near the California border, 58 miles N.E. of Lake Tahoe and 32 miles N. of Carson City).

Reno may be best known for its neon arch on Virginia Street which welcomes visitors to "The Biggest Little City in the World." The current arch is actually the fourth one since the original arch was built in 1927. The area also houses the nation's largest car collection at the National Automobile Museum. For Reno information call the Reno/Sparks Convention & Visitors Authority at (800) FOR-RENO.

Here's information, as supplied by Nevada's State Gaming Control Board, showing the slot machine payback percentages for all of the Reno area casinos for the fiscal year beginning July 1, 2002 and ending June 30, 2003:

Denomination	Payback %
5¢ Slots	92.47
25¢ Slots	94.12
$1 Slots	95.81
$1 Megabucks	88.44
$5 Slots	96.46
All Slots	94.93

These numbers reflect the percentage of money returned on each denomination of machine and encompass all electronic machines including slots, video poker and video keno.

Optional games in the casino listings include: sports book (SB), race book (RB), Spanish 21 (S21), baccarat (B), mini-baccarat (MB), pai gow (PG), poker (P), pai gow poker (PGP), Caribbean stud poker (CSP), let it ride (LIR), three-card poker (TCP), big 6 wheel (B6), keno (K) and bingo (BG).

Atlantis Casino Resort
3800 S. Virginia Street
Reno, Nevada 89502
(775) 825-4700
Website: www.atlantiscasino.com

Reservation Number: (800) 723-6500
Rooms: 1,000 Price Range: $29-$169
Suites: 30 Price Range: $129-$425
Restaurants: 7 (1 open 24 hours)
Buffets: B-$7.99/$8.99 (Sat)/$15.99 (Sun)
L-$9.99 D-$12.99/$20.99 (Fri-Sat)/$13.99 (Sun)
Casino Size: 51,000 Square Feet
Other Games: SB, RB, MB, P, PGP, LIR, TCP, K
Senior Discount: 10% off buffet, if 55 or older
Special Features: Health spa, salon.

Bonanza Casino
4720 N. Virginia Street
Reno, Nevada 89506
(775) 323-2724
Website: www.bonanzacasino.com

Restaurants: 2 (1 open 24 hours)
Buffets: B-$7.95 (Sun)/$6.95 (Sat)
L-$5.95 D-$7.95/$9.95 (Fri-Sat)
Casino Size: 12,583 Square Feet
Other Games: SB, RB, K
Senior Discount: 10% off food, if 60,or older
Fun Book: Show out-of-town ID
Special Features: $1 single-deck BJ. 25¢ craps and roulette.

Bordertown Casino RV Resort
19575 Highway 395
N. Reno, Nevada 89506
(775) 972-1309
Website: www.bordertowncasinorv.com

Toll-Free Number: (800) 443-4383
RV Reservations: (800) 218-9339
Restaurants: 2
Casino Size: 4,650 Square Feet
Other Games: No Craps or Roulette
Fun Book: Ask at cashier's cage
Special Features: 50-space RV park.

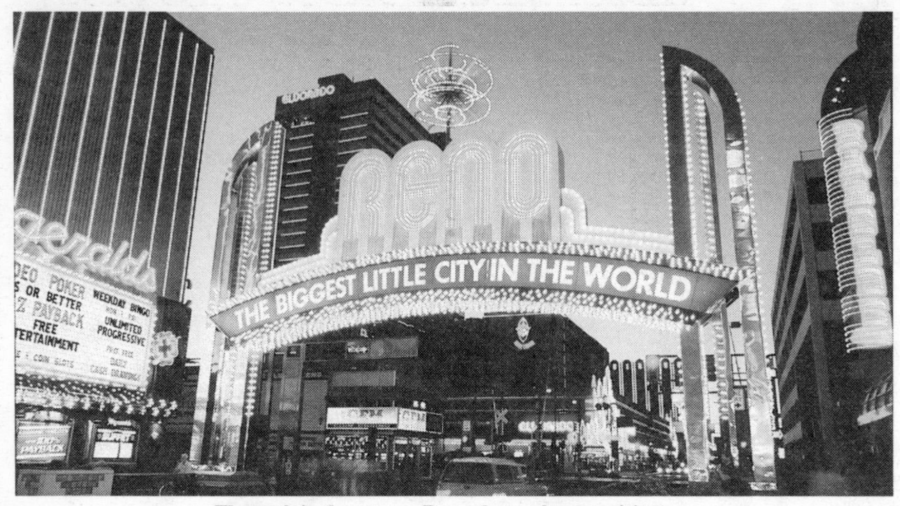

The arch in downtown Reno that welcomes visitors to "The Biggest Little City in the World" is the city's most famous landmark.

Circus Circus Hotel Casino/Reno
500 N. Sierra Street
Reno, Nevada 89503
(775) 329-0711
Website: www.circusreno.com

Reservation Number: (800) 648-5010
Rooms: 1,464 Price Range: $39-$199
Suites: 108 Price Range: $69-$239
Restaurants: 6 (1 open 24 hours)
Buffets: B-$6.99/$9.99 (Sat-Sun) L-$7.99
D-$9.99/$13.99 (Thu-Sat)/10.49 (Sun)
Casino Size: 61,260 Square Feet
Other Games: SB, RB, MB, P, PGP, TCP, LIR, K
Fun Book: Only given to hotel guests
Special Features: Free circus acts. Carnival games. 24-hour gift shop/liquor store.

Club Cal-Neva/Virginian Hotel and Casino
38 E. Second Street
Reno, Nevada 89505
(775) 323-1046
Website: www.clubcalneva.com

Toll-Free Number (877) 777-7303
Rooms: 303 Price Range: $29-$119
Suites: 6 Price Range: $99-$450
Restaurants: 5 (1 open 24 hours)
Casino Size: 44,760 Square Feet
Other Games: SB, RB, P, PGP, LIR, TCP, K

Diamond's Casino at Holiday Inn
1010 E. 6th Street
Reno, Nevada 89512
(775) 786-5151

Reservation Number: (800) 648-4877
Rooms: 280 Price Range: $69-$109
Suites: 6 Price Range: $99-$175
Restaurants: 2 (1 open 24 hours)
Casino Size: 10,000 Square Feet
Other Games: SB, RB, No Roulette or Craps
Fun Book: Only given to hotel guests
Special Features: Located next to Holiday Inn. Free airport and downtown shuttle.

Eldorado Hotel Casino
345 N. Virginia Street
Reno, Nevada 89501
(775) 786-5700
Website: www.eldoradoreno.com

Reservation Number: (800) 648-5966
Rooms: 817 Price Range: $49-$119
Suites: 127 Price Range: $110-$750
Restaurants: 9 (1 open 24 hours)
Buffets: B-$6.99/$8.99 (Sat-Sun)
L-$7.99 D-$12.99/$14.99 (Fri)/$17.99 (Sat)
Casino Size: 76,500 Square Feet
Other Games: SB, RB, MB, PG, P, PGP, CSP, LIR, TCP, B6, K
Casino Marketing: (800) 648-4597
Special Features: In-house coffee roasting. Pasta shop. Microbrewery. Bakery. Butcher shop. Gelato factory. Video arcade.

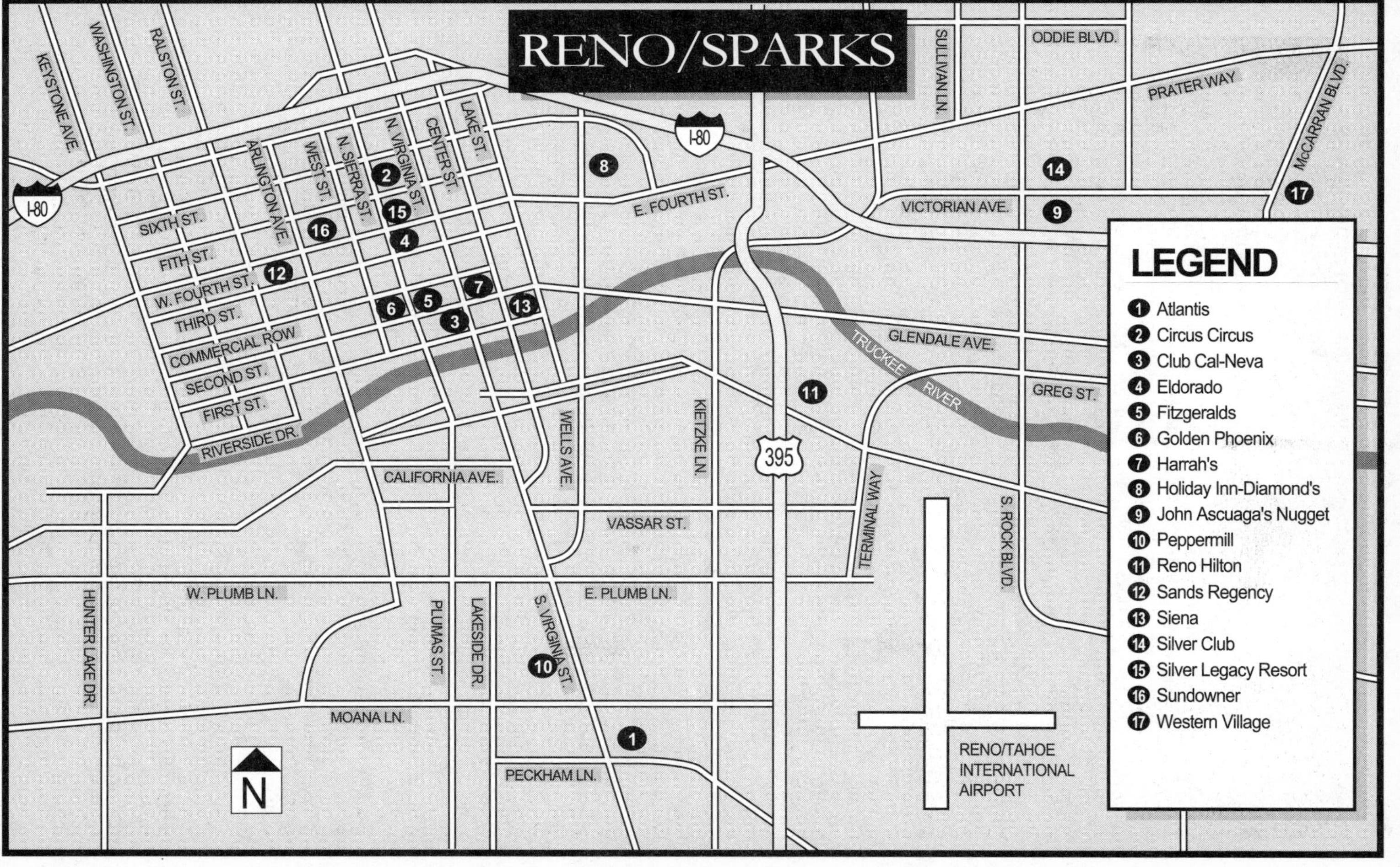
RENO/SPARKS
LEGEND
1 Atlantis
2 Circus Circus
3 Club Cal-Neva
4 Eldorado
5 Fitzgeralds
6 Golden Phoenix
7 Harrah's
8 Holiday Inn-Diamond's
9 John Ascuaga's Nugget
10 Peppermill
11 Reno Hilton
12 Sands Regency
13 Siena
14 Silver Club
15 Silver Legacy Resort
16 Sundowner
17 Western Village
KEYSTONE AVE.
WASHINGTON ST.
RALSTON ST.
I-80
ARLINGTON AVE.
WEST ST.
N. SIERRA ST.
N. VIRGINIA ST.
CENTER ST.
LAKE ST.
SIXTH ST.
FITH ST.
W. FOURTH ST.
THIRD ST.
COMMERCIAL ROW
SECOND ST.
FIRST ST.
RIVERSIDE DR.
E. FOURTH ST.
SULLIVAN LN.
ODDIE BLVD.
PRATER WAY
McCARRAN BLVD.
VICTORIAN AVE.
GLENDALE AVE.
TRUCKEE RIVER
GREG ST.
CALIFORNIA AVE.
WELLS AVE.
KIETZKE LN.
395
TERMINAL WAY
S. ROCK BLVD.
VASSAR ST.
W. PLUMB LN.
E. PLUMB LN.
HUNTER LAKE DR.
PLUMAS ST.
LAKESIDE DR.
S. VIRGINIA ST.
MOANA LN.
PECKHAM LN.
RENO/TAHOE INTERNATIONAL AIRPORT
N

Fitzgeralds Casino/Hotel - Reno
255 N. Virginia Street
Reno, Nevada 89504
(775) 785-3300
Website: www.fitzgeraldsreno.com

Toll-Free Number: (800) 535-LUCK
Room Reservations: (800) 648-5022
Rooms: 351 Price Range: $24-$150
Suites: 8 Price Range: $100-$240
Restaurants: 3 (1 open 24 hours)
Buffets: B-$5.49/$6.49 (Sat-Sun)
L-$6.49/$7.49 (Fri-Sat)
D-$10.88/$11.88 (Sat)
Casino Size: 26,380 Square Feet
Other Games: SB, RB, LIR, TCP, K
Special Features: Irish-themed casino. Room discount for AAA members.

Golden Phoenix Hotel & Casino
255 N. Sierra Street
Reno, Nevada 89501
(775) 785-7100
Website: www.phoenixreno.com

Reservation Number: (800) 648-1828
Rooms: 604 Price Range: $33-$89
Restaurants: 3 (1 open 24 hours)
Casino Size: 40,000 Square Feet
Other Games: SB, RB, MB, PG, PGP, TCP, LIR, K
Special Features: Benihana Steak House.

Harrah's Reno
219 N. Center Street
Reno, Nevada 89501
(775) 786-3232
Website: www.harrahsreno.com

Toll-Free Number: (800) 423-1121
Reservation Number: (800) HARRAHS
Rooms: 456 Price Range: $39-$149
Suites: 60 Price Range: $69-$195
Restaurants: 7 (1 open 24 hours)
Buffets: B-$7.99 L-$8.99/$10.99 (Sat-Sun)
D-$12.99/$17.99 (Fri-Sat)/$13.99 (Sun)
Casino Size: 51,500 Square Feet
Other Games: SB, RB, S21, B, MB, PG, PGP, LIR, TCP, K
Special Features: Some rooms are at Hampton Inn which is connected to Harrah's.

Peppermill Hotel Casino Reno
2707 S. Virginia Street
Reno, Nevada 89502
(775) 826-2121
Website: www.peppermillcasinos.com

Toll-Free Number: (800) 648-6992
Reservation Number: (800) 282-2444
Rooms: 1,070 Price Range: $39-$149
Suites: 185 Price Range: $79-$399
Restaurants: 6 (1 open 24 hours)
Buffets: B-$7.99/$15.99 (Sun)
L-$9.99/$15.99 (Sat)
D-$14.99/$26.99 (Fri)/$23.99 (Sat)
Casino Size: 65,502 Square Feet
Other Games: SB, RB, MB, PG, P, PGP, CSP, LIR, TCP, B6, K
Casino Marketing: (800) 648-5555
Fun Book: Only given to hotel guests
Senior Discount: Various discounts if 55+

Reno Hilton Casino Resort
2500 E. Second Street
Reno, Nevada 89595
(775) 789-2000
Website: www.renohilton.com

Reservation Number: (800) 648-5080
Rooms: 1,847 Price Range: $69-$209
Suites: 154 Price Range: $275-$1,000
Restaurants: 10 (1 open 24 hours)
Buffets: B-$7.99 L-$8.99 D-$13.99
Casino Size: 117,400 Square Feet
Other Games: SB, RB, B, MB, PG, P, PGP, LIR, TCP, B6, K
Fun Book: Only given to hotel guests
Senior Discount: Join Club Magic/Club 55 if 55+ for various discounts
Special Features: Largest hotel in Reno. Two movie theaters. 265-space RV park. KOA campground. 50-lane bowling center. Health club. Shopping mall. 8 tennis courts. Family amusement center. Laketop golf driving range. Indoor simulated golf. Free airport shuttle.

The Best Places To Play in Reno/Tahoe

Roulette - The best roulette game in the Reno/Tahoe area can be found at Club Cal-Neva in downtown Reno which offers a single-zero roulette wheel but only on the weekends. Single-zero roulette has only a 2.70% edge as compared to the usual 5.26% edge on a double-zero roulette wheel. Club Cal-Neva has three roulette wheels in the casino but only one of them is single-zero. The minimum bet is $2.

Craps - Almost all Reno/Tahoe area casino offer double odds on their crap games. The casinos offering the highest odds are the Sands Regency in Reno and the Lakeside Inn in Lake Tahoe which both offer 10 times odds.

Blackjack - There's good news and bad news for blackjack players in Northern Nevada. The good news is that there is an abundance of single-deck and double-deck games available. The bad news though is that unlike Las Vegas, where many Strip-area casinos stand on soft 17 in their blackjack games, all casinos in the Reno/Tahoe area hit soft 17, except for CaesarsTahoe. This results in a slightly higher advantage (.20%) for the casinos. Additionally, some casinos may also restrict your double-downs to two-card totals of 9, 10 or 11 only. The following recommendations apply to basic strategy players.

For single-deck players the best game is at the Alamo Travel Center in Sparks which has the following rules: double down on any first two cards, split any pair, resplit any pair, late surrender, and they will count a Six-Card Charlie as an automatic winner. The casino edge here is .10%.

Next best is the game at the Sundowner where they will only allow you to double down on two-card-totals of 9, 10 or 11 but they will give you a "push" if your cards total 21 and the dealer has a blackjack with an ace in the hole. The casino edge in this game is .15% and it's offered at all of their blackjack tables.

Next best are nine casinos that offer single-deck with the basic Northern Nevada rules: double down on any first two cards, split any pair and resplit any pair (except aces): Baldini's, Peppermill, Atlantis, Siena, Rail City, John Ascuaga's Nugget, Western Village, Boomtown and Silver Club. The casino edge here is .18%. (NOTE: There are numerous casinos that offer a game similar to this one except they will only allow you to double down on totals of 10 or more. This raises the casino edge in this game to .44%)

There are six casinos that tie for best place to play double-deck blackjack: Silver Legacy, Eldorado, Atlantis, Reno Hilton, Club Cal-Neva and John Ascuaga's Nugget. Their two-deck games have the following rules: double down on any first two cards, split any pair, and resplit any pair (except aces). This works out to a casino edge of .53%

For six-deck shoe games the best place is Caesars in Lake Tahoe which is the only casino where the delaer stands on soft 17 (six-deck game only). Additional rules are: split any pair, resplit any pair (including aces) and double down after splitting. The casino edge in this game is .26% and there's a $25 minimum bet required..

Next best is John Ascuaga's Nugget in Sparks where they offer a similar game except: they don't offer surrender, they hit soft 17, and they will allow you to double down with any number of cards (not just the first two). The casino advantage is .31% and minimum bets are $5.

The next best places to play six-deck games are all in Lake Tahoe: Caesars ($5 minimum tables), Harrah's and Lakeside Inn. The game's edge is .56% with these rules: double down on any two cards, split any pair, resplit any pair (including aces) and double allowed after split.

If you take away resplitting of aces from the above rules you have a game with a casino edge of .63% that's offered in Reno at the Eldorado, Reno Hilton, Siena and Circus Circus. It's also offered in Lake Tahoe at Horizon, Bill's and Harvey's.

Video Poker - Smart video poker players know that the three best varieties of machines to look for are: 9/6 Jacks or Better, 10/7 Double Bonus and full-pay Deuces Wild. By only playing these three kinds of machines, playing the maximum coin and using perfect strategy you can achieve, theoretically, the following payback percentages: 99.54% on 9/6 Jacks or Better, 100.17% on 10/7 Double Bonus and 100.76% on full-pay Deuces Wild.

Fortunately, excellent video poker opportunities are available in Northern Nevada with nickel, quarter and dollar 9/6 Jacks or Better games available at almost every casino in Reno. John Ascuaga's Nugget, Atlantis and the Horizon in Lake Tahoe, also offer some quarter 9/6 games with 4,700 coin (rather than the standard 4,000) for the royal flush jackpot. In Lake Tahoe only Harrah's and Horizon offer quarter 9/6 games, while many casinos offer the game at the $1 level. Fifty-play 9/6 at denominations from nickel to quarters is offered at Circus Circus, Atlantis, Hilton, Peppermill and Silver Legacy.

10/7 Double Bonus in quarters (some with progressive jackpots) is widely available in Reno and Sparks. $1 10/7 Double Bonus can be found at: Atlantis, John Ascuaga's Nugget, Cal-Neva, Eldorado, Silver Legacy, Siena, Peppermill, Hilton and Western Village.

Full-pay Deuces Wild is offered in quarter denominations in Reno at the Hilton and Silver Legacy (progressive) but it is not available anywhere in Lake Tahoe. The best Deuces game in Lake Tahoe is Deuces Deluxe (100.32% return) which can be found at Harvey's in quarters and at Caesars and Harrah's in dollars.

Another popular video poker game, Pick'em (99.95% return) is offered in quarters and dollars at Harrah's, Boomtown, Hilton and John Ascuaga's Nugget. Pick'em is also offered in Lake Tahoe at Harvey's (nickels, quarters and $1) and Harrah's ($1 and $5).

Slots - For slot players it pays to play where the machines are set to return the most. According to the Nevada Gaming Control Board, for the fiscal year ending June 30, 2003 the average north Lake Tahoe slot machine returned 94.88% while the average south Lake Tahoe machine returned 94.20%. In Reno the average return was 94.93% but the highest return of all was 95.36% in Sparks. Additionally, Sparks seems to be an especially good spot for low limit players because the city's nickel machines had the highest returns in the state: 94.69%.

The Sands Regency Hotel Casino
345 North Arlington Avenue
Reno, Nevada 89501
(775) 348-2200
Website: www.sandsregency.com

Reservation Number: (800) 648-3553
Rooms: 811 Price Range: $69-$109
Suites: 27 Price Range: $89-$159
Restaurants: 3 (1 open 24 hours)
Casino Size: 29,000 Square Feet
Other Games: SB, PGP, LIR, TCP, K, BG
Special Features: Arby's, Tony Roma's and Pizza Hut Express.

Siena Hotel Spa Casino
1 S. Lake Street
Reno, Nevada 89501
(775) 337-6260
Website: www.sienareno.com

Toll-Free Number: (877) 743-6233
Rooms: 214 Price Range: $49-$199
Suites: 27 Price Range: $129-$229
Restaurants: 3 (1 open 24 hours)
Casino Size: 20,900 Square Feet
Other Games: SB, RB, MB, PGP, TCP
Fun Book: Given with slot club sign-up
Special Features: Business center. Health spa. Wine cellar.

Silver Legacy Resort Casino
407 N. Virginia Street
Reno, Nevada 89501
(775) 325-7401
Website: www.silverlegacy.com

Reservation Number: (800) 687-8733
Rooms: 1,720 Price Range: $55-$169
Suites: 150 Price Range: $100-$260
Restaurants: 5 (1 open 24 hours)
Buffets: B-$6.99/$9.99 (Sat-Sun)
L-$7.99 D-$10.99/$14.99 (Fri-Sat)
Casino Size: 88,400 Square Feet
Other Games: SB, RB, S21, B, PG, PGP,
CSP, LIR, TCP, B6, K
Casino Marketing: (800) 215-7721
Special Features: Automated mining machine above casino floor. Comedy club. Rum bar.

Sundowner Hotel Casino
450 N. Arlington Avenue
Reno, Nevada 89503
(775) 786-7050
Website: www.sundowner-casino.com

Reservation Number: (800) 648-5490
Rooms: 583 Price Range: $35-$69
Suites: 10 Price Range: $109-$200
Restaurants: 3 (1 open 24 hours)
Buffets: B-$5.95 (Sun) L-$5.95 D-$6.95
Casino Size: 19,640 Square Feet
Other Games: SB, RB, K, No Roulette
Casino Marketing: (800) 648-5490

Searchlight

Map Location: **#25** (58 miles S. of Las Vegas on Hwy. 95)

Searchlight Nugget Casino
100 N. Highway 95
Searchlight, Nevada 89046
(702) 297-1201

Casino Size: 3,260 Square Feet
Other Games: P, No Craps or Roulette

Sparks

Map Location: **#4** (Sparks is a suburb of Reno and is located one mile east of Reno on I-80)

Here's information, as supplied by Nevada's State Gaming Control Board, showing the slot machine payback percentages for all of the Sparks area casinos for the fiscal year beginning July 1, 2002 and ending June 30, 2003:

Denomination	Payback %
5¢ Slots	94.69
25¢ Slots	95.30
$1 Slots	96.18
$1 Megabucks	89.19
$5 Slots	96.66
All Slots	95.36

These numbers reflect the percentage of money returned on each denomination of machine and encompass all electronic machines including slots, video poker and video keno. For nickel slot players Sparks' casinos offer the highest returns in the state.

Alamo Travel Center
1959 East Greg Street
Sparks, Nevada 89431
(775) 355-8888
Website: www.thealamo.com

Reservation Number: (800) 800-8000
Rooms: 71 Price Range: $57-$80
Restaurants: 1
Casino Size: 7,150 Square Feet
Other Games: TCP, No Craps or Roulette
Special Features: Motel is Super 8. Truck stop. Video arcade. Post office and service station.

Baldini's Sports Casino
865 South Rock Boulevard
Sparks, Nevada 89431
(775) 358-0116
Website: www.baldinissportscasino.com

Restaurants: 4 (1 open 24 hours)
Buffets: B-$3.99/$4.99 (Sat/Sun)
L-$5.99/$6.99 (Sat-Sun) D-$6.99
Casino Size: 14,340 Square Feet
Other Games: SB, RB, K, TCP, No Roulette
Senior Discount: 15% off food, if 55 or older
Special Features: Convenience store. Gas station. Free six-pack of Pepsi awarded with natural 4-of-a-kind, or better, in video poker with maximum coins bet.

John Ascuaga's Nugget
1100 Nugget Avenue
Sparks, Nevada 89431
(775) 356-3300
Website: www.janugget.com

Toll-Free Number: (800) 648-1177
Rooms: 1,600 Price Range: $36-$155
Suites: 150 Price Range: $99-$295
Restaurants: 8 (1 open 24 hours)
Buffets: B-$9.50 (Sat)/$12.95 (Sun) L-$7.99
D-$12.95 /$19.95 (Fri-Sun)
Casino Size: 82,600 Square Feet
Other Games: SB, RB, P, PGP,
LIR, TCP, K, BG
Special Features: Wedding chapel. Video arcade. Health club.

Rail City Casino
2121 Victorian Avenue
Sparks, Nevada 89431
(775) 359-9440
Website: www.railcity.com

Restaurants: 1
Buffets: B/ L-$5.95 D-$6.95/$9.95 (Fri)
Casino Size: 16,620 Square Feet
Other Games: SB, RB, K
Senior Discount: 20% off buffet, if 50 or older

Silver Club Hotel/Casino
1040 Victorian Avenue
Sparks, Nevada 89432
(775) 358-4771
Website: www.silverclub.com

Reservation Number: (800) 905-7774
Rooms: 204 Price Range: $39-$79
Suites: 8 Price Range: $85-$225
Restaurants: 4 (1 open 24 hours)
Buffets: B-$4.95 L-$5.95 D-$7.95
Casino Size: 16,200 Square Feet
Other Games: SB, RB, LIR, TCP, K
Senior Discount: 10% off food, if 55 or older

Western Village Inn & Casino
815 Nichols Boulevard
Sparks, Nevada 89432
(775) 331-1069
Website: www.westernvillagecasino.com

Reservation Number: (800) 648-1170
Rooms: 280 Price Range: $22-$50
Suites: 5 Price Range: $110-$135
Restaurants: 3 (1 open 24 hours)
Casino Size: 26,973 Square Feet
Other Games: SB
Fun Book: Given to hotel guests, or
at cage after cashing a check
Senior Discount: Room discount, if 55 or older

Tonopah

Map Location: **#26** (200 miles N.W. of Las Vegas on Hwy. 95 where it meets Hwy. 6)

The Station House
P.O. Box 1351
Tonopah, Nevada 89049
(775) 482-9777

Rooms: 75 Price Range: $60-$80
Suites: 3 Price Range: $136
Restaurants: 1
Casino Size: 4,800 Square Feet
Other Games: No Roulette
Special Features: 20-space RV park.

Verdi

Map Location: **#4** (4 miles W. of Reno on I-80 at the California border)

Boomtown Hotel & Casino
P.O. Box 399
Verdi, Nevada 89439
(775) 345-6000
Website: www.boomtownreno.com

Reservation Number: (800) 648-3790
Rooms: 318 Price Range: $49-$150
Suites: 20 Price Range: $99-$279
Restaurants: 4 (1 open 24 hours)
Buffets: B-$7.49/$11.99 (Sat-Sun) L-$7.49
D-$11.99/$23.99 (Fri-Sun)
Casino Size: 39,650 Square Feet
Other Games: SB, RB, P, PGP, LIR, K
Special Features: 203-space RV park. 24-hour mini-mart. Indoor family fun center with rides and arcade games. Free shuttle to/from Reno.

Wells

Map Location: **#27** (338 miles N.E. of Reno on I-80)

Four Way Bar/Cafe & Casino
U.S. 93 & Interstate 80
Wells, Nevada 89835
(775) 752-3344

Restaurants: 1
Casino Size: 4,500 Square Feet
Other Games: No Craps or Roulette
Fun Book: Ask at cage

Lucky J's Casino
PO Box 515/U.S. 93 & Interstate 80
Wells, Nevada 89835
(775) 752-2252

Restaurants: 1
Casino Size: 900 Square Feet
Other Games: No Craps or Roulette
Special Features: Located in Flying J Truck Stop. Blackjack open 7:30am-11:30 pm.

W. Wendover

Map Location: **#28** (Just W. of the Utah border on I-80)

Here's information, as supplied by Nevada's State Gaming Control Board, showing the slot machine payback percentages for all of the Sparks area casinos for the fiscal year beginning July 1, 2002 and ending June 30, 2003:

Denomination	Payback %
5¢ Slots	93.61
25¢ Slots	94.73
$1 Slots	97.02
$1 Megabucks	89.94
$5 Slots	97.35
All Slots	95.70

These numbers reflect the percentage of money returned on each denomination of machine and encompass all electronic machines including slots, video poker and video keno.

Montego Bay Casino Resort
100 Wendover Boulevard
W. Wendover, Nevada 89883
(775) 664-9100

Toll-Free Number: (877) 666-8346
Rooms: 250 Price Range: $35-$100
Suites: 29 Price Range: $70-$140
Restaurants: 2 (1 open 24 hours)
Buffets: B-$6.95 (Sat-Sun)
D-$9.95/$13.95 (Fri)
Casino Size: 25,538 Square Feet
Other Games: PGP, TCP
Fun Book: Given to hotel guests
Special Features: 56-space RV Park. Connected by sky bridge to State Line Nugget Casino & Gambling Hall. Gift shop. Liquor Store. Video arcade. Golf packages.

Peppermill Inn & Casino
680 Wendover Boulevard
W. Wendover, Nevada 89883
(775) 664-2255
Website: www.peppermillwendover.com

Reservation Number: (800) 648-9660
Rooms: 302 Price Range: $31-$90
Suites: 42 Price Range: $70-$215
Restaurants: 2 (1 open 24 hours)
Buffets: B-$7.95 L-$8.95/$9.95 (Sat)
D-$15.95/$18.95 (Fri-Sat)
Casino Size: 24,880 Square Feet
Other Games: PGP, LIR, TCP, K
Fun Book: Given to hotel guests at check-in
Special Features: Single-zero roulette.

Rainbow Hotel Casino
1045 Wendover Boulevard
W. Wendover, Nevada 89883
(775) 664-4000
Website: www.rainbowwendover.com

Toll-Free Number: (800) 217-0049
Rooms: 298 Price Range: $28-$100
Suites: 72 Price Range: $70-$250
Restaurants: 2
Buffets: B-$7.95 L-$8.95/$9.95 (Sat-Sun)
D-$15.95/$18.95 (Fri-Sat)
Casino Size: 47,560 Square Feet
Other Games: SB, RB, PGP, P, LIR, TCP
Fun Book: Given to hotel guests
Senior Discount: $2 off buffet, if 65 or older

Red Garter Hotel & Casino
P.O. Box 2399
W. Wendover, Nevada 89883
(775) 664-3315
Website: www.fh-inc.com

Toll-Free Number: (800) 982-2111
Rooms: 46 Price Range: $22-$65
Restaurants: 1
Casino Size: 13,600 Square Feet
Other Games: SB
Fun Book: Ask at Welcome Center

State Line Nugget Hotel & Gambling Hall
101 Wendover Boulevard
W. Wendover, Nevada 89883
(775) 664-2221
Website: www.statelinenugget.com

Toll-Free Number: (800) 848-7300
Rooms: 498 Price Range: $35-$90
Suites: 50 Price Range: $99-$199
Restaurants: 1 (open 24 hours)
Buffets: B-$8.95 (Sat) /$9.95 (Sun)
D-$10.95/$14.95 (Fri)
Casino Size: 47,358 Square Feet
Other Games: SB, RB, MB, P, PGP,
LIR, TCP, K
Special Features: Connected by sky bridge to Montego Bay. Gift shop. Golf packages.

Winnemucca

Map Location: **#29** (164 miles N.E. of Reno on I-80)

Model T Hotel/Casino/RV Park
1130 W. Winnemucca Blvd.
Winnemucca, Nevada 89446
(775) 623-2588
Website: www.modelt.com

Reservation Number: (800) 645-5658
Rooms: 75 Price Range: $45-$75
Restaurants: 4 (1 open 24 hours)
Casino Size: 9,482 Square Feet
Other Games: TCP, K, No Craps or Roulette
Fun Book: Given to hotel and RV park guests
Special Features: 58-space RV park. Food court with Baskin-Robbins, A&W, Taco Bell Express and gourmet coffee shop. Country store.

Red Lion Inn & Casino
741 W. Winnemucca Boulevard
Winnemucca, Nevada 89445
(775) 623-2565
Website: www.redlionwinn.com

Reservation Number: (800) 633-6435
Rooms: 100 Price Range: $55-$94
Suites: 7 Price Range: $105-$165
Restaurants: 1
Casino Size: 3,050 Square Feet
Other Games: SB, RB, No Craps or Roulette
Fun Book: Given to hotel guests and also distributed by local motels.

Winners Hotel/Casino
185 W. Winnemucca Boulevard
Winnemucca, Nevada 89445
(775) 623-2511
Website: www.winnerscasino.com

Reservation Number: (800) 648-4770
Rooms: 125 Price Range: $35-$60
Suites: 3 Price Range: $70-$80
Restaurants: 2
Buffets: B-$5.49 (Sat-Sun) D-$9.95 (Fri)
Casino Size: 11,340 Square Feet
Other Games: LIR, TCP, BG
Fun Book: Given to hotel guests
Senior Discount: 10% room discount, if 55+
Special Features: Courtesy car service to motels and airport. Gift shop. Video arcade.

Yerington

Map Location: **#30** (60 miles S.E. of Reno on Hwy. Alt. 95)

Casino West
11 N. Main Street
Yerington, Nevada 89447
(775) 463-2481
Website: www.casino-west.net

Reservation Number: (800) 227-4661
Rooms: 79 Price Range: $44-$56
Restaurants: 1
Buffets: B-$5.50 (Sun)
D-$5.50 - $12.95
Casino Size: 4,950 Square Feet
Other Games: K, No Craps or Roulette
Senior Discount: Room discounts, if 55+
Special Features: Movie theater. 12-lane bowling alley. Slot club members get $1 off buffets.

Indian Casino

Avi Hotel & Casino
10000 Aha Macav Parkway
Laughlin, Nevada 89029
(702) 535-5555
Website: www.avicasino.com
Map Location: **#2**

Toll-Free Number: (800) AVI-2-WIN
Rooms: 301 Price Range: $19-$119
Suites: 29 Price Range: $59-$175
Restaurants: 3 (1 open 24 hours)
Buffets: B-$5.99/$6.99 (Sat-Sun)
L-$6.99/$5.99 Sat-Sun)
D-$8.49/$9.49 (Sat)/$11.49 (Fri)
Casino Size: 25,000 Square Feet
Other Games: SB, P, CSP, TCP, LIR, K, BG
Special Features: 300-space RV park. On Colorado River with boat dock, launch and private beach. Baskin-Robbins. Subway. Gas station. Smoke shop. Kid's Quest childcare center.

NEW JERSEY

Map Location: **#1** (on the Atlantic Ocean in southeast New Jersey, 130 miles south of New York City and 60 miles southeast of Philadelphia)

Once a major tourist destination that was world-famous for its steel pier and boardwalk attractions, Atlantic City gradually fell into decline and casino gambling was seen as its salvation when voters approved it there in 1976.

The first casino (Resorts International) opened to "standing-room-only crowds" in 1978. Since then 12 more casinos have opened and all but three are located along the boardwalk. Those three, Borgata, Harrah's and Trump Marina, are located in the marina section.

In mid-1997 Bally's Wild Wild West casino (Atlantic City's first themed casino) opened, but due to a quirk in the licensing law, this casino is only considered part of Bally's Park Place and not a separate casino.

If you fly into Atlantic City it's a 12 to 14-mile drive from the airport to the casinos and there are only two choices of transportation. The taxi charges are regulated and it's a flat $27 to any casino. That price include all tolls and luggage.

The other option is a rental car and the only three rental car companies at the airport are Hertz, Avis and Budget. Rental rates are in the range of $50 to $60 per day but you can usually get a discount off of those rates by booking online or using a coupon. In addition to the daily rental fee there's about another 22% in taxes and fees.

If you do rent a car there is a charge of $3 to $5 per 24 hours (6 a.m. to 6 a.m.) for parking in a garage at any casino hotel in Atlantic City. Whenever you pay the fee you are issued a receipt which you can then use to park for free at *one* other casino. When you leave the second garage you have to give them the receipt from the first garage.

For transportation among the casinos there are two options, besides taxis. A 24-hour jitney service makes stops along Pacific Avenue and will drop you off by any casino including those in the Marina. The jitneys are very efficient and you will probably never have a wait of more than five minutes for one to arrive. The cost for one ride is $1.50 per person. Frequent rider tickets are offered for $12.50 per 10 rides and senior citizen can buy 10 rides for only $5. For jitney information call (609) 344-8642.

On the Atlantic City Boardwalk itself, there are the famous rolling chairs. These are covered two-seater wicker chairs on wheels that are pushed by an attendant as he walks you to your destination. They are all owned by the same company so the rates are the same: $5 for up to five blocks, $10 for six to 13 blocks, and $15 for 14 to 21 blocks. For more information on the rolling chairs call (609) 347-7500.

The Best Places To Play in Atlantic City

Blackjack: The blackjack games offered at Atlantic City casinos are pretty much all the same: eight-deck shoe games with double down on any first two cards, dealers stands on soft 17, pairs can be split up to three times and doubling after splitting is allowed.

This works out to a casino edge of .44% against a player using perfect basic strategy and virtually every casino in Atlantic City offers this game. The two exceptions are the Claridge (which doesn't allow any replits) and Borgata (which only offers six-deck games).

Both the Tropicana and Claridge offer this same game, without resplitting of pairs, which brings the advantage up to .48%. Bally's, Caesars, Claridge and Taj Mahal also offer an identical game in a multiple action format with a similar .48% edge.

If you're willing to make higher minimum bets you can find slightly better games. Most casinos offer six-deck games with minimum bets of $25, $50 or $100 per hand (Borgata has $10 minimums during the day).

A six-deck game, with the standard rules in place, lowers the casino edge from .44% to .42% The casinos offering this game are: Borgata, Bally's, Caesars, Hilton, Resorts, Showboat, Tropicana and all three Trump casinos.

Roulette: When choosing roulette games it's usually best to play in a casino offering a single-zero wheel because the casino advantage is 2.70% versus a double-zero wheel which has a 5.26% advantage. However, that situation is somewhat different in Atlantic City because of certain gaming regulations.

On double-zero wheels the casinos can only take one-half of a wager on even-money bets (odd/even, red/black, 1-18/19-36) when zero or double-zero is the winning number. This lowers the casino edge on these particular bets to 2.63%, while the edge on all other bets remains at 5.26%. This rule is not in effect on single-zero wheels and virtually all bets on that game have a 2.70% house edge.

There are nine casinos that have single-zero roulette wheels: Harrah's, Trump Marina, Bally's, Borgata, Trump Taj Mahal, Hilton, Tropicana, Sands and Caesars. You should be aware, however, that almost all of these games are only open on weekends and they usually require $25 minimum bets ($50 at Plaza, $100 at Taj Mahal). The lone exception is the Sands which always has one table open and requires a $10 minimum bet.

Craps: Trump Marina and the Sands are the only casinos to offer 10 times odds. It's offered at some (not all) of their tables and the minimum bet is $25.

Resorts, Taj Mahal, Tropicana and the Hilton offer five times odds on all of their crap games ($10 minimums). The Claridge and Sands offer five times odds on some (not all) of their games.

Video Poker: One of the better video poker games available in Atlantic City is a Double Joker machine with a 99.97% payback. The paytable to look for is one that offers 9-for-1 on 4-of-a-kind (rather than 8-for-1 which lowers the payback to 98.10%). Other good games to look for are: 9/6 Jacks or Better (99.5%) and Pick'em (99.99%). When Borgata opened in mid-2003 they introduced All American poker but the return is so good (100.72%) that it's doubtful the game will last very long (especially, the dollar version). Look for it in Bally Game Maker machines.

Quarter Games - Borgata's All American is the best play in town. Next best is the Tropicana which has almost 19 full-pay Double Joker machines. No 9/6 Jacks or Better games are offere for quarters. At the 50-cent level some 9/6 games can be found at the Sands, Borgata and Tropicana. Quarter full-pay Pick'em can be found at Bally's (16 machines) and Trump Plaza (8 machines). Be careful whenplaying this game as there is a short-paying version offered in other casinos.

Dollar Games - Borgata's All American, once again, is the best play in town. Next best is the Claridge which has one 9/5 Double Joker game. There are quite a few casinos offering 9/6 Jacks or Better: Borgata, Harrah's, Resorts (one machine), Sands, Taj Mahal, Wild Wild West, Tropicana and Trump Marina. Additionally, Bally's has the best 9/6 game because they offer it with a progressive. Atlantic City's only $1 Pick'em game can be found at Bally's and the city's only 10/7 Double Bonus machine can be found at Trump Plaza. $5 and higher 9/6 games are widely available throughout the city but the best $5 game is the full-pay Double Joker available at Trump Plaza.

Unlike video poker games, when it comes to slot machines you really can't tell what they're set to pay back. Therefore, you need to rely on statistics from the state's gaming regulators to see where the best-paying machines are located. Just take a look at the statistics below to see which casinos offer the best returns on their machines.

Following is information from the New Jersey Casino Control Commission regarding average slot payout percentages for the 12-month period from July 1, 2002 through June 30, 2003:

CASINO	PAYBACK %
Caesars	92.3
Resorts	92.2
Bally's A.C.	92.2
A.C. Hilton	92.1
Harrah's	92.0
Sands	91.9
Trump's Marina	91.9
Trump Plaza	91.9
Tropicana	91.8
Trump Taj Mahal	91.8
Showboat	91.4
Claridge	91.4

These figures reflect the total percentages returned by each casino for all of their electronic machines which includes slot machines, video poker, etc.

All Atlantic City casinos are open 24 hours and, unless otherwise noted, the games offered at every casino are: slots, video poker, big six, craps, blackjack, roulette, baccarat, mini-baccarat, Caribbean stud poker, let it ride, pai gow poker and keno. Additional games offered include: simulcasting (S), poker (P), pai gow tiles (PG), sic bo (SB), Spanish 21 (S21), three-card poker (TCP) and casino war (CW). The minimum gambling age is 21.

For more information on visiting New Jersey you can contact the state's Travel & Tourism Department at (800) 537-7397. For information only on Atlantic City call (800) VISIT-NJ.

Atlantic City Hilton Casino Resort
Boston & The Boardwalk
Atlantic City, New Jersey 08401
(609) 347-7111
Website: www.hiltonac.com

Reservation Number: (800) 257-8677
Rooms: 675 Price Range: $125-$375
Suites: 54 Price Range: $220-$600
Restaurants: 6 (1 open 24 hours)
Buffets: L/D-$16.95
Casino Size: 59,440 Square Feet
Other Games: S, PG, SB
Casino Marketing: (800) THE-GRAND
Senior Discount: $99 AARP midweek room rate (when available)
Special Features: Beachside resort with water sports and beachfront bar. Spa facilities with indoor pool. 2,000-seat entertainment theater. Unisex salon.

Bally's Atlantic City
Park Place and the Boardwalk
Atlantic City, New Jersey 08401
(609) 340-2000
Website: www.ballysac.com

Reservation Number: (800) 225-5977
Rooms: 1,162 Price Range: $109-$400
Suites: 92 Price Range: $279-$620
Restaurants: 15 (1 open 24 hours)
Buffets (Bally's): B-$11.99 L/D-$13.99
Buffets (W.W. West): L-$14.99 D-$18.99
Casino Size (P. Place): 80,809 Square Feet
Casino Size: (W.W. West) 73,935 Square Feet
Other Games: S, PG, SB, TCP, S21
Casino Marketing: (800) 772-7777 ext. 2700
Special Features: Walkway connects to second casino - Wild Wild West - a fully-themed casino which features an animated mountain, waterfalls, 17 animated robotic figures, three western restaurants and three retail shops. Spa.

The Borgata
One Borgata Way
Atlantic City, NJ 08401
(609) 667-1000
Website: www.the borgata.com

Toll-Free Number: (866) 692-6742
Rooms: 1,600 Prices Range: $99-$425
Suites: 400 Price Range: $175-$1,000
Restaurants: 11
Buffets: B-$12.95 L-$16.95 D-$24.95
Buffets: B-$12.95 L-$16.95 D-$24.95
Casino Size: 135,000 Square Feet
Other Games: S21, P, PG, TCP, SB, S
Special Features: Health spa. Outdoor pool.

Caesars Atlantic City
2100 Pacific Avenue
Atlantic City, New Jersey 08401
(609) 348-4411
Website: www.caesarsac.com

Toll-Free Number: (800) 443-0104
Reservation Number: (800) 524-2867
Rooms: 1,479 Price Range: $125-$375
Suites: 198 Price Range: $175-$700
Restaurants: 12 (1 open 24 hours)
Buffets: B-$10.95 L-$14.95/$19.95 (Sat-Sun) D-$19.95
Casino Size: 120,231 Square Feet
Casino Marketing: (800) 367-3767
Other Games: S, P, PG, SB
Special Features: Roman theme throughout hotel and casino. Smoke-free sections. Planet Hollywood restaurant. Health spa. Shopping arcade. Outdoor pool. Rooftop tennis. Unisex beauty salon.

Claridge Casino Hotel
Boardwalk & Park Place
Atlantic City, New Jersey 08401
(609) 340-3400
Website: www.claridge.com

Reservation Number: (800) 257-8585
Rooms: 449 Price Range: $110-$310
Suites: 53 Price Range: $210-$540
Restaurants: 5 (1 open 24 hours)
Casino Size: 58,565 Square Feet
Other Games: SB
Casino Marketing: (800) 847-LUCK
Special Features: Indoor pool and health spa. Unisex salon. Gift shop.

Harrah's Casino Hotel
777 Harrah's Boulevard
Atlantic City, New Jersey 08401
(609) 441-5000
Website: www.harrahs.com

Reservation Number: (800) 2-HARRAH
Rooms: 1,312 Price Range: $99-$275
Suites: 318 Price Range: Casino Use Only
Restaurants: 8 (1 open 24 hours)
Buffets: B-$12.99 D-$19.99
Casino Size: 89,617 Square Feet
Other Games: P, CW
Casino Marketing: (800) 2-HARRAH
Special Features: Largest hotel in New Jersey. 65-slip marina. Fitness center. Two retail shops. Beauty salon. Video arcade. Miniature golf course (in season).

Resorts Casino Hotel
1133 Boardwalk
Atlantic City, New Jersey 08401
(609) 344-6000
Website: www.resortsac.com

Toll-Free Number: (800) 336-6378
Reservation Number: (800) 334-6378
Rooms: 644 Price Range: $89-$250
Suites: 30 Price Range: $150-$500
Restaurants: 10 (1 open 24 hours)
Buffets: B-$9.95 L-$11.95/$14.95 (Sun)
D-$14.95/$8.95 (Wed/Fri)/$17.95 (Sat)
Casino Size: 77,000 Square Feet
Other Games: S, P, PG, TCP
Casino Marketing: (800) 438-7424
Special Features: Health Spa. Indoor/outdoor pool with saunas and Jacuzzis. Squash club. Game room. Nightclub. Beachfront shops. Slot club members get $2 off buffets.

Sands Hotel & Casino
Indiana Avenue & Brighton Park
Atlantic City, New Jersey 08401
(609) 441-4000
Website: www.acsands.com

Reservation Number: (800) 257-8580
Rooms: 476 Price Range: $79-$275
Suites: 58 Price Range: $375-$600
Restaurants: 5 (1 open 24 hours)
Buffets (Boardwalk): B-$10.95 L/D-$15.95
Casino Size: 57,296 Square Feet
Other Games: S, P, PG, SB
Casino Marketing: (800) AC-SANDS

Showboat Casino-Hotel
801 Boardwalk
Atlantic City, New Jersey 08401
(609) 343-4000
Website: www.harrahs.com

Reservation Number: (800) 621-0200
Rooms: 731 Price Range: $79-$199
Suites: 69 Price Range: Casino Use Only
Restaurants: 8 (1 open 24 hours)
Buffets: L-$17.99 D-$21.99
Casino Size: 80,707 Square Feet
Other Games: S, P, PG

Tropicana Casino & Resort
Brighton Avenue and the Boardwalk
Atlantic City, New Jersey 08401
(609) 340-4000
Website: www.tropicana.net

Reservation Number: (800) THE-TROP
Rooms: 1,426 Price Range: $75-$350
Suites: 340 Price Range: $175-$475
Restaurants: 8 (1 open 24 hours)
Buffets: B/L-$12.99 D-$18.99
Casino Size: 114,320 Square Feet
Other Games: S, P, PG
Senior Discount: Slot club 55 offers various discounts to member 55, and older.
Casino Marketing: (800) 338-5553
Special Features: Single-zero roulette game offered on weekends ($50 minimum bet). New tower to open by spring 2004. Called "The Quarter," it will add 502 new rooms, 200,000 square feet of meeting space and a retail-dining entertainment complex.

Trump Marina Hotel Casino
Huron Avenue & Brigantine Boulevard
Atlantic City, New Jersey 08401
(609) 441-2000
Website: www.trumpmarina.com

Reservation Number: (800) 365-8786
Rooms: 568 Price Range: $99-$425
Suites: 160 Price Range: $175-$450
Restaurants: 7 (1 open 24 hours)
Buffets: B-$8.50 L/D-$13.50
Casino Size: 73,734 Square Feet
Other Games: P, PG, SB
Casino Marketing: (800) 777-8477
Special Features: Adjacent to state marina with 640 slips.

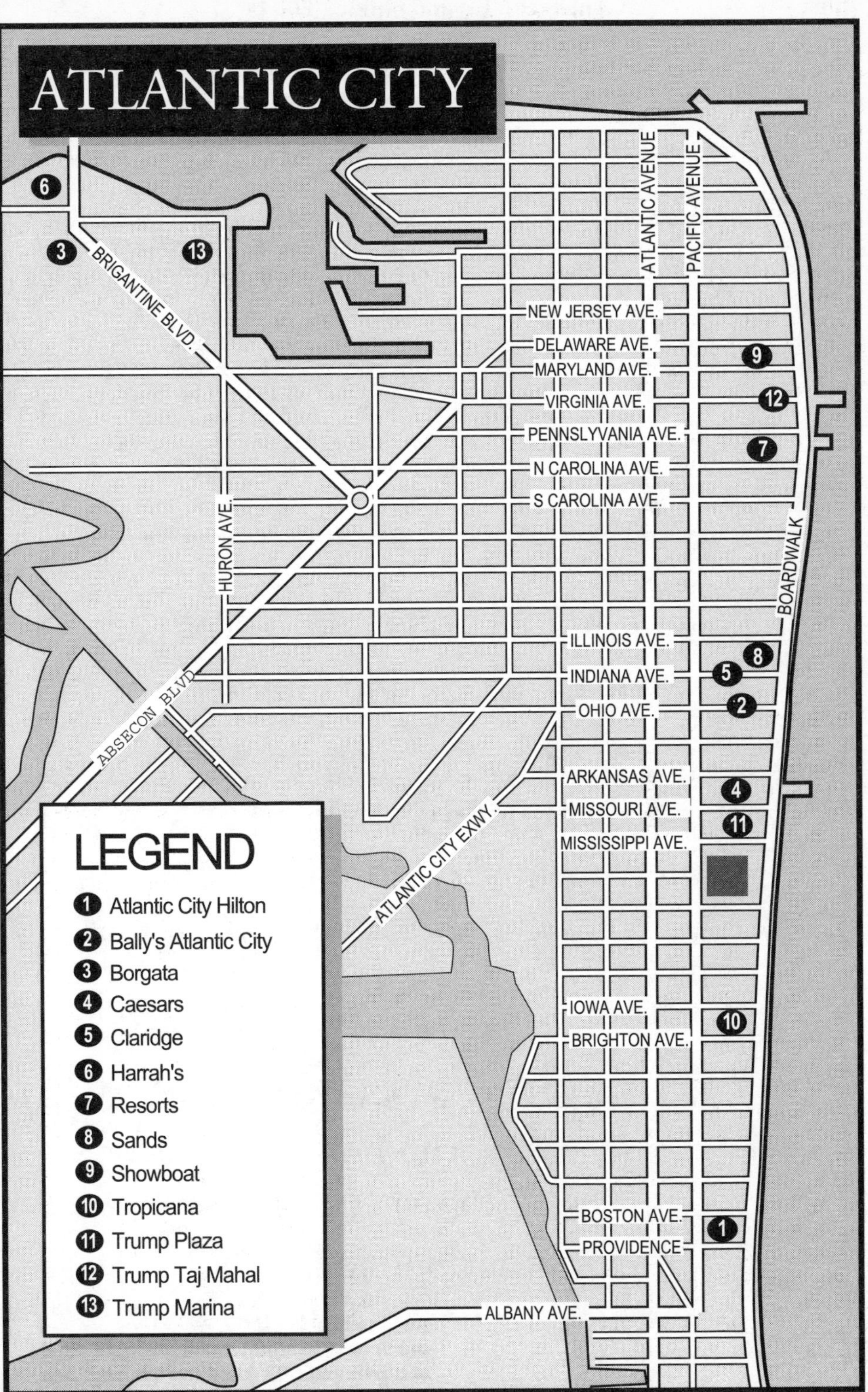
ATLANTIC CITY
BRIGANTINE BLVD.
ATLANTIC AVENUE
PACIFIC AVENUE
NEW JERSEY AVE.
DELAWARE AVE.
MARYLAND AVE.
VIRGINIA AVE.
PENNSLYVANIA AVE.
N CAROLINA AVE.
S CAROLINA AVE.
HURON AVE.
BOARDWALK
ILLINOIS AVE.
INDIANA AVE.
OHIO AVE.
ABSECON BLVD
ARKANSAS AVE.
MISSOURI AVE.
MISSISSIPPI AVE.
ATLANTIC CITY EXWY.
IOWA AVE.
BRIGHTON AVE.
BOSTON AVE.
PROVIDENCE
ALBANY AVE.
LEGEND
1 Atlantic City Hilton
2 Bally's Atlantic City
3 Borgata
4 Caesars
5 Claridge
6 Harrah's
7 Resorts
8 Sands
9 Showboat
10 Tropicana
11 Trump Plaza
12 Trump Taj Mahal
13 Trump Marina

Trump Plaza Hotel and Casino
The Boardwalk at Mississippi Avenue
Atlantic City, New Jersey 08401
(609) 441-6000
Website: www.trumpplaza.com

Reservation Number: (800) 677-7378
Rooms: 1,331 Price Range: $95-$400
Suites: 73 Price Range: $250-$325
Restaurants: 11 (1 open 24 hours)
Buffets: L-$13.95 D-$16.95
Casino Size: 138,295 Square Feet
Other Games: PG, SB
Casino Marketing: (800) 677-0711
Special Features: Health spa with massage, herbal wraps and salt-glo loofah cleansing. Indoor pool. East Side Lounge offers live entertainment nightly with no cover and one drink minimum.

Trump Taj Mahal Casino Resort
1000 Boardwalk at Virginia Avenue
Atlantic City, New Jersey 08401
(609) 449-1000
Website: www.trumptaj.com

Reservation Number: (800) 825-8888
Rooms: 1,013 Price Range: $125-$395
Suites: 237 Price Range: $300-$550
Restaurants: 9 (1 open 24 hours)
Buffets: L/D-$15.95
Casino Size: 116,199 Square Feet
Casino Marketing: (800) 234-5678
Other Games: S, P, PG, SB, S21, TCP
Senior Discount: Half off buffets Mon-Thu if 50, or older, with Trump Card.
Special Features: Health spa and indoor Olympic-size pool. Hard Rock cafe.

NEW MEXICO

New Mexico's Indian casinos offer an assortment of table games and electronic gaming machines. Additionally, slot machines are allowed at four of the state's race tracks as well as at about 30 various fraternal and veterans clubs.

New Mexico gaming regulations require that electronic machines at racetracks and fraternal/veterans organizations be set to return a minimum of 80% and a maximum of 96%.

New Mexico's Indian tribes do not make their slot machine payback percentages a matter of public record but the terms of the compact between the state and the tribes require all electronic gaming machines to return a minimum of 80%.

Unless otherwise noted, all New Mexico Indian casinos are open 24 hours and offer: blackjack, craps, roulette, video slots and video poker. Some casinos also offer: mini-baccarat (MB), poker (P), pai gow poker (PGP), three-card poker (TCP), Caribbean stud poker (CSP), let it ride (LIR), big 6 wheel (B6), keno (K), bingo (BG) and Simulcasting (S). The minimum gambling age is 21 but some casinos will allow you to play bingo if you are 18 or older.

For information on visiting New Mexico call the state's tourism department at (800) 733-6396.

Best Western Jicarilla Inn and Casino
U.S. Highway 64
Dulce, New Mexico 87529
(505) 759-3663
Map Location: **#12** (95 miles N.W. of Santa Fe)

Room Reservations Number: (800) 428-2627
Rooms: 43 Price Range: $65-$95
Restaurants: 1 Liquor: Yes
Other Games: Only electronic Machines

Big Rock Casino Bowl
419 N. Riverside Drive
Espanola, New Mexico 87532
(505) 747-3100
Website: www.bigrockcasino.com
Map Location: **#7** (25 miles N. of Santa Fe)

Toll-Free Number: (866) 244-7625
Restaurants: 2 Liquor: Yes
Hours: 8am-4am/24 hours (Fri-Sat)
Other Games: No roulette
Special Features: 24-lane bowling center. $1.99 breakfast special.

Camel Rock Casino
17486-A Highway 84/285
Santa Fe, New Mexico 87504
(505) 984-8414
Website: www.camelrockcasino.com
Map Location: **#2**

Toll-Free Number: (800) GO-CAMEL
Restaurants: 1 Liquor: No
Buffets: B-$4.95 L-$6.95 D-$7.95/$9.95 (Fri)
Casino Size: 60,000 Square feet
Other Games: CSP, BG (Thu-Mon)
Senior Discount: Bingo discount on Thursday, if 55, or older

Casino Apache
P.O Box 205
Mescalero, New Mexico 88340
(505) 630-4100
www.innofthemountaingods.com/casino.htm
Map Location: **#4** (90 miles N.E. of Las Cruces)

Toll-Free Number: (877) 277-5677
Room Reservations: (800) 545-9011
Rooms: Opening Nov 2004
Restaurants: 3 Liquor: Yes
Buffets: B-$6.35 L-$7.42
D-$10.95/$12.95 (Wed)
Hours: 7am-2:30am/24 hours (Thu-Sat)
Casino Size: 45,000 Square Feet
Other Games: P, CSP, K
Senior Discount: 20% off buffet, if 62, or older
Special Features: Casino is located in Inn of the Mountain Gods.

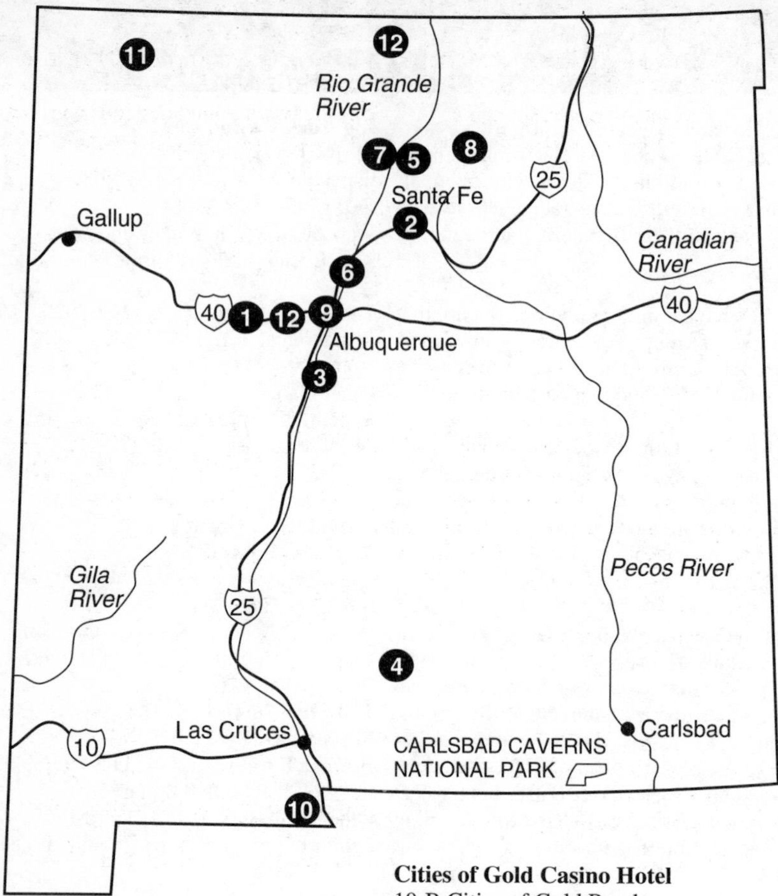

Casino Apache Travel Center
25845 U.S. Highway 70
Ruidoso, New Mexico 88340
(505) 464-6960
Map Location: **#4** (90 miles N.E. of Las Cruces)

Restaurants: 1 Liquor: Yes
Casino Size: 10,000 Square Feet
Other Games: No Craps
Senior Discount: 20% off buffet, if 62, or older
Special Features: Free shuttle service to Inn of the Mountain Gods. Truck stop. Discount smoke shop.

Cities of Gold Casino Hotel
10-B Cities of Gold Road
Santa Fe, New Mexico 87501
(505) 455-3313
Website: www.citiesofgold.com
Map Location: **#2**

Toll-Free Number: (800) 455-3313
Room Reservations: (877) 455-0515
Rooms: 122 Price Range: $65-$95
Suites: 2 Price Range: $136
Restaurants: 2 Liquor: Yes
Buffets: B-$4.24 L-$5.95 D-$6.95
Hours: 8am-4am/24 hours (Fri-Sat)
Casino Size: 40,000 Square Feet
Other Games: P, LIR, BG, S, TCP
Fun Book: Given when you first get club card
Special Features: They also operate the Pojoaque Sports Bar which is one block away from main casino. Liquor is served there but they only have slots - no table games. AAA and AARP room discounts. 27-hole golf course.

Dancing Eagle Casino
P.O. Box 520
Casa Blanca, New Mexico 87007
(505) 552-1111
Website: www.dancingeaglecasino.com
Map Location: **#1** (40 miles W. of Albuquerque)

Toll-Free Number: (877) 440-9969
Buffets: B-$5.99 L-$7.99 D-$10.99
Restaurants: 1 Liquor: No
Hours: 8am-4am/24 hours (Fri-Sun)
Casino Size: 21,266 Square Feet
Other Games: TCP, CSP
Fun Book: Given to new slot club members and birthday celebrants
Special Features: Video arcade. Truck stop. RV park.

Isleta Casino Resort
11000 Broadway S.E.
Albuquerque, New Mexico 87105
(505) 724-3800
Website: www.isletacasinoresort.com
Map Location: **#3**

Toll-Free Number: (800) 843-5156
Restaurants: 5 Liquor: Yes
Buffets: B-$7.95 (Sat-Sun) L-$6.95/$8.95 (Sat-Sun) D-$8.95/$16.95 (Fri)/$10.95 (Sat)
Hours: 8am-4am/24 hours (Fri-Sat)
Casino Size: 30,000 Square Feet
Other Games: P, BG, K
Senior Discount: 13% buffet discount, if 55+
Special Features: Convenience store. Gas station. 27-hole golf course. Alcohol is only served at sports bar in casino.

Ohkay Casino Resort
P.O. Box 1270
San Juan Pueblo, New Mexico 87566
(505) 747-1668
Website: www.ohkay.com
Map Location: **#5** (24 miles N. of Santa Fe)

Toll-Free Number: (800) PLAY-AT-OK
Room Reservation (877) 829-2865
Rooms: 101 Price Range: $65-$99
Suites: 24 Price Range: $95-$135
Restaurants: 2 (1 open 24 hours) Liquor: Yes
Buffets: B-$6.25 L-$7.25 D-$8.25
Casino Size: 35,000 Square Feet
Senior Discount: 10% off room, if 55 or older
Special Features: Hotel is Best Western.

Route 66 Casino
14500 Central Avenue
Rio Puerco, New Mexico 87121
(505) 352-7866
Website: www.route66casinos.com
Map Location: **#12** (20 miles W. of Albuq.)

Toll-Free Number: (866) 352-7866
Restaurants: 2 Liquor: No
Hours: 8am-4am/24 hours (Fri-Sun)
Other Games: Bingo

San Felipe Casino Hollywood
25 Hagan Road
Algodones, New Mexico 87001
(505) 867-6700
Website: www.sanfelipecasino.com
Map Location: **#6** (17 miles N. of Albuq.)

Toll-Free Number: (877) 529-2946
Restaurants: 2 Liquor: No
Buffets: B-$4.25 L-$6.25 D-$7.50
Hours: 8am-4am/24 hours (Fri-Sun)
Other Games: PGP

Sandia Casino
30 Rainbow Road
Albuquerque, New Mexico 87113
(505) 796-7500
Website: www.sandiacasino.com
Map Location: **#9**

Toll-Free Number: (800) 526-9366
Restaurants: 3 Liquor: Yes
Buffets: B-$5.50 L-$6.95/$9.95 (Sun) D-$8.95/$16.95 (Fri)/$10.95 (Sat)
Hours: 8am-4am/24 hours (Thu-Sun)
Casino Size: 65,000 Square feet
Other Games: P, CSP, LIR, K, BG, TCP
Senior Discount: Bingo discounts, if 65, or older
Special Features: Subway sandwich shop.

Santa Ana Star Casino
54 Jemez Dam Canyon Road
Bernalillo, New Mexico 87004
(505) 867-0000
Website: www.santaanastar.com
Map Location: **#6** (17 miles N. of Albuq.)

Restaurants: 4 Liquor: No
Buffets: L-$6.95 D-$8.95/$15.95(Thu)
Hours: 8am-4am/24 hours (Fri-Sat)
Casino Size: 19,000 Square Feet
Other Games: P, LIR
Special Features: 36-lane bowling alley.

Sky City Casino
P.O. Box 519
San Fidel, New Mexico 87049
(505) 552-6017
Website: www.skycitycasino.com
Map Location: **#1** (50 miles W. of Albuquerque)

Toll-Free Number: (888) SKY-CITY
Rooms: 134 Price Range: $50-$70
Suites: 15 Price Range: $90-$135
Restaurants: 1 Liquor: No
Buffets: B-$6.95 (Sun) L-$7.95 D-$9.95
Hours: 8am-4am/24 hours (Thu-Sat)
Casino Size: 30,000 Square Feet
Other Games: P, BG, S
Senior Discount: 10% off buffet, if 55, or older

Taos Mountain Casino
P.O. Box 1477
Taos, New Mexico 87571
(505) 758-4460
Website: www.taosmountaincasino.com
Map Location: **#8** (50 miles N.E. of Santa Fe)

Toll-Free Number: (888) WIN-TAOS
Restaurants: 1 Deli Liquor: No
Buffets: B-$7.95 (Sun)
Hours: 8am-1am/2am (Thu-Sun)
Other Games: No craps
Special Features: Entire casino is nonsmoking.

Pari-Mutuels

Downs at Albuquerque
P.O. Box 8510
Albuquerque, NM 87198
(505) 266-5555
Website: www.abqdowns.com
Map Location: **#9**

Restaurants: 1
Buffets: L-$7.95 D-$7.95
Hours: Noon-Midnight Daily
Other Games: Only gaming machines
Senior Discount: $2 off buffets, if 55+
Special Features: Live horse racing late March through early June and during New Mexico State Fair in September. Horse race simulcasting all year.

Ruidoso Downs & Billy The Kid Casino
P.O. Box 449
Ruidoso Downs, NM 88346
(505) 378-4431
Website: www.btkcasino.com
Map Location: **#4** (90 miles N.E. of Las Cruces)

Restaurants: 1
Buffets: B-$6.50 (Sun) L-$6.50 D-$7.95
Hours: 11am-11pm/12pm-12am (Fri)
Other Games: Only gaming machines
Senior Discount: 10% off buffets, if 55 or older
Special Features: Live horse racing (Thu-Sun) during season which runs from late May through early September. Horse race simulcasting all year.

Sunland Park
1200 Futurity Drive
Sunland Park, NM 88063
(505) 874-5200
Website: www.sunland-park.com
Map Location: **#10** (5 miles W. of El Paso, TX)

Restaurants: 1
Buffets: L-$7.95 D-$7.95
Hours: Noon-Midnight
Other Games: Only gaming machines
Senior Discount: Special coupon book, if 55+
Special Features: Live thoroughbred and quarter-horse racing during season which runs from November through April. Simulcasting of horse racing all year.

SunRay Park and Casino
#39 Road 5568
Farmington, NM 87401
(505) 566-1200
Website: www.sunraygaming.com
Map Location: **#11** (150 miles N.W. of Santa Fe)

Restaurants: 1
Hours: 1pm-1am/2pm-2am (Fri-Sat)
Other Games: Only gaming machines
Special Features: Live horse racing during season which runs from September through November. Simulcasting of horse racing all year.

NEW YORK

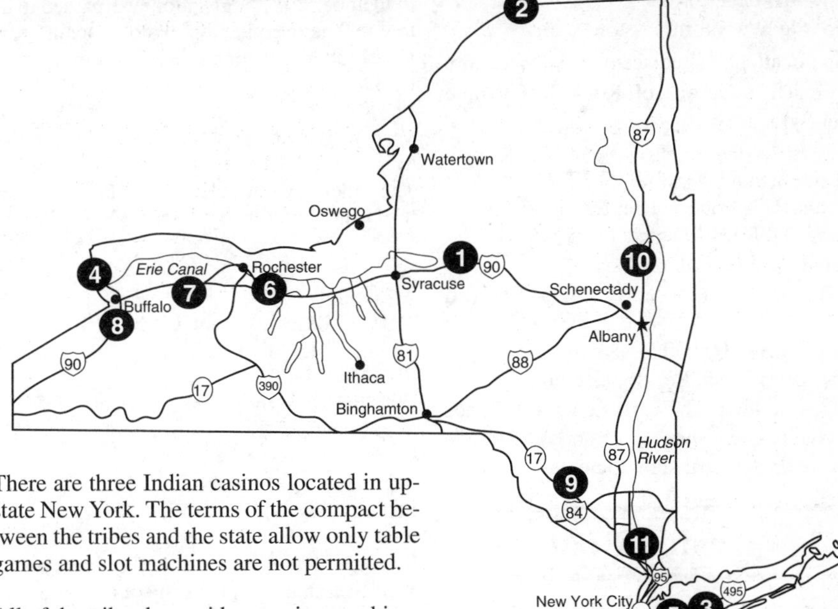

There are three Indian casinos located in upstate New York. The terms of the compact between the tribes and the state allow only table games and slot machines are not permitted.

All of the tribes have video gaming machines which offer slot-style games, plus keno and poker. These machines do not pay out in cash. Instead, they print out a receipt which must be exchanged for cash.

In October 2001 the New York Assembly passed legislation to expand gambling within the state by allowing up to six Indian casinos. Three of the casinos would be located in the western half of the state and the other three would be located in the Catskills (about a three-hour drive from midtown Manahattan).

As of August 2003 the only Indian casino to open was in Niagara Falls and the other casinos were still in the planning stages.

All New York Indian casinos are open 24 hours and offer the following games: blackjack, craps, roulette, pai gow poker, mini-baccarat, Caribbean stud poker, let it ride, money (big six) wheel and poker. The minimum gambling age is 21 at Niagara and 18 at the others.

For more information on visiting New York call the state's travel information center at (800) 225-5697.

Akwesasne Mohawk Casino
Route 37, Box 670
Hogansburg, New York 13655
(518) 358-2222
Web Site: www.mohawkcasino.com
Map Location: **#2** (65 miles W. of Champlain)

Toll-Free Number: (888) 622-1155
Restaurants: 2 Liquor: Yes
Buffets: B-$3.95 (Sat-Sun) L-$7.95 D-$11.95
Casino Size: 40,000 Square Feet

Seneca Niagara Casino
310 Fourth Street
Niagara Falls, New York 14303
(716) 299-1100
Web Site: www.snfgc.com
Map Location: **#4**

Toll-Free Number: (877) 873-6322
Restaurants: 4 Liquor: Yes
Buffets: L/D-$14.99
Other Games: Baccarat, No Poker

Special Features: $8.99 late night buffet

Turning Stone Casino Resort
5218 Patrick Road
Verona, New York 13478
(315) 361-7711
Web Site: www.turning-stone.com
Map Location: **#1** (adjacent to NY State Thruway exit 33 at Verona, off Route 365, 30 miles E. of Syracuse)

Toll-Free Number: (800) 771-7711
Rooms: 277 Price Range: $96-$175
Suites: 28 Price Range: $126-$395
Restaurants: 9 Liquor: No
Buffets: B-$6.95 (Sat-Sun) L-$8.95/$9.95 (Fri)
D-$8.95/$12.95 (Fri/Sat)
Casino Size: 100,000 Square Feet
Other Games: Sic Bo, Bingo, Keno
Special Features: Three golf courses. Gift shop. Discount smoke shop. AAA and AARP room discounts. 800-seat showroom.

Casino Boat

New York has one casino boat which travels three miles out into international waters where gambling is permitted. The boat offers: blackjack, craps, roulette, Caribbean stud poker, let it ride, slots and video poker.

Freeport Casino Cruises
361 Woodcleft Avenue
Freeport, New York 11520
(516) 377-7400
Map Location **#3**

Reservation Number: (516) 377-7400
Gambling Age: 21
Ship's Registry: U.S.A.
Food Service: Free Snacks
Schedule:
11:30am - 4:30pm/5:00pm (Fri-Sat)
7:00pm - 11:30pm/12:30am (Fri-Sat)
Price: Free
Port Charges: Included
Parking: Free
Special Features: 500-passenger, *Midnight Gambler II* departs from Freeport's Nautical Mile. You must be 21 or older to board.

Pari-Mutuels

In October 2001, legislation was passed to allow for the introduction of slot machine-type video lottery terminals (VLTs) at eight racetracks.

Vernon Downs, was expected to be the first to have the VLT's in operation by late 2003. The other seven tracks should all have their VLT's in operation by mid-2004.

Aqueduct
110-00 Rockaway Boulevard
Jamaica, New York 11417
(718) 641-4700
Website: www.nyra.com/aqueduct
Map Location: **#5** (15 miles E. of Manhattan)

Admission: $1 Clubhouse: $3
Self-Parking: $1 Valet: $5
Restaurants: 2
Special Features: Live thoroughbred racing Wed-Sat. Daily simulcasting of thoroughbred racing.

Batavia Downs Race Track
8315 Park Road
Batavia, New York 14010
(585) 343-3750
Website: www.batavia-downs.com
Map Location: **#7** (35 miles E. of Buffalo)

Admission: Free
Parking: Free
Restaurants: 1
Special Features: Live harness racing Mon/Wed/Fri/Sat from mid-July through mid-December. Daily simulcasting of throroughbred and harness racing.

Buffalo Raceway
5600 McKinley Parkway
Hamburg Fairgrounds
Hamburg, New York 14075
(716) 649-1280
Website: www.buffaloraceway.com
Map Location: **#8** (15 miles S. of Buffalo)

Admission: Free
Parking: Free
Restaurants: 1
Special Features: Live harness racing Wed/Fri/Sat from February through July. Daily simulcasting of throroughbred and harness racing.

Finger Lakes Race Track
5857 Route 96
Farmington, NY 14425
(585) 924-3232
Website: www.fingerlakesracetrack.com
Map Location: **#6** (25 miles S. of Rochester)

Admission: Free
Parking: Free
Restaurants: 2
Special Features: Live thoroughbred horse racing (Fri-Tue) mid-April through late November. Simulcasting offered every day.

Monticello Raceway
Route 17B
Monticello, New York 12701
(845) 794-4100
Website: www.monticelloraceway.com
Map Location: **#9** (50 miles W. of Newburgh)

Admission: Free/$1.50 (Sun)
Self-Parking: Free
Restaurants: 1
Special Features: Year-round live harness racing Sun-Wed. Daily simulcast of throroughbred and harness racing.

Saratoga Raceway
Crescent Avenue
Saratoga Springs, New York 12866
(518) 584-2110
Website: www.saratogaraceway.com
Map Location: **#10** (25 miles N. of Schenectady)

Admission: Free
Parking: Free
Restaurants: 1
Special Features: Live harness racing on various evenings from November through September. Daily simulcasting of throroughbred and harness racing.

Vernon Downs
14 Ruth Street
Vernon, New York 13476
(315) 829-2201
Website: www.vernondowns.com
Map Location: **#1** (30 miles E. of Syracuse)

Toll-Free Number: (877) 777-8559
Room Reservations: (866) 829-3400
Suites: 87 Price Range: $79-$250
Admission: Free
Parking: Free
Restaurants: 1
Special Features: Live harness racing Thu-Sun evenings May through November. Daily simulcasting of throroughbred and harness racing.

Yonkers Raceway
8100 Central Avenue
Yonkers, New York 10704
(914) 968-4200
Website: www.yonkersraceway.com
Map Location: **#11** (20 miles N. of Manhattan)

Restaurants: 1
Self-Parking: $2 Valet: $5
Special Features: Year-round live harness racing Mon/Tue/Thu/Sat evenings. Daily simulcasting of throroughbred and harness racing.

NORTH CAROLINA

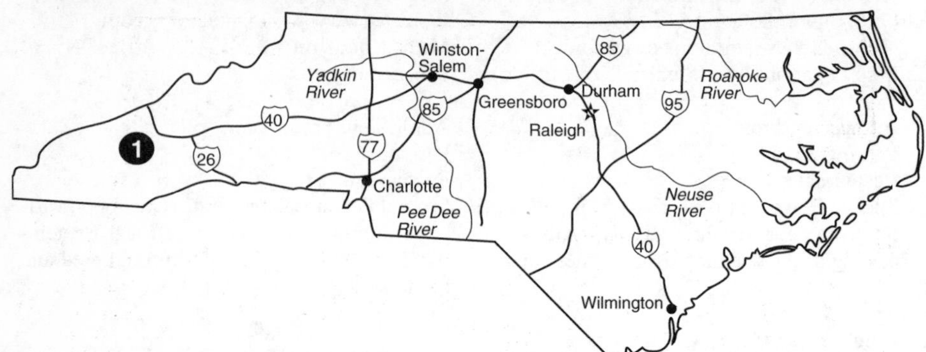

North Carolina has one Indian casino. In August, 1994 the state's Eastern Band of Cherokee Indians signed a compact with the governor to allow forms of video gambling. According to the terms of the compact, the video machines must be games of skill and they are required to return a minimum of 83% and a maximum of 98%.

No table games are offered at the Cherokee Casino, only video slots, video poker, and video versions of craps and blackjack. The slots are different than slots you will find in other casinos because of the required "skill" factor. With these "skill" slots you have two opportunities to spin the reels. The "skill" factor comes into play because after seeing the results of your first spin you then have to decide whether to keep none, one, two, or all three of the symbols on each reel before you spin them again.

The casino is open 24 hours and the minimum gambling age is 21.

For more information on visiting North Carolina call the state's division of travel & tourism at (800) 847-4862.

Harrah's Cherokee Casino
P.O. Box 1959
Cherokee, North Carolina 28719
(828) 497-7777
Website: www.harrahs.com
Map Location: **#1** (55 miles S.W. of Asheville)

Toll-Free Number: (800) HARRAHS
Rooms 252 Price Range: $59-$179
Restaurants: 5 Liquor: No
Buffets: B-$8.00 L-$10.00 D-$14.50
Special Features: Offers "Play and Stay" packages at five nearby hotels (call 800-HARRAHS to book). Planet-4-Kidz childcare center. 1,500-seat entertainment pavilion.

NORTH DAKOTA

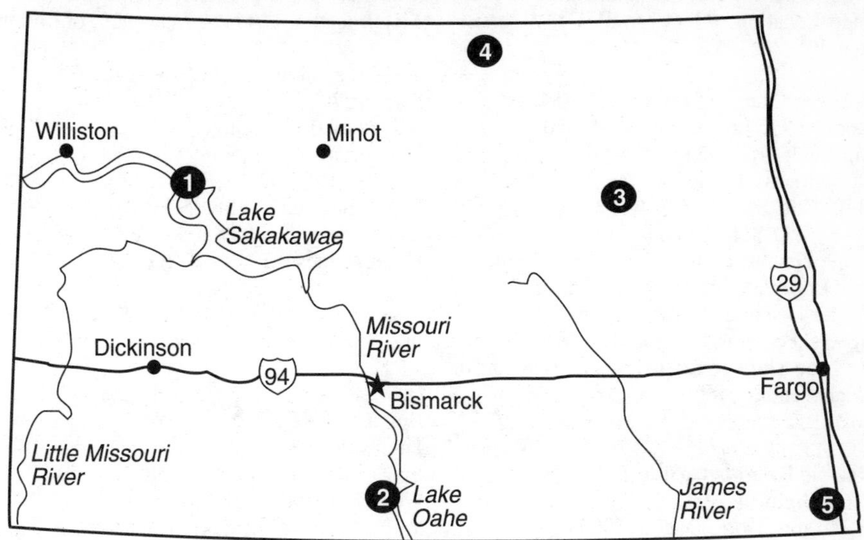

North Dakota has more than 800 sites throughout the state that offer blackjack, with a $25 maximum bet, for the benefit of charities.

There are also six Indian casinos which, although not restricted to that same $25 amount, are limited by law to the following maximum bets: blackjack-$100 (two tables in a casino may have limits up to $250), craps-$60, roulette-$50, slots/video poker-$25 and poker-$50 per bet, per round with a maximum of three rounds.

The terms of the state's compact with the tribes require gaming machines to return a minimum of 80% and a maximum of 100%. However, if a machine is affected by skill, such as video poker or video blackjack, the machines must return a minimum of 83%.

All casinos are open 24 hours and offer: blackjack, craps, roulette, poker, slots, video poker, video keno and video blackjack. Optional games include: Caribbean stud poker (CSP), let it ride (LIR), keno (K), bingo (BG), big-6 wheel (B6) and simulcasting (S). The minimum gambling age is 21.

For information on visiting North Dakota call the state's tourism office at (800) 435-5663.

Dakota Magic Casino
16849 102nd Street SE
Hankinson, North Dakota 58041
(701) 634-3000
Website: www.dakotamagic.com
Map Location: **#5** (50 miles S. of Fargo)

Toll-Free Number: (800) 325-6825
Rooms: 76 Price Range: $40-$85
Suites: 8 Price Range: $90-$95
Restaurants: 1 Liquor: Yes
Buffets: B-$4.95 L-$5.95 D-$5.95/$9.95(Fri)
Casino Size: 24,000 Square Feet
Other Games: P, K
Fun Book: Given to hotel guests
Senior Discount: Various on Mon, if 55 or older

Four Bears Casino & Lodge
202 Frontage Rd
New Town, North Dakota 58763
(701) 627-4018
Website: www.4bearscasino.com
Map Location: **#1** (150 miles N.W. of Bismarck)

Toll-Free Number: (800) 294-5454
Rooms: 97 Price Range: $55-$70
Suites: 3 Price Range: $99
Restaurants: 2 Liquor: Yes
Buffets: L-$4.95 (Mon-Fri)
D-$11.95 (Thu-Sun)
Other Games: P, BG
Fun Book: Inquire at slot club desk
Senior Discount: Various, if 55+
Special Features: 85-space RV park with laundry and shower facilities. Nearby marina. Event center.

Prairie Knights Casino & Resort
7932 Highway 24
Fort Yates, North Dakota 58538
(701) 854-7777
Website: www.prairieknights.com
Map Location: **#2** (60 miles S. of Bismarck)

Toll-Free Number: (800) 425-8277
Rooms: 96 Price Range: $60-$75
Suites: 4 Price Range: $85-$130
Restaurants: 2 Liquor: Yes
Buffets: L/D-$9.25/$14.95 (Sun)
Casino Size: 42,000 Square Feet
Other Games: S21, TCP, LIR
Senior Discount: $6.75 buffet from
11am - 5pm (Mon-Sat), if 55 or older
Special Features: Marina with boat slips and 32 RV sites. $45 rooms for slot club members.

Sky Dancer Hotel & Casino
Highway 5 West
Belcourt, North Dakota 58316
(701) 244-2400
Website: www.skydancercasino.com
Map Location: **#4** (120 miles N.E. of Minot)

Toll-Free Number: (866) 244-9467
Rooms: 70 Price Range: $45-$55
Suites: 27 Price Range: $75-$85
Restaurants: 2 Liquor: Yes
Buffets: B-$2.99/$5.95 (Sat-Sun) L-$4.95/ $6.95 (Sat-Sun) D-$8.95-$14.90
Casino Size: 25,000 Square Feet
Other Games: LIR, TCP, BG, S,
P, No Roulette
Special Features: Gift shop. 12 Free RV hookups. $5.99 late night weekend buffet.

Spirit Lake Casino & Resort
Highway 57
Spirit Lake, North Dakota 58370
(701) 766-4747
Website: www.spiritlakecasino.com
Map Location: **#3** (6 miles S. of Devil's Lake)

Toll-Free Number: (800) WIN-U-BET
Rooms: 108 Price Range: $70
Suites: 16 Price Range: $80-$125
Restaurants: 3 Liquor: No
Buffets: B-$5.50/$7.95 (Sun) L-$6.50
D-$9.95/$16.95 (Wed)
Casino Size: 45,000 Square Feet
Other Games: P, LIR, BG
Senior Discount: 10% off room, if 55 or older
Special Features: 15-space RV park. Gift shop. Discount smoke shop. 10% room discount for AAA members. Marina.

Turtle Mountain Chippewa Mini-Casino
Highway 5 West
Belcourt, North Dakota 58316
(701) 477-6438
Map Location: **#4** (120 miles N.E. of Minot)

Restaurants: 1 Liquor: Yes
Other Games: Only Machines - No Table Games
Special Features: Located four miles east of Sky Dancer Hotel and Casino.

OREGON

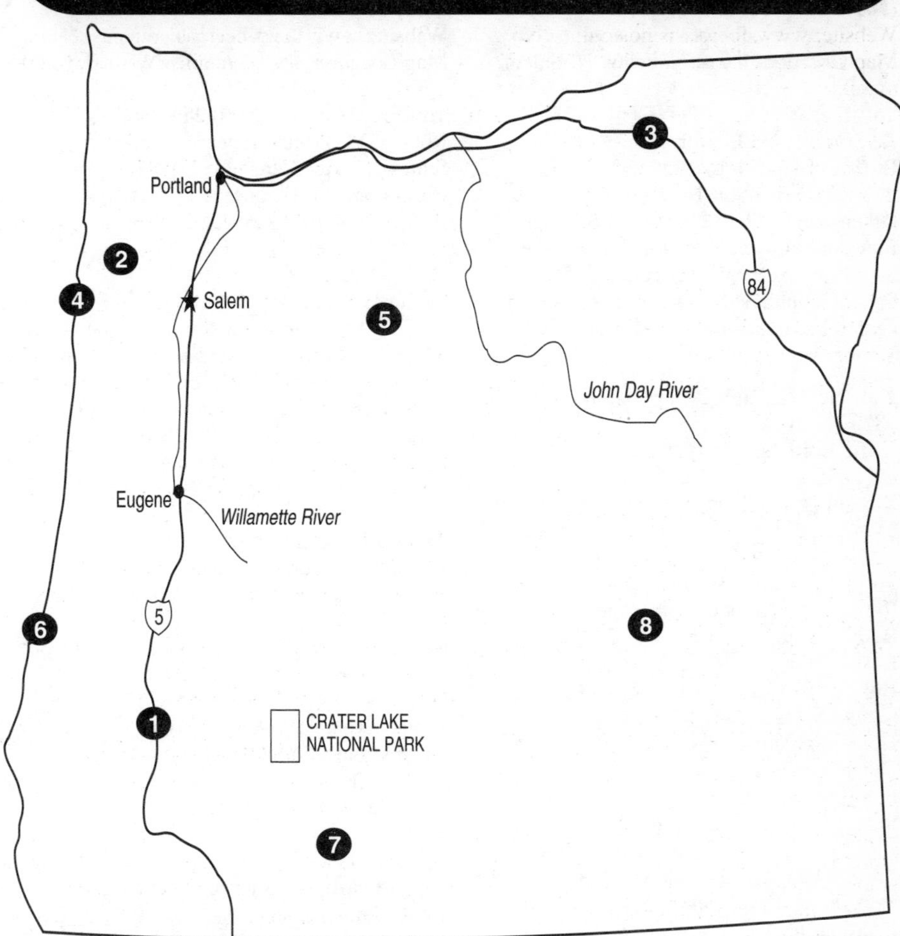

Oregon law permits bars and taverns to have up to five video lottery terminals that offer various versions of video poker. The maximum bet allowed is $2 and the maximum payout on any machine is capped at $600.

These machines are the same as regular video gaming devices but are called lottery terminals because they are regulated by the state's lottery commission which receives a share of each machine's revenue. The machines accept cash but do not pay out in cash; instead, they print out a receipt which must be taken to a cashier.

During the Oregon Lottery's fiscal year from July 1, 2002 through June 30, 2003, the VLT's had an approximate return of 93.90%.

There are eight Indian casinos in operation in Oregon. According to the governor's office which regulates the Tribe's compacts, "there is no minimum payback percentage required on the Tribe's machines. Each Tribe is free to set their own limits on their machines."

All casinos offer blackjack, video slots, video poker, video keno, video blackjack and pull tabs. Some casinos also offer: craps (C), roulette (R), poker (P), Pai Gow Poker (PGP), let it ride (LIR), big 6 wheel (B6), bingo (BG), keno (K) and simulcasting. Unless otherwise noted, all casinos are open 24 hours and the minimum gambling age is 21.

For Oregon tourism information call (800) 547-7842.

Chinook Winds Gaming Center
1777 N.W. 44th Street
Lincoln City, Oregon 97367
(541) 996-5700
Website: www.chinookwindscasino.com
Map Location: **#4** (45 miles W. of Salem)

Toll-Free Number: (888) CHINOOK
Restaurants: 3 Liquor: Yes
Buffets: B-$6.50 L-$7.50
D-$11.50/$14.50 (Fri/Sat)
Other Games: P, BG, K, LIR, CSP, PGP
Fun Book: Given with slot club membership.
Senior Discount: Buffet discount, if 55, or older
Special Features: Smoke-free area. Childcare center. Video arcade. Gift shop.

Kah-Nee-Ta High Desert Resort & Casino
6823 Highway 8
Warm Springs, Oregon 97761
(541) 553-1112
Website: www.kahneeta.com
Map Location: **#5** (100 miles E. of Portland)

Toll-Free Number: (800) 238-6946
Reservation Number: (800) 554-4786
Rooms: 169 Price Range: $139-$260
Restaurants: 2 Liquor: Yes
Buffets: B-$7.95 L-$9.95 D-$18.95
Casino Size: 25,000 Square Feet
Hours: 8:30am-2am
Other Games: P
Fun Book: Given to lodge guests, bus groups,
Senior Discount: Free fun Book on Mon,
10% room discount, if 55+
Special Features: 18-hole golf course. Horseback riding. European spa. Campground, miniature golf.

Kla-Mo-Ya Casino
34333 Hwy 97 North
Chiloquin, Oregon 97624
(541) 783-7529
Website: www.klamoya.com
Map Location: **#7** (20 miles N. of Klamath Falls)

Toll-Free Number: (888) 552-6692
Restaurants: 2 Liquor: No
Buffets: L-$6.99 D-$8.99
Hours: 7am-1am/24 Hours (Fri-Sat)
Other Games: P
Senior Discount: $2 buffet discount. Various promotions on Mondays, if 55 or older

The Mill Casino Hotel
3201 Tremont Avenue
North Bend, Oregon 97459
(541) 756-8800
Website: www.themillcasino.com
Map Location: **#6** (75 miles S.W. of Eugene)

Toll-Free Number: (800) 953-4800
Rooms: 112 Price Range: $69-$145
Suites: 3 Price Range: $125-$210
Restaurants: 4 Liquor: Yes
Buffets: B-$13.95 (Sun) L-$9.95
D-$14.95/$17.95 (Fri-Sat)
Other Games: BG
Senior Discount: 10% off food, if 55 or older
Fun Book: Given when you join slot club
Special Features: Free shuttle bus from airport and local motels. Video arcade. Room and food discounts for slot club members. Free RV parking. Buffet discount for slot club members.

The Old Camp Casino
2205 W. Monroe Street
Burns, Oregon 97720
(541) 573-1500
Map Location: **#8** (250 miles S. of Pendleton)

Restaurants: 1 Liquor: Yes
Hours: 11am-11pm/2am (Fri-Sat)
Other Games: P, BG
Special Features: Liquor sold in lounge and restaurant only. RV park.

Seven Feathers Hotel & Casino Resort
146 Chief Miwaleta Lane
Canyonville, Oregon 97417
(541) 839-1111
Website: www.sevenfeathers.com
Map Location: **#1** (80 miles S. of Eugene)

Toll-Free Number: (800) 548-8461
Rooms: 145 Price Range: $89-$109
Suites: 1 Price Range: $175-$225
Restaurants: 3 Liquor: Yes
Buffets: B-$16.50 (Sun) D-$10.95
Casino Size: 27,300 Square Feet
Other Games: C, R, P, K, BG, LIR, PGP
Fun Book: Ask during birth month
Senior Discount: 10% off room, if 55, or older
Special Features: RV park. 18-hole golf course. 10% room discount for AAA/AARP members.

Spirit Mountain Casino
P.O. Box 39
Grand Ronde, Oregon 97347
(503) 879-2350
Website: www.spiritmountain.com
Map Location: **#2** (85 miles S.W. of Portland)

Toll-Free Number: (800) 760-7977
Reservation Number: (888) 668-7366
Rooms: 94 Price Range: $99-$119
Suites: 6 Price Range: $169-$235
Restaurants: 5 Liquor: Yes
Buffets: B-$5.75 L-$6.75 D-$9.75/$11.95 (Wed)
Fun Book: Ask Tue. at Player Services Desk
Other Games: C, R, P, PGP, LIR, B6, K, BG, S
Special Features: Separate nonsmoking casino and bingo area. Liquor sold in lounge only. Childcare center. Video arcade. Slot club members receive a $20 room discount. The slot club can be signed up for online.

Wildhorse Resort & Casino
72777 Highway 331
Pendleton, Oregon 97801
(541) 278-2274
Website: www.wildhorseresort.com
Map Location: **#3** (211 miles E. of Portland)

Toll-Free Number: (800) 654-9453
Rooms: 100 Price Range: $65-$95
Suites: 5 Price Range: $90- $175
Restaurants: 4 (1 open 24 hours) Liquor: No
Casino Size: 80,000 Square Feet
Other Games: P, K, BG, S, S21, TCP
Senior Discount: 10% off room, if 55, or older
Special Features: RV park. 18-hole golf course. Health spa. Cultural Institute. 10% hotel discount if 55, or older. Child care center, video arcade.

RHODE ISLAND

Rhode Island has two pari-mutuel facilities which both feature video lottery terminals (VLT's). These machines are the same as regular video gaming devices but are called lottery terminals because they are regulated by the state's lottery commission which receives a share of each machine's revenue. The machines accept cash but don't pay out in cash; instead, they print out a receipt which must be taken to a cashier.

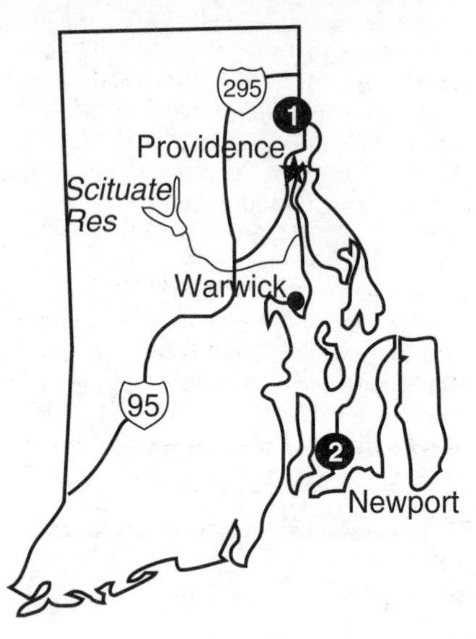

All VLT's are programmed to play at least six different games: blackjack, keno, slots and three versions of poker (jacks or better, joker poker and deuces wild).

The Rhode Island Lottery does not provide figures to determine the actual paybacks on its VLT's, however, according to Dennis Tripodi, finance administrator for the Rhode Island Lottery, the VLT's are programmed to pay back the following amounts over time:

Blackjack - 99.1%
5¢, 10¢, 25¢ Video Poker - 95%
50¢ Video Poker - 96.5%
$1 Video Poker - 98%
5¢, 10¢, 25¢ Slots - 92%
50¢ Slots - 94%
$1 Slots - 96%
25¢ Keno - 92%
50¢ Keno - 94%
$1 Keno - 96%.

The minimum gambling age in Rhode Island is 18. For information on visiting Rhode Island call the state's tourism division at (800) 556-2484.

Lincoln Park
1600 Louisquisset Pike
Lincoln, Rhode Island 02865
(401) 723-3200
Web Site: www.lincolnparkri.com
Map Location: **#1** (10 miles N. of Providence)

Toll-Free Number: (800) 720-7275
Restaurants: 3
Hours: 9am-1am Daily
Admission: Free
Valet Parking: Free
Special Features: Live dog racing (Mon/Wed/Fri/Sat) throughout the year. Daily (except Tuesday) simulcasting of horse and dog racing.

Newport Grand Jai-Alai
150 Admiral Kalbfus Road
Newport, Rhode Island 02840
(401) 849-5000
Web Site: www.newportgrand.com
Map Location: **#2**

Toll-Free Number: (800) 451-2500
Restaurants: 1
Hours: 10am-1am Daily
Admission: Free
Valet Parking: $1.50
Special Features: Daily simulcasting of horse and dog racing.

SOUTH CAROLINA

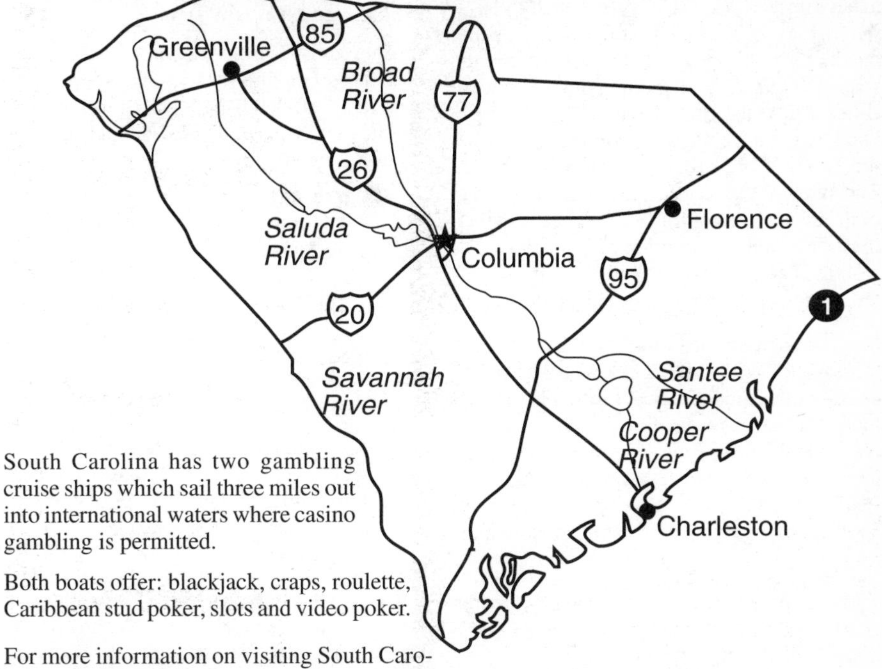

South Carolina has two gambling cruise ships which sail three miles out into international waters where casino gambling is permitted.

Both boats offer: blackjack, craps, roulette, Caribbean stud poker, slots and video poker.

For more information on visiting South Carolina call the state's tourism department at (800) 872-3505.

Southern Elegance Casino Cruises
4491 Waterfront Avenue
Little River, South Carolina 29566
(843) 249-9811
Website: www.southernelegancecasino.com
Map Location: **#1** (35 miles N. of M. Beach)

Reservation Number: (877) 250-5825
Meal Service: Deli
Schedule:
11:00am - 4:30pm (Mon-Thu)
7:00pm- 12:30am (Daily)
12:00pm- 5:30pm (Sat-Sun)
Prices: Free
Port Charges: None Parking: Free
Senior Discount: Mon-Fri receive free deli selection on morning cruise, if 55+
Special Features: 401-passenger boat sails from Little River waterfront. Free shuttle available from Myrtle Beach. Must be 21, or older, to board. Dinner served before sailing at $7 per person.

SunCruz Casino - Myrtle Beach
4491 Waterfront Drive
Little River, South Carolina 29566
(843) 280-2933
Website: www.suncruzcasino.com
Map Location: **#1** (35 miles N. of Myrtle Beach)

Reservation Number: (800) 474-DICE
Gambling Age: 18
Buffets: L-$5 D-$7
Schedule:
11:00am - 4:15pm (Mon-Fri)
Noon - 5:15pm (Sat-Sun)
7:00pm - 12:15am (Sun-Thu)
7:00pm - 1:00am (Fri/Sat/Holidays)
Prices: $10
Port Charges: Included Parking: Free
Other Games: Mini-Baccarat, Let It Ride
Special Features: 600-passenger *SunCruz VII* sails from Little River waterfront. Must be 18, or older, to board. Reservations recommended.

SOUTH DAKOTA

South Dakota's bars and taverns are allowed to have up to 10 video lottery terminals (VLT's) that offer the following games: poker, keno, blackjack and bingo. These machines are the same as regular video gaming devices but are called lottery terminals because they are regulated by the state's lottery commission which receives a share of each machine's revenue. The machines accept cash but don't pay out in cash; instead, they print out a receipt which must be taken to a cashier. Slot machines, as well as blackjack and poker are only permitted at Indian casinos and in Deadwood.

Deadwood was once most famous for being the home of Wild Bill Hickok who was shot to death while playing cards in the No. 10 Saloon. The hand he held at the time was two pairs: black aces and eights, which is now commonly referred to as a "dead man's hand." Wild Bill is buried in the local cemetery along with another local celebrity: Calamity Jane.

The first casinos in Deadwood opened on November 1, 1989. All of the buildings in the downtown area are required to conform with the city's authentic 1880's architecture. Many of the casinos are located in historic structures but there are also some new structures which were designed to be compatible with the historic theme of the town. The old No. 10 Saloon is still operating and you can actually gamble in the same spot where old Wild Bill bit the dust! One of the casinos, Midnight Star, is owned by movie actor Kevin Costner and his brother, Dan.

South Dakota law limits each casino licensee to a maximum of 30 machines and no one person is allowed to hold more than three licenses. Some operators combine licenses with other operators to form a cooperative which may look like one casino but in reality it's actually several licensees operating under one name.

The state's gaming laws originally limited blackjack, poker, let it ride and three-card poker bets to a maximum of $5, however, in late 2000 the law was changed to allow maximum bets of $100.

In addition to the Deadwood casinos, there are also nine Indian casinos in South Dakota. These casinos are also subject to the $100 maximum bet restrictions.

Here are statistics from the South Dakota Commission on Gaming for the payback percentages on all of Deadwood's slot machines for the six-month period from January 1, 2003 through June 30, 2003:

Denomination	Payback %
1¢ Slots	90.85
5¢ Slots	91.14
10¢ Slots	92.23
25¢ Slots	90.99
50¢ Slots	91.83
$1 Slots	91.96
$5 Slots	94.26
$25 Slots	94.44

Some of the larger casinos are open 24 hours but most of the smaller ones are open from 8am until midnight Sunday through Thursday and 8am until 2am on the weekends.

There is a scheduled shuttle service to all of the casinos that operates from 8am to midnight weekdays and 7am to 3 am weekends. (During the summer months the weekday hours are extended to 7am to 1:30am). The cost is 50 cents per ride.

Unless otherwise noted, all casinos offer slot machines and video poker. Some casinos also offer: blackjack (BJ), let it ride (LIR), three-card poker (TCP), Caribbean stud poker (CSP) and poker (P). Most of the Indian casinos also offer bingo (BG).

The minimum gambling age is 21 (18 at Indian casinos that don't serve alcohol). South Dakota's casinos have very liberal rules about allowing minors into casinos and virtually all of the casinos will allow children to enter with their parents until about 8 p.m. Additionally, South Dakota is the only jurisdiction that will allow children to stand next to their parents while they are gambling.

For South Dakota tourism information call (800) 732-5682. For information on visiting Deadwood call the city's Chamber of Commerce at (800) 999-1876, or visit their website at www.deadwood.org.

Deadwood

Map Location: **#1** (in the Black Hills, 41 miles N.W. of Rapid City. Take I-90 W. Get off at the second Sturges exit and take Hwy. 14-A into Deadwood)

B. B. Cody's
681 Main Street
Deadwood, SD 57732
(605) 578-2209

Restaurants: 2 (1 open 24 hours)
Other Games: BJ
Special Features: Video arcade. Pizza Hut Express.

Best Western Hickok House
137 Charles Street
(605) 578-1611
Website: www.bestwestern.com

Best Western Reservations: 800-528-1234
Rooms: 38 Price Range: $39-$109
Restaurants: 1
Special Features: Hot tub and sauna. AAA and AARP room discount.

Bodega Bar
662 Main Street
(605) 578-1162

Restaurants: 1
Other Games: BJ

Buffalo Saloon
658 Main Street
(605) 578-1162

Other games: BJ (Thu-Sat)

Bullock Express
68 Main Street
(605) 578-3476

Reservation Number: 800-526-8277
Rooms: 38 Price Range: $65-$95
Restaurants: 1
Hours: 6am-2am
Special Features: AARP room discount.

Bullock Hotel
633 Main Street
(605) 578-1745
Website: www.bullockhotel.com

Reservation Number: 800-336-1876
Rooms: 29 Price Range: $65-$99
Suites: 7 Price Range: $135-$159
Restaurants: 1
Hours: 24 hours daily
Special Features: Deadwood's oldest hotel. 10% room discount for AAA members.

Cadillac Jacks's Gaming Resort
360 Main Street
(605) 578-1500
Website: www.cadillacjacksgaming.com

Toll Free Number: (866) 332-3966
Rooms: 103 Price Range: $47-$99
Suites: 11 Price Range: $99-$189
Restaurants: 1
Hours: 24 hours daily
Casino Size: 10,000 Square Feet
Other Games: BJ, TCP
Senior Discount: Free meal Mon-Sat, if 50+ and slot club member
Special Features: Hotel is AmericInn. Denny's restaurant. Video arcade.

Celebrity Hotel & Casino
629 Main Street
(605) 578-1909
Website: www.celebritycasinos.com

Toll-Free Number: (888) 399-1886
Rooms: 9 Price Range: $49-$99
Suites: 3 Price Range: $79-$139
Hours: 24 Hours Daily
Special Features: Car and motorcycle museum. Free to hotel guests, otherwise admission charge. 10% AAA room discount. Includes **Mint** casino.

Dakota Frontier/Deadwood Stage
670 Main Street
(605) 578-1515

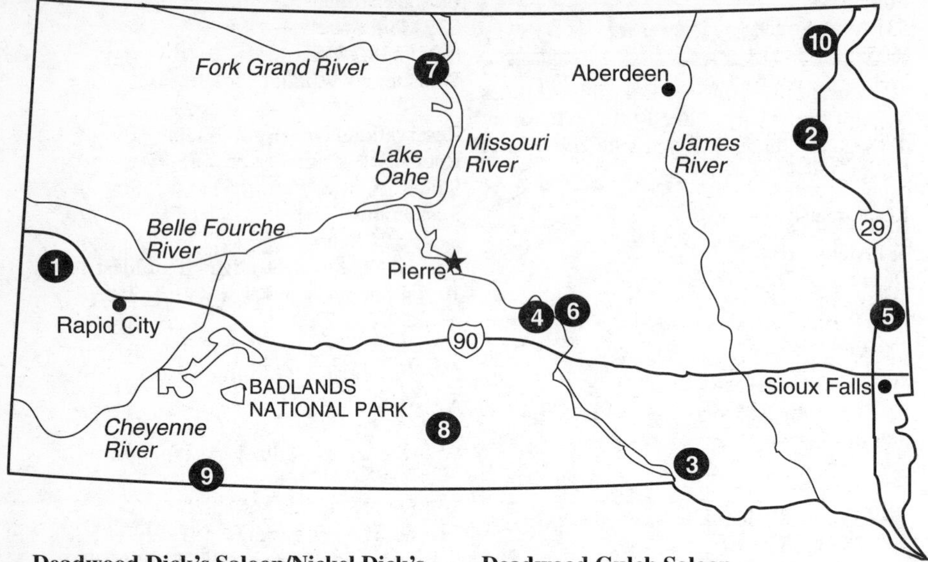

Deadwood Dick's Saloon/Nickel Dick's
51-55 Sherman Street
(605) 578-3224
Website: www.deadwooddicks.com

Toll Free Number: (877) 882-4990
Rooms: 5 Price Range: $59-$69
Suites: 6 Price Range: $85-$125
Restaurants: 1
Special Features: Antiques mall. 30% room discount for stays of 3 or more days.

Deadwood Gulch Resort
Highway 85 South/P.O. Box 643
(605) 578-1294
Website: www.deadwoodgulch.com

Reservation Number: (800) 695-1876
Rooms: 95 Price Range: $62-$109
Suites: 3 Price Range: $85-$125
Restaurants: 2
Hours: 24 hours daily
Casino Size: 7,000 Square Feet
Other Games: BJ
Special Features: Hotel is Days Inn. 10% room discount to AAA/AARP members. Convenience store and gas station. Family fun park with go-carts, bumper boats, miniature golf, batting cages, kiddie playland and arcade.

Deadwood Gulch Saloon
560 Main Street
(605) 578-1207

Deadwood Inn
27 Deadwood Street
(605) 578-7700

Toll Free Number: (877) 815-7974
Rooms: 19 Price Range: $59-$99
Suites: 4 Price Range: $89-$175
Casino Size: 1,000 Square Feet
Special Features: 10% room discount for AAA members and seniors 65 or older.

First Gold Hotel & Gaming
270 Main Street
(605) 578-9777
Website: www.firstgold.com

Reservation Number: (800) 274-1876
Rooms: 132 Price Range: $39-$199
Suites: 2 Price Range: $79-$250
Restaurants: 1
Hours: 24 hours daily
Casino Size: 7,000 Square Feet
Other Games: BJ, TCP
Casino Marketing: (800) 410-3732
Fun Book: Given to hotel and RV park guests
Senior Discount: 10% off room, if 60, or older
Special Features: 79¢ breakfast and $1.99 lunch specials. RV park located next door. Also contains **Horseshoe** and **Blackjack** casinos.

Four Aces
531 Main Street
(605) 578-2323
Website: www.fouracesdeadwood.com

Toll Free Number: (800) 834-4384
Rooms: 59 Price Range: $99-$139
Suites: 5 Price Range: $150-$350
Restaurants: 1
Buffets: B-$4.99 (Sun) L-$6.99
D-$8.99/$11.99 (Fri-Sat)
Hours: 24 hours daily
Casino Size: 24,000 Square Feet
Other Games: BJ, LIR, TCP
Senior Discount: 10% off room, if 55, or older

Gold Country Inn
801 Main Street
Deadwood, SD
(605) 578-2393

Reservation Number: (800) 287-1251
Rooms: 53 Price Range: $45-$59
Restaurants: 1

Gold Dust Gaming & Entertainment Complex
688 Main Street
(605) 578-2100
Website: www.golddustgaming.com

Toll-Free Number: 800-456-0533
Rooms: 56 Price Range: $59-$150
Suites: 22 Price Range: $150-$250
Restaurants: 1
Buffets: B-$4.99 L-$5.99
D-$9.99/$10.99 (Sat)/$11.95 (Fri)
Hours: 24 hours Daily
Casino Size: 30,000 Square Feet
Other Games: BJ, P
Fun Book: Call or write to request in advance
Senior Discount: $1 off buffets, if 55, or older
Special Features: Hotel is Holiday Inn Express. Largest gaming complex in Deadwood with nine casinos including: **Legends, French Quarter and Silver Dollar.** AARP discount, free continental breakfast, indoor pool, gym, whirlpool, arcade.

Gulches of Fun
225 Cliff Street
(605) 578-7550
Website: www.gulchesoffun.com

Reservation Number: (800) 961-3096
Rooms: 70 Price Range: $79-$279
Restaurants: 1
Other Games: BJ
Hours: 24 hours daily
Special Features: Hotel is Comfort Inn. AAA/AARP room discounts.

Hickok's Saloon
685 Main Street
(605) 578-2222

Other Games: BJ, TCP
Special Features: Video arcade.

Historic Franklin Hotel
700 Main Street
(605) 578-2241
Website: www.deadwood.net/franklin

Reservation Number: 800-688-1876
Rooms: 80 Price Range: $59-$105
Suites: 15 Price Range: $90-$175
Restaurants: 1
Other Games: BJ, P
Senior Discount: 10% off room, if 65, or older
Special Features: Historic old hotel. Three lounges. Wedding chapel.

Lady Luck
660 Main Street
(605) 578-1162

Lucky 8 Gaming Hall/Super 8 Lodge
196 Cliff Street
(605) 578-2535
Website: www.deadwoodsuper8.com

Reservation Number: (800) 800-8000
Rooms: 51 Price Range: $40-$90
Suites: 4 Price Range: $80-$130
Restaurants: 1
Hours: 24 hours daily
Fun Book: Given to guests at check-in
Senior Discount: 10% AARP room discount
Special Features: Casino claims highest percentage payback chips installed on their games. Video arcade. Free breakfast for room guests.

Nestled in the Black Hills of South Dakota, the entire city of Deadwood has been designated a national historic landmark. Free historic walking tours are offered daily.

McKenna's Gold
470 Main Street
(605) 578-3207
Website: www.deadwoodattractions.com

Midnight Star
677 Main Street
(605) 578-1555
Website: www.themidnightstar.com

Toll-Free Number: (800) 999-6482
Restaurants: 2
Other Games: BJ, LIR, TCP
Fun Book: Call to receive by mail
Special Features: Kevin Costner is part-owner and the property features a museum with authentic costumes and memorabilia from his movies. Sports Bar & Grill.

Mineral Palace Hotel & Gaming Complex
601 Main Street
(605) 578-2036
Website: www.mineralpalace.com

Reservation Number: (800) 84-PALACE
Rooms: 63 Price Range: $69-$109
Suites: 4 Price Range: $89-$225
Restaurants: 1
Hours: 24 hours daily
Other Games: BJ
Special Features: Contains **Cousin Jack's**, **Carrie Nation's** and **Deadwood Livery** casinos. Cappuccino/espresso bar. Liquor store.

Miss Kitty's Gaming Emporium
647 Main Street
(605) 578-1811

Restaurants: 2
Hours: 24 Hours Daily
Other Games: BJ, P
Special Features: Chinese and Mexican restaurants.

Mustang Sally's
634 Main Street
(605) 578-2025

Old Style Saloon #10
657 Main Street
(605) 578-3346
Website: www.saloon10.com

Toll-Free Number: (800) 952-9398
Restaurants: 1
Casino Size: 4,000 Square Feet
Other Games: BJ, P, TCP
Special Features: During summer there is a reenactment of the "Shooting of Wild Bill Hickok" at 1, 3, 5 and 7 p.m. Wild Bill's chair and other Old West artifacts on display.

Oyster Bay/Fairmont Hotel
628 Main Street
(605) 578-2205

Restaurants: 1
Special Features: Historic restoration of 1895 brothel and spa. Oyster bar.

Silverado Gaming & Restaurant
709 Main Street
(605) 578-3670
Website: www.silveradocasino.com

Toll-Free Number: (800) 584-7005
Restaurants: 1
Buffets: B-$5.95 (Sat-Sun) L-$5.95
D-$10.95/$11.95 (Fri-Sat)
Hours: 8am-2am/24 hours (Fri-Sat)
Casino Size: 20,000 Square Feet
Other Games: BJ, LIR, TCP, CSP
Fun Book: Call or write for information
Special Features: 50-cent breakfast special.

Tin Lizzie Gaming
555 Main Street
(605) 578-1715
Web Sit: www.tinlizzie.com

Toll-Free Number: (800) 643-4490
Restaurants: 1
Buffets: B-$1.99 L-$1.99
Hours: 24 hours daily
Casino Size: 8,300 Square Feet
Other Games: BJ
Fun Book: Request online or write
Senior Discount: Various, if 50 or older

Veteran's Of Foreign War
10 Pine Street
(605) 578-9914

Wild West Winners Casino
608-622 Main Street
(605) 578-1100
Website: www.wildwestwinners.com

Toll-Free Number: (800) 873-1876
Restaurants: 1
Fun Book: Call or write for information
Special Features: Also contains **Green Door** and **Jackpot Charlie's** casinos. Steakhouse restaurant.

Wooden Nickel
9 Lee Street
(605) 578-1952

Indian Casinos

Dakota Connection
RR 1, Box 177-B
Sisseton, South Dakota 57262
(605) 698-4273
Website: www.dakotaconnection.net
Map Location: **#10** (165 miles N. of Sioux Falls)

Toll-Free Number: (800) 542-2876
Restaurants: 1 Liquor: No
Buffets: B-$5.95 (Sat-Sun) L-$6.95 (Sat-Sun)
Hours: 24 Hours Daily
Other Games: BJ, BG
Senior Discount: Various on Tue, if 55 or older

Dakota Sioux Casino
16415 Sioux Conifer Road
Watertown, South Dakota 57201
(605) 882-2051
Website: www.dakotasioux.com
Map Location: **#2** (104 miles N. of Sioux Falls)

Toll-Free Number: (800) 658-4717
Restaurants: 1 Liquor: Yes
Buffets: L/D-$5.95
Hours: 24 Hours Daily
Other Games: BJ, P, BG (Fri-Tue)
Senior Discount: Specials on Mon, if 55+

Fort Randall Casino Hotel
East Highway 46
Pickstown, South Dakota 57367
(605) 487-7871
Website: www.fortrandall.com
Map Location: **#3** (100 miles S.W. of Sioux Falls)

Room Reservations: (800) 362-6333
Rooms: 57 Price Range: $49.80
Suites: 2 Price Range: $71.80
Restaurants: 1 Liquor: Yes
Buffets: B-$5.95 L-$6.95
D-$9.95/$13.95 (Sat)
Hours: 24 hours daily
Other Games: BJ, P, BG
Special Features: Buffet is only open Fri--Sun.

Golden Buffalo Casino
P.O. Box 204
Lower Brule, South Dakota 57548
(605) 473-5577
Map Location: **#4** (45 miles S.E. of Pierre)

Room Reservations: (605) 473-5506
Rooms: 38 Price Range: $48-$55
Restaurants: 1 Liquor: Yes
Hours: 8am-1am Daily
Other Games: BJ, P, TCP, BG (Wed)

Grand River Casino
P.O. Box 639
Mobridge, South Dakota 57601
(605) 845-7104
Website: www.grandrivercasino.com
Map Location: **#7** (240 miles N.E. of Rapid City)

Toll-Free Number: (800) 475-3321
Restaurants: 1 Liquor: Yes
Hours: 8am-3am/24 hours (Fri-Sat)
Other Games: BJ, P

Lode Star Casino
P.O. Box 140
Fort Thompson, South Dakota 57339
(605) 245-6000
Website: www.lodecasino.com
Map Location: **#6** (150 miles N.W. of Sioux Falls)

Room Reservations: (605) 245-2176
Restaurants: 1 Liquor: Yes
Rooms: 50 Price Range: $45-$62
Hours: 8am-2am/7am-2am (Fri-Sat)
Other Games: BJ, P
Senior Discount: 10% off room for AAA and AARP members.

Prairie Wind Casino
HC 49, Box 10
Pine Ridge, South Dakota 57770
(605) 867-6300
Website: www.prairiewindcasino.net
Map Location: **#9** (85 miles S.E. of Rapid City)

Toll-Free Number: (800) 705-9463
Restaurants: 1 Liquor: No
Buffets: B-$3 L-$6.95 D-$7.95
Hours: 24 Hours Daily
Other Games: BJ, TCP
Special Features: Casino is located 12 miles East of Oelrichs off Hwy. 385 and 8 miles West of Oglala on Hwy. 18.

Rosebud Casino
Highway 83 (on SD/NE stateline)
Mission, South Dakota 57555
(605) 378-3800
Website: www.rosebudcasino.com
Map Location: **#8** (22 miles S. of Mission)

Toll-Free Number: (800) 786-7673
Room Reservations: (877) 521-9913
Rooms: 60 Price Range: $50-$79
Suites: 2 Price Range: $79-$99
Restaurants: 2 Liquor: Yes
Buffets: D-$9.99
Hours: 24 hours daily
Other Games: BJ, P, BG
Senior Discount: Various, if 55 or older
Fun Book: Ask at marketing office
Special Features: Hotel is a Quality Inn. AAA, AARP and Internet discounts available.

Royal River Casino Bingo & Motel
607 S. Veterans Street
Flandreau, South Dakota 57028
(605) 997-3746
Website: www.royalrivercasino.com
Map Location: **#5** (35 miles N. of Sioux Falls on I-29)

Toll-Free Number: (800) 833-8666
Rooms: 60 Price Range: $55-$60
Suites: 6 Price Range: $90-$95
Restaurants: 2 Liquor: Yes
Hours: 24 Hours Daily
Casino Size: 17,000 Square Feet
Other Games: BJ, BG
Special Features: RV parking for $10 per day. AAA and AARP room discounts.

TEXAS

In mid-2002 Texas had three Indian casinos. However, the state's Attorney General started legal action against two of those operations and he was successful in closing them. The two affected tribes are attempting to work with the Texas legislature to allow them to reopen but as of August 2003 no arrangements had been made to allow them to reopen.

If you would like to check the status of those two casinos you can call them directly:

Speaking Rock Casino
122 S. Old Pueblo Road
El Paso, Texas 79907
(915) 860-7777
Website: www.speakingrockcasino.com
Map Location: **#2**

Alabama-Coushatta Entertainment Center
710 State Park Road
Livingston, Texas 77351
(936) 563-1500
Map Location: **#4** (75 miles N.E. of Houston)

Indian Casino

There is one Texas Indian casino which offers poker, pull tab machines, bingo and a player-pool-banked blackjack game where each player must pay a commission to the house for each bet that is made. The minimum gambling age is 21 and the casino is open 24 hours daily.

For more information on visiting Texas call (800) 888-8TEX.

Kickapoo Lucky Eagle Casino
Rt 1, Box 7777
Eagle Pass, Texas 78852
(830) 758-1995
Website: www.kickapooluckyeaglecasino.com
Map Location: **#1** (150 miles S.W. of San Antonio)

Toll-Free Number: (888) 255-8259
Restaurants: 1 Liquor: Yes
Casino Size: 16,000 Square Feet
Special Features: Blackjack commission is 50¢ per $25 bet.

Casino Boats

There are two casino boats in Texas which both sail nine miles out into the Gulf of Mexico where casino gambling is permitted. The boats offers: blackjack, craps, roulette, Caribbean stud poker, pai gow poker, let it ride, slots and video poker.

Texas Treasure Casino Cruises
1401 W. Wheeler Avenue
Aransas Pass, Texas 78336
(361) 758-4444
Website: www.txtreasure.com
Map Location: **#3** (10 miles N.E. of Corpus Christi)

Reservation Number: (800) 472-5215
Gambling Age: 21 Ship's Registry: Panama
Meal Service: Buffet Included
Schedule:
12:00pm - 6pm (Sun-Mon)
11:00 am - 5pm (Tue-Thu)
11:00 am - 4:30pm (Fri-Sat)
6:30pm - 12:00am (Tue-Wed)
6:30pm - 12:30am (Thu)
6:30pm - 1am (Fri-Sat)
Prices:
$19.95 Labor Day to Memorial Day
$29.95 Memorial Day to Labor Day
Port Charges: Included Parking: Free
Senior Discount: $5 off any cruise, if 55+
Special Features: 1,200-passenger *Texas Treasure* sails from dock near ferry in Aransas Pass. Restaurant upgrade is available for $15 per person. Must be 21 or older to board.

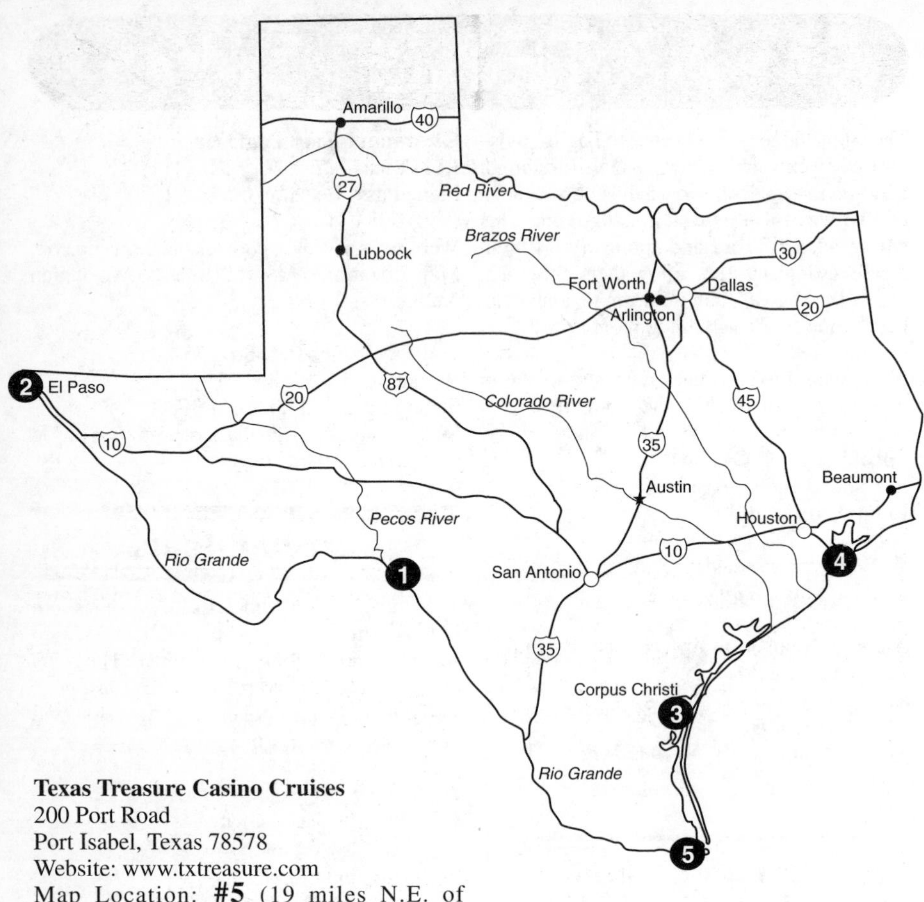

Texas Treasure Casino Cruises
200 Port Road
Port Isabel, Texas 78578
Website: www.txtreasure.com
Map Location: **#5** (19 miles N.E. of Brownsville)

Reservation Number: (800) 472-5215
Gambling Age: 21 Ship's Registry: Panama
Meal Service: Buffet Included
Schedule:
12:00pm - 6pm (Sun-Mon)
11:00 am - 5pm (Tue-Thu)
11:00 am - 4:30pm (Fri-Sat)
6:30pm - 12:00am (Tue-Wed)
6:30pm - 12:30am (Thu)
6:30pm - 1am (Fri-Sat)
Prices:
$19.95 Labor Day to Memorial Day
$29.95 Memorial Day to Labor Day
Port Charges: Included Parking: Free
Senior Discount: $5 off any cruise, if 55+
Special Features: 800-passenger *Texas Treasure II.* Restaurant upgrade is available for $15 per person. Must be 21 or older to board.

WASHINGTON

There are 26 Indian casinos operating in Washington. Twenty-two casinos are affiliated with tribes that have compacts with the state that allow them to offer table games, as well as special video poker and video slot machines. These machines aren't allowed to accept cash. Instead, a cashless system is used whereby you have to go to a cashier cage, or a kiosk, and buy a smart card which then deducts losses from, or credits wins to, your account.

Of the state's remaining four casinos, they are affiliated with the Spokane Tribe which has an ongoing dispute with the state and are operating without a compact. All four of their casinos offer regular spinning-reel slots that accept cash, plus an assortment of table games.

Most Washington casinos are not open on a 24-hour basis and the hours of operation are noted in each casino's listing. All casinos offer slots, video poker, blackjack, craps, roulette and pull tabs. Optional games offered include: baccarat (B), mini-baccarat (MB), poker (P), pai gow poker (PGP), Caribbean stud poker (CSP), three-card poker (TCP), Spanish 21 (S21), big 6 wheel (B6), keno (K) and bingo (BG). The minimum gambling age is 18 (21 if liquor is served).

Although most of the casinos have toll-free numbers many of these numbers will only work for calls within Washington. For more information on visiting Washington call the state's tourism department at (800) 544-1800.

Chewelah Casino
2555 Smith Road
Chewelah, Washington 99109
(509) 935-6167
Website: www.chewelahcasino.com
Map Location: **#13** (50 miles N. of Spokane)

Toll-Free Number: (800) 322-2788
Restaurants: 1 Deli Liquor: No
Buffets: B-$3.95 (Sat)/$6.95 (Sun)
D-$7.95 (Sun)
Hours: 9am-2am Daily
Casino Size: 22,000 Square Feet
Senior Discount: Various on Wed if 55 or older
Fun Book: Given out on Fridays
Special Features: Regular slots. One block from Double Eagle Casino.

Clearwater Casino
15347 Suquamish Way N.E
Suquamish, Washington 98392
(360) 598-8700
Website: www.clearwatercasino.com
Map Location: **#14** (15 miles W. of Seattle via Bainbridge Ferry)

Toll-Free Number: (800) 375-6073
Restaurants: 2 Liquor: Yes
Buffets: B-$7.50 (Sun) L-$6.00
D-$8.00/$13.00 (Sat)/$16 (Fri)
Hours: 10am-4am Daily
Casino Size: 22,000 Square Feet
Other Games: S21, MB, P, PGP, CSP,
TCP, LIR, K, BG
Senior Discount: 50% off Sun buffets if 55+
Special features: Closest casino to Seattle. Free shuttle service.

Coulee Dam Casino
515 Birch Street
Coulee Dam, Washington 99155
(509) 633-0766
Website: www.couleecasino.com
Map Location: **#11** (190 miles E. of Seattle)

Toll-Free Number: (800) 556-7492
Restaurants: 1 Deli Liquor: No
Hours: 9am-Mid/24 Hours (Fri/Sat)
Other Games: No craps or roulette
Casino Marketing: (800) 648-2946
Special features: BJ tables only open 2pm-12am (Fri-Sat)/12pm-10pm (Sun-Mon). Gift shop.

Double Eagle Casino
2539 Smith Road
Chewelah, Washington 99109
(509) 935-4406
Map Location: **#13** (50 miles N. of Spokane)

Restaurants: 1 Deli Liquor: No
Hours: 9am-1am/2am (Fri-Sat)
Other Games: PGP, No Craps
Special Features: Regular slots. One block from Chewelah Casino.

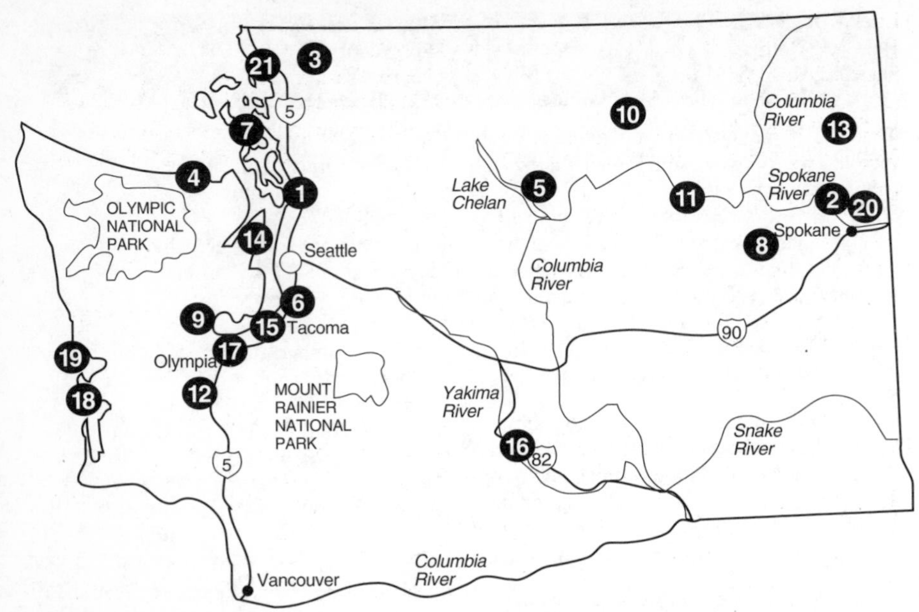

Emerald Queen Casino - Riverboat
2102 Alexander Avenue
Tacoma, Washington 98421
(206) 594-7777
Website: www.emeraldqueen.com
Map Location: **#15**

Toll-Free Number: (888) 831-7655
Restaurants: 3 Liquor: Yes
Buffets: L-$9.95/$12.95 (Sat)/$14.95 (Sun)
D-$15.95/$19.95 (Mon/Sat)
Hours: 10am-6am/24 Hours (Fri-Mon)
Other Games: MB, P, PGP, CSP, LIR, K, S21
Special Features: Property has two casinos. One is on a riverboat and the other is in a shoreside facility.

Emerald Queen Casino - I-5
2024 East 29th Street
Tacoma, Washington 98404
(206) 383-1572
Website: www.emeraldqueen.com
Map Location: **#15**

Toll-Free Number: (888) 831-7655
Restaurants: 1 Liquor: Yes
Hours: 10am-6am/24 Hours (Fri-Mon)
Other Games: No table games
Special Features: Sports bar.

Li'l Chiefs Casino
P.O. Box 130
Wellpinit, Washington 99040
(509) 258-4544
Map Location: **#2** (25 miles N.W. of Spokane)

Restaurants: 1 Liquor: No
Hours: 9am-1am/2am (Fri-Sat)
Other Games: Only Slots and Video Poker
Special Features: Regular slots. Casino is in city of Ford.

Little Creek Casino
West 91 Highway 108
Shelton, Washington 98584
(360) 427-7711
Website: www.little-creek.com
Map Location: **#9** (23 miles N. of Olympia off Hwy 101/108 interchange)

Toll-Free Number: (800) 667-7711
Restaurants: 3 Liquor: Yes
Buffets: L-$5.95 (Tue/Sat/Sun)
D-$8.95 (Tue)/$9.95/$12.95 (Fri-Sun)
Hours: 10am-4am/6am (Fri-Sat)
Casino Size: 49,000 Square Feet
Other Games: P, PGP, LIR, K, BG
Senior Discount: Specials Tue/Wed, if 50+
Special Features: Gift shop.

Lucky Dog Casino
19330 N. Highway 101
Shelton, Washington 98584
(360) 877-5656
Website: www.theluckydogcasino.com
Map Location: **#9** (23 miles N. of Olympia)

Restaurants: 1 Deli Liquor: No
Hours: 10am-Midnite/2am (Fri-Sat)
Other Games: No table games

Lucky Eagle Casino
12888 188th Avenue SW
Rochester, Washington 98579
(360) 273-2000
Website: www.luckyeagle.com
Map Location: **#12** (26 miles S. of Olympia)

Toll-Free Number: (800) 720-1788
Restaurants: 5 Liquor: Yes
Buffets: L-$7.95/$16.95 (Sun)
D-$13.95/$18.95 (Fri/Sat)
Hours: 10am-4am/6am (Fri/Sat)
Casino Size: 75,000 Square Feet
Other Games: P, PGP, LIR, TCP, K, BG
Fun Book: Given to new slot club members
Senior Discount: Buffets discounts, plus various discounts on Mondays if 55+
Special Features: 20-space RV park.

Mill Bay Casino
455 E. Wapato Lake Road
Manson, Washington 98831
(509) 687-2102
Website: www.colvillecasinos.com/millbay
Map Location: **#5** (200 miles N.E. of Seattle on the N. shore of Lake Chelan)

Toll-Free Number: (800) 648-2946
Restaurants: 1 Liquor: No
Buffets: B-$10.75 (Sun)
Other Games: PGP
Senior Discount: Various discounts, if 55+
Fun Book: Ask at customer service booth

Muckleshoot Casino
2402 Auburn Way South
Auburn, Washington 98002
(253) 804-4444
Website: www.muckleshootcasino.com
Map Location: **#6** (20 miles S. of Seattle)

Toll-Free Number (800) 804-4944
Restaurants: 5 Liquor: Yes
Buffets: L-$8.95 (Sat-Sun) D-$16.95
Hours: 10am-5:45am Daily
Other Games: B, P, PGP, CSP, LIR, TCP, S21, K, BG, Simulcasting (seasonal)
Senior Discount: $3 off Sat lunch, if 55+

Nooksack River Casino
5048 Mt. Baker Highway
Deming, Washington 98244
(360) 592-5472
Website: www.nooksackcasino.com
Map Location: **#3** (14 miles E. of Bellingham)

Restaurants: 1 Liquor: Yes
Buffets: L-$7.95/$12.95 (Sun)
D-$13.95/$11.95 (Thu)/$12.95 (Sun)/$15.95 (Fri)
Hours: 10am-3am/6am (Fri-Sat)
Casino Size: 21,500 Square Feet
Other Games: MB, PGP, CSP, LIR
Senior Discount: $2 off buffets, if 55+

Northern Quest Casino
100 N. Hayford Road
Airway Heights, Washington 99001
(509) 242-7000
Website: www.northernquest.net
Map Location: **#20** (10 miles N. of Spokane)

Restaurants: 1 Liquor: Yes
Buffets: B-$5.95/$9.95 (Sun) L-$7.95 D-$10.95
Hours: 9am-5am
Casino Size: 21,500 Square Feet
Other Games: S21, P, LIR, PGP, K, Simulcasting
Senior Discount: Buffet discounts, if 55+

Okanogan Bingo and Casino
41 Appleway Road
Okanogan, Washington 98840
Website: www.okanoganbingocasino.com
(509) 422-4646
Map Location: **#10** (165 miles E. of Seattle)

Toll-Free Number: (800) 559-4643
Restaurants: 1 Snack Bar Liquor: No
Hours: 9am-Mid/2am (Fri/Sat)
Other Games: BG, No Craps or Roulette
Special Features: Blackjack opens 4pm/2pm (Sun)

Point No Point Casino
7989 Salish Lane NE
Kingston, Washington 98346
(360) 297-0070
Website: www.pointnopointcasino.com
Map Location: **#14** (18 miles W. of Seattle via Bainbridge Ferry)

Restaurants: 2 Liquor: Yes
Casino Size: 12,000 Square Feet
Hours: 10am-2am/4am (Fri-Sat)
Other Games: PGP, S21
Seniro Discounts: Various on Sunday, if 55+

Quinault Beach Resort
78 Route 115
Ocean Shores, Washington 98569
(360) 289-9466
Website: www.quinaultbchresort.com
Map Location: **#19** (90 miles W. of Tacoma)

Toll-Free Number: (888) 461-2214
Rooms: 159 Price Range: $99-$159
Suite: 9 Price Range: $300-$750
Restaurants: 2 Liquor: Yes
Casino Size: 16,000 Square Feet
Hours: 9am-2am/4:30am (Fri-Sat)
Other Games: B, PGP, LIR, CSP, S21, K
Senior Discount: Various on Wed, if 55+
Special Features: Full service spa. AARP room discount.

Red Wind Casino
12819 Yelm Highway
Olympia, Washington 98513
(360) 412-5000
Website: www.redwindcasino.net
Map Location: **#17**

Toll-Free Number: (866) 946-2444
Restaurants: 1 Liquor: Yes
Hours: 9am-5am Daily
Casino Size: 12,000 Square Feet
Other Games: PGP, CSP, LIR, K, S21
Senior Discount: Various Mon-Wed, if 55+
Fun Book: Ask at promotions booth

7 Cedars Casino
270756 Highway 101
Sequim, Washington 98382
(360) 683-7777
Website: www.7cedarscasino.com
Map Location: **#4** (70 miles N.W. of Seattle via ferry)

Toll-Free Number: (800) 4-LUCKY-7
Restaurants: 2 Liquor: Yes
Buffets: L-$6.95 D-$16.95 (Fri)/$10.95 (Sat)
Hours: 10am-1am/3am (Fri-Sat)
Other Games: BG
Special Features: $4.95 Steak special.

Shoalwater Bay Casino
4112 Highway 105
Tokeland, Washington 98590
(360) 267-2048
Map Location: **#18** (75 miles S.W. of Olympia)

Toll-Free Number: (888) 332-2048
Restaurants: 1 Liquor: No
Hours: 10am-12am/2am (Fri-Sat)
Casino Size: 10,000 Square Feet
Other Games: P, No Craps or Roulette
Senior Discount: Various on Tue, if 55 or older
Special Features: Daily food specials.

Silver Reef Casino
4876 Haxton Way
Ferndale, Washington 98248
(360) 383-0777
Website: www.silverreefcasino.com
Map Location: **#14** (7 miles N. of Bellingham)

Toll-Free Number: (866) 383-0777
Restaurants: 2 Liquor: Yes
Buffets: L-$8.95 D-$14.95
Casino Size: 28,000 Square Feet
Hours: 10am-4am/6am (Fri-Sat)
Other Games: TCP, PGP, MB, CW

Skagit Valley Casino
590 Dark Lane
Bow, Washington 98232
(360) 724-7777
Website: www.theskagit.com
Map Location: **#7** (75 miles N. of Seattle)

Toll-Free Number: (877) 275-2448
Room Reservations: (800) 895-3423
Rooms: 86 Price Range: $79-$109
Rooms: 23 Price Range: $159-$215
Restaurants: 3 Liquor: Yes
Buffets: B-$5.75 (Sat) L-$8.95/$12.95 (Sun)
D-$13.95/$15.95 (Fri-Sat)/$16.95 (Wed)
Hours: 9am-3am/5am (Fri-Sat)
Casino Size: 26,075 Square Feet
Other Games: PGP, LIR, TCP
Senior Discount: Various on Mon, if 55 or older

Swinomish Northern Lights Casino
837 Casino Drive
Anacortes, Washington 98221
(360) 293-2691
Website: www.swinomishcasino.com
Map Location: **#7** (70 miles N. of Seattle, between I-5 and Anacortes on Hwy. 20)

Restaurants: 2 Liquor: Yes
Buffets: L-$7.49/$10.95 (Sun)
D-$9.95/$10.95 (Wed)/$16.95 (Fri)/$15.95 (Sat)
Hours: 11am-4am/6am (Fri-Sat)
Casino Size: 73,000 Square Feet
Other Games: P, PGP, LIR, TCP, BG, K,
Red Dog, Simulcasting
Senior Discount: Buffet discount, if 55+
Special Features: Gift shop.

Tulalip Casino
10200 Quil Ceda Boulevard
Marysville, Washington 98271
(360) 651-1111
Website: www.tulalipcasino.com
Map Location: **#1** (30 miles N. of Seattle)

Toll-Free Number: (888) 272-1111
Restaurants: 4 Liquor: Yes
Buffets: L-$9.95 D-$16.95
Hours: 10am-6am/24 Hours (Wed-Sun)
Casino Size: 45,000 Square Feet
Other Games: MB, P, PGP, K, BG
Special Features: Gift shop.

Two Rivers Casino & Resort
6828-B Highway 25 South
Davenport, Washington 99122
(509) 722-4000
Website: www.tworiverscasinoandresort.com
Map Location: **#8** (60 miles W. of Spokane)

Toll-Free Number: (877) 7-COME-11
Restaurants: 1 Liquor: No
Buffets: B-$5.95 (Sat/Sun) L-$5.95 (Tue)
D-$5.95 (Thu)/$13.95 (Fri)
Hours: 12pm-10pm/11pm-1am (Fri-Sun)
Casino Size: 10,000 Square Feet
Special Features: Regular slots. 35-space RV park. 200-slip marina and beach.

Yakama Nation Legends Casino
580 Fort Road
Toppenish, Washington 98948
(509) 865-8800
Website: www.yakamalegends.com
Map Location: **#16** (20 miles S. of Yakima)

Toll-Free Number: (877) 7-COME-11
Restaurants: 2 Liquor: No
Buffets: L-$5.99/$7.99 (Sat)/$9.99 (Fri/Sun)
D-$7.99-$9.99/$16.99 (Fri)/$12.99 (Sat)
Hours: 9am-4am Daily
Casino Size: 45,000 Square Feet
Other Games: P, LIR, CSP, K, No Roulette
Fun Book: Given to out-of-state visitors, Birthday Club members and for special events
Senior Discount: 10% off buffets, if 55 or older and Fun Book on Tuesdays
Special Features: Childcare center. Indoor waterfall. Gift shop.

Card Rooms

Card rooms have been legal in Washington since 1974. Initially limited to just five tables per location, the law was changed in 1996 to allow up to 15 tables. Then, one year later, a provision was added to allow house-banked games. Permissible games include: blackjack, Caribbean stud poker, pai gow poker, let it ride and casino war. The games of baccarat, craps, roulette and keno are not allowed.

The maximum bet at each card room is dependant on certain licensing requirements and is capped at either $3, $25 or $100. Additionally, the rooms can be open no more than 20 hours per day. These card rooms are now commonly called "mini-casinos."

Each city and county has the option to ban the card rooms so they are not found in every major city (Seattle has none). Due to space limitations we don't list all of the Washington card rooms in this book but we do list them on our website: www.americancasinoguide.com

When you get to the American Casino Guide website look on the left side for "U.S. Casino Directory," click on that link and when you get to the next page just click on "Washington."

WEST VIRGINIA

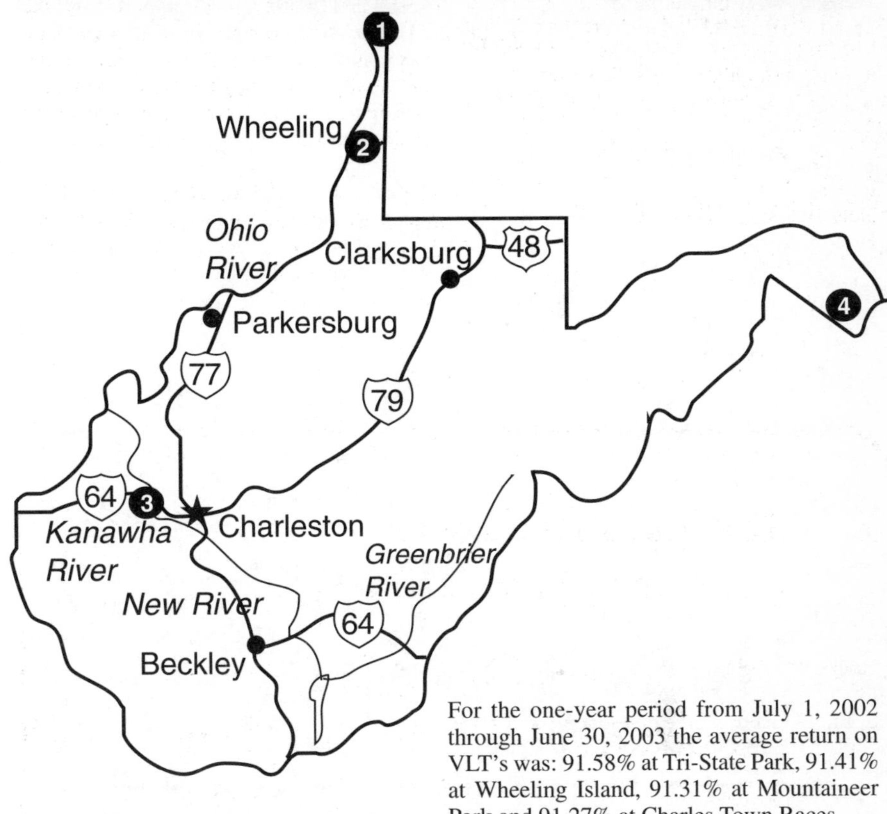

West Virginia has four pari-mutuel facilities that feature video lottery terminals. The VLT's are the same as regular video gaming devices but are called lottery terminals because they are regulated by the state's lottery commission which receives a share of each machine's revenue.

The maximum allowable bet on a machine is $2. Most of the gaming machines pay out coins or tokens but there are also some machines which will only print out a receipt which must be taken to a cashier. West Virginia law requires that VLT's return a minimum of 80% to a maximum of 95%. VLT games include: slots, blackjack, keno and numerous versions of poker. The minimum gambling age is 18.

For the one-year period from July 1, 2002 through June 30, 2003 the average return on VLT's was: 91.58% at Tri-State Park, 91.41% at Wheeling Island, 91.31% at Mountaineer Park and 91.27% at Charles Town Races.

For West Virginia tourism information call (800) 225-5982.

Charles Town Races & Slots
P.O. Box 551
Charles Town, West Virginia 25414
(304) 725-7001
Website: www.ctownraces.com
Map Location: **#4**

Toll-Free Number: (800) 795-7001
Restaurants: 4
Buffets: L-$8.95
D-$8.95/$14.95 (Mon/Fri/Sat)/$22.95 (Wed)
Hours: 7am-3:30am/3am (Sat)
10am-3:30am (Sun)
Special Features: Live horse racing Wed-Sun. Daily simulcasting of horse and dog racing. Food court with five fast-food outlets.

Mountaineer Race Track & Gaming Resort
State Route #2
Chester, West Virginia 26034
(304) 387-2400
Website: www.mtrgaming.com
Map Location: **#1** (35 miles N. of Wheeling)

Toll-Free Number: (800) 804-0468
Room Reservations: (800) 489-8192
Rooms: 337 Price Range: $75-$119
Suites: 22 Price Range: $155-$185
Restaurants: 8
Buffets: B-$4.95 L-$7.95 D-$9.95
Hours: 7:30am-3:30am/3am (Sat)
10am-3:30am (Sun)
Special Features: 18-hole golf course. Health spa. Live horse racing Thu-Mon. Daily simulcasting of horse and dog racing.

Tri-State Racetrack & Gaming Center
1 Greyhound Lane
Cross Lanes, West Virginia 25356
(304) 776-1000
Map Location: **#3** (10 miles N.W. of Charleston)

Toll-Free Number: (800) 224-9683
Restaurants: 1
Hours: 11am-3am/1pm-3am (Sun)
Casino Size: 30,000 Square Feet
Special Features: Live dog racing Wed-Mon. Daily simulcasting of horse and dog racing.

Wheeling Island
Racetrack & Gaming Center
1 S. Stone Street
Wheeling, West Virginia 26003
(304) 232-5050
Website: www.wheelingdowns.com
Map Location: **#2**

Toll-Free Number: (877) WIN-HERE
Restaurants: 2
Buffets: L-$8.95 D-$12.95
Hours: 9am-3am/10am-3am (Sun)
Casino Size: 50,000 Square Feet
Special Features: Live dog racing Wed-Mon. Daily simulcasting of horse and dog racing.

WISCONSIN

All Wisconsin casinos are located on Indian reservations and originally, blackjack was the only table game permitted. However, in mid-2003, a compact between the state and the Tribes was negotiated to allow the games of roulette, craps, keno, poker and other card games such as let it ride, Caribbean stud and three-card poker. As this book went to press no casinos had started offering the new games but they were all expected to do so in the future.

The Indian tribes are not required to release information on their slot machine percentage paybacks, but according to the terms of the compact between the state and the tribes "for games not affected by player skill, such as slot machines, the machine is required to return a minimum of 80% and a maximum of 100% of the amount wagered."

Unless otherwise noted, all casinos are open 24 hours and the only games offered are: blackjack, slots, video poker and video keno. The minimum gambling age is 21 at all casinos (18 for bingo).

For visitor information call the state's department of tourism at (800) 432-8747.

Bad River Lodge Casino and Convention Center
U.S. Highway 2
Odanah, Wisconsin 54861
(715) 682-7121
Website: www.badriver.com
Map Location: **#1** (halfway between Ironwood, MI and Ashland, WI; 45 miles east of Duluth, MN on US 2)

Toll-Free Number: (800) 777-7449
Lodge Reservations: (800) 795-7121
Rooms: 42 Price Range: $45-$72
Suites: 8 Price Range: $55-$97
Restaurants: 2 Liquor: Yes
Buffets: B-$4.95 L-$6.95 D-$8.95
Casino Size: 19,200 Square Feet
Hours: 8am-2am /4am (Fri-Sat in summer)
Special Features: 20-space RV park. Gas station. Grocery store. AAA and AARP members get 10% room discount.

Ho Chunk Casino Hotel and Convention Center
S3214 Highway 12
Baraboo, Wisconsin 53913
(608) 356-6210
Website: www.ho-chunk.com
Map Location: **#4** (40 miles N. of Madison. On Hwy. 12 just S. of Delton)

Toll-Free Number: (800) 746-2486
Rooms: 295 Price Range: $29-$150
Suites: 20 Price Range: $89-$305
Restaurants: 5 (1 open 24 hrs) Liquor: Yes
Buffets: B-$6.95 L-$8.95
D-$11.95/$21.95 (Wed)
Casino Size: 90,000 Square Feet
Other Games: Bingo
Senior Discount: Bingo discount if 55+
Special Features: Gift shop. Discount smoke shop. Shuttle service from local area motels. Kid's Quest childcare center.

Hole In The Wall Casino & Hotel
P.O. Box 98, Highways 35 & 77
Danbury, Wisconsin 54830
(715) 656-3444
Map Location: **#5** (26 miles E. of Hinckley, MN)

Toll-Free Number: (800) BET-U-WIN
Rooms: 45 Price Range: $55-$100
Restaurants: 1 Liquor: Yes
Casino Size: 22,500 Square Feet
Hours: 8am-2am/4am (Fri/Sat)
Special Features: 35-space RV park. Gift shop. $10 off room for slot club members.

Isle Vista Casino
Highway 13 North, Box 1167
Bayfield, Wisconsin 54814
(715) 779-3712
Map Location: **#6** (70 miles E. of Duluth, MN on Hwy. 13, 3 miles N. of Bayfield)

Toll-Free Number: (800) 226-8478
Restaurants: 1 Liquor: Yes
Hours: 10am-12am/2am (Thu-Sat)
Other Games: Bingo (Thu/Sat/Sun)
Senior Discount: Seniors program on Mondays if 55, or older.

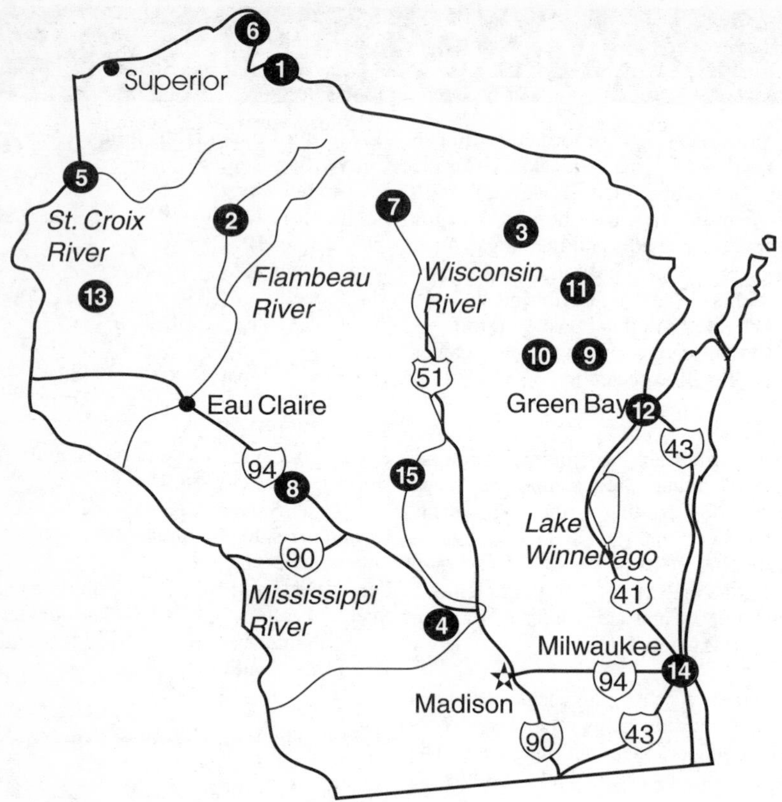

Lake of the Torches Resort Casino
510 Old Abe Road
Lac du Flambeau, Wisconsin 54538
(715) 588-7070
Website: www.180025torch.com
Map Location: **#7** (160 miles N.W. of Green Bay. Heading N. on Hwy. 51, go left on Hwy. 47, 12 miles to casino)

Toll-Free Number: (800) 25-TORCH
Room Reservations: (888) 599-9200
Rooms: 88 Price Range: $100-$110
Suites: 13 Price Range: $107-$150
Restaurants: 2 Liquor: Yes
Buffets: B-$5.95/$6.95 (Sat-Sun) L-$7.95 D-$10.95/$11.95 (Thu)/$12.95 (Sun)/$16.50 (Fri)
Other Games: Bingo (Tue-Sun)
Special Features: Slot club members get 20% off room and other discounts. Room rates include free breakfast and $20 match play.

LCO Casino, Lodge & Convention Center
13767 W County Road B
Hayward, Wisconsin 54843
(715) 634-5643
Website: www.lcocasino.com
Map Location: **#2** (55 miles S.E. of Duluth, MN. 3 miles N.E. of Hayward on county trunk B)

Toll-Free Number: (800) LCO-CASH
Room Reservations: (800) LCO-LODGE
Rooms: 41 Price Range: $54-$74
Suites: 14 Price Range: $75-$105
Restaurants: 2 Liquor: Yes
Buffets: B-$4.95 L-$6.95 D-$7.95
Casino Size: 35,000 Square Feet
Hours: 9am-4am Daily
Other Games: Bingo (Sun-Fri)
Senior Discount: 5% discount at Lodge and free prize spin on Sundays if 55, or older
Special Features: Sports lounge. Gift shop.

Majestic Pines Casino, Bingo & Hotel
W9010 Highway 54 East
Black River Falls, Wisconsin 54615
(715) 284-9098
Website: www.ho-chunk.com
Map Location: **#8** (110 miles M.W. of Madison on Hwy. 54, 4 miles E. of I-94)

Toll-Free Number: (800) 657-4621
Rooms: 60 Price Range: $59-$75
Suites: 6 Price Range: $95-$105
Restaurants: 2 Liquor: Yes
Buffets: L-$7.95 D-$9.95/$21.95 (Thu)
Hours: 8am-2am/24 hrs (Memorial-Labor Day)
Size: 75,000 Square Feet
Other Games: Bingo (Thu-Tue)
Senior Discount: $5 off bingo Sun, if 55+
Special Features: 10% off buffets and hotel rates with slot club card. Heated pool.

Menominee Casino Bingo & Hotel
P.O. Box 760, Highways 47 & 55
Keshena, Wisconsin 54135
(715) 799-3600
Website: www.menomineecasinoresort.com
Map Location: **#9** (40 miles N.W. of Green Bay on Hwy. 47, 7 miles N. of Shawano)

Toll-Free Number: (800) 343-7778
Rooms: 100 Price Range: $60-$70
Suites: 8 Price Range: $80-$125
Restaurants: 1 Liquor: Yes
Buffets: L-$6.95/$8.95 (Sun)
D-$9.95/$10.95 (Wed-Thu)/$14.50 (Fri/Sat)
Casino Size: 36,000 Square Feet
Other Games: Bingo, LIR, TCP, P
Senior Discount: $5 matchplay on Tues if 55+
Special Features: 60-space RV park. Gift shop. Smoke shop. 10% room discount for AAA and AARP members. $10 matchplay and free continental breakfast with rooms.

Mohican North Star Casino & Bingo
W12180A County Road A
Bowler, Wisconsin 54416
(715) 787-3110
Website: www.mohicannorthstar.com
Map Location: **#10** (50 miles N.W. of G. Bay)

Toll-Free Number: (800) 952-0195
Restaurants: 2 Liquor: Yes
Hours: 8am-2am/24 Hours (Fri-Sat)
Other Games: Bingo (Sun-Mon/Wed-Fri)
Special Features: 57-space RV park. Smoke shop.

Mole Lake/Regency Casino
Highway 55
Mole Lake, Wisconsin 54520
(715) 478-5290
Website: www.molelake.com
Map Location: **#3** (100 miles N.W. of Green Bay on Hwy. 55, 7 miles S. of Crandon)

Toll-Free Number: (800) 236-WINN
Motel Reservations: (800) 457-4312
Rooms: 25 Price Range: $46-$55
Restaurants: 1 Cafeteria Liquor: Yes
Hours: 10am-1am/3am (Fri/Sat)
Other Games: Bingo (Fri-Tue)
Senior Discount: $5 matchplay Wed if 50+
Special Features: Two casinos housed in separate buildings. Motel is two blocks from casino. Blackjack opens at 12 p.m. $10 match play given to hotel guests. 8-space RV park.

Oneida Bingo & Casino
2020/2100 Airport Drive
Green Bay, Wisconsin 54313
(920) 494-4500
Website: www.oneidabingoandcasino.net
Map Location: **#12** (across from Austin Straubel Airport, take Interstate 43 to Highway 172)

Toll-Free Number: (800) 238-4263
Reservation Number: (800) 333-3333
Rooms: 301 Price Range: $79-$159
Suites: 29 Price Range: $159-$229
Restaurants: 3 Liquor: No
Buffets (at Radisson Inn): B-$7.95 L-$7.95
Hours: 10am-4am (Tables)/24 Hours (Slots)
Other Games: Bingo
Senior Discount: Free early bird bingo pack on Wednesday, if 55, or older
Special Features: Two casinos. One is connected to Radisson Inn where hotel rooms are located. Free local shuttle bus service. Gift shop. Discount smoke shop.

Potawatomi Bingo Casino
1721 W. Canal Street
Milwaukee, Wisconsin 53233
(414) 645-6888
Website: www.paysbig.com
Map Location: **#14**

Toll-Free Number: (800) PAYS-BIG
Restaurants: 3 Liquor: No
Buffets: L-$9.99 D-$13.99/$15.99 (Fri-Sat)
Other Games: Bingo
Casino Size: 38,400 Square Feet
Special Features: Alcohol only served in sports bar.

Potawatomi Bingo/Northern Lights Casino
Highway 32
Wabeno, Wisconsin 54566
(715) 473-2021
Website: www.cartercasino.com
Map Location: **#11** (85 miles N. of Green Bay on Hwy. 32)

Toll-Free Number: (800) 487-9522
Lodge Reservations: (800) 777-1640
Rooms: 70 Price Range: $65-$85
Suites: 29 Price Range: $75-$115
Restaurants: 2 Liquor: Yes
Buffets: B-$7.99 (Sat-Sun)
D-$13.99 (Fri)/$8.99 (Sat)
Casino Size: 12,000 Square Feet
Hours: 9am-2am/4am (Fri/Sat)
Other Games: Bingo
Senior Discount: Specials on Wed if 55+
Special Features: Lodge is across parking lot from casino and offers casino packages. 10% room discount for AAA/AARP members. 24-hour gas station and convenience store.

Rainbow Casino & Bingo
949 County Road G
Nekoosa, Wisconsin 54457
(715) 886-4560
Website: www.rbcwin.com
Map Location: **#15** (50 miles S. of Wausau)

Toll-Free Number: (800) 782-4560
Restaurants: 2 Liquor: Yes
Buffets (only Sundays): L-$8.95 D-$9.95
Hours: 8am-2am/24 hours (Fri-Sat)
Other Games: Bingo
Senior Discount: Specials on Thu. if 55+
Special Features: Smoke and gift shop. Motel and tour packages. Convenience store.

St. Croix Casino & Hotel
777 US Highway 8
Turtle Lake, Wisconsin 54889
(715) 986-4777
Website: www.stcroixcasino.com
Map Location: **#13** (105 miles S. of Duluth, MN on Hwy. 8)

Toll-Free Number: (800) 846-8946
Room Reservations: (800) 782-9987
Rooms: 158 Price Range: $55-$73
Suites: 8 Price Range: $110-$135
Restaurants: 3 Liquor: Yes
Buffets: B-$4.20 L-$8.40 D-$11.60/$19 (Thu)
Casino Size: 95,000 Square Feet
Other Games: Bingo
Special Features: 20% off rooms for slot club member.

Casino Index

G

H

I

J

Coupon Directory

About Your Coupons

Due to past problems with our coupons being abused and/or counterfeited, it is now required that you remove the coupons from this book ONLY at the time of redemption.

The only exception to this requirement is for the first five coupons which appear on pages 351 through 354.

All other redemptions will require you to remove the coupon from this book in the presence of the participating merchant. This will allow the merchant to know that you have a legitimate coupon. This protective feature will also allow us to continue to provide you with the excellent coupons offers that you have come to expect.

We apologize for any inconvenience that this situation may cause you and we thank you for your cooperation!

AMERICAN CASINO GUIDE

$15 Off!

Alamo

alamo.com

1-800-354-2322

Alamo features GM vehicles

- Reserve a midsize car through a sport utility vehicle in the United States, Canada, Latin America or the Caribbean
- Valid for a rental of at least four days
- Valid through 12/31/04
- Book with your travel agent or Alamo at 1-800-354-2322. Or, book online at ***alamo.com*** Be sure to request ID #641394, Rate Code BY, and Coupon Code D39B at time of reservation..

See terms and conditions on reserve side of this coupon.

D39B

CASINO COUPON

AMERICAN CASINO GUIDE

One FREE Upgrade!

Alamo

alamo.com

1-800-354-2322

Alamo features GM vehicles

- Reserve a compact through midsize 4-door car in the U.S. or Canada, or an economy through fullsize car.in Europe
- No minimum rental required
- Valid through 12/31/04
- Book with your travel agent or Alamo at 1-800-354-2322. Or, book online at ***alamo.com***
- Be sure to request ID #641394, Rate Code BY and Coupon Code U26B at time of reservations

See terms and conditions on reserve side of this coupon.

U26B

CASINO COUPON

AMERICAN CASINO GUIDE

Save on Your Car Rental with Alamo-Rent-A-Car!

Alamo

alamo.com

1-800-354-2322

See the world one stop at a time with special rates from Alamo. As an American Casino Guide reader, you'll receive up up to 15% off our great rates year-round, unlimited mileage and no fee for the first additional driver. We'll always go that extra mile to make your car rental experince a fun part of your trip. Book with your travel agent or Alamo. Be sure to request ID #641394 and Rate Code BY. Alamo features GM vehicles. This is not a coupon.

See terms and conditions on reserve side.

CASINO COUPON

Terms and Conditions

- One coupon per Alamo rental and void once redeemed.
- Original coupon must be presented at counter upon arrival.
- Discount applies to base rate, which does not include taxes (including GST), governmentally-authorized or imposed surcharges, llicense recoupment/air tax recovery and concession recoupoment fees, or optional items.
- Offer is subject to standard rental conditions.
- Blackout dates may apply.
- Not valid with any other discount or promotional rate.
- Subject to availability and good only at participating Alamo locations.
- Offer not valid in San Jose, California.
- Travel Agents GDS: /ID-XA641394//RC-BY/SI-C-D39B APOLLO only: /ID-XA641394 XPBY/SI-C-D39B

Terms and Conditions

- One coupon per Alamo rental and void once redeemed.
- Original coupon must be presented at counter upon arrival.
- Upgrade is subject to availability at time of rental pick up.
- Offer is subject to standard rental conditions.
- Blackout dates may apply.
- Not valid with any other discount or promotional rate.
- Subject to availablility and good only at participating Alamo locations.
- Coupon is valid for one free upgrade to the next car category (same transmission in Europe).
- Travel Agents GDS: /ID-XA641394//RC-BY/SI-C-U26B APOLLO only: /ID-XA641394 XPBY/SI-C-U26B

Terms and Conditions

Discount applies to basic rate, which does not include taxes (including GST/VAT), governmentally-authorized or imposed surcharges, license recoupment/air tax recovery and concession recoupment fees, vehicle license fee, road fee, premium location charges, airport and airport facility fees, fuel, one-way rental charge and optional items. Renter must meet standard age, driver and credit requirements (may vary by country). 24-hour advance reservation required (up to 72 hours for licensee locations). May not be combined with other discounts. Availability is limited. Subject to change without notice. Black out dates may apply. In United States, offer valid only at airport-serving locations. This is not a coupon. Percentage discount is reflected in the reserved rate.

Alamo
alamo.com
1-800-354-2322

AMERICAN CASINO GUIDE

$100 Off Per Person

This coupon entitles the bearer to a $100 discount, per person, on the regular registration fee for the 16th Annual World Championship Bingo Tournament & Gaming Cruise, a spectacular 8-day Caribbean adventure aboard Carnival Cruise Line's *Conquest* sailing from New Orleans, October 31st through November 7th, 2004. Call 1-800-326-0373 for a free full-color brochure. Offer expires 10/1/04.

CASINO COUPON

AMERICAN CASINO GUIDE

FREE Copy of *The Crapshooter* Newsletter! A $7 Value!

This coupon entitles you to receive one FREE copy of *The Crapshooter* newsletter. The only publication devoted exclusively to the game of casino craps! You'll also receive a FREE catalog and a special FREE offer! See reverse for full details.

CASINO COUPON

AMERICAN CASINO GUIDE

Free Casino Fun Money

Please present this coupon at the Casino Cashier Cage to receive a FREE Casino Fun Money sheet loaded with valuable offers. See reverse side for full details.

Offer void if detached from book. This coupon should only be removed at time of redemption.

More than $100,000 in gaming prizes!

- Offer valid for 2 adults (18 or older) per coupon. Advance reservations are required for this world class event. Book early for best accomodations.
- Call 1-800-326-0373 and mention the "American Casino Guide" coupon when making reservations to receive this discount.
- Space subject to availability. Offer valid through 10/1/04. Offer not valid with any other promotion. Program subject to change or cancellation without notice.

Just send this coupon and two first-class stamps for postage to:
The Crapshooter • P.O. Box 421440 • San Diego, CA 92142-1440
You'll also receive a FREE catalog and a special FREE offer!

Name

Address

City, St, Zip

Offer good only with this coupon. One offer per address. Offer expires 12/31/04.

111 Country Club Drive
Incline Village, NV 89451
(775) 832-1234
(800) 327-3910

Limit one coupon per guest. Must be 21 years of age, or older. No cash value. Not valid with any other offer. Management reserves the right to cancel or modify this offer. Expires 12/30/04.

AMERICAN CASINO GUIDE

Reno Hilton

Buy One Buffet Get One FREE

Buy one breakfast, lunch or dinner at *The Lodge* and receive the second for FREE. See back for full details.

Offer void if detached from book. This coupon should only be removed at time of redemption.

AMERICAN CASINO GUIDE

Reno Hilton

$10 Room Discount

Save $10 on our prevailing daily room rate with this coupon. See reverse for full details.

Offer void if detached from book. This coupon should only be removed at time of redemption.

AMERICAN CASINO GUIDE

Baldini's SPORTS CASINO

Free Buffet!

Present this coupon to the cashier at Baldini's Buffet to buy one buffet at regular price and receive another FREE!

Offer void if detached from book. This coupon should only be removed at time of redemption.

2500 E. Second St.
Reno, NV 89595
(702) 789-2000
(800) 648-5080

Present this coupon to the cashier at *The Lodge*. Not valid in conjunction with any other offer or discounts. Must be 21 years or older.

Management reserves the right to change or cancel this offer at any time. Offer expires 12/24/04.

D-53

Reno Hilton

2500 E. Second St.
Reno, NV 89595
(702) 789-2000
(800) 648-5080

Call 1-800-648-5080 to make your ADVANCE reservations. Ask for reservation code ACG. Coupon must be presented on arrival. Promotional offer not available for groups or conventions. Must be 21 years or older. Limited availability. Excludes special events & holiday periods. Management reserves the right to change or cancel this offer at any time. Offer expires 12/24/04.

Baldini's
SPORTS CASINO

856 S. Rock Blvd.
Sparks, NV 89431
(702) 358-0116

"Reno's Premier International Buffet"

Must be 21 years of age or older. Not valid on holidays. Not valid with any other offer. Management reserves the right to cancel or alter this coupon at any time without prior notice. Offer expires 12/30/04.

AMERICAN CASINO GUIDE

Buy One, Get One FREE

Redeem this coupon at the Broadway Buffet to enjoy two buffets for the price of one, or half-price for one person. See back for full details.

TRUMP PLAZA

Offer void if detached from book. This coupon should only be removed at time of redemption.

AMERICAN CASINO GUIDE

Receive $10 Off at the French Quarter Buffet!

($5 per person, up to two people)

Valid through December 30, 2004 (excluding December 31, 2003)
See reverse for details. FC-ACG04-10

SHOWBOAT
THE MARDI GRAS CASINO®

Offer void if detached from book. This coupon should only be removed at time of redemption.

AMERICAN CASINO GUIDE

Ripley's Believe It or Not!®

Two-For-One Admission

Present this coupon and get one free admission with the purchase of one adult admission at Ripley's Believe It or Not.® Located on the famous Atlantic City Boardwalk. See back for full details.

Offer void if detached from book. This coupon should only be removed at time of redemption.

Coupon must be presented at the Broadway Buffet in Trump Plaza.
Must be 21 years of age. May not be used in conjunction with any other offers.
Not valid on Saturdays or Sundays or holidays. Limit one coupon per person.
Offer subject to cancellation without notice.
Valid thru 12/30/04.

TRUMP PLAZA

Must have Total Rewards® Card to redeem offer. Gratuity and tax not included. Valid only for the French Quarter Buffet at Showboat, Atlantic City, NJ. Not good with any other offer, complimentaries or Total Rewards® discount. Must be 21 or older to gamble, enter and remain in a New Jersey casino or participate in any Showboat promotion. Know When To Stop Before You Start. Gambling Problem? Call 1-800-GAMBLER. ©2003, Harrah's Operating Company, Inc.

Ripley's Believe It or Not!®

On the Boardwalk at
New York Avenue
Atlantic City, NJ 08401
(609) 347-2001

Open year 'round
Call for operating hours

Adults: $10.95
Children (5-12) $6.95
4 and under Free

Not valid with any other offer. Limit: two free tickets per coupon. Expires December 30, 2004.

CP263

REVUE SHOW

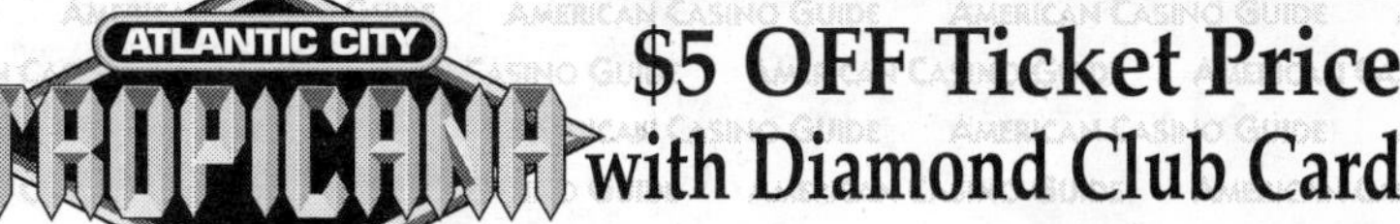

$5 OFF Ticket Price with Diamond Club Card

Redeem this coupon at the Tropicana Box Office for $5 OFF regularly priced adult ticket. Not valid on holidays, based upon availability. See reverse for complete details.

ACG

Offer void if detached from book. This coupon should only be removed at time of redemption.

AMERICAN CASINO GUIDE

STARBUCKS COFFEE ®

ONE FREE BISCOTTI OR TWO SHORTBREAD COOKIES

WITH ANY VENTI SIZE COFFEE PURCHASE

ATLANTIC CITY TROPICANA

Present this coupon to the Starbucks cashier prior to your purchase to redeem. See reverse for complete details.

ACG

Offer void if detached from book. This coupon should only be removed at time of redemption.

AMERICAN CASINO GUIDE

James'® SALT WATER TAFFY

$1 OFF The Purchase

Of A Pound Of Fudge Or A Pound of Salt Water Taffy

Present this coupon to the James' cashier prior to your purchase to redeem. See reverse for complete details.

ATLANTIC CITY TROPICANA

ACG

Offer void if detached from book. This coupon should only be removed at time of redemption.

Brighton and the Boardwalk
Atlantic City, NJ 08401-6390
1-800-THE-TROP
www.tropicana.net

Present this coupon and your Diamond Club Card to the Tropicana Box Office to receive $5 off the regularly priced adult admission to Tropciana's Revue Show only.Limit of two discounts per coupon. Not valid on holidays, previously purchased admissions, telephone orders or Ticketmaster purchases. No cash value. Not valid in conjunction with any other offer. Copies of coupon not accepted. Show and offer subject to availability and change. Valid November 1, 2003 through December 30, 2004.

Brighton and the Boardwalk
Atlantic City, NJ 08401-6390
1-800-THE-TROP
www.tropicana.net

Present this coupon to the Starbucks cashier, prior to your purchase to receive one free biscotti or two shortbread cookies with the purchase of any Venti size coffee. Coupon redeemable any day from November 1, 2003 through December 31, 2004. Not valid in conjunction with any other offer. Subject to availability and change without notice. This coupon is non-transferable and has no cash value. Original coupon must be presented, no photocopies will be accepted. Limit one offer per customer. Valid only at Starbucks in the Tropicana Casino and Resort, Atlantic City.

Brighton and the Boardwalk
Atlantic City, NJ 08401-6390
1-800-THE-TROP
www.tropicana.net

Present this coupon to the James' cashier, prior to your purchase to receive one dollar off the purchase of one pound of fudge or one pound of salt water taffy. Coupon redeemable Sunday through Thursday only from November 1, 2003 through December 31, 2004. Not valid in conjunction with any other offer. Subject to availablility and change without notice. This coupon is non-transferable and has no cash value.Original coupon must be presented, no photocopies will be accepted. Limit one offer per customer.Valid only at James' in the Tropicana Casino and Resort, Atlantic City.

AMERICAN CASINO GUIDE

$25 Match Play Voucher

Present this voucher and your valid Wampum Card at any Wampum Club Center in exchange for one $25 Match Play coupon. Valid for even money bets on designated games. Must be at least 21. One coupon per person, per account.

ACG25

Offer void if detached from book. This coupon should only be removed at time of redemption.

AMERICAN CASINO GUIDE

Majestic Star™ CASINO

$5 CASH for New Members!

Just sign up for a Club Majestic® card and you will receive $5 in chips or tokens! Simply present this coupon at our Club Majestic booth to redeem. Club Majestic members get great benefits including Weekly Club Cash©, invitations to exclusive events and more! Join the hottest club on the Lake today and get lucky using your Club Majestic card. See back for complete details.

ACG04

Offer void if detached from book. This coupon should only be removed at time of redemption.

AMERICAN CASINO GUIDE

Receive 150 Bonus Points When You Earn 150 Points!

Use your Club Greektown Card and when you earn 150 points we'll give you 150 bonus points! See reverse for full details.

Offer void if detached from book. This coupon should only be removed at time of redemption.

Route 2
Mashantucket, CT 06339
(860) 312-3000
(800) FOXWOODS

Can be used only once • Non-negotiable • No cash value • Coupons will be retained by the dealer after each wager • One coupon per person, per account • Must have a valid Wampum Card • Non-transferable • Cannot be sold • Non-replaceable • Considered void if altered in any fashion • Must be at least 21 • Subject to change or cancellation at any time • Other restrictions may apply • Offer expires December 30, 2004.

Majestic Star™
CASINO

One Buffington Harbor Drive
Gary, IN 46406
1-888-2B-LUCKY
www.majesticstar.com

Present this coupon at the Club Majestic booth when signing up for a card. Must be at least 21 and present a valid photo ID. Limit one per person. Valid for new accounts only. Program may be discontinued at any time. Management reserves all rights. Expires December 31, 2004.

Gambling Problem?
Call 1-800-9-WITH-IT.

555 E. Lafayette Avenue
Detroit, MI 48226
(313) 223-2999
(888) 771-4386
www.greektowncasino.com

One coupon per person. Must be 21 years of age or older. Management reserves all rights Club Greektown membership rules apply. No cash value. No reproductions. Not valid with any other offer. Management reserves the right to modify or cancel this promotion at any time. Offer valid through December 30, 2004.

AMERICAN CASINO GUIDE

Buy One Buffet Get One FREE!

Present this coupon to the cashier at the Queen's Courtyard Buffet to receive one FREE buffet upon the purchase of another buffet at the regular price. Offer expires 12/30/04.

#881161

Offer void if detached from book. This coupon should only be removed at time of redemption.

AMERICAN CASINO GUIDE

Casino Magic® Biloxi

Your Host On The Coast.℠

Two FREE Show Tickets!

Present this voucher at the Casino Magic® Biloxi Players Club to receive two FREE admission tickets to any Show Room performance (up to $20 value). Call 1-800-5-MAGIC-5 Biloxi extension 3995 for current performance schedules.

Offer void if detached from book. This coupon should only be removed at time of redemption.

AMERICAN CASINO GUIDE

TUNICA CASINO & HOTEL

Two-For-One Buffet

Present this coupon, along with your Harrah's Total Rewards Card, to the cashier at the Fresh Market Square Buffet at Harrah's Tunica Casino & Hotel to receive one FREE buffet upon the purchase of another buffet of equal or greater value.

Total Rewards# ____________________

CG **0170-7000-402**

Offer void if detached from book. This coupon should only be removed at time of redemption.

200 South Front Street
East St. Louis, IL 62201
(618) 874-5000
(800) 777-0777

Purchase one buffet and receive the second buffet FREE! This offer may not be combined with any other offer, is non-transferable, not valid on holidays, and does not apply to the purchase of alcoholic beverages. One coupon per couple, per day. Tax and gratuity are not included. Casino Queen reserves the right to change or revoke this offer without prior notice.

Casino Magic® Biloxi

Your Host On The Coast.℠

1-800-5-MAGIC-5

195 Beach Boulevard
Biloxi, MS 39530
(228) 387-4600
www.casinomagic-biloxi.com

Magic Money℠ Players Club membership required to redeem this offer (membership is free). Offer is based on availability and valid for general admission seating only. Must be 21. No reproductions. No refunds. Not valid with any other offer. Management reserves the right to modify or cancel this promotion at any time. Offer valid at Casino Magic® Biloxi only through December 23, 2004.

TUNICA CASINO & HOTEL
1100 Casino Strip Resorts Blvd.
Robinsonville, MS
662-363-7777

You must have a Harrah's Total Rewards Card when using this coupon. To become a Harrah's Total Rewards Card member simply present a valid ID at the Total Rewards Card Center.

This offer is only valid at Harrah's Tunica Casino and Hotel. It is nontransferable and cannot be used in conjunction with any other offer or promotion. Management reserves the right to withdraw this offer without prior notice. Must be 21 years of age or older. Valid through 12/30/04. No photocopies accepted.

AMERICAN CASINO GUIDE

Tunica, MS

Buy One Epic Buffet and Get One Free!

Enjoy two buffets for the price of one at Hollywood's Epic Buffet! Dine and play among movie memorabilia in an authentic Hollywood atmosphere 7 days a week! See reverse side for full details.

Offer void if detached from book. This coupon should only be removed at time of redemption.

AMERICAN CASINO GUIDE

Buy 1 Buffet Get 1 FREE!

Present this coupon along with your Club Fitz Card to the Hostess at the Castle Court Buffet MONDAY thru THURSDAY 7 a.m. to 11 p.m. and receive one FREE buffet when you purchase one. See other side for full terms and conditions.

MKTG

Offer void if detached from book. This coupon should only be removed at time of redemption.

AMERICAN CASINO GUIDE

25% Off at Fitzgeralds Gift Shoppe

Present this coupon with any purchase of $10 or more and receive 25% off your total purchase price at Fitzgeralds Gift Shoppe (exclusive of tobacco, food, drug and sale items). See other side for full terms and conditions.

MKTG

Offer void if detached from book. This coupon should only be removed at time of redemption.

Sign up for a Screen Test card at the Club Hollywood Booth on the casino floor. Then present this coupon at Club Hollywood to receive your buy-one-get-one-free Epic Buffet coupon.

Hollywood Casino Tunica reserves the right to modify or cancel this promotion at anytime without prior notice. Offer not valid on Friday or Saturday from 6p.m. to midnight. This coupon cannot be combined with any other promotion. Offer expires 12/31/04. Valid only at Hollywood Casino Tunica.

YOUR PLACE TO SHINE™

1150 Casino Strip Resorts Blvd.
Tunica Resorts, MS 38664
(800) 871-0711
(662) 357-7700

711 Lucky Lane
Tunica Resorts, MS 38664
1-800-766-LUCK
For Hotel Reservations
1-888-766-LUCK

Gratuity and alcoholic beverages not included. Limit one coupon per guest per day. Not valid with any other coupon or offer. Management reserves the right to change or discontinue this coupon at any time. Must be 21 years or older with valid I.D. Offer expires 12/30/04.

711 Lucky Lane
Tunica Resorts, MS 38664
1-800-766-LUCK
For Hotel Reservations
1-888-766-LUCK

Limit one coupon per person per day. Not valid with any other coupon or offer. Management reserves the right to change or discontinue this coupon at any time. Must be 21 years or older with valid I.D. Offer expires 12/30/04.

AMERICAN CASINO GUIDE

FREE Bahamas Trip

GOLF RESORT AND CASINO
GRAND BAHAMA ISLAND
from Fort Lauderdale, FL

Offer includes roundtrip 727 jet air from Ft. Lauderdale, Florida, roundtrip taxi transfers (airport/casino/airport). Does not include $78 U.S. & Bahamas departure/APHIS/ Airport facility taxes and fees, 15% gratuity on all food and beverages (figured before discount), all items not specified. See reverse for full details. Offer valid through 12/20/04. Ask for "Day-A-Way."

For reservations and information about special rates from Grand Bahama Vacations/Laker Airways departure cities call (800) 432-2294.

Offer void if detached from book. This coupon should only be removed at time of redemption.

AMERICAN CASINO GUIDE

FREE Bahamas Trip

GOLF RESORT AND CASINO
GRAND BAHAMA ISLAND
from Fort Lauderdale, FL

Offer includes roundtrip 727 jet air from Ft. Lauderdale, Florida, roundtrip taxi transfers (airport/casino/airport). Does not include $78 U.S. & Bahamas departure/APHIS/ Airport facility taxes and fees, 15% gratuity on all food and beverages (figured before discount), all items not specified. See reverse for full details. Offer valid through 12/20/04. Ask for "Day-A-Way."

For reservations and information about special rates from Grand Bahama Vacations/Laker Airways departure cities call (800) 432-2294.

Offer void if detached from book. This coupon should only be removed at time of redemption.

AMERICAN CASINO GUIDE

Free Cruise For Two

aboard

"Florida's Best Value Casino Ships"

Use this coupon for a FREE cruise aboard SunCruz Casino in
Hollywood • Key Largo • Port Canaveral
Daytona Beach • Jacksonville
John's Pass, T.I. • N. Myrtle Beach, S.C.

Ships' registry U.S.

Offer void if detached from book. This coupon should only be removed at time of redemption.

Offer subject to availability and expires December 20, 2004. Must be 18 years of age or older. Limit one person per coupon. **VALID PROOF OF CITIZENSHIP IS REQUIRED. All taxes**, fees, airport facilities charges, etc. must be paid at airport in cash. Credit cards and checks are not accepted at airport.

Reservations are highly recommended. Stand-bys are subject to availability only. **Instruct** reservationist you are requesting the "American Casino Guide Day-A-Way" promotion to receive this offer.

Terms & Conditions: Taxes and fees are subject to change, valid on Laker Airways (Bahamas) Ltd., no cash value on offer or any of its parts, no checked baggage allowed. Offer may be withdrawn without notice.

Availability: Offer available on day excursions Monday through Friday, night excursions on Thursday, not available on weekends or holidays. Other blackout dates may apply.

All bookings are subject to the General Conditions of Grand Bahama Vacations. All bookings will be confirmed on a space available basis only. The Casino at The Royal Oasis Golf Resort & Casino and/or Grand Bahama Vacations reserves the right to deny reservation and/or boarding to any person deemed unsuitable or previously denied travel for any reason. Grand Bahama Vacations acts only as marketing agent for The Casino at The Royal Oasis Golf Resort & Casino in the U.S.

Offer subject to availability and expires December 20, 2004. Must be 18 years of age or older. Limit one person per coupon. **VALID PROOF OF CITIZENSHIP IS REQUIRED. All taxes**, fees, airport facilities charges, etc. must be paid at airport in cash. Credit cards and checks are not accepted at airport.

Reservations are highly recommended. Stand-bys are subject to availability only. **Instruct** reservationist you are requesting the "American Casino Guide Day-A-Way" promotion to receive this offer.

Terms & Conditions: Taxes and fees are subject to change, valid on Laker Airways (Bahamas) Ltd., no cash value on offer or any of its parts, no checked baggage allowed. Offer may be withdrawn without notice.

Availability: Offer available on day excursions Monday through Friday, night excursions on Thursday, not available on weekends or holidays. Other blackout dates may apply.

All bookings are subject to the General Conditions of Grand Bahama Vacations. All bookings will be confirmed on a space available basis only. The Casino at The Royal Oasis Golf Resort & Casino and/or Grand Bahama Vacations reserves the right to deny reservation and/or boarding to any person deemed unsuitable or previously denied travel for any reason. Grand Bahama Vacations acts only as marketing agent for The Casino at The Royal Oasis Golf Resort & Casino in the U.S.

1-800-474-DICE

No other ships pay out more!

Hollywood • Key Largo
Jacksonville • Port Canaveral
Daytona Beach • John's Pass, T.I.
N. Myrtle Beach, South Carolina

Just like Las Vegas only offshore!

Offer valid for two persons on SunCruz CASINOS at any of the above locations. Coupon cannot be combined with any other offers. Reservations are required. Government tax per person is additional. For reservations or information call 1-800-474-DICE. Offer expires 12/30/04.

AMERICAN CASINO GUIDE

VALLEY VIEW CASINO

$15 in Free MOREPLAY™

Present this coupon at the VIP Players Club, sign up for a Players Club card and receive $15 in Free MOREPLAY™ **NEW MEMBERS ONLY.** See reverse for more details.

Offer void if detached from book. This coupon should only be removed at time of redemption.

AMERICAN CASINO GUIDE

Go Greyhound. Lucky Streak

$5 Discount on a Greyhound Casino Ticket

This coupon entitles the bearer to a $5 discount on the purchase of a round-trip Greyhound casino ticket at any Greyhound office in California or Arizona. For more information on Greyhound travel call (800) 231-2222

Offer void if detached from book. This coupon should only be removed at time of redemption.

AMERICAN CASINO GUIDE

Double Game Play Up To $50!

Present this coupon at the GameWorks location in Las Vegas and when you purchase from $10 to $50 of game play it will be matched with an equal amount of game play for FREE! See reverse for complete details.

Offer void if detached from book. This coupon should only be removed at time of redemption.

An Enterprise of the San Pasqual Band of Mission Indians

16300 Nyemii Pass Road
Valley Center, CA 92082
(760) 291-5500
1-866-VIEW-WIN
www.valleyviewcasino.com

Must present this original coupon (no photocopies). Limit one coupon per person at time of sign-up. Cannot be combined with any other offer or discount. No cash value. Non transferable. See the VIP Players Club for full details. MUST BE 21 OR OLDER TO ENTER THE FACILITY. Management reserves all rights. EXPIRES 12-30-04.

It should all be fun and games. If you or someone you know has a gambling problem please call 1-800-GAMBLER (1-800-522-4700) for help.

Go Greyhound.
Lucky Streak
(800) 231-2222

Convenient Daily Schedules To All
Major Casino Gaming Destinations!

- Special open ended tickets allow you to return anytime within 5 or 7 days from the day you leave.
- Special room rates for Greyhound customers at each casino property.

Offer valid for one adult (21 or older), per coupon, at any Greyhound ticket office in Arizona or California. Offer not valid with any other discount or promotion. Program subject to change or cancellation without notice. Offer valid through 12/30/04.

3785 Las Vegas Blvd. S.
Las Vegas, NV 89109
(702) 432-4263
www.gameworks.com
On the Strip next to the MGM Grand

Only valid at GameWorks Las Vegas. This coupon is valid for an equal amount of game play FREE upon $10 minimum purchase (valid up to $50 maximum). Original coupon (no photocopies) must be presented at time of purchase. Value 1/20th of a cent. Not valid with any other value added pricing offer. This video game play offer does not include photo or prize games. Limit one coupon per person, per day. Offer expires 12-30-04.

AMERICAN CASINO GUIDE

ALADDIN™

RESORT • CASINO • LAS VEGAS

$10 in FREE Slot Play With $20 Coin-in

Bring this original coupon (no photocopies) to the Club Aladdin Center to receive your $10 Gaming Bonus. Limit one coupon per person. See reverse for more details.

Offer void if detached from book. This coupon should only be removed at time of redemption.

AMERICAN CASINO GUIDE

ALADDIN™

RESORT • CASINO • LAS VEGAS

Free Ceramic Aladdin Mug

Bring this original coupon (no photocopies) to the Club Aladdin Center to receive your FREE Aladdin Souvenir Mug. Limit one coupon per person. See reverse for more details.

Offer void if detached from book. This coupon should only be removed at time of redemption.

AMERICAN CASINO GUIDE

ALADDIN™

RESORT • CASINO • LAS VEGAS

$5 Off Zanzibar Cafe with $20 Purchase

Present this original coupon (no photocopies) to your server at the Zanazibar Cafe before ordering to receive $5 off any purchase of $20 or more. Limit one coupon per table. See reverse for more details.

Offer void if detached from book. This coupon should only be removed at time of redemption.

ALADDIN™
RESORT · CASINO · LAS VEGAS

3667 Las Vegas Blvd. S.
Las Vegas, NV 89109
(702) 785-5555 • (877) 333-9475
www.aladdincasino.com

Restrictions apply. See Club Aladdin for complete rules. This offer is non-transferable, non-refundable, and has no cash value. Offer cannot be used in conjunction with any other promotions offering Free Slot play. Must be 21 years of age or older. Subject to change or cancellation at any time without notice. This offer is available to current and new Club Aladdin members. Management reserves all rights. Expires December 24, 2004.

ALADDIN™
RESORT · CASINO · LAS VEGAS

3667 Las Vegas Blvd. S.
Las Vegas, NV 89109
(702) 785-5555 • (877) 333-9475
www.aladdincasino.com

Restrictions apply. See Club Aladdin for complete rules. This offer is non-transferable, non-refundable, and has no cash value. Offer cannot be used in conjunction with any other promotions offering Free Slot play. Must be 21 years of age or older. Subject to change or cancellation at any time without notice. This offer is available to current and new Club Aladdin members. Management reserves all rights. Expires December 24, 2004.

ALADDIN™
RESORT · CASINO · LAS VEGAS

3667 Las Vegas Blvd. S.
Las Vegas, NV 89109
(702) 785-5555 • (877) 333-9475
www.aladdincasino.com

Coupon is not valid with any other offer and has no cash value. Subject to change or cancellation at anytime without notice. Must relinquesh this coupon upon redemption. Aladdin Management reserves all rights. Gratuity not included. Expires December 24, 2004.

AMERICAN CASINO GUIDE

2-For-1 Buffet

Present this coupon to the buffet cashier at either Arizona Charlie's Decatur or Arizona Charlie's Boulder to receive one FREE buffet when you purchase one buffet at the regular price. See reverse for more details.

Offer void if detached from book. This coupon should only be removed at time of redemption.

AMERICAN CASINO GUIDE

$5 Dining Comp at the Sourdough or Yukon Grille

Present this coupon to the cashier at the Sourdough Cafe or Yukon Grille Steakhouse at either Arizona Charlie's Decatur or Arizona Charlie's Boulder to receive $5 off your check of $10 or more. See reverse for more details.

Offer void if detached from book. This coupon should only be removed at time of redemption.

AMERICAN CASINO GUIDE

FREE FUNBOOK!

Present this coupon at either the Market Express across from THE Steakhouse, or Headliners located on the Promenade level. Must be 21 years old.

CIRCUS CIRCUS
LAS VEGAS

One coupon per person per day. Offer may be cancelled/revised by management at any time. No cash value. Expires 12-23-04.

Offer void if detached from book. This coupon should only be removed at time of redemption.

4575 Boulder Highway
Las Vegas, NV 89121
(702) 951-9000 • (800) 362-4040
www.arizonacharlies.com

740 S. Decatur Boulevard
Las Vegas, NV 89107
(702) 258-5200 • (800) 342-2695
www.arizonacharlies.com

Must be 21 years of age or older. Must present your Ultimate Rewards card and surrender this original coupon (no photocopies) to the cashier before being seated. Limit one coupon per person. Resale prohibited. Management reserves all rights. Valid thru December 31, 2004.

Decatur - 131-100-1100-60100-003
Boulder - 141-100-1100-60100-003

4575 Boulder Highway
Las Vegas, NV 89121
(702) 951-9000 • (800) 362-4040
www.arizonacharlies.com

740 S. Decatur Boulevard
Las Vegas, NV 89107
(702) 258-5200 • (800) 342-2695
www.arizonacharlies.com

Must be 21 years of age or older. Must present your Ultimate Rewards card and surrender this original coupon (no photocopies) to the cashier before being seated. Minimum $10 purchase. Limit one coupon per check. Resale prohibited. Management reserves all rights. Valid thru December 31, 2004.

Decatur - 131-100-1100-60100-003
Boulder - 141-100-1100-60100-003

CIRCUS CIRCUS®

2880 Las Vegas Boulevard South
Las Vegas, NV 89109
(702) 734-0410
Reservations (800) 444-2472

AMERICAN CASINO GUIDE

2-For-1 Feast Buffet

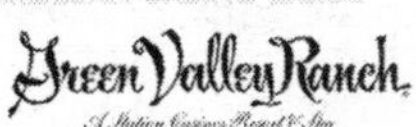

Valid once at Sunset Station, Boulder Station, Texas Station or Green Valley Ranch. Present this coupon to the cashier. Pay for one Feast Buffet and get the second Feast Buffet free! Valid Sunday through Thursday only. Offer expires December 26, 2004. Settle to comp BS 11-942, GVR 413-214, SS 413-279, TS 82-295.

Offer void if detached from book. This coupon should only be removed at time of redemption.

AMERICAN CASINO GUIDE

2-For-1 Room

Offer valid Monday-Thursday, based on availability. Black out dates may apply. Must have advance reservations. Limit one coupon per check in. No exceptions. Holiday and convention periods excluded. Management reserves all rights. No cash value. For reservations call: 1-866-767-7772 and ask for operator #16. Offer expires December 30, 2004. See reverse for more details.

Offer void if detached from book. This coupon should only be removed at time of redemption.

AMERICAN CASINO GUIDE

2-For-1 Laugh Trax

Pay for one admission to Laugh Trax and get another admission FREE! Laugh Trax is Las Vegas' hottest new Comedy Club featuring great new comedians. Offer valid Tuesday through Saturday. See reverse for more details.

Offer void if detached from book. This coupon should only be removed at time of redemption.

Offer valid one time at any of the above Station Casinos Properties

This ticket entitles bearer to one free breakfast, lunch, or dinner in The Feast Buffet when accompanied by a paying guest. Tax and gratuity not included. One coupon per person. Coupon must be presented to cashier. Coupons are not transferable and are not redeemable for cash. Must be 21 years of age or older. Not a line pass. Valid Sunday through Thursday only. Not valid on holidays. Not valid with any other offer. Offer may be changed or discontinued at any time at the discretion of management. Offer expires 12/26/04.

2411 W. Sahara Avenue
Las Vegas, NV 89102
(702) 367-2411
(800) 634-3101
www.stationcasinos.com

This voucher entitles the bearer to one free room night at Palace Station Hotel & Casino, with the purchase of one night at the prevailing rate. Must have advance reservations. Must present voucher upon check-in. Not valid in conjunction with any other offer. Management reserves the right to cancel this promotion at any time. Credit card or cash deposit required. Guest is responsible for tax, telephone, room service and all other additional charges. Must be 21 or older. Limit one free room per person.

2411 W. Sahara Avenue
Las Vegas, NV 89102
(702) 367-2411
(800) 634-3101
www.stationcasinos.com

Redeem this original coupon (no photocopies) at the Palace Station Rewards Center one hour prior to showtime.

Based on availability. Must be 21 years or older to redeem. Tax not included. Valid Tuesday - Saturday. One drink minimum per person. Laugh Trax is a non-smoking showroom. Management reserves all rights. No cash value. Offer expires December 30, 2004.

AMERICAN CASINO GUIDE

2-For-1 Room

Pay for one night and get the second night FREE! Good Sunday through Thursday. Holidays and convention periods excluded. Black out dates may apply. Subject to availability. For reservations call 1-866-767-7776 and ask for operator 717. Offer expires December 26, 2004. See reverse for complete details.

Offer void if detached from book. This coupon should only be removed at time of redemption.

AMERICAN CASINO GUIDE

One FREE Game of Bowling Anytime!

The bearer of this coupon is entitled to one FREE game of bowling anytime. One coupon per person, per day. Management reserves all rights. Offer expires December 30, 2004. See reverse for complete details.

Offer void if detached from book. This coupon should only be removed at time of redemption.

AMERICAN CASINO GUIDE

One FREE Skate during Public Skating Sessions!

The bearer of this coupon is entitled to one FREE skate during any public skating session. One coupon per person, per day. Management reserves all rights. Offer expires December 30, 2004. See reverse for complete details.

Offer void if detached from book. This coupon should only be removed at time of redemption.

4949 N. Rancho Drive
N. Las Vegas, NV 89130
(702) 658-4900
(866) 767-7770
www.santafecasino.com

This voucher entitles the bearer to one free room night at Santa Fe Station, with the purchase of one night at the prevailing rate. Must have advance reservations. Must present voucher upon check-in. Not valid in conjunction with any other offer. Management reserves all rights to cancel this promotion at any time. Credit card or cash deposit required. Guest is responsible for tax, telephone, room service and all other additional charges. Must be 21 years or older. Limit one free room per person. Offer expires December 26, 2004.

4949 N. Rancho Drive
N. Las Vegas, NV 89130
(702) 658-4900
(866) 767-7770
www.santafecasino.com

The bearer of this coupon is entitled to 1 free Game of Bowling anytime!

One coupon per person, per day. Must present original coupon (no photocopies). Management reserves all rights. Offer expires December 30, 2004.

GL #34007

4949 N. Rancho Drive
N. Las Vegas, NV 89130
(702) 658-4900
(866) 767-7770
www.santafecasino.com

The bearer of this coupon is entitled to 1 free Skate during Public Skating Sessions!

One coupon per person, per day. Must present original coupon (no photocopies). Management reserves all rights. Call 702 658-4983 for Public Skating Sessions. Offer expires December 30, 2004.

GL #63042-15

AMERICAN CASINO GUIDE

2-For 1 Room

Pay for one night and get the second night FREE! Good Sunday through Thursday. Holidays and convention periods excluded. Black out dates may apply. Subject to availability. Offer expires December 26, 2004. For reservations call: 1-888-786-7389 and ask for Operator #205. See reverse for complete details.

Offer void if detached from book. This coupon should only be removed at time of redemption.

AMERICAN CASINO GUIDE

Buy one Breakfast, Lunch or Dinner entrée, get the second entrée FREE!

Buy one entrée at the Gambler's Grill and enjoy a second entree of equal or lesser value FREE! See reverse for more details.

Offer void if detached from book. This coupon should only be removed at time of redemption.

AMERICAN CASINO GUIDE

Pay for one night at prevailing rate, get a second night at half-price!

Present this coupon when you check in at the front desk Monday through Thursday. Pay for one night at the prevailing rate and get the second night at half-price. For reservations call (702) 367-2441 and ask for Operator #623. See reverse for more details.

Offer void if detached from book. This coupon should only be removed at time of redemption.

1301 W. Sunset Road
Henderson, NV 89014
(702) 547-7777
(888) 786-7389
www.sunsetstation.com

This voucher entitles the bearer to one free room night at the Sunset Station Hotel & Casino, with the purchase of one night at the prevailing rate. Must have advance reservations. Must present original voucher (no photocopies) upon check-in. Not valid in conjunction with any other offer. Management reserves the right to cancel this promotion at any time. Credit card or cash deposit required. Guest is responsible for tax, telephone, room service and all other additional charges. Must be 21 or older. Limit one free room per person. Offer expires 12/26/04.

3330 W. Tropicana Ave.
Las Vegas, NV 89103
(702) 740-0000
(800) 634-3488
www.stationcasinos.com

- Present original coupon (no photocopies) to server prior to ordering.
- Limit one coupon per person.
- Management reserves all rights.
- No Cash Value.
- Offer expires December 31, 2004.
- Settle to comp #10187

3330 W. Tropicana Ave.
Las Vegas, NV 89103
(702) 740-0000
(800) 634-3488

Offer good Monday-Thursday. Holidays and convention periods are excluded. Must have advance reservations.

Limit one coupon per check in. No exceptions. Must present original voucher upon check-in (no photocopies). Management reserves all rights. No cash value. Offer expires December 31, 2004.

AMERICAN CASINO GUIDE

$5 - $10 Blackjack Matchplay

Present this coupon and your Barley's Player Rewards Card to any Blackjack table prior to the start of a game and **we'll match your bet of $5 to $10** if you win. See reverse for complete details.

Offer void if detached from book. This coupon should only be removed at time of redemption.

AMERICAN CASINO GUIDE

2-For-1 Sub Sandwich Combo

Bring this coupon directly to the *Brickhouse Pizza Kitchen*, show your Barley's Player Rewards Card, pay for one sub sandwich and a regular-size soft drink and get a second sub sandwich FREE! Chips included with both subs at no additional charge. See reverse for complete details.

Offer void if detached from book. This coupon should only be removed at time of redemption.

AMERICAN CASINO GUIDE

One FREE Game of Bowling Anytime!
(including Cosmic Bowling)

The bearer of this coupon is entitled to one FREE game of bowling anytime (including Cosmic Bowling). One coupon per person, per day. Management Reserves All Rights. Offer expires December 26, 2004. See reverse for complete details.

Offer void if detached from book. This coupon should only be removed at time of redemption.

4500 E. Sunset Road #30
Henderson, NV 89014
(702) 458-2739
www.stationcasinos.com

One coupon per person, per day. Cannot be redeemed for cash. Must be 21 or older. Non-transferable. Cannot be combined with any other offer or promotion.

Must be a Barleys Player Rewards member and must present original coupon (no photocopies). Not responsible for lost or stolen coupon. Management reserves all rights. Offer may be changed or discontinued at anytime at the discretion of management. Offer expires December 26, 2004.

4500 E. Sunset Road #30
Henderson, NV 89014
(702) 458-2739
www.stationcasinos.com

Must be 21 or older. Must be a Barley's Player Reward member and must present original coupon (no photocopies). Offer expires December 31, 2004.

Offer valid daily during normal pizza kitchen hours. Tax & Gratuity not included. Offer has no cash value. Non-transferable. Not responsible for lost or stolen coupon. Management reserves all rights. Not valid with any other offer or promotion. Offer may be changed or discontinued at anytime at the discretion of management. Settle to #151-140

Gambling Hall & Hotel

2101 Texas Star Lane
N. Las Vegas, NV 89032
(702) 631-1000
(800) 654-8888
www.texasstation.com

This coupon entitles the bearer to one FREE game of bowling anytime at the Texas Station Hotel & Casino Bowling Center.

Must present original voucher (no photocopies). Not valid in conjunction with any other offer. Management reserves the right to cancel this promotion at any time. Limit one free game per person, per day. Offer expires 12/26/04.

AMERICAN CASINO GUIDE

2-For-1 Room

Pay for one night and get the second night FREE! Good Sunday through Thursday. Holidays and convention periods excluded. Subject to availability. For reservations call 1-800-654-8888 and ask for operator #325. Offer expires December 26, 2004. See reverse for more details.

Offer void if detached from book. This coupon should only be removed at time of redemption.

AMERICAN CASINO GUIDE

FREE 1/2 lb. Burger & Fries

with purchase of a beverage

Bring this coupon to Dante's Restaurant, show your Wildfire Player's Card, and receive a FREE 1/2 lb. burger with fries when you purchase a beverage! See reverse for more details.

Offer void if detached from book. This coupon should only be removed at time of redemption.

AMERICAN CASINO GUIDE

Up to $100 in FREE Slot Play!

with new slot club card sign-up

Get up to $100 in FREE slot play, when you sign up for a new Wildfire Player's Card. Simply insert your Player's Card into any machine to receive your Free Slot Play. See reverse for more details.

Offer void if detached from book. This coupon should only be removed at time of redemption.

2101 Texas Star Lane
N. Las Vegas, NV 89032
(702) 631-1000
(800) 654-8888
www.texasstation.com

This voucher entitles the bearer to one free room night at the Texas Station Hotel & Casino, with the purchase of one night at the prevailing rate. Must have advance reservations. Must present original voucher (no photocopies) upon check-in. Not valid in conjunction with any other offer. Management reserves the right to cancel this promotion at any time. Credit card or cash deposit required. Guest is responsible for tax, telephone, room service and all other additional charges. Must be 21 or older. Limit one free room per person. Offer expires 12/26/04.

1901 N. Rancho Drive
Las Vegas, NV 89106
(702) 648-1182

Must be 21 or older. Must be a member of the Wildfire Player's Club. Valid one time. Not valid with any other offer or promotion.

Valid Sunday through Thursday only. Tax and gratuity not included. Must purchase a beverage. Non-transferable. Must present original coupon (no photocopies). Offer has no cash value. Management reserves all rights. Coupon expires December 26, 2004.

1901 N. Rancho Drive
Las Vegas, NV 89106
(702) 648-1182

Offer valid for first time sign up for Wildfire Player's Card. Original coupon (no photocopies) must be presented to the Player's Club. Must be 21 or older. Non-transferable.

Offer has no cash value. Management reserves all rights. One coupon per person. Offer may be changed or discontinued at anytime at the discretion of management. Offer expires December 31, 2004.

AMERICAN CASINO GUIDE

2-For 1 Room

Pay for one night and get the second night FREE! Good Sunday through Thursday. Holidays and convention periods excluded. Black out dates may apply. Subject to availability. Offer expires December 26, 2004. For reservations call: 1-800-683-7777 and ask for Operator #103.

Offer void if detached from book. This coupon should only be removed at time of redemption.

AMERICAN CASINO GUIDE

$5 Match Play on any Table Game

Make a minimum $5 bet with this coupon at any table game and you'll receive an extra $5 if you win! Coupon must be surrendered after bet wins or loses. See reverse for more details.

Offer void if detached from book. This coupon should only be removed at time of redemption.

AMERICAN CASINO GUIDE

2-For-1 Lunch or Dinner Buffet

Buy one lunch or dinner buffet and get a second one FREE! Offer valid Sunday-Thursday, excludes Sunday brunch and Thursday dinner. Both buffets must be redeemed on same visit. See reverse for more details.

Offer void if detached from book. This coupon should only be removed at time of redemption.

4111 Boulder Highway
Las Vegas, NV 89121
(702) 432-7777
(800) 683-7777
www.stationcasinos.com

This voucher entitles the bearer to one free room night at Boulder Station Hotel & Casino, with the purchase of one night at the prevailing rate. Must have advance reservations. Must present voucher upon check-in. Not valid in conjunction with any other offer. Management reserves the right to cancel this promotion at any time. Credit card or cash deposit required. Guest is responsible for tax, telephone, room service and all other additional charges. Must be 21 or older. Limit one free room per person. Offer expires 12/26/04.

2121 E. Craig Road
N. Las Vegas, NV 89030
(702) 507-5700
(866) 999-4899
www.cannerycasinos.com

Make a $5 minimum bet at any table game, along with this coupon, and receive a $5 match bet. Even-money bets only. Coupon must be surrendered after bet wins or loses. Cannot be redeemed for cash. Not valid with any other offer. Must be 21or older to redeem. Limit one coupon per person, per year. No photocopies accepted. Management reserves all rights. Offer expires12/31/04.

2121 E. Craig Road
N. Las Vegas, NV 89030
(702) 507-5700
(866) 999-4899
www.cannerycasinos.com

Present this coupon to the cashier at time of purchase. Must be 21 or older to reeem. Tax and gratuity not included. Coupon not redeeemable for cash. Original coupon (no photocopies) must be presented to the cashier. One coupon per customer. Management reserves all rights. Valid through 12/31/04.

AMERICAN CASINO GUIDE

2-For-1 Room Offer!

Buy one room night (Sunday-Thursday) at the regular rate and receive the second night FREE! See reverse for details.

Offer void if detached from book. This coupon should only be removed at time of redemption.

AMERICAN CASINO GUIDE

FREE Funbook

includes Free Breakfast!

Present this coupon at the Promotions Desk inside the El Cortez Hotel & Casino for your FREE Funbook. See reverse for details.

Offer void if detached from book. This coupon should only be removed at time of redemption.

AMERICAN CASINO GUIDE

FREE Draft Beer or Wine!

Present this coupon to the server at any bar or lounge in the El Cortez Hotel & Casino to receive one FREE glass of draft beer or wine.See reverse for details.

Offer void if detached from book. This coupon should only be removed at time of redemption.

600 E. Fremont Street
Las Vegas, NV 89101
(702) 385-5200
(800) 634-6703
www.elcortezhotelcasino.com

Offer valid for adults 21 years of age or older. Advance reservations required. Call 1-800-634-6703 to make your reservations and ask for the **American Casino Guide** 2-For-1 discount. Not valid with any other offers or discounts. Management reserves all rights. Coupon must be presented upon check-in. Offer expires 12/23/04.

600 E. Fremont Street
Las Vegas, NV 89101
(702) 385-5200
(800) 634-6703
www.elcortezhotelcasino.com

Offer valid for adults 21 years of age or older. Coupon must be presented at promotions desk to receive FREE funbook. Limited to one funbook per person, per day. This offer is subject to change or cancellation without notice. Offer expires 12/31/04.

600 E. Fremont Street
Las Vegas, NV 89101
(702) 385-5200
(800) 634-6703
www.elcortezhotelcasino.com

Offer valid for adults 21 years of age or older. Coupon must be presented to server to receive FREE drink. Limited to one FREE glass of draft beer or wine per person, per day. This offer is subject to change or cancellation without notice. Offer expires 12/30/04.

AMERICAN CASINO GUIDE

Second Room Night FREE!

Buy one room night at the regular rate and receive the second night FREE! See reverse for details.

Offer void if detached from book. This coupon should only be removed at time of redemption.

AMERICAN CASINO GUIDE

Two Meals For The Price of One!

Get one meal FREE when you buy one meal of equal or greater value at the Diner in the Gold Spike Hotel & Casino. See reverse for more details.

Offer void if detached from book. This coupon should only be removed at time of redemption.

AMERICAN CASINO GUIDE

FREE Drink at the Casino Bar

Draft Beer, Wine or Soft Drink

Present this coupon at the Casino Bar to receive your FREE glass of draft beer or wine, or the Snack Bar to receive your FREE soft drink. See reverse for more details.

Offer void if detached from book. This coupon should only be removed at time of redemption.

400 E. Ogden Avenue
Las Vegas, NV 89101
(702) 384-8444
(800) 634-6703
www.goldspikehotelcasino.com

Offer valid on a space available basis for adults 21 years of age or older. Advance reservations required. Call 1-800-634-6703 to make your reservations and ask for the **American Casino Guide second night FREE offer.** Not valid with any other offers or discounts. Management reserves all rights. Original coupon (no photocopies) must be presented upon check-in. Limit: one coupon per customer. Offer expires 12/25/04.

400 E. Ogden Avenue
Las Vegas, NV 89101
(702) 384-8444
(800) 634-6703
www.goldspikehotelcasino.com

Offer valid for adults 21 years of age or older 24 hours a day. Original coupon (no photocopies) must be presented to server to receive your FREE meal. This offer is limited to one FREE meal (includes: one entree, one drink and one dessert) per person, per day. This offer is subject to change or cancellation without notice. Management reserves all rights. Offer expires 12/25/04.

400 E. Ogden Avenue
Las Vegas, NV 89101
(702) 384-8444
(800) 634-6703
www.goldspikehotelcasino.com

Offer valid for adults 21 years of age or older. Original coupon (no photocopies) must be presented to attendant at the Casino Bar or the Snack Bar to receive your FREE drink. This offer is limited to one FREE glass of draft beer, wine, or soft drink, per person, per day. This offer is subject to change or cancellation without notice. Management reserves all rights. Offer expires 12/25/04.

AMERICAN CASINO GUIDE

Second Room Night FREE!

Buy one room night at the regular rate and receive the second night FREE! See reverse for details.

Offer void if detached from book. This coupon should only be removed at time of redemption.

AMERICAN CASINO GUIDE

FREE Drink at Any Casino Bar

Present this coupon at any Plaza Casino Bar to receive your FREE glass of draft beer, wine, or bottle of water. See reverse for more details.

Offer void if detached from book. This coupon should only be removed at time of redemption.

AMERICAN CASINO GUIDE

One FREE Progressive Bonanza (with any buy-in)

8 sessions daily from 9:00 a.m. until 11:00 p.m.

Present this coupon in our Bingo Room to receive a FREE Progressive Bonanza Card with any buy-in. See reverse for more details.

Offer void if detached from book. This coupon should only be removed at time of redemption.

1 Main Street
Las Vegas, NV 89101
(702) 386-2110
(800) 634-6575
www.plazahotelcasino.com

Offer valid on a space available basis for adults 21 years of age or older. Advance reservations required. Call 1-800-634-6575 to make your reservations and ask for the **American Casino Guide** 2-For-1 discount. Not valid with any other offers or discounts. Management reserves all rights. Original coupon (no photocopies) must be presented upon check-in. Limited to one coupon per customer. Offer expires 12/25/04.

1 Main Street
Las Vegas, NV 89101
(702) 386-2110
(800) 634-6575
www.plazahotelcasino.com

Offer valid for adults 21 years of age or older. Original coupon (no photocopies) must be presented to bartender to receive your FREE drink. Limited to one FREE glass of draft beer, wine, or bottle of water, per person, per day. This offer is subject to change or cancellation without notice. Management reserves all rights. Offer expires 12/25/04.

1 Main Street
Las Vegas, NV 89101
(702) 386-2110
(800) 634-6575
www.plazahotelcasino.com

Offer valid for adults 21 years of age or older. Limit one coupon per person per session. Original coupon (no photocopies) must be presented to attendant to receive FREE Progressive Bonanza Card . Coupon has no cash value. This offer is subject to change or cancellation without notice and is not valid with any other offer. Management reserves all rights. Offer expires 12/25/04.

AMERICAN CASINO GUIDE

2-For-1 Room Offer!

Buy one room night (Sunday-Wednesday) at the regular rate and receive the second night FREE! See reverse for details.

Offer void if detached from book. This coupon should only be removed at time of redemption.

AMERICAN CASINO GUIDE

Buy one Breakfast, Lunch or Dinner entrée and get a second entrée FREE!

Buy one entrée at the Upper Deck restaurant at the Las Vegas Club Casino Hotel and enjoy a second entree of equal or lesser value FREE! See reverse for details.

Offer void if detached from book. This coupon should only be removed at time of redemption.

AMERICAN CASINO GUIDE

FREE Draft Beer or Wine!

Present this coupon to the server at any bar or lounge in the Las Vegas Club Casino Hotel to receive one FREE glass of draft beer or wine. See reverse for details.

Offer void if detached from book. This coupon should only be removed at time of redemption.

18 E. Fremont Street
Las Vegas, NV 89101
(702) 385-1664
(800) 634-6532
www.playatlvc.com

Offer valid on a space available basis for adults 21 years of age or older. Advance reservations required. Call 1-800-634-6532 to make your reservations and ask for the **American Casino Guide** 2-For-1 discount. Not valid with any other offers or discounts. Management reserves all rights. Original coupon must be presented upon check-in. Limited to one coupon per customer. Offer expires 12/25/04.

18 E. Fremont Street
Las Vegas, NV 89101
(702) 385-1664
(800) 634-6532
www.playatlvc.com

- Offer valid for adults 21 years of age or older.
- Present original coupon (no photocopies) to server prior to ordering.
- Limit one coupon per person.
- Management reserves all rights.
- No Cash Value.
- Offer expires 12/25/04.

18 E. Fremont Street
Las Vegas, NV 89101
(702) 385-1664
(800) 634-6532
www.playatlvc.com

Offer valid for adults 21 years of age or older. Original coupon (no photocopies) must be presented to server to receive FREE drink.

Limited to one FREE glass of draft beer or wine per person, per day. This offer is subject to change or cancellation without notice. Management reserves all rights. Offer expires 12/25/04.

AMERICAN CASINO GUIDE

THE NEW FRONTIER LAS VEGAS • NEVADA

$5 Match Play On Any Blackjack Table

Present this coupon to the New Frontier Rewards Club to validate prior to use. Must be a Rewards Club member to redeem coupon. Membership is free. See reverse for more details.

Offer void if detached from book. This coupon should only be removed at time of redemption.

AMERICAN CASINO GUIDE

THE NEW FRONTIER LAS VEGAS • NEVADA

2-For-1 Breakfast Buffet

Present this coupon to the New Frontier Rewards Club to validate prior to use. Must be a Rewards Club member to redeem coupon. Membership is free. See reverse for more details.

Offer void if detached from book. This coupon should only be removed at time of redemption.

AMERICAN CASINO GUIDE

THE NEW FRONTIER LAS VEGAS • NEVADA

One FREE admission to Gilley's for any Friday or Saturday night. A $10 value! See reverse for details.

Offer void if detached from book. This coupon should only be removed at time of redemption.

THE NEW
FRONTIER
LAS VEGAS • NEVADA

3120 Las Vegas Blvd. South
Las Vegas, NV 89109
(702) 794-8200
www.frontierlv.com

Present this coupon to the New Frontier Rewards Club to validate prior to use. Then, present this validated coupon and $5 to receive $10 when you win any even money bet at any blackjack table at The New Frontier. Must bet table minimum. Management reserves all rights. Coupon has no cash value and may not be combined with any other offer. Must be 21 years old to redeem. Not responsible for lost or stolen coupons. Expires:12/26/04.

THE NEW
FRONTIER
LAS VEGAS • NEVADA

3120 Las Vegas Blvd. South
Las Vegas, NV 89109
(702) 794-8200
www.frontierlv.com

Present this coupon to the New Frontier Rewards Club to validate prior to use. Then, present this validated coupon to the cashier or server at the Orchard Café to receive one free breakfast buffet with the purchase of one breakfast buffet at regular price. Management reserves all rights. Coupon has no cash value and may not be combined with any other offer. Does not include beverage, tax or gratuity. Must be 21 years old to redeem. Not responsible for lost or stolen coupons. Expires:12/26/04

CODE 531

THE NEW
FRONTIER
LAS VEGAS • NEVADA

3120 Las Vegas Blvd. South
Las Vegas, NV 89109
(702) 794-8200
www.frontierlv.com

Present this coupon to the door person at The New Frontier Gilley's to receive one free admission. Limited to one coupon per person. Management reserves all rights. Coupon has no cash value and may not be combined with any other offer. Must be 21 years old to redeem. Not responsible for lost or stolen coupons. Expires: 12/26/04.

CODE 532

AMERICAN CASINO GUIDE

$10 Match Play for Any Even-Money Table Game Bet

(with your Passport Players Club Card)

Make a $10 even-money bet at blackjack, craps or roulette with this coupon and your Passport Players Club Card and receive a FREE $10 Match Bet!

Offer void if detached from book. This coupon should only be removed at time of redemption.

AMERICAN CASINO GUIDE

2-For-1 Menu Item

Present this coupon, along with your Passport Players Club Card, at the Restaurant or BBQ in the Ellis Island Casino & Brewery to receive one FREE menu item when you purchase one item at the regular price. See reverse for more details.

Offer void if detached from book. This coupon should only be removed at time of redemption.

AMERICAN CASINO GUIDE

4 FREE Cocktails at the Casino Bar!

Present this coupon, along with your Passport Players Club Card, at the Casino Bar inside the Ellis Island Casino & Brewery to receive four FREE cocktails of your choice. See reverse for more details.

Offer void if detached from book. This coupon should only be removed at time of redemption.

4178 Koval Lane
Las Vegas, NV 89109
(702) 733-8901
www.ellisislandscasino.com

Must be 21 years of age or older and a Passport Players Club member. Make a $10 minimum even-money bet at any Ellis Island Casino blackjack, craps or roulette game, along with this original coupon (no photocopies), and receive a $10 Match Bet. Valid for one bet only and coupon must be surrendered after play. No Cash Value. Limit: one coupon per customer. Not valid with any other offer. Management reserves all rights. Offer expires 12/30/04.

4178 Koval Lane
Las Vegas, NV 89109
(702) 733-8901
www.ellisislandscasino.com

Present this original coupon (no photocopies) to the hostess in the restaurant or the BBQ, along with your Passport Players Club Card, to receive one FREE menu item from the regular menu with the purchase of another menu item at the regular price. The FREE item must be of equal of lesser value. Limit: one coupon per customer. No cash value. Must be 21 years of age or older. Tax and gratuity not included. Management reserves all rights. Offer expires 12/30/04.

4178 Koval Lane
Las Vegas, NV 89109
(702) 733-8901
www.ellisislandscasino.com

Must be 21 years of age or older. No restrictions on brands. Gratuity not included.

Please present before ordering. Original coupon must be presented (no photocopies) along with your Passport Players Club Card. Resale prohibited. Management reserves the right to cancel or alter this coupon without prior notice. Offer expires 12/30/04.

AMERICAN CASINO GUIDE

Hit Four-of-a-Kind and Receive a FREE Buffet Dinner!

Present this coupon to the Slot Supervisor when you win a four-of-a-kind (no wild cards) on any denomination video poker machine at the Suncoast Hotel and Casino. Your Club Denaro card must be properly inserted while playing and you must be playing maximim coins in order to receive this buffet bonus. See reverse for complete details.

Offer void if detached from book. This coupon should only be removed at time of redemption.

AMERICAN CASINO GUIDE

Join Club Denaro and receive 1,000 FREE Bonus Points!

Present this coupon to the Club Denaro desk at the Suncoast Hotel and Casino to recive 1,000 FREE bonus points when you join!. Valid for new enrollments only. See reverse for complete details.

Offer void if detached from book. This coupon should only be removed at time of redemption.

AMERICAN CASINO GUIDE

$4 Bingo Bucks FREE with purchase!

Present this coupon at the Bingo Hall at the Suncoast Hotel and Casino to receive $4 in Bingo Bucks FREE with the purchase of one regular price pack. Excludes Bonanza, Cashball or any validation. Use this coupon for credit towards additional bingo packs. See reverse for complete details.

Offer void if detached from book. This coupon should only be removed at time of redemption.

9090 Alta Drive
Las Vegas, NV 89145
(702) 636-7111 • (877) 677-7111
www.suncoastcasino.com

Four-of-a-kind must be verified by slot supervisor at time of jackpot and original coupon must be presented (no photocopies). No game recalls. Based on maximum coins played. No wild cards. Multi-line poker machines must hit on base line only. One bonus per player only. Cannot be used with any other offers. Must be 21 years of age or older. Offer expires 12-30-04.

9090 Alta Drive
Las Vegas, NV 89145
(702) 636-7111 • (877) 677-7111
www.suncoastcasino.com

One 1,000-point bonus per player. Original coupon (no photocopies) must be presented at time of enrollment. Cannot be used in conjunction with any other offer. Coupon has no cash value. Must be 21 years of age or older. Offer expires 12-30-04.

9090 Alta Drive
Las Vegas, NV 89145
(702) 636-7111 • (877) 677-7111
www.suncoastcasino.com

Limit: one per guest. Coupon has no cash value. Original coupon (no photocopies) must be presented at time of purchase. Cannot be used in conjunction with any other offer. Must be 21 years of age or older. Offer expires 12-30-04.

AMERICAN CASINO GUIDE

2-For-1 Buffet

Present this coupon to the cashier at the *Ports O' Call Buffet* to purchase one breakfast, lunch or dinner buffet at regular price and receive a second buffet for FREE (or 50% off when dining alone). See reverse for full details.

Offer void if detached from book. This coupon should only be removed at time of redemption.

AMERICAN CASINO GUIDE

2-For-1 Show Tickets

Present this coupon at the Gold Coast Box Office to purchase one ticket to either *Serendipity* or *Honky Tonk Angels* and receive a second ticket for FREE (or 50% off one ticket). Admission includes two FREE drinks (one during and one after the show). See reverse for full details.

Offer void if detached from book. This coupon should only be removed at time of redemption.

AMERICAN CASINO GUIDE

Two FREE Cocktails at any Casino Bar

Present this coupon to the server at any casino bar in the Gold Coast Hotel & Casino to receive two FREE cocktails. See reverse for full details.

Offer void if detached from book. This coupon should only be removed at time of redemption.

Gold Coast Hotel & Casino
4000 W. Flamingo Road
Las Vegas, NV 89103
(702) 367-7111 • (800) 331-5334
www.goldcoastcasino.com

Must be 21 years of age or older. Not valid on holidays. Not valid with any other offer. Limit one coupon per person. Resale prohibited. Original coupon must be presented (no photocopies). Discount is 50% off when dining alone. Gratuity not included. Management reserves the right to cancel or alter this coupon without prior notice. Offer expires 12-30-04.

Gold Coast Hotel & Casino
4000 W. Flamingo Road
Las Vegas, NV 89103
(702) 367-7111 • (800) 331-5334
www.goldcoastcasino.com

Must be 21 years of age or older. Not valid with any other offer. Limit one coupon per person. Resale prohibited. Original coupon must be presented (no photocopies). Discount is 50% off when attending alone. Offer not valid on dinner and show package. Management reserves all rights. Offer expires 12-30-04.

Gold Coast Hotel & Casino
4000 W. Flamingo Road
Las Vegas, NV 89103
(702) 367-7111 • (800) 331-5334
www.goldcoastcasino.com

Must be 21 years of age or older. Excludes specialty drinks in souvenir glasses. Excludes Showroom and restaurant bars. Gratuity not included. Please present before ordering. Original coupon must be presented (no photocopies). Resale prohibited. Management reserves the right to cancel or alter this coupon without prior notice. Offer expires 12-30-04.

AMERICAN CASINO GUIDE

2-For-1 Buffet

Present this coupon to the cashier at the *French Market Buffet* to purchase one breakfast, lunch or dinner buffet at regular price and receive a second buffet for FREE (or 50% off when dining alone). See reverse for more details.

Offer void if detached from book. This coupon should only be removed at time of redemption.

AMERICAN CASINO GUIDE

2-For-1 Fajita Dinner

Present this coupon to your server at *Don Miguel's* to purchase one beef or chicken fajita dinner at regular price and receive a second beef or chicken fajita dinner of equal or lesser value for FREE (or 50% off when dining alone). See reverse for complete details.

Offer void if detached from book. This coupon should only be removed at time of redemption.

AMERICAN CASINO GUIDE

Two FREE Cocktails at any Casino Bar

Present this coupon to the server at any casino bar in the Orleans Hotel & Casino to receive two FREE cocktails. See reverse for details.

Offer void if detached from book. This coupon should only be removed at time of redemption.

4500 W. Tropicana Ave.
Las Vegas, NV 89103
(702) 365-7111
(800) ORLEANS
www.orleanscasino.com

Must be 21 years of age or older. Not valid on holidays. Not valid with any other offer. Limit one coupon per person. Resale prohibited. Original coupon must be presented (no photocopies). Discount is 50% off when dining alone. Gratuity not included. Management reserves the right to cancel or alter this coupon without prior notice. Offer expires 12-30-04.

4500 W. Tropicana Ave.
Las Vegas, NV 89103
(702) 365-7111
(800) ORLEANS
www.orleanscasino.com

Must be 21 years of age or older. Not valid on holidays. Not valid with any other offer. Limit one coupon per person. Resale prohibited. Original coupon must be presented (no photocopies). Discount is 50% off when dining alone. Gratuity not included. Management reserves the right to cancel or alter this coupon without prior notice. Offer expires 12-30-04.

4500 W. Tropicana Ave.
Las Vegas, NV 89103
(702) 365-7111
(800) ORLEANS
www.orleanscasino.com

Must be 21 years of age or older. Excludes specialty drinks in souvenir glasses. Excludes Showroom and restaurant bars. Gratuity not included.

Please present before ordering. Original coupon must be presented (no photocopies). Resale prohibited. Management reserves the right to cancel or alter this coupon without prior notice. Offer expires 12-30-04.

AMERICAN CASINO GUIDE

FREE Hot Dog and a Beer!

Present this coupon at the hot dog cart located in the Sports Lounge and receive one free hot dog and a beer. See reverse for complete details.

Offer void if detached from book. This coupon should only be removed at time of redemption.

AMERICAN CASINO GUIDE

One FREE Cocktail at any Casino Bar

Present this coupon to the server at any casino bar in the Barbary Coast Hotel & Casino to receive one FREE cocktail. See reverse for details.

Offer void if detached from book. This coupon should only be removed at time of redemption.

AMERICAN CASINO GUIDE

$10 in FREE Slot Play!

New members only, present this coupon at the Club Palms booth, sign up for the Club Palms card and receive $10 in FREE slot play. See reverse for complete details.

Offer void if detached from book. This coupon should only be removed at time of redemption.

3595 Las Vegas Blvd. S.
Las Vegas, NV 89109
(702) 737-7111
(888) 227-2279
www.barbarycoastcasino.com

Must be 21 years of age or older. Not valid with any other offer. Resale prohibited. Limit one coupon per person. Gratuity not included. Original coupon must be presented (no photocopies).

Management reserves the right to cancel or alter this coupon without prior notice. Offer expires 12-30-04.

3595 Las Vegas Blvd. S.
Las Vegas, NV 89109
(702) 737-7111
(888) 227-2279
www.barbarycoastcasino.com

Must be 21 years of age or older. Excludes specialty drinks in souvenir glasses. Excludes restaurant bars. Gratuity not included. Please present before ordering. Original coupon must be presented (no photocopies accepted). Resale prohibited.

Management reserves the right to cancel or alter this coupon without prior notice. Offer expires 12-30-04.

Las Vegas' Newest Resort Destination
(702) 942-7777 • 1-866-942-7777
On Flamingo West of the Strip
Easy Access Convenient Parking
www.palms.com

New members present this voucher to the Club Palms booth and receive $10 in FREE slot play.

Must be 21 years of age or older. Not valid in conjunction with any other offer. Management reserves the right to cancel or change this offer at any time. Offer expires 12/31/04.

AMERICAN CASINO GUIDE

Las Vegas Hilton
Like no other.

$10 in FREE Promotional Chips

Play anywhere you like on your favorite table game! Present this coupon and your Park Place Connection card at the Casino Cage for $10 in non-negotiable gaming chips. If you do not have a Park Place Connection card, sign-up at our Park Place Connection Booth to begin earning player rewards. See reverse for more details. #1072

Offer void if detached from book. This coupon should only be removed at time of redemption.

AMERICAN CASINO GUIDE

THE BUFFET

Buy One Buffet Get One FREE

Present this coupon to the cashier at the buffet at the Las Vegas Hilton to buy one buffet and get one FREE. See reverse for more details. #1073

Offer void if detached from book. This coupon should only be removed at time of redemption.

AMERICAN CASINO GUIDE

Las Vegas Hilton
Like no other.

$45 Room Rate

Stay at the Las Vegas Hilton for only $45 per night (Sunday through Thursday). Just call (800) 457-3307 and ask for the American Casino Guide exclusive room offer. See reverse for more details.

Offer void if detached from book. This coupon should only be removed at time of redemption.

AMERICAN CASINO GUIDE

2 for 1 Buffet

Present to buffet cashier. Must purchase one buffet
to receive the second one free.
Settle to public comp # 404.

Expires December 30, 2004

Casino Guide

Offer void if detached from book. This coupon should only be removed at time of redemption.

AMERICAN CASINO GUIDE

$10 off next stay

Sunday - Thursday. Based on availability.
Not valid during holidays or conventions. Reservations required.
Must present coupon at check-in.

Expires December 30, 2004

Casino Guide

Offer void if detached from book. This coupon should only be removed at time of redemption.

AMERICAN CASINO GUIDE

Join the Player's Club and receive

1,000 FREE points

Must join club. Please allow 72 hours before points will be available.
Existing club members receive 250 points free. One coupon per person.

Expires December 30, 2004

Casino Guide

Offer void if detached from book. This coupon should only be removed at time of redemption.

www.SilvertonCasino.com • (800) 588-7711
3333 BBlue Diamond Rd. at I-15

www.SilvertonCasino.com • (800) 588-7711
3333 BBlue Diamond Rd. at I-15

www.SilvertonCasino.com • (800) 588-7711
3333 BBlue Diamond Rd. at I-15

AMERICAN CASINO GUIDE

2 for 1 BUFFET

Brunch - Monday through Friday. 7a.m. to 3p.m.
Not valid for weekends or holiday brunch.
Dinner - Good seven days a week, 4p.m. to 10p.m.

One coupon per person.Coupon may not be duplicated and has no cash value. Coupon cannot be combined with any other offer. Management reserves the right to modify or cancel this promotion at any time. Each member of party must be 21. Offer expires December 23, 2004.

Comp #183

Offer void if detached from book. This coupon should only be removed at time of redemption.

AMERICAN CASINO GUIDE

$5 Blackjack Matchplay

Present this coupon and your Club Sahara Card at any blackjack table prior to the start of a game and **we'll match your bet of $5** if you win. See reverse for complete details.

Offer void if detached from book. This coupon should only be removed at time of redemption.

AMERICAN CASINO GUIDE

$5.00 OFF THRILL PASS

Unlimited Rides, All Day Long!

Quicken your pulse with unlimited rides on these great attractions!
Regular price $19.95

One coupon per person. Coupon may not be duplicated. Coupon has no cash value. Coupon cannot be combined with any other offer. Management reserves the right to modify or cancel this promotion at any time. Offer expires December 23, 2004.

Offer void if detached from book. This coupon should only be removed at time of redemption.

Sahara Hotel and Casino
2535 Las Vegas Blvd., South
Las Vegas, NV 89109

1-888-696-2122

www.saharavegas.com

Sahara Hotel and Casino
2535 Las Vegas Blvd. S.
Las Vegas, NV 89109
(702) 737-2111
(800) 634-6645

Limit: one coupon per person, per day. Cannot be redeemed for cash. Must be 21 or older. Cannot be combined with any other offer or promotion.

Must be a Sahara Club member and must present original coupon (no photocopies). Not responsible for lost or stolen coupon. Management reserves all rights. Offer may be changed or discontinued at anytime at the discretion of management. Offer expires December 23, 2004.

NASCAR Cafe
2535 Las Vegas Blvd., South
Las Vegas, NV 89109

1-702-734-7223

www.saharavegas.com

AMERICAN CASINO GUIDE

2-For-1 Entree at Mahoney's Cafe

Buy one entreee at Mahoney's Cafe and receive the second entree of equal or lesser value for FREE. Valid for breakist, lunch or dinner. Cafe open from 6:00 a.m. to Midnight. See reverse for more details.

Offer void if detached from book. This coupon should only be removed at time of redemption.

AMERICAN CASINO GUIDE

$10 Refund For New Slot Club Members

Present this coupon at the Club Center and become a new Silver Nugget slot club member. Then, if you should lose $20.00 in slot, video poker or keno machines on the day you join the club, you will receive a $10 refund! See reverse for more details.

Offer void if detached from book. This coupon should only be removed at time of redemption.

AMERICAN CASINO GUIDE

2-For-1 Bowling

Buy one game of bowling and receive one game FREE! Also, receive shoe rental for only $1.00 with this coupon. See reverse for more details.

Offer void if detached from book. This coupon should only be removed at time of redemption.

2140 Las Vegas Blvd N.
N. Las Vegas, NV 89030
(702) 399-1111
www.mahoneyscasino.com

- Must be 21 years of age or older.
- Present original coupon (no photocopies) to server before ordering.
- Cannot be used with any other offer.
- Management reserves all rights.
- Offer expires 12/30/04.

2140 Las Vegas Blvd N.
N. Las Vegas, NV 89030
(702) 399-1111
www.mahoneyscasino.com

- Must be 21 years of age or older.
- Present original coupon (no photocopies) at Club Center. Membership is FREE and the Club is open from 8:00 a.m until Midnight.
- Valid for new slot club members only.
- Receive $10 refund after play is verified.
- Management reserves all rights.
- Offer expires 12/30/04.

2140 Las Vegas Blvd N.
N. Las Vegas, NV 89030
(702) 399-1111
www.mahoneyscasino.com

- Present original coupon (no photocopies) at bowling desk.
- Valid 9 a.m. to 5 p.m. Monday through Friday.
- Valid for up to four players per coupon.
- Cannot be used with any other offer.
- Management reserves all rights.
- Offer expires 12/30/04.

Al Aleman presents
La Cage
Starring
FRANK MARINO
as Joan Rivers
and an All-Star cast of Female Impersonators

Crazy Girls

Las Vegas' Sexiest Topless Revue
Voted #1 Showgirls

2-For-1 Show Tickets!

All of these shows have been voted the best in Las Vegas. Make sure to check out the greatest female impersonators, the sexiest topless review, and the funniest club in town. Shows perform nightly. Please call the Riviera box office at 702-794-9433 for performance schedule. See reverse for more details.

Offer void if detached from book. This coupon should only be removed at time of redemption.

AMERICAN CASINO GUIDE

$2 off the World's Fare Buffet

$2 off The Buffet of Taste! Your choice of Breakfast, Lunch, or Dinner – 7 Days a Week! Present this coupon to the Buffet Cashier prior to purchase to receive discount. See reverse for more details.

Offer void if detached from book. This coupon should only be removed at time of redemption.

AMERICAN CASINO GUIDE

Riviera
HOTEL & CASINO
LAS VEGAS
The Entertainment Center of Las Vegas

Blackjack
$7-for-$5 Match Play
$2 Value

Bet this coupon with five dollars. When you win, we pay you seven dollars. See reverse for more details.

Offer void if detached from book. This coupon should only be removed at time of redemption.

2901 Las Vegas Blvd. S.
Las Vegas, NV 89109
(702) 734-5110
(800) 634-3420

Original coupon must be presented to Riviera box office (no photocopies) to buy one ticket at regular price and get another FREE! Your choice of three shows: Crazy Girls, La Cage or Comedy Club. Must be 21 or older. Not valid Saturdays, or Saturdays and Sundays of a holiday weekend, or with any other offer. One coupon per person. Offer may be cancelled at any time without notice. No cash value. Offer expires 12/30/04.

Riviera
HOTEL & CASINO
LAS VEGAS
The Entertainment Center of Las Vegas
2901 Las Vegas Blvd. S.
Las Vegas, NV 89109
(702) 734-5110
(800) 634-3420

Present this original coupon (no photocopies) to the Buffet Cashier. Limit one coupon per day. Valid for up to four people. Not valid on prior purchases. Management may revoke this offer at any time without notice. Cannot be combined with any other offer or promotion. Must be at least 21. Offer expires 12/30/04.

Riviera
HOTEL & CASINO
LAS VEGAS
The Entertainment Center of Las Vegas
2901 Las Vegas Blvd. S.
Las Vegas, NV 89109
(702) 734-5110
(800) 634-3420

Bet this coupon with five dollars. When you win, we pay you seven dollars. Playable at "21" tables only and for even money bets only. One coupon per day per person. We retain the coupon. Management may revoke this offer at any time without notice. Must be at least 21. Offer expires 12/30/04.

AMERICAN CASINO GUIDE

$20 Match Play

Play this coupon, along with your Club Uno Card, and a minimum of $20 on any even-money bet on any of our table games and we'll match it with a FREE $20 bet. See reverse for details.

Offer void if detached from book. This coupon should only be removed at time of redemption.

AMERICAN CASINO GUIDE

1,000 FREE Slot Points

Join Club Uno and receive 1,000 Free Points. Existing club members receive 250 points. Limit one coupon per person, per calendar year (January 1-December 31). See reverse for details.

Offer void if detached from book. This coupon should only be removed at time of redemption.

AMERICAN CASINO GUIDE

One FREE Cocktail at any Casino Bar

Present this original coupon to our server at any casino bar to receive one FREE cocktail. See reverse for details.

Offer void if detached from book. This coupon should only be removed at time of redemption.

8 Strada Di Villaggio
Henderson, NV 89011
(702) 939-8888
www.casinomontelago.com

Must be a Club Uno member to participate. Coupon to be played with a minimum of $20 wager. Match play valid on all even-money bets on table games only. Limited to one coupon at a time and to one $20 play per person, per day. Coupon will be replaced with $20 in gaming tokens on all winning bets. Must be 21 or older. Non-transferable or refundable. Not replaced if lost or stolen. Coupon cannot be redeemed for cash. Management reserves all rights to alter, change or cancel without notice. Void if duplicated or altered. Offer expires December 30, 2004.

8 Strada Di Villaggio
Henderson, NV 89011
(702) 939-8888
www.casinomontelago.com

One 1,000-point bonus per player. Allow 72 hours before points will be available. Original coupon (no photocopies) must be presented at time of enrollment. Cannot be used in conjunction with any other offer. Coupon has no cash value. Existing club members receive 250 points. Bonuses are limited to one per account, per calendar year (January 1 - December 31). Must be 21 years of age or older. Offer expires December 30, 2004.

8 Strada Di Villaggio
Henderson, NV 89011
(702) 939-8888
www.casinomontelago.com

Must be 21 years of age or older. Limited to one free drink per person, per day. Excludes specialty drinks. Excludes restaurant bars. Gratuity not included. Present original coupon (no photocopies) before ordering. Resale is prohibited. Management reserves all rights to cancel or alter this coupon without notice. Offer expires December 30, 2004.

AMERICAN CASINO GUIDE

40 Coin Bonus on Four-of-a-Kind

Present this coupon to the floorperson when you win a four-of-a-kind (no wild cards) on any denomination video poker machine at the Nevada Palace Hotel and Casino. Your Players Circle Card must be properly inserted while playing and you must be playing maximim coins in order to receive this bonus. See reverse for more details.

Offer void if detached from book. This coupon should only be removed at time of redemption.

AMERICAN CASINO GUIDE

$5 Match Play on any Table Game

Make a minimum $5 bet with this coupon at any table game and you'll receive an extra $5 if you win! Coupon must be surrendered after bet wins or loses. See reverse for more details.

Offer void if detached from book. This coupon should only be removed at time of redemption.

AMERICAN CASINO GUIDE

2-For-1 Dinner Buffet

Buy one dinner buffet and get a second one FREE! Offer valid Sunday through Thursday. Both buffets must be redeemed on same visit. See reverse for more details.

Offer void if detached from book. This coupon should only be removed at time of redemption.

5255 Boulder Highway
Las Vegas, NV 89122
(702) 458-8810
(800) 634-6283
www.nvpalace.com

Must be 21 or older to redeem. Natural four-of-a-kind only. Maximum coins bet. Players Circle Card must be in machine. Floor person must verify. Management reserves the right to cancel, alter or discontinue any promotion at their discretion. See casino for details. Original coupon (no photocopies) must be presented. Limit one coupon per person per year. Valid through 12/31/04.

5255 Boulder Highway
Las Vegas, NV 89122
(702) 458-8810
(800) 634-6283
www.nvpalace.com

Make a $5 minimum bet at any table game, along with this coupon, and receive a $5 match bet. Even-money bets only. Coupon must be surrendered after bet wins or loses. Cannot be redeemed for cash. Not valid with any other offer. Must be 21or older to redeem. Limit one coupon per person, per year. No photocopies accepted. Management reserves all rights. Offer expires12/31/04.

5255 Boulder Highway
Las Vegas, NV 89122
(702) 458-8810
(800) 634-6283
www.nvpalace.com

Present this coupon to the cashier at time of purchase. Must be 21 or older to reeem. Tax and gratuity not included. Coupon not redeeemable for cash. Original coupon (no photocopies) must be presented to the cashier. One coupon per customer. Management reserves all rights. Valid through 12/31/04.

AMERICAN CASINO GUIDE

FREE Super Value Coupon Book

Present this coupon and your Poker Palace Gold Club Card at the main cage to receive your FREE coupon book containing $9 in matchplays, four FREE drinks, 2-for-1 menu items and more!.See reverse for complete details.

Offer void if detached from book. This coupon should only be removed at time of redemption.

AMERICAN CASINO GUIDE

$5 Blackjack Matchplay

Present this coupon and your Poker Palace Gold Club Card at any blackjack table prior to the start of a game and **we'll match your bet of $5** if you win. See reverse for complete details.

Offer void if detached from book. This coupon should only be removed at time of redemption.

AMERICAN CASINO GUIDE

Double Slot Club Points Up to 2,000 FREE Points!

Present this coupon at the Poker Palace Gold Club booth to receive double slot club points during any 24-hour period of play. Get up to 2,000 FREE points! See reverse for complete details.

Offer void if detached from book. This coupon should only be removed at time of redemption.

The Poker Palace
2757 Las Vegas Blvd. N.
N. Las Vegas, NV 89030
(702) 649-3799

Limit: one FREE coupon book per person, per month. Must be 21 or older and present picture ID. Cannot be combined with any other offer or promotion.

Must join or be a Poker Palace Gold Club member and must present original coupon (no photocopies). Not responsible for lost or stolen coupon. Management reserves all rights. Offer may be changed or discontinued at anytime at the discretion of management. Offer expires December 30, 2004.

Gold Club Member #________________

The Poker Palace
2757 Las Vegas Blvd. N.
N. Las Vegas, NV 89030
(702) 649-3799

Limit: one coupon per person, per day. Cannot be redeemed for cash. Must be 21 or older and present picture ID. Non-transferable. Cannot be combined with any other offer or promotion.

Must join or be a Poker Palace Gold Club member and must present original coupon (no photocopies). Not responsible for lost or stolen coupon. Management reserves all rights. Offer may be changed or discontinued at anytime at the discretion of management. Offer expires December 30, 2004.

Gold Club Member #________________

The Poker Palace
2757 Las Vegas Blvd. N.
N. Las Vegas, NV 89030
(702) 649-3799

One time use only. Limited to one coupon per account. Points must be earned within a 24-hour period. Cannot be redeemed for cash. Must be 21 or older and present picture ID. Non-transferable. Cannot be combined with any other offer or promotion.

Must be a Poker Palace Gold Club member and must present original coupon (no photocopies). Not responsible for lost or stolen coupon. Management reserves all rights. Offer may be changed or discontinued at anytime at the discretion of management. Offer expires December 30, 2004.

Gold Club Member #________________

AMERICAN CASINO GUIDE

One FREE Entry into Thursday Video Poker Tournament

Present this original coupon (no photocopies) to the Horseshoe Club for your FREE entry. $1,750 in cash prizes. See reverse side for more details. Offer expires 12/31/04

Offer void if detached from book. This coupon should only be removed at time of redemption.

AMERICAN CASINO GUIDE

One FREE Entry into Tuesday Slot Tournament

Present this original coupon (no photocopies) to the Horseshoe Club for your FREE entry. $1,750 in cash prizes, plus session money. See reverse side for more details. Offer expires 12/31/04

Offer void if detached from book. This coupon should only be removed at time of redemption.

AMERICAN CASINO GUIDE

Binion's HORSESHOE

5,000 Bonus Points

Present this coupon to the Horseshoe Club to receive your 5,000 Free Bonus points. **Offer valid for new members only**. See reverse side for more details

Offer void if detached from book. This coupon should only be removed at time of redemption.

128 E. Fremont St.
Las Vegas, NV 89101
(702) 382-1600
1-800-937-6537
www.binions.com

Must have a Horseshoe Club card to participate. Must be 21 years of age or older. Sessions times start at 6:00pm with new sessions every half-hour. Finals are at 9:00 pm depending on number of participants. Call ahead to reserve your spot (702) 382-1600. Management reserves all rights. Offer expires 12/31/04.

128 E. Fremont St.
Las Vegas, NV 89101
(702) 382-1600
1-800-937-6537
www.binions.com

Must have a Horseshoe Club card to participate. Must be 21 years of age or older. Sessions times start at 7:00pm. Maximum of 100 participants. Call ahead to reserve your spot (702) 382-1600. Management reserves all rights. Offer expires 12/31/04.

128 E. Fremont St.
Las Vegas, NV 89101
(702) 382-1600
1-800-937-6537
www.binions.com

Must present this original coupon (no photocopies) to the Horseshoe Club. Must be 21 years of age or older. **New enrollments only**. Not valid with any other offer. Management reserves all rights. Offer expires 12/31/04.

AMERICAN CASINO GUIDE

2-For-1 Festival Buffet!

Present this coupon to the cashier at the Festival Buffet at either Fiesta Rancho or Fiesta Henderson. Pay for one buffet and get the second buffet FREE! Valid Sunday through Thursday only. Offer expires 12/30/04. Settle to FH 41-353/FR 33-513

Offer void if detached from book. This coupon should only be removed at time of redemption.

AMERICAN CASINO GUIDE

Sign up for an Amigo Card and receive 1,500 bonus points!

Present this coupon to the Amigo Club when you sign up for an Amigo Card and receive 1,500 bonus points! Valid at either Fiesta Rancho or Fiesta Henderson. See reverse for details.

Offer void if detached from book. This coupon should only be removed at time of redemption.

AMERICAN CASINO GUIDE

FREE Entry! Tequila Willie's Tournaments

Tuesday Video Poker Tournaments. Wednesday Pai Gow Tournaments. Thursday Blackjack Tournaments. Tournament Times: 11am-3pm or 3pm-7pm (last session begins at 6:30pm). Valid at either Fiesta Rancho or Fiesta Henderson.

Amigo Club # ____________________

Offer void if detached from book. This coupon should only be removed at time of redemption.

777 W. Lake Mead Drive
Henderson, NV 89015
(702) 558-7000 • (866) 469-7666
www.stationcasinos.com

2400 N. Rancho Drive
Las Vegas, NV 89130
(702) 631-7000 • (866) 731-7333
www.stationcasinos.com

Must be 21 or older. Management reserves all rights. Not a line pass. Tax and gratuity not included. Coupons are not transferable and not redeeemable for cash. Original coupon (no photocopies) must be presented to the cashier. Not valid on holidays. Valid through 12/30/04. Settle to FH 41-353/ FR 33-513

777 W. Lake Mead Drive
Henderson, NV 89015
(702) 558-7000 • (866) 469-7666
www.stationcasinos.com

2400 N. Rancho Drive
Las Vegas, NV 89130
(702) 631-7000 • (866) 731-7333
www.stationcasinos.com

Offer only valid for first time sign up for the Amigo Card. Original coupon (no photocopies) must be presented at Amigo Club. Must be 21 or older. Management reserves all rights. One coupon per person. Valid through 12/31/04.

777 W. Lake Mead Drive
Henderson, NV 89015
(702) 558-7000 • (866) 469-7666
www.stationcasinos.com

2400 N. Rancho Drive
Las Vegas, NV 89130
(702) 631-7000 • (866) 731-7333
www.stationcasinos.com

One coupon per person. Must be an Amigo Club Member. Amigo Club membership is free. Must be 21 or older. Valid only for Tequila Willie's Tournaments. Coupon cannot be used for re-buys. Rebuys only $5. Complete rules available at the Amigo Club. Not valid with any other offer. Not valid at Fiesta Henderson's Tuesday Blackjack Tournaments. Management reserves all rights. Expires 12/30/04.

AMERICAN CASINO GUIDE

2 FREE Shows and 2 FREE Drinks

Present this coupon at the Fitzgeralds' Showroom to receive 2 FREE show admissions, plus 2 FREE drinks. See reverse for more details.

Offer void if detached from book. This coupon should only be removed at time of redemption.

AMERICAN CASINO GUIDE

250 Bonus Points When you join Club Fitz

Present this coupon at Club Fitz on the second floor to receive your 250 bonus points. Offer valid for new club members only and is valid through 12/31/04.

Offer void if detached from book. This coupon should only be removed at time of redemption.

AMERICAN CASINO GUIDE

SHOWGIRLS OF MAGIC

Magic Never Looked So Good!

2-For-1 Show Tickets!

Get one FREE *Showgirls of Magic* ticket with the purchase of one ticket at the regular price. Coupon must be presented at the box office at the Hotel San Remo. See back for full details.

Offer void if detached from book. This coupon should only be removed at time of redemption.

301 Fremont St.
Las Vegas, NV 89101
(702) 388-2400
1-800-274-LUCK
fitzgeraldslasvegas.com

Must be 21 years of age or older. Show times are 5, 7, 9 and 10:30 p.m. Thursday through Monday nights. Limit one offer per coupon. Shows and performers subject to change or cancellation at any time. Management reserves all rights. Offer expires 12/30/04.

301 Fremont St.
Las Vegas, NV 89101
(702) 388-2400
1-800-274-LUCK
fitzgeraldslasvegas.com

Must be 21 years of age or older. Coupon has no cash value and may be revoked/cancelled at any time. Employees of Fitzgeralds not eligible. Offer valid through 12/30/04. Gambling problem? Call 1-800-522-4700.

SHOWGIRLS OF MAGIC
Magic Never Looked So Good!

Hotel San Remo
115 E. Tropicana Avenue
Las Vegas, NV 89109
(702) 597-6028

Call Box Office For Showtimes and Reservations (702) 597-6028

Only valid with the purchase of a show ticket at the Hotel San Remo box office. May not be used in conjunction with any other offer. Limit one coupon per customer. Offer expires 12-30-04.

AMERICAN CASINO GUIDE

JERRY'S NUGGET

Blackjack $5 Match Play with your More Club Plus Card

Make a $5 bet at a "21" table and receive a $5 Match Bet ($5 minimum bet required). See reverse for full details.

Offer void if detached from book. This coupon should only be removed at time of redemption.

AMERICAN CASINO GUIDE

JERRY'S NUGGET

FREE Gift <u>and</u> FREE 100 BONUS POINTS For New Members! Join More Club Plus today, the only player's club that gives you more!

See reverse for full details.

Offer void if detached from book. This coupon should only be removed at time of redemption.

AMERICAN CASINO GUIDE

JERRY'S NUGGET

FREE Bingo With your More Plus Card!

Redeem this coupon for a FREE $3 BLUE CARD. Sessions at 11am, 1pm, 3pm, 7pm, 9pm and 11pm See reverse for full details.

Offer void if detached from book. This coupon should only be removed at time of redemption.

1821Las Vegas Boulevard North
N. Las Vegas, NV 89030
(702) 399-3000 • www.jerrysnugget.com

Blackjack $5 Match Play

Limit one coupon per customer. Must be a More Club Plus member. Make a $5 minimum bet at a Jerry's Nugget '21' table, along with this coupon and receive a $5 match bet. Coupon surrendered after first hand. Good for one hand, one wager. Cannot be redeemed for cash. Not valid with any other offer. Must be 21 years of age or older to redeem. Management reserves all rights. Offer expires 12/30/04.

1821Las Vegas Boulevard North
N. Las Vegas, NV 89030
(702) 399-3000 • www.jerrysnugget.com

FREE Gift and FREE 100 BONUS POINTS!

Limit one coupon per customer. New More Club Plus members only. Must be 21 years of age or older to redeem. Present this coupon at the More Club Center, sign up for the More Club Plus and receive your free gift and 100 bonus points. Must present valid ID. Offer expires 12/30/04.

1821Las Vegas Boulevard North
N. Las Vegas, NV 89030
(702) 399-3000 • www.jerrysnugget.com

FREE $3 BINGO

Limit one coupon per customer. Must be a More Club Plus member. T.E.D. purchase includes $1.25 extra charge. Valid only during regular sessions. Cannot be redeemed for cash. Not valid with any other offer. Not valid on holidays. Must be 21 years of age or older to redeem. Management reserves all rights. Offer expires 12/30/04.

AMERICAN CASINO GUIDE

2-for-1 Lunch Entrée in Magnolia's

Buy one lunch entrée in Magnolia's and get one lunch entrée FREE! See reverse for full details.

Offer void if detached from book. This coupon should only be removed at time of redemption.

AMERICAN CASINO GUIDE

Double Points (Up to 100) for members of the REEL WINNERS Club®

Double your REEL WINNERS Club® points (up to 100) with this coupon! See reverse for full details.

Offer void if detached from book. This coupon should only be removed at time of redemption.

AMERICAN CASINO GUIDE

20% Discount on any tour!

Book a half-day or full-day tour with Scenic Airlines and receive a 20% discount. Please present this coupon at check-in to receive discount. Coupon only valid by calling Scenic directly at (800) 634-6801 or (702) 638-3300. Not valid with any other offer or promotion. Offer expires 12/31/04.

Grand Canyon • Monument Valley • Bryce Canyon

mention code: ACG

Offer void if detached from book. This coupon should only be removed at time of redemption.

202 Fremont Street
Las Vegas, NV 89101
(702) 385-4011
(800) 634-6045
www.fourqueens.com

Limit one coupon per person. Must be 21 years or older. Purchase one lunch entrée (equal or greater value) to receive the second one free. Offer valid only in Magnolia's. Coupon is void if altered or duplicated. Tax, alcoholic beverages and gratuity are not included. Not valid with any other offers or discounts. Management reserves the right to cancel or modify offer at any time. Coupon has no cash value. Offer expires December 30, 2004.

202 Fremont Street
Las Vegas, NV 89101
(702) 385-4011
(800) 634-6045
www.fourqueens.com

Limit one coupon per person. Coupon has no cash value. Must be 21 years or older. Points must be earned on day of redemption. Offer valid for REEL WINNERS Club® members only. Double points will be added to account within 48 hours. Management reserves the right to cancel or modify offer at any time without notice. Coupon is void if altered or duplicated. Offer expires December 30, 2004.

Available now...**One Day White Water Rafting**...Call now

Grand Canyon • Monument Valley • Bryce Canyon

20% Discount 20% Discount

- Half-day or full-day tours
- High wings & giant windows for best view
- Digital quality tour narration en route
- Tour facility located two blocks from "Strip"
- Free flight certificate

Reservations: (800) 634-6801 • (702) 638-3300 www.scenic.com

AMERICAN CASINO GUIDE

KEY LARGO
CASINO

FREE Fun Book

Present this coupon at our Front Desk to receive a FREE Fun Book - a $100 value! Offer expires 12/30/04.

Offer void if detached from book. This coupon should only be removed at time of redemption.

AMERICAN CASINO GUIDE

KEY LARGO
CASINO

One FREE Beer or Well Drink

Present this coupon to the server at the casino bar in the Key Largo Hotel & Casino to receive one FREE beer or well drink. See reverse for full details.

Offer void if detached from book. This coupon should only be removed at time of redemption.

AMERICAN CASINO GUIDE

BIG SAVINGS
On Heli USA's Ultimate
Grand Canyon &
Wild West Ranch
Adventures By Helicopter!
Heli USA Airways
LAS VEGAS • GRAND CANYON • HAWAII
$50
OFF ANY GRAND CANYON FLIGHT
MUST MENTION CODE "ACG" AT TIME OF BOOKING TO RECEIVE APPLICABLE DISCOUNT. NOT VALID WITH ANY OTHER OFFER. MUST CALL DIRECT.

Offer void if detached from book. This coupon should only be removed at time of redemption.

377 E. Flamingo Rd • Las Vegas, NV 89109
(702) 733-7777 • (800) 634-6617

Must be at least 21 years of age. This offer subject to change or cancellation without prior notice.

377 E. Flamingo Rd
Las Vegas, NV 89109
(702) 733-7777 • (800) 634-6617

Offer valid for adults 21 years of age or older. Coupon must be presented to server to receive FREE drink. Limited to one FREE beer or well drink per person, per day. This offer is subject to change or cancellation without notice. Offer expires 12/30/04.

The Ultimate Grand Canyon & Wild West Ranch Adventures By Helicopter – Call Today!

Heli USA Airways®

LAS VEGAS • GRAND CANYON • HAWAII

RESERVATIONS 6 A.M. TO 10 P.M. (PST)

702.736.8787

Toll Free 1.800.359.8727

275 E. Tropicana Ave., Suite 200, Las Vegas, NV 89109
Web Site: www.HeliUSA.com ★ Email: Res1@HeliUSA.net
Offer valid through 12/31/04.

AMERICAN CASINO GUIDE

2 FOR 1 Breakfast or Lunch Buffet

Use this coupon to receive your second buffet meal FREE.

Offer void if detached from book. This coupon should only be removed at time of redemption.

AMERICAN CASINO GUIDE

pay $49 for your first night

TERRIBLE'S HOTEL · CASINO

get your second night FREE

Offer void if detached from book. This coupon should only be removed at time of redemption.

AMERICAN CASINO GUIDE

Two-For-One Admission

Present this coupon and get one free admission when a second admission of equal or greater value is purchased.

Offer void if detached from book. This coupon should only be removed at time of redemption.

733.7000
4100 Paradise Rd.
Las Vegas, NV • 89109
www.terribleherbst.com

Present this coupon along with your Terrible's Player Card to the Cashier at the Buffet when paying for your meal. Receive one FREE breakfast or lunch buffet with the purchase of another at the regular price. Must be a Players Cub Member. One coupon for up to a party of two. Non-transferable. No cash value. Must be 21 years of age or older. Tax and gratuity not included. Management reserves the right to modify, change or cancel this offer at anytime without prior notice. Expires 12/31/04.

call1.800.640.9777
for **RESERVATIONS**
4100 Paradise Rd.
Las Vegas, NV • 89109

Call 1-800-640-9777 to make your reservation. Offer is good only after purchasing first nights stay at $49. This offer is valid Sunday through Wednesday arrival only. No cash value. One coupon per customer. Must be 21 years of age or older. Based on availability. Management reserves the right to modify, change or cancel this offer at anytime without prior notice. Expires 12/31/04.

www.terribleherbst.com

2780 Las Vegas Blvd. S.
Las Vegas, NV 89109
(702) 792-0640

Open 7 days a week, including holidays, 9 a.m. to 6 p.m. Located 1/2 block north of the Circus Cicus Hotel on the Las Vegas Strip

This wacky, weird and wonderful museum brings The Guinness Book of Records to life with color videos, hands-on displays and life-sized replicas.

Not valid with any other offer.
Expires December 30, 2004.

AMERICAN CASINO GUIDE

2-For-1 Lunch or Dinner Buffet

Buy one lunch or dinner buffet and get a second one FREE! Offer valid Sunday-Thursday, excludes Sunday brunch and Thursday dinner. Both buffets must be redeemed on same visit. See reverse for more details.

Offer void if detached from book. This coupon should only be removed at time of redemption.

AMERICAN CASINO GUIDE

RAMPART CASINO
AT THE RESORT AT SUMMERLIN

$5 Match Play on any Table Game

Make a minimum $5 bet with this coupon at any table game and you'll receive an extra $5 if you win! Coupon must be surrendered after bet wins or loses. See reverse for more details.

Offer void if detached from book. This coupon should only be removed at time of redemption.

AMERICAN CASINO GUIDE

2-For-1 General Admission

After 5:00 p.m.

Receive one FREE ticket with the purchase of a full-price general admission ticket at Madame Tussauds Interactive Wax Museum located in front of the Venetian Resort on Las Vegas Boulevard. **Valid after 5:00 p.m. only.**

Offer void if detached from book. This coupon should only be removed at time of redemption.

221 N. Rampart Boulevard
Las Vegas, NV 89128
(702) 507-5900
(877) 869-8777

Present this coupon to the cashier at time of purchase. Must be 21 or older to reeem. Tax and gratuity not included. Coupon not redeeemable for cash. Original coupon (no photocopies) must be presented to the cashier. One coupon per customer. Management reserves all rights. Valid through 12/31/04.

221 N. Rampart Boulevard
Las Vegas, NV 89128
(702) 507-5900
(877) 869-8777

Make a $5 minimum bet at any table game, along with this coupon, and receive a $5 match bet. Even-money bets only. Coupon must be surrendered after bet wins or loses. Cannot be redeemed for cash. Not valid with any other offer. Must be 21or older to redeem. Limit one coupon per person, per year. No photocopies accepted. Management reserves all rights. Offer expires12/31/04.

Located in front of the Venetian Resort on Las Vegas Boulevard (The Strip)
(702) 862-7800
www.madame-tussauds.com

At Madame Tussauds Interactive Wax, you have the unique opportunity to hug, touch, and take pictures with over 100 of your favorite stars, including The Rock, Lucille Ball, Whoopi Goldberg, Princess Diana and John Wayne all masterfully portrayed in wax. You'll be amazed at how lifelike they are (and your friends back home won't be able to tell the difference). Open daily at 10a.m.

Maximum of two free tickets. Not valid with any other discount or promotion. Expires December 31, 2004.

AMERICAN CASINO GUIDE

FREE $45 in Slot Play!

Present this original coupon to the Mad Money Booth in the Lady Luck Casino Hotel and get $50 of slot play for only $5! See reverse for complete details.

Offer void if detached from book. This coupon should only be removed at time of redemption.

AMERICAN CASINO GUIDE

FREE Fun Book and Souvenir

for new slot club members only

Sign up for a Mad Money Players Card and receive a FREE Lady Luck Souvenir, plus a FREE Fun Book! For new slot club members only. See reverse for complete details.

Offer void if detached from book. This coupon should only be removed at time of redemption.

AMERICAN CASINO GUIDE

Established 1906

GOLDEN GATE

HOTEL & CASINO • ONE FREMONT STREET • LAS VEGAS

FREE Deck of Cards

Receive a FREE deck of cards from Las Vegas' most historic hotel at One Fremont Street.

See reverse side for full details.

Offer void if detached from book. This coupon should only be removed at time of redemption.

206 N. Third Street
Las Vegas, NV 89101
(702) 477-3000
(800) 634-6580
www.ladyluck.com

For only $5 you receive an additional $45 free for a grand total of $50 in slot play in our Big Bucks slot machine area. Present this original coupon to the Mad Money Booth. Guaranteed gift for every player! Must be 21 or older to redeem coupon. Coupon has no cash value. Management reserves the right to cancel or modify this offer at any time. Offer expires December 30, 2004.

206 N. Third Street
Las Vegas, NV 89101
(702) 477-3000
(800) 634-6580
www.ladyluck.com

Present this original coupon to the Mad Money Booth and sign up for a Mad Money Players Card to receive a FREE Lady Luck Souvenir, plus a FREE Fun Book! Must be 21 or older. Valid for new slot club members only. Coupon has no cash value. Management reserves the right to cancel or modify this offer at any time. Offer expires December 30, 2004.

One Fremont Street
Las Vegas, NV 89101
(702) 385-1906
Reservations (800) 426-1906

Present this coupon at our hotel desk and receive a FREE deck of cards. Limit: one deck of cards per person. Must be 21 years of age or older. Subject to change or cancellation without notice. While supplies last. Offer expires December 30, 2004.

AMERICAN CASINO GUIDE

FREE T-Shirt!

Join the Park Place Connection Club at the Flamingo, earn 15 points and we'll give you a FREE t-shirt! See the Connection Club for more details.

Offer void if detached from book. This coupon should only be removed at time of redemption.

AMERICAN CASINO GUIDE

$2 Keno Ticket For just $1 Win up to $11,000!

This coupon, plus $1 cash, is good for one $2 7-Spot Keno ticket. Present coupon at the keno booth at the Flamingo Las Vegas. See reverse for more details.

Offer void if detached from book. This coupon should only be removed at time of redemption.

AMERICAN CASINO GUIDE

Manhattan Express® Roller Coaster Up to $6 Off

Please present this pass at the Manhattan Express® ticket booth prior to boarding the ride and receive $3 off each paid admission up to (2) people.

Expires 12/22/04

Offer void if detached from book. This coupon should only be removed at time of redemption.

3555 Las Vegas Blvd. S.
Las Vegas, NV 89109
(702) 733-3111
(800) 732-2111
www.flamingolasvegas.com

For new Connection Card members only. Must be 21 years of age or older to gamble or consume alcohol. Please present this coupon at the Park Place Connection Club booth at the Flamingo Las Vegas. Original coupon must be presented (no photocopies).

Management reserves the right to cancel or alter offer without prior notice. Offer expires 12/27/04.

3555 Las Vegas Blvd. S.
Las Vegas, NV 89109
(702) 733-3111
(800) 732-2111
www.flamingolasvegas.com

Please present this coupon at the keno booth at the Flamingo Las Vegas. Non-transferable. Not redeemable for cash.

Management reserves the right to modify or cancel this promotion at any time. Must be 21 years of age or older to gamble or consume alcohol. Original coupon must be presented (no photocopies). Offer expires 12/27/04.

Height restrictions apply. Limit one coupon per guest, for use up to (2) people. To be used only at designated locations. Not for resale or transfer. May not be copied. Cash value: 1/10 of 1¢. Offer not valid on holidays, special events, conventions, or in conjunction with any other offer. Offer may be withdrawn by management at any time without notice. Provider of products or services retains the right to substitute items of equal value. All other trademarks and registered trademarks are property of their respective owner. Must be 21 years of age or older for all alcohol and gaming offers. Expires 12/22/04.

AMERICAN CASINO GUIDE

Free Deck of Cards and Fun Book

Present this coupon at the Slots-A-Fun Gift Shop to receive a FREE deck of cards. FREE Fun Book is available at the Free Pull Booth and "One Club" Booth. See reverse for more details.

Offer void if detached from book. This coupon should only be removed at time of redemption.

AMERICAN CASINO GUIDE

FREE Show For Two!

Voted Best Afternoon Show

Free Viva Las Vegas Show Ticket With Purchase of One Drink for $5.95 plus tax, per person. Coupon must be presented at the Stratosphere's Ticket Center. See back for full details.

Offer void if detached from book. This coupon should only be removed at time of redemption.

AMERICAN CASINO GUIDE

Two-For-One Show Tickets

Voted Las Vegas' Best Entertainment Value!*

Get one FREE "American Superstars" Show with the purchase of one American Superstars Show ticket. Coupon must be presented at the Stratosphere's Ticket Center. See back for full details.

**by Las Vegas Advisor*

Offer void if detached from book. This coupon should only be removed at time of redemption.

SLOTS A FUN
CASINO
LAS VEGAS
LOCATED NEXT TO
CIRCUS CIRCUS

Must be 21 years or older to receive this promotion. Limit one free offer per person. Must present original coupon (no photocopies).

Management may revoke this offer at any time without notice. Offer valid through December 31, 2004.

2000 Las Vegas Blvd. S. • Las Vegas, NV 89104
(800) 99-TOWER • (702) 380-7777

Must be at least 5 years of age to attend show. Some material may be inappropriate for children; parental discretion recommended. Minors must be accompanied by an adult. Subject to availability. Show times subject to change. Offers cannot be combined. Management reserves all rights. Not for resale. Valid through December 27, 2004. **(Coupon must be presented at the Stratosphere's Ticket Center.)**

2000 Las Vegas Blvd. S. • Las Vegas, NV 89104
(800) 99-TOWER • (702) 380-7777

Must be at least 5 years of age to attend show. Some material may be inappropriate for children; parental discretion recommended. Minors must be accompanied by an adult. Subject to availability. Show times subject to change. Offers cannot be combined. Management reserves all rights. Not for resale. Valid through December 27, 2004. **(Coupon must be presented at the Stratosphere's Ticket Center.)**

AMERICAN CASINO GUIDE

Buy One Night, Stay Second Night FREE!

Buy one room night (Sunday-Thursday) at the regular rate and receive the second night FREE! See reverse for details.

Offer void if detached from book. This coupon should only be removed at time of redemption.

AMERICAN CASINO GUIDE

2-For-1 Cocktail

Present this coupon at *The Deck*, or at any *Casino Bar* to receive one FREE well drink or domestic beer with the purchase of one at the regular price. See reverse for more details.

Offer void if detached from book. This coupon should only be removed at time of redemption.

AMERICAN CASINO GUIDE

Gigantic 56-ounce Margarita in *The Deck* Logo Glass just $10 and You Keep the Glass!

Present this coupon at *The Deck* to receive a 56-ounce strawberry or regular Margarita in *The Deck* souvenir logo glass for just $10. See reverse for more details.

Offer void if detached from book. This coupon should only be removed at time of redemption.

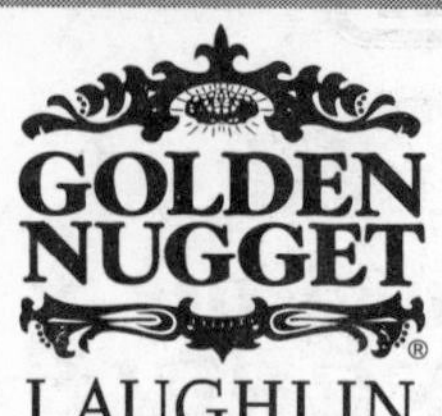

LAUGHLIN

2300 S. Casino Drive
Laughlin, NV 89028
(702) 298-7111
(800) 955-7568
www.gnlaughlin.com

Offer valid on a space available basis for adults 21 years of age or older. Advance reservations required. Call 1-800-950-7700 to make your reservations and ask for the **American Casino Guide** 2-For-1 discount. Must present original coupon (no photocopies) upon check-in. Limit one coupon per person, per promotion. Credit card or incidental deposit required. Based on prevailing room rate. Nights must be consecutive. Valid Sunday-Thursday (based on availability), excluding holidays. Offer expires 12-15-04.

LAUGHLIN

2300 S. Casino Drive
Laughlin, NV 89028
(702) 298-7111
(800) 955-7568
www.gnlaughlin.com

Must be 21 years of age or older to redeem coupon. Present this original coupon (no photocopies) at *The Deck* or any Golden Nugget Laughlin *Casino Bar* to receive one free well drink or domestic beer with the purchase of one well drink or domestic beer at the regular price. Must present coupon before ordering. Cannot be combined with any other offer. Management reserves all rights. Offer expires 12/15/04.

LAUGHLIN

2300 S. Casino Drive
Laughlin, NV 89028
(702) 298-7111
(800) 955-7568
www.gnlaughlin.com

Must be 21 years of age or older to redeem coupon. This coupon good at *The Deck* only. Must present original coupon (no photocopies) before ordering. Cannot be combined with any other offer. Management reserves all rights. Offer expires 12/15/04

AMERICAN CASINO GUIDE

Fresh Market Square BUFFET

Buy One Buffet - Get One FREE!

Present this coupon at the Fresh Market Square Buffet at Harrah's Laughlin at time of purchase. Buy one buffet (breakfast, lunch, or dinner) and receive one buffet free! Valid at Harrah's Laughlin only. Offer code: 176

Offer void if detached from book. This coupon should only be removed at time of redemption.

AMERICAN CASINO GUIDE

BAJA BLUE •RESTAURANT & CANTINA•

Buy One Entree - Get One FREE!

Present this coupon at the Baja Blue Restaurant & Cantina at Harrah's Laughlin at time of seating. Buy one dinner entree at Baja Blue and receive one entree of equal or lesser value FREE! Valid at Harrah's Laughlin only. Offer code: 176

Offer void if detached from book. This coupon should only be removed at time of redemption.

AMERICAN CASINO GUIDE

Buy One Appetizer - Get One FREE!

Present this coupon at the Range Steakhouse at Harrah's Laughlin at time of seating. Buy one appetizer at the Range and receive one appetizer of equal or lesser value FREE. Valid only at Harrah's Laughlin. Offer code: 176

Offer void if detached from book. This coupon should only be removed at time of redemption.

2900 South Casino Drive
Laughlin, Nevada 89029
(702) 298-4600 • (800) HARRAHS
www.harrahs.com

Management reserves the right to modify this offer at any time without prior notice. Original coupon must be presented (no photocopies). Not valid on weekends (Friday/Saturday) or holidays. Cannot be combined with any other offer, advertisement or mailing. Must be 21 years of age or older. Limit one coupon per person per visit. Subject to availability. Gratuity not included. Offer valid through 12/15/04.

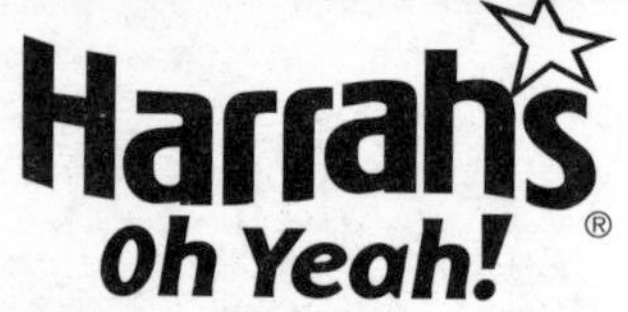

2900 South Casino Drive
Laughlin, Nevada 89029
(702) 298-4600 • (800) HARRAHS
www.harrahs.com

Management reserves the right to modify this offer at any time without prior notice. Original coupon must be presented (no photocopies). Not valid on weekends (Friday/Saturday) or holidays. Cannot be combined with any other offer, advertisement or mailing. Must be 21 years of age or older. Limit one coupon per person per visit. Subject to availability. Gratuity not included. Offer valid through 12/15/04.

2900 South Casino Drive
Laughlin, Nevada 89029
(702) 298-4600 • (800) HARRAHS
www.harrahs.com

Management reserves the right to modify this offer at any time without prior notice. Original coupon must be presented (no photocopies). Not valid on weekends (Friday/Saturday) or holidays. Cannot be combined with any other offer, advertisement or mailing. Must be 21 years of age or older. Limit one coupon per person per visit. Subject to availability. Gratuity not included. Offer valid through 12/15/04.

Warman's® Depression Glass

FIELD GUIDE

2nd Edition

Ellen T. Schroy

Values and Identification

Published by

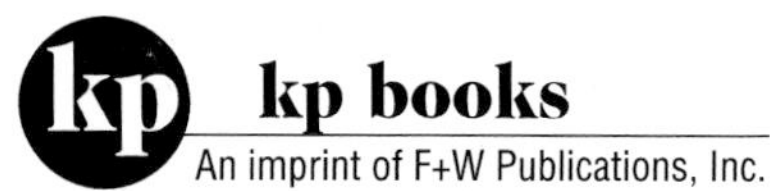

700 East State Street • Iola, WI 54990-0001
715-445-2214 • 888-457-2873

Our toll-free number to place an order or obtain
a free catalog is (800) 258-0929.

The prices contained within are intended to serve merely as a guide. Many factors, such as region and supply and demand, influence values. We suggest that users do further research in their own locale to see the impact of these variables on item values.

Library of Congress Catalog Number: 2004114145

ISBN: 0-89689-164-X

Designed by Jamie Griffin
Edited by Tracy L. Schmidt

Printed in the United States of America

CONTENTS

Using this Book

In this second edition, we have added color swatches to the included patterns. Due to variations within batches, patterns, and thickness, glass colors are a bit subjective. We have done our best to represent what is available. We do hope that this added feature will aid readers in identifying items.

*Ships, cobalt blue dinner plate **$27.50**.*

Company Timeline

19th C Ohio Flint Glass founded, later becomes part of National Glass Company conglomerate.
Indiana Glass Company established in 1907.
Bottle plant at Jeannette, Pennsylvania, which becomes Jeannette Glass Company.

1853 McKee and Brothers founded in Pittsburgh, Pennsylvania.

1887 Fostoria Glass Company, founded in Fostoria, Ohio, but moves to Moundsville, West Virginia, when fuel supply is depleted.

1888 McKee moves to Jeannette, Pennsylvania.

1890 Westmoreland Specialty Company established in Grapeville, Pennsylvania. Early manufacture includes bottles and food containers. During World War I, glass candy containers are made. The plant continues on to make colored and opaque glassware in both Depression patterns and later a giftware line.

1891 U.S. Glass Company organizes by combining 18 different glass houses located in Pennsylvania, Ohio, and West Virginia. The main offices are in Pittsburgh, as well as some manufacturing.

1899 Macbeth merges with Evans, creating Macbeth-Evans. Main factory located in Charleroi, Pennsylvania, with others located in Marion, Bethevan, and Elwood, Indiana, as well as Toledo, Ohio.

1900 Federal Glass Company opens Columbus, Ohio, plant. First wares are crystal with needle etching, various decorations, and crackle finish. After switching to automation, they soon begin production of tumblers and many Depression-era patterns, as well as restaurant wares, all at an economical price.

1901 Imperial Glass Company organizes. Produces first glass at Bellaire, Ohio, plant in 1904.

Morgantown Glass Works begins production in Morgantown, West Virginia.

New Martinsville Glass Manufacturing Company is established at New Martinsville, West Virginia.

1902 Hazel Atlas Glass Company established in Washington, Pennsylvania, a result of the merger of the Hazel Glass Company and its neighboring factory, Atlas Glass and Metal Company. Corporate offices are later established at Wheeling, West Virginia.

1903 Morgantown Glass Works reorganizes as Economy Tumbler Company and operates using that name.

Liberty Cut Glass Works established in Egg Harbor, New Jersey. Primarily a cutting house for years, pressed glass is also made.

McKee Brothers reorganizes into McKee Glass Company and continues until 1951.

1905 Anchor Hocking Glass Company established in Lancaster, Ohio. Well known by the mid-1920s for their tumbler and tableware production.

1906 Fenton Art Glass Company builds new factory, Williamstown, West Virginia. While their giftware lines are well known, some Depression-era glassware is produced.

1907 Indiana Glass Company established at Dunkirk, Indiana. Early production is hand pressed. Assembly line patterns evolve during the 1920s, although some still require hand work. Later produce automobile glassware items, become a subsidiary of Lancaster Colony.

1908 Lancaster Glass Company, Lancaster, Ohio, built by first president of Fostoria.

1911 L.E. Smith begins in the glass trade. A lot of the production of this company remains utilitarian in nature as well as making lenses for automobiles.

1916 Paden City Glass Manufacturing Company established at Paden City, West Virginia. Production includes some Depression-era patterns, but is more well known for their elegant lines, vases, lamps and restaurant wares.

1923 Economy Tumbler Company changes name to Economy Glass Company.

1924 Fostoria introduces color and starts national magazine advertising campaign.

Jeannette touted by trade as "one of the most complete automatic factories in the country."

Lancaster becomes subsidiary of Hocking Glass Company. Continues to make kitchenware, cut and dec tableware under the Lancaster name until 1937. Also makes colored blanks for Standard Glass Company, another Hocking subsidiary, where the glass is etched and cut. Known as Plant #2 to Anchor Hocking.

1927 Jeannette management ceases all hand operations.

1928 Jeannette makes green and pink glass automatically in a continuous tank, a first!

Trade journals proclaim Clarksburg, West Virginia, Hazel-Atlas factory the "World's Largest Tumbler Factory," which accurately describes the fully automated factory.

1929 Economy Glass Company changes name back to Morgantown Glass Works, Inc.

1932 Liberty Cut Glass Works destroyed by fire, never to rebuild.

1937 Corning Glass Works purchases Macbeth-Evans.
Hocking Glass Company merges with Anchor Cap and Closure Corporation, Long Island City, New York, creating the huge Anchor-Hocking Glass Company, which has continued to have a major impact on the glassware industry.
Morgantown Glass Works, Inc., closes.

1938 U.S. Glass moves main offices to Tiffin, Ohio, and production decreases.

1939 Morgantown Glassware Guild organizes and reopens factory.

1944 New Martinsville sold and reorganizes as Viking Glass Company.

1949 Westmoreland Glass Company begins to use impressed intertwined "W" and "G" mark.

1951 The only operating company of the former U.S. Glass is Tiffin. The rest have all closed.
McKee sold to Thatcher Manufacturing Co.

1952 Fire destroys Belmont plant, Bellaire, Ohio, and with the fire go company records.

1955 Duncan and Miller molds acquired by Tiffin, who begins to produce colors and crystal wares with these molds.

1956 Continental Can purchases Hazel-Atlas and continues to sell tableware under name "Hazelware."

1958 Federal Glass becomes a division of Federal Paper Board Company, and continues glassware production.

1961 Jeannette buys old McKee factory in Jeannette and moves there to continue production.

1964 Brockway Glass Company buys out Continental Can's interest in Hazel-Atlas and begins operation.

1965 Fostoria Glass Company purchases Morgantown Glassware Guild.

1966 Continental Can takes over operation of Tiffin until 1969, with glass production continuing.

1971 Glass production terminated at Fostoria's Morgantown facility, ending the Morgantown Glassware Guild.

1973 Imperial Glass Company sold to Lenox, Inc.

1980 Tiffin Glass discontinues operation.

1982 Westmoreland Glass Company closes factory in May. Reorganizes in July.

1983 Lancaster Glass purchases Fostoria.
Westmoreland begins to use full name as imprinted mark.

1984 Westmoreland Glass Company again closes Grapeville plant.

1999 L.G. Wright discontinues operation. Molds, factory equipment liquidated at public auction in May.

2000 Indiana Glass goes out of business in November.

2004 L.E. Smith ceases production in June.

*Forest Green, cup and saucer **$10**.*

Color Timeline

Amber

1923: McKee

1923: New Martinsville

1924: Paden City

1924: Westmoreland's Transparent Amber

1924-1941: Fostoria

1925: Indiana

Mid-1920s: Hocking, Imperial and L.E. Smith

1926: Jeannette

Late 1920s: Liberty

1931-1942: Federal's Golden Glow

1960: Westmoreland's Golden Sunset

Amethyst

1923: McKee

1924: New Martinsville

Mid-1920s: L.E. Smith

1926: Morgantown's Old Amethyst

1933: Paden City

1939: Morgantown's Light Amethyst

Apple Green

1925: Jeannette

Black

1920s-1930s: L.E. Smith

1922: Morgantown's India Black

1923 and 1930s: Paden City

1923: New Martinsville

1924: Fostoria

1930: McKee

1931: Hazel-Atlas, Imperial, Lancaster

Blue

1920s: Lancaster

1923: McKee's Jap Blue and Transparent Blue

1923: New Martinsville

1924: Paden City

1924-1928: Fostoria

1925: McKee's Sky Blue and Westmoreland's

Mid-1920s: Hocking

1926: Imperial, Morgantown's Azure and transparent blue

1927: Imperial's Blue-Green, Morgantown's Ritz

1928: New Martinsville's Alice Blue (medium shade)

1928-1943: Fostoria's Azure Blue (lighter shade)

Late 1920s: Liberty's pale shade

1930: Hocking's Mayfair Blue (medium shade), McKee's Ritz Blue and Chalaine Blue

1931: Imperial's Ritz Blue, Lancaster's pale blue, Westmoreland's Belgian Blue

1933: Fostoria's Regal Blue

1933-1934: Federal's Madonna Blue (medium shade)

1933-1942: New Martinsville's Ritz Blue

Mid 1930s: MacBeth-Evans' Ritz Blue

1936: Hazel-Atlas's Ritz Blue, McKee's opaque Poudre Blue, Paden City's Ceylon Blue

1939: Morgantown's Copen Blue and Gloria Blue

1940: Anchor-Hocking's Fire King

1950s: Indiana's Blue-Green

Burgundy

1933: Fostoria

1936: Hazel-Atlas (deep shade)

Canary Yellow

1923: McKee

Mid-1920s: Hocking, L.E. Smith

1924: New Martinsville

1924-1927: Fostoria

1925: Lancaster

Cobalt Blue

1930: Liberty

1936: Paden City

1939: Morgantown

Cremax

1939: MacBeth-Evans

Crystal

1923: Paden City

1930s: Imperial

1935: New Martinsville and Westmoreland—most companies produced crystal throughout their years of production

Delphite, Delfite

1936: Jeannette

Fired-On Colors

1920s: Federal and Lancaster

1923: Westmoreland

1926: New Martinsville

Mid-1930s: MacBeth-Evans

French Ivory (Opaque)

1933: McKee

Green

1920s: Lancaster

1921: Morgantown's Venetian Green

1922: Morgantown's Meadow Green

1923: McKee

1924: Paden City

1924-1941: Fostoria

Mid-1920s: Hocking, Imperial and L.E. Smith

1925: Indiana, McKee's Grass Green and New Martinsville

1926: New Martinsville's Emerald Green

1926-1936: Federal's Springtime Green

1928: MacBeth-Evans' Emerald

Late 1920s: Liberty

1929: Hazel-Atlas, Imperial

1931: Morgantown's Stiegel Green

1931-1933: New Martinsville's Stiegel Green

1933: Fostoria's Empire Green, Hazel-Atlas's Killarney Green, New Martinsville's Evergreen (dark shade)

1936: Paden City's Forest Green

1939: Morgantown's Shamrock Green

1950s: Anchor-Hocking's Forest Green

Iridescent

1920s: Federal

1920s to present: Jeannette

1934-1935: Federal's Iridescent Amber

Ivory

1929: Imperial

1933: Indiana (opaque)

1940: Anchor-Hocking

Ivrene

1930s: MacBeth-Evans

Jade

1930: McKee

1931: New Martinsville

Jade Yellow

1923: McKee

Jadite

1932: Jeannette

Monax

1920s: MacBeth-Evans

Mulberry

1924: Paden City

Opalescent

1923: Morgantown's Alabaster

1931: Westmoreland's Moonstone (blue)

1942: Anchor-Hocking's Moonstone

Orchid

1927: McKee

1927-1929: Fostoria

1929: Imperial

Pink

Mid-1920s: Imperial's Rose Marie, Rose

1925: Paden City's Cheriglo

1926: McKee's Rose Pink, Morgantown's Anna

1926-1942: Hocking's Rose (later called Flamingo or Cerise), New Martinsville's Peach Melba (later known as Rose)

1927: Jeannette's Wild Rose, L.E. Smith

1928: MacBeth-Evans

1928-1941: Fostoria's Rose or Dawn

Late 1920s: Liberty

1930: Hazel-Atlas, Lancaster's deep pink

1931-1942: Federal's Rose Glow

1933: Hazel-Atlas's Sunset Pink

1939: Morgantown's Pink Champagne

1947-1949: Jeannette

Red-Amber

1930: Liberty

Rose

1926: Indiana and Westmoreland

Royal Blue

1932: Paden City

Ruby

1925: Morgantown

1927: McKee

Yellow #1, from left: Madrid, Patrick, Jubilee, Mayfair, Orchid, Madrid, and Roxana.

Yellow #2, from left: Crow's Foot, Princess (apricot grill plate), Daisy, Rock Crystal (front).

Shape Guide

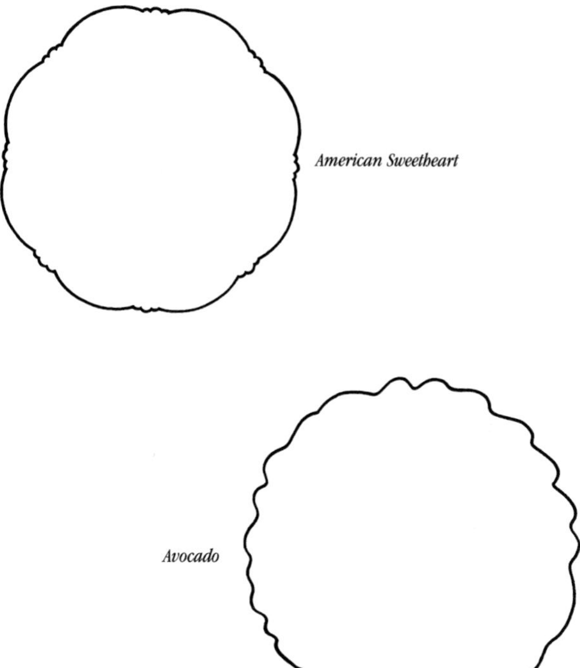

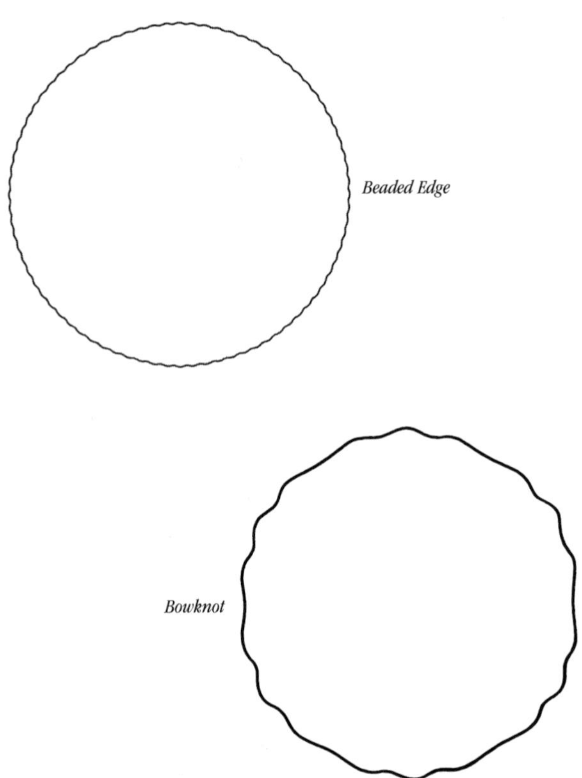
Beaded Edge
Bowknot

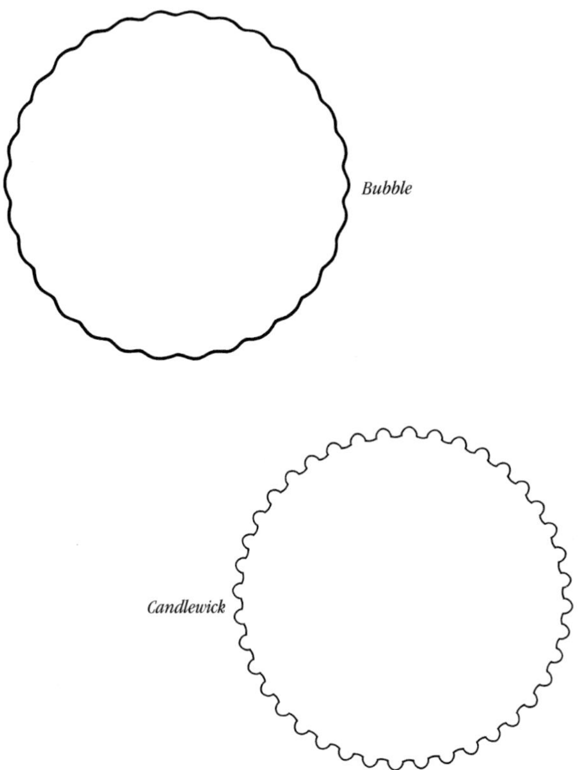
Bubble
Candlewick

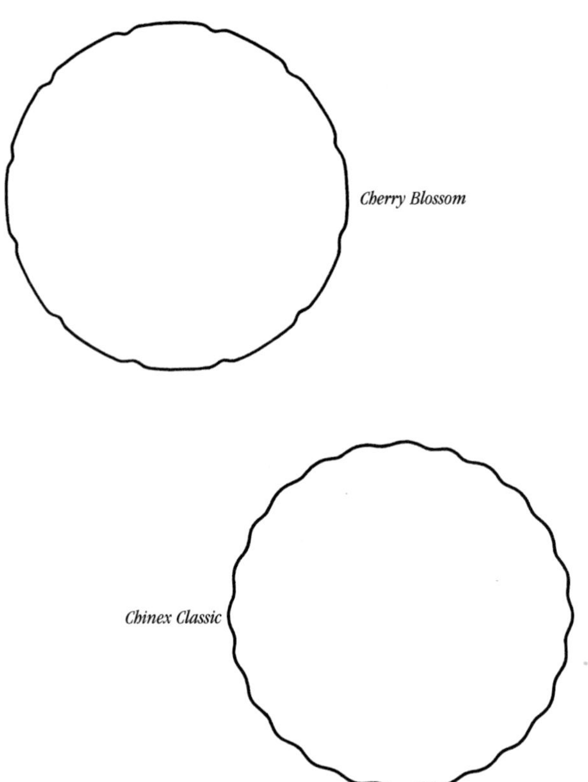
Cherry Blossom
Chinex Classic

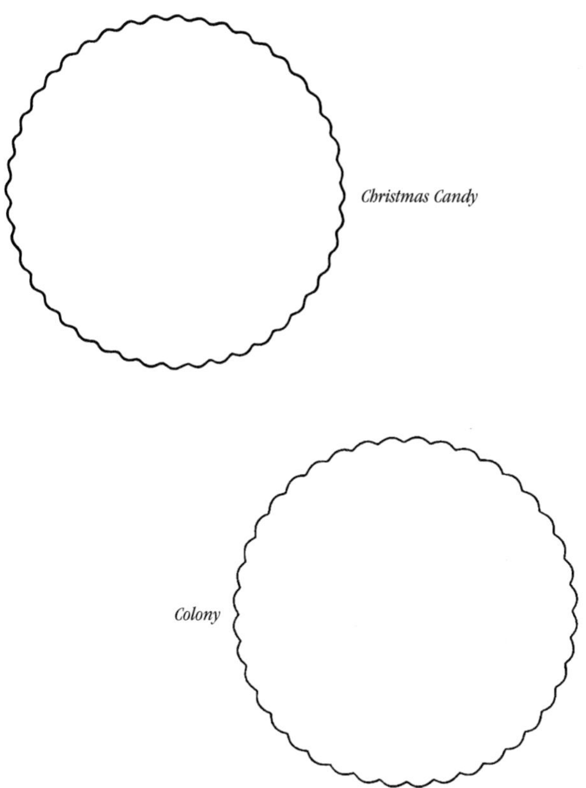
Christmas Candy
Colony

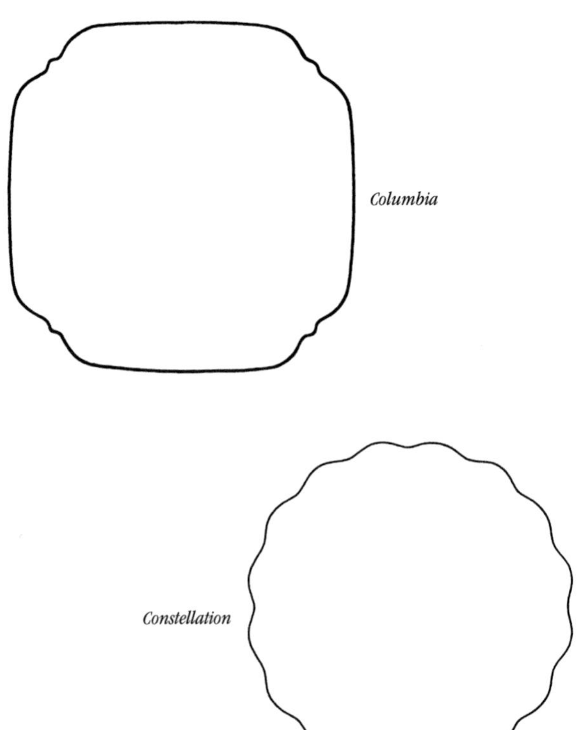
Columbia
Constellation

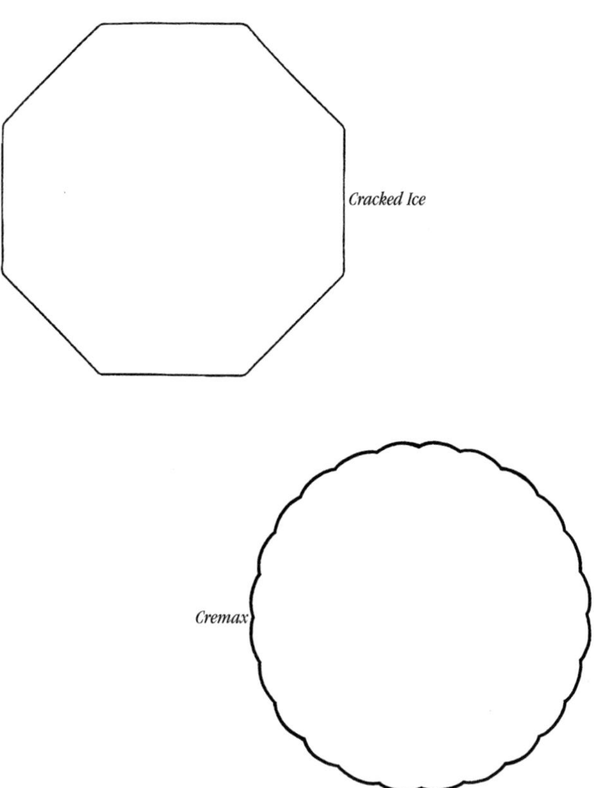
Cracked Ice
Cremax

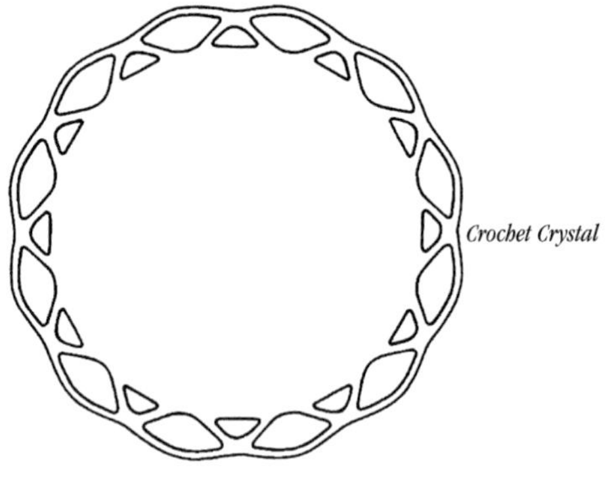

Crochet Crystal

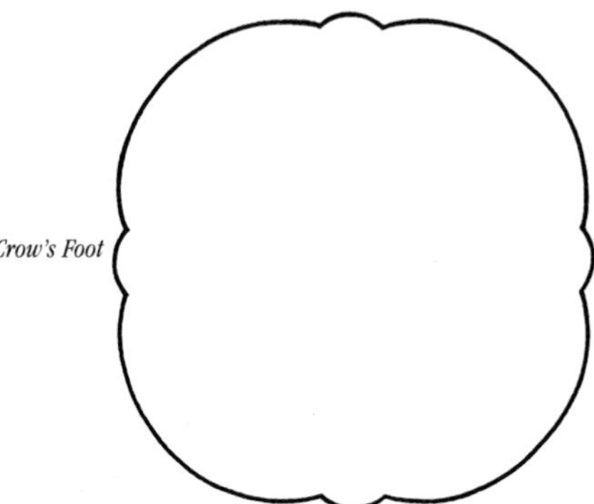

Crow's Foot

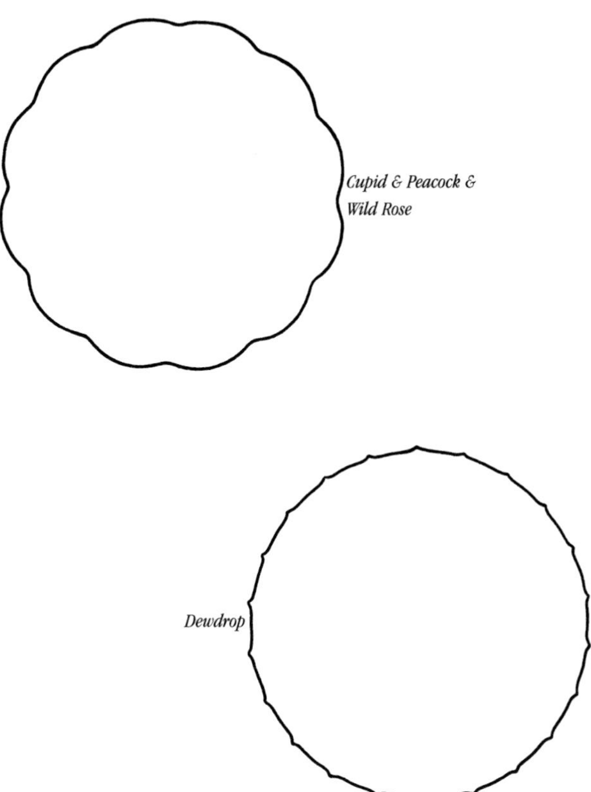
Cupid & Peacock &
Wild Rose
Dewdrop

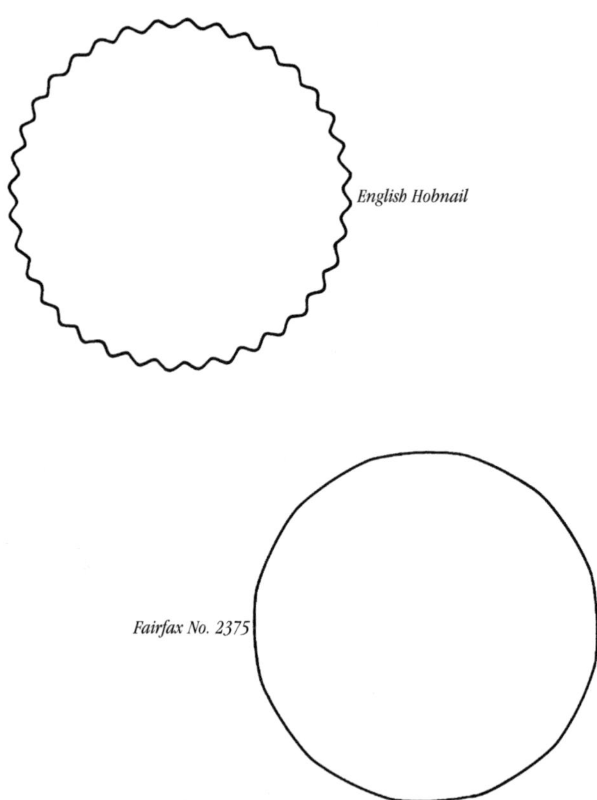
English Hobnail
Fairfax No. 2375

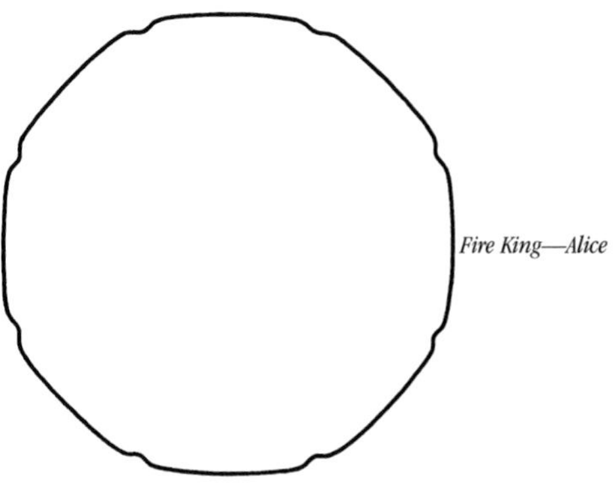

Fire King—Alice

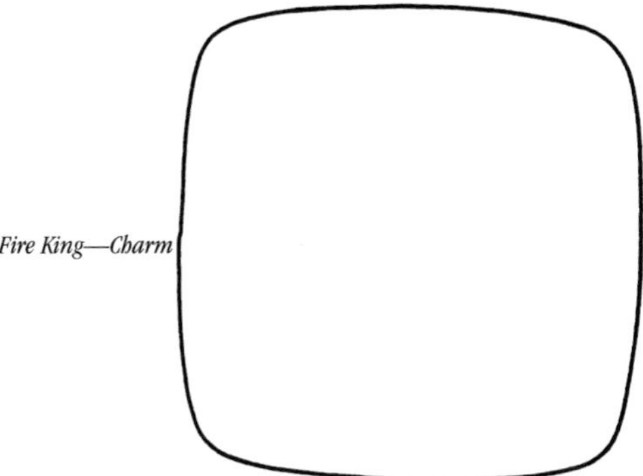

Fire King—Charm

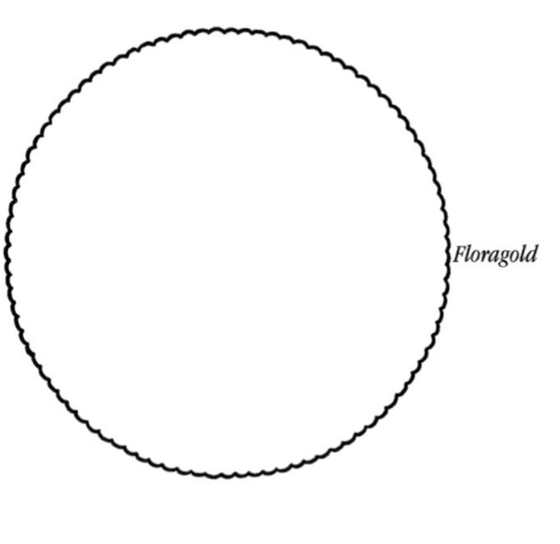

Floragold

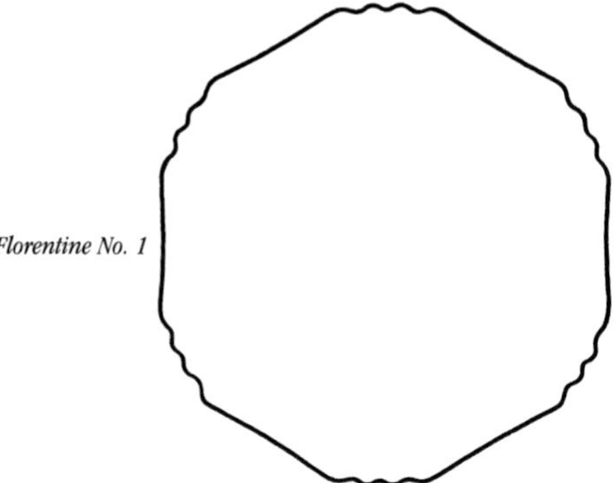

Florentine No. 1

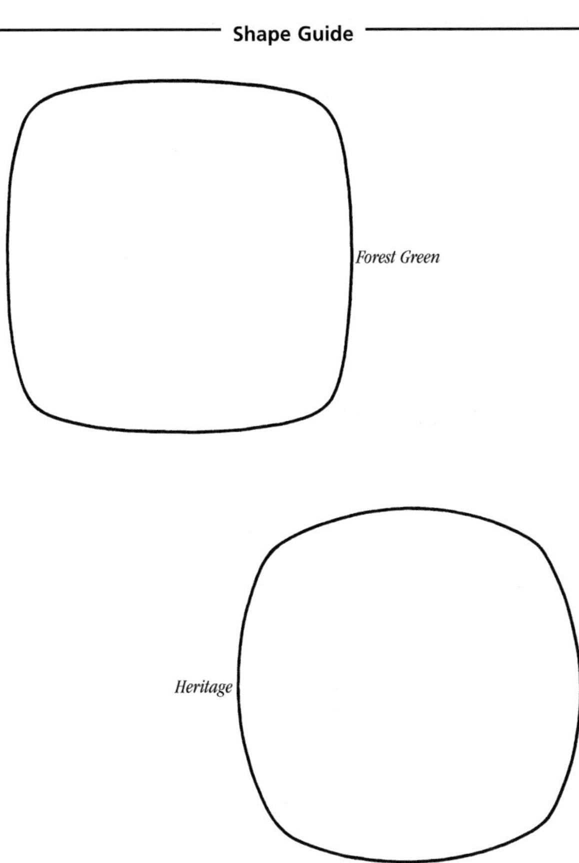
Forest Green
Heritage

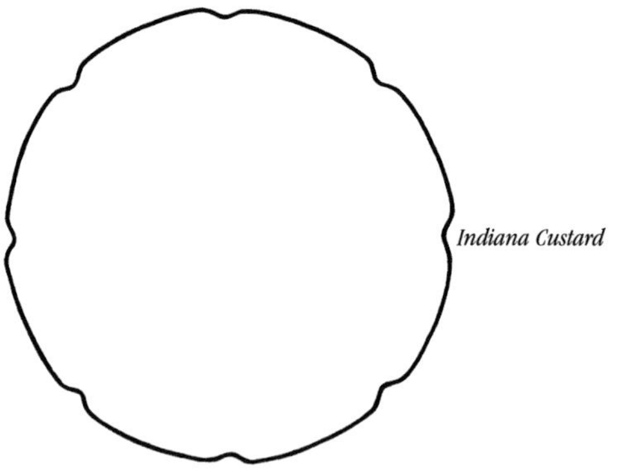
Indiana Custard

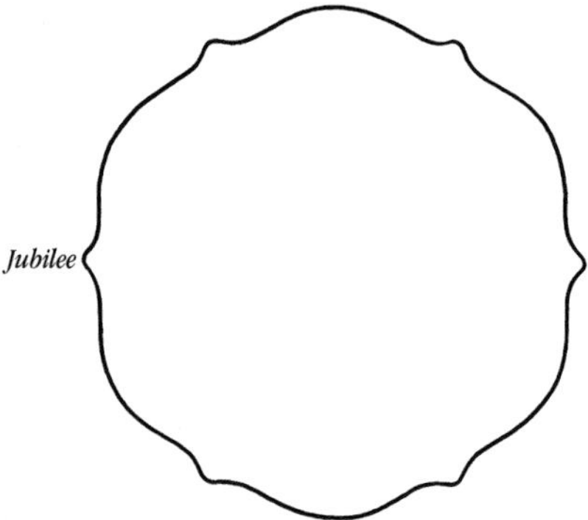
Jubilee

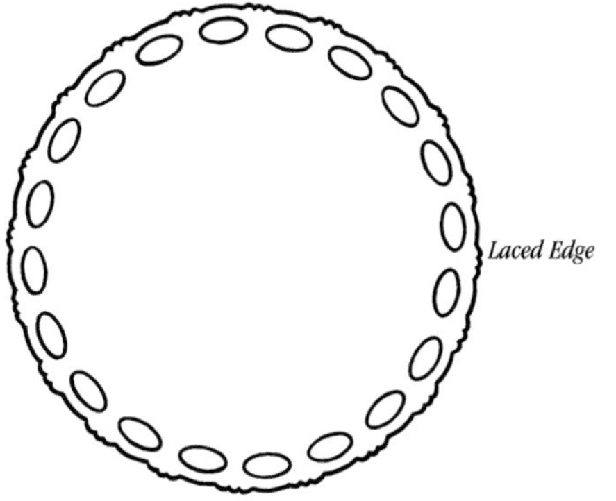
Laced Edge

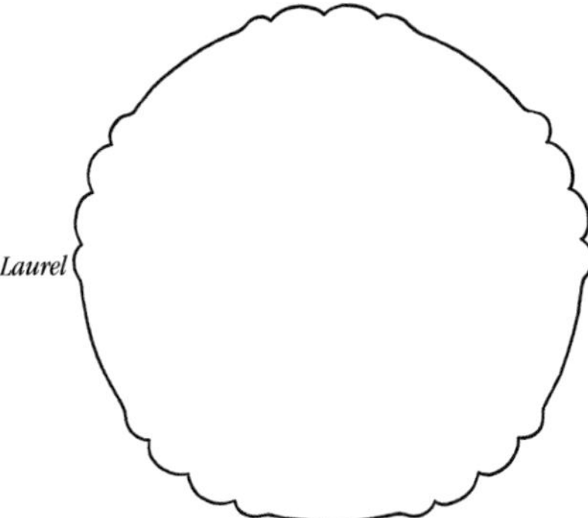
Laurel

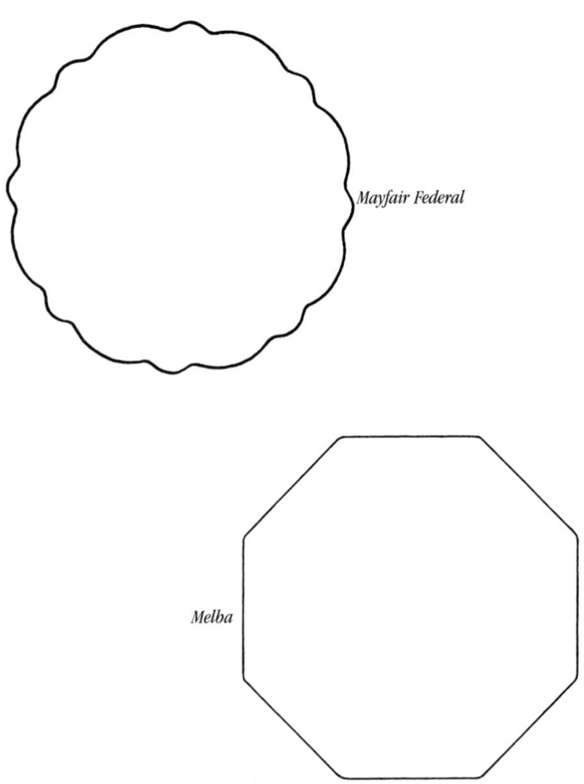
Mayfair Federal
Melba

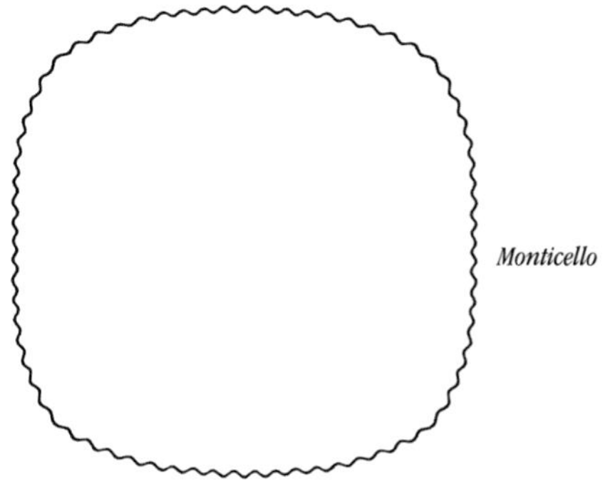

Monticello

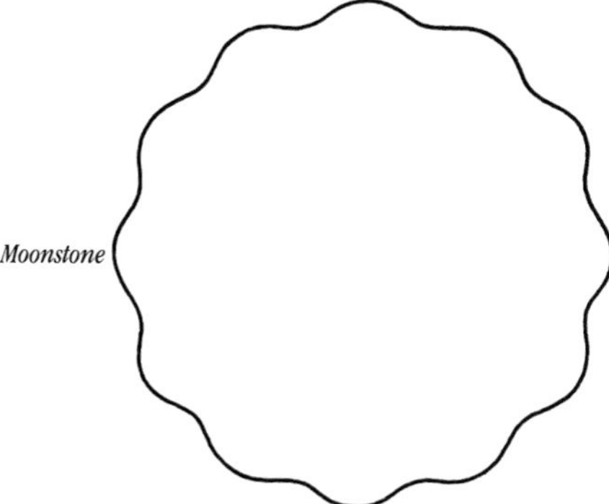

Moonstone

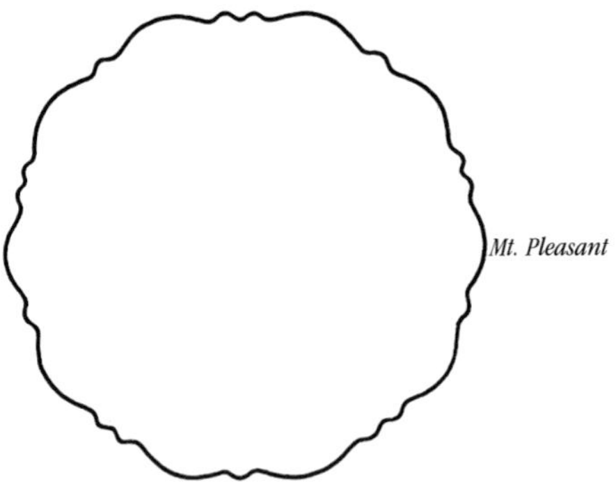
Mt. Pleasant

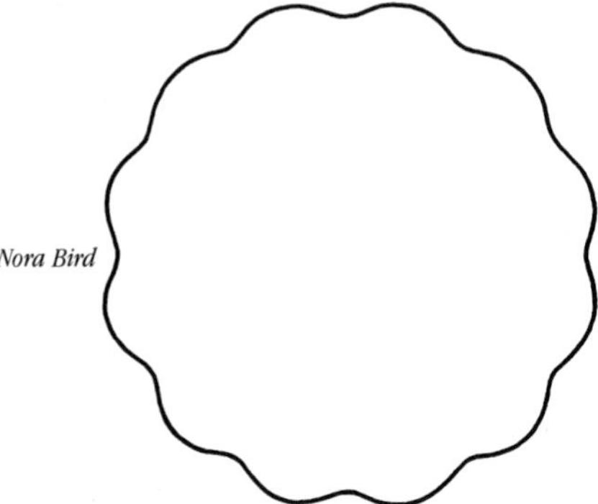
Nora Bird

Old Café
Orchid

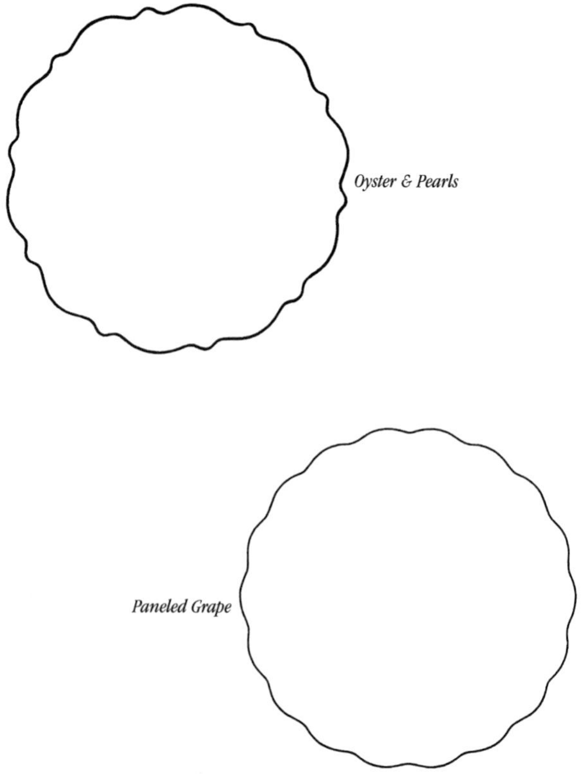
Oyster & Pearls
Paneled Grape

Parrot

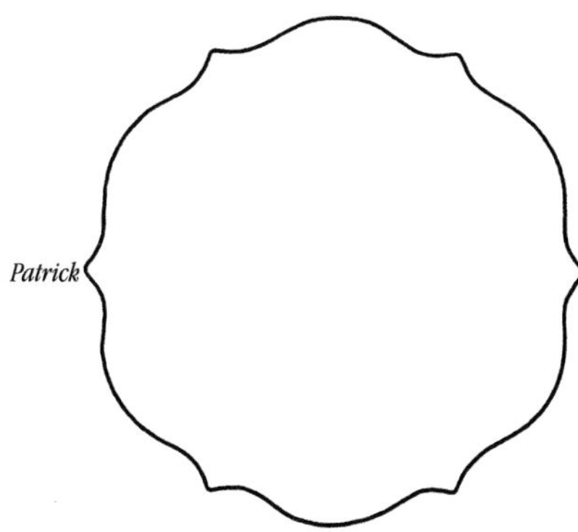
Patrick

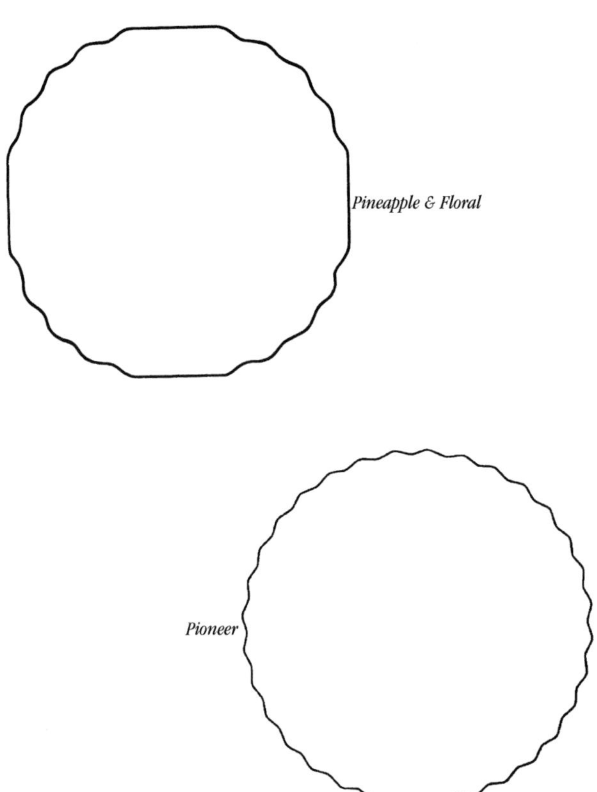
Pineapple & Floral
Pioneer

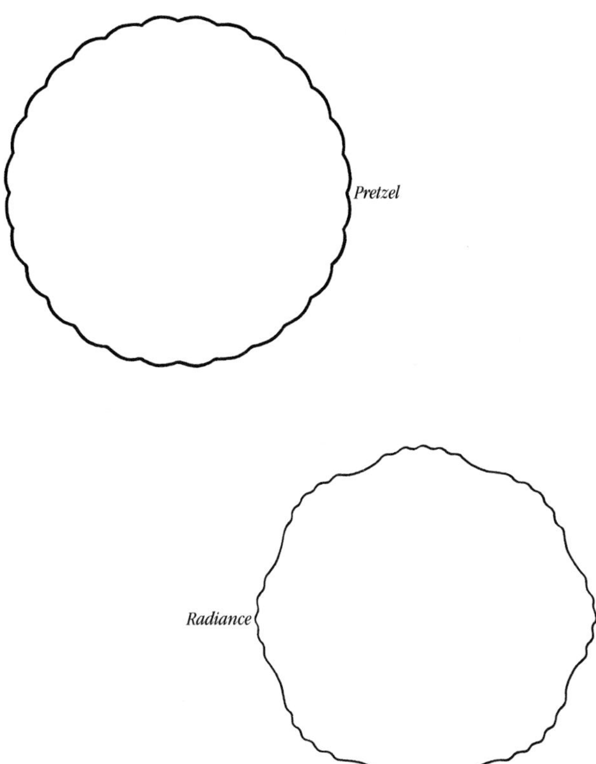
Pretzel
Radiance

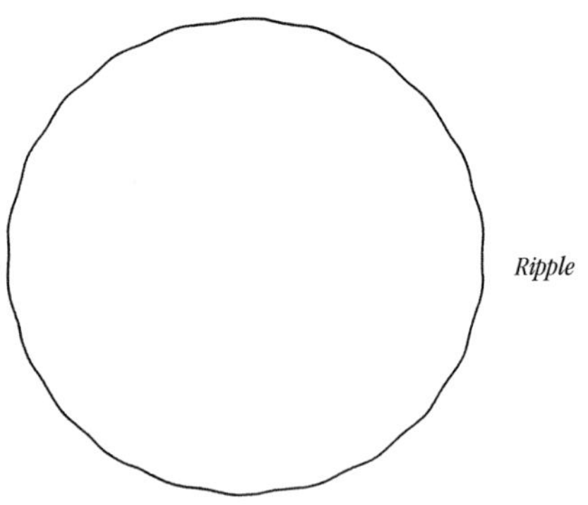

Ripple

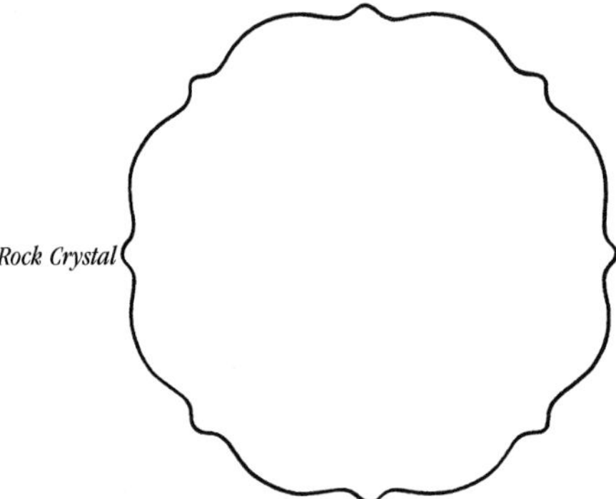

Rock Crystal

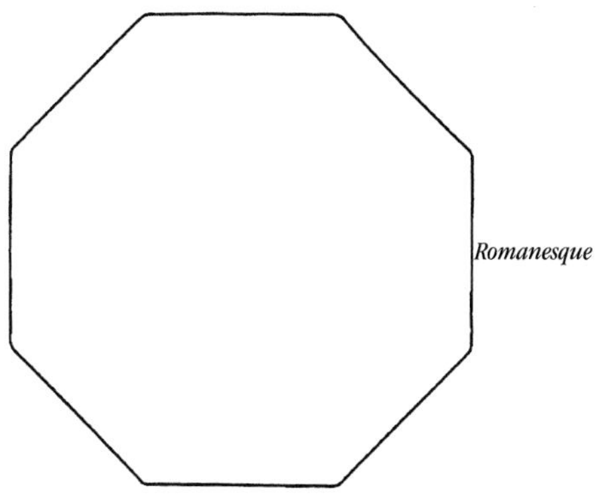

Romanesque

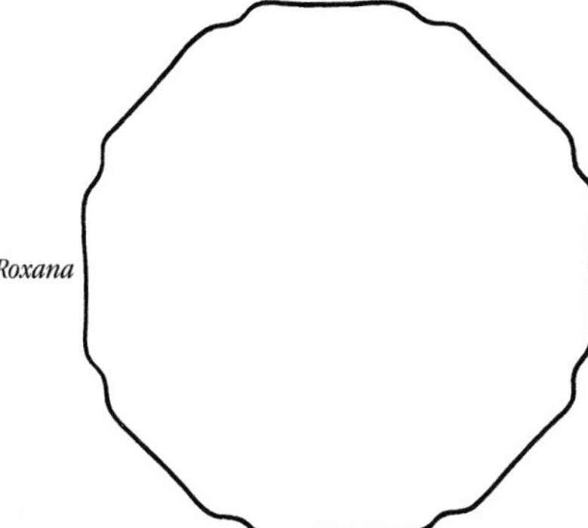

Roxana

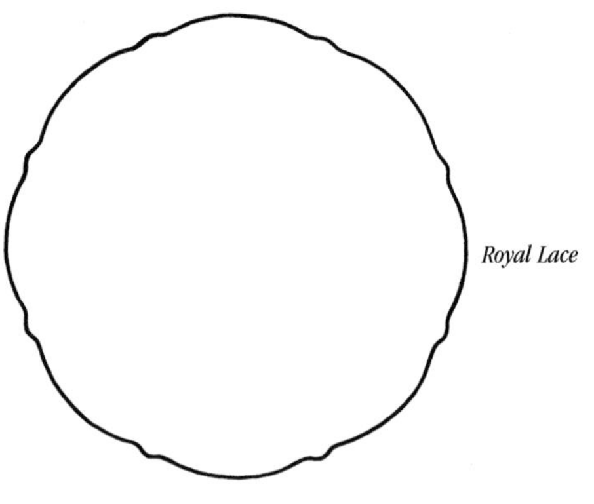

Royal Lace

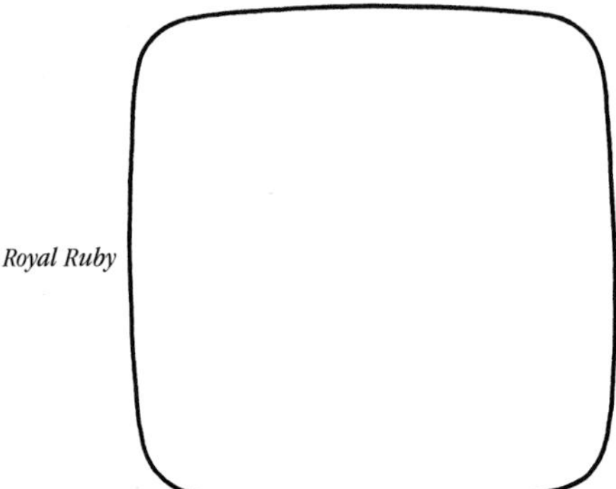

Royal Ruby

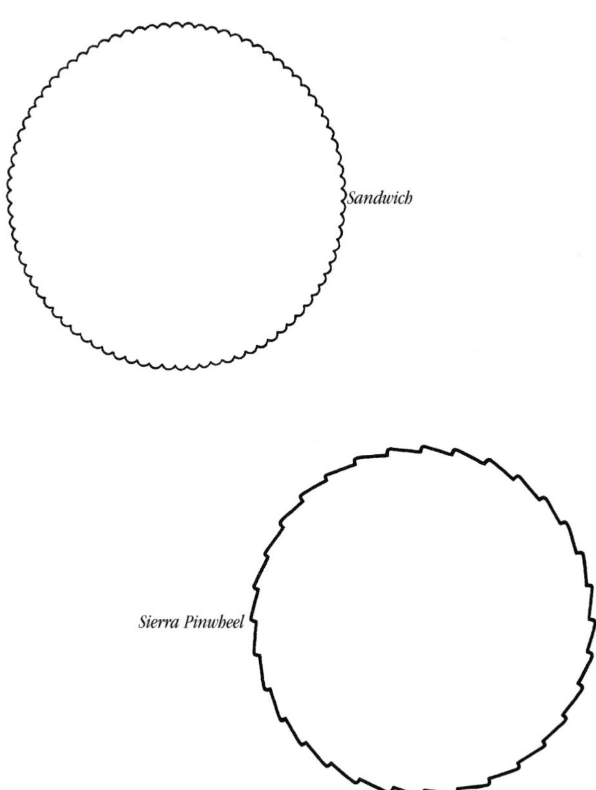
Sandwich
Sierra Pinwheel

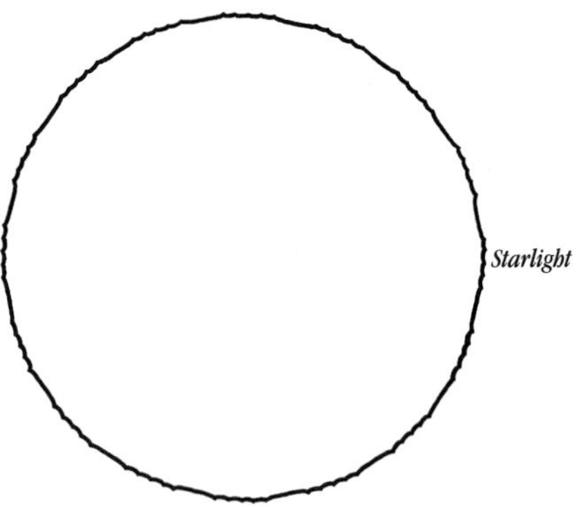
Starlight

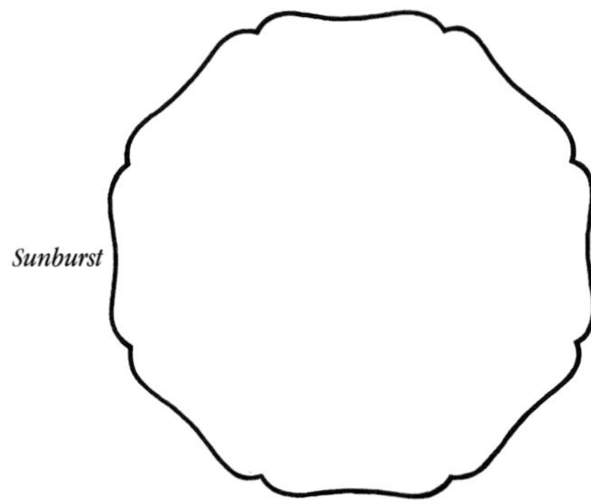
Sunburst

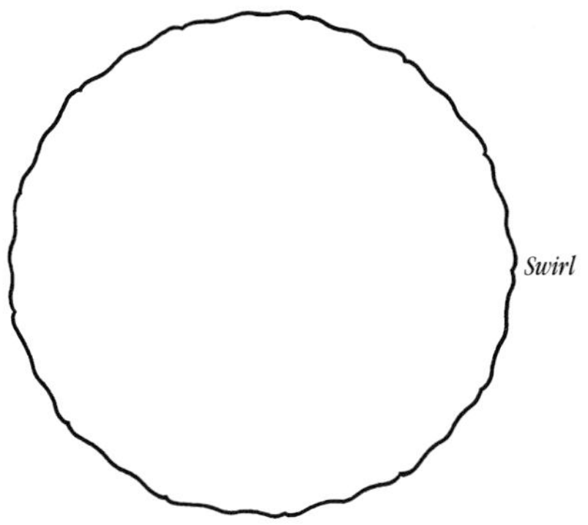
Swirl

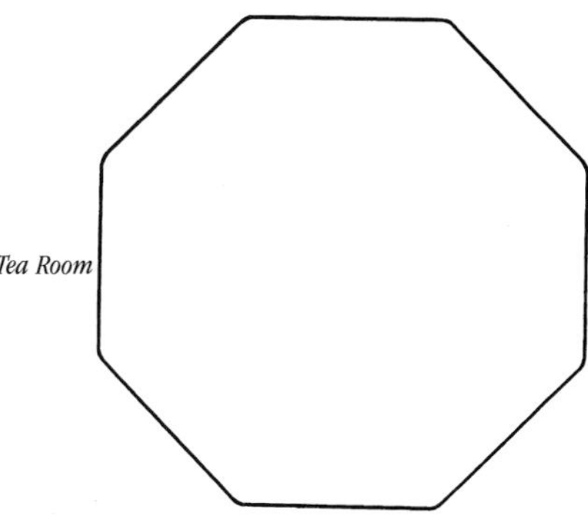
Tea Room

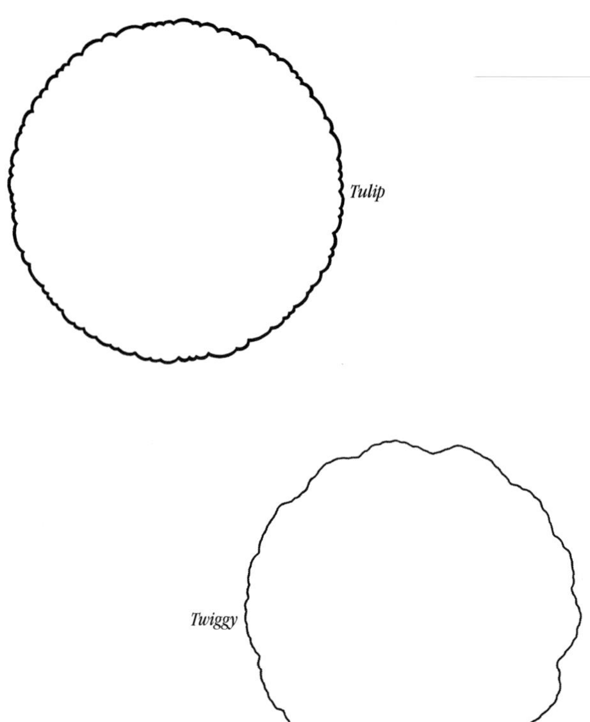
Tulip
Twiggy

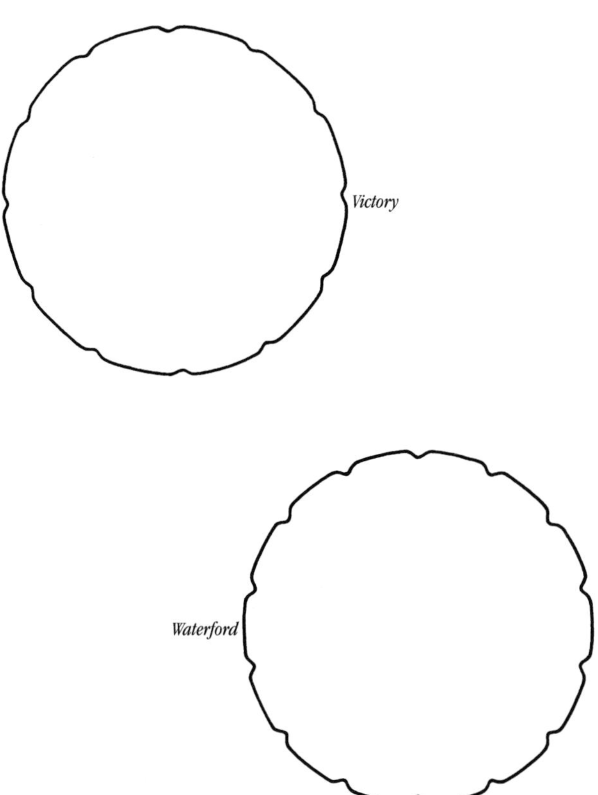
Victory
Waterford

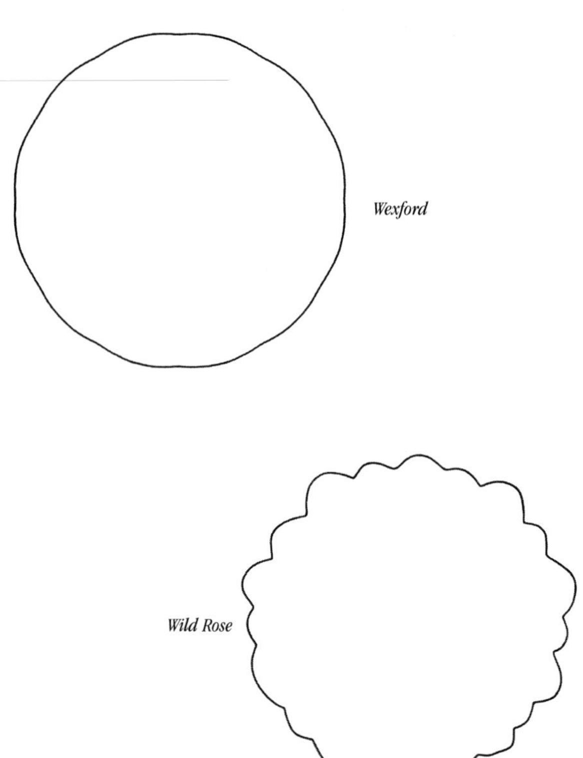
Wexford
Wild Rose

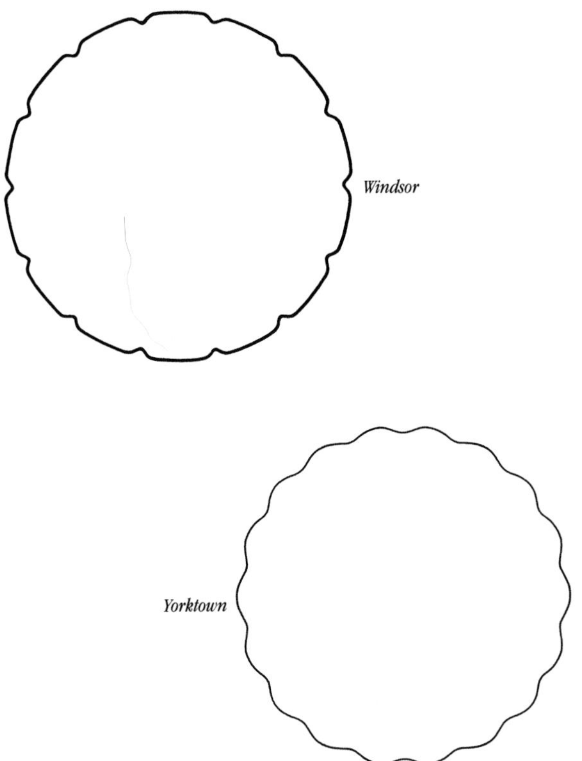
Windsor
Yorktown

THUMBNAIL GUIDE

The thumbnail guide included in this edition has been enhanced for easier referencing. All of the thumbnails from our comprehensive *Warman's Depression Glass, 3rd edition,* have been included. They appear in alphabetical order within the subgroupings. Patterns that have been included in the field guide will have cross-reference page numbers underneath the pattern names.

ART DECO

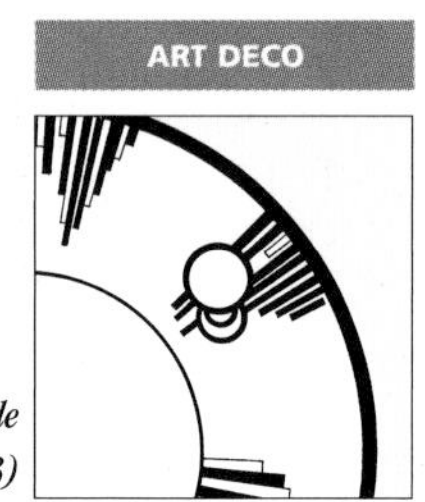

Ovide
(see page 333)

BASKETS

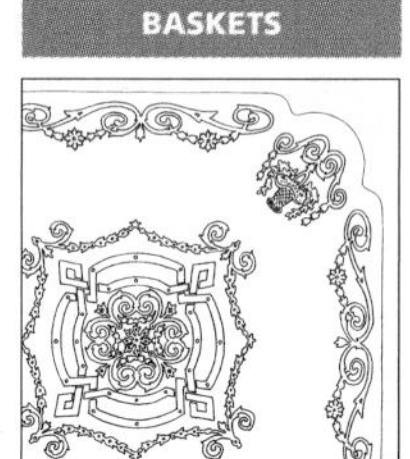

Lorain
(see page 275)

BEADED EDGES

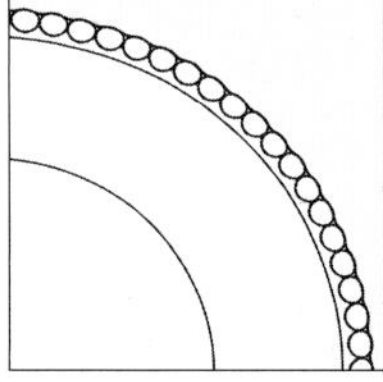

Beaded Edge

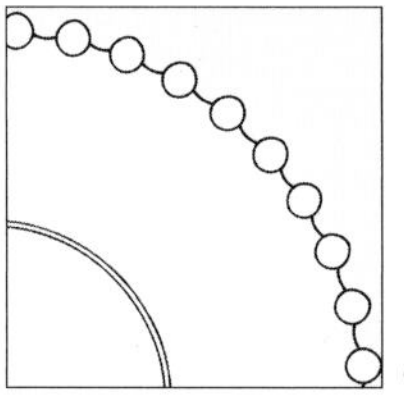

Candlewick

BIRDS

Delilah Bird

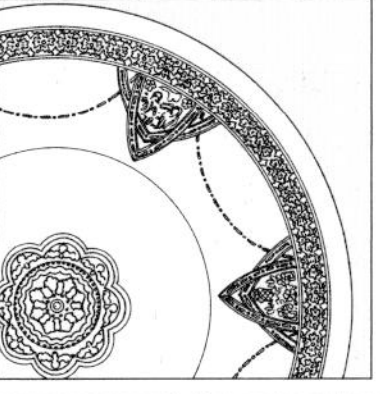
Georgian *(see page 237)*

Nora Bird

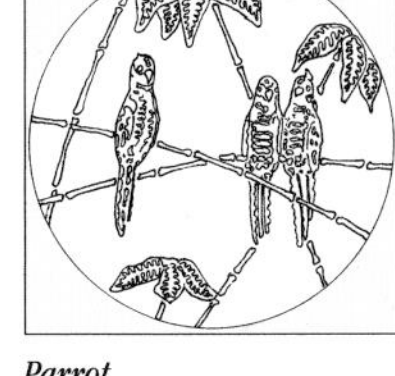
Parrot *(see page 339)*

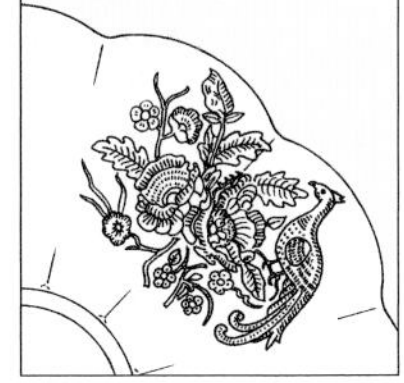
Peacock & Wild Rose

BLOCKS

Beaded Block *(see page 105)*

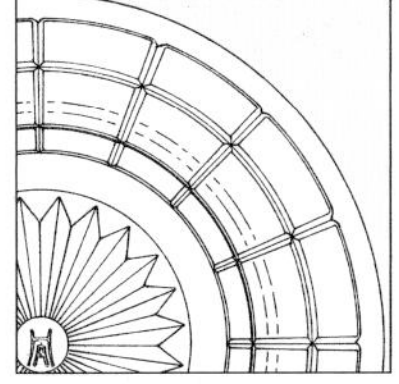
Colonial Block *(see page 148)*

BOWS

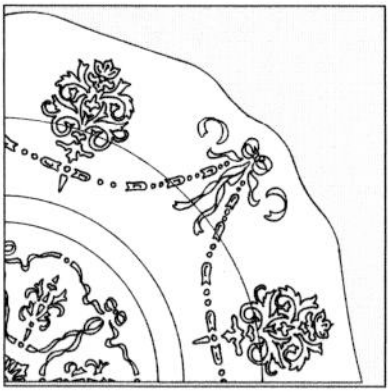

COINS

Bowknot
(see page 114)

Coin

CUBES

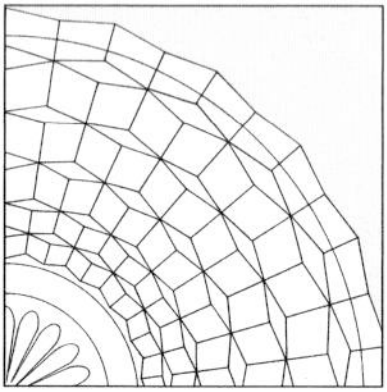

CUBES

American

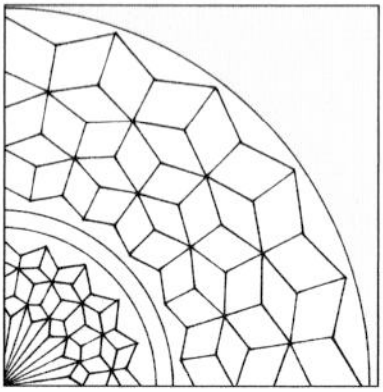

Cube
(see page 160)

DIAMONDS

Cape Cod

Diamond Quilted
(see page 176)

DIAMONDS

English Hobnail
(see page 194)

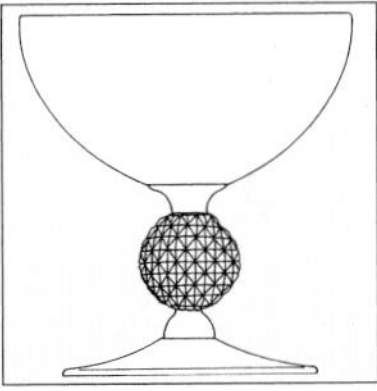

Golf Ball

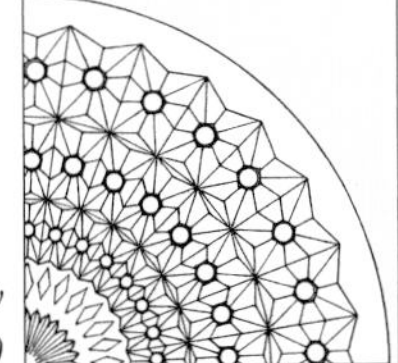

Holiday
(see page 248)

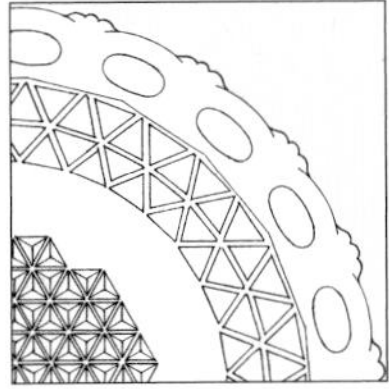

Laced Edge
(see page 265)

Miss America
(see page 297)

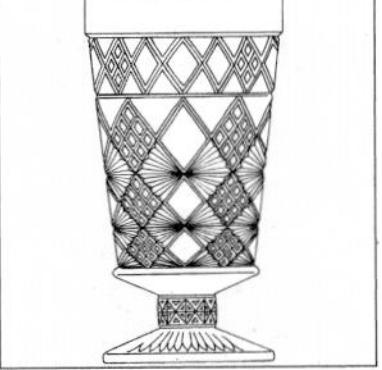

Peanut Butter

DIAMONDS

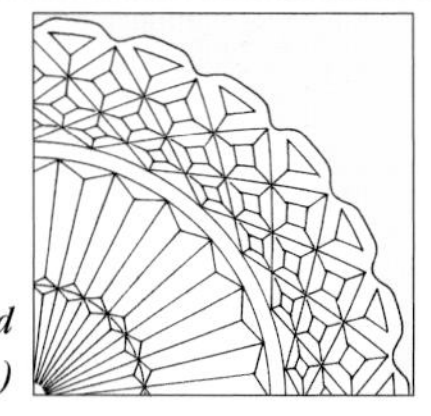

Waterford
(see page 453)

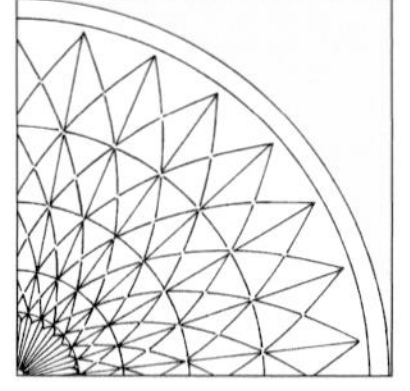

Windsor
(see page 460)

ELLIPSES

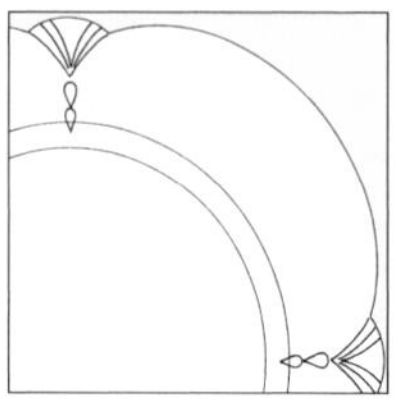

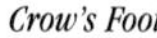

Crow's Foot

Newport
(see page 321)

Romanesque

FLORALS

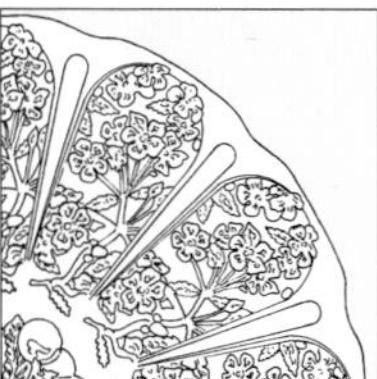

Cherry Blossom
(see page 129)

Cloverleaf
(see page 142)

FLORALS

Daisy
(see page 165)

Dogwood
(see page 183)

Doric
(see page 186)

Doric & Pansy
(see page 188)

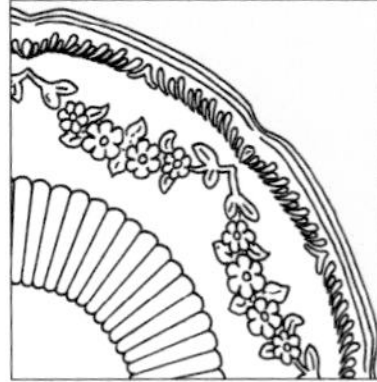

Fire-King Alice

Floragold
(see page 209)

FLORALS

Floral
(see page 212)

Floral &
Diamond Band
(see page 216)

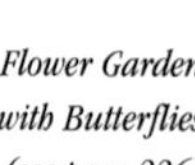

Flower Garden
with Butterflies
(see page 226)

Indiana Custard
(see page 257)

Iris
(see page 259)

Jubilee
(see page 262)

FLORALS

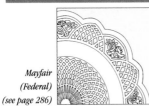

Mayfair (Federal) *(see page 286)*

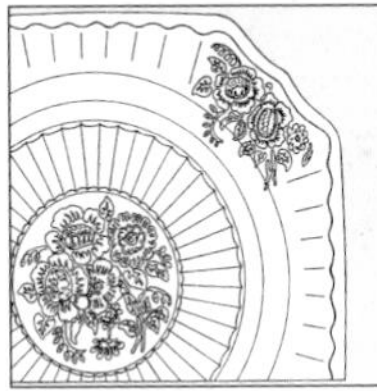

Mayfair (Open Rose) *(see page 288)*

Normandie *(see page 323)*

Orange Blossom

Orchid

Pineapple & Floral *(see page 348)*

FLORALS

Primrose

Rosemary
(see page 374)

Rose Cameo
(see page 372)

Royal Lace
(see page 382)

Seville

Sharon
(see page 407)

FLORALS

Sunflower
(see page 425)

Thistle
(see page 433)

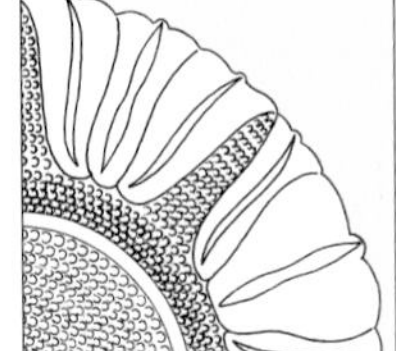

Tulip
(see page 437)

Vitrock
(see page 451)

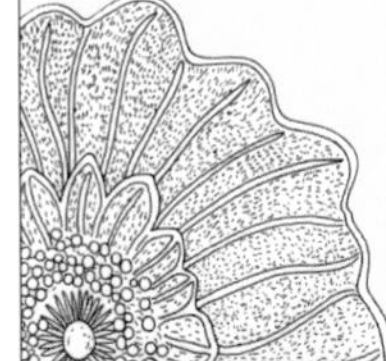

Wild Rose

FIGURES

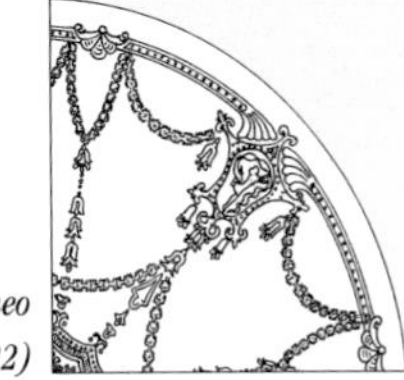

Cameo
(see page 122)

Cupid
(see page 162)

FRUITS

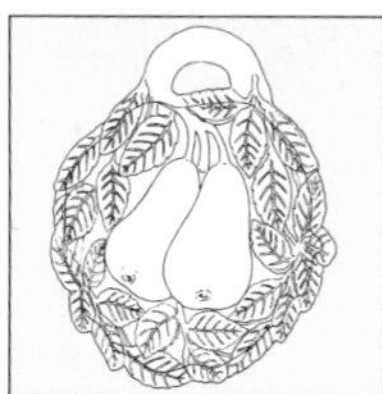

Avocado
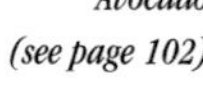
(see page 102)

Cherryberry
(see page 133)

Della Robbia
(see page 169)

Fruits
(see page 235)

Paneled Grape

Strawberry
(see page 421)

GEOMETRIC & LINE DESIGNS

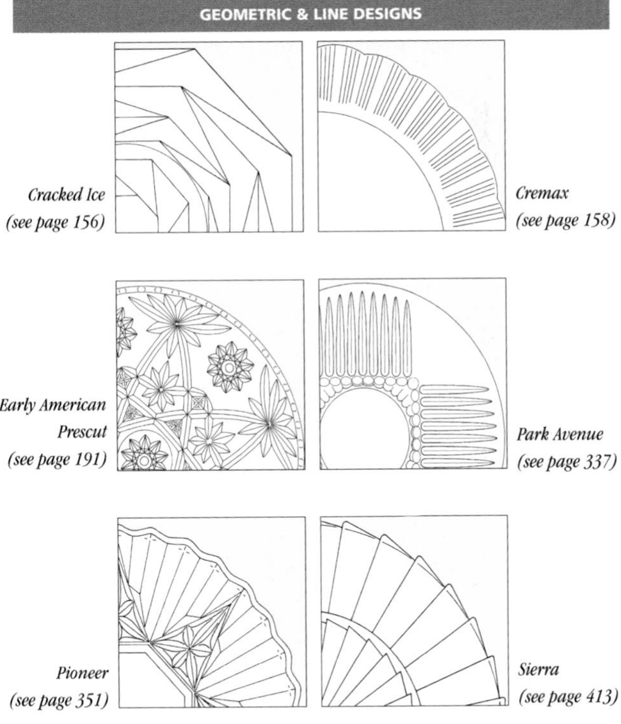

Cracked Ice *(see page 156)*

Cremax *(see page 158)*

Early American Prescut *(see page 191)*

Park Avenue *(see page 337)*

Pioneer *(see page 351)*

Sierra *(see page 413)*

GEOMETRIC & LINE DESIGNS

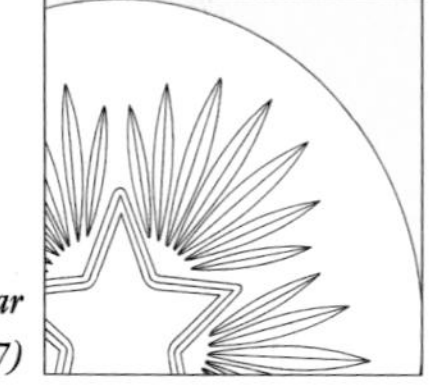

Star
(see page 417)

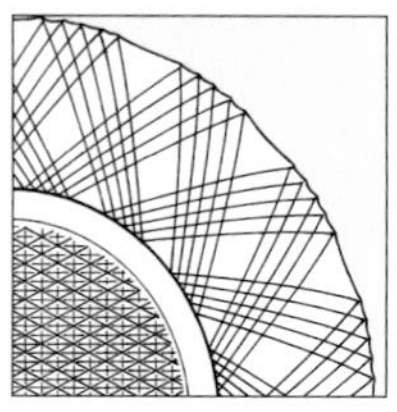

Starlight
(see page 419)

Wexford
(see page 456)

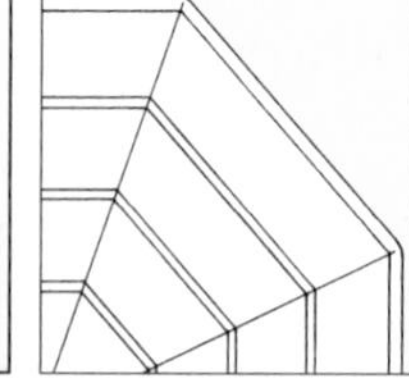

Tea Room
(see page 430)

HONEYCOMB

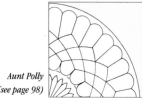

Aunt Polly
(see page 98)

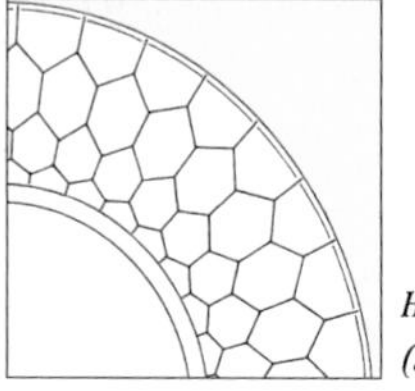

Hex Optic
(see page 243)

HORSESHOE

Horseshoe

(see page 254)

INDENTED CIRCLES

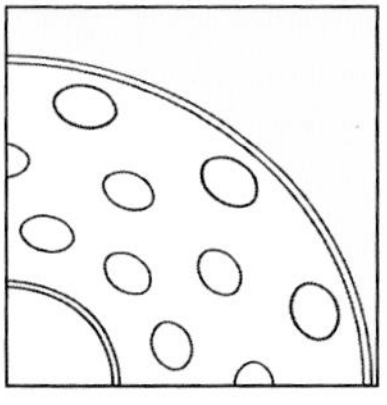

Capri

(see page 126)

LACY DESIGNS

Harp

(see page 239)

LACY DESIGNS

Heritage

(see page 241)

S-Pattern

(see page 390)

Sandwich (Duncan & Miller)

(see page 393)

Sandwich (Hocking)

(see page 399)

Sandwich (Indiana)

(see page 404)

LEAVES

Fire-King Peach Luster

Laurel
(see page 269)

Sunburst
(see page 423)

LOOPS

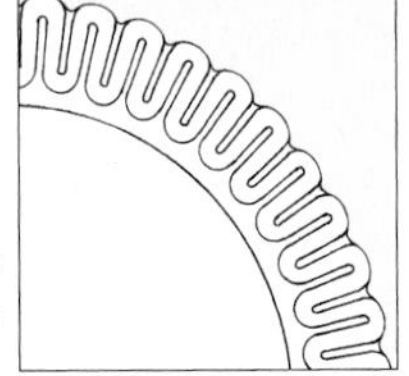

Christmas Candy
(see page 137)

Crocheted Crystal

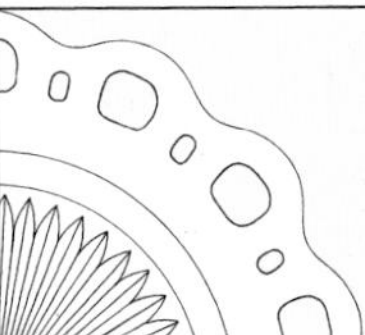

Old Colony
(see page 331)

Pretzel
(see page 328)

PETALS

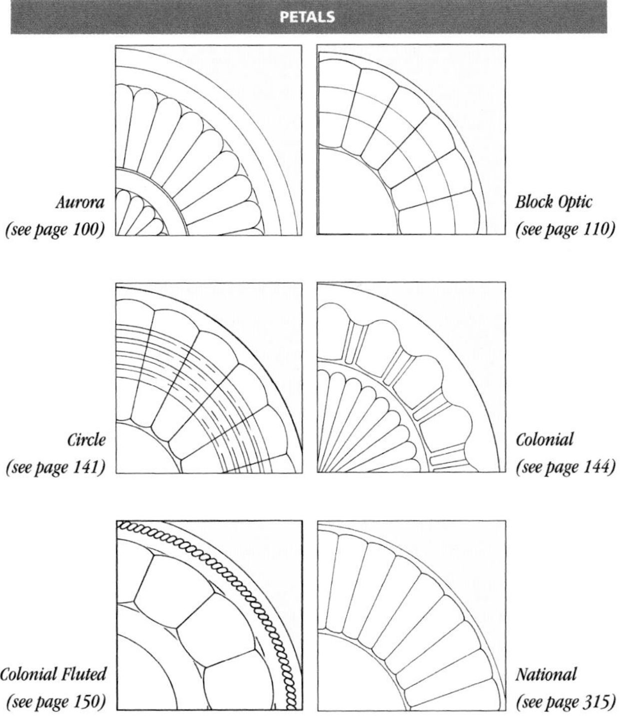

Aurora
(see page 100)

Block Optic
(see page 110)

Circle
(see page 141)

Colonial
(see page 144)

Colonial Fluted
(see page 150)

National
(see page 315)

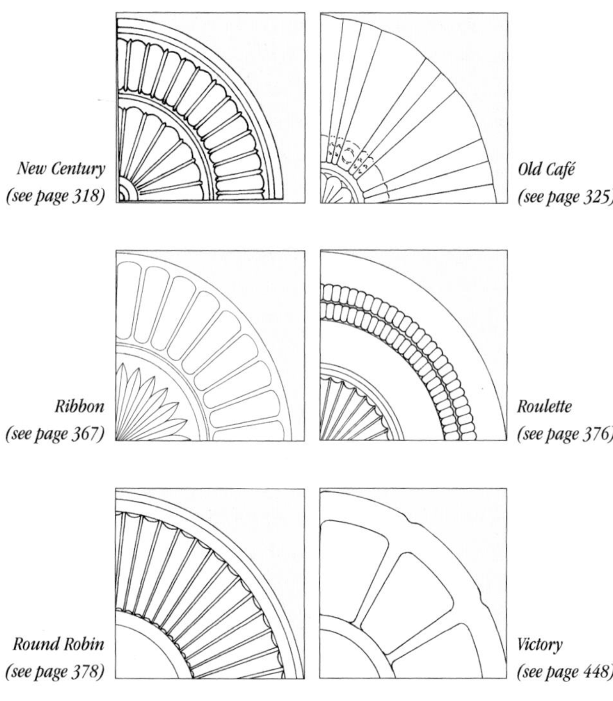

New Century
(see page 318)

Old Café
(see page 325)

Ribbon
(see page 367)

Roulette
(see page 376)

Round Robin
(see page 378)

Victory
(see page 448)

PETALS OR RIDGES WITH DIAMOND ACCENTS

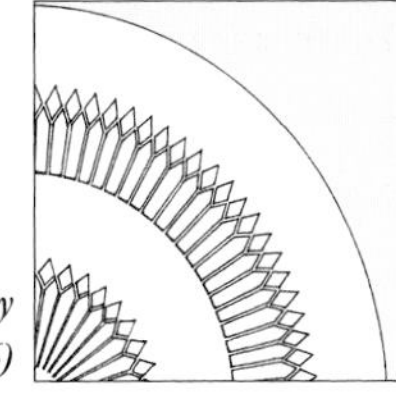
Anniversary
(see page 96)

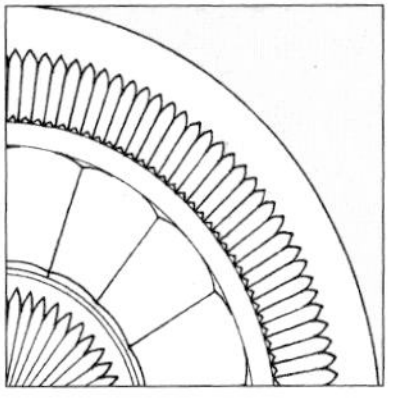
Coronation
(see page 154)

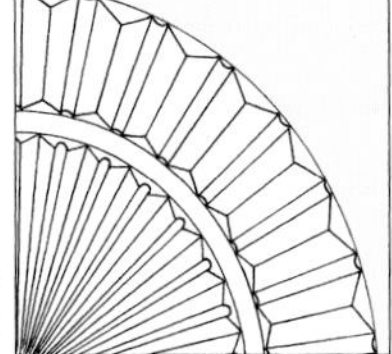
Fortune
(see page 233)

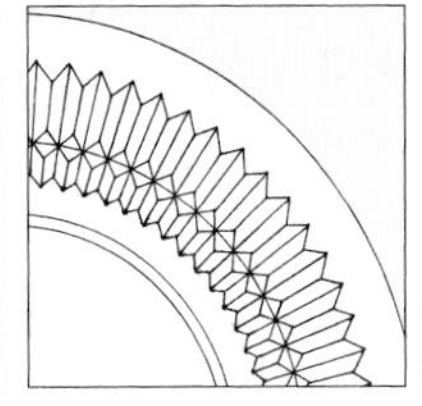
Lincoln Inn
(see page 272)

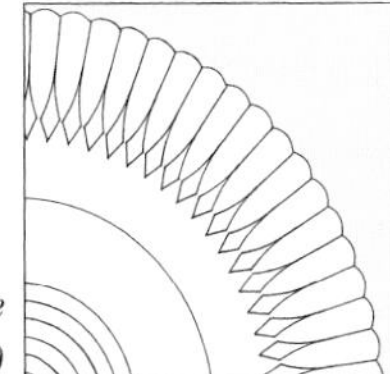
Petalware
(see page 345)

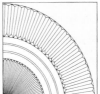

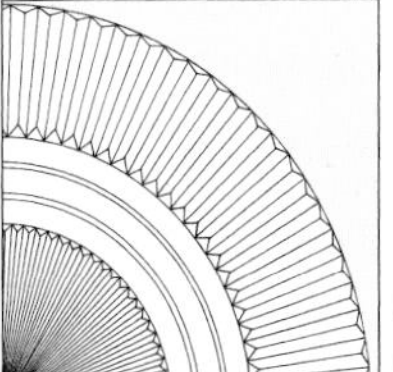
Queen Mary
(see page 362)

PLAIN

PYRAMIDS

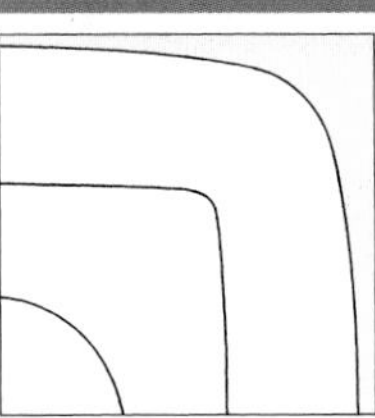

Fire-King Charm

Mt. Pleasant

(see page 312)

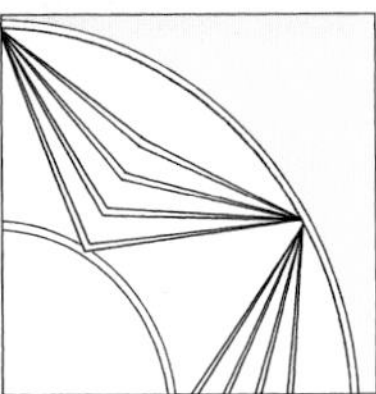

Pyramid

(see page 360)

RAISED BAND

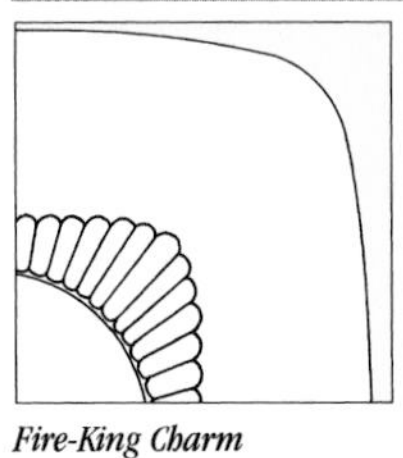

Fire-King Charm

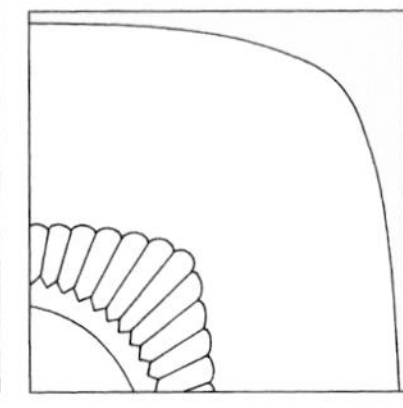

Forest Green

(see page 229)

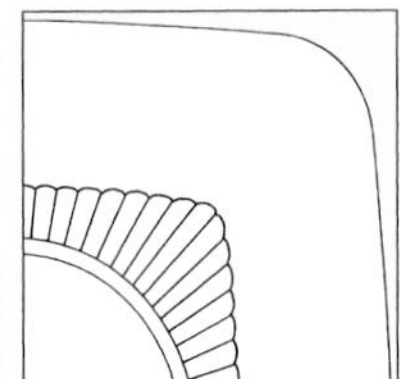

Royal Ruby

(see page 385)

RAISED CIRCLES

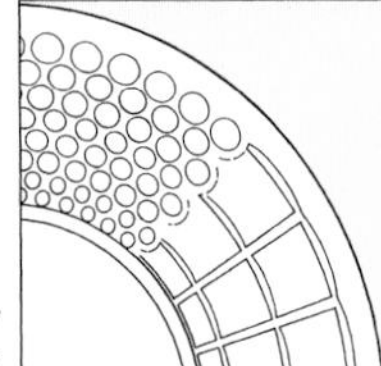

American Pioneer

(see page 89)

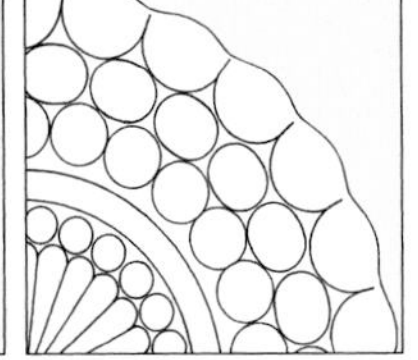

Bubble

(see page 116)

RAISED CIRCLES

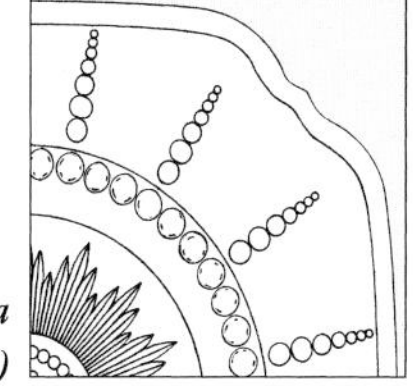
Columbia
(see page 152)

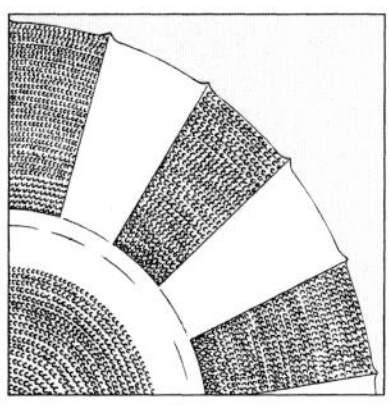
Dewdrop
(see page 173)

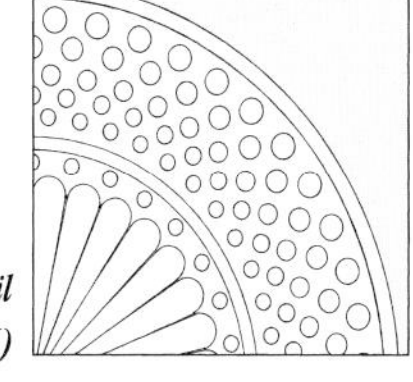
Hobnail
(see page 246)

Moonstone
(see page 306)

Oyster & Pearls
(see page 335)

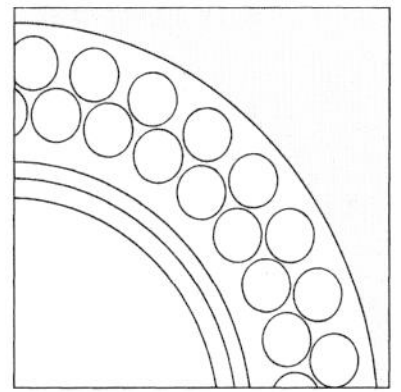
Raindrops
(see page 365)

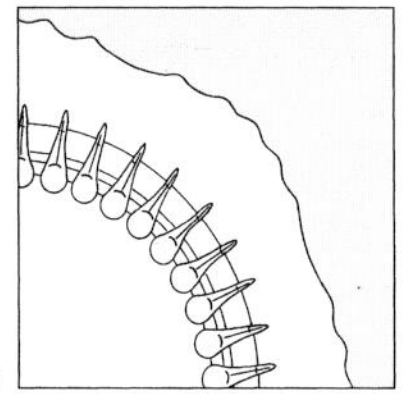

Radiance

Ships
(see page 410)

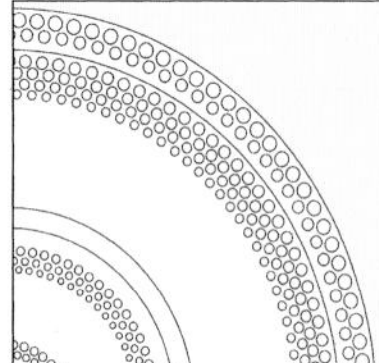

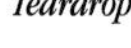

Teardrop

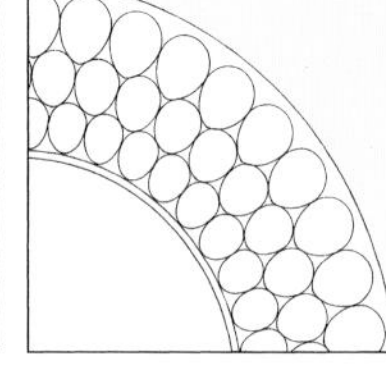

Thumbprint
(see page 435)

RIBS

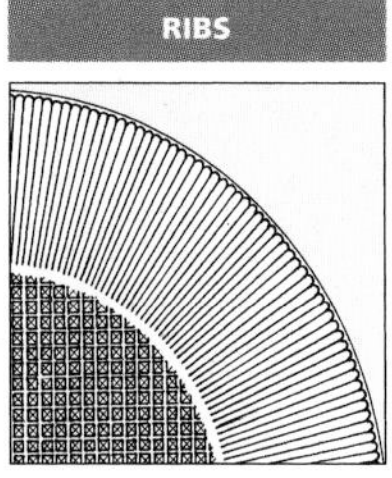

Homespun
(see page 251)

RINGS (CIRCLES)

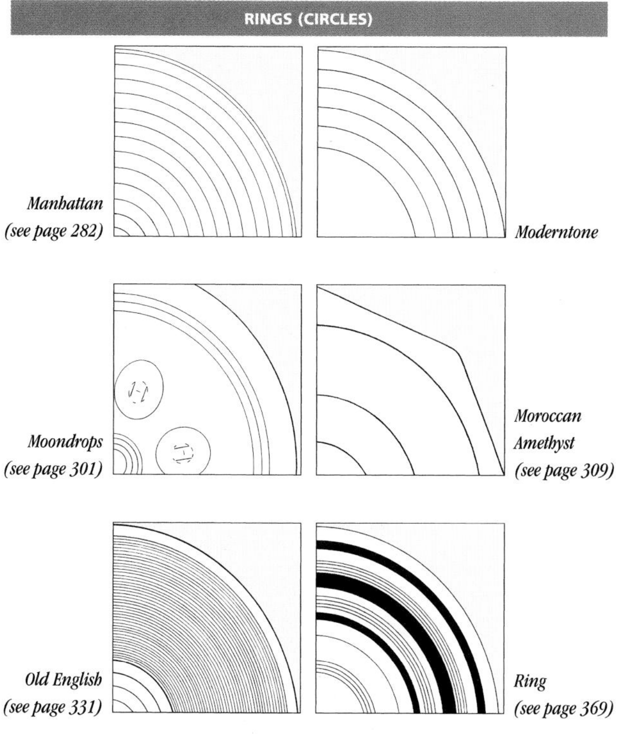

Manhattan
(see page 282)
Moderntone
Moondrops
(see page 301)
Moroccan
Amethyst
(see page 309)
Old English
(see page 331)
Ring
(see page 369)

SCENES

Chinex Classic
(see page 135)

Lake Como
(see page 267)

SCROLLING DESIGNS

Adam
(see page 86)

American Sweetheart
(see page 92)

Fire-King Philbe

Florentine No.1
(see page 218)

SCROLLING DESIGNS

Florentine No.2
(see page 221)

Madrid
(see page 277)

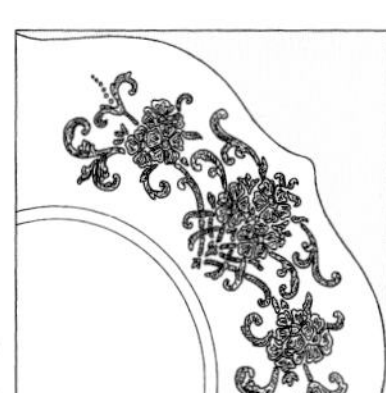

Patrick
(see page 343)

Primo
(see page 355)

Princess
(see page 357)

Rock Crystal

Roxana
(see page 380)

Vernon
(see page 446)

SWIRLS

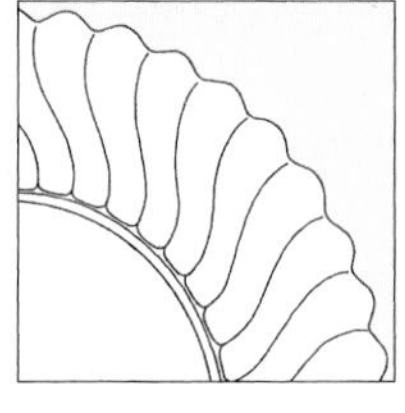

Colony

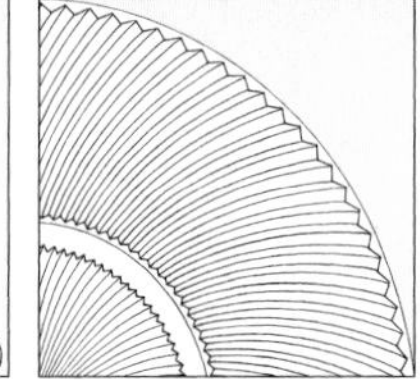

Diana
(see page 180)

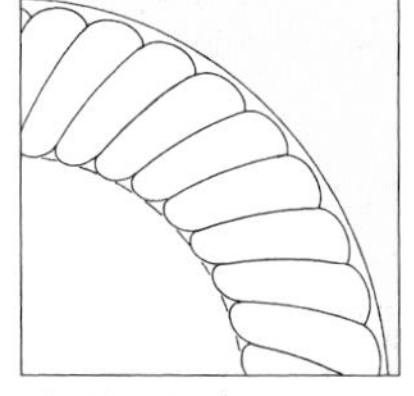

Fire-King Swirl

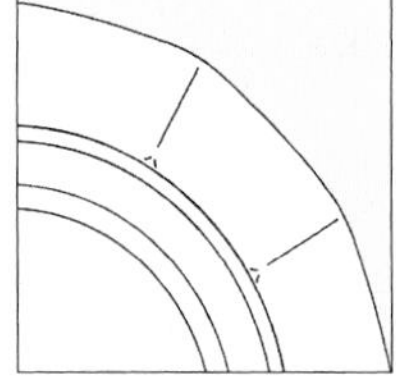

Fairfax
(see page 204)

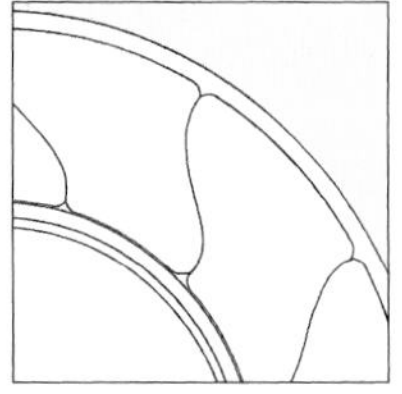

Jamestown

SWIRLS

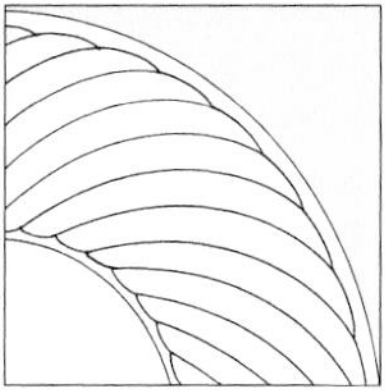

Spiral
(see page 415)

Swirl
(see page 427)

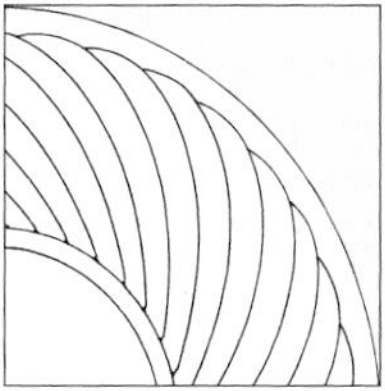

Twisted Optic
(see page 442)

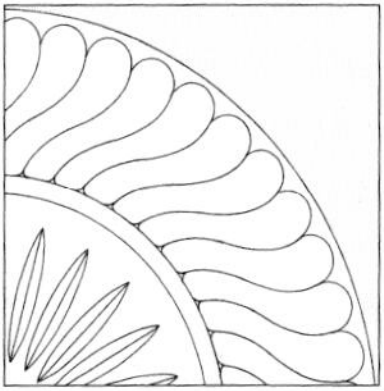

U.S. Swirl
(see page 444)

TEXTURED

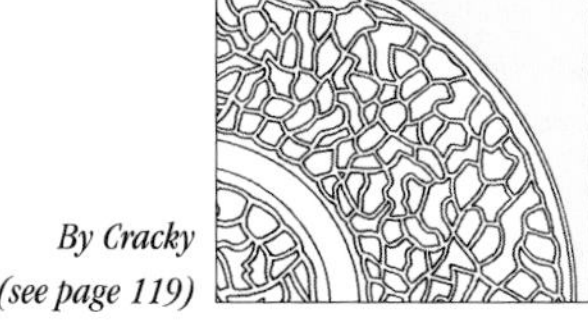

By Cracky
(see page 119)

Twiggy
(see page 439)

ADAM

Swatches

Crystal

Delphite Blue

Green

Pink

Topaz Yellow

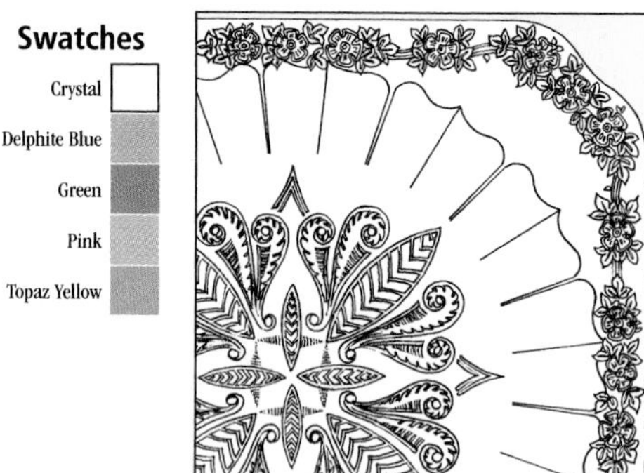

Manufactured by Jeannette Glass Company, Jeannette, Pa., from 1932 to 1934.

Made in crystal, Delphite blue, green, pink, some topaz and yellow. Delphite 4" h candlesticks are valued at $250 a pair. A yellow cup and saucer are valued at $200, and a 7-3/4" d yellow plate is valued at $115. Production in topaz and yellow was very limited. Crystal prices would be approximately 50 percent of the prices listed for green.

Reproductions: † Butter dish in pink and green.

Item	Green	Pink
Ashtray, 4-1/2" d	**$28**	**$32**
Berry bowl, small	**20**	**18.50**
Bowl, 9" d, cov	**95**	**80**
Bowl, 9" d, open	**45**	**30**
Bowl, 10" l, oval	**40**	**40**

Item	Green	Pink
Butter dish, cov †	400	145
Cake plate, 10" d, ftd	38	35
Candlesticks, pr, 4" h	125	100
Candy jar, cov, 2-1/2" h	120	115
Casserole, cov	95	80
Cereal bowl, 5-3/4" d	50	48
Coaster, 3-1/4" d	25	35
Creamer	30	28
Cup	28	30
Dessert bowl, 4-3/4" d	25	25
Iced tea tumbler, 5-1/2" h	70	75

*Adam, green salad plate **$20**.*

Item	Green	Pink
Lamp	500	500
Pitcher, 32 oz, round base	-	125
Pitcher, 32 oz, 8" h	48	45
Plate, 6" d, sherbet	15	18
Plate, 7-3/4" d, salad, sq	20	24
Plate, 9" d, dinner, sq	35	40
Plate, 9" d, grill	35	35
Platter, 11-3/4" l, rect	38	35
Relish dish, 8" l, divided	27	20
Salt and pepper shakers, pr, 4" h	130	95
Sherbet, 3"	40	35
Sugar, cov	48	42
Tumbler, 4-1/2" h	35	38
Vase, 7-1/2" h	60	250
Vegetable bowl, 7-3/4" d	30	30

*Adam, green ashtray **$28**, and pink pitcher **$45**.*

AMERICAN PIONEER

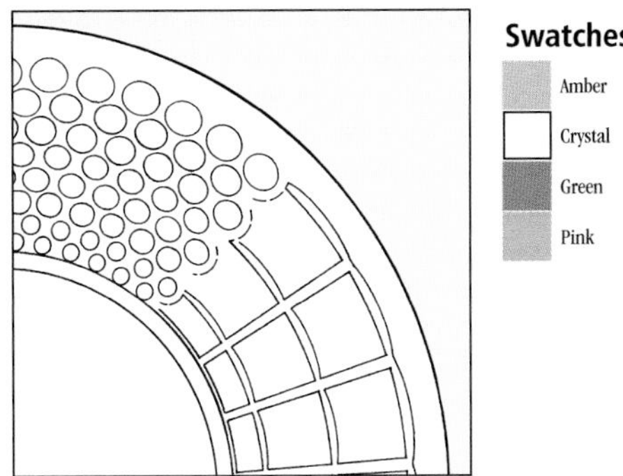

Swatches

Amber

Crystal

Green

Pink

Manufactured by Liberty Works, Egg Harbor, N.J., from 1931 to 1934. Made in amber, crystal, green, and pink.

Item	Amber	Crystal	Green	Pink
Bowl, 5" d, handle	$45	$24	$27.50	$24
Bowl, 8-3/4" d, cov	-	115	125	115
Bowl, 9" d, handle	-	24	30	24
Bowl, 9-1/4" d, cov	-	120	150	120
Bowl, 10" d	-	50	70	60
Candlesticks, pr, 6-1/2" h	-	75	95	75
Candy jar, cov, 1 pound	-	100	115	110
Candy jar, cov, 1-1/2 pound	-	70	125	95
Cheese and cracker set, indented plate and compote	-	50	65	55

Item	Amber	Crystal	Green	Pink
Coaster, 3-1/2" d	-	30	35	32
Cocktail, 3 oz, 3-13/16" h	45	-	-	-
Cocktail, 3-1/2 oz, 3 -15/16" h	45	-	-	-
Console bowl, 10-3/4" d	-	50	75	60
Creamer, 2-3/4" h	-	20	22	25
Creamer, 3-1/2" h	60	30	32	30
Cup	24	12	15	12
Dresser set, 2 cologne bottles, powder jar, 7-1/2" tray	-	300	345	365
Goblet, 8 oz, 6" h, water	-	40	45	40
Ice bucket, 6" h	-	50	80	65
Juice tumbler, 5 oz	-	40	45	40
Lamp, 1-3/4", metal pole, 9-1/2"	-	-	85	-
Lamp, 5-1/2" round, ball shape	175	-	-	70
Lamp, 8-1/2" h	-	90	115	110
Mayonnaise, 4-1/4"	-	60	90	60
Pilsner, 5-3/4" h, 11 oz	-	100	110	100
Pitcher, cov, 5" h	295	150	225	165
Pitcher, cov, 7" h	325	175	250	195
Plate, 6" d	-	12.50	17.50	12.50
Plate, 6" d, handle	25	12.50	17.50	12.50
Plate, 8" d	28	10	13	14
Plate, 11-1/2" d, handle	40	20	24	20
Rose bowl, 4-1/4" d, ftd	-	40	50	45
Saucer, 6" sq	10	4	5	5.50
Sherbet, 3-1/2" h	-	18	22	20
Sherbet, 4-3/4" h	-	32.50	40	30
Sugar, 2-3/4" h	-	20	27.50	25
Sugar, 3-1/2" h	50	20	27.50	25
Tumbler, 8 oz, 4" h	-	32	55	35

Item	Amber	Crystal	Green	Pink
Tumbler, 12 oz, 5" h	-	40	55	40
Vase, 7" h, 4 styles	-	115	145	115
Vase, 9" h, round	-	-	245	-
Whiskey, 2 oz., 2-1/4" h	-	50	100	50

*American Pioneer, green plate **$13**, cup **$15**, and saucer **$5**.*

AMERICAN SWEETHEART

Swatches

Blue

Cremax

Monax

Pink

Red

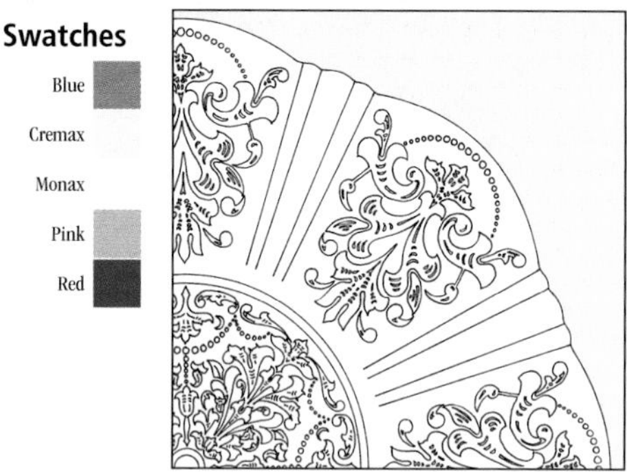

Manufactured by Macbeth-Evans Glass Company, Charleroi, Pa., from 1930 to 1936.

Made in blue, Monax, pink, and red. Limited production in Cremax and color-trimmed Monax.

Item	Blue	Cremax	Monax
Berry bowl, 3-1/4"d, flat	$-	$-	$-
Berry bowl, 9" d	-	50	75
Cereal bowl, 6" d	-	19.50	20
Chop plate, 11" d	-	-	24
Console bowl, 18" d	1,400	-	475
Cream soup, 4-1/2" d	-	-	135
Creamer, ftd	195	-	11.50
Cup	160	-	15
Lamp shade	-	450	500

Item	Blue	Cremax	Monax
Pitcher, 60 oz, 7-1/2" h	-	-	-
Pitcher, 80 oz, 8" h	-	-	-
Plate, 6" d, bread and butter	-	-	7.50
Plate, 8" d, salad	125	-	10
Plate, 9" d, luncheon	-	-	14
Plate, 9-3/4" d, dinner	-	-	25
Plate, 10-1/4" d, dinner	-	-	30
Platter, 13" l, oval	-	-	85
Salt and pepper shakers, pr, ftd	-	-	395
Salver plate, 12" d	275	-	30
Saucer	25	-	7
Serving plate, 15-1/2" d	425	-	250
Sherbet, 4-1/4" h, ftd	-	-	25
Soup bowl, flat, 9-1/2" d	-	-	95
Sugar lid	-	-	300
Sugar, open, ftd	195	-	15

*American Sweetheart, Monax open sugar **$15**, and creamer **$11.50**.*

Item	Blue	Cremax	Monax
Tidbit, 2 tiers	350	-	95
Tidbit, 3 tiers	750	-	275
Tumbler, 5 oz, 3-1/2" h	-	-	-
Tumbler, 9 oz, 4-1/4" h	-	-	-
Tumbler, 10 oz, 4-3/4" h	-	-	-
Vegetable bowl, 11"	-	-	90

American Sweetheart, Monax 10-1/4" dinner plate $30.

Item	Monax w/ color trim	Pink	Red
Berry bowl, 3-1/4"d, flat	$-	$80	$-
Berry bowl, 9" d	200	65	-
Cereal bowl, 6" d	50	24	-
Console bowl, 18" d	-	-	1,100
Cream soup, 4-1/2" d	-	85	-
Creamer, ftd	110	18	175
Cup	100	20	95
Pitcher, 60 oz, 7-1/2" h	-	995	-
Pitcher, 80 oz, 8" h	-	795	-
Plate, 6" d, bread and butter	24	8	-
Plate, 8" d, salad	30	12	125
Plate, 9" d, luncheon	45	-	-
Plate, 9-3/4" d, dinner	90	42	-
Plate, 10-1/4" d, dinner	-	45	-
Platter, 13" l, oval	225	70	-
Salt and pepper shakers, pr, ftd	-	500	-
Salver plate, 12" d	-	30	200
Saucer	18	5.75	45
Serving plate, 15-1/2" d	-	-	350
Sherbet, 3-3/4" h, ftd	-	25	-
Sherbet, 4-1/4" h, ftd	110	25	-
Soup bowl, flat, 9-1/2" d	170	85	-
Sugar, open, ftd	110	15	175
Tidbit, 2 tiers	-	-	250
Tidbit, 3 tiers	-	-	600
Tumbler, 5 oz, 3-1/2" h	-	110	-
Tumbler, 9 oz, 4-1/4" h	-	85	-
Tumbler, 10 oz, 4-3/4" h	-	185	-
Vegetable bowl, 11"	-	80	-

ANNIVERSARY

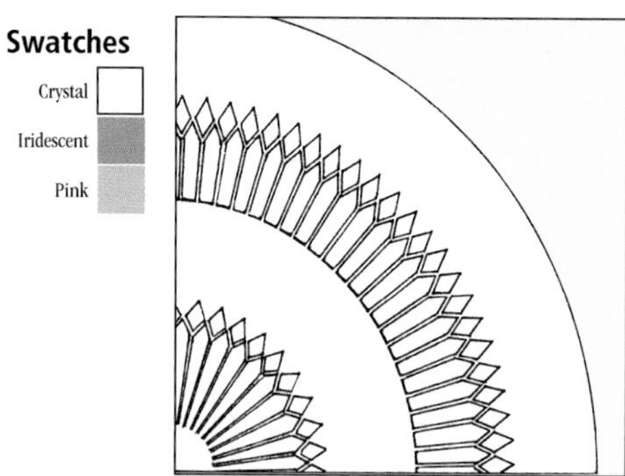

Manufactured by Jeannette Glass Company, Jeannette, Pa., from 1947 to 1949, and late 1960s to mid-1970s.

Made in crystal, iridescent, and pink.

Item	Crystal	Irid.	Pink
Berry bowl, 4-7/8" d	$3.50	$4.50	$11
Butter dish, cov	25	-	50
Cake plate, 12-3/8" w, square	7	-	16.50
Cake plate, 12-1/2" d, round	8	-	18.50
Cake plate, metal cover	15	-	-
Candlesticks, pr, 4-7/8" h	20	25	-
Candy jar, cov	24	-	45
Compote, open, 3 legs	5	5	16
Compote, ruffled, 3 legs	6.50	-	-
Creamer, ftd	6	6.50	14
Cup	5	4	9

Item	Crystal	Irid.	Pink
Fruit bowl, 9" d	10	14	24
Pickle dish 9" d	5.50	7.50	12
Plate, 9" d, dinner	5	8	17
Relish dish, 8" d	5.60	7.50	14
Saucer	1	1.50	6
Sherbet, ftd	7	-	10
Soup bowl, 7-3/8" d	8	7.50	18
Sugar, cov	12	10	20
Sugar, open, gold trim	4.50	-	-
Vase, 6-1/2" h	16	-	30
Wine, 2-1/2 oz	10	-	20

*Anniversary, iridescent dinner plate **$8**.*

AUNT POLLY

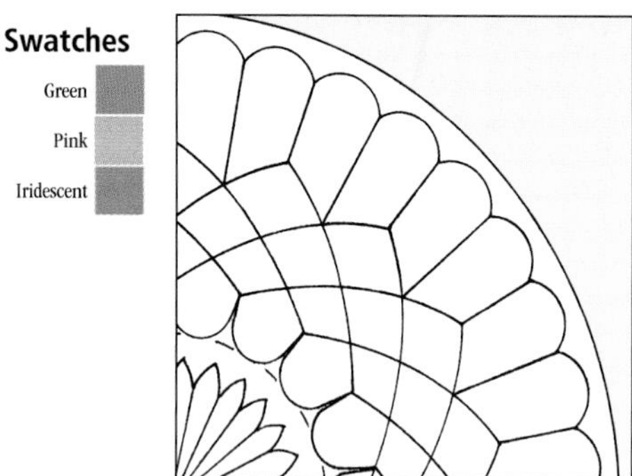

Manufactured by U.S. Glass Company, Pittsburgh, Pa., in the late 1920s.

Made in blue, green, and iridescent.

Item	Blue	Green	Irid.
Berry bowl, 4-3/4" d, individual	$18	$10	$10
Berry bowl, 7-1/8" d, master	45	22	22
Bowl, 4-3/4" d, 2" h	-	15	15
Bowl, 5-1/2" d, one handle	25	15	15
Bowl, 8-3/8" l, oval	100	42	42
Butter dish, cov	245	200	200
Candy jar, cov, two handles	50	30	30
Candy jar, ftd, two handles	-	27.50	27.50
Creamer	60	32	32
Pickle, 7-1/4" l, oval, handle	42	17.50	17.50
Pitcher, 48 oz, 8" h	200	-	-

Item	Blue	Green	Irid.
Plate, 6" d, sherbet	12	6	6
Plate, 8" d, luncheon	20	-	-
Salt and pepper shakers, pr	245	-	-
Sherbet	15	12	12
Sugar	195	95	95
Tumbler, 8 oz, 3-5/8" h	30	-	-
Vase, 6-1/2" h, ftd	48	30	30

Aunt Polly, blue sherbet ***$15.***

AURORA

Swatches

Cobalt Blue

Crystal

Green

Pink

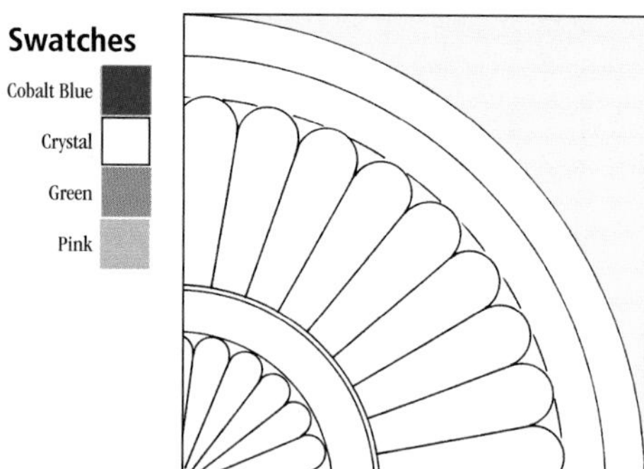

Manufactured by Hazel Atlas Glass Company, Clarksburg, W.V., and Zanesville, Ohio, in the late 1930s.

Made in cobalt (Ritz) blue, crystal, green, and pink.

Item	Cobalt Blue	Crystal	Green	Pink
Bowl, 4-1/2" d	**$60**	**$-**	**$-**	**$60**
Breakfast set, 24 pcs, service for 4	**500**	**-**	**-**	**-**
Cereal bowl, 5-3/8" d	**20**	**12**	**10**	**15**
Cup	**20**	**6**	**10**	**15**
Milk pitcher	**27.50**	**-**	**-**	**25**
Plate, 6-1/2" d	**12.50**	**-**	**-**	**12.50**
Saucer	**6**	**2**	**3**	**6**
Tumbler, 10 oz, 4-3/4" h	**27.50**	**-**	**-**	**27.50**

*Aurora, blue bowl (deep) 4-1/2"d **$60**, cereal bowl 5-3/8"d **$20**, and milk pitcher **$27.50**.*

AVOCADO

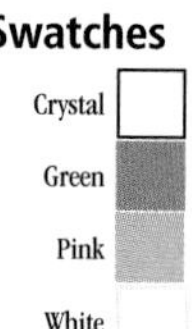

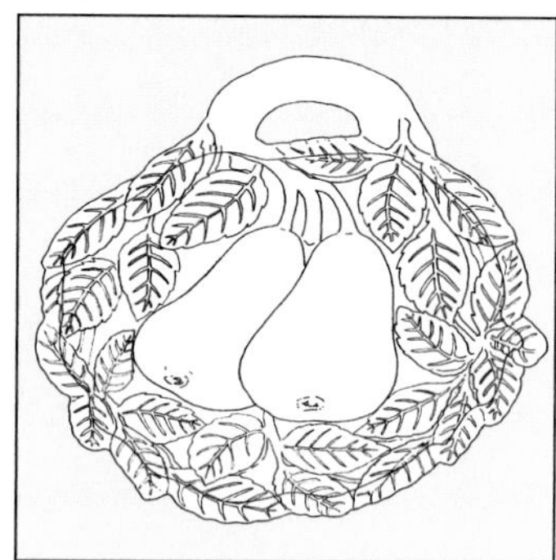

Manufactured by Indiana Glass Company, Dunkirk, Ind., from 1923 to 1933.

Made in crystal, green, pink, and white.

Reproductions: † Creamer, 8" pickle, 64 oz. pitcher, plates, sherbet, sugar, and tumblers. Reproductions can be found in amethyst, blue, dark green, frosted green, frosted pink, pink, red, and yellow, representing several colors not made originally.

Item	Crystal	Green	Pink	White
Bowl, 5-1/4" d, two handles	$12	$38	$27.50	$-
Bowl, 8" d, two handles, oval	17.50	30	25	-
Bowl, 8-1/2" d	20	60	50	-
Bowl, 9-1/2" d, 3-1/4" deep	35	175	150	-
Cake plate, 10-1/4" d, two handles	17.50	60	40	-
Creamer, ftd †	17.50	40	35	-

Item	Crystal	Green	Pink	White
Cup, ftd	-	36	30	-
Pickle bowl, 8" d, two handles, oval†	17.50	30	25	-
Pitcher, 64 oz †	385	1,100	900	425
Plate, 6-3/8" d, sherbet †	6	22	15	-
Plate, 8-1/4" d, luncheon †	7.50	25	20	-
Preserve bowl, 7" l, handle	10	32	28	-
Relish, 6" d, ftd	10	35	28	-
Salad bowl, 7-1/2" d	9	55	37.50	-
Saucer	6	24	15	-
Sherbet, ftd †	-	75	55	-
Sugar, ftd †	17.50	40	35	-
Tumbler †	25	250	150	35

*Avocado, green creamer, ftd, **$40**, and sugar, ftd **$40**.*

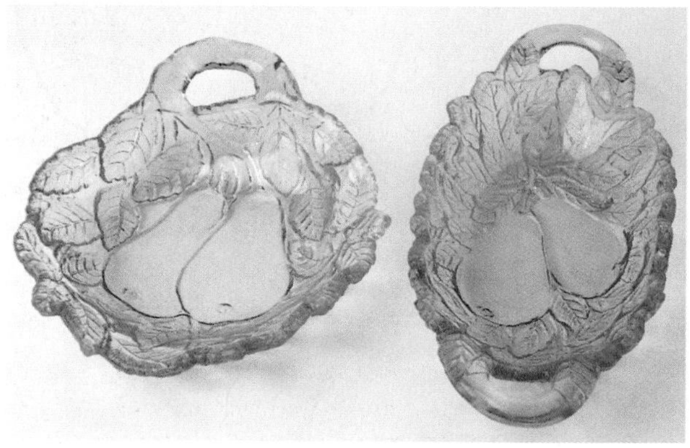

*Avocado, green, preserve bowl, handle **$32**, and bowl, two handles **$30**.*

BEADED BLOCK

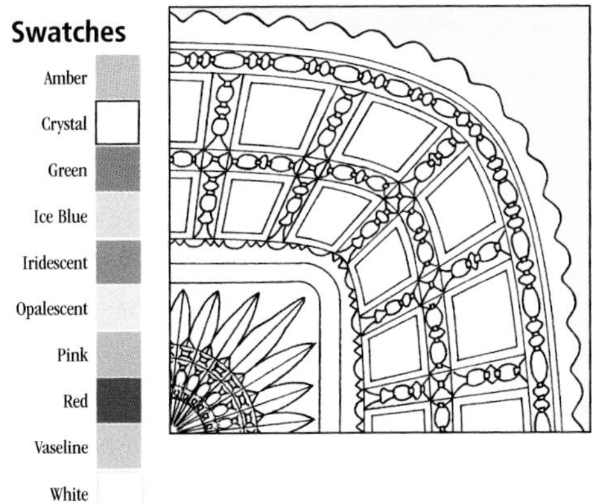

Manufactured by Imperial Glass Company, Bellaire, Ohio, from 1927 to the 1930s.

Made in amber, crystal, green, ice blue, iridescent, milk white (1950s), opalescent, pink, red, and Vaseline. Some pieces are still being made in pink and are embossed with the "IG" trademark. The only form known in red is the 4-1/2" lily bowl, valued at $300. The secondary market for milk white is still being established.

Item	Amber	Crystal	Green	Ice Blue
Bowl, 4-1/2" d, lily	$20	$15	$22	$24
Bowl, 4-1/2" d, two handles	18	10	22	28
Bowl, 5-1/2" sq	18	8	20	12

Item	Amber	Crystal	Green	Ice Blue
Bowl, 5-1/2" d, 1 handle	18	8	20	12
Bowl, 6" deep	24	12	24	15
Bowl, 6-1/4" d	24	8.50	20	12
Bowl, 6-1/2" d, two handles	24	8.50	20	12
Bowl, 6-3/4" d	28	12	28	14

*Beaded Block, ice blue vase **$35**, and crystal jelly, stemmed, **$10**.*

Item	Amber	Crystal	Green	Ice Blue
Bowl, 7-1/4" d, flared	30	12	28	14
Bowl, 7-1/2" d, fluted	30	22	30	24
Bowl, 7-1/2" plain	30	20	30	22
Candy dish, cov, pear shaped	-	-	395	-
Celery, 8-1/4" d	35	18	35	18
Creamer, ftd	25	25	25	24
Jelly, 4-1/2" h, stemmed	20	10	20	12
Jelly, 4-1/2" h, stemmed, flared lid	24	20	24	30
Pitcher, 1 pt, 5-1/4" h	95	115	125	115
Plate, 7-3/4" sq	20	7.50	20	10
Plate, 8-3/4"	30	24	30	30
Sugar, ftd	25	24	30	30
Syrup	-	-	-	-
Vase, 6" h, ftd	25	20	35	35

Additional Colors:

Item	Irid.	Opal	Pink	Vaseline
Bowl, 4-1/2" d, lily	$18	$30	$18	$24
Bowl, 4-1/2" d, two handles	20	30	12	28
Bowl, 5-1/2" sq	10	15	10	12
Bowl, 5 -1/2 d, 1 handle	10	15	20	12
Bowl, 6" deep	12	24	18	15
Bowl, 6-1/4" d	12	18	10	12
Bowl, 6-1/2" d, two handles	12	18	28	12
Bowl, 6-3/4" d	15	20	14	14
Bowl, 7-1/4" d, flared	15	20	14	14
Bowl, 7-1/2" d, fluted	20	24	24	24
Bowl, 7-1/2" plain	24	24	20	22

Item	Irid.	Opal	Pink	Vaseline
Candy dish, cov, pear shaped	-	-	-	650
Celery, 8-1/4" d	18	30	16.50	18
Creamer, ftd	24	50	30	24
Jelly, 4-1/2" h, stemmed	12	15	12	12
Jelly, 4-1/2" h, stemmed, flared lid	15	24	15	12
Pitcher, 1 pt, 5-1/4" h	115	125	195	115
Plate, 7-3/4" sq	10	15	8	10
Plate, 8-3/4"	20	24	20	20
Sugar, ftd	20	60	30	20
Syrup	-	-	-	165
Vase, 6" h, ftd	25	110	36	30

Beaded Block is a very popular pattern with those who collect only depression glass. It is also popular with those who specialize in collecting patterns made by the Imperial Glass Co., long known for their intricate and interesting patterns and shapes.

*Beaded Block, Vaseline square plate **$10**, and iridescent round plate **$20**.*

BLOCK OPTIC

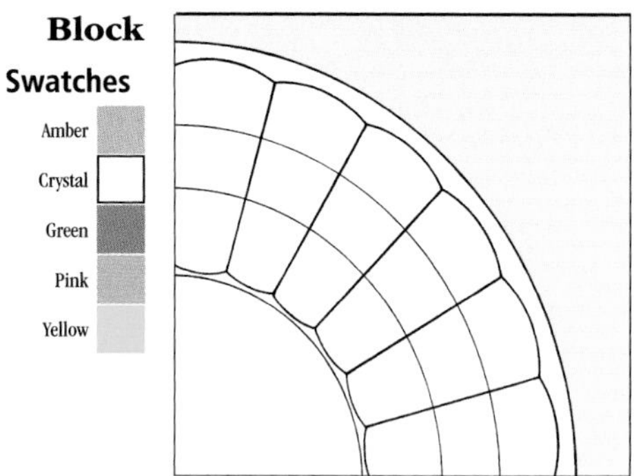

Manufactured by Hocking Glass Company, Lancaster, Ohio, from 1929 to 1933.

Made in amber, crystal, green, pink, and yellow. Production in amber was very limited. A 11-3/4" d console bowl is valued at $50, while a pair of matching 1-3/4" h candlesticks is valued at $110.

* There are five styles of creamers and four styles of cups, each have a relative value.

Item	Crystal	Green	Pink	Yellow
Berry bowl, 8-1/2" d	$20	$35	$40	$-
Bowl, 4-1/4" d, 1-3/8" h	6	15	10	-
Bowl, 4-1/2" d, 1-1/2" h	-	28	-	-
Bowl, 8-5/8" d, low, ruffled	-	150	-	-
Butter dish, cov	-	50	-	-
Cake plate, 10" d, ftd	18	-	-	-

*Block Optic, green, large berry bowl, 8-1/2" d **$35,** cereal bowl, 5-1/4" d **$12** and individual berry bowl, 4-1/4" d **$15**.*

Item	Crystal	Green	Pink	Yellow
Candlesticks, pr, 1-3/4" h	-	120	100	-
Candy jar, cov, 2-1/4" h	30	60	55	75
Candy jar, cov, 6-1/4" h	40	80	60	-
Champagne, 4-3/4" h	10	27.50	16.50	20
Cocktail, 4" h	-	35	35	-
Compote, 4" wide	-	36	70	-
Console bowl, 11-3/4" d, rolled	55	75	95	-
Creamer*	12	17.50	20	20
Cup*	7.50	9	7	10
Goblet, 9 oz, 5-3/4" h	12	40	45	-

Item	Crystal	Green	Pink	Yellow
Goblet, 9 oz, 7-1/2" h, thin	15	-	30	40
Ice bucket	-	40	48	-
Ice tub, open	-	60	-	-
Pitcher, 54 oz, 7-5/8" h, bulbous	-	75	75	-
Pitcher, 54 oz, 8-1/2" h	-	42	40	-
Pitcher, 80 oz, 8" h	-	90	85	-
Plate, 6" d, sherbet	1.50	5	5	6.50
Plate, 8" d, luncheon	3.50	8	7.50	8.50
Plate, 9" d, dinner	11	27.50	35	45
Plate, 9" d, dinner, snowflake center	-	16.50	-	-
Plate, 9" d, grill	15	27.50	30	60
Salad bowl, 7-1/4" d	-	155	-	-
Salad bowl, 7-1/4" d	-	155	-	-
Salt and pepper shakers, pr, ftd	-	42	90	95
Salt and pepper shakers, pr, squatty	-	100	-	-
Sandwich plate, 10-1/4" d	-	27.50	30	-
Sandwich server, center handle	-	65	50	-
Saucer, 5-3/4" d	-	12	10	-
Saucer, 6-1/8" d	2	10	10	3.50
Sherbet, 5-1/2 oz, 3-1/4" h	-	12	9.50	7.50
Sherbet, 6 oz, 4-3/4" h	7	28	17.50	18
Sugar, cone	-	17.50	15	15
Sugar, flat	-	10	10	-
Sugar, round, ftd	10	12	18	-
Tumbler, 3 oz, 2-5/8" h	-	30	28	-
Tumbler, 3 oz, 3-1/4" h, ftd	-	27.50	25	-
Tumbler, 5 oz, 3-1/2" h, flat	-	20	17.50	-
Tumbler, 5-3/8" h, ftd	-	-	24	18
Tumbler, 9" h, ftd	-	-	17.50	22
Tumbler, 9-1/2 oz, 3-13/16" h, flat	-	17.50	15	-

Item	Crystal	Green	Pink	Yellow
Tumbler, 10 oz, 6" h, ftd	12	-	-	-
Tumbler, 10 or 11 oz, 5" h, flat	-	30	35	-
Tumbler, 12 oz, 4-7/8" h, flat	-	35.50	30	-
Tumbler, 15 oz, 5-1/4" h, flat	-	32.50	30	-
Vase, 5-3/4" h, blown	-	350	-	-
Whiskey, 2 oz, 2-1/4" h	15	35	30	-
Wine, 3-1/2" h	-	415	415	-

*Block Optic, green sherbet **$28**, sugar **$12**, and creamer **$17.50**, and Hazel Atlas look-alike covered candy dish.*

BOWKNOT

Swatches

Green

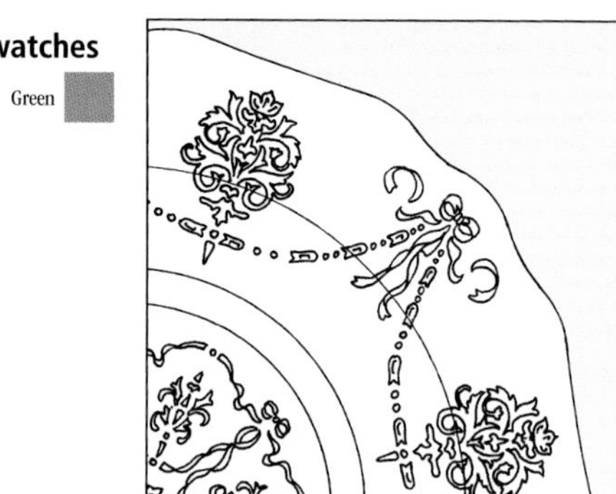

Unknown maker, late 1920s.
Made in green.

Item	Green
Berry bowl, 4-1/2" d	$25
Cereal bowl, 5-1/2" d	30
Cup	20
Plate, 7" d, salad	15
Sherbet, low, ftd	25
Tumbler, 10 oz, 5" h, flat	20
Tumbler, 10 oz, 5" h, ftd	20

*Bowknot, green tumbler **$20**, and footed berry bowl **$25**.*

Bullseye, Provincial

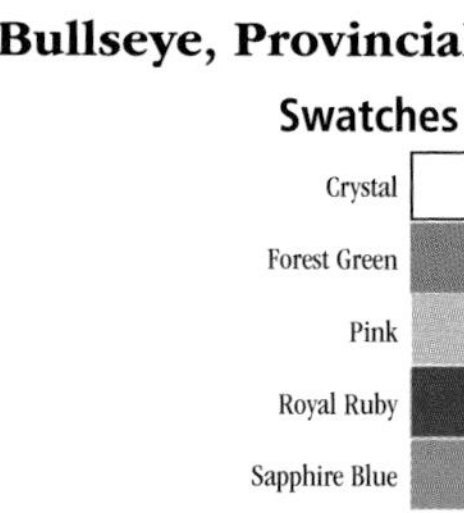

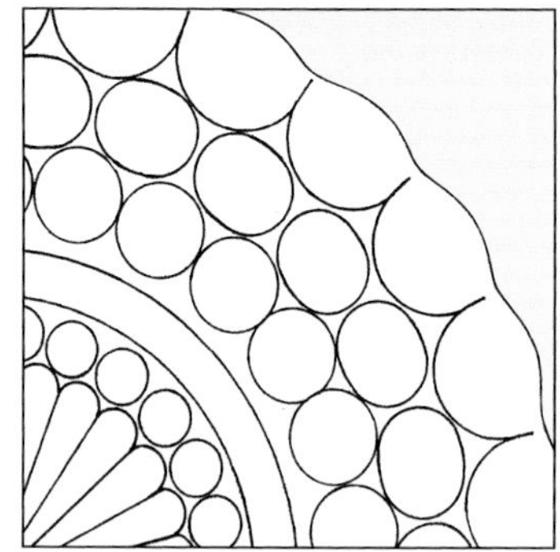

Manufactured originally by Hocking Glass Company, and followed by Anchor Hocking Glass Corporation, Lancaster, Ohio, from 1937 to 1965.

Made in crystal (1937); forest green (1937); pink, Royal Ruby (1963); and sapphire blue (1937). Production in pink was limited. The current value for a pink cup and saucer is $175.

Item	Crystal	Forest Green	Royal Ruby	Sapph. Blue
Berry bowl, 4" d	**$5**	**$-**	**$6.50**	**$24**
Berry bowl, 8-3/4" d	**12**	**15**	**18**	**20**
Bowl, 9" d, flanged	**8**	**-**	**-**	**335**
Candlesticks, pr	**24**	**40**	**-**	**-**
Cereal bowl, 5-1/4" d	**8**	**20**	**-**	**17.50**
Cocktail, 3-1/2 oz	**4.50**	**10**	**10**	**-**
Cocktail, 4-1/2 oz	**4.50**	**12.50**	**12.50**	**-**
Creamer	**7.50**	**15**	**18**	**45**

*Bubble, blue grill plate **$22**, platter **$18**, and soup bowl **$16**, berry bowl, 4" d $24.*

Item	Crystal	Forest Green	Royal Ruby	Sapph. Blue
Cup	4.50	8.75	12.50	15
Fruit bowl, 4-1/2" d	5	11	9	12
Goblet, 9 oz, stem, 5-1/2" h	7.50	15	15	-
Goblet, 9-1/2 oz, stem	7.50	15	15	-
Iced tea goblet, 14 oz	8	17.50	-	-
Iced tea tumbler, 12 oz, 4-1/2" h	12.50	-	19.50	-
Juice goblet, 4 oz	3	14	-	-
Juice goblet, 5-1/2 oz	5	12.50	12.50	-
Juice tumbler, 6 oz, ftd	4	12	10	-

Item	Crystal	Forest Green	Royal Ruby	Sapph. Blue
Lamp, 3 styles	42	-	-	-
Lemonade Tumbler, 16 oz, 5-7/8" h	16	-	16	-
Old Fashioned Tumbler, 8 oz, 3-1/4" h	6.50	16	16	-
Pitcher, 64 oz, ice lip	60	-	65	-
Plate, 6-3/4" d, bread and butter	4	4.50	-	3.75
Plate, 9-3/8" d, dinner	7.50	28	27.50	8
Plate, 9-3/8" d, grill	-	20	-	22
Platter, 12" l, oval	10	-	-	18
Sandwich Plate, 9-1/2" d	7.50	25	22	8
Saucer	1.50	5	5	1.50
Sherbet, 6 oz	4.50	9.50	12	-
Soup Bowl, flat, 7-3/4" d	10	-	-	16
Sugar	6	14.50	-	30
Tidbit, 2 tiers	-	-	35	-
Tumbler, 9 oz, water	6	-	16	-

BY CRACKY

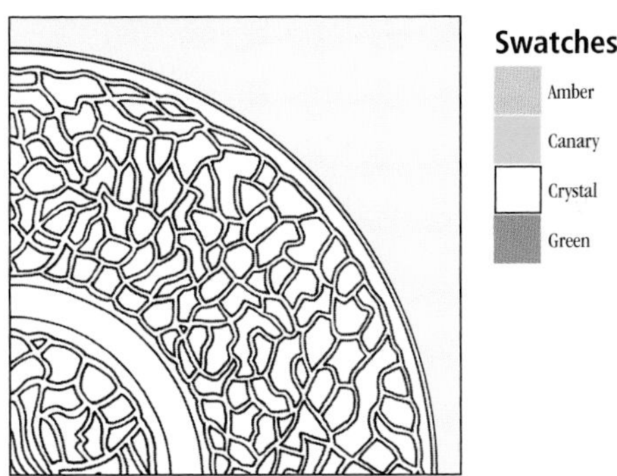

Swatches

Amber

Canary

Crystal

Green

Manufactured by L.E. Smith Glass Company, Mount Pleasant, Pa., in the late 1920s.

Made in amber, canary, crystal, and green.

Item	Amber	Canary	Crystal	Green
Cake plate, ftd	$35	$40	$30	$30
Candleholder, octagonal base	7.50	10	5	5
Candleholder, round base	5	7.50	5	5
Candy box, cov	17.50	20	15	17.50
Candy jar, cov	20	25	17.50	17.50
Center bowl, 12", octagonal	15	17.50	12	15
Cup	5	5	5	5
Goblet	18	18	10	15
Flower block, 3"	15	17.50	7.50	10
Plate, 8", octagonal	15	17.50	7.50	10
Saucer	3	5	2	2

Item	Amber	Canary	Crystal	Green
Sherbet	7.50	10	5	5
Sherbet plate	12	15	5	7.50
Vase, fan shape	20	25	15	15
Violet bowl	20	25	15	15

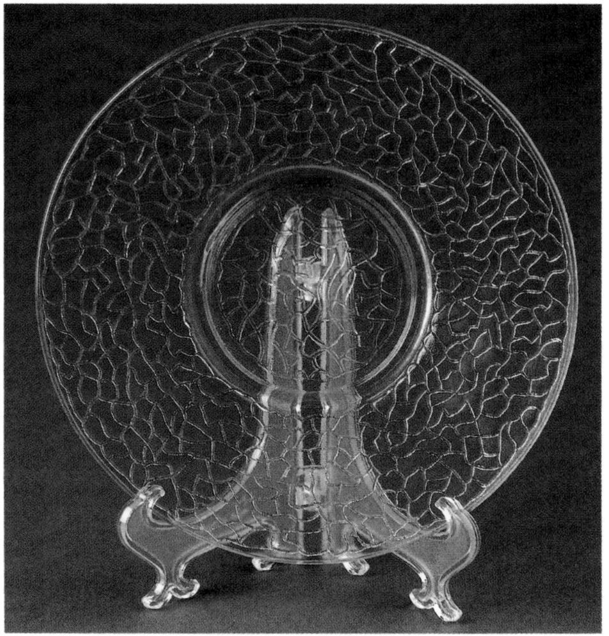

By Cracky, crystal sherbet plate ***$5***.

By Cracky, green goblet ***$15***.

CAMEO

Ballerina, Dancing Girl

Swatches

Crystal

Green

Pink

Yellow

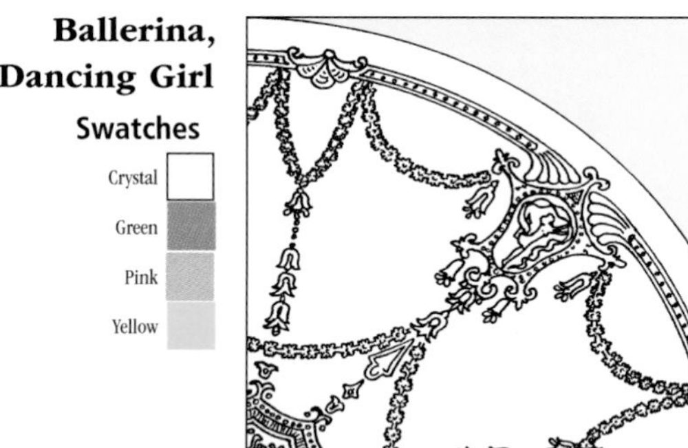

Manufactured by Hocking Glass Company, Lancaster, Ohio, from 1930 to 1934.

Made in crystal, green, pink, and yellow. Only the crystal has a platinum rim.

Reproductions: † Salt shakers made in blue, green and pink. Children's dishes have been made in green and pink, but were never part of the original pattern. Recently, a squatty candy dish in cobalt blue has also been made. This was not an original color.

Item	Crystal	Green	Pink	Yellow
Berry bowl, 8-1/4" d	**$-**	**$48**	**$175**	**$-**
Butter dish, cov	**-**	**250**	**-**	**1,500**
Cake plate, 10" d, 3 legs	**-**	**28**	**-**	**-**
Cake plate, 10-1/2" d, flat	**-**	**120**	**165**	**-**
Candlesticks, pr, 4" h	**-**	**150**	**-**	**-**

*Cameo, green vegetable bowl **$50**.*

Item	Crystal	Green	Pink	Yellow
Candy jar, cov, 4" h	-	100	495	125
Candy jar, cov, 6-1/2" h	-	195	-	-
Cereal bowl, 5-1/2" d	8.50	40	160	35
Cocktail shaker	600	-	-	-
Comport, 5" w	-	50	200	-
Console bowl, 3 legs, 11" d	-	90	45	125
Cookie jar, cov	-	65	-	-
Cream soup, 4-3/4" d	-	185	-	-
Creamer, 3-1/4" h	-	30	110	25
Creamer, 4-1/4" h	-	30	115	-
Decanter, 10" h	225	215	-	-
Domino tray, 7" l	150	175	250	-
Goblet, 6" h, water	-	95	195	-

Item	Crystal	Green	Pink	Yellow
Ice bowl, 3" h, 5-1/2" d	265	300	750	-
Jam jar, cov, 2" h	175	225	-	-
Juice pitcher, 6" h, 36 oz	-	110	-	-
Juice tumbler, 3 oz, ftd	-	65	90	-
Pitcher, 8-1/2" h, 56 oz	550	70	1,450	-
Plate, 7" d, salad	12	13.50	-	-
Plate, 8" d, luncheon	8	18	36	12.50
Plate, 8-1/2", luncheon, sq	-	60	-	250
Plate, 9-1/2" d, dinner	-	28	85	15
Plate, 10-1/2" d, dinner, rimmed	-	115	175	-
Plate, 10-1/2" d, grill	-	20	55	10
Platter, 12" l	-	30	-	42
Relish, 7-1/2" l, ftd, 3 parts	175	35	-	-
Salad bowl, 7-1/4" d	-	70	-	-
Salt and pepper shakers, pr, ftd †	-	95	90	-
Saucer	4	4	90	4.50
Sherbet, 3-1/8" h, blown	-	18	75	-
Sherbet, 3-1/8" h, molded	-	16	75	40
Sherbet, 4-7/8" h	-	40	100	45
Soup bowl, rimmed, 9" d	-	95	135	85
Sugar, 3-1/4" h	-	24	-	22
Sugar, 4-1/4" h	-	32.50	125	-
Syrup pitcher, 20 oz, 5-3/4" h	-	250	-	2,000
Tumbler, 9 oz, 4" h	16	32	80	-
Tumbler, 9 oz, 5" h, ftd	-	30	115	20
Tumbler, 10 oz, 4-3/4" h, flat	-	35	95	-
Tumbler, 11" oz, 5" h, flat	-	30	90	60
Tumbler, 11 oz, 5-3/4" h, ftd	-	75	135	-
Tumbler, 15 oz, 5-1/4" h	-	80	145	-
Tumbler, 15 oz, 6-3/8" h, ftd	-	495	-	-

Item	Crystal	Green	Pink	Yellow
Vase, 5-3/4" h	-	375	-	-
Vase, 8" h	-	70	-	-
Vegetable, oval, 10" l	-	50	-	45
Wine, 3-1/2" h	-	1,200	950	-
Wine, 4" h	-	95	250	-

Cameo, crystal tumbler with platinum trim ***$16***.

CAPRI

Swatches

Azure Blue

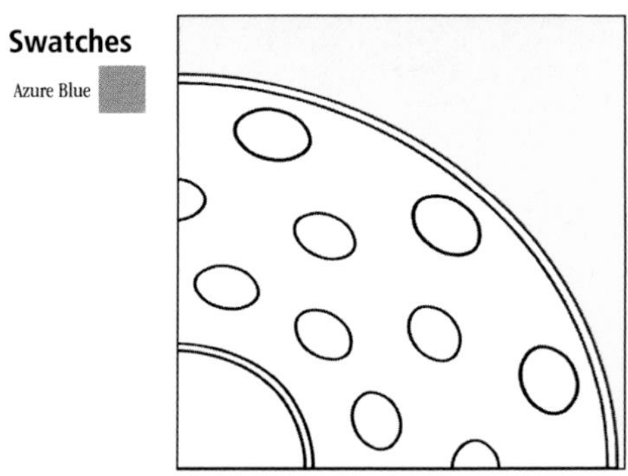

Manufactured by Hazel Ware, division of Continental Can, 1960s. Collectors are starting to divide these wares into several distinct patterns, based on the shape. All are the same pretty azure blue color and have the same market value. Original "Capri" paper labels are found on most of the styles.

Made in azure blue.

Item	Azure Blue
Ashtray, 3-1/2" sq, emb flower center	$15
Ashtray, 3-1/4" w, triangular or round	5
Ashtray, 5" d, round	7.50
Ashtray, 6-7/8" w, triangular	10
Bowl, 4-3/4" d, octagonal or swirled	7.50
Bowl, 4-7/8" d, round, Dots	7.50
Bowl, 5-3/4" w, sq	9.50

Item	Azure Blue
Bowl, 5-5/8", Colony Swirl	8.50
Bowl, 6" d, Dots, Colony Swirl	8
Bowl, 6" d, Tulip	12
Bowl, 7-3/4" l, oval	12
Bowl, 8-3/4" d, swirled	12
Bowl, 9-1/2" d	18
Candy jar, cov, ftd	30
Chip and dip set, metal rack	30
Creamer	12
Cup, octagonal	6.50
Iced tea tumbler, 5" h, 12 oz	10
Old fashioned tumbler, 3-5/8" h, Dots	7.50
Plate, 5-3/4" d, bread and butter	5
Plate, 7" d, salad	6.50
Plate, 8" w, sq	7.50
Plate, 9-3/4", dinner	10
Salad bowl, 5-3/8" d	7.50
Saucer, round, sq, or octagonal	1.50
Sherbet	7.50
Snack plate, fan shape	12
Snack plate, round	9.50
Sugar, cov	20
Tidbit, two bowl tiers, Colony Swirl	45
Tumbler, 2-3/4" h, Colony Swirl	7.50
Tumbler, 3" h, Dots	7.50
Tumbler, 3-1/16", Colony, Colony Swirl	8.50
Tumbler, 4-1/4" h, 9 oz	7.50
Vase, 8" h, Dots	20
Vase, 8-1/2" h, ruffled rim	30

Capri, azure blue candy dish with metal handle, 7-3/4" l ***$12***.

CHERRY BLOSSOM

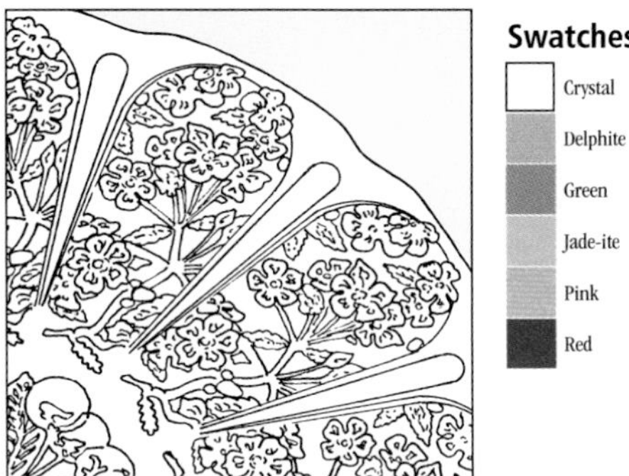

Swatches

- Crystal
- Delphite
- Green
- Jade-ite
- Pink
- Red

Manufactured by Jeannette Glass Company, Jeannette, Pa., from 1930 to 1939.

Made in Crystal, Delphite, green, jade-ite, pink, and red (production was very limited in crystal, jade-ite and red).

Reproductions: † Reproductions include: small berry bowl, 8-1/2" d bowl, covered butter dish, cake plate, cereal bowl, cup, pitcher, 6" and 9" plates, divided 13" platter, salt shaker, sandwich tray, saucer, and 3-3/4" and 4-1/2" h ftd tumblers. Reproductions have been made in cobalt blue, Delphite, green, pink, and red. A children's butter dish has also been made, which was never included in the original production.

Item	Delphite	Green	Pink
Berry bowl, 4-3/4" d †	$17.50	$25	$22.50
Berry bowl, 8-1/2" d †	55	50	65
Bowl, 9" d, two handles	27.50	95	48

Item	Delphite	Green	Pink
Butter dish, cov †	-	115	75
Cake plate, 10-1/4" d, 3 legs †	-	38	25
Cereal bowl, 5-3/4" d †	-	35	32
Coaster	-	20	15
Creamer	30	35	35
Cup †	28	25	28
Fruit bowl, 10-1/2" d	32	90	90
Juice tumbler, 1 oz, 3-1/2"	-	35	24
Mug, 7 oz	-	195	265
Pitcher, 36 oz, 6-3/4" h, 36 oz †	95	60	72
Pitcher, 36 oz, 8", PAT, ftd	-	65	60
Pitcher, 42 oz, 8", PAT, flat	-	65	60
Plate, 6" d, sherbet †	12.50	10	12
Plate, 7" d, salad	-	27.50	24
Plate, 9" d, dinner †	18	28	35
Plate, 9" d, grill	-	35	32.50
Plate, 10" d, grill	-	32.50	-
Platter, 11" l, oval	40	48	35
Platter, 13" d	-	72	100
Platter, 13" divided †	-	72	75
Salt and pepper shakers, pr, scallop base †	-	995	1,250
Sandwich tray, 10-1/2" d †	20	30	45
Saucer †	6	7.50	6
Sherbet	18	30	19.50
Soup, flat, 7-3/4" d	-	90	80
Sugar, cov	24	37.50	35
Tumbler, 3-3/4" h, AOP, ftd †	-	22	24
Tumbler, 5" h	20	70	72
Tumbler, 8 oz, 4-1/2" h, scalloped ftd base, AOP	-	40	35
Tumbler, 9 oz, 4-1/4" h	-	24	22

Item	Delphite	Green	Pink
Tumbler, 9 oz, 4-1/2" h †	20	30	32
Vegetable bowl, 9" l, oval	45	42	40

Children's

Item	Delphite	Pink
Creamer	$50	$50
Cup †	42	42
Plate, 6" d	15	15
Saucer	7.50	7.50
Sugar	50	50

*Cherry Blossom, delphite berry bowls, 4-3/4" d, each **$17.50**.*

CHERRYBERRY

Swatches

- Crystal
- Green
- Iridescent
- Pink

Manufactured by U.S. Glass Company, Pittsburgh, Pa., early 1930s. Made in crystal, green, iridescent, and pink.

Item	Crystal	Green	Irid.	Pink
Berry bowl, 4" d	$7	$8.75	$7	$8.75
Berry bowl, 7-1/2" d, deep	17.50	20	20	20
Bowl, 6-1/4" d, 2" deep	50	55	40	55
Butter dish, cov	150	175	150	175
Comport, 5-3/4"	17.50	25	17.50	25
Creamer, large, 4-5/8"	40	45	40	45
Creamer, small	15	20	15	20
Olive dish, 5" l, one handle	10	15	10	15
Pickle dish, 8-1/4" l, oval	10	15	10	15
Pitcher, 7-3/4" h	165	175	165	175
Plate, 6" d, sherbet	6.50	11	6.50	11
Plate, 7-1/2" d, salad	8.50	15	9	15

Item	Crystal	Green	Irid.	Pink
Salad bowl, 6-1/2" d, deep	17.50	22	17.50	22
Sherbet	10	12	12	14
Sugar, large, cov	45	75	45	75
Sugar, small, open	15	20	15	20
Tumbler, 9 oz, 3-5/8" h	20	35	20	35

*Cherryberry, crystal, berry bowl **$17.50**.*

CHINEX CLASSIC

Swatches

Chinex

Chinex Classic
Bouquet decal

Chinex, Classic
Castle decal

Manufactured by Macbeth-Evans Division of Corning Glass Works, from the late 1930s to early 1940s.

Made in Chinex (ivory) and Chinex with Classic Bouquet or Classic Castle decal.

Item	Chinex	Chinex Classic Bouquet decal	Chinex, Classic Castle decal
Bowl, 11" d	$20	$36	$48
Butter dish, cov	55	80	135
Cake plate, 11-1/2" d	10	15	25
Cereal bowl, 5- 3/4" d	6	8.50	15
Creamer	8.50	12	20
Cup	6	9.50	17.50
Plate, 6-1/4" d, sherbet	8	6.50	10
Plate, 9-3/4" d, dinner	16	10	18
Sandwich plate, 11-1/2" d	8	15	25

Item	Chinex	Chinex Classic Bouquet decal	Chinex, Classic Castle decal
Saucer	2	4	7
Sherbet, low, ftd	9.50	12	30
Soup bowl, 7-3/4" d	14	25	40
Sugar, open	7.50	12.50	20
Vegetable bowl, 7" d	15	25	35
Vegetable bowl, 9" d	15	25	35

Chinex Classic, plate with castle decal $18.

CHRISTMAS CANDY

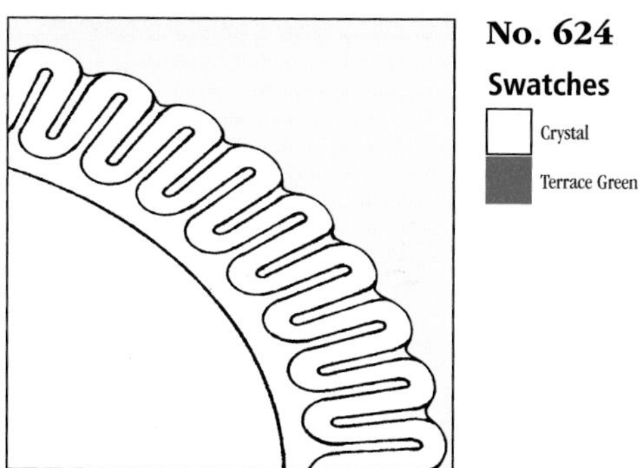

No. 624

Swatches

Crystal

Terrace Green

Manufactured by Indiana Glass Company, Dunkirk, Ind., 1950s. Made in crystal and Terrace Green (teal).

Item	Crystal	Terrace Green
Bowl, 5-3/4" d	$6.50	$-
Creamer	15	30
Cup	8	35
Mayonnaise, ladle, liner	24	-
Plate, 6" d, bread and butter	6	16
Plate, 8-1/4" d, luncheon	8	28
Plate, 9-5/8"d, dinner	12	36
Sandwich plate, 11-1/4" d	24	65
Saucer	5	15
Soup bowl, 7-3/8" d	12	75
Sugar	15	35

Item	Crystal	Terrace Green
Tidbit, two tiers	20	-
Vegetable bowl, 9-1/2" d	-	235

*Christmas Candy, crystal sugar **$15**, and creamer **$15**.*

CIRCLE

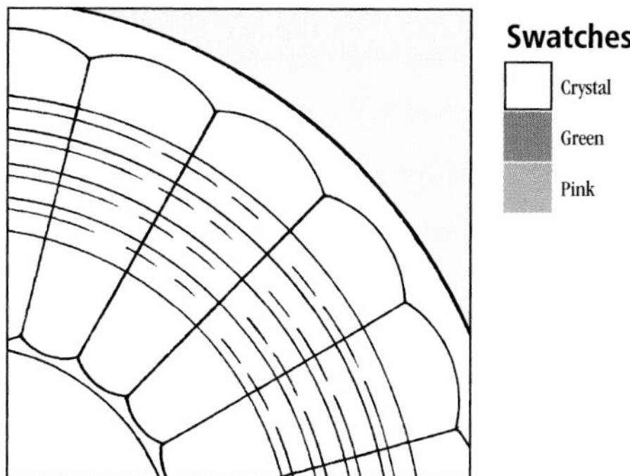

Swatches

Crystal

Green

Pink

Manufactured by Hocking Glass Company, Lancaster, Ohio, in the 1930s.

Made in crystal, green, and pink. Crystal is listed in the original catalogs, but few pieces have surfaced to date. A 3-1/8" d sherbet is known and valued at $4.

Item	Green	Pink
Bowl, 4-1/2" d	**$15**	**$15**
Bowl, 5-1/2" d, flared	**17.50**	**17.50**
Bowl, 8" d	**16**	**16**
Bowl, 9-3/8" d	**18.50**	**18.50**
Creamer, ftd	**9**	**16**
Cup	**6**	**7.50**
Goblet, 8 oz, 5-3/4" h	**16.50**	**15**
Iced tea tumbler, 10 oz	**17.50**	**17.50**
Juice tumbler, 4 oz	**9.50**	**9**

Item	Green	Pink
Pitcher, 60 oz	35	35
Pitcher, 80 oz	30	32
Plate, 6" d, sherbet	3	3
Plate, 8-1/4" d, luncheon	11	11
Plate, 9-1/2" d, dinner	12	12
Sandwich plate, 10" d	15	17.50
Saucer, 6" d	2.50	2.50
Sherbet, 3-1/8"	5	5
Sherbet, 4-3/4"	12	12
Sugar, ftd	12	16
Tumbler, 8 oz	10	10
Tumbler, 15 oz, flat	17.50	17.50
Wine, 4-1/2" h	15	15

Circle, green cup ***$6.***

CLOVERLEAF

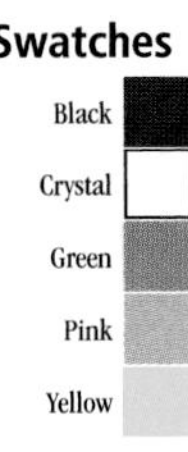

Manufactured by Hazel Atlas Glass Company, Clarksburg, W.V., and Zanesville, Ohio, from 1930 to 1936.

Made in black, crystal, green, pink, and yellow. Collector interest in crystal is minimal; prices would be about 50 percent of those listed for green.

Item	Black	Green	Pink	Yellow
Ashtray, match holder 4" d	$65	$-	$-	$-
Ashtray, match holder, 5-3/4" d	90	-	-	-
Bowl, 8" d	-	95	-	-
Candy dish, cov	-	65	-	130
Cereal bowl, 5" d	-	50	-	55
Creamer, 3-5/8" h, ftd	25	12	-	24
Cup	18.50	9	8	12
Dessert bowl, 4" d	-	30	30	35
Plate, 6" d, sherbet	40	6.50	-	10

Item	Black	Green	Pink	Yellow
Plate, 8" d, luncheon	16	9	12	18
Salad bowl, 7" d	-	60	-	65
Salt and pepper shakers, pr	100	40	-	140
Saucer	7	6	6	5
Sherbet, 3" h, ftd	22	15	10	12
Sugar, 3-5/8" h, ftd	25	12	-	24
Tumbler, 9 oz, 4" h, flat	-	65	26.50	35
Tumbler, 10 oz, 3-3/4" h, flat	-	50	30	-
Tumbler, 10 oz, 5-3/4" h, ftd	-	30	-	42

*Cloverleaf, green saucer **$7**, pink plate **$12**, and cup **$8**.*

Knife and Fork

Swatches

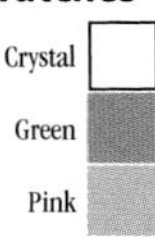

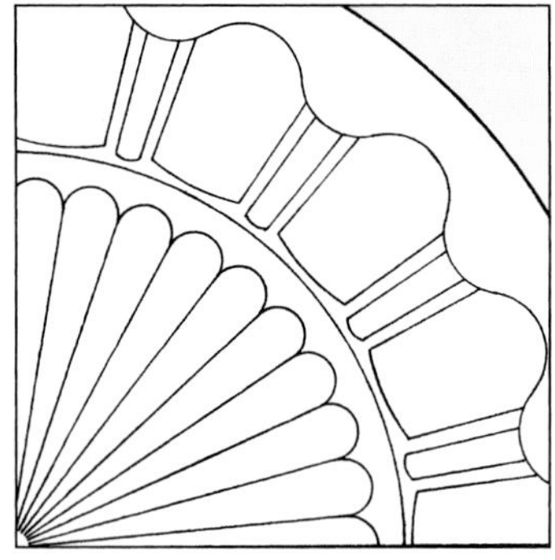

Manufactured by Hocking Glass Company, Lancaster, Ohio, from 1934 to 1938.

Made in crystal, green, and pink.

Item	Crystal	Green	Pink
Berry bowl, 3-3/4" d	$-	$-	$60
Berry bowl, 4-1/2"	12	22	18
Berry bowl, 9" d	24	30	35
Butter dish, cov	40	60	700
Cereal bowl, 5-1/2" d	32	85	60
Claret, 4 oz, 5-1/4" h	20	25	-
Cocktail, 3 oz, 4" h	15	25	-
Cordial, 1 oz, 3-3/4" h	20	30	-
Cream soup bowl, 4-1/2" d	70	85	72
Creamer, 8 oz, 5" h	25	25	65
Cup	8	15	12

Item	Crystal	Green	Pink
Goblet, 8-1/2 oz, 5-3/4" h	25	35	40
Ice tea tumbler, 12 oz	28	55	45
Juice tumbler, 5 oz, 3" h	17.50	27.50	22
Lemonade tumbler, 15 oz	47.50	75	65
Milk pitcher, 8 oz, 5" h	25	25	65
Mug, 12 oz, 5-1/2" h	-	825	500
Pitcher, 54 oz, 7" h, ice lip	40	45	48
Pitcher, 54 oz, 7" h, no lip	40	45	48
Pitcher, 68 oz, 7-3/4" h, ice lip	35	72	65
Pitcher, 68 oz, 7-3/4" h, no lip	45	72	65
Plate, 6" d, sherbet	4.50	8	7
Plate, 8-1/2" d, luncheon	6	8	10
Plate, 10" d, dinner	35	65	55

*Colonial, green creamer **$25**, and sugar **$12**.*

Item	Crystal	Green	Pink
Plate, 10" d, grill	17.50	27	27.50
Plate, 12" d, oval	17.50	25	30
Platter, 12" l, oval	17.50	25	35
Salt and pepper shakers, pr	65	160	150
Saucer	4.50	7.50	6.50
Sherbet, 3" h	-	-	24
Sherbet, 3-3/8" h	10	15	16
Soup bowl, 7" d	30	85	85
Spoon holder or celery vase	105	130	135
Sugar, cov	90	48	50
Sugar, 5", open	10	12	15
Tumbler, 3 oz, 3-1/4" h, ftd	11	15	14
Tumbler, 5 oz, 4" h, ftd	15	35	30

*Colonial, crystal wine **$17**, and cocktail **$15**.*

Item	Crystal	Green	Pink
Tumbler, 9 oz, 4" h	15	20	25
Tumbler, 10 oz, 5-1/4" h, ftd	30	46.50	50
Tumbler, 11 oz, 5-1/8" h	25	37	40
Vegetable bowl, 10" l, oval	18	25	30
Whiskey, 2-1/2" h, 1-1/2 oz	9	20	15
Wine, 4-1/2" h, 2-1/2 oz	16	28	11

Colonial, green saucer ***$7.50.***

COLONIAL BLOCK

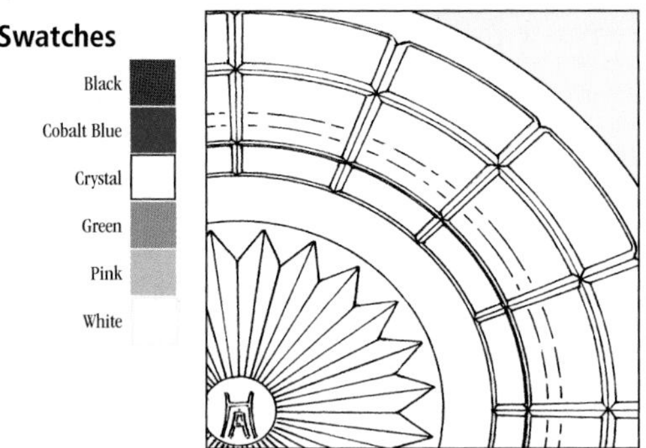

Manufactured by Hazel Atlas Glass Company, Clarksburg, W.V., and Zanesville, Ohio, early 1930s.

Made in black, cobalt blue (rare), crystal, green, pink, and white (1950s).

Item	Black	Crystal	Green	Pink	White
Bowl, 4" d	$-	$6	$10	$10	$-
Bowl, 7" d	-	16	20	20	-
Butter dish, cov	-	35	50	45	-
Butter tub, cov	-	35	40	40	-
Candy jar, cov	-	30	40	40	-
Compote, 4" h, 4-3/4" w	-	12	-	-	-
Creamer	-	15	16	15	7.50
Goblet, 5-3/4" h	-	9	12	15	-
Pitcher, 20 oz, 5-3/4" h	-	40	50	50	-
Powder jar, cov	30	20	24	24	-

Item	Black	Crystal	Green	Pink	White
Sherbet	-	6	10	9.50	-
Sugar, cov	-	20	25	25	20
Sugar, open	-	6	8	8	10

*Colonial Block, green covered butter dish **$50**.*

COLONIAL FLUTED

Rope

Swatches

Crystal

Green

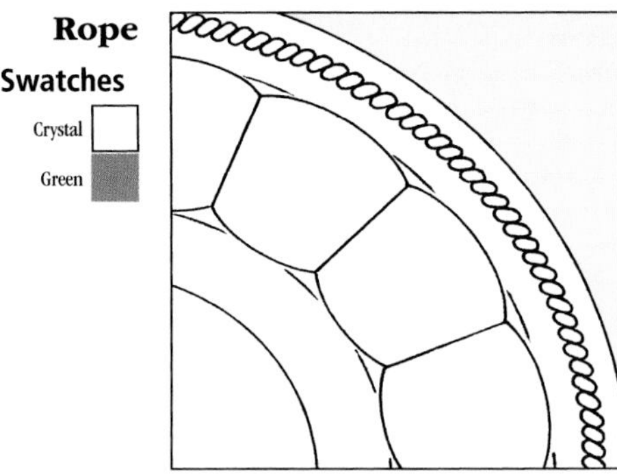

Manufactured by Federal Glass Company, Columbus, Ohio, from 1928 to 1933.

Made in crystal and green.

Item	Crystal	Green
Berry bowl, 4" d	**$11**	**$12**
Berry bowl, 7-1/2" d	**16**	**18**
Cereal bowl, 6" d	**15**	**18**
Creamer, ftd	**12**	**14**
Cup	**5**	**7.50**
Plate, 6" d, sherbet	**2.50**	**4**
Plate, 8" d, luncheon	**5**	**10**
Salad bowl, 6-1/2" d, 2-1/2" deep	**22**	**35**
Saucer	**2.50**	**4**
Sugar, cov	**21**	**25**
Sugar, open	**8**	**10**

*Colonial Fluted, green sugar **$10** and creamer **$14**.*

COLUMBIA

Swatches

Crystal

Pink

Flashed Colors

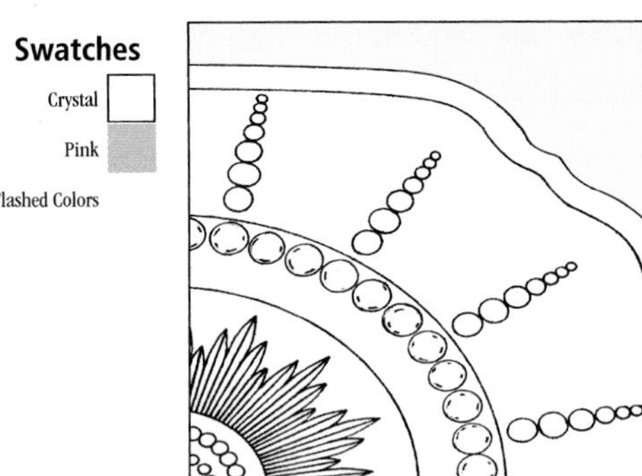

Manufactured by Federal Glass Company, Columbus, Ohio, from 1938 to 1942.

Made in crystal and pink. Several flashed (stained) colors are found, and some decaled pieces are known.

Reproductions: † The 2-7/8" h juice tumbler has been reproduced. Look for the "France" on the base to clearly identify the reproductions.

Item	Crystal	Flashed	Pink
Bowl, 10-1/2" d, ruffled edge	**$24**	**$20**	**$-**
Butter dish, cov	**20**	**25**	**-**
Cereal bowl, 5" d	**18**	**-**	**-**
Chop plate, 11" d	**17**	**12**	**-**
Crescent shaped salad	**27**	**-**	**-**
Cup	**9.50**	**10**	**25**

Item	Crystal	Flashed	Pink
Juice tumbler, 4 oz, 2-3/4" h †	30	-	-
Plate, 6" d, bread & butter	5	4	14
Plate, 9-1/2" d, luncheon	22	12	32
Salad bowl, 8-1/2" d	20	-	-
Saucer	4.50	4	10
Snack tray, cup	35	-	-
Soup bowl, 8" d, low	25	-	-
Tumbler, 9 oz	42.50	-	-

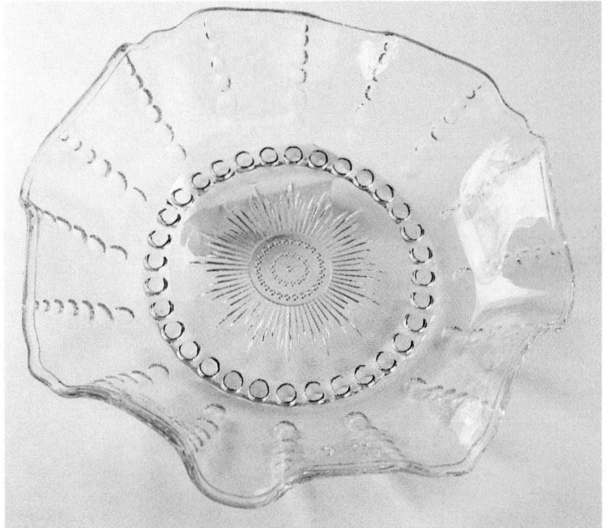

*Columbia, crystal ruffled bowl **$24.***

CORONATION

Banded Fine Rib, Saxon

Swatches

Crystal

Green

Pink

Royal Ruby

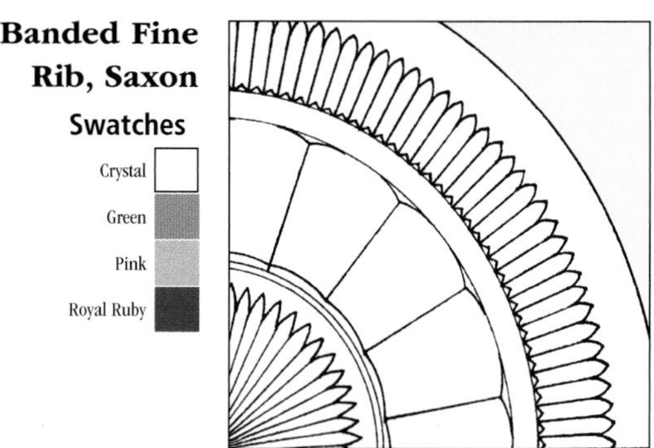

Manufactured by Hocking Glass Company, Lancaster, Ohio, from 1936 to 1940.

Made in crystal, green, pink, and Royal Ruby.

Item	Crystal	Green	Pink	Royal Ruby
Berry bowl, 4-1/4" d	$-	$50	$8.50	$6.50
Berry bowl, 8" d, handle	-	-	18	20
Berry bowl, 8" d	-	195	-	-
Cup	5	-	6	7.50
Nappy bowl, 6-1/2" d	15	-	7.50	15
Pitcher, 68 oz, 7-3/4" h	-	-	500	-
Plate, 6" d, sherbet	2	-	4.50	-
Plate, 8-1/2" d, luncheon	5	60	12	8.50

Item	Crystal	Green	Pink	Royal Ruby
Saucer	2	-	4	-
Sherbet	-	85	7	-
Tumbler, 10 oz, 5" h, ftd	-	195	35	-

*Coronation, ruby handled berry bowl **$20**.*

CRACKED ICE

Swatches

Green

Pink

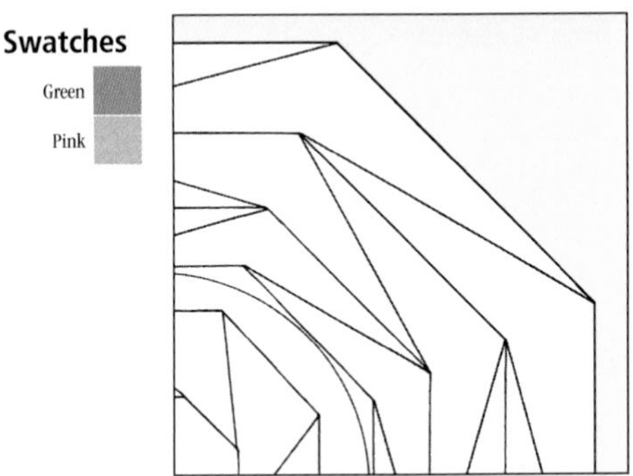

Manufactured by Indiana Glass, Dunkirk, Ind., in the 1930s.

Made in pink and green. Often mistaken for Tea Room, look for the additional diagonal line, giving it a more Art Deco style.

Item	Green	Pink
Creamer	$30	$35
Plate, 6-1/2" d	15	18
Sherbet	12	15
Sugar, cov	30	35
Tumbler	30	32.50

*Cracked Ice, pink creamer **$35**, and covered sugar **$35**.*

CREMAX

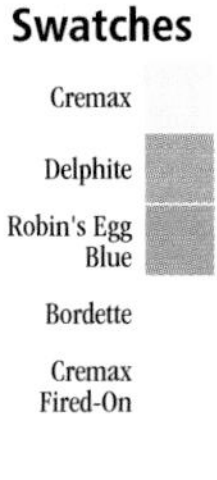

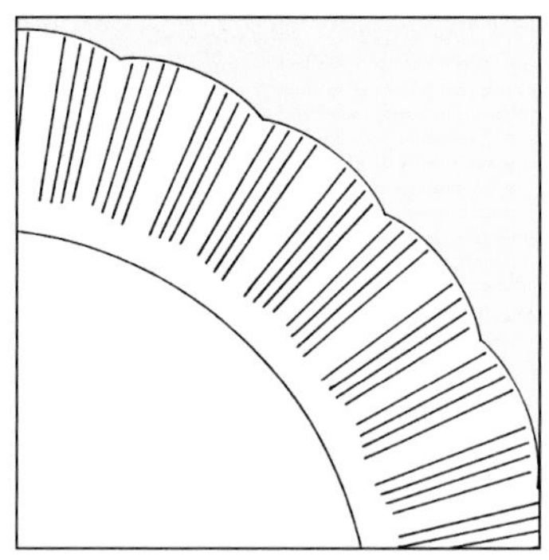

Manufactured by Macbeth-Evans Division of Corning Glass Works, late 1930s to early 1940s.

Made in Cremax, Cremax with fired-on colors, Delphite, and Robin's Egg Blue. One set is known as Bordette.

Item	Bordette	Cremax	Cremax Fired-On	Delphite	Robin's Egg Blue
Cereal bowl, 5-3/4" d	$5	$6	$9	$10	$10
Creamer	6	6.50	6	11	11
Cup	5	6	8	7	7
Demitasse cup	10	16	18	26	26
Demitasse saucer	6	7	8	12	20
Egg cup, 2-1/4" h	12	-	-	-	-
Plate, 6-1/4" d, bread and butter	4	4.50	5.50	7	7

Item	Bordette	Cremax	Cremax Fired-On	Delphite	Robin's Egg Blue
Plate, 9-3/4" d, dinner	14	7	11	12	12
Sandwich plate, 11-1/2" d	9.50	10	15	17	17
Saucer	3.50	4	4	6	6
Sugar, open	6	6.50	6	11	11
Vegetable bowl, 9" d	10	11	10	20	20

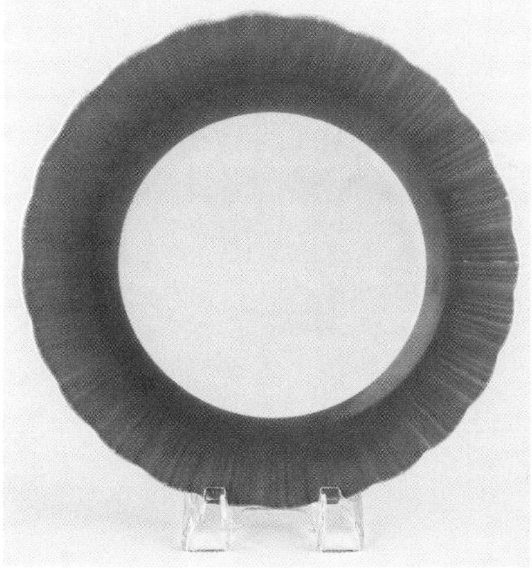

*Cremax, dinner plate, Bordette, blue edge **$11**.*

CUBE

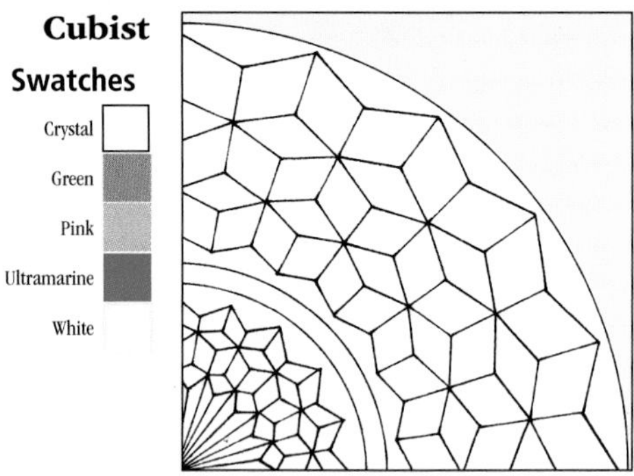

Manufactured by Jeannette Glass Company, Jeannette, Pa., from 1929 to 1933.

Made in amber, crystal, green, pink, ultramarine, and white. Production in amber and white is limited to the 2-3/8" h sugar bowl, and is valued at $3.

Item	Crystal	Green	Pink	Ultramarine
Bowl, 4-1/2" d, deep	$-	$7	$9.50	$35
Butter dish, cov	-	60	65	-
Candy jar, cov, 6-1/2" h	-	35	30	-
Coaster, 3-1/4" d	-	10	10	-
Creamer, 2-5/8" h	5	10	10	70
Creamer, 3-9/16" h	-	9	9	-
Cup	-	7	8	-
Dessert bowl, 4-1/2" d, pointed rim	4	8.50	9.50	-

Item	Crystal	Green	Pink	Ultramarine
Pitcher, 8-3/4" h, 45 oz	-	235	215	-
Plate, 8" d, luncheon	-	8.50	7.50	-
Powder Jar, cov, 3 legs	-	30	35	-
Salt and Pepper Shakers, pr	-	35	36	-
Saucer	1.50	3	3.50	-
Sherbet, ftd	-	8.50	12	-
Sugar, cov, 2-3/8" h	4	22	6	-
Sugar, cov, 3" h	-	25	25	-
Sugar, open, 3"	5	8	7	-
Tumbler, 9 oz, 4" h	-	70	65	-

*Cube, pink luncheon plate **$7.50**.*

CUPID

Swatches

Black

Canary Yellow

Crystal

Green

Light Blue

Peacock Blue

Pink

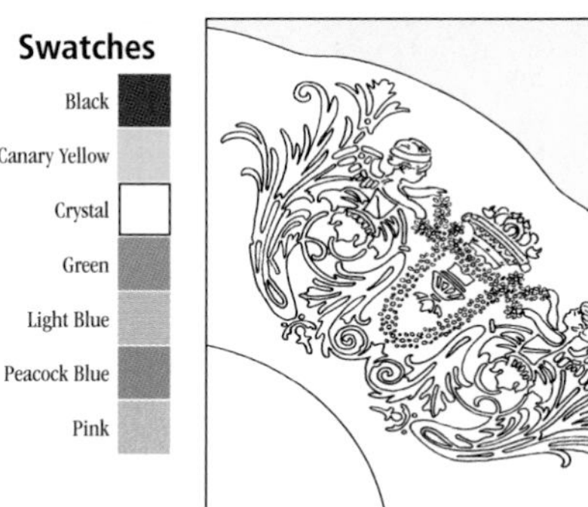

Manufactured by Paden City Glass Company, Paden City, W.V., 1930s.

Made in amber, black, canary yellow, crystal, green, light blue, peacock blue, and pink. Prices for colors like amber, black, canary yellow, and light blue are still being established as more pieces of this pattern arrive on the secondary market. This expensive pattern is one to keep your eyes open for while searching at flea markets and garage sales.

Item	Crystal	Green	Peacock Blue	Pink
Bowl, 8-1/2" l, oval, ftd	$-	$300	$-	$300
Bowl, 9-1/4" d, center handle	-	275	-	275
Bowl, 10-1/2" d, rolled edge	-	250	-	250
Cake plate, 11-3/4" h	-	200	-	200

Item	Crystal	Green	Peacock Blue	Pink
Cake stand, 2" h, ftd	-	235	-	235
Candlesticks, pr, 5" h	-	245	-	245
Candy, cov, 3 part	-	385	-	385
Candy, cov, 5-1/4" h	-	295	-	295
Champagne, 5-7/8" h	35	-	-	-
Cocktail, 5-1/8" h	25	-	-	-
Comport, 4-1/2" h, ftd	-	175	-	175
Comport, 6-1/4" h, ftd	-	185	225	290
Console bowl, 11" d	-	250	-	250
Creamer, 4-1/2" h, ftd	45	150	-	150
Creamer, 5" h, ftd	-	150	-	150
Fruit bowl, 9-1/4" d, ftd	-	360	-	360
Fruit bowl, 10-1/4" d	-	245	-	275
Ice bucket, 6" h	-	325	-	325
Ice tub, 4-3/4" h	-	325	-	325
Mayonnaise, 6" d, spoon, 8" d plate	-	275	295	275
Plate, 10-1/2" d	-	150	175	150
Samovar	-	990	-	990
Sugar, 4-1/4" h, ftd	-	150	-	150
Sugar, 5" h, ftd	-	150	-	150
Tray, 10-3/4" d, center handle	-	200	-	200
Tray, 10-7/8" l, oval, ftd	-	250	-	250
Vase, 8-1/4" h, elliptical	-	650	-	650
Vase, 10" h	-	315	-	315
Wine, 5-1/8" h	12.50	-	-	-

Cupid, pink low pedestal-foot comport, 6-1/4" h, ***$290.***

DAISY

No. 620

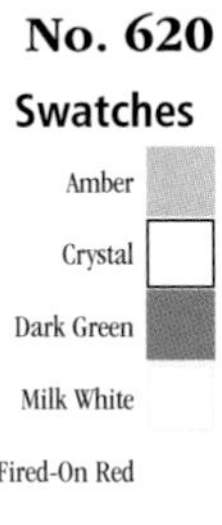

Manufactured by Indiana Glass Company, Dunkirk, Ind., from late 1930s to 1980s.

Made in amber (1940s), crystal (1933-40), dark green (1960s-80s), fired-on red (late 1930s), and milk glass (1960s-80s).

Item	Amber or Fired On Red	Crystal	Dark Green or Milk White
Berry bowl, 4-1/2" d	$11	$6	$6
Berry bowl, 7-3/8" d, deep	17.50	8.50	9.50
Berry bowl, 9-3/8" d, deep	35	14	14
Cake plate, 11-1/2" d	16.50	14	14
Cereal bowl, 6" d	25	10	10
Cream soup bowl, 4-1/2" d	13.50	7.50	7.50
Creamer, ftd	10	8	8
Cup	8	6	6
Plate, 6" d, sherbet	5	4.50	5

Item	Amber or Fired On Red	Crystal	Dark Green or Milk White
Plate, 7-3/8" d, salad	8.50	8.50	9
Plate, 8-3/8" d, luncheon	10	10	12
Plate, 9-3/8" d, dinner	12	12	15
Plate, 10-3/8" d, grill	15	15	18
Platter, 10-3/4" d	18	11	11
Relish dish, 8-3/8" d, 3 part	24	12	12
Sandwich plate, 11-1/2" d	17.50	14	14

Daisy, amber creamer ***$10.***

Item	Amber or Fired On Red	Crystal	Dark Green or Milk White
Saucer	2	6	2
Sherbet, ftd	9	5	5
Sugar, ftd	10	8	8
Tumbler, 9 oz, ftd	16	10	10
Tumbler, 12 oz, ftd	40	15	15
Vegetable bowl, 10" l, oval	25	18	18

*Daisy, green luncheon plate **$12**.*

*Daisy, crystal luncheon plate **$10.***

*Daisy, amber luncheon plate **$10.***

DELLA ROBBIA

#1058

Swatches

Crystal

Manufactured by Westmoreland Glass Company, Grapeville, Pa., from late 1920s to 1940s.

Made in crystal, with applied luster colors and milk glass. Examples of milk white prices are: hand-painted decorated candy jar, $45; creamer, $18; goblet, $20; tumbler, $22.50; wine, $18.

Item	Crystal
Basket, 9"	$210
Basket, 12"	300
Bowl, 8" d, bell, handle	48
Bowl, 8" d, heart shape, handle	95
Bowl, 12" d, ftd	12
Bowl, 13" d, rolled edge	115
Bowl, 14" d, oval, flange	155
Bowl, 15" d, bell	175
Cake salver, 14" d, ftd	120

Item	Crystal
Candlesticks, pr, 4" h	65
Candlesticks, pr, 4" h, two-lite	160
Candy jar, cov, scalloped edge	85
Champagne, 6 oz.	25
Chocolate candy, round, flat	75
Cocktail, 3-1/4 oz.	15
Comport, 12" d, ftd, bell	115
Comport, 13" d, flanged	125
Creamer, ftd	18
Cup, coffee	18.50
Finger bowl, 5" d	30
Ginger ale tumbler, 5 oz	25
Goblet, 8 oz., 6" h	28
Iced tea tumbler 11 oz., ftd	35
Iced tea tumbler 12 oz., 5-3/16" h, straight	40
Iced tea tumbler 12 oz., bell	32
Iced tea tumbler, 12 oz., bell, ftd	32
Mint comport, 6-1/2" d, 3-5/8" h, ftd	45
Nappy, 7-1/2" d	42
Nappy, 8" d, bell	45
Nappy, 4-1/2" d	30
Nappy, 6" d, bell	35
Nappy, 6-1/2" d, one handle	32
Nappy, 9" d	60
Pitcher, 32 oz.	200
Plate, 6" d, finger bowl liner	12
Plate, 6-1/8" d, bread and butter	14
Plate, 7-1/4" d, salad	22
Plate, 9" d, luncheon	35
Plate, 10-1/2" d, dinner	95

Item	Crystal
Plate, 18" d	195
Platter, 14" l, oval	195
Punch bowl, 14" d	225
Punch bowl liner, 18" d plate, upturned edge	200
Punch cup	15
Salt and pepper shakers, pr	55
Saucer	10
Sherbet, 5 oz, low foot	22
Sherbet, 5 oz, 4-3/4" h, ftd	24
Sugar, ftd	27.50
Sweetmeat comport, 8" d	115
Torte plate, 14" d	125
Tumbler 8 oz., ftd	30

*Della Robbia, crystal salad plate **$22**.*

Item	Crystal
Tumbler, 8 oz, water	32
Wine, 3 oz	25

*Della Robbia, luster-decorated compote **$145**.*

DEWDROP

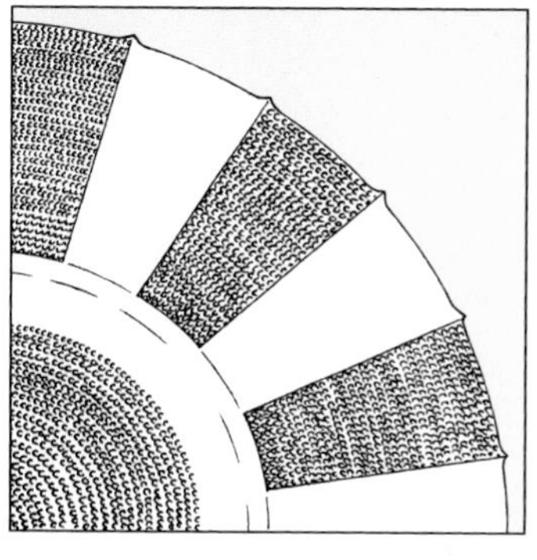

Swatches

Crystal

Manufactured by Jeannette Glass Company, Jeannette, Pa., from 1953 to 1956.

Made in crystal.

Item	Crystal
Bowl, 4-3/4" d	$9
Bowl, 8-1/2" d	22
Bowl, 10-3/8" d	24
Butter, cov	32
Candy dish, cov, 7" d	30
Casserole, cov	27.50
Creamer	8.50
Iced tea tumbler, 15 oz	17.50
Lazy Susan, 13" d tray	32
Pitcher, 1/2 gallon, ftd	48
Plate, 11-1/2" d	20

Item	Crystal
Punch cup	4
Punch bowl set, bowl, 12 cups	75
Snack cup	4
Snack plate, indent for cup	5
Relish, leaf-shape, handle	9
Sugar, cov	14
Tray, 10" d	22
Tumbler, 9 oz	15

*Dewdrop, crystal sugar **$8.50**, and creamer **$8.50**.*

*Dewdrop, crystal tumbler **$15**, and iridescent pitcher **$48**.*

DIAMOND QUILTED

Flat Diamond

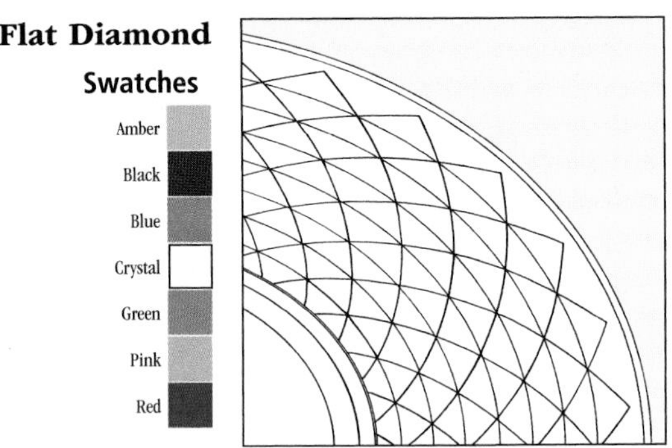

Manufactured by Imperial Glass Company, Bellaire, Ohio, from late 1920 to early 1930s.

Made in amber, black, blue, crystal, green, pink, and red. Amber and red prices would be valued slightly higher than black.

Item	Black	Blue	Crystal
Bowl, 5-1/2" d, one handle	$20	$-	$-
Bowl, 7" d, crimped edge	22	-	-
Cake salver, 10" d, tall	-	-	-
Candlesticks, pr	60	-	50
Candy jar, cov, ftd	-	-	25
Cereal bowl, 5" d	15	-	8
Champagne, 9 oz, 6" h	-	-	-
Compote, 6" h, 7-1/4" w	-	-	-
Compote, cov, 11-1/2" d	-	-	-
Console bowl, 10-1/2" d, rolled edge	65	60	15

Item	Black	Blue	Crystal
Cordial, 1 oz	-	-	-
Cream soup bowl, 4-3/4" d	22	20	20
Creamer	18.50	20	15
Cup	18	18.50	7
Ice bucket	90	90	-
Iced tea tumbler, 12 oz	-	-	-
Mayonnaise set, comport, plate, ladle	60	65	25
Pitcher, 64 oz	-	-	-
Plate, 6" d, sherbet	10	8.50	7.50
Plate, 7" d, salad	10	10	8
Plate, 8" d, luncheon	12	12	9
Punch bowl and stand	-	-	-
Sandwich plate, 14" d	-	-	-
Sandwich server, center handle	50	50	20
Saucer	5	5	2
Sherbet	16	16	14
Sugar	20	25	12
Tumbler, 6 oz, ftd	-	-	-
Tumbler, 9 oz	-	-	-
Tumbler, 9 oz, ftd	-	-	-
Tumbler, 12 oz, ftd	-	-	-
Vase, fan	80	75	-
Whiskey, 1-1/2 oz	-	-	-
Wine, 2 oz	-	-	-
Wine, 3 oz	-	-	-

Additional Colors

Item	Green	Pink
Bowl, 5-1/2" d, one handle	$15	$18
Bowl, 7" d, crimped edge	18	20
Cake salver, 10" d, tall	60	65
Candlesticks, pr	32	28
Candy jar, cov, ftd	65	65
Cerealbowl, 5" d	9	8.50
Champagne, 9 oz, 6" h	12	-
Compote, 6" h, 7-1/4" w	45	48
Compote, cov, 11-1/2" d	80	75

*Diamond Quilted, pink sugar **$13.50**, and creamer **$12**.*

Item	Green	Pink
Console bowl, 10-1/2" d, rolled edge	20	24
Cordial, 1 oz	12	15
Cream soup bowl, 4-3/4" d	12	14
Creamer	12	12
Cup	10	12
Ice bucket	50	50
Iced tea tumbler, 12 oz	10	10
Mayonnaise set, comport, plate, ladle	37.50	40
Pitcher, 64 oz	50	55
Plate, 6" d, sherbet	7	7.50
Plate, 7" d, salad	8.50	8.50
Plate, 8" d, luncheon	6.50	8.50
Punch bowl and stand	450	450
Sandwich plate, 14" d	15	15
Sandwich server, center handle	25	25
Saucer	4	4
Sherbet	12	10
Sugar	15	13.50
Tumbler, 6 oz, ftd	9	10
Tumbler, 9 oz	14	16
Tumbler, 9 oz, ftd	14	16
Tumbler, 12 oz, ftd	15	15
Vase, fan	50	50
Whiskey, 1-1/2 oz	10	12
Wine, 2 oz	12.50	12.50
Wine, 3 oz	15	15

DIANA

Swatches

Amber

Crystal

Pink

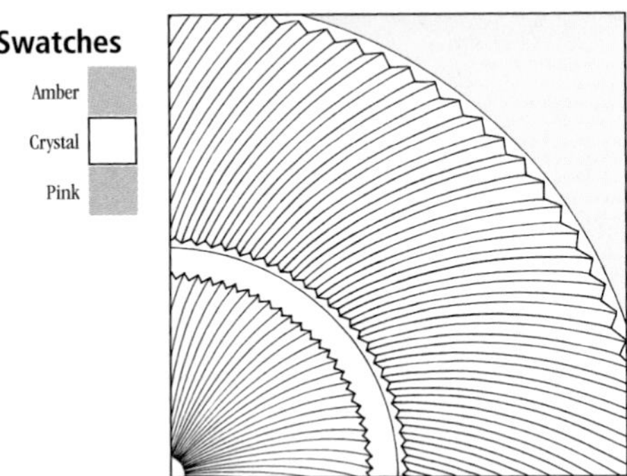

Manufactured by Federal Glass Company, Columbus, Ohio, from 1937 to 1941.

Made in amber, crystal, and pink.

Reproductions: † A 13-1/8" d scalloped pink bowl has been made, which was not original to the pattern.

Item	Amber	Crystal	Pink
Ashtray, 3-1/2" d	$-	$4	$5
Bowl, 12" d, scalloped edge	20	10	32
Candy jar, cov, round	40	18.50	48
Cereal bowl, 5" d	15	6.50	13
Coaster, 3-1/2" d	12	4	7
Console/fruit bowl, 11" d	10	20	44
Cream soup bowl, 5-1/2" d	18	14	24
Creamer, oval	9	4	12.50
Cup	7	4	19

Item	Amber	Crystal	Pink
Junior set, six cups and saucers, rack	-	125	300
Plate, 6" d, bread and butter	3.50	3	5.50
Plate, 9-1/2" d, dinner	9	7	18.50
Platter, 12" l, oval	15	12	28
Salad bowl, 9" d	18	15	20
Salt and pepper shakers, pr	100	30	75
Sandwich plate, 11-3/4" d	10	9.50	28
Saucer	2.25	2	6
Sherbet	10	7	12
Sugar, open, oval	10	10	16
Tumbler, 9 oz, 4-1/8" h	27.50	18	45

*Diana, pink sherbet **$12**.*

*Diana, crystal tumbler **$18.***

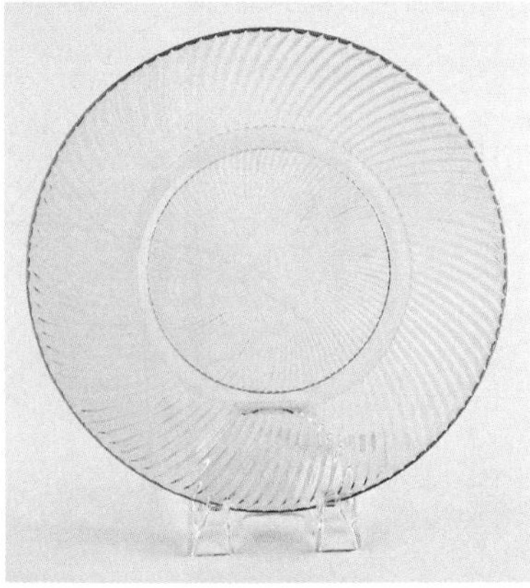

*Diana, pink plate **$18.50.***

DOGWOOD

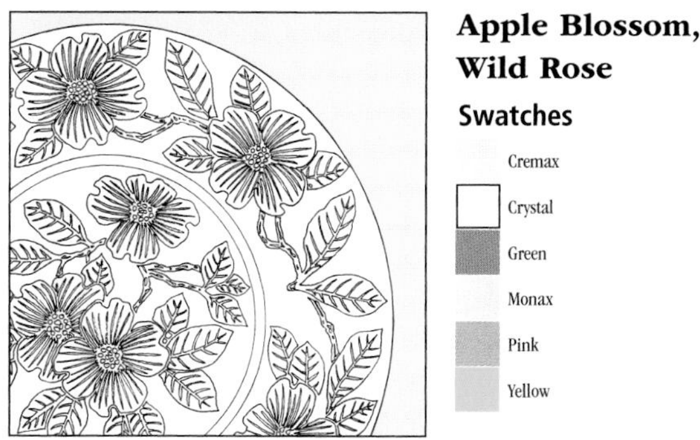

Apple Blossom, Wild Rose

Swatches

Cremax

Crystal

Green

Monax

Pink

Yellow

Manufactured by Macbeth-Evans Company, Charleroi, Pa., from 1929 to 1932.

Made in Cremax, crystal, green, Monax, pink and yellow. Yellow is rare; a cereal bowl is known and valued at $95. Crystal items are valued at 50 percent less than green.

Item	Cremax or Monax	Green	Pink
Berry bowl, 8-1/2" d	$40	$100	$65
Cake plate, 11" d, heavy solid foot	-	-	650
Cake plate, 13" d, heavy solid foot	185	135	165
Cereal bowl, 5-1/2" d	12	35	40
Coaster, 3-1/4" d	-	-	500
Creamer, 2-1/2" h, thin	-	48	30
Creamer, 3-1/4" h, thick	-	-	25
Cup, thin	-	32	24

Item	Cremax or Monax	Green	Pink
Cup, thick	36	40	25
Fruit bowl, 10-1/4" d	100	250	600
Pitcher, 8" h, 80 oz, (American Sweetheart style)	-	-	1,350
Pitcher, 8" h, 80 oz, decorated	-	550	265
Plate, 6" d, bread and butter	25	10	9.50
Plate, 8" d, luncheon	-	12	12
Plate, 9-1/4" d, dinner	-	-	42
Plates, 10-1/2" d, grill, AOP or border design only	-	22	55
Platter, 12" d, oval	-	-	735
Salver, 12" d	185	-	40
Saucer	20	10	8.50
Sherbet, low, ftd	-	95	40
Sugar, 2-1/2" h, thin	-	50	22.50
Sugar, 3-1/4" h, thick, ftd	-	-	25
Tidbit, 2 tier	-	-	90
Tumbler, 10 oz, 4" h, decorated	-	100	55
Tumbler, 11 oz, 4-3/4" h, decorated	-	95	75
Tumbler, 12 oz, 5" h, decorated	-	125	75
Tumbler, molded band	-	-	25

*Dogwood, pink sugar **$25**, creamer **$25**, and luncheon plate **$12**.*

DORIC

Swatches

Delphite

Green

Pink

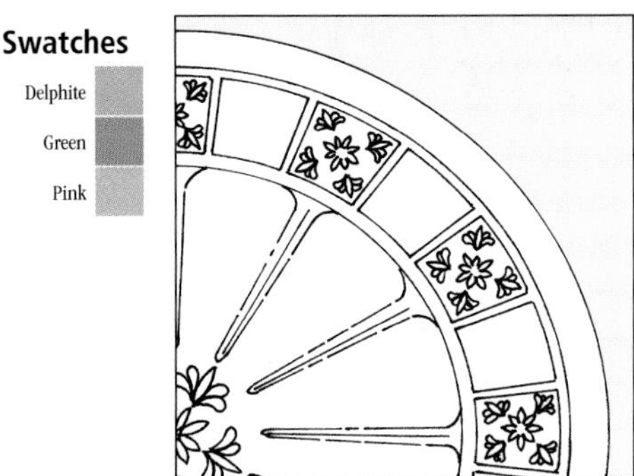

Manufactured by Jeannette Glass Company, Jeannette, Pa., from 1935 to 1938.

Made in Delphite, green, pink, and yellow. Yellow is rare.

Item	Delphite	Green	Pink
Berry bowl, 4-1/2" d	$50	$12	$12
Berry bowl, 8-1/4" d	150	32	17
Bowl, 9" d, two handles	-	45	45
Butter dish, cov	-	90	75
Cake plate, 10" d, three legs	-	30	30
Cereal bowl, 5-1/2" d	-	65	90
Coaster, 3" d	-	28	20
Cream soup, 5" d, two handles	-	385	-
Creamer, 4" h	-	17	14
Cup	-	10	10
Pitcher, 36 oz, 6" h, flat	1,200	50	45

Item	Delphite	Green	Pink
Plate, 6" d, sherbet	-	7.50	7.50
Plate, 9" d, dinner	-	24	12
Plate, 9" d, grill	-	20	25
Platter, 12" l, oval	-	32	35
Relish tray, 4" x 8"	-	20	17.50
Salt and pepper shakers, pr	-	40	45
Saucer	-	7	7
Sherbet, footed	12	17.50	15
Sugar, cov	-	35	32
Tumbler, 9 oz, 4-1/2" h, flat	-	100	75
Tumbler, 12 oz, 5" h, ftd.	-	125	85
Vegetable bowl, 9" l, oval	-	45	40

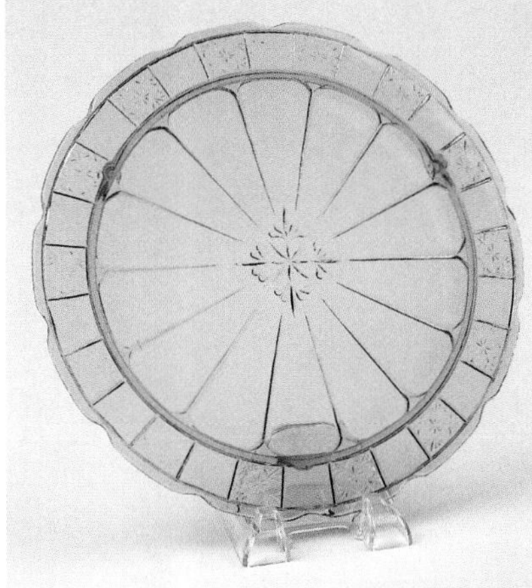

*Doric, green cake plate **$30**.*

DORIC & PANSY

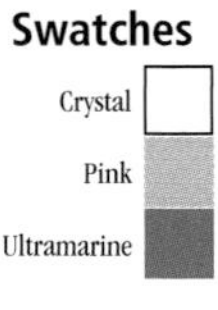

Manufactured by Jeannette Glass Company, Jeannette, Pa., from 1937 to 1938.

Made in ultramarine, with limited production in pink and crystal.

Item	Crystal	Pink	Ultramarine
Berry bowl, 4-1/2" d	$12	$12	$24
Berry bowl, 8" d	-	24	75
Bowl, 9" d, handle	15	20	35
Butter dish, cov	-	-	600
Candy, cov, three parts	-	-	22.50
Cup	12	14	20
Creamer	72	90	145
Plate, 6" d, sherbet	8	12	14.50
Plate, 7" d, salad	-	-	40
Plate, 9" d, dinner	7.50	8	30
Salt shaker, orig top	-	-	325

Item	Crystal	Pink	Ultramarine
Saucer	4.50	4.50	5.50
Sugar, open	80	85	145
Tray, 10" l, handles	45	-	25
Tumbler, 9 oz, 4-1/2" h	-	-	500

*Doric and Pansy, pink dinner plate **$8**.*

Children's

Item	Pink	Ultramarine
Creamer	$35	$50
Cup	35	48
Plate	12	12.50
Saucer	7	8.50
Sugar	35	50
14-pc set, orig box	400	425

*Doric and Pansy, ultramarine, child's sugar **$50**, and creamer **$50**.*

EARLY AMERICAN PRESCUT

Swatches

Crystal

Other Colors

Manufactured by Anchor Hocking, Lancaster, Ohio, from 1960 and 1999. Made in crystal, with some limited production in colors.

Item	Crystal
Ashtray, 4" d	$4
Ashtray, 5" d	8
Ashtray, 7-3/4" d	12
Basket, 6" x 4-1/2"	20
Bowl, 4-1/4" d, plain rim	20
Bowl, 4-1/4" d, scalloped	7.50
Bowl, 5-1/4" d, scalloped	7.50
Bowl, 6-3/4" d, three legs	5
Bowl, 7-1/4" d, scalloped	20
Bowl, 8-3/4" d	9
Bowl, 9" d, oval	8
Bowl, 11-3/4" d, paneled	225

Item	Crystal
Bud vase, 5" h, ftd	475
Butter, cov, 1/4 lb	7.50
Butter, cov, metal handle, knife	15
Cake plate	25
Candlesticks, pr, two-lite	28.50
Candy, cov, 5-1/4"	12
Candy, cov, 7-1/4"	14.50
Chip and dip, 10-1/4" bowl, metal holder	25
Coaster	6
Cocktail shaker, 30 oz	300
Console bowl, 9" d	15
Creamer	3.50
Deviled egg plate, 11-3/4" d	42
Hostess tray, 6-1/2" x 12"	14
Iced tea tumbler, 15 oz, 6" h	20
Juice tumbler, 5 oz, 4" h	5
Lamp, oil	315
Lazy Susan, 9 pcs	60
Pitcher, 18 oz	15
Pitcher, 40 oz, sq	60
Plate, 6-3/4" d, salad	55
Plate, 6-3/4" d, snack, ring for cup	40
Plate, 10" d, snack	15
Plate, 11" d	15
Punch cup	3
Punch set, 15 pcs	35
Relish, two parts, 10" l, tab handle	7.50
Relish, three parts, 8-1/2" l, oval	6.50
Relish, five parts, 13-1/2" d	30
Salad bowl, 10-3/4" d	15

Item	Crystal
Salt and pepper shakers, pr, individual size	72
Salt and pepper shakers, pr, metal tops	10
Salt and pepper shakers, pr, plastic tops	12
Serving plate, 11" d, four parts	90
Serving plate, 13-1/2" d	15
Sherbet, 6 oz	90
Snack cup	3
Sugar, cov	4.50
Syrup pitcher, 12 oz	24
Tumbler, 10 oz, 4-1/2" h	6.50
Vase, 10" h	15

*Early American Prescut, 11" d crystal cake plate **$25**.*

ENGLISH HOBNAIL

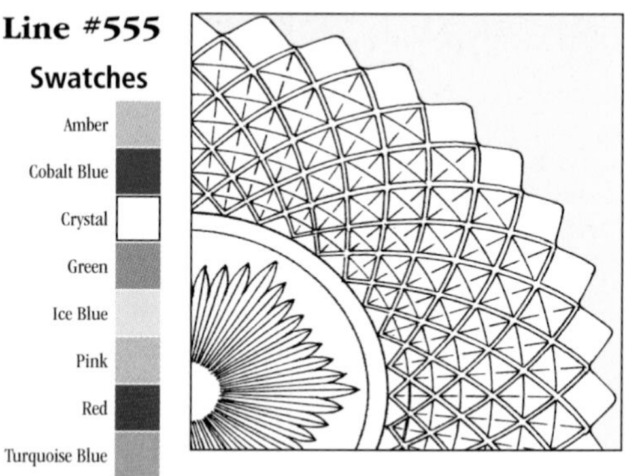

Manufactured by Westmoreland Glass Company, Grapeville, Pa., from the 1920s to 1983.

Made in amber, cobalt blue, crystal, crystal with various color treatments, green, ice blue, pink, red, and turquoise blue. Values for cobalt blue, red or turquoise blue pieces would be about 25 percent higher than ice blue values. Currently, a turquoise basket is valued at $150; a red basket at $100. Crystal pieces with a color accent would be slightly higher than crystal values.

Reproductions: † A creamer and sugar with a hexagonal foot have been reproduced, as well as a nut bowl and pickle dish.

Item	Amber	Crystal	Green	Ice Blue	Pink
Ashtray, 3" d	$20	$20	$22	$-	$22
Ashtray, 4-1/2" d	9	9	15	24	15
Ashtray, 4-1/2" sq	9.50	9.50	15	-	15
Basket, 5" d, handle	20	20	-	-	-
Basket, 6" d, handle, tall	40	40	-	-	43
Bonbon, 6-1/2" h, handle	15	17.50	30	40	30
Bowl, 7" d, six parts	17.50	17.50	-	-	-
Bowl, 7" d, oblong spoon	17.50	17.50	-	-	-
Bowl, 8" d, ftd	30	30	48	-	48
Bowl, 8" d, hexagonal foot, two handles	38	38	75	115	75
Bowl, 8", 6 pt	24	24	-	-	-
Bowl, 9-1/2" d, round, crimped	30	30	-	-	-
Bowl, 10" d, flared	35	35	40	-	40
Bowl, 10" l, oval, crimped	40	40	-	-	-
Bowl, 11" d, rolled edge	35	35	40	85	40
Bowl, 12" d, flared	32	32	40	-	95
Bowl,12" l, oval crimped	32	32	-	-	-
Candelabra, two lite	20	20	-	-	-
Candlesticks, pr, 3-1/2" h, round base	24	32	36	-	60
Candlesticks, pr, 5-1/2" h, sq base	30	32	-	-	-
Candlesticks, pr, 9" h, round base	50	40	72	-	125
Candy dish, three feet	45	38	50	-	50
Candy dish, cov, 1/2 lb, cone shape	45	40	55	-	90
Celery, 12" l, oval	24	45	36	-	36

*English Hobnail, crystal tumbler **$10**.*

Item	Amber	Crystal	Green	Ice Blue	Pink
Celery, 9" d	18	20	32	-	32
Champagne, two ball, round foot	8	7	20	-	20
Chandelier, 17" shade, 200 prisms	425	400	-	-	-
Cheese, cov, 6" d	40	42	-	-	-
Cheese, cov, 8-3/4" d	50	48	-	-	-
Cigarette box, cov, 4-1/2" x 2-1/2"	24.50	24.50	30	-	55
Cigarette jar, cov, round	16	18	25	-	65
Claret, 5 oz, round	15	17.50	-	-	-
Coaster, 3"	5	5	-	-	-
Cocktail, 3 oz, round	8.50	12	-	-	37.50
Cocktail, 3-1/2 oz, round, ball	15	17.50	-	-	-
Compote, 5" d, round, round foot	22	20	25	-	25
Compote, 5" d, round, sq foot	24	24	-	-	-
Compote, 5-1/2" d, bell	12	15	-	-	-
Compote, 5-1/2" d, bell, sq foot	20	20	-	-	-
Console bowl, 12" d, flange	30	30	40	-	40
Cordial, 1 oz, round, ball	16.50	17.50	-	-	-
Cordial, 1 oz, round, foot	16.50	16.50	-	-	-
Cream soup bowl, 4-5/8" d	15	15	-	-	-
Cream soup liner, round, 6-1/2" d	5	5	-	-	-
Creamer, hexagonal foot †	20	20	25	-	48
Creamer, low, flat	10	10	-	-	-

Item	Amber	Crystal	Green	Ice Blue	Pink
Creamer, sq foot	24	24	45	-	45
Cruet, 12 oz	-	25	-	-	-
Cup	8	12	18	-	25
Decanter, 20 oz	55	55	-	-	-
Demitasse cup	17.50	17.50	55	-	55
Dish, 6" d, crimped	15	15	-	-	-
Egg cup	15	15	-	-	-
Finger bowl, 4-1/2" d	7.50	7.50	15	35	15
Finger bowl, 4-1/2" sq, foot	9.50	9.50	18	40	18
Finger bowl liner, 6" sq	6.50	7	20	-	20
Finger bowl liner, 6-1/2" d, round	12	12	10	-	10
Ginger ale tumbler, 5 oz, flat	10	10	18	-	20
Ginger ale tumbler, 5 oz, round foot	10	10	-	-	-
Ginger ale tumbler, 5 oz, sq foot	8	8	32	-	35
Goblet, 8 oz, 6-1/4" h, round, water	12	12	-	50	35
Goblet, 8 oz, sq foot, water	10	10	-	-	50
Grapefruit bowl, 6-1/2" d	12	12	22	-	24
Hat, high	18	18	-	-	-
Hat, low	15	15	-	-	-
Honey compote, 6" d, round foot	18	18	35	-	35
Honey compote, 6" d, sq foot	18	18	-	-	-
Ice tub, 4" h	18	18	50	-	85
Ice tub, 5-1/2" h	36	36	65	-	100

Item	Amber	Crystal	Green	Ice Blue	Pink
Iced tea tumbler, 10 oz	14	14	30	-	30
Iced tea tumbler, 11 oz, round, ball	12	12	-	-	-
Iced tea tumbler, 11 oz, sq foot	13.50	13.50	-	-	-
Iced tea tumbler, 12-1/2 oz, round foot	14	14	-	-	-
Iced tea tumbler, 12 oz, flat	14	14	32	-	32
Icer, sq base, patterned insert	45	45	-	-	-
Ivy bowl, 6-1/2" d, sq foot, crimp top	35	35	-	-	-
Juice tumbler, 7 oz, round foot	27.50	27.50	-	-	-
Juice tumbler, 7 oz, sq foot	6.50	6.50	-	-	-
Lamp shade, 17" d	175	165	-	-	-
Lamp, 6-1/2" h, electric	45	45	50	-	50
Lamp, 9-1/2" d, electric	45	45	115	-	115
Lamp, candlestick	32	32	-	-	-
Marmalade, cov	40	40	45	-	70
Mayonnaise, 6"	12	12	22	-	22
Mustard, cov, sq, foot	18	18	-	-	-
Nappy, 4-1/2" d, round	8	8	15	30	15
Nappy, 4-1/2" w, sq	8.50	8.50	-	-	-
Nappy, 5" d, round	10	10	15	35	15
Nappy, 5-1/2" d, bell	12	12	-	-	-
Nappy, 6" d, round	10	10	17.50	-	17.50
Nappy, 6" d, sq	10	10	17.50	-	17.50
Nappy, 6-1/2" d, round	12.50	12.50	20	-	20
Nappy, 6-1/2" d, sq	14	14	-	-	-

Item	Amber	Crystal	Green	Ice Blue	Pink
Nappy, 7" d, round	14	14	24	-	24
Nappy, 7-1/2" d, bell	15	15	-	-	-
Nappy, 8" d, cupped	22	22	30	-	30
Nappy, 8" d, round	22	22	35	-	35
Nappy, 9" d, bell	25	25	-	-	-
Nut, individual, ftd †	6	6	14.50	-	14.50
Oil bottle, 2 oz, handle	25	25	-	-	-
Oil bottle, 6 oz, handle	27.50	27.50	-	-	-
Old fashioned tumbler, 5 oz	15	15	-	-	-
Oyster cocktail, 5 oz, sq foot	12	12	17.50	-	17.50
Parfait, round foot	17.50	17.50	-	-	-
Pickle, 8" d †	15	15	-	-	-
Pitcher, 23 oz, rounded	48	48	150	-	165
Pitcher, 32 oz, straight side	50	50	175	-	175
Pitcher, 38 oz, rounded	65	65	215	-	215
Pitcher, 60 oz, rounded	70	70	295	-	295
Pitcher, 64 oz, straight side	75	75	310	-	310
Plate, 5-1/2" d, round	7	7	10	-	10
Plate, 6-1/2" d, round	6.25	6.25	10	-	10
Plate, 6-1/2" d, round, depressed center	6	6	-	-	-
Plate, 8" d, round	9	9	14	-	14
Plate, 8" d, round, ftd	13	13	-	-	-
Plate, 8-1/2" d, plain edge	9	9	-	-	-
Plate, 8-1/2" d, round	7	9	17.50	-	28
Plate, 8-3/4" w, sq	9.25	9.25	-	-	-
Plate, 10" d, round	15	15	45	-	65
Plate, 10" w, sq	15	15	-	-	-

*English Hobnail, crystal nappy with handle **$22**.*

Item	Amber	Crystal	Green	Ice Blue	Pink
Plate, 10-1/2" d, round, grill	18	18	-	-	-
Plate, 12" w, sq	20	20	-	-	-
Plate, 15" w, sq	28	28	-	-	-
Preserve, 8" d	15	15	-	-	-
Puff box, cov, 6" d, round	20	20	47.50	-	80
Punch bowl and stand	215	215	-	-	-
Relish, 8" d, three parts	18	18	-	-	-
Rose bowl, 4" d	17.50	17.50	48	-	50
Rose bowl, 6" d	20	20	-	-	-
Salt and pepper shakers, pr, round foot	27.50	27.50	150	-	165
Salt and pepper shakers, pr, sq foot	20	20	-	-	-
Saucer, demitasse, round	10	10	15	-	17.50
Saucer, demitasse, sq	10	10	-	-	-
Saucer, round	2	2	6	-	6
Saucer, sq	2	2	-	-	-
Sherbet, high, round foot	7	7	18	-	37.50
Sherbet, high, sq foot	8	8	18	-	-
Sherbet, high, two ball, round foot	10	10	-	-	-
Sherbet, low, one ball, round foot	12	10	-	-	15
Sherbet, low, round foot	12.50	7	-	-	-
Sherbet, low, sq foot	6.50	6	15	-	17.50
Straw jar, 10" h	65	60	-	-	-
Sugar, hexagonal, ftd †	9	9	25	-	48
Sugar, low, flat	8	8	45	-	-
Sugar, sq foot	9	9	48	-	55

Item	Amber	Crystal	Green	Ice Blue	Pink
Sweetmeat, 5-1/2" d, ball stem	30	30	-	-	-
Sweetmeat, 8" d, ball stem	40	40	60	-	65
Tidbit, two tiers	27.50	27.50	65	85	80
Toilet bottle, 5 oz	25	25	40	65	40
Torte plate, 14" d, round	35	30	48	-	48
Torte plate, 20-1/2" round	55	50	-	-	-
Tumbler, 8 oz, water	10	10	24	-	24
Tumbler, 9 oz, round, ftd water	10	10	-	-	-
Tumbler, 9 oz, sq foot, water	10	10	-	-	-
Urn, cov, 11" h	35	35	350	-	350
Vase, 6-1/2" h, sq foot	24	24	-	-	-
Vase, 7-1/2" h, flip	27.50	27.50	70	-	70
Vase, 7-1/2" h, flip jar with cov	55	55	85	-	85
Vase, 8" h, sq foot	35	35	-	-	-
Vase, 8-1/2" h, flared top	40	40	120	-	235
Whiskey, 3 oz	12	15	-	-	-
Wine, 2 oz, round foot	15	15	-	-	-
Wine, 2 oz, sq ft	24	24	35	-	65
Wine, 2-1/2 oz, ball, foot	20	20	-	-	-

FAIRFAX

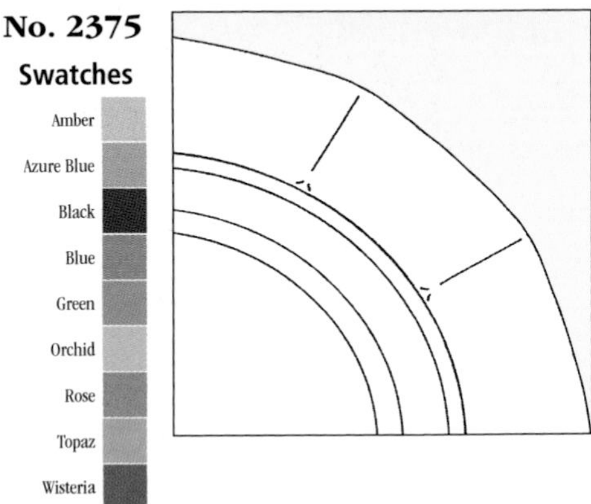

Manufactured by Fostoria Glass Company, Moundsville, Va., from 1927 to 1944. While this pattern is collected as Fairfax by many, the blanks were also used for some Fostoria etchings, such as June, Trojan, and Versailles. The values listed below are for the Fairfax pattern; expect to pay more for the etched patterns.

Made in amber, azure blue, black, blue, green, orchid, rose, topaz, and wisteria, with limited production in ruby.

Item	Amber	Azure Blue, Black, and Blue	Green	Orchid, Rose, Wist.	Topaz
After dinner cup and saucer	$15	$30	$18	$30	$18
Ashtray, 2-1/2" d	9	15	12	15	12
Ashtray, 4"	10	17.50	12.50	17.50	12.50
Ashtray, 5-1/2"	12	20	15	20	15
Baker, oval, 9" l	17.50	35	24	35	24
Baker, oval, 10-1/2" l	20	42	25	42	25
Bonbon	10	12.50	12	12.50	12
Bouillon, ftd	8.50	14.50	10	14.50	10
Bowl, 7" d, three ftd	10	15	14	15	14
Bowl, 12" d	22	42	24	42	24
Bread plate, 12" d	27.50	45	30	45	30
Butter dish, cov	80	140	100	140	100
Cake plate, 10" d	15	24	15	24	15
Canapé plate	12	20	15	20	15
Candlesticks, pr, 3" h	20	35	30	35	30
Candy, cov, three parts	40	65	50	65	50
Candy, cov, ftd	45	70	60	70	60
Celery tray, 11-1/4" l	12	25	17.50	25	17.50
Centerpiece bowl, 12" d	20	40	25	40	25
Centerpiece bowl, 13" l, oval	24	45	35	45	35
Centerpiece bowl, 15" d	27.50	48	37.50	48	40
Cereal bowl, 6" d	12	24	14.50	24	18
Cheese and cracker set	20	45	25	45	25
Chop plate, 13" d	15	25	17.50	25	17.50
Cigarette box	20	48	24	48	24
Claret, 4 oz, 6" h	25	40	35	40	35
Cocktail, 3 oz, 5-1/4" h	12	24	20	24	20

Item	Amber	Azure Blue, Black, and Blue	Green	Orchid, Rose, Wist.	Topaz
Comport, 5"	15	30	20	30	20
Comport, 7"	15	30	24	30	24
Cordial, 3/4 oz, 4" h	25	65	45	65	45
Cream soup, ftd	10	20	15	20	15
Cream soup underplate	5	8	5	8	5
Creamer, flat	12	-	15	-	15
Creamer, ftd	10	24	12	15	12
Creamer, tea size	9	18.50	12.50	18.50	12.50
Cup, flat	4.50	-	6.50	-	6.50
Cup, ftd	7.50	15	9	10	9
Dessert bowl, large, handle	15	40	24	40	24
Flower holder, oval	25	85	40	85	40
Fruit bowl, 5" d	8	15	9	15	9
Goblet, 10 oz, 8-1/4" h	17.50	32	22	35	22
Grapefruit	17.50	35	25	35	25
Grapefruit liner	15	32	20	32	22
Ice bowl	12	20	14.50	20	14.50
Ice bowl liner	12	22	12	22	14.50
Ice bucket	32	50	35	50	35
Juice tumbler, 2-1/2 oz, ftd	12	32	18.50	32	18.50
Lemon bowl, two handles, ftd	6.50	12.50	7.50	12.50	7.50
Mayonnaise	10	15	10	15	10
Mayonnaise ladle	20	30	24	30	24
Mayonnaise underplate	5	8	4	8	5
Nappy, 8" d	18	40	24	40	24
Nut cup	15	32	20	32	20

Item	Amber	Azure Blue, Black, and Blue	Green	Orchid, Rose, Wist.	Topaz
Oil bottle, ftd, os	85	150	110	150	110
Pickle, 8-1/2" l	10	25	15	25	15
Pitcher	115	200	145	200	145
Plate, 6" d, bread and butter	2.50	4.50	3	4.50	3
Plate, 7-1/2" d, salad	5	5.50	4.50	5.50	5
Plate, 8-3/4" d, salad	4.50	12	5.50	7.50	5.50
Plate, 9-1/2" d, luncheon	8	12	7.50	12	7.50
Plate, 10-1/4" d, dinner	18	40	30	40	30
Plate, 10-1/4" d, grill	17.50	40	27.50	40	27.50
Platter, 10-1/2" l	18	35	25	35	25
Platter, 12" l	20	40	32	40	32
Platter, 15" l	30	70	42	70	42
Relish, three parts, 8-1/2" l	12	22	14	22	14
Relish, 11-1/2" l	14	24	17.50	24	17.50
Salad dressing bowl	75	180	90	180	90
Salt and pepper shakers, pr, ftd	32	60	40	60	40
Salt and pepper shakers, pr, individual size	20	-	25	-	25
Sauce boat and underplate	30	65	38	65	40
Saucer	3	6.50	3	4.50	3
Sherbet, 6 oz, 6" h	10	20	12.50	20	12.50
Soup bowl, 7" d	18	40	24	40	24
Sugar bowl, flat	12	-	14	-	14
Sugar bowl, ftd	8	24	10	12	10
Sugar bowl, tea size	10	20	14.50	20	14.50

Item	Amber	Azure Blue, Black, and Blue	Green	Orchid, Rose, Wist.	Topaz
Sugar bowl lid	20	35	25	35	25
Sugar pail	25	60	40	60	40
Sweetmeat	12	17.50	15	17.50	15
Tray, 11" d, center handle	15	25	20	25	20
Tumbler, 5 oz, 4-1/2" h, ftd	10	17.50	12	17.50	12
Tumbler, 9 oz, 5-1/4" h, ftd	14.50	20	17.50	20	17.50
Tumbler, 12 oz, 6", ftd	17.50	27.50	25	27.50	25
Vase, 8" h	35	50	35	50	35
Whipped cream pail	25	55	40	55	40
Whipped cream underplate	9	12	10	12	10
Wine, 3 oz, 5-1/2" h	20	30	25	30	25

FLORAGOLD

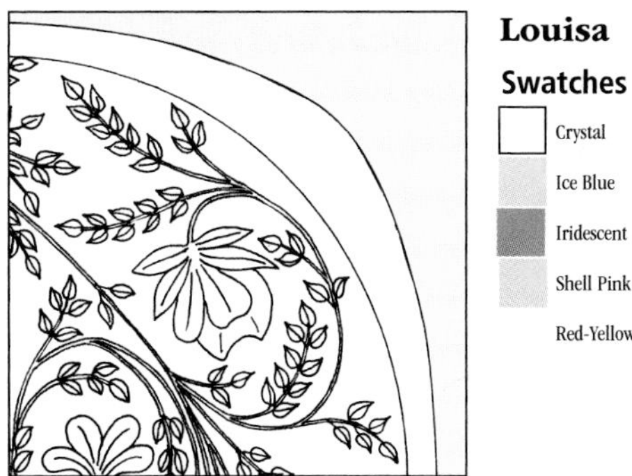

Louisa

Swatches

Crystal

Ice Blue

Iridescent

Shell Pink

Red-Yellow

Manufactured by Jeannette Glass Company, Jeannette, Pa., 1950s.

Made in iridescent. Some large comports were later made in ice blue, crystal, red-yellow, and shell pink.

Item	Iridescent
Ashtray, 4" d	**$10**
Bowl, 4-1/2" sq	**6.50**
Bowl, 5-1/4" d, ruffled	**16**
Bowl, 8-1/2" d, sq	**22**
Bowl, 8-1/2" d, ruffled	**14**
Butter dish, cov, 1/4 pound, oblong	**30**
Butter dish, cov, round, 5-1/2" w sq base	**800**
Butter dish, cov, round, 6-1/4" w sq base	**55**
Candlesticks, pr, double branch	**60**
Candy dish, one handle	**16.50**

*Floragold, iridescent dinner plate **$40** and ruffled berry bowl, 5-1/4" d **$16**.*

Item	Iridescent
Candy or cheese dish, cov, 6-3/4" d	130
Candy, 5-3/4" l, four feet	12
Celery vase	420
Cereal bowl, 5-1/2" d, round	40
Coaster, 4" d	10
Comport, 5-1/4", plain top	795
Comport, 5-1/4", ruffled top	895
Creamer	21
Cup	8
Fruit bowl, 5-1/2" d, ruffled	8.50
Fruit bowl, 12" d, ruffled, large	15
Nappy, 5" d, one handle	12
Pitcher, 64 oz	45
Plate, 5-1/4" d, sherbet	15
Plate, 8-1/2" d, dinner	40
Platter, 11-1/4" d	30
Salad bowl, 9-1/2" d, deep	42.50
Salt and pepper shakers, pr, plastic tops	60
Saucer, 5-1/4" d	12
Sherbet, low, ftd	16
Sugar	22
Sugar lid	15
Tidbit, wooden post	35
Tray, 13-1/2" d	75
Tray, 13-1/2" d, with indent	65
Tumbler, 11 oz, ftd	20
Tumbler, 10 oz, ftd	20
Tumbler, 15 oz, ftd	110
Vase	420

Poinsettia

Swatches

Delphite

Green

Jade-ite

Pink

Red

Yellow

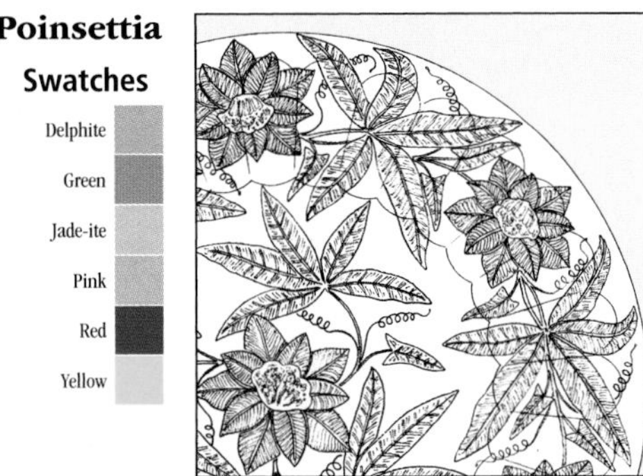

Manufactured by Jeannette Glass Company, Jeannette, Pa., from 1931 to 1935.

Made in amber, crystal, Delphite, green, Jad-ite, pink, red, and yellow. Production in amber, crystal, red, and yellow was limited. A crystal 6-7/8" h vase would be valued at $295.

Reproductions: † Reproduction salt and pepper shakers have been made in cobalt blue, dark green, green, pink and red.

Item	Delphite	Green	Jad-ite	Pink
Berry bowl, 4" d	$50	$25	$-	$25
Butter dish, cov	-	95	-	90
Candlesticks, pr, 4" h	-	90	-	95
Candy jar, cov	80	45	-	45
Canister set	-	-	60	-
Casserole, cov	-	45	-	28

*Floral, pink dinner plate **$27.50**.*

Item	Delphite	Green	Jad-ite	Pink
Coaster, 3-1/4" d	-	15	-	-
Comport, 9"	-	875	-	795
Cream soup, 5-1/2" d	-	735	-	735
Creamer, flat	-	24	-	24
Cup	-	15	-	15
Dresser set	-	1,350	-	-
Dresser tray, 9-1/4" l, oval	-	200	-	-
Flower frog	-	695	-	-
Ice tub, 3-1/2" h, oval	-	850	-	825
Juice tumbler, ftd	-	28	-	27.50
Juice tumbler, 5 oz, 4" h, flat	-	35	-	35
Lamp	-	295	-	260
Lemonade pitcher, 48 oz, 10-1/4" h	-	295	-	350
Lemonade tumbler, 9 oz, 5-1/4" h, ftd	-	60	-	55
Pitcher, 23 or 24 oz, 5-1/2" h	-	595	-	-
Pitcher, 32 oz, ftd, cone, 8" h	-	45	-	60
Plate, 6" d, sherbet	-	8.50	-	8.50
Plate, 8" d, salad	-	15	-	17
Plate, 9" d, dinner	145	30	-	27.50
Plate, 9" d, grill	-	185	-	-
Plate, 10-3/4" l, oval	-	20	-	17.50
Platter, 11" l	150	30	-	30
Refrigerator dish, cov, 5" sq	-	-	15	-
Relish, two parts, oval	165	24	-	20
Rose bowl, three legs	-	500	-	-
Salad bowl, 7-1/2" d	-	40	-	40
Salad bowl, 7-1/2" d, ruffled	65	125	-	120
Salt and pepper shakers, pr, 4" h, ftd †	-	60	-	50
Salt and pepper shakers, pr, 6" flat	-	-	-	60

Item	Delphite	Green	Jad-ite	Pink
Saucer	-	12.50	-	12.50
Sherbet	90	20	-	20
Sugar, cov	-	32	-	35
Sugar, open	75	-	-	-
Tray, 6" sq, closed handles	-	195	-	-
Tumbler, 3 oz, 3-1/2" h, ftd	-	18	-	25
Tumbler, 7 oz, 4-1/2", ftd	175	25	-	25
Tumbler, 5-1/4" h, ftd	-	60	-	55
Vase, flared, three legs	-	485	-	-
Vase, 6-7/8" h	-	475	-	-
Vegetable bowl, 8" d, cov	-	50	-	65
Vegetable bowl, 8" d, open	80	-	-	40
Vegetable bowl, 9" l, oval	-	35	-	35

FLORAL AND DIAMOND BAND

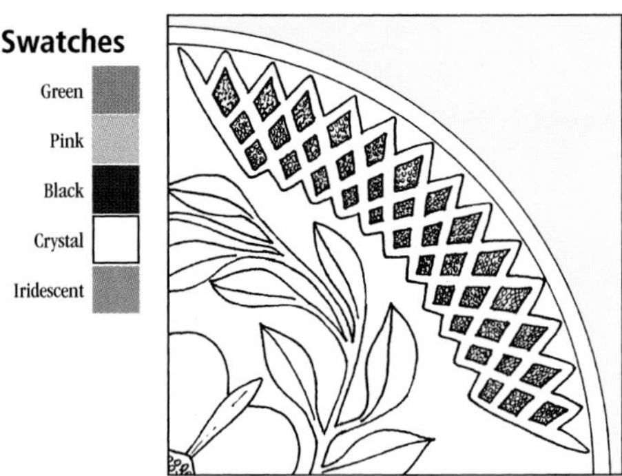

Manufactured by U.S. Glass Company, Pittsburgh, Pa., in the late 1920s.

Made in pink and green with limited production in black, crystal, and iridescent.

Item	Green	Pink
Berry bowl, 4-1/2" d	$12	$15
Berry bowl, 8" d	15	18
Butter dish, cov	140	175
Compote, 5-1/2" h	18	17.50
Creamer, 4-3/4"	20	17.50
Iced tea tumbler, 5" h	45	50
Nappy, 5-3/4" d, handle	12	11
Pitcher, 42 oz, 8" h	95	90
Plate, 8" d, luncheon	40	40
Sherbet	8	9.50

Item	Green	Pink
Sugar, 5-1/4"	15	15
Tumbler, 4" h, water	25	25

*Floral and Diamond Band, green luncheon plate **$40**.*

FLORENTINE NO. 1

Old Florentine, Poppy No. 1

Swatches

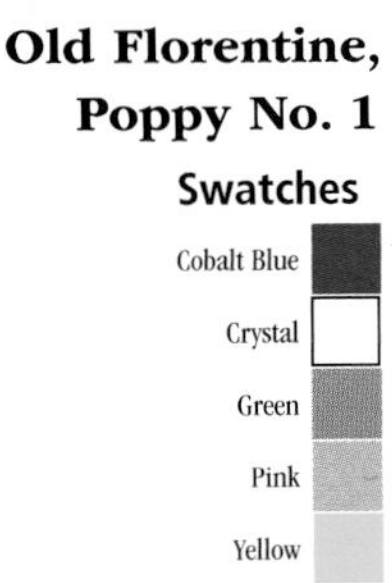

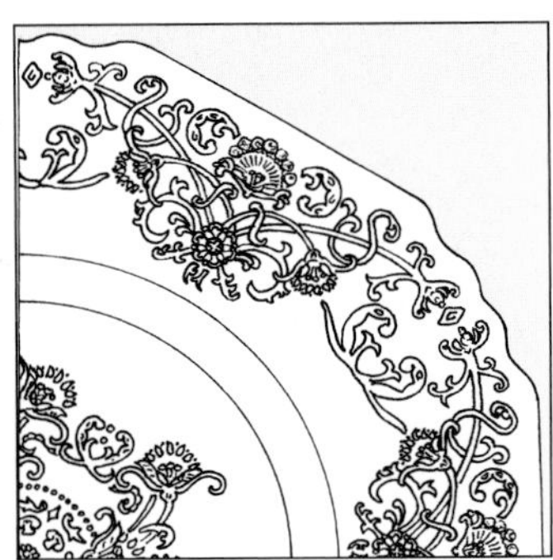

Manufactured by Hazel Atlas Glass Company, Clarksburg, W.V., and Zanesville, Ohio, from 1932 to 1935.

Made in crystal, green, pink, yellow, and limited production in cobalt blue.

Reproductions: † Salt and pepper shakers have been reproduced in cobalt blue, pink, and red.

Item	Cobalt Blue	Crystal	Green	Pink	Yellow
Ashtray, 5-1/2" d	$-	$24	$24	$28	$28
Berry bowl, 5" d	24	12	12	15	15
Berry bowl, 8-1/2" d	-	24	25	28	28
Butter dish, cov	-	110	115	165	160
Cereal bowl, 6" d	-	32	32	35	35
Coaster/ashtray, 3-3/4" d	-	18	20	25	25
Comport, 3-1/2" h, ruffled	60	25	25	15	-

Item	Cobalt Blue	Crystal	Green	Pink	Yellow
Cream soup, 5" d, ruffled	50	12	14	20	-
Creamer	-	10	12	25	20
Creamer, ruffled	65	45	35	37	-
Cup	85	10	8	12	10
Iced tea tumbler, 12 oz, 5-1/4" h, ftd	-	28	28	30	24
Juice tumbler, 5 oz, 3-3/4" h, ftd	-	16	16	20	22
Lemonade tumbler, 9 oz, 5-1/4" h	-	-	-	100	-
Pitcher, 36 oz, 6-1/2", ftd	850	45	45	65	50
Pitcher, 48 oz, 7-1/2", flat, with or without ice lip	-	75	75	135	195
Plate, 6" d, sherbet	-	7.50	9	7.50	9
Plate, 8-1/2" d, salad	-	8	10	12	12
Plate, 10" d, dinner	-	16	16	22	24
Plate, 10" d, grill	-	12	12.50	20	22
Platter, 11-1/2" l, oval	-	19	10	22	28
Salt and pepper shakers, pr, ftd †	-	22	32	55	58
Saucer	18	3.50	3.50	4	3
Sherbet, 3 oz, ftd	-	10	10	13	16
Sugar, cov	-	10	12.50	25	12
Sugar, ruffled	55	35	30	42.50	-
Tumbler, 4 oz, 3-1/4" h, ftd	-	15	16	-	-
Tumbler, 9 oz, 4" h, ribbed	-	14	14	22	-
Tumbler, 10 oz, 4-3/4" h, ftd	-	22	20	22	24
Vegetable bowl, cov, 9-1/2" l, oval	-	42	42	60	60

*Florentine No. 1, green creamer **$12**, and covered sugar **$12.50**.*

FLORENTINE NO. 2

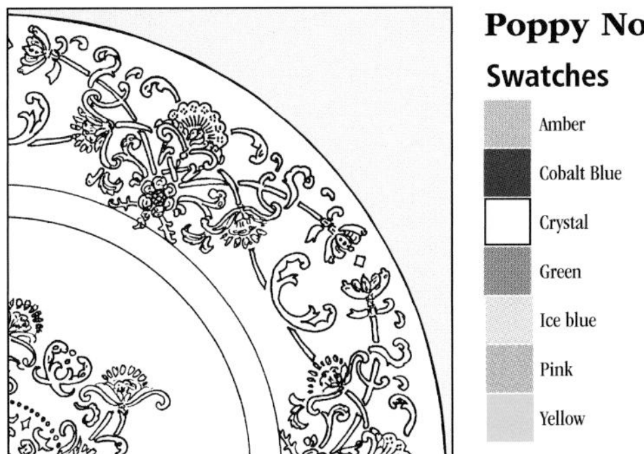

Poppy No. 2

Swatches

- Amber
- Cobalt Blue
- Crystal
- Green
- Ice blue
- Pink
- Yellow

Manufactured by Hazel Atlas Glass Company, Clarksburg, W.V., and Zanesville, Ohio, from 1932 to 1935.

Made in amber, cobalt blue, crystal, green, ice blue, pink, and yellow. Ice blue production is limited to 7-1/2" h pitcher, valued at $525. Amber production is limited to 9 oz and 12 oz tumblers, both currently valued at $80; cup and saucer, valued at $75; and sherbet, valued at $45. Cobalt blue production is limited to 3-1/2" comport, valued at $60, and 9 oz tumbler, valued at $80.

Reproductions: † 7-1/2" h cone-shaped pitcher and 4" h footed tumbler. Reproductions are found in amber, cobalt blue, crystal, deep green, and pink.

Item	Crystal	Green	Pink	Yellow
Ashtray, 3-1/2" d	$18.50	$18.50	$-	$25
Ashtray, 5-1/2" d	20	25	-	35

Item	Crystal	Green	Pink	Yellow
Berry bowl, 4-1/2" d	14.50	16.50	17.50	22.50
Berry bowl, 8" d	24	26	30	35
Bowl, 5-1/2" d	32	35	-	42
Bowl, 7-1/2" d, shallow	-	-	-	85
Bowl, 9" d, flat	27.50	27.50	-	-
Butter dish, cov	115	125	-	165
Candlesticks, pr, 2-3/4" h	45	48	-	70
Candy dish, cov	110	100	150	165
Cereal bowl, 6" d	28	28	-	40
Coaster, 3-1/4" d	-	-	-	25
Coaster, 3-3/4" d	18.50	18.50	-	25
Coaster, 5-1/2" d	20	25	-	35
Cocktail, 3-1/4" h, ftd	-	-	-	14.50
Comport, 3-1/2" d, ruffled	25	25	25	-
Condiment tray, round	-	-	-	65
Cream soup, 4-3/4" d, two handles	16.50	16	18.50	20
Creamer	8	12	-	14.50
Cup	7.50	8	-	12
Custard cup	60	60	-	85
Gravy boat	-	-	-	65
Gravy boat underplate, 11-1/2" l	-	-	-	115
Iced tea tumbler, 12 oz, 5" h	35	35	-	45
Juice tumbler, 5 oz, 3-1/8" h, flat	14.50	14.50	14.50	22
Juice tumbler, 5 oz, 3-1/8" h, ftd	13	15	-	21
Parfait, 6" h	30	32	-	65
Pitcher, 28 oz, ftd, 7-1/2" h †	60	40	-	50
Pitcher, 48 oz, 7-1/2" h	60	70	120	32
Pitcher, 76 oz, 8-1/4" h	90	95	225	400
Plate, 6" d, sherbet	6	6	-	7.50

Item	Crystal	Green	Pink	Yellow
Plate, 6-1/2" d, indent	16	17.50	-	30
Plate, 8-1/2" d, salad	8.50	9.50	9	10
Plate, 10" d, dinner	16.50	16	-	19
Plate, 10-1/4" d, grill	15	15	-	14.50
Plate, 10-1/4" d, grill, cream soup ring	35	35	-	-
Platter, 11" oval	15	16	18.50	24
Relish, 10" d, divided, three parts	22.50	24	26	32
Relish, 10" d, plain	22.50	24	26	32

*Florentine No. 2, yellow cup **$12.***

Butterflies and Roses

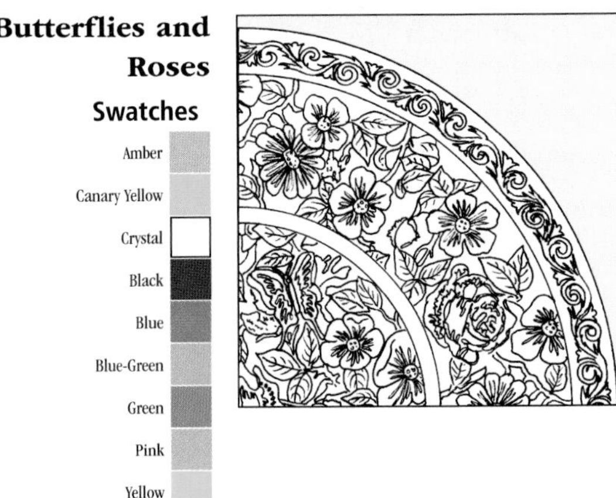

Manufactured by U.S. Glass Company, Pittsburgh, Pa., in the late 1920s.

Made in amber, black, blue, blue-green, canary yellow, crystal, green, and pink.

Item	Amber or Crystal	Black	Blue-Green, Green or Pink	Blue or Canary Yellow
Ashtray	$175	$-	$185	$225
Bonbon, cov, 6-5/8" d	-	265	-	-
Bowl, 9" d, rolled edge	-	225	-	-
Candlesticks, pr, 4" h	50	-	60	100

Item	Crystal	Green	Pink	Yellow
Salt and pepper shakers, pr	48	48	-	65
Saucer	5	4	-	3.50
Sherbet, ftd	10	12.50	-	14.50
Sugar, cov	8.50	9	-	38
Tumbler, 5 oz, 3-1/4" h, ftd	18	15	15	-
Tumbler, 5 oz, 4" h, ftd †	15	15	18	20
Tumbler, 5 oz, 3-5/16" h, blown	18.50	18.50	-	-
Tumbler, 6 oz, 3-9/16" h, blown	16	18.50	-	-
Tumbler, 9 oz, 4" h	14.50	18.50	16	22.50
Tumbler, 9 oz, 4-1/2" h, ftd	25	25	-	38
Tumbler, 10 oz, 4-11/16" h, blown	19	19	-	-
Tumbler, 12 oz, 5" h, blown	20	20	-	20
Vase, 6" h	30	32	-	65
Vegetable bowl, cov, 9" l, oval	55	60	-	85

Butterflies and Roses

Swatches

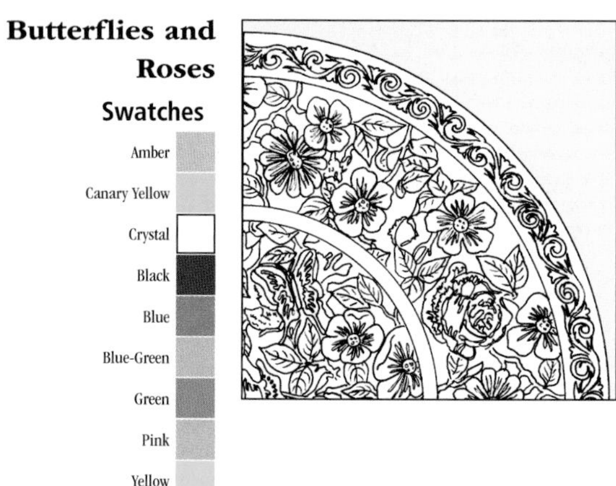

Manufactured by U.S. Glass Company, Pittsburgh, Pa., in the late 1920s.

Made in amber, black, blue, blue-green, canary yellow, crystal, green, and pink.

Item	Amber or Crystal	Black	Blue-Green, Green or Pink	Blue or Canary Yellow
Ashtray	$175	$-	$185	$225
Bonbon, cov, 6-5/8" d	-	265	-	-
Bowl, 9" d, rolled edge	-	225	-	-
Candlesticks, pr, 4" h	50	-	60	100

Item	Crystal	Green	Pink	Yellow
Plate, 6-1/2" d, indent	16	17.50	-	30
Plate, 8-1/2" d, salad	8.50	9.50	9	10
Plate, 10" d, dinner	16.50	16	-	19
Plate, 10-1/4" d, grill	15	15	-	14.50
Plate, 10-1/4" d, grill, cream soup ring	35	35	-	-
Platter, 11" oval	15	16	18.50	24
Relish, 10" d, divided, three parts	22.50	24	26	32
Relish, 10" d, plain	22.50	24	26	32

*Florentine No. 2, yellow cup **$12.***

REPRODUCTION! Florentine No. 2, green pitcher and tumbler.

Item	Amber or Crystal	Black	Blue-Green, Green or Pink	Blue or Canary Yellow
Candlesticks, pr, 8" h	90	325	145	145
Candy, cov, 6" d, flat	135	-	165	-
Candy, cov, 7-1/2" cone shape	90	100	165	175
Candy, cov, heart shape	-	-	1,250	1,500
Cologne bottle, 7-1/2" h	-	-	225	365
Comport, 2-7/8" h	-	250	40	45
Comport, 3" h	25	-	30	35
Comport, 4-1/4" h, 4-3/4" w	-	-	-	65

*Flower Garden with Butterflies, blue comport **$90.***

Item	Amber or Crystal	Black	Blue-Green, Green or Pink	Blue or Canary Yellow
Comport, 4-3/4" h, 10-1/4" w	50	250	70	90
Comport, 5-7/8" h, 11" w	60	-	-	95
Comport, 7-1/4" h, 8-1/4" w	65	175	85	-
Creamer	-	-	75	-
Cup	-	-	70	-
Orange bowl, 11" d, ftd	-	250	-	-
Plate, 7" d	20	-	25	30
Plate, 8" d	17.50	-	20	27.50
Plate, 10" d	-	-	45	50
Plate, 10" d, indent	35	150	45	50
Powder jar, 3-1/2", flat	-	-	75	-
Powder jar, 6-1/4" h, ftd	225	-	130	175
Powder jar, 7-1/2" h, ftd	85	-	135	195
Sandwich server, center handle	55	135	75	100
Saucer	-	-	30	-
Tray, 5-1/2" x 10", oval	50	-	75	9
Tray, 11-3/4" x 7-3/4", rect	50	-	75	90
Tumbler, 7-1/2 oz	175	-	-	-
Vase, 6-1/4" h	75	145	135	145
Vase, 8" h, Dahlia, cupped	-	275	-	-
Vase, 10" h, two handles	-	250	-	-
Vase, 10-1/2" h	-	-	150	225
Wall pocket, 9" l	-	365	-	-

FOREST GREEN

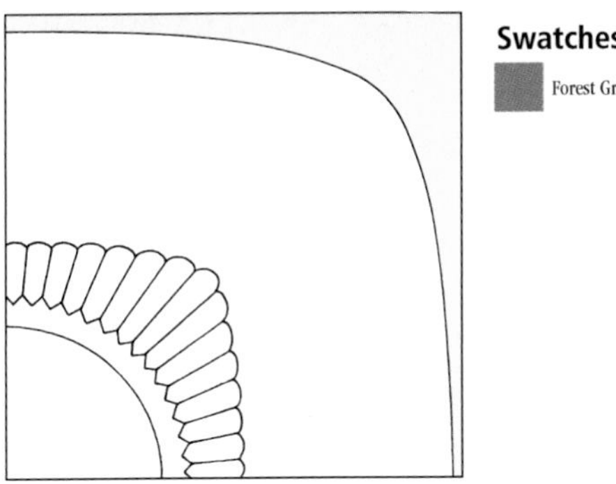

Swatches

Forest Green

Manufactured by Anchor Hocking Glass Company, Lancaster, Ohio, and Long Island City, N.Y., from 1950 to 1957.

Made only in forest green.

Item	Forest Green
Ashtray, 3-1/2" sq	$5
Ashtray, 4-5/8" sq	5.50
Ashtray, 5-3/4" hexagon	8
Ashtray, 5-3/4" sq	7.50
Batter bowl, spout	25
Berry bowl, large	15
Berry bowl, small	7.50
Bonbon, 6-1/4" w, tricorn	12
Bowl, 4-1/2" w, sq	7
Bowl, 5-1/4" deep	8.50
Bowl, 6" w, sq	18

Item	Forest Green
Bowl, 6-1/2" d, scalloped	9
Bowl, 6-3/8" d, three toes	15
Bowl, 7-3/8" w, sq	30
Bowl, 7-1/2" d, crimped	10
Cocktail, 3-1/2 oz	12
Cocktail, 4-1/2 oz	14
Creamer, flat	7.50
Cup, sq	7
Dessert bowl, 4-3/4" d	7
Goblet, 9 oz	10
Goblet, 9-1/2 oz	14
Iced tea tumbler, 13 oz	8
Iced tea tumbler, 14 oz, Boopie	8
Iced tea tumbler, 15 oz, tall	10
Iced tea tumbler, 32 oz, giant	18
Ivy ball, 4" h	5
Juice roly-poly tumbler, 3-3/8" h	6
Juice tumbler, 4 oz	10
Juice tumbler, 5-1/2 oz	12.50
Ladle, all green glass	80
Mixing bowl, 6" d	9.50
Pitcher, 22 oz	22.50
Pitcher, 36 oz	25
Pitcher, 86 oz, round	45
Plate, 6-3/4" d, salad	7.50
Plate, 7" w, sq	6.75
Plate, 8-3/8" d, luncheon	9
Plate, 9-1/4" d, dinner	33.50
Platter, 11" l, rect	22
Popcorn bowl, 5-1/4" d	10

Item	Forest Green
Punch bowl	25
Punch bowl and stand	60
Punch cup	4.25
Relish tray, 4-3/4" x 6-3/4" l, two handles	25
Roly-poly tumbler, 5 1/8" h	7.50
Salad bowl, 7-3/8" d	15
Sandwich plate, 13-3/4" d	45
Saucer, 5-3/8" w	3
Sherbet, 6 oz	9
Sherbet, 6 oz, Boopie	7
Sherbet, flat	7.50

*Forest Green, cup **$7**, and saucer **$3**.*

Item	Forest Green
Soup bowl, 6" d	17
Sugar, flat	7
Tray, 6" x 10", two handles	30
Tumbler, 5 oz, 3-1/2" h	4
Tumbler, 7 oz	4.50
Tumbler, 5-1/4" h	4
Tumbler, 9-1/2 oz, tall	8
Tumbler, 9 oz, fancy	7
Tumbler, 9 oz, table	5
Tumbler, 10 oz, 4-1/2" h, ftd	7.50
Tumbler, 11 oz	7
Tumbler, 14 oz, 5" h	8
Tumbler, 15 oz, long boy	10
Vase, 6-3/8" h, Harding	10
Vase, 7" h, crimped	15
Vase, 9" h	12
Vegetable bowl, 8-1/2" l, oval	24

FORTUNE

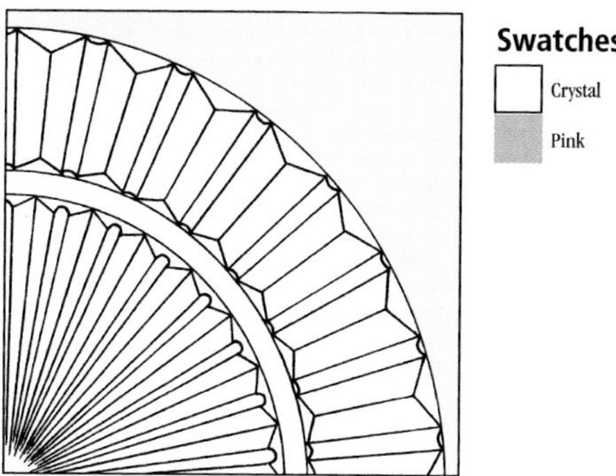

Swatches

Crystal

Pink

Manufactured by Hocking Glass Company, Lancaster, Ohio, from 1937 to 1938.

Made in crystal and pink.

Item	Crystal	Pink
Berry bowl, 4" d	$10	$12
Berry bowl, 7-3/4" d	25	28
Bowl, 4-1/2" d, handle	12	15
Bowl, 5-1/4" d, rolled edge	20	22
Candy dish, cov, flat	28	30
Cup	12	15
Dessert bowl, 4-1/2" d	12	15
Juice tumbler, 5 oz, 3-1/2" h	12	12
Plate, 6" d, sherbet	8	15
Plate, 8" d, luncheon	25	25
Salad bowl, 7-3/4" d	25	25

Item	Crystal	Pink
Saucer	5	8.50
Tumbler, 9 oz, 4" h	15	18.50

*Fortune, pink berry bowl, 7-3/4" d, **$28**.*

FRUITS

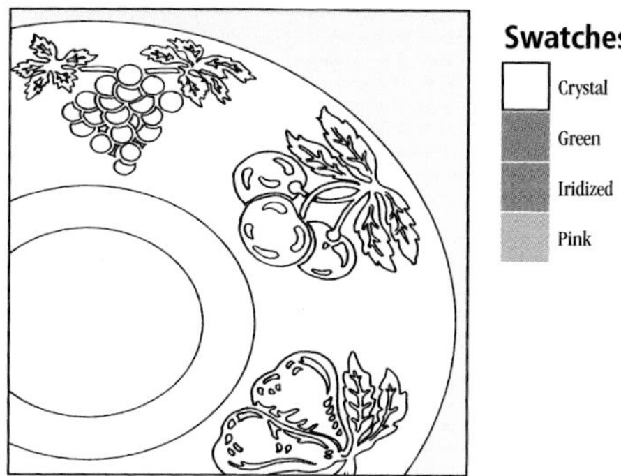

Swatches

Crystal

Green

Iridized

Pink

Manufactured by Hazel Atlas Company, and several other small glass companies, from 1931 to 1935.

Made in crystal, green, iridized, and pink. Iridized production includes only a 4" tumbler, valued at $10.

Item	Crystal	Green	Pink
Berry bowl, 5" d	$17.50	$32	$28
Berry bowl, 8" d	40	85	45
Cup	5	10	7
Juice tumbler, 5 oz, 3-1/2" h	20	60	22
Pitcher, 7" h	50	95	-
Plate, 8" d, luncheon	12	15	12
Saucer	2.50	5	4.50
Sherbet	10	15	12
Tumbler, 4" h, multiple fruits	15	24	22

Item	Crystal	Green	Pink
Tumbler, 4" h, single fruit	20	30	25
Tumbler, 12 oz, 5" h	70	200	95

*Fruits, green cup **$10**, and saucer **$5**.*

GEORGIAN

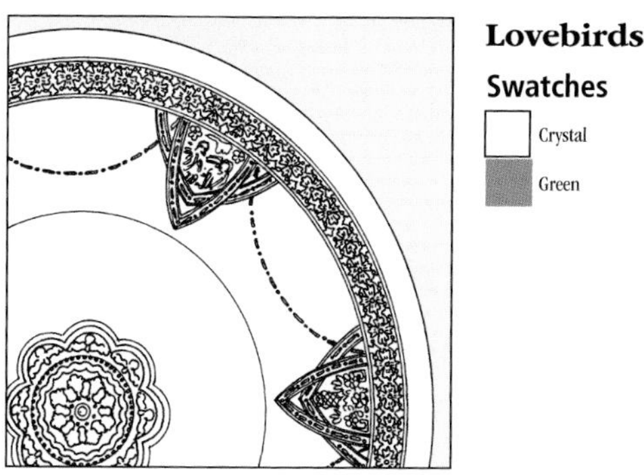

Lovebirds

Swatches

Crystal

Green

Manufactured by Federal Glass Company, Columbus, Ohio, from 1931 to 1936.

Made in green. A crystal hot plate is valued at $25.

Item	Green
Berry bowl, 4-1/2" d	$10
Berry bowl, 7-1/2" d, large	65
Bowl, 6-1/2" d, deep	65
Butter dish, cov	80
Cereal bowl, 5-3/4" d	30
Cold cuts server, 18-1/2" d, wood, seven openings for 5" d coasters	875
Creamer, 3" d, ftd	16
Creamer, 4" d, ftd	16.50
Cup	10
Hot plate, 5" d, center design	48
Plate, 6" d, sherbet	6.50

Item	Green
Plate, 8" d, luncheon	10
Plate, 9-1/4" d, center design only	25
Plate, 9-1/4" d, dinner	36
Platter, 11-1/2" l, closed handle	70
Saucer	4
Sherbet, ftd	16
Sugar cover, 3" d	12
Sugar cover, 4" d	12
Sugar, 3" d, ftd	15
Sugar, 4" d, ftd	15
Tumbler, 9 oz, 4" h, flat	80
Tumbler 12 oz, 5-1/4" h, flat	135
Vegetable bowl, 9" l, oval	65

*Georgian, green sherbet **$16**.*

HARP

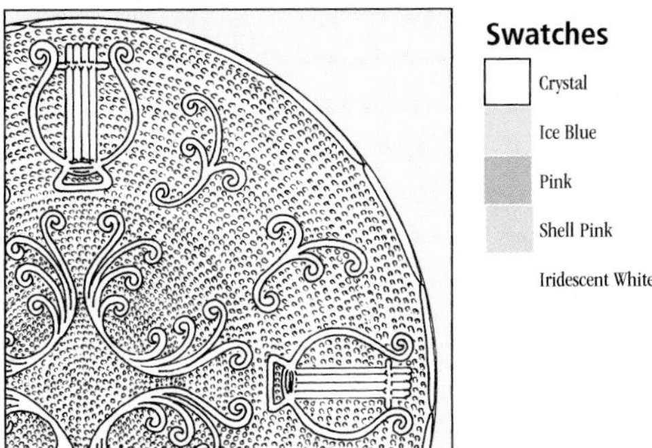

Swatches

- Crystal
- Ice Blue
- Pink
- Shell Pink
- Iridescent White

Manufactured by Jeannette Glass Company, Jeannette, Pa., from 1954 to 1957.

Made in crystal and crystal with gold trim; limited pieces made in ice blue, iridescent white, pink, and shell pink.

Item	Crystal	Ice Blue	Shell Pink
Ashtray	$6	$-	$-
Cake stand, 9" d	35	45	45
Coaster	6	-	-
Cup	30	-	-
Parfait	20	-	-
Plate, 7" d	20	25	-
Saucer	12	-	-
Snack set, cup, saucer, 7" plate	48	-	-
Tray, two handles, rectangular	35	35	65
Vase, 7-1/2" h	35	-	-

*Harp, crystal with gold trim, 7" plate **$20** and cake stand **$35**.*

HERITAGE

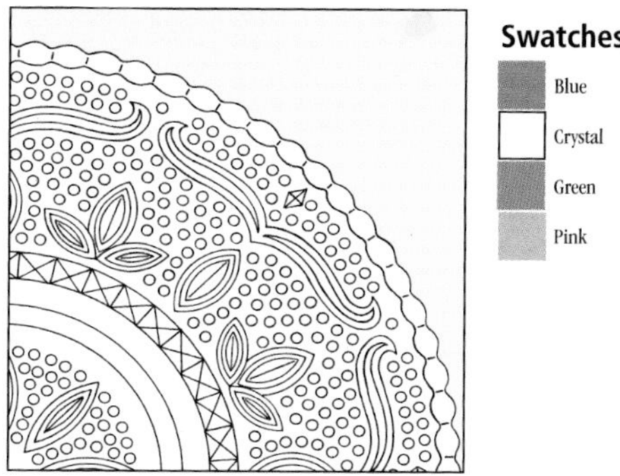

Swatches

- Blue
- Crystal
- Green
- Pink

Manufactured by Federal Glass Company, Columbus, Ohio, from 1940 to 1955.

Made in blue, crystal, green, and pink.

Reproductions: † Bowls have been reproduced in amber, crystal, and green. Some are marked with N or MC.

Item	Blue	Crystal	Green	Pink
Berry bowl, 5" d †	**$80**	**$12**	**$75**	**$75**
Berry bowl, 8-1/2" d †	**250**	**48**	**200**	**195**
Creamer, ftd	-	**32**	-	-
Cup	-	**8**	-	-
Fruit bowl, 10-1/2" d	-	**18**	-	-
Plate, 9-1/4" d, dinner	-	**12**	-	-
Sandwich plate, 12" d	-	**18**	-	-
Saucer	-	**5**	-	-
Sugar, open, ftd	-	**25**	-	-

Heritage, crystal plate, 9-1/4" d, ***$12***.

HEX OPTIC

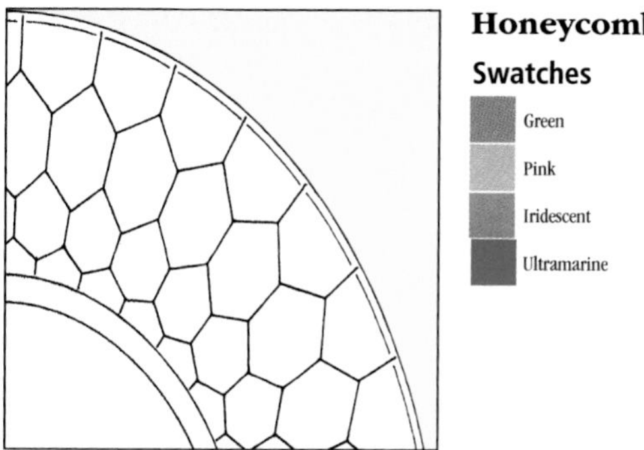

Honeycomb

Swatches

Green

Pink

Iridescent

Ultramarine

Manufactured by Jeannette Glass Company, Jeannette, Pa., from 1928 to 1932.

Made in green and pink. Ultramarine tumblers have been found. Iridescent tumblers and pitchers were made about 1960 and it is assumed that they were made by Jeannette.

Item	Green	Pink
Berry bowl, 4-1/4" d, ruffled	$9.50	$8.50
Berry bowl, 7-1/2" d	15	12
Bucket reamer	65	60
Butter dish, cov, rect, 1-lb size	90	90
Creamer, two style handles	8	7
Cup, two style handles	5	5
Ice bucket, metal handle	30	30
Mixing bowl, 8-1/4" d	18	18
Mixing bowl, 9" d	20	20

Item	Green	Pink
Mixing bowl, 10" d	20	20
Pitcher, 32 oz, 5" h	25	25
Pitcher, 48 oz, 9" h, ftd	48	50
Pitcher, 96 oz, 8" h	235	245
Plate, 6" d, sherbet	3	3
Plate, 8" d, luncheon	6	6
Platter, 11" d, round	14	16
Refrigerator dish, 4" x 4"	20	18
Refrigerator stack set, 4 pcs	75	75
Salt and pepper shakers, pr	30	30
Saucer	4	4
Sherbet, 5 oz, ftd	5	5
Sugar, two styles of handles	6	6
Sugar shaker	225	225
Tumbler, 12 oz, 5" h	8	8
Tumbler, 5-3/4" h, ftd	10	10
Tumbler, 7" h, ftd	12	12
Tumbler, 7 oz, 4-3/4" h, ftd	8	8
Tumbler, 9 oz, 3-3/4" h	5	5
Whiskey, 1 oz, 2" h	8.50	8.50

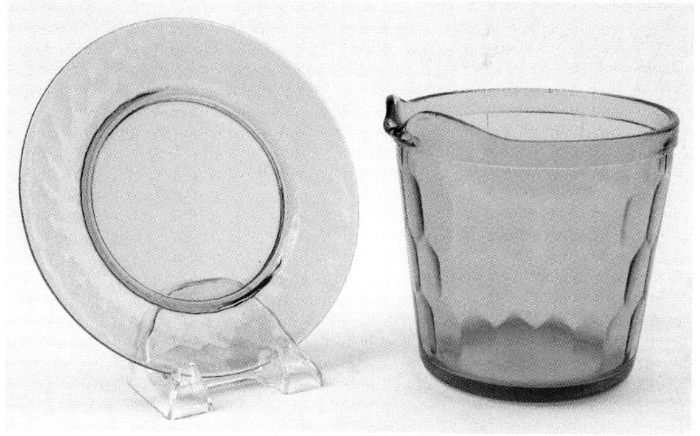

*Hex Optic, green luncheon plate **$6,** and bucket reamer base **$45**.*

HOBNAIL

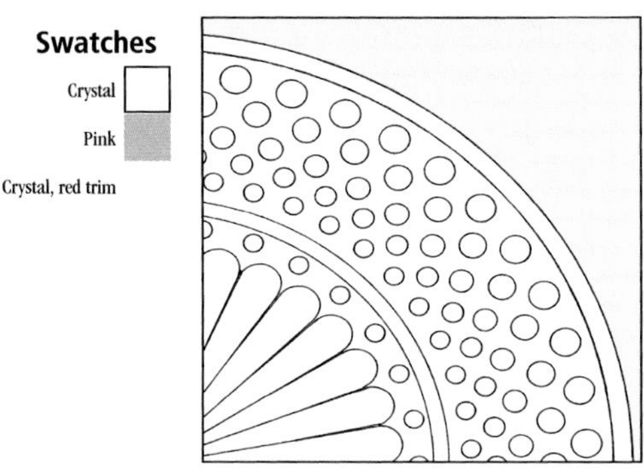

Manufactured by Hocking Glass Company, Lancaster, Ohio, from 1934 to 1936.

Made in crystal, crystal with red trim, and pink.

Item	Crystal	Crystal, red trim	Pink
Cereal bowl, 5-1/2" d	**$4.25**	**$4.25**	**$-**
Cordial, 5 oz, ftd	**6**	**6**	**-**
Creamer, ftd	**4**	**4**	**-**
Cup	**5**	**5**	**6**
Decanter and stopper, 32 oz	**27.50**	**27.50**	**-**
Goblet, 10 oz	**7.50**	**7.50**	**-**
Iced tea goblet, 13 oz	**8.50**	**8.50**	**-**
Iced tea tumbler, 15 oz	**8.50**	**8.50**	**-**
Juice tumbler, 5 oz	**4**	**4**	**-**

Item	Crystal	Crystal, red trim	Pink
Milk pitcher, 18 oz	22	22	-
Pitcher, 67 oz	25	25	-
Plate, 6" d, sherbet	2.50	2.50	3.50
Plate, 8-1/2" d, luncheon	5.50	5.50	7.50
Salad bowl, 7" d	5	5	-
Saucer	2	2	3
Sherbet	4	4	5
Sugar, ftd	4	4	-
Tumbler, 9 oz, 4-3/4" h, flat	5	5	-
Whiskey, 1-1/2 oz	5	5	-
Wine, 3 oz, ftd	6.50	6.50	-

*Hobnail, pink sherbet **$5**.*

Button and Bows

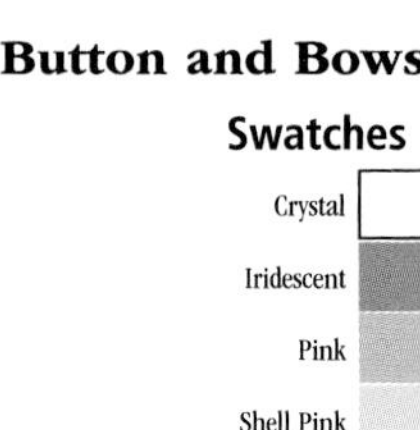

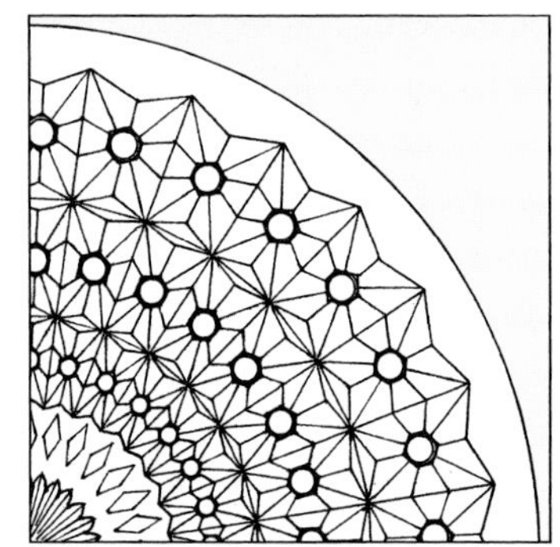

Manufactured by Jeannette Glass Company, Jeannette, Pa., from 1947 to the 1950s.

Made in crystal, iridescent, pink, and shell pink. Shell pink production was limited to the console bowl, valued at $48.

Item	Crystal	Irid.	Pink
Berry bowl, 5-1/8" d	$-	$-	$16
Berry bowl, 8-1/2" d	-	-	55
Butter dish, cov	-	-	60
Cake plate, 10-1/2" d, three legs	-	-	220
Candlesticks, pr, 3" h	-	-	125
Chop plate, 13-3/4" d	-	-	140
Console bowl, 10-1/4" d	-	-	225
Creamer, ftd	-	-	20
Cup, plain	-	-	15
Cup, rayed bottom, 2" d base	-	-	12

Item	Crystal	Irid.	Pink
Cup, rayed bottom, 2-3/8" d base	-	-	16
Juice tumbler, 5 oz, 4" h, ftd	-	-	60
Pitcher, 16 oz, 4-3/4" h	17.50	35	85
Pitcher, 52 oz, 6-3/4" h	-	-	45
Plate, 6" d, sherbet	-	-	8.50
Plate, 9" d, dinner	-	-	25
Platter, 11-3/8" l, oval	-	17.50	30
Sandwich tray, 10-1/2" l	-	20	28
Saucer, plain center	-	-	5
Saucer, rayed center, 2-1/8" d ring	-	-	7.50
Saucer, rayed center, 2-1/2" d ring	-	-	7.50
Sherbet	-	-	12
Soup bowl, 7-3/4" d	-	-	82
Sugar, cov	-	-	30
Sugar lid	-	-	20
Tumbler, 5 oz, 4" h, ftd	-	15	35
Tumbler, 5-1/4 oz, 4-1/4" h, ftd	8	-	45
Tumbler, 6" h, ftd	-	-	195
Tumbler, 9 oz, 4" h, ftd	-	-	55
Tumbler, 10 oz, 4" h, flat	-	-	28
Vegetable bowl, 9-1/2" l, oval	-	-	36

Holiday, pink pitcher, 4-3/4" h ***$85.***

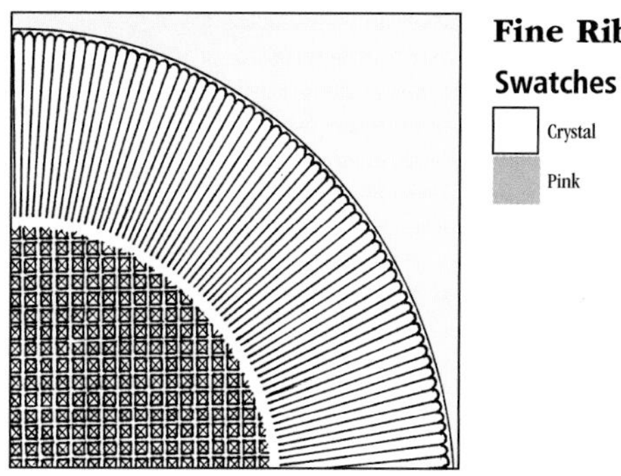

Fine Rib

Swatches

Crystal

Pink

Manufactured by Jeannette Glass Company, Jeannette, Pa., from 1939 to 1949.

Made in crystal and pink.

Item	Crystal	Pink
Ashtray	$6	$6
Berry bowl, 4-1/2" d, closed handles	15	15
Berry bowl, 8-1/4" d	20	20
Butter dish, cov	55	60
Cereal bowl, 5" d, closed handles	30	30
Coaster	6	6
Creamer, ftd	12.50	12.50
Cup	12	12
Iced tea tumbler, 13 oz, 5-1/4" h	32	32
Plate, 6" d, sherbet	7.50	7.50
Plate, 9-1/4" d, dinner	18	18

Item	Crystal	Pink
Platter, 13" d, closed handles	20	20
Saucer	5.50	5.50
Sherbet, low, flat	17.50	19
Sugar, ftd	12.50	12.50
Tumbler, 5 oz, 4" h, ftd	8	8
Tumbler, 6 oz, 3-7/8" h, straight	7	7
Tumbler, 9 oz, 4" h, flared top	17.50	17.50
Tumbler, 9 oz, 4-1/4" h, top band	17.50	17.50
Tumbler, 15 oz, 6-1/4" h, ftd	38	38
Tumbler, 15 oz, 6-3/8" h, ftd	36	36

Children's

Item	Crystal	Pink
Cup	$25	$35
Plate	10	15
Saucer	9	12
Teapot	-	125

*Homespun, pink sugar **$12.50**, and look-alike tumbler.*

HORSESHOE

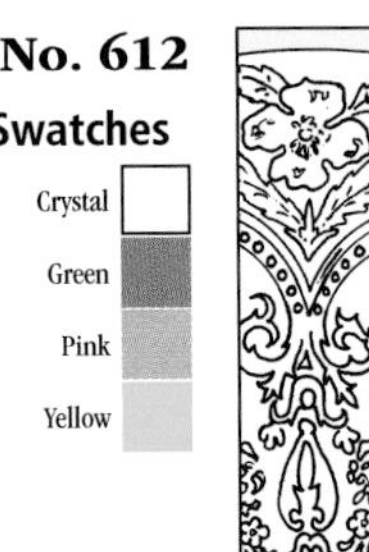

Manufactured by Indiana Glass Company, Dunkirk, Ind., from 1930 to 1933.

Made in crystal, green, pink, and yellow. There is limited collector interest in crystal and pink at the current time.

Item	Green	Yellow
Berry bowl, 4-1/2" d	$30	$25
Berry bowl, 9-1/2" d	40	35
Butter dish, cov	750	-
Candy dish, metal holder	175	-
Cereal bowl, 6-1/2" d	25	35
Creamer, ftd	18	20
Cup and saucer	20	24
Pitcher, 64 oz, 8-1/2" h	295	350
Plate, 6" d, sherbet	9	9
Plate, 8-3/8" d, salad	10	10

Item	Green	Yellow
Plate, 9-3/8" d, luncheon	15	20
Plate, 10-3/8" d, grill	125	150
Platter, 10-3/4" l, oval	25	25
Relish, three parts, ftd	20	24
Salad bowl, 7-1/2" d	24	24
Sandwich plate, 11-1/2" d	24	27.50
Saucer	6	6.50
Sherbet	16	18.50
Sugar, open	16.50	17
Tumbler, 9 oz, ftd	25	28
Tumbler, 9 oz, 4-1/4" h	150	-

*Horseshoe, yellow cup **$17.50**.*

Item	Green	Yellow
Tumbler, 12 oz, ftd	140	150
Tumbler, 12 oz, 4-3/4" h	150	-
Vegetable bowl, 8-1/2" d	30	30
Vegetable bowl, 10-1/2" d, oval	25	28.50

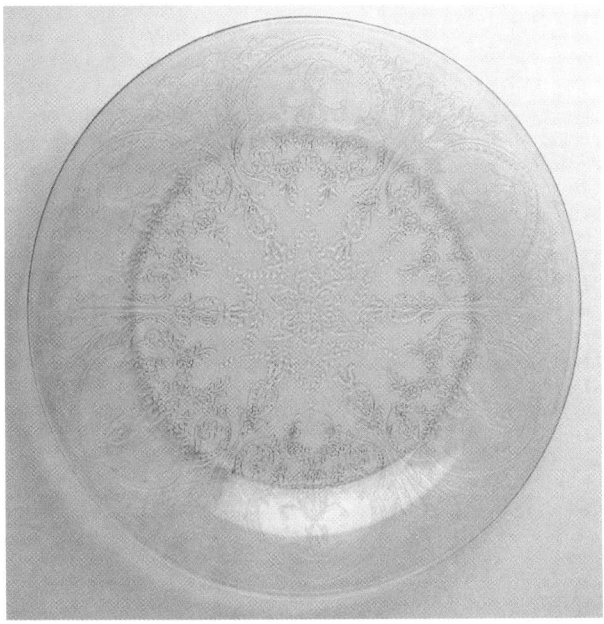

*Horseshoe, yellow luncheon plate **$20**.*

Flower and Leaf Band

Swatches

French Ivory

Manufactured by Indiana Glass Company, Dunkirk, Ind., in the 1930s and in the 1950s.

Made in custard color, known as French Ivory.

Item	French Ivory
Berry bowl, 5-1/2" d	$16.50
Berry bowl, 9" d, 1-3/4" deep	36
Butter dish, cov	68
Cereal bowl, 6-1/2" d	8
Creamer	20
Cup	38
Plate, 5-3/4" d, bread and butter	7
Plate, 7-1/2" d, salad	16
Plate, 8-7/8" d, luncheon	18
Plate, 9-3/4" d, dinner	28
Platter, 11-1/2" l, oval	30

Item	French Ivory
Saucer	12
Sherbet	90
Soup bowl, 7-1/2" d, flat	32
Sugar, cov	35

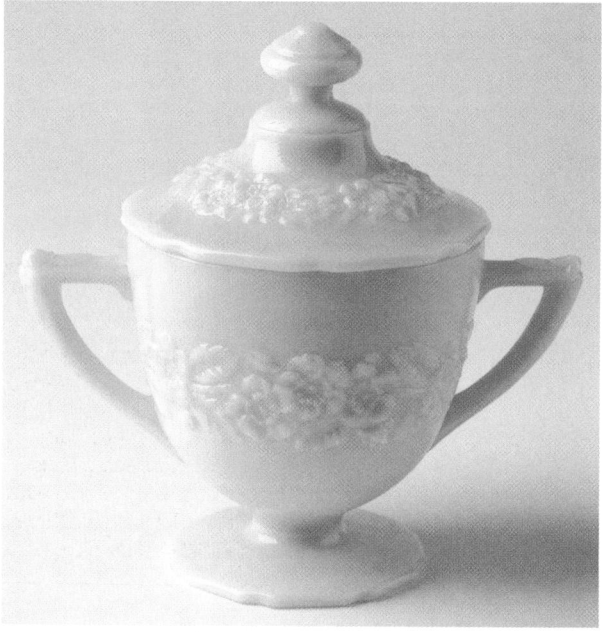

Indiana Custard, covered sugar ***$35.***

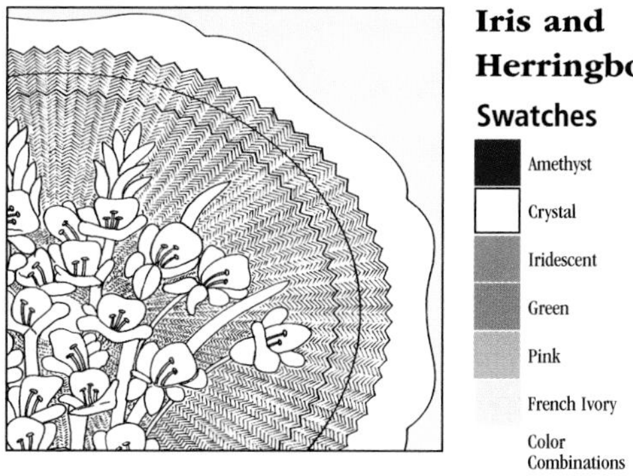

Iris and Herringbone

Swatches

Amethyst

Crystal

Iridescent

Green

Pink

French Ivory

Color Combinations

Manufactured by Jeannette Glass Company, Jeannette, Pa., from 1928 to 1932 and in the 1950s and 1970s.

Made in crystal, iridescent, some green, and pink. Recent color combinations of red with yellow, blue with green, and white have been made. A record price of $495 is noted for a rare amethyst demitasse cup and saucer.

Reproductions: † Some collectors and dealers feel strongly that the newer re-issues of this pattern are actually reproductions. Forms that have the potential to fool buyers are the 4-1/2" berry bowl, covered candy jar, 10" d dinner plate, 6-1/2" h footed tumbler, and vase. Careful examination of the object, plus careful consideration of the color, should help determine age.

Item	Crystal	Green	Iridescent	Pink
Berry bowl, 4-1/2" d, beaded edge †	$50	$-	$20	$-
Berry bowl, 8" d, beaded edge	135	-	30	-
Bowl, 5-1/2" d, scalloped	10	-	23	-
Bowl, 9-1/2" d, scalloped	17.50	-	14	-
Bread plate, 11-3/4" d	20	-	38	-
Butter dish, cov	60	-	65	-
Candlesticks, pr	50	-	55	-
Candy jar, cov †	195	-	-	-
Cereal bowl, 5" d	150	-	-	-
Coaster †	120	-	-	-
Cocktail, 4 oz, 4-1/4" h	32	-	-	-
Creamer, ftd	25	150	17.50	150
Cup	22	-	20	-
Demitasse cup and saucer	225	-	350	-
Fruit bowl, 11" d, straight edge	75	-	-	-
Fruit bowl, 11-1/2" d, ruffled	25	-	18	-
Fruit set	110	-	-	-
Goblet, 4 oz, 5-3/4" h	30	-	135	-
Goblet, 8 oz, 5-3/4" h	35	-	175	-
Iced tea tumbler, 6-1/2" h, ftd	42	-	-	-
Lamp shade, 11-1/2"	100	-	-	-
Nut set	115	-	-	-
Pitcher, 9-1/2" h, ftd	50	-	50	-
Plate, 5-1/2" d, sherbet	16	-	15	-
Plate, 7" d	95	-	-	-
Plate, 8" d, luncheon	130	-	115	-
Plate, 9" d, dinner †	65	-	48	-
Salad bowl, 9-1/2" d, ruffled	20	150	20	135
Sandwich plate, 11-3/4" d	55	-	40	-
Sauce, 5" d, ruffled	12.50	-	30	-

Item	Crystal	Green	Iridescent	Pink
Saucer	15	-	11	-
Sherbet, 2-1/2" h, ftd	35	-	15.50	-
Sherbet, 4" h, ftd	30	-	15.50	-
Soup bowl, 7-1/2" d	185	-	90	-
Sugar, cov	32	150	23	150
Tumbler, 4" h, flat †	150	-	18	-
Tumbler, 6" h, ftd †	30	-	25	-
Tumbler, 6-1/2" h, ftd †	40	-	-	-
Tumbler, flat, water †	135	-	-	-
Vase, 9" h †	38	-	35	225
Wine, 4" h	20	-	33.50	-
Wine, 4-1/4" h, 3 oz	24	-	-	-
Wine, 5-1/2" h	27.50	-	-	-

*Iris, crystal candlesticks **$50**, and iridescent dinner plate **$48**.*

JUBILEE

Swatches

Pink

Yellow

Manufactured by Lancaster Glass Company, Lancaster, Ohio, early 1930s.

Made in pink and yellow.

Item	Pink	Yellow
Bowl, 8" d, 5-1/8" h, three legs	$275	$225
Bowl, 11-1/2" d, three legs	265	250
Bowl, 11-1/2" d, three legs, curved in	-	250
Bowl, 13" d, three legs	250	245
Cake tray, 11" d, two handles	75	85
Candlesticks, pr	190	195
Candy jar, cov, three legs	325	325
Cheese and cracker set	265	255
Cordial, 1 oz, 4" h	-	245
Creamer	45	30
Cup	40	17.50

Item	Pink	Yellow
Fruit bowl, 9" d, handle	-	125
Fruit bowl, 11-1/2" h, flat	200	165
Goblet, 3 oz, 4-7/8" h	-	150
Goblet, 11 oz, 7-1/2" h	-	75
Iced tea tumbler, 12-1/2 oz, 6 1/8" h	-	135
Juice tumbler, 6 oz, 5" h, ftd	-	100
Mayonnaise, plate, orig ladle	315	285
Mayonnaise underplate	125	110

*Jubilee, yellow saucer **$8**, and cup **$17.50**.*

Item	Pink	Yellow
Plate, 7" d, salad	25	14
Plate, 8-3/4" d, luncheon	30	16.50
Plate, 14" d, three legs	-	210
Sandwich plate, 13-1/2" d	95	85
Sandwich tray, 11" d, center handle	215	250
Saucer	15	8
Sherbet, 8 oz, 3" h	-	75
Sherbet/champagne, 7 oz, 5-1/2" h	-	75
Sugar	40	24
Tumbler, 10 oz, 6" h, ftd	75	35
Vase, 12" h	-	385

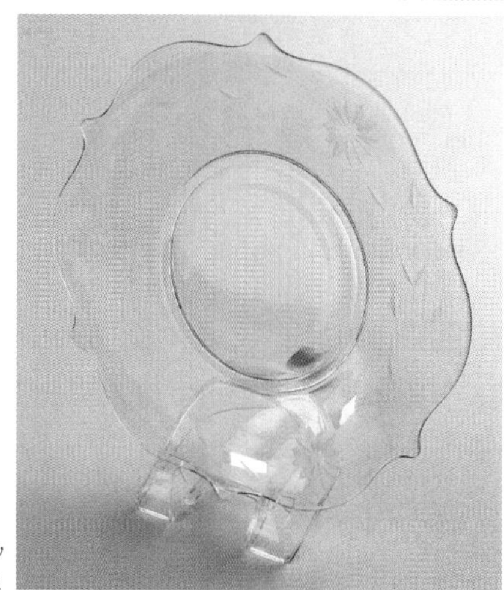

*Jubilee, yellow luncheon plate **$16.50**.*

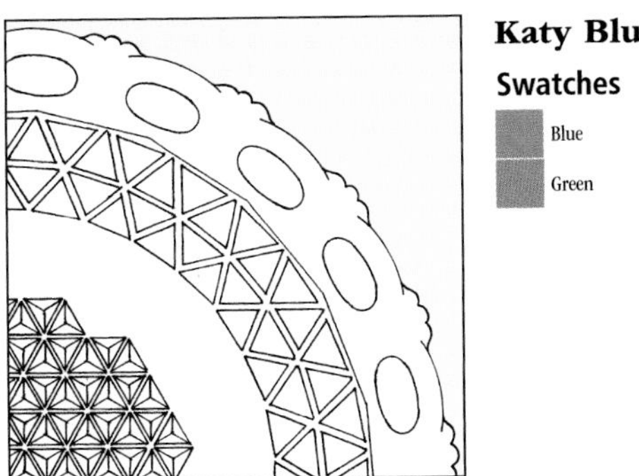

Katy Blue

Swatches

Blue

Green

Manufactured by Imperial Glass Company, Bellaire, Ohio, early 1930s.

Made in blue and green with opalescent edges.

Item	Blue	Green
Basket, 9" d	$265	$-
Bowl, 5" d	40	40
Bowl, 5-1/2" d	42	42
Bowl, 5-7/8" d	42	42
Bowl, 11" l, oval	295	285
Bowl, 11" l, oval, divided	165	165
Candlesticks, pr, double lite	175	180
Creamer	45	40
Cup	35	35
Fruit bowl, 4-1/2" d	32	30
Mayonnaise, three pieces	100	125

Item	Blue	Green
Plate, 6-1/2" d, bread and butter	24	24
Plate, 8" d, salad	35	35
Plate, 10" d, dinner	95	95
Plate, 12" d, luncheon	90	90
Platter, 13" l	185	165
Saucer	18	15
Soup bowl, 7" d	85	80
Sugar	45	40
Tidbit, two tiers, 8" and 10" plates	110	100
Tumbler, 9 oz	60	60
Vegetable bowl, 9" d	95	95

Laced Edge, blue bowl, 5-1/2" d, ***$42.***

LAKE COMO

Swatches

White

Manufactured by Hocking Glass Company, Lancaster, Ohio, from 1934 to 1937.

Made in opaque white with a blue scene.

Item	White
Cereal bowl, 6" d	$30
Creamer, ftd	35
Cup, regular	32
Cup, St. Denis	35
Plate, 7-1/4" d, salad	30
Plate, 9-1/4" d, dinner	35
Platter, 11" d	70
Salt and pepper shakers, pr	48
Saucer	12
Saucer, St. Denis	12
Soup bowl, flat	100

Item	White
Sugar, ftd	35
Vegetable bowl, 9-3/4" l	65

*Lake Como, blue and white salad plate **$30**.*

LAUREL

Swatches

French Ivory

Jade-ite

Poudre Blue

White Opal

Manufactured by McKee Glass Company, Pittsburgh, Pa., 1930s. Made in French Ivory, Jade Green, Poudre Blue, and White Opal.

Item	French Ivory	Jade-ite	Poudre Blue	White Opal
Berry bowl, 4-3/4" d	$9	$15	$16	$14
Berry bowl, 9" d	28.50	40	55	30
Bowl, 6" d, three legs	15	25	-	15
Bowl, 10-1/2" d, three legs	37.50	50	68	45
Bowl, 11" d	40	55	85	37.50
Candlesticks, pr, 4" h	50	65	-	45
Cereal bowl, 6" d	12	25	28	20
Cheese dish, cov	60	95	-	75
Creamer, short	12	25	-	18
Creamer, tall	15	28	40	24
Cup	9.50	15	20	12

Item	French Ivory	Jade-ite	Poudre Blue	White Opal
Plate, 6" d, sherbet	6	15	10	8
Plate, 7-1/2" d, salad	10	20	17.50	12
Plate, 9-1/8" d, dinner	15	25	30	18.50
Plate, 9-1/8" d, grill, round	15	25	-	18.50
Plate, 9-1/8" d, grill, scalloped	15	25	-	18.50
Platter, 10-3/4" l, oval	32	48	45	30
Salt and pepper shakers, pr	60	85	-	65
Saucer	3.25	4.50	7.50	3.50
Sherbet	12.50	20	-	18
Sherbet/champagne, 5"	50	72	-	60
Soup bowl, 7-7/8" d	35	40	-	40
Sugar, short	12	25	-	18
Sugar, tall	15	28	40	24
Tumbler, 9 oz, 4-1/2" h, flat	40	60	-	60
Tumbler, 12 oz, 5" h, flat	60	-	-	-
Vegetable bowl, 9-3/4" l, oval	18.50	480	45	20

Children's

Item	Plain	Green or Decorated	Scotty Dog Green	Scotty Dog Ivory
Creamer	$30	$100	$250	$125
Cup	25	50	100	50
Plate	15	20	75	40
Saucer	12	14	75	40
Sugar	30	100	250	125

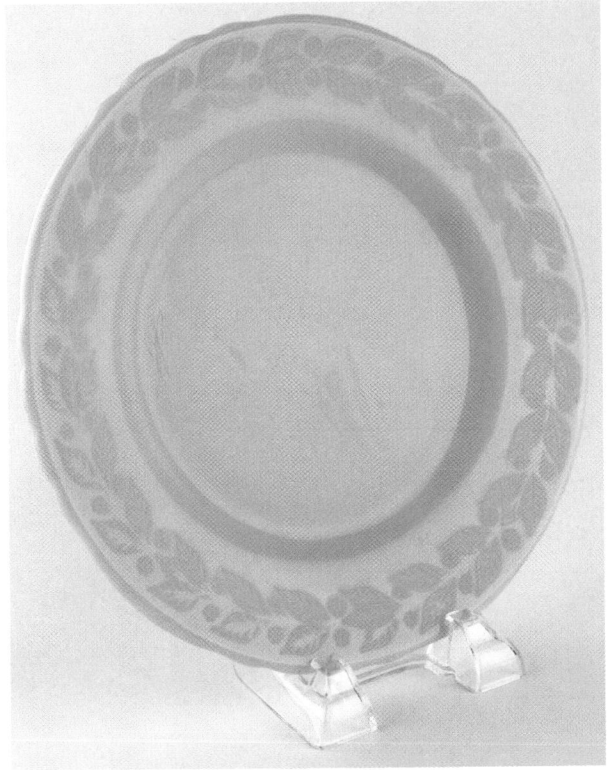

*Laurel, Jade-ite dinner plate **$25**.*

LINCOLN INN

Swatches

Amethyst

Cobalt Blue

Crystal

Red

Other Colors

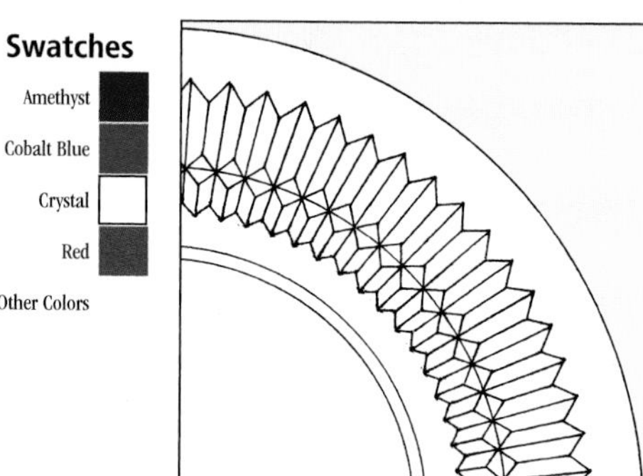

Manufactured by Fenton Art Glass Company, Williamstown, W.V., late 1920s.

Made in amber, amethyst, black, cobalt blue, crystal, green, green opalescent, light blue, opaque jade, pink, and red. Production in black was limited to salt and pepper shakers, valued at $325. Some rare pieces have been identified in several other colors.

Item	Cobalt Blue	Crystal	Other Colors	Red
Ashtray	$17.50	$12	$12	$17.50
Bonbon, oval, handle	17.50	12	14	18
Bonbon, sq, handle	15	12	14	15
Bowl, 6" d, crimped	14.50	7.50	10	14.50
Bowl, 9-1/4" d, ftd	42	18	20	45
Bowl, 10-1/2" d, ftd	50	28	30	50
Candy dish, ftd, oval	24	14.50	14.50	24

Item	Cobalt Blue	Crystal	Other Colors	Red
Cereal bowl, 6" d	12.50	7.50	9.50	12.50
Comport	25	14	15	25
Creamer	24	12	15	24
Cup	17.50	8.50	9.50	18
Finger bowl	20	14	14.50	20
Fruit bowl, 5" d	14	7	9	14
Goblet, 6" h	30	18.50	16	30
Iced tea tumbler, 12 oz, ftd	40	22	24	40
Juice tumbler, 4 oz, flat	27.50	9	14	27.50
Nut dish, ftd	20	14.50	16	20
Pitcher, 46 oz, 7-1/4" h	820	700	715	820
Plate, 6" d	19.50	12	12.50	19.50
Plate, 8" d	27.50	15	14	27.50

Lincoln Inn, pink plate, 8" d ***$14.***

Item	Cobalt Blue	Crystal	Other Colors	Red
Plate, 9-1/4" d	30	15	16.50	30
Plate, 12" d	35	16	18	35
Salt and pepper shakers, pr	265	175	175	265
Sandwich server, center handle	175	110	110	175
Saucer	5	4	4.50	5
Sherbet, 4-1/2" h, cone shape	18	12	14	18
Sherbet, 4-3/4" h	20	14	14.50	20
Sugar	24	12	15	24
Tumbler, 5 oz, ftd	24	14	14.50	24
Tumbler, 9 oz, flat	-	14	15	15
Tumbler, 9 oz, ftd	28	32	35	30
Vase, 9-3/4" h	160	85	95	145
Vase, 12" h, ftd	225	115	125	175
Wine	35	20	24	40

*Lincoln Inn, cobalt blue goblet **$30**.*

LORAIN

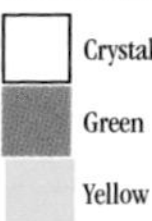

Basket, No. 615

Swatches

Crystal

Green

Yellow

Manufactured by Indiana Glass Company, Dunkirk, Ind., from 1929 to 1939.

Made in crystal, green, and yellow.

Reproductions: † A fantasy sherbet has been reported in both milk white and avocado green.

Item	Crystal	Green	Yellow
Berry bowl, 8" d	$125	$190	$250
Cereal bowl, 6" d	45	50	65
Creamer, ftd	20	20	30
Cup and saucer	32	32	25
Plate, 5-1/2" d, sherbet	10	12	15
Plate, 7-3/4" d, salad	15	18	24
Plate, 8-3/4" d, luncheon	20	24	32.50
Plate, 10-1/4" d, dinner	30	40	90
Platter, 11-1/2" l	32.50	32.50	48

Item	Crystal	Green	Yellow
Relish, 8" d, four parts	32	32	40
Salad bowl, 7-3/4" d	40	40	75
Saucer	6	6	8
Sherbet, ftd †	32	20	40
Snack tray, crystal trim	32	37.50	-
Sugar, ftd	20	24	30
Tumbler, 9 oz, 4-3/4" h, ftd	32	35	40
Vegetable bowl, 9-3/4" l, oval	5000	60	75

*Lorain, yellow luncheon plate **$32.50**, and tumbler **$40**.*

MADRID

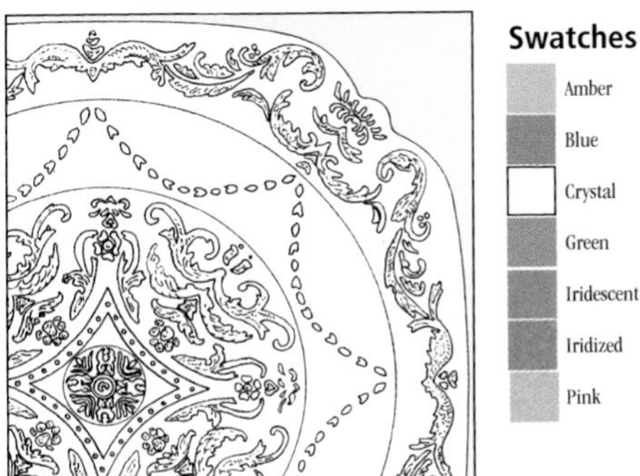

Manufactured by Federal Glass Company, Lancaster, Ohio, from 1932 to 1939.

Made in amber, blue, crystal, green, iridescent, and pink. Iridized pieces are limited to a console set, consisting of a low bowl and pair of candlesticks, valued at $40.

Reproductions: † Reproductions include candlesticks, cups, saucers and vegetable bowl. Reproductions are found in amber, blue, crystal, and pink. Federal Glass Company reissued this pattern under the name "Recollection." Some of these pieces were dated 1976. When Federal went bankrupt, the molds were sold to Indiana Glass, which removed the date and began production of crystal, then pink. Several pieces were made recently that were not part of the original production and include a footed cake stand, goblet, two-section grill plate, preserves stand, squatty salt and pepper shakers, 11-oz tumbler and vase.

Item	Amber	Blue	Crystal	Green	Pink
Ashtray, 6" sq	$300	$-	$-	$295	$-
Berry bowl, small	7.50	-	6.50	-	-
Berry bowl, 9-3/8" d	25	-	25	-	25
Bowl, 7" d	17.50	-	12	17.50	-
Butter dish, cov	80	-	65	90	-
Cake plate, 11-1/4" d	24	-	20	-	28
Candlesticks, 2-1/4" h, pr †	18.50	-	14.50	-	28
Coaster, 5" d	40	-	40	35	-
Console bowl, 11" d	20	-	18	-	36
Cookie jar	50	-	45	-	40
Creamer	12	18	7	10	-
Cream soup, 4 3/4" d	18	-	15.50	-	-
Cup †	14	20	6.50	12	8.50
Gravy boat	1,950	-	900	-	-
Gravy boat platter	900	-	900	-	-
Hot dish coaster, 3-1/2" d	95	-	40	45	-
Iced tea tumbler, round	24	-	24	22	-
Jam dish, 7" d	24	35	12	25	-
Juice pitcher	50	-	45	-	-
Juice tumbler, 5 oz, 3-7/8" h, ftd	16.50	40	35	30	-
Pitcher, jug-type	60	-	24	190	-
Pitcher, 60 oz, 8" h, sq	50	225	150	145	50
Pitcher, 80 oz, 8-1/2" h, ice lip	75	-	30	225	-
Plate, 6" d, sherbet	5.50	12	4	4.50	4
Plate, 7-1/2" d, salad	12	17	12	9	9
Plate, 8-7/8" d, luncheon	10	20	7.50	12	10
Plate, 10-1/2" d, dinner	48	60	24	45	-

Item	Amber	Blue	Crystal	Green	Pink
Plate, 10-1/2" d, grill	12	-	10	18.50	-
Platter, 11-1/2" oval	20	32	20	18	18
Relish dish, 10-1/2" d	14.50	-	7	16	20
Salad bowl, 8" d	17	-	9.50	15.50	-
Salad bowl, 9-1/2" d	32	-	30	-	-
Salt and pepper shakers, 3-1/2" h	135	145	95	110	-
Sauce bowl, 5" d	9	-	7.50	8.50	11
Saucer †	5	8	4	7	5
Sherbet, cone	7.50	18	6.50	14	-
Sherbet, ftd	8.50	15	6	11	-
Soup bowl, 7" d †	15	20	6	15.50	-
Sugar, cov †	46	175	32.50	48	-

*Madrid, amber sugar **$10**, and creamer **$12**.*

Item	Amber	Blue	Crystal	Green	Pink
Sugar, open †	10	15	8	10	-
Tumbler, 9 oz, 4-1/2" h	20	40	17.50	25	25
Tumbler, 12 oz, 5-1/4" h, ftd or flat	35	-	30	40	-
Vegetable bowl, 10" l, oval †	28	35	24	24	30

*Madrid, amber grill plate **$12**, berry bowl **$7.50**, and cup **$14**.*

*Madrid, amber bowl **$17.50**.*

MANHATTAN

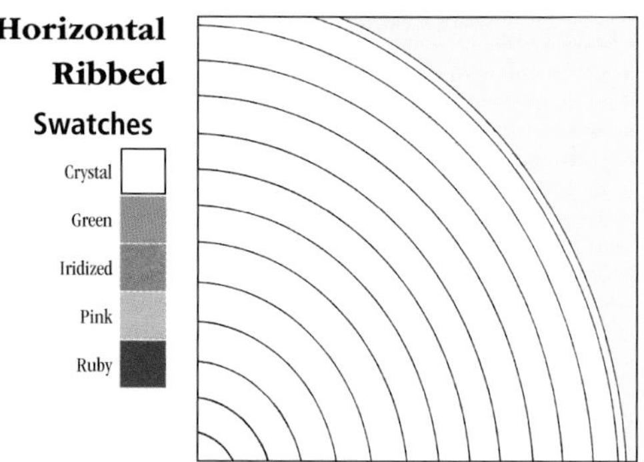

Manufactured by Anchor Hocking Glass Company, from 1938 to 1943.

Made in crystal, green, iridized, pink, and ruby. Ruby pieces are limited to relish tray inserts, currently valued at $8 each. Green and iridized production was limited to footed tumblers, currently valued at $17.50.

Anchor Hocking introduced a similar pattern, Park Avenue, in 1987. Anchor Hocking was careful to preserve the Manhattan pattern. Collectors should pay careful attention to measurements if they are uncertain of the pattern.

Item	Crystal	Pink
Ashtray, 4" d, round	$12	$10
Ashtray, 4-1/2" w, sq	25	-
Berry bowl, 5-3/8" d, handles	24	24

Item	Crystal	Pink
Berry bowl, 7-1/2" d	28	-
Bowl, 4-1/2" d	9	-
Bowl, 8" d, closed handles	28	25
Bowl, 8" d, metal handle	25	-
Bowl, 9-1/2" d, handle	-	45
Candlesticks, pr, 4-1/2" h	25	-
Candy dish, three legs	-	16
Candy dish, cov	40	-
Cereal bowl, 5-1/4" d, no handles	95	-
Coaster, 3-1/2"	20	-
Cocktail	18	-
Comport, 5-3/4" h	35	65
Creamer, oval	9	20
Cup	20	160
Fruit bowl, 9-1/2" d, two open handles	40	50
Juice pitcher, 24 oz	40	-
Pitcher, 80 oz, tilted	55	85
Plate, 6" d, sherbet	7	50
Plate, 8-1/2" d, salad	24	-
Plate, 10-1/4" d, dinner	30	120
Relish tray insert	2.50	6
Relish tray, 14" d, inserts	85	50
Relish tray, 14" d, four parts	65	-
Salad bowl, 9" d	20	-
Salt and pepper shakers, pr, 2" h, sq	50	60
Sandwich plate, 14" d	22	-
Sauce bowl, 4-1/2" d, handles	12	-
Saucer	7	50

Item	Crystal	Pink
Sherbet	14	20
Sugar, oval	12	17.50
Tumbler, 10 oz, 5-1/4" h, ftd	22	25
Vase, 8" h	30	-
Wine, 3-1/2" h	15	-

*Manhattan, relish tray with ruby inserts and crystal base **$85** and crystal comport **$35**, vase **$30**, and fruit bowl with open handles **$40**.*

Manhattan, small crystal bowl (on pedestal) ***$9****; pink creamer* ***$20*** *and sugar* ***$17.50****; crystal salt and pepper shakers* ***$50****; crystal cereal bowl* ***$95****; crystal iced tea tumbler* ***$22****; crystal pitcher* ***$55****; relish with metal stand* ***$30****; and pink ftd candy dish* ***$16****.*

MAYFAIR

Federal

Swatches

Amber

Crystal

Green

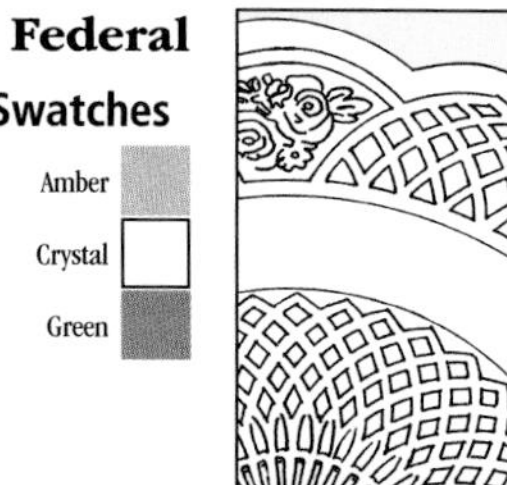

Manufactured by Federal Glass Company, Columbus, Ohio, 1934. Made in amber, crystal, and green.

Item	Amber	Crystal	Green
Cereal bowl, 6" d	$18.50	$15	$22
Cream soup, 5" d	22	12	20
Creamer, ftd	17.50	14	16
Cup	8.50	5	8.50
Plate, 6-3/4" d, salad	7	4.50	8.50
Plate, 9-1/2" d, dinner	14	12	14.50
Plate, 9-1/2" d, grill	17.50	15	17.50
Platter, 12" l, oval	27.50	22	30
Sauce bowl, 5" d	8.50	7	12
Saucer	4.50	2.50	4.50
Sugar, ftd	14	12	14

Item	Amber	Crystal	Green
Tumbler, 9 oz, 4-1/2" h	27.50	16.50	32
Vegetable, 10" l, oval	32	32	32

Mayfair, amber dinner plate ***$14***.

MAYFAIR

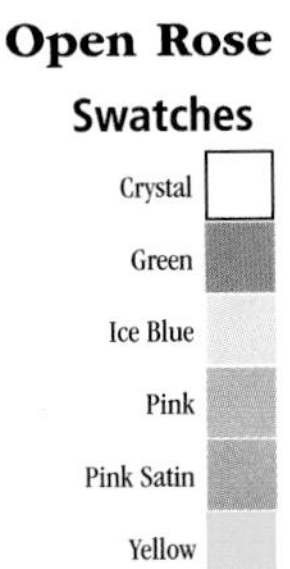

Manufactured by Hocking Glass Company, Lancaster, Ohio, from 1931 to 1937.

Made in crystal, green, ice blue, pink, pink satin, and yellow.

Reproductions: † This pattern has been plagued with reproductions since 1977. Items reproduced include cookie jars, salt and pepper shakers, juice pitchers, and whiskey glasses. Reproductions are found in amethyst, blue, cobalt blue, green, pink, and red.

Item	Crystal	Green	Ice Blue	Pink	Pink Satin	Yellow
Bowl, 11-3/4" l, flat	$-	$35	$75	$65	$70	$195
Butter dish, cov	-	1,295	325	80	95	1,295
Cake plate, 10" d, ftd	-	115	75	40	45	-

Item	Crystal	Green	Ice Blue	Pink	Pink Satin	Yellow
Cake plate, 12" d, handles	-	40	95	65	50	-
Candy dish, cov	-	575	325	70	85	475
Celery dish, 9" l, divided	-	155	60	-	-	150
Celery dish, 10" l, divided	-	-	90	295	-	-
Celery dish, 10" l, not divided	-	115	80	55	50	115
Cereal bowl, 5-1/2" d	-	24	48	30	35	75
Claret, 4-1/2 oz, 5-1/4" h	-	950	-	1,150	-	-
Cocktail, 3 oz, 4" h	-	975	-	125	-	-

*Mayfair, pink 11 oz tumbler **$225**, and pink satin-finish covered cookie jar **$37**.*

Item	Crystal	Green	Ice Blue	Pink	Pink Satin	Yellow
Console bowl, 9" d, 3-1/8" h, three legs	-	5,000	-	5,000	-	-
Cookie jar, cov †	-	575	295	75	37	860
Cordial, 1 oz, 3-3/4" h	-	950	-	1,100	-	-
Cream soup, 5" d	-	-	-	65	68	-
Creamer, ftd	-			35	30	
Cup	-	150	55	24	27.50	150
Decanter, stopper, 32 oz	-	-	-	225	-	-
Fruit bowl, 12" d, scalloped	-	50	125	90	75	215
Goblet, 2-1/2 oz, 4-1/8"	-	950	-	950	-	-
Goblet, 9 oz, 5-3/4" h	-	465	-	90	-	-
Goblet, 9 oz, 7-1/4" h, thin	-	-	225	250	-	-
Iced tea tumbler, 13-1/2 oz, 5-1/4" h			225	70		
Iced tea tumbler, 15 oz, 6-1/2" h, ftd	-	250	285	65	65	-

Item	Crystal	Green	Ice Blue	Pink	Pink Satin	Yellow
Juice pitcher, 37 oz, 6" h †	24.50	525	150	70	65	525
Juice tumbler, 3 oz, 3-1/4" h, ftd	-	-	-	80	-	-
Juice tumbler, 5 oz, 3-1/2" h	-	-	225	80	-	-
Pitcher, 60 oz, 8" h	-	475	195	95	100	425
Pitcher, 80 oz, 8-1/2" h	-	725	295	130	135	725
Plate, 5-3/4" d	-	90	25	15	15	90
Plate, 6-1/2" d, off-center indent	-	115	42	30	35	-

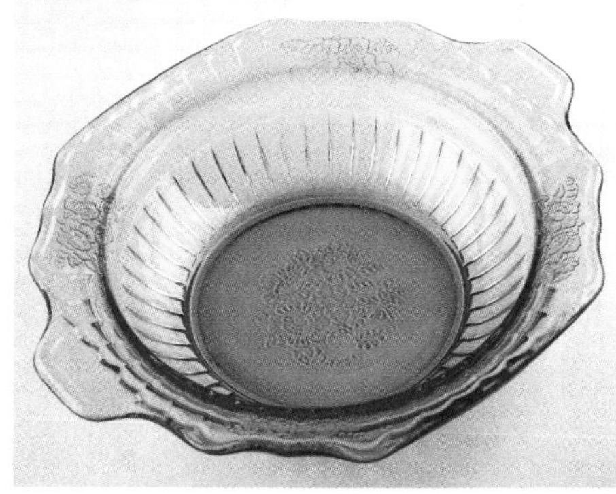

*Mayfair, blue handled vegetable bowl **$75**.*

Item	Crystal	Green	Ice Blue	Pink	Pink Satin	Yellow
Plate, 6-1/2" d, sherbet	-	-	24	14.50	-	-
Plate, 8-1/2" d, luncheon	-	85	55	40	35	80
Plate, 9-1/2" d, dinner	-	150	90	65	62	150
Plate, 9-1/2" d, grill	-	75	70	50	35	80
Plate, 11-1/2" d, grill, handles	-	-	-	-	-	100
Platter, 12" l, oval, open handles	17.50	175	60	40	35	115

Mayfair, crystal, platter, oval, open handles ***$17.50.***

Item	Crystal	Green	Ice Blue	Pink	Pink Satin	Yellow
Platter, 12-1/2" oval, 8" wide, closed handles	-	245	-	-	-	245
Relish, 8-3/8" d, four parts	-	160	65	37.50	37.50	160
Relish, 8-3/8" d, non-partitioned	-	275	-	200	-	275
Salt and pepper shakers, pr, flat †	20	1,000	295	65	70	800
Sandwich server, center handle	-	48	85	65	50	130

REPRODUCTION! Mayfair, green and blue cookie jars.

Item	Crystal	Green	Ice Blue	Pink	Pink Satin	Yellow
Saucer	-	90	30	45	35	140
Sherbet, 2-1/4" flat	-	-	135	185	-	-
Sherbet, 3" ftd	-	-	-	20	-	-
Sherbet, 4-3/4" ftd	-	150	75	75	75	150
Sugar, ftd	-	195	85	35	40	185
Sweet pea vase	-	285	135	250	145	-
Tumbler, 9 oz, 4-1/4" h	-	-	100	30	-	-
Tumbler, 10 oz, 5-1/4" h	-	-	145	65	-	185
Tumbler, 11 oz, 4-3/4" h	-	200	250	225	225	215
Vegetable bowl, 7" d, two handles	-	33	75	65	70	195
Vegetable bowl, 9-1/2" l, oval	-	110	70	40	30	125
Vegetable bowl, 10" d cov	-	-	120	120	120	900
Vegetable bowl, 10" d open	-	-	85	20	19	200
Whiskey, 1-1/2 oz, 2-1/4" h †	-	-	-	58	-	-
Wine, 3 oz, 4-1/2" h	-	450	-	120	-	-

MELBA

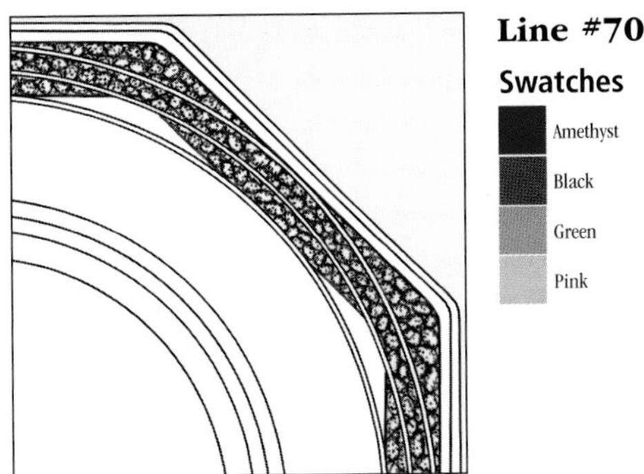

Line #707

Swatches

Amethyst
Black
Green
Pink

Manufactured by L.E. Smith Glass Company, Mount Pleasant, Pa., in the early 1930s.

Made in amethyst, black, green, and pink.

Items	Amethyst	Black	Green	Pink
Baker, oval	$20	$22	$18	$18
Bowl, 10-1/2" d, ruffled	18	20	15	15
Candleholder	15	17	12	12
Creamer	15	18	12	12
Cup	6.50	8.50	5	5
Dessert bowl	4.50	5	3.50	3.50
Plate, 6" d, bread and butter	5	7.50	4	4
Plate, 7" d, salad	7	9.50	6	6
Plate, 9" d, luncheon	9	12	8	8
Platter	15	18	12	12
Salad bowl	18	20	15	15

Items	Amethyst	Black	Green	Pink
Saucer	3.50	4.50	3	3
Serving plate, 9" d, handles	15	18	12	12
Sugar	15	18	12	12
Vegetable bowl, 9-1/2" l	18	20	15	15

*Melba, amethyst luncheon plate **$9**.*

MISS AMERICA

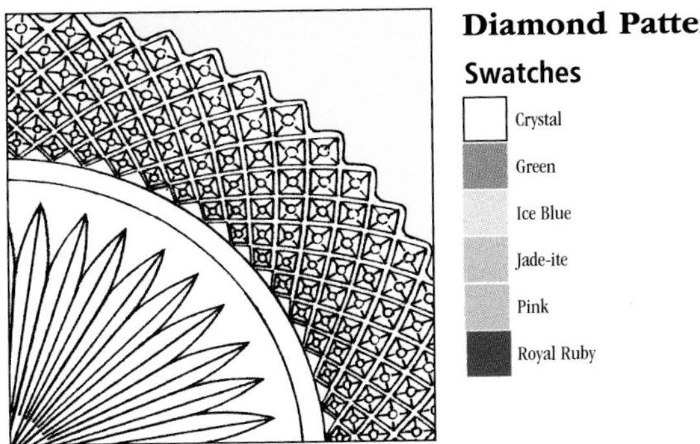

Manufactured by Hocking Glass Company, Lancaster, Ohio, from 1935 to 1938.

Made in crystal, green, ice blue, jade-ite, pink, and royal ruby.

Reproductions: † Reproductions include the butter dish (including a new importer), creamer, 8" pitcher, salt and pepper shakers, sugar, and tumbler. Reproductions are found in amberina, blue, cobalt blue, crystal, green, pink, and red.

Item	Crystal	Green	Ice Blue	Pink	Royal Ruby
Berry bowl, 4-1/2" d	$-	$15	$-	$-	$-
Bowl, 8" d, curved at top	48	-	-	95	-
Bowl, 8" d, straight sides	-	-	-	85	-
Bowl, 11" d, shallow	-	-	-	-	850
Butter dish, cov †	200	-	-	550	-

Item	Crystal	Green	Ice Blue	Pink	Royal Ruby
Cake plate, 12" d, ftd	27.50	-	-	45	-
Candy jar, cov, 11-1/2"	65	-	-	200	-
Celery dish, 10-1/2" l, oval	19.50	-	160	42	-
Cereal bowl, 6-1/4" d	12	18	-	35	-
Coaster, 5-3/4" d	19.50	-	-	45	-
Comport, 5" d	20	-	-	40	-
Creamer, ftd †	12.50	-	-	24	215
Cup	12.50	12	14	30	235
Fruit bowl, 8-3/4" d	39.50	-	-	60	450
Goblet, 10 oz, 5-1/2" h	22.50	-	-	70	250
Iced tea tumbler, 14 oz, 5-3/4" h	25	-	-	85	-
Juice goblet, 5 oz, 4-3/4" h	27.50	-	-	125	250
Juice tumbler, 5 oz, 4" h	27.50	-	150	60	200
Pitcher, 65 oz, 8-1/2" h, ice lip	75	-	-	135	50
Plate, 5-3/4" d, sherbet	7.50	9	55	18	-
Plate, 8-1/2" d, salad	9	14	-	32	150
Plate, 10-1/4" d, dinner	16.50	-	150	45	-
Plate, 10-1/4" d, grill	15	-	-	37.50	-
Platter, 12-1/4" l, oval	18	-	-	50	-
Relish, 8-3/4" l, 4 part	30	-	-	40	-
Relish, 11-3/4" d, divided	35	-	-	40	-
Salt and pepper shakers, pr †	35	300	-	65	-
Saucer	4	-	-	10	60
Sherbet	10	-	60	20	175
Sugar †	12	-	-	25	225
Tumbler, 10 oz, 4-1/2" h, flat †	20	45	-	40	-

Item	Crystal	Green	Ice Blue	Pink	Royal Ruby
Tumbler, 14 oz, 5-3/4" h	28	-	-	-	-
Vegetable bowl, 10" l, oval	18	-	-	47.50	-
Whiskey	24	-	-	-	-
Wine, 3 oz, 3-3/4" h	25	-	-	85	250

*Miss America, pink goblet **$70**, comport **$40**, and tumbler 10 oz, with original label **$40**.*

*Miss America, green plate **$9,** and berry bowl **$15**.*

MOONDROPS

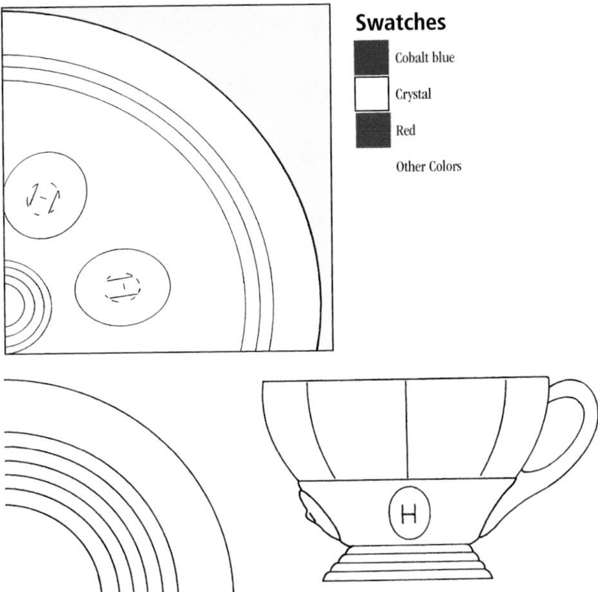

Swatches

Cobalt blue

Crystal

Red

Other Colors

Manufactured by New Martinsville Glass Company, New Martinsville, W.V., from 1932 to 1940.

Made in amber, amethyst, black, cobalt blue, crystal, dark green, green, ice blue, Jade-ite, light green, pink, red, and smoke.

Item	Cobalt Blue	Crystal	Other Colors	Red
Ashtray	$30	$-	$18	$30
Berry bowl, 5-1/4" d	20	-	12	20
Bowl, 8-1/2" d, ftd, concave top	40	-	25	40
Bowl, 9-1/2" d, three legs, ruffled	60	-	-	60
Bowl, 9-3/4" l, oval, handles	50	-	30	50
Butter dish, cov	425	-	275	295
Candlesticks, pr, 2" h, ruffled	40	-	25	40
Candlesticks, pr, 4" h, sherbet style	30	-	18	30
Candlesticks, pr, 5" h, ruffled	32	-	22	32
Candlesticks, pr, 5" h, wings	90	-	60	90
Candlesticks, pr, 5-1/4" h, triple light	100	65	65	100
Candlesticks, pr, 8-1/2" h, metal stem	40	-	32	40
Candy dish, 8" d, ruffled	40	-	20	40
Casserole, cov, 9-3/4" d	185	-	100	185
Celery bowl, 11" l, boat-shape	30	-	24	30
Cocktail shaker, metal top	60	-	35	60
Comport, 4" d	25	-	15	25
Comport, 11-1/2" d	60	-	30	60
Console bowl, 13" d, wings	-	-	80	120
Cordial, 3/4 oz, 2-7/8" h	55	-	25	48
Cream soup, 4-1/4" d	90	-	35	90
Creamer, 2-3/4" h	15	-	10	20
Creamer, 3-3/4" h	12	-	12	16
Cup	14	8	10	16
Decanter, 7-3/4" h	70	-	40	70
Decanter, 10-1/4" h, rocket-shape	425	-	375	425
Goblet, 5 oz, 4-3/4" h	25	-	15	22

Item	Cobalt Blue	Crystal	Other Colors	Red
Goblet, 8 oz, 5-3/4" h	35	-	20	33
Goblet, 9 oz, 6-1/4" h, metal stem	15	-	17.50	15
Gravy boat	120	-	90	125
Juice tumbler, 3 oz, 3-1/4" h, ftd	15	-	10	15
Mayonnaise, 5-1/4" h	32.50	-	30	32.50
Mug, 12 oz, 5-1/8" h	40	-	24	42
Perfume bottle, rocket-shape	200	-	150	210

*Moondrops, pink saucer **$4**, and cup **$10**.*

Item	Cobalt Blue	Crystal	Other Colors	Red
Pickle, 7-1/2" d	25	-	15	25
Pitcher, 22 oz, 6-7/8" h	175	-	90	175
Pitcher, 32 oz, 8-1/8" h	195	-	110	195
Pitcher, 50 oz, 8" h, lip	200	-	115	200
Pitcher, 53 oz, 8-1/8" h	195	-	120	195
Plate, 5-7/8" d	12	-	7.50	12
Plate, 6" d, round, off center indent	12.50	-	10	12.50
Plate, 6-1/8" d, sherbet	8	-	6	8
Plate, 7-1/8" d, salad	12	-	10	12
Plate, 8-1/2" d, luncheon	15	-	12	15
Plate, 9-1/2" d, dinner	25	-	15	25
Platter, 12" l, oval	35	-	20	35
Powder jar, three ftd	175	-	100	185
Relish, 8-1/2" d, 3 ftd, divided	30	-	20	30
Sandwich plate, 14" d	40	-	20	40
Sandwich plate, 14" d, with handles	44	-	24	45
Saucer	6	2	4	6.50
Sherbet, 2-5/8" h	15	10	11	20
Sherbet, 3-1/2" h	25	-	15	25
Shot glass, 2 oz, 2-3/4" h	17.50	-	12	17.50
Shot glass, 2 oz, 2-3/4" h, handle	17.50	-	15	17.50
Soup bowl, 6-3/4" d	80	-	-	80
Sugar, 2-3/4" h	10	-	10	18
Tray, 7-1/2" l	15	-	20	16
Tumbler, 5 oz, 3-5/8" h	15	-	10	15
Tumbler, 8 oz, 4-3/8" h	17.50	-	12	22
Tumbler, 9 oz, 4-7/8" h, handle	30	-	15	28
Tumbler, 12 oz, 5-1/8" h	30	-	15	33
Vase, 7-1/4" h, flat, ruffled	60	-	60	60

Item	Cobalt Blue	Crystal	Other Colors	Red
Vase, 8-1/2" h, bud, rocket-shape	245	-	185	245
Vase, 9-1/4" h, rocket-shape	240	-	125	240
Vegetable bowl, 9-3/4" l, oval	48	-	24	48
Wine, 4-3/4" h, rocket-shape	27.50	-	30	85
Wine, 4 oz, 5-1/2" h, metal stem	20	-	12	20

*Moondrops, ruby sugar **$18**, and creamer **$16**.*

MOONSTONE

Swatches

Crystal

Ocean Green

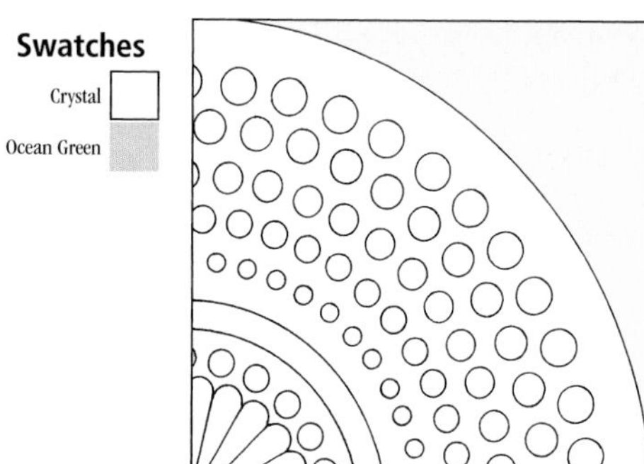

Manufactured by Anchor Hocking Glass Company, Lancaster, Ohio, from 1941 to 1946.

Made in crystal with opalescent hobnails and Ocean Green with opalescent hobnails.

Item	Crystal	Ocean Green
Berry bowl, 5-1/2" d	$25	$-
Bonbon, heart shape, handle	16	-
Bowl, 6-1/2" d, crimped, handle	20	-
Bowl, 7-1/4" d, flat	25	-
Bowl, 9-1/2" d, crimped	30	-
Bud vase, 5-1/2" h	15	-
Candleholder, pr	25	-
Candy jar, cov, 6" h	30	-
Cigarette box, cov	25	-

Item	Crystal	Ocean Green
Creamer	10	9.50
Cup	10	10
Dessert bowl, 5-1/2" d, crimped	12.50	-
Goblet, 10 oz	28	24
Plate, 6-1/4" d, sherbet	7	9
Plate, 8-3/8" d, luncheon	17.50	17.50
Puff box, cov, 4-3/4" d, round	25	-
Relish, 7-1/4" d, divided	12.50	-
Relish, cloverleaf	14	-
Sandwich plate, 10-3/4" d	45	-
Saucer	6	6
Sherbet, ftd	8	7
Sugar, ftd	10	12.50
Vase, 6-1/2" h, ruffled	12	-

Moonstone, crystal luncheon plate with opalescent hobnails ***$17.50.***

MOROCCAN AMETHYST

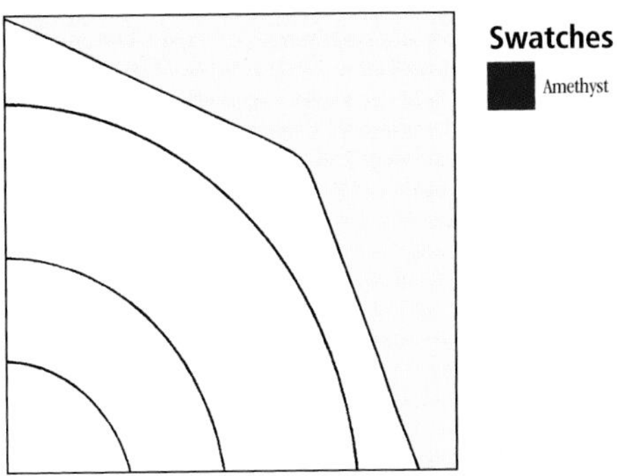

Swatches

Amethyst

Manufactured by Hazel Ware, division of Continental Can, 1960s. Made in amethyst.

Item	Amethyst
Ashtray, 3-1/4" d, round	$5.75
Ashtray, 3-1/4" w, triangular	5.75
Ashtray, 6-7/8" w, triangular	12.50
Ashtray, 8" w, square	14
Bowl, 5-3/4" w, deep, square	12
Bowl, 6" d, round	12.50
Bowl, 7-3/4" l, oval	18.50
Bowl, 7-3/4" l, rectangular, metal handle	17.50
Bowl, 10-3/4" d	30
Candy, cov, short	35
Candy, cov, tall	32
Chip and dip, 10-3/4" and 5-3/4" bowls in metal frame	40

Item	Amethyst
Cocktail shaker, chrome lid	30
Cocktail, stirrer, 16 oz, 6-1/4" h, lip	30
Cup	7.50
Fruit bowl, 4-3/4" d, octagonal	9.50
Goblet, 9 oz, 5-1/2" h	12.50
Ice bucket, 6" h	35
Iced tea tumbler, 16 oz, 6-1/2" h	18.50
Juice goblet, 5-1/2 oz, 4-3/8" h	12
Juice tumbler, 4 oz, 2-1/2" h	12.50
Old fashioned tumbler, 8 oz, 3-1/4" h	15
Plate, 5-3/4" d, sherbet	4.50
Plate, 7-1/4" d, salad	4.75
Plate, 9-3/4" d, dinner	7
Punch bowl	85
Punch cup	6
Relish, 7-3/4" l	14
Salad fork and spoon	12
Sandwich plate, 12" d, metal handle	15
Saucer	3
Sherbet, 7-1/2 oz, 4-1/4" h	8
Snack plate, 10" l, fan shaped, cup rest	8
Snack set, square plate, cup	12
Tidbit, three tiers	75
Tumbler, 9 oz	12.50
Tumbler, 11 oz, 4-1/4" h, crinkled bottom	12
Tumbler, 11 oz, 4-5/8" h	12
Vase, 8-1/2" h, ruffled	40
Wine, 4-1/2 oz, 4" h	12.50

Moroccan Amethyst, cup ***$7.50****, and saucer* ***$3****.*

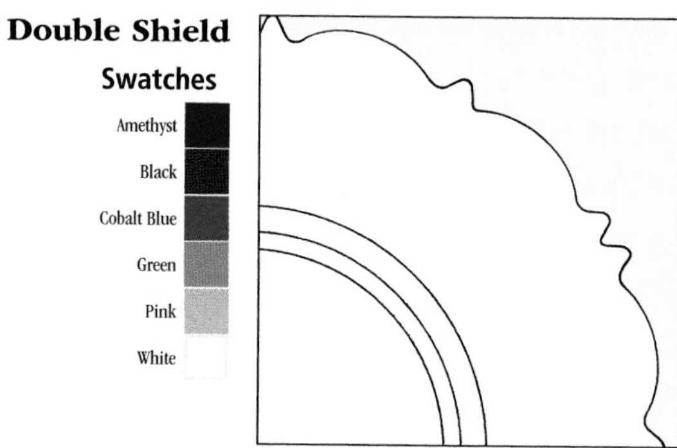

Manufactured by L.E. Smith, Mt. Pleasant, Pa., from the 1920s to 1934.

Made in amethyst, black, cobalt blue, crystal, green, pink, and white.

Item	Ameth.	Black	Cobalt Blue	Green	Pink
Bonbon, 7" d, rolled edge	$24	$24.50	$24	$16	$16
Bowl, 6" d, three legs	-	25	-	-	-
Bowl, 6" w, sq, handles	27.50	18	24	15	15
Bowl, 7" d, three ftd, rolled out edge	18.50	24.50	18.50	17.50	17.50
Bowl, 8" d, scalloped, two handles	37.50	35	37.50	20	20
Bowl, 8" d, sq, two handles	38	40	38	20	20
Bowl, 9" d, scalloped, 1-3/4" deep, ftd	28	32	30	-	-

Item	Ameth.	Black	Cobalt Blue	Green	Pink
Cake plate, 10-1/2" d, 1-1/4" h, ftd	45	47	40	-	-
Cake plate, 10-1/2" d, two handles	26	40	28	17.50	17.50
Candlesticks, pr, single lite	28	42.50	30	24	28
Candlesticks, pr, two lite	48	55	50	30	32
Creamer	21	20	22.50	20	24
Cup	15	15	14	12.50	12.50
Fruit bowl, 4-7/8" sq	16	20	18	12	12.50
Fruit bowl, 9-1/4" sq	30	50	35	20	20
Fruit bowl, 10" d, scalloped	40	40	40	-	-
Leaf, 8" l	12.50	17.50	16	-	-
Leaf, 11-1/4" l	25	30	28	-	-
Mayonnaise, 5-1/2" h, three ftd	25	28	25	17.50	17.50
Mint, 6" d, center handle	25	26.50	25	16	16
Plate, 8" d, scalloped	16	15	16	12.50	12.50
Plate, 8" d, scalloped, three ftd	17.50	27	17.50	12.50	12.50
Plate, 8" w, sq	17.50	25	17.50	12.50	12.50
Plate, 12" d, two handles	35	35	35	20	20
Salt and pepper shakers, pr	50	50	45	25	25
Sandwich server, center handle	40	37.50	40	-	-
Saucer	5	5	5	3.50	3.50
Sherbet	15	16.50	16.50	12.50	12.50
Sugar	9	20	15	20	20
Tumbler, ftd	25	27.50	27.50	-	-
Vase, 7-1/4" h	30	35	40	-	35

*Mt. Pleasant, black creamer **$20**, sugar (on pedestal) **$20**, cup **$15**, and bowl with handles **$35**.*

NATIONAL

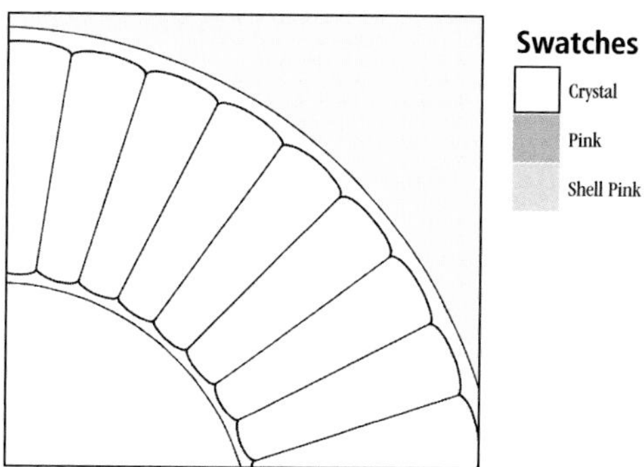

Swatches

Crystal

Pink

Shell Pink

Manufactured by Jeannette Glass Company, Jeannette, Pa., from the late 1940s to the mid-1950s.

Made in crystal, pink, and shell pink. Collector interest is primarily with crystal. Prices for pink and shell pink are not yet firmly established, but usually command slightly higher than crystal.

Item	Crystal
Ashtray	$4.50
Berry bowl, 4-1/2" d	4
Berry bowl, 8-1/2" d	8
Bowl, 12" d	15
Candleholders, pr	30
Candy dish, cov, ftd	20
Cigarette box	15
Creamer	6.50
Creamer and sugar tray	6

Item	Crystal
Cup	4
Jar, cov	15
Lazy Susan	40
Milk pitcher, 20 oz	20
Plate, 8" d	6.50
Punch bowl stand	10
Punch bowl, 12" d	25
Punch cup	3.50
Relish, three parts	15
Salt and pepper shakers, pr	10
Saucer	1
Sugar, open	6.50
Serving plate, 15" d	17.50

*National, crystal candleholders **$30**.*

Item	Crystal
Tray, two handles	17.50
Tumbler, ftd	8.50
Vase, 9"	20
Water pitcher, 64 oz	30

*National, crystal sugar bowl **$6.50**.*

NEW CENTURY

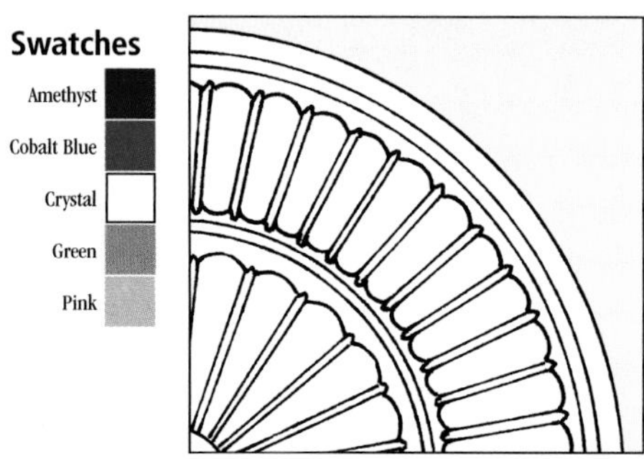

Manufactured by Hazel Atlas Company, Clarksburg, W.V., and Zanesville, Ohio, from 1930 to 1935.

Made in crystal and green, with limited production in amethyst, cobalt blue, and pink.

Item	Ameth.	Cobalt Blue	Crystal	Green	Pink
Ashtray/coaster, 5-3/8" d	$-	$-	$30	$30	$-
Berry bowl, 4-1/2" d	-	-	35	35	-
Berry bowl, 8" d	-	-	30	30	-
Butter dish, cov	-	-	75	75	-
Casserole, cov, 9" d	-	-	115	115	-
Cocktail, 3-1/4 oz	-	-	42	42	-
Cream soup, 4-3/4" d	-	-	25	25	-
Creamer	-	-	12	14	-
Cup	20	20	10	12	20

Item	Ameth.	Cobalt Blue	Crystal	Green	Pink
Decanter, stopper	-	-	90	90	-
Pitcher, with or without ice lip, 60 oz	55	55	45	48	50
Pitcher, with or without ice lip, 80 oz	55	55	45	48	50
Plate, 6" d, sherbet	-	-	5.50	6.50	-
Plate, 8-1/2" d, salad	-	-	12	12	-
Plate, 10" d, dinner	-	-	24	24	-
Plate, 10" d, grill	-	-	15	18	-
Platter, 11" l, oval	-	-	30	30	-
Salt and pepper shakers, pr	-	-	45	45	-

*New Century, green dinner plate **$24**.*

Item	Ameth.	Cobalt Blue	Crystal	Green	Pink
Saucer	7.50	7.50	5	6.50	8
Sherbet, 3" h	-	-	9	9	-
Sugar, cov	-	-	40	45	-
Tumbler, 5 oz, 3-1/2" h	12	16.50	15	18	18
Tumbler, 5 oz, 4" h, ftd	-	-	30	32.50	-
Tumbler, 8 oz, 3-1/2" h	-	-	25	27.50	-
Tumbler, 9 oz, 4-1/4" h	15	15	18	20	15
Tumbler, 9 oz, 4-7/8" h, ftd	-	-	25	25	-
Whiskey, 2-1/2" h, 1-1/2 oz	-	-	18	20	-
Wine, 2-1/2 oz	-	-	35	40	-

*New Century, green salt and pepper shakers **$45**.*

NEWPORT

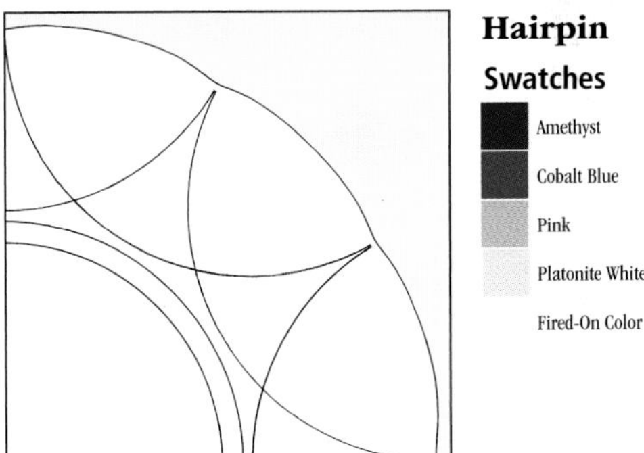

Hairpin

Swatches

Amethyst

Cobalt Blue

Pink

Platonite White

Fired-On Color

Manufactured by Hazel Atlas Glass Company, Clarksburg, W.V., and Zanesville, Ohio, from 1936 to the early 1950s.

Made in amethyst, cobalt blue, pink (from 1936 to 1940), Platonite white, and fired-on colors (from the 1940s to early 1950s).

Item	Ameth.	Cobalt Blue	Fired-On	Pink	Platon.
Berry bowl, 8-1/4" d	$50	$50	$16	$25	$10
Cream soup, 4-3/4" d	25	25	10	17.50	8.50
Creamer	20	22	8.50	10	3
Cup	12	15	9	6	4.50
Plate, 6" d, sherbet	7.50	10	5	3.50	2
Plate, 8-1/2" d, luncheon	15	22	9	8	4.50
Plate, 8-13/16" d, dinner	32	35	15	15	12
Platter, 11-3/4" l, oval	42	48	18	20	12

Item	Ameth.	Cobalt Blue	Fired-On	Pink	Platon.
Salt and pepper shakers, pr	60	65	32	30	18
Saucer	5.25	6	3	2.50	2
Sherbet	15	18.50	10	8	4
Sugar	20	22	9.50	10	5
Tumbler, 9 oz, 4-1/2" h	40	48	15	20	-

*Newport, amethyst dinner plate **$32**, sugar **$20**, creamer **$20**, and cream soup bowl **$25**.*

NORMANDIE

Bouquet and Lattice

Swatches

Amber

Crystal

Iridescent

Pink

Manufactured by Federal Glass Company, Columbus, Ohio, from 1933 to 1940.

Made in amber, crystal, iridescent, and pink.

Item	Amber	Crystal	Iridescent	Pink
Berry bowl, 5" d	$9.50	$6	$6.50	$12
Berry bowl, 8-1/2" d	35	24	30	80
Cereal bowl, 6-1/2" d	30	20	10	35
Creamer, ftd	20	10	8	18
Cup	8	4	6	9.50
Iced tea tumbler, 12 oz, 5" h	40	-	-	-
Juice tumbler, 5 oz, 4" h	38	-	-	-
Pitcher, 80 oz, 8" h	115	-	-	245
Plate, 7-3/4" d, salad	10	5	55	14
Plate, 9-1/4" d, luncheon	12.50	6	16.50	100
Plate, 11" d, dinner	32	15	10	18

Item	Amber	Crystal	Iridescent	Pink
Plate, 11" d, grill	15	8	10	25
Platter, 11-3/4" l	24	10	12	80
Salt and pepper shakers, pr	50	20	-	4
Saucer	4	1.50	3.50	10
Sherbet	7.50	6.50	9	9
Sugar	8	6	7	12
Tumbler, 9 oz, 4-1/4" h	25	10	-	50
Vegetable bowl, 10" l, oval	27.50	12	25	45

*Normandie, iridescent dinner plate **$10**.*

OLD CAFÉ

Swatches

Crystal

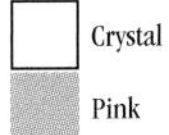
Pink

Royal Ruby

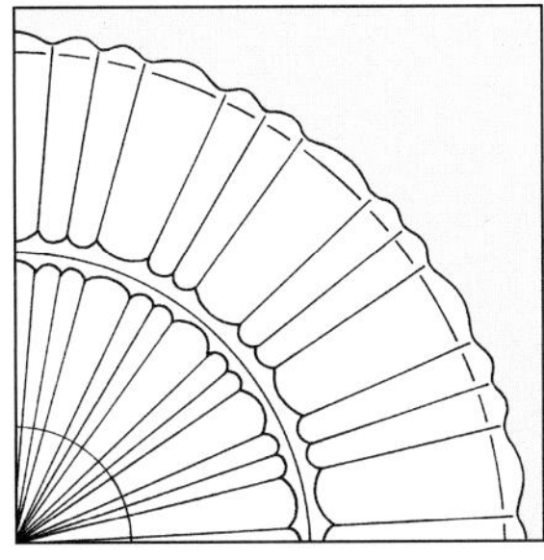

Manufactured by Hocking Glass Company, Lancaster, Ohio, from 1936 to 1940.

Made in crystal, pink, and royal ruby.

Item	Crystal	Pink	Royal Ruby
Berry bowl, 3-3/4" d	$9.50	$10	$9
Bowl, 6-1/2" d	15	18	-
Bowl, 9" d, closed handles	10	10	15
Candy dish, 8" d, low	18	15	20

Item	Crystal	Pink	Royal Ruby
Candy jar, 5-1/2" d, crystal with ruby cover	-	-	25
Cereal bowl, 5-1/2" d	30	30	15
Cup	12	12	15
Juice tumbler, 3" h	18	18	20
Lamp	100	100	150
Olive dish, 6" l, oblong	7.50	8.50	-
Pitcher, 36 oz, 6" h	125	145	-
Plate, 6" d, sherbet	5	5	-
Plate, 10" d, dinner	60	65	-
Saucer	5	5	-
Sherbet, low, ftd	15	12	12
Tumbler, 4" h	18	20	18
Vase, 7-1/4" h	40	45	50

*Old Café, ruby berry bowl **$9**.*

*Old Café, ruby bowl with handles and original label **$15**.*

OLD COLONY

Lace Edge, Open Lace

Swatches

Crystal

Pink

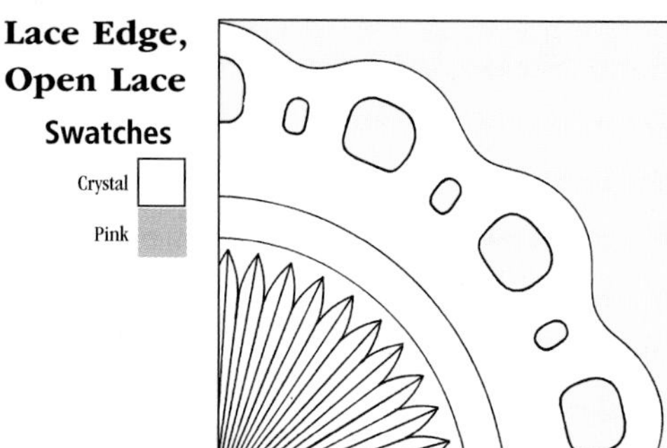

Manufactured by Hocking Glass Company, Lancaster, Ohio, from 1935 to 1938.

Made in crystal and pink.

Crystal Old Colony pieces are valued at about 50 percent of pink, as are frosted or satin finish prices. Many other companies made a look-alike to Old Colony, so care must be exercised.

Item	Pink
Bonbon, cov	$65
Bowl, 9-1/2" d, plain	40
Bowl, 9-1/2" d, ribbed	35
Butter dish, cov	70
Candlesticks, pr	350
Candy jar, cov, ribbed	65
Cereal bowl, 6-3/8" d	24
Comport, 7" d, cov	60

Item	Pink
Comport, 9" d	950
Console bowl, 10-1/2" d, three legs	250
Cookie jar, cov	75
Creamer	25
Cup	24
Flower bowl, crystal frog	30
Plate, 7-1/4" d, salad	27.50
Plate, 8-1/4" d, luncheon	32
Plate, 10-1/2" d, dinner	36
Plate, 10-1/2" d, grill	28
Plate, 13" d, four parts, solid lace	65
Plate, 13" d, solid lace	65
Platter, 12-3/4" l	42
Platter, 12-3/4" l, five parts	40
Relish dish, 7-1/2" d, three parts, deep	60

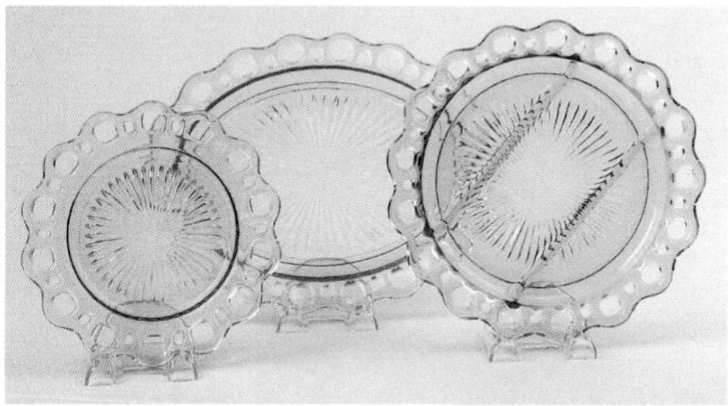

*Old Colony, pink luncheon plate **$32**, platter **$42**, and divided relish **$60**.*

Item	Pink
Relish plate, 10-1/2" d, three parts	25
Salad bowl, 7-3/4" d, ribbed	60
Saucer	15
Sherbet, ftd	112
Sugar	25
Tumbler, 5 oz, 3-1/2" h, flat	120
Tumbler, 9 oz, 4-1/2" h, flat	22
Tumbler, 10-1/2 oz, 5" h, ftd	95
Vase, 7" h	650

Old Colony, pink satin-finish candlestick ***$350*** *pair.*

OLD ENGLISH

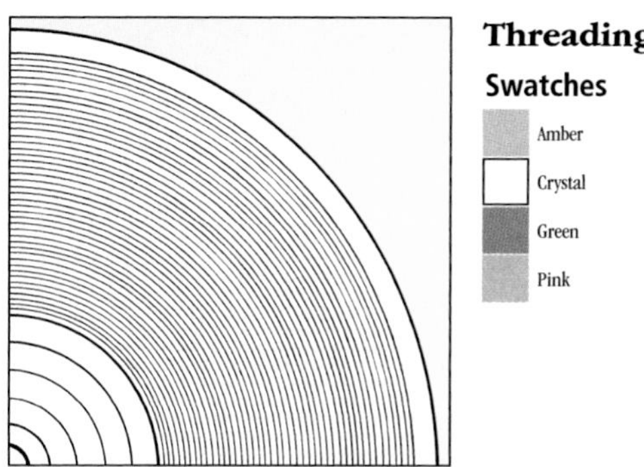

Threading

Swatches

Amber
Crystal
Green
Pink

Manufactured by Indiana Glass Company, Dunkirk, Ind., late 1920s. Made in amber, crystal, green, and pink.

Item	Amber	Crystal	Green	Pink
Bowl, 4" d, flat	$20	$18	$22	$20
Bowl, 9-1/2" d, flat	35	25	35	35
Candlesticks, pr, 4" h	35	25	35	35
Candy dish, cov, flat	50	40	50	50
Candy jar, cov	55	45	55	55
Cheese compote, 3-1/2" h	17.50	12	17.50	17.50
Cheese plate, indent	20	10	20	20
Compote, 3-1/2" h, 6-3/8" w, two handles	24	12	24	24
Compote, 3-1/2" h, 7" w	24	12	24	24
Creamer	18	10	18	18
Egg cup	-	10	-	-

Item	Amber	Crystal	Green	Pink
Fruit bowl, 9" d, ftd	30	20	30	30
Fruit stand, 11" h, ftd	40	18	40	40
Goblet, 8 oz, 5-3/4" h	30	15	30	30
Pitcher	70	35	70	70
Pitcher, cov	125	55	125	125
Sandwich server, center handle	60	-	60	60
Sherbet	20	10	20	20
Sugar, cov	38	14	38	38
Tumbler, 4-1/2" h, ftd	24	12	28	24
Tumbler, 5-1/2" h, ftd	40	20	40	40
Vase, 5-3/8" h, 7" w, fan-shape	48	24	48	48
Vase, 8" h, 4-1/2" w, ftd	45	20	45	45
Vase, 8-1/4" h, 4-1/4" w, ftd	45	20	45	45
Vase, 12" h, ftd	72	35	72	72

*Old English, green fruit stand **$40**.*

OVIDE

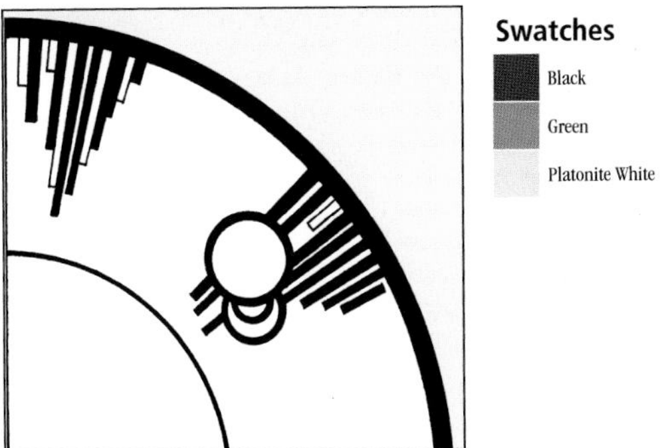

Swatches

Black

Green

Platonite White

Manufactured by Hazel Atlas Glass Company, Clarksburg, W.V., and Zanesville, Ohio, 1930-35 and in the 1950s.

Made in black, green, and Platonite white with fired-on colors in the 1950s.

Item	Black	Green	Platonite
Berry bowl, 4-3/4" d	$-	$-	$10
Berry bowl, 8" d	-	-	22
Candy dish, cov	45	24	35
Cereal bowl, 5-1/2" d	10	-	12
Creamer	7	6	18
Cup	6.50	4.50	15
Egg cup	-	-	22
Fruit cocktail, ftd	5	4.50	-
Plate, 6" d, sherbet	-	2.50	6
Plate, 8" d, luncheon	-	3.50	15

Item	Black	Green	Platonite
Plate, 9" d, dinner	-	-	25
Platter, 11" d	-	-	24
Salt and pepper shakers, pr	28	28	25
Saucer	3.50	4.50	6
Sherbet	6.50	3.50	15
Sugar, open	9	7	20
Tumbler	18	-	20

*Ovide, pink and gray platonite luncheon plate **$15**.*

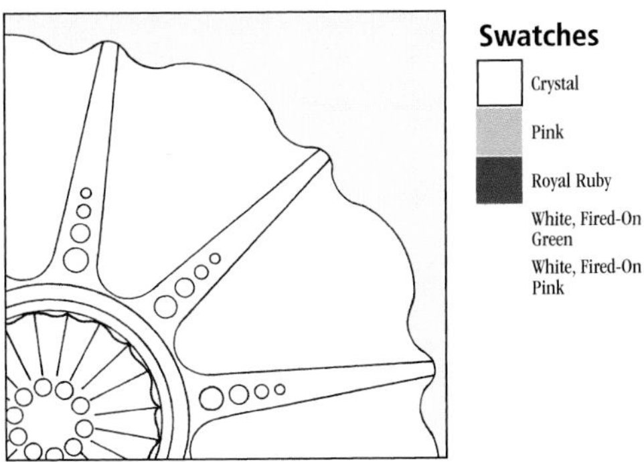

Swatches

Crystal

Pink

Royal Ruby

White, Fired-On Green

White, Fired-On Pink

Manufactured by Anchor Hocking Glass Corporation, from 1938 to 1940.

Made in crystal, pink, royal ruby, and white with fired-on green or pink.

Item	Crystal	Pink	Royal Ruby	White, Fired-On Green	White, Fired-On Pink
Bowl, 5-1/2" d, handle	$8	$15	$20	$-	$-
Bowl, 5-1/4" w, handle, heart-shape	12	21	-	12	-
Bowl, 6-1/2" d, handle	12	15	28	-	-
Candleholders, pr, 3-1/2" h	35	45	65	25	25
Fruit bowl, 10-1/2" d, deep	20	25	50	30	30

Item	Crystal	Pink	Royal Ruby	White, Fired-On Green	White, Fired-On Pink
Relish dish, 10-1/4" l, divided	10	35	-	-	-
Sandwich plate, 13-1/2" d	20	40	50	-	-

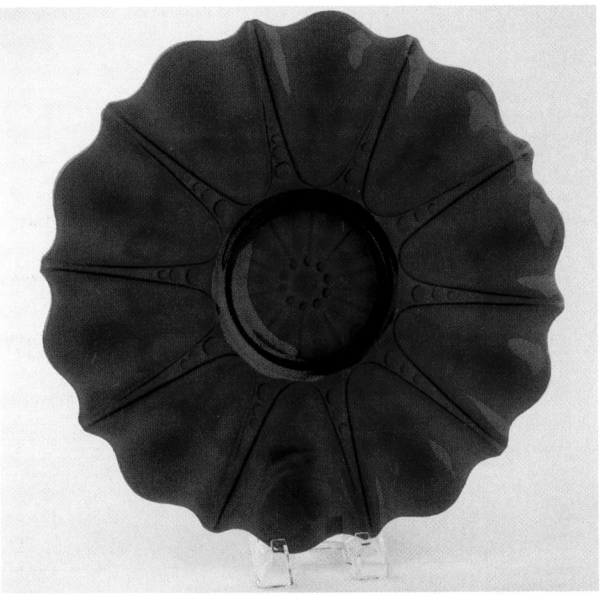

*Oyster and Pearl, ruby sandwich plate **$50**.*

PARK AVENUE

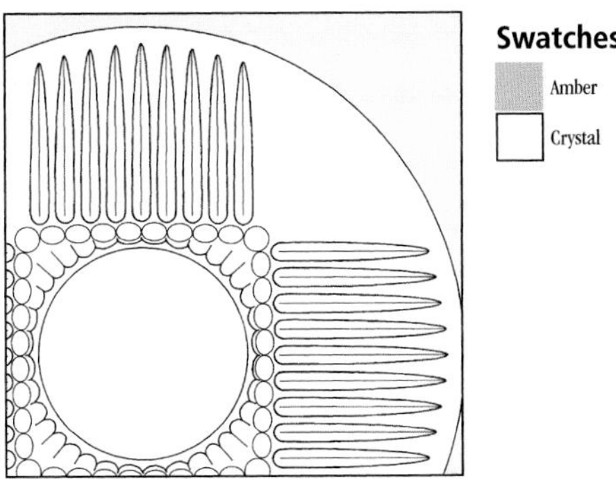

Swatches

Amber

Crystal

Manufactured by Federal Glass Company, Columbus, Ohio, 1941 to the early 1970s.

Made in amber, crystal, and crystal with gold trim. Values for crystal and crystal with gold trim are the same.

Item	Amber	Crystal
Ashtray, 3-1/2" sq	$-	$5
Ashtray, 4-1/2" sq	-	6.50
Candleholder, pr, 5" d	-	9
Dessert bowl, 5" d	6.50	3
Iced tea tumbler, 12 oz	12	6.50
Juice tumbler, 4-1/2 oz	5	5
Tumbler, 9 oz	8	6
Tumbler, 10 oz	9	6
Vegetable bowl, 8-1/2" d	18	10
Whiskey tumbler, 1-1/4 oz	-	4.50

Park Avenue, juice tumbler, crystal with gold band ***$5***.

PARROT

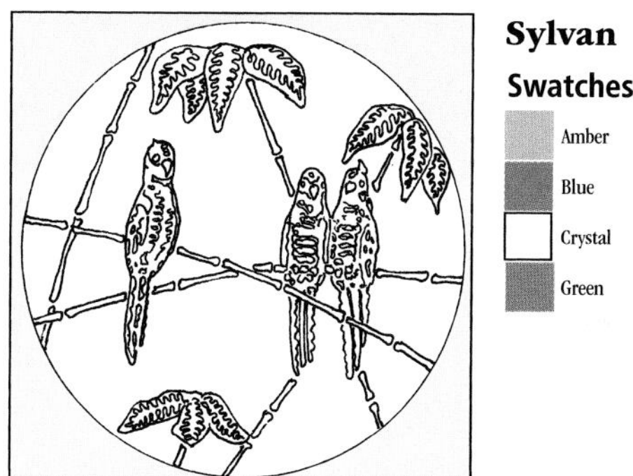

Sylvan

Swatches

Amber

Blue

Crystal

Green

Manufactured by Federal Glass Company, Columbus, Ohio, from 1931 to 1932.

Made in amber and green, with limited production in blue and crystal.

Item	Amber	Green
Berry bowl, 8" d	$75	$80
Butter dish, cov	1,250	475
Creamer, ftd	65	55
Cup	35	35
Hot plate, 5" d, pointed	875	900
Hot plate, round	-	950
Pitcher, 80 oz, 8-1/2" h	-	2,500
Plate, 5-3/4" d, sherbet	24	35
Plate, 7-1/2" d, salad	-	40
Plate, 9" d, dinner	50	50

Item	Amber	Green
Plate, 10-1/2" d, grill, round	35	-
Plate, 10-1/2" d, grill, square	-	30
Platter, 11-1/4" l, oblong	65	70
Salt and pepper shakers, pr	-	270
Saucer	18	18
Sherbet, ftd, cone	30	27.50
Sugar, cov	450	175
Tumbler, 10 oz, 4-1/4" h	100	130
Tumbler, 10 oz, 5-1/2" h, ftd, Madrid mold	145	-
Tumbler, 12 oz, 5-1/2" h	115	160
Tumbler, 5-3/4" h, ftd, heavy	100	120
Vegetable bowl, 10" l, oval	75	65

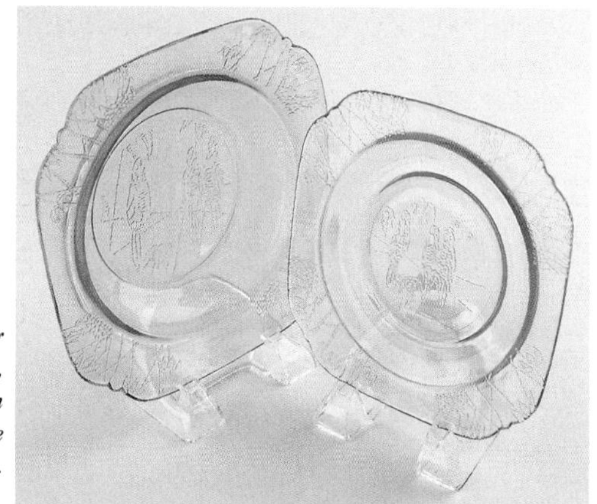

*Parrot, amber jam dish **$35**, and green sherbet plate **$35**.*

PATRICIAN

Spoke

Swatches

Amber

Crystal

Green

Pink

Manufactured by Federal Glass Company, Columbus, Ohio, from 1933 to 1937.

Made in amber (also called Golden Glo), crystal, green, and pink.

Item	Amber	Crystal	Green	Pink
Berry bowl, 5" d	$12.50	$10	$12.50	$18.50
Berry bowl, 8-1/2" d	50	15	37.50	35
Butter dish, cov	95	100	215	225
Cereal bowl, 6" d	32	27.50	27.50	25
Cookie jar, cov	90	80	500	-
Cream soup, 4-3/4" d	28	25	24.50	22
Creamer, ftd	12.50	9	12.50	12.50
Cup	12.50	12	15	12.50
Pitcher, 75 oz, 8" h, molded handle	120	125	125	115
Pitcher, 75 oz, 8-1/4" h, applied handle	150	140	150	145
Plate, 6" d, sherbet	10	8.50	10	10

Item	Amber	Crystal	Green	Pink
Plate, 7-1/2" d, salad	17.50	15	12.50	15
Plate, 9" d, luncheon	14	12.50	12	12.50
Plate, 10-1/2 d, dinner	10	12.75	32	36
Platter, 11-1/2" l, oval	32.50	30	30	28
Salt and pepper shakers, pr	65	65	65	85
Saucer	10	9.25	9.50	9.50
Sherbet	15	10	14	16
Sugar	12.50	9	12.50	12.50
Tumbler, 8 oz, 5-1/4" h, ftd	50	42	50	-
Tumbler, 14 oz, 5-1/2" h	42	38	40	46
Vegetable bowl, 10" l, oval	38	30	38.50	30

*Patrician, amber cream soup bowl **$28**, sherbet **$15**, and cup **$12.50**.*

PATRICK

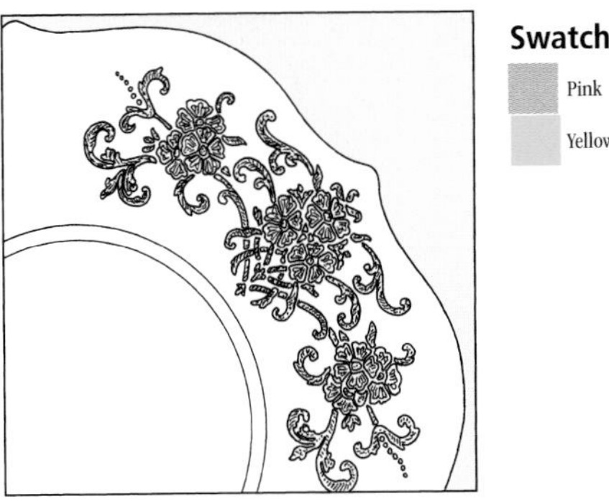

Swatches

Pink

Yellow

Manufactured by Lancaster Glass Company, Lancaster, Ohio, early 1930s.

Made in pink and yellow.

Item	Pink	Yellow
Candlesticks, pr	$200	$160
Candy dish, three ftd	175	175
Cheese and cracker set	150	130
Cocktail, 4" h	85	85
Console bowl, 11" d	150	150
Creamer	75	40
Cup	70	40
Fruit bowl, 9" d, handle	175	130
Goblet, 10 oz, 6" h	85	75
Juice goblet, 6 oz, 4-3/4" h	85	75
Mayonnaise, three pieces	200	140

Item	Pink	Yellow
Plate, 7" d, sherbet	20	15
Plate, 7-1/2" d, salad	25	20
Plate, 8" d, luncheon	45	30
Saucer	20	12
Sherbet, 4-3/4" d	72	60
Sugar	75	40
Tray, 11" d, center handle	165	120
Tray, 11" d, two handles	80	65

*Patrick, yellow tray with caned center **$65**.*

PETALWARE

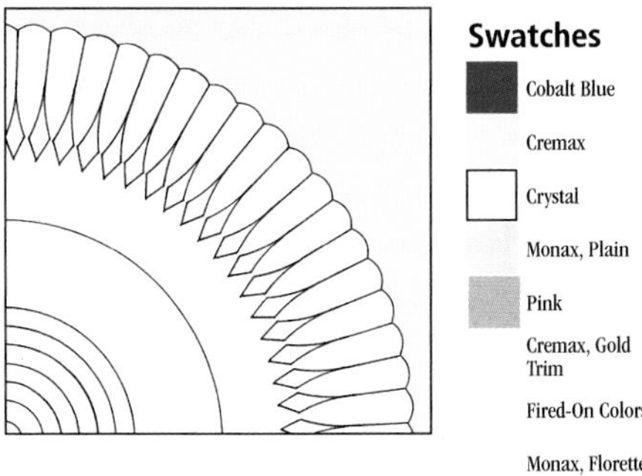

Swatches

Cobalt Blue

Cremax

Crystal

Monax, Plain

Pink

Cremax, Gold Trim

Fired-On Colors

Monax, Florette

Manufactured by Macbeth-Evans Glass Company, Charleroi, Pa., from 1930 to 1940.

Made in cobalt blue, Cremax, crystal, fired-on red, blue, green and yellow, Monax and pink. Florette is the name given to a floral decorated with a pointed petal. There are other patterns, such as red flower with a red rim, fruit and other floral patterns.

Crystal values are approximately 50 percent less than those listed for Cremax. Cobalt blue production was limited and the mustard is currently valued at $15 when complete with its metal lid. Monax Regency is priced the same as Monax Florette.

Item	Cremax	Cremax, Gold Trim	Fired-On Colors
Berry bowl, 9" d	$30	$32	$-
Cereal bowl, 5-1/4" d	15	17.50	8.50

Item	Cremax	Cremax, Gold Trim	Fired-On Colors
Cream soup liner	-	-	-
Cream soup, 4-1/2" d	12.50	12	12
Creamer, ftd	12.50	15	8.50
Cup	8	10	9.50
Lamp shade, 9" d	17	-	-
Plate, 6" d, sherbet	4.50	50	6
Plate, 8" d, salad	8	8	7.50
Plate, 9" d, dinner	15.50	14	8.50
Platter, 13" l, oval	25	20	20
Saucer	3.50	4	4
Sherbet, 4" h, low ftd	-	-	-
Sherbet, 4-1/2" h, low ftd	15	12	8
Soup bowl, 7" d	65	60	70
Sugar, ftd	7.50	11	12
Tumbler, 12 oz, 4-5/8" h	-	-	-

*Petalware, pink dinner plate **$16**, creamer **$10**, and sugar **$10**.*

Item	Monax, Florette	Monax, Plain	Pink
Berry bowl, 9" d	$35.50	$18	$25
Cereal bowl, 5-1/4" d	15.50	9	15
Cream soup liner	-	18.75	-
Cream soup, 4-1/2" d	15	11.25	17
Creamer, ftd	12	10	10
Cup	12	4.50	10
Lamp shade, 9" d	14	18	-
Plate, 6" d, sherbet	6	2.50	4.50
Plate, 8" d, salad	10	4.50	10
Plate, 9" d, dinner	16.50	10	16
Platter, 13" l, oval	25	20	17.50
Saucer	5	4.50	5
Sherbet, 4" h, low ftd	-	32	-
Sherbet, 4-1/2" h, low ftd	12	10	8.50
Soup bowl, 7" d	65	60	-
Sugar, ftd	12	10	10
Tumbler, 12 oz, 4-5/8" h	-	-	25

*Petalware, pink sugar **$10**, creamer **$10**, and two dinner plates **$16** ea.*

PINEAPPLE & FLORAL

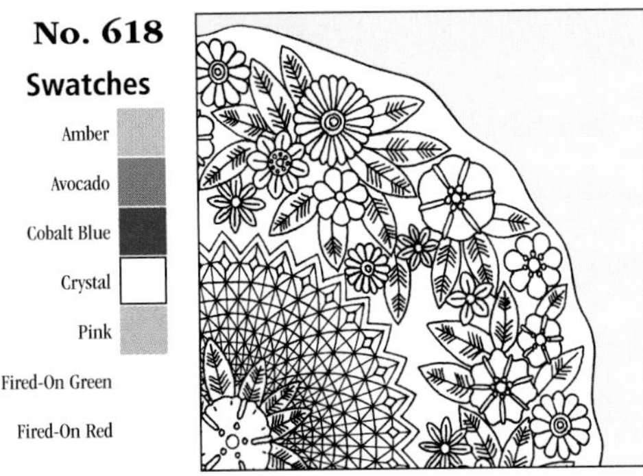

Manufactured by Indiana Glass Company, Dunkirk, Ind., from 1932 to 1937.

Made in amber, avocado (late 1960s), cobalt blue (1980s), crystal, fired-on green, fired-on red, and pink (1980s).

Reproductions: † Salad bowl and diamond-shaped comport have been reproduced in several different colors, including crystal, pink, and avocado green.

Item	Amber	Crystal	Fired-On Red
Ashtray, 4-1/2" d	$20	$17.50	$20
Berry bowl, 4-3/4" d	24	20	22
Cereal bowl, 6" d	24	30	22
Comport, diamond-shape	10	5	10
Creamer, diamond-shape	10	7.50	10

Item	Amber	Crystal	Fired-On Red
Cream soup	16.50	18	16.50
Cup	10	12	10
Plate, 6" d, sherbet	8	6.50	8
Plate, 8-3/8" d, salad	12	10	12
Plate, 9-3/8" d, dinner	17.50	18	17.50
Plate, 9-3/4" d, indentation	-	25	-
Plate, 11" d, closed handles	24	20	24
Plate, 11-1/2" d, indentation	-	25	-
Platter, 11" l, closed handles	20	18	20
Relish, 11-1/2" d, divided	28	24	28
Salad bowl, 7" d †	10	5	10
Sandwich plate, 11-1/2" d	24	20	24
Saucer	7.50	6	7.50
Sherbet, ftd	28	24	28
Sugar, diamond-shape	10	7.50	10

*Pineapple & Floral, crystal sugar **$7.50**, and creamer **$7.50**.*

Item	Amber	Crystal	Fired-On Red
Tumbler, 8 oz, 4-1/4" h	40	40	40
Tumbler, 12 oz, 5" h	48	47.50	48
Vase, cone shape	45	42.50	45
Vegetable bowl, 10" l, oval	32	30	32

Pineapple & Floral, amber cream soup ***$16.50.***

PIONEER

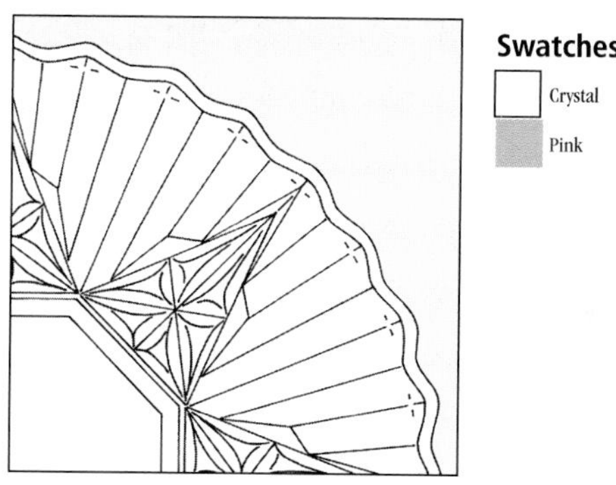

Swatches

Crystal

Pink

Manufactured by Federal Glass Co., Columbus, Ohio, starting in the 1940s.

Originally made in pink, crystal was added later. The crystal 11" fluted bowl and 12" dinner plate were made until 1973.

Item	Crystal	Pink
Bowl, 7" d, low, fruits center	**$8**	**$10**
Bowl, 7-3/4" d, ruffled, fruits center	**10**	**12**
Bowl, 10-1/2" d, fruits center	**12**	**14**
Bowl, 10-1/2" d, plain center	**10**	**12**
Bowl, 11" d, ruffled, fruits center	**15**	**18**
Bowl, 11" d, ruffled, plain center	**12**	**15**
Nappy, 5-3/8" d, fruits center	**8**	**10**
Nappy, 5-3/8" d, plain center	**6**	**8**
Plate, 8" d, luncheon, fruits center	**6**	**8**
Plate, 8" d, luncheon, plain center	**6**	**8**

Item	Crystal	Pink
Plate, 12" d, fruit center	10	12
Plate, 12" d, plain center	10	12

*Pioneer, pink plate with fruit center **$12**.*

PRETZEL

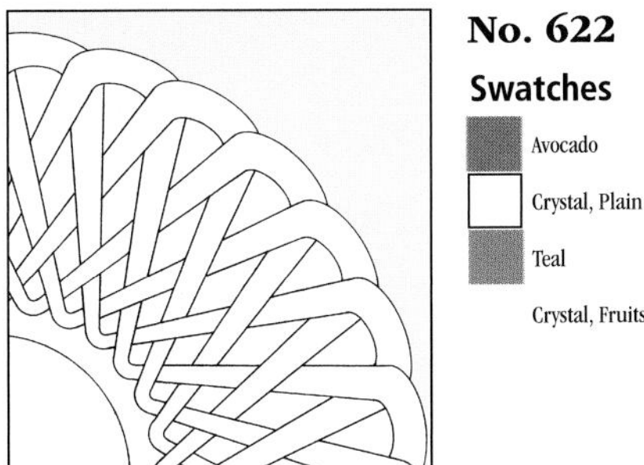

No. 622

Swatches

Avocado

Crystal, Plain

Teal

Crystal, Fruits

Manufactured by Indiana Glass Company, Dunkirk, Ind., from late 1930s to 1960s.

Made in avocado, crystal, and teal. Some crystal pieces have a fruit decoration. Recent amber, blue, and opaque white issues. A teal cup and saucer is valued at $165.

Item	Crystal, Plain	Crystal, Fruits
Berry bowl, 9-3/8" d	**$18**	**$-**
Celery tray, 10-1/4" l	**7.50**	**-**
Creamer	**7**	**-**
Cup	**7.50**	**-**
Iced tea tumbler, 12 oz, 5-1/2" h	**70**	**-**
Juice tumbler	**35**	**-**
Pitcher, 39 oz	**250**	**-**
Plate, 6" d	**3.50**	**5**
Plate, 6" d, tab handle	**7**	**-**

Item	Crystal, Plain	Crystal, Fruits
Plate, 7-1/4" w, sq, indent	8	-
Plate, 7-1/4" w, sq, indent, three parts	10	-
Plate, 8-3/8" d, salad	7.50	4
Plate, 9-3/8" d, dinner	10	12
Plate, 10" d, dinner	12	15
Relish, 7", three parts	10	-
Sandwich plate, 11-1/2" d	12.50	12
Saucer	1.50	-
Sugar	8	-
Tumbler, 5 oz, 3-1/2" h	50	-
Tumbler, 9 oz, 4-1/2" h	70	-

*Pretzel, crystal sugar **$8**, and sugar **$7**.*

PRIMO

Paneled Aster

Swatches

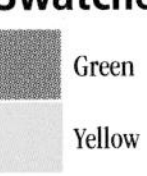

Manufactured by U.S. Glass Company, Pittsburgh, Pa., early 1930s. Made in green and yellow.

Item	Green	Yellow
Bowl, 4-1/2" d	$20	$25
Bowl, 7-3/4" d	38	40
Cake plate, 10" d, 3 ftd	40	45
Coaster/ashtray	8.75	8.75
Creamer	12	15
Cup	14.50	14.50
Hostess tray, 5-3/4" d, handles	42	45
Plate, 7-1/2" d	10.25	12
Plate, 10" d, dinner	27.50	30
Plate, 10" d, grill	18	20
Saucer	3.25	3.25
Sherbet	14.25	14.50
Sugar	12	12
Tumbler, 9 oz, 5-3/4" h, ftd	22	45

*Primo, yellow cup **$14.50**.*

PRINCESS

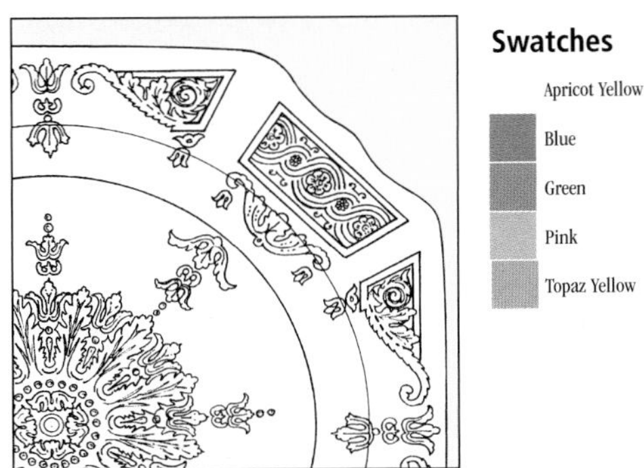

Swatches

Apricot Yellow

Blue

Green

Pink

Topaz Yellow

Manufactured by Hocking Glass Company, Lancaster, Ohio, from 1931 to 1935.

Made in apricot yellow, blue, green, pink, and topaz yellow.

Reproductions: † The candy dish and salt and pepper shakers have been reproduced in blue, green and pink.

Item	Apricot Yellow	Blue	Green	Pink	Topaz Yellow
Ashtray, 4-1/2" d	**$110**	**$-**	**$72**	**$90**	**$110**
Berry bowl, 4-1/2" d	55	-	40	32	55
Butter dish, cov	700	-	110	115	700
Cake plate, 10" d, ftd	-	-	37.50	100	-
Candy dish, cov †	-	-	75	85	-
Cereal bowl, 5" d	-	-	48	45	-
Coaster	100	-	65	65	100
Cookie jar, cov	-	875	65	75	-

Item	Apricot Yellow	Blue	Green	Pink	Topaz Yellow
Creamer, oval	25	-	15	17.50	22.50
Cup	7.50	120	14	15.50	10
Hat-shaped bowl, 9-1/2" d	125	-	45	50	125
Iced tea tumbler, 13 oz, 5-1/2" h	45	-	125	115	40
Juice tumbler, 5 oz, 3" h	28	-	25	28	28
Pitcher, 37 oz, 6" h	775	-	60	75	775
Plate, 8" d, salad	10	-	15	15	10
Plate, 9-1/2" d, dinner	25	-	33.50	45	25
Plate, 9-1/2" d, grill	10	175	15	15	10
Plate, 10-1/2" d, grill, closed handles	10	-	15	15	10
Platter, 12" l, closed handles	60	-	25	25	60
Relish, 7-1/2" l, divided, four parts	100	-	35	30	100
Relish, 7-1/2" l, plain	225	-	195	195	225
Salad bowl, 9" d, octagonal	125	-	55	40	125
Salt and pepper shakers, pr, 4-1/2" h †	75	-	60	65	85
Sandwich plate, 10-1/4" d, closed handles	175	-	30	35	175
Saucer, 6" sq	2.75	65	10	10	3.75
Sherbet, ftd	40	-	28	25	40
Spice shakers, pr, 5-1/2" h	-	-	20	-	-
Sugar, cov	30	-	35	65	30
Tumbler, 9 oz, 4" h	25	-	28	25	25
Tumbler, 9 oz, 4-3/4" h, sq, ftd	-	-	65	25	-

Item	Apricot Yellow	Blue	Green	Pink	Topaz Yellow
Tumbler, 12-1/2 oz, 6-1/2" h, ftd	25	-	180	95	25
Vase, 8" h	-	-	45	50	-
Vegetable bowl, 10" l, oval	60	-	30	30	65

*Princess, green cookie jar **$65**.*

PYRAMID

No. 610

Swatches

Crystal

Green

Pink

White

Yellow

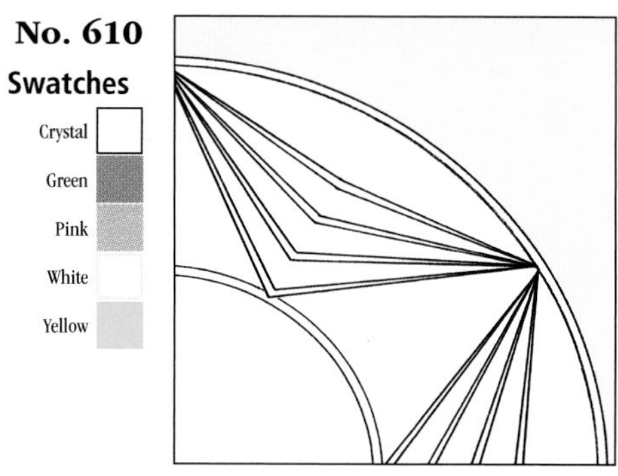

Manufactured by Indiana Glass Company, Dunkirk, Ind., from 1926 to 1932.

Made in crystal, green, pink, white, and yellow. Later production in 1974 to 1975 by Tiara produced black and blue pieces. Production limited in blue and white. Prices for black not firmly established in secondary market at this time.

Item	Crystal	Green	Pink	Yellow
Berry bowl, 4-3/4" d	$20	$35	$35	$55
Berry bowl, 8-1/2" d	30	65	55	75
Bowl, 9-1/2" l, oval	30	45	40	65
Creamer	20	35	35	40
Ice tub	95	145	155	225
Pickle dish, 9-1/2" l, 5-3/4" w	30	35	35	65
Pitcher	395	265	400	550
Relish, four parts, handles	25	65	60	70

Item	Crystal	Green	Pink	Yellow
Sugar	20	35	35	40
Tray for creamer and sugar	25	30	30	35
Tumbler, 8 oz, ftd	55	50	55	75
Tumbler, 11 oz, ftd	70	75	50	95

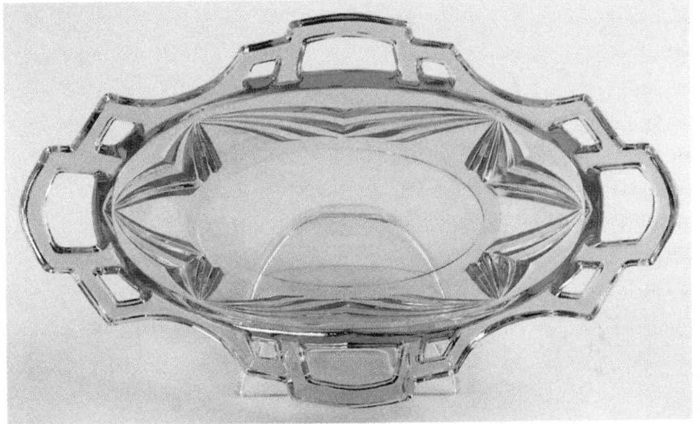

Pyramid, green pickle dish ***$35***.

QUEEN MARY

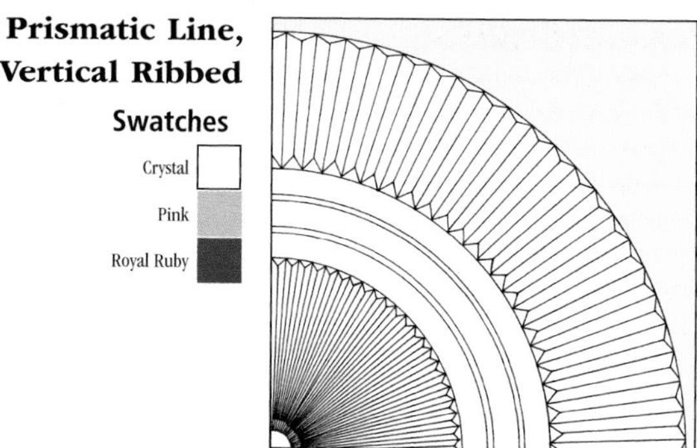

Manufactured by Hocking Glass Company, Lancaster, Ohio, from 1936 to 1948.

Made in crystal, pink, and royal ruby.

Item	Crystal	Pink	Royal Ruby
Ashtray, 2" x 3-3/4" l, oval	$4	$5.50	$5
Ashtray, 3-1/2" d, round	4	-	-
Berry bowl, 4-1/2" d	3	5	-
Berry bowl, 5" d	5	10	-
Berry bowl, 8-3/4" d	10	17.50	-
Bowl, 4" d, one handle	4	12.50	-
Bowl, 5-1/2" d, two handles	6	15	-
Bowl, 7" d	7.50	35	-
Butter dish, cov	42	125	-
Candlesticks, pr, two lite, 4-1/2" h	24	-	70

Item	Crystal	Pink	Royal Ruby
Candy dish, cov	30	42	-
Celery tray, 5" x 10"	10	24	-
Cereal bowl, 6" d	8	24	-
Cigarette jar, 2" x 3" oval	6.50	7.50	-
Coaster, 3-1/2" d	4	5	-
Coaster/ashtray, 4-1/4" sq	4	6	-
Comport, 5-3/4"	9	14	-
Creamer, ftd	6	40	-
Creamer, oval	6	12	-
Cup, large	6.50	10	-
Cup, small	8.50	12.50	-
Juice tumbler, 5 oz, 3-1/2" h	9.50	15	-
Pickle dish, 5" x 10"	10	24	-
Plate, 6" d, sherbet	4	5	-
Plate, 6-1/2" d, bread and butter	6	-	-
Plate, 8-1/4" d, salad	6	-	-
Plate, 9-1/2" d, dinner	15	65	-
Preserve, cov	30	125	-
Relish, clover-shape	15	17.50	-
Relish, 12" d, three parts	10	15	-
Relish, 14" d, four parts	15	17.50	-
Salt and pepper shakers, pr	25	-	-
Sandwich plate, 12" d	20	17.50	-
Saucer	2	5	-
Serving tray, 14" d	15	9	-
Sherbet, ftd	6.50	10	-
Sugar, ftd	-	40	-
Sugar, oval	6	12	-
Tumbler, 9 oz, 4" h	6	19.50	-
Tumbler, 10 oz, 5" h, ftd	35	70	-

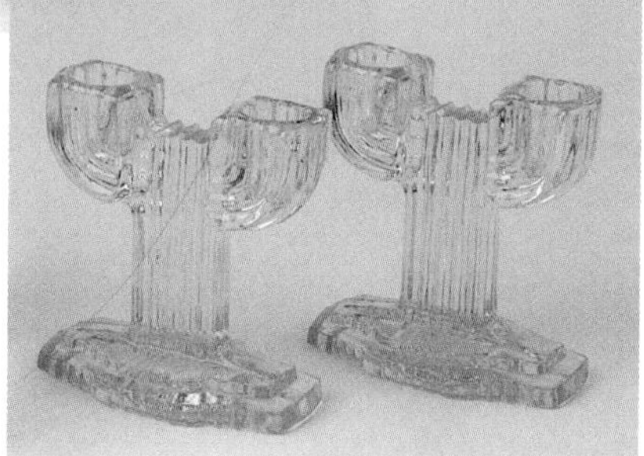

Queen Mary, crystal bowl ***$7.50****, and candlesticks* ***$24*** *pair.*

RAINDROPS

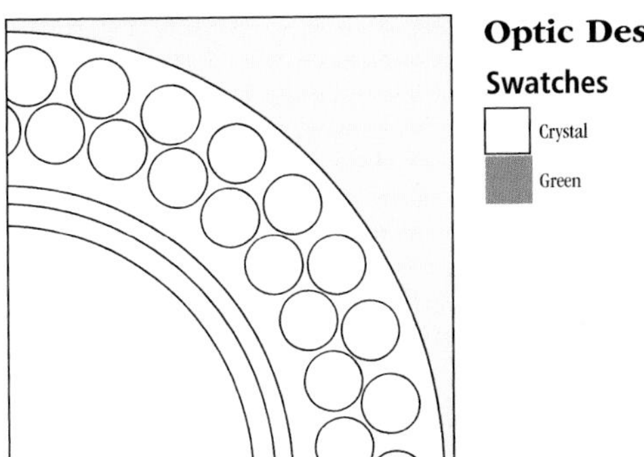

Optic Design

Swatches

Crystal

Green

Manufactured by Federal Glass Company, Columbus, Ohio, from 1929 to 1933.

Made in crystal and green.

Item	Crystal	Green
Berry bowl, 7-1/2" d	**$30**	**$45**
Cereal bowl, 6" d	**10**	**15**
Creamer	**8**	**10**
Cup	**8.50**	**6.50**
Fruit bowl, 4-1/2" d	**5**	**11**
Plate, 6" d, sherbet	**1.50**	**3**
Plate, 8" d, luncheon	**4**	**7.50**
Salt and pepper shakers, pr	**200**	**350**
Saucer	**3**	**3.50**
Sherbet	**4.50**	**7.50**
Sugar, cov	**7.50**	**15**

Item	Crystal	Green
Tumbler, 4 oz, 3" h	4	7
Tumbler, 5 oz, 3-7/8" h	5.50	9.50
Tumbler, 9-1/2 oz, 4-1/8" h	6	12
Tumblers, 10 oz, 5" h	6	12
Tumblers, 14 oz, 5-3/8" h	7.50	15
Whiskey, 1 oz, 1-7/8" h	7.50	10

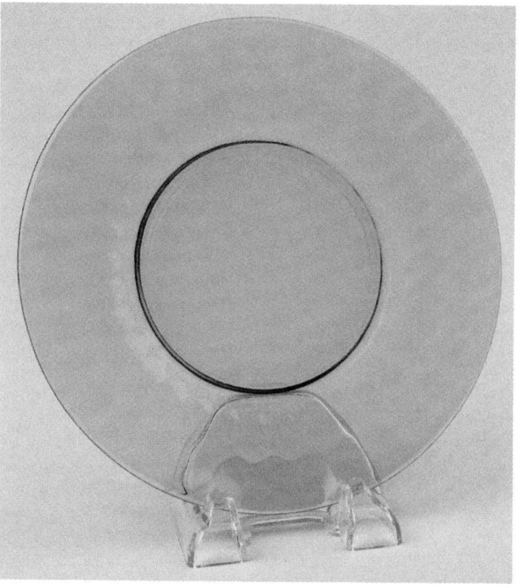

*Raindrops, green luncheon plate **$7.50**.*

RIBBON

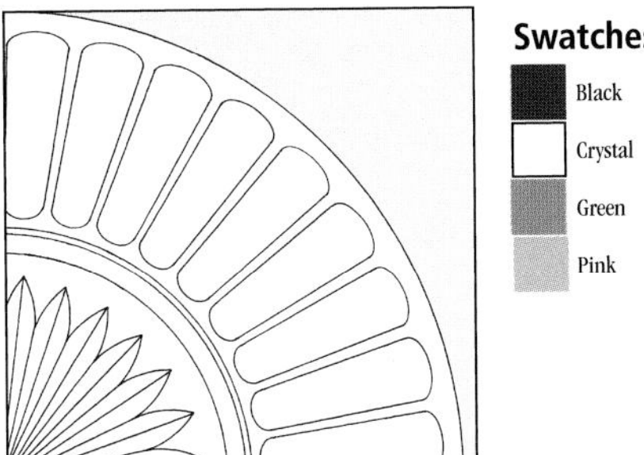

Swatches

- Black
- Crystal
- Green
- Pink

Manufactured by Hazel Atlas Glass Company, Clarksburg, W.V., and Zanesville, Ohio, early 1930s.

Made in black, crystal, green, and pink. Production in pink was limited to salt and pepper shakers, valued at $40.

Item	Black	Crystal	Green
Berry bowl, 4" d	$-	$20	$22
Berry bowl, 8" d	-	27.50	30
Bowl, 9" d, wide bands	-	-	35
Candy dish, cov	45	35	45
Cereal bowl, 5" d	-	20	25
Creamer, ftd	-	10	15
Cup	-	4.50	6.50
Plate, 6-1/4" d, sherbet	-	3.50	4.50
Plate, 8" d, luncheon	15	7	10
Salt and pepper shakers, pr	45	22	32
Saucer	-	2	3.50
Sherbet	-	6	8

Item	Black	Crystal	Green
Sugar, ftd	-	12	16.50
Tumbler, 10 oz, 6" h	-	28	30

*Ribbon, green cup **$6.50**, and creamer **$15**.*

RING

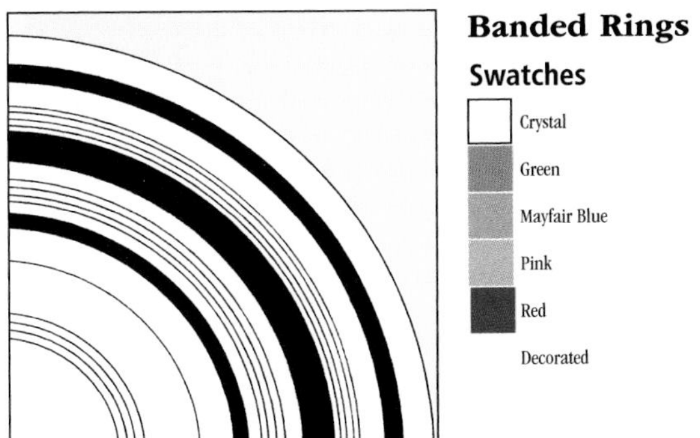

Banded Rings

Swatches

Crystal
Green
Mayfair Blue
Pink
Red
Decorated

Manufactured by Hocking Glass Company, Lancaster, Ohio, from 1927 to 1933.

Made in crystal, crystal with rings of black, blue, pink, red, orange, silver and yellow; and green, Mayfair blue, pink and red. Prices for decorated pieces are quite similar to each other.

Item	Crystal	Decorated	Green
Berry bowl, 5" d	$4	$9	$8
Berry bowl, 8" d	7.50	16	16
Bowl, 5-1/4" d, divided	12.50	-	-
Butter tub	24	25	20
Cereal bowl	-	5	8
Cocktail shaker	20	30	27.50
Cocktail, 3-1/2 oz, 3-3/4" h	12	18	18
Creamer, ftd	5	10	10
Cup	5	3	5

Item	Crystal	Decorated	Green
Decanter, stopper	30	35	32
Ice bucket	24	33	30
Ice tub	24	25	20
Iced tea tumbler, 6-1/2" h	10	15	15
Juice tumbler, 3-1/2" h, ftd	6.50	10	15
Old fashioned tumbler, 8 oz, 4" h	15	17.50	17.50
Pitcher, 60 oz, 8" h	22	25	25
Pitcher, 80 oz, 8-1/2" h	25	30	36
Plate, 6-1/2" d, off-center ring	6.50	8.50	8
Plate, 6-1/4" d, sherbet	3	4.50	4
Plate, 8" d, luncheon	3	7	9
Salt and pepper shakers, pr, 3" h	20	40	42
Sandwich plate, 11-3/4" d	8	15	15
Sandwich server, center handle	15	27.50	27.50
Saucer	1.50	2.50	2.50
Sherbet, 4-3/4" h	6.50	10	12

*Ring, green ice tub **$20**.*

Item	Crystal	Decorated	Green
Sherbet, flat, 6-1/2" d underplate	12	18	21
Soup bowl, 7" d	10	9	8
Sugar, ftd	5	10	3
Tumbler, 4 oz, 3" h	4	6.50	6
Tumbler, 5-1/2" h, ftd	6	10	10
Tumbler, 5 oz, 3-1/2" h	6.50	6.50	12
Tumbler, 9 oz, 4-1/4" h	7.50	7	9
Tumbler, 10 oz, 4-3/4" h	8.50	-	9
Tumbler, 12 oz, 5-1/8" h, ftd	10	12	20
Vase, 8" h	20	35	37.50
Whiskey, 1-1/2 oz, 2" h	8.50	10	12
Wine, 3-1/2 oz, 4-1/2" h	17.50	20	24

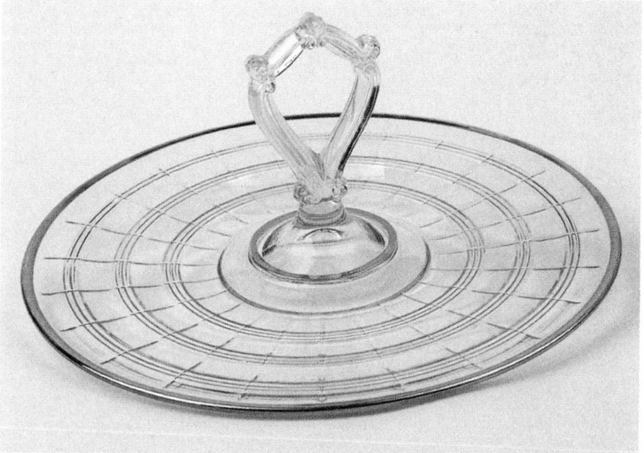

Ring, crystal sandwich server ***$15.***

ROSE CAMEO

Swatches

Green

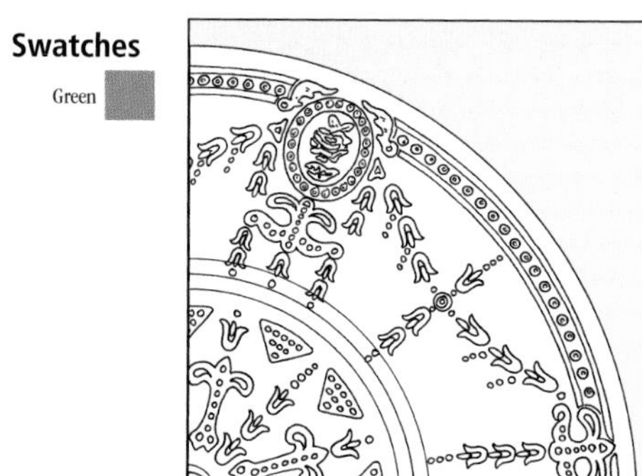

Manufactured by Belmont Tumbler Company, Bellaire, Ohio, in 1931. Made in green.

Item	Green
Berry bowl, 4-1/2" d	$15
Cereal bowl, 5" d	27.50
Bowl, 6" d, straight sides	30
Plate, 7" d, salad	16
Sherbet	16
Tumbler, 5" h, ftd	28
Tumbler, 5" h, ftd, sterling silver trim	30

*Rose Cameo, green tumbler **$28**.*

ROSEMARY

Dutch Rose

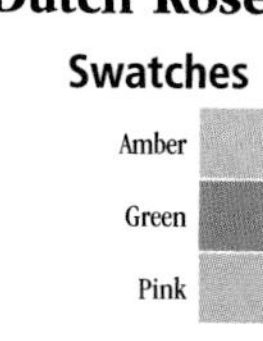

Manufactured by Federal Glass Company, Columbus, Ohio, from 1935 to 1937.

Made in amber, green, and pink.

Item	Amber	Green	Pink
Berry bowl, 5" d	**$7**	**$17.50**	**$17.50**
Cereal bowl, 6" d	**30**	**32**	**35**
Cream soup, 5" d	**18**	**25**	**30**
Creamer, ftd	**10**	**16**	**20**
Cup	**9**	**12.50**	**15**
Plate, 6-3/4" d, salad	**6.50**	**12**	**12.50**
Plate, 9-1/2" d, dinner	**10**	**15**	**22**
Plate, 9-1/2" d, grill	**12**	**15**	**22**
Platter, 12" l, oval	**18.50**	**24**	**35**
Saucer	**5**	**8.50**	**9.50**
Sugar, ftd	**10**	**16**	**20**

Item	Amber	Green	Pink
Tumbler, 9 oz, 4-1/4" h	35	38	50
Vegetable bowl, 10" l, oval	18	40	45

*Rosemary, green platter **$24**.*

ROULETTE

Many Windows

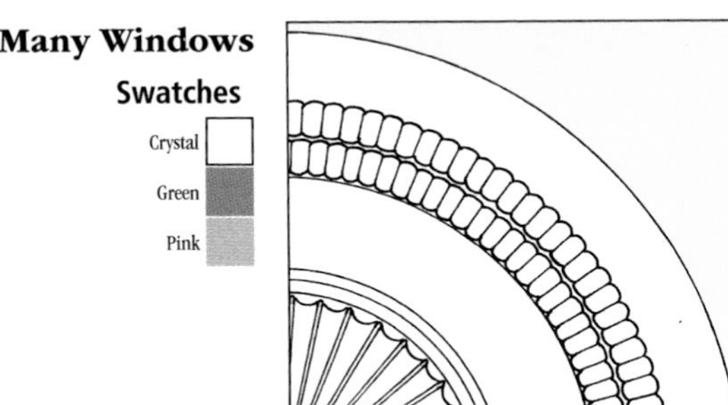

Manufactured by Hocking Glass Company, Lancaster, Ohio, from 1935 to 1939.

Made in crystal, green, and pink.

Item	Crystal	Green	Pink
Cup	$35	$8	$8.50
Fruit bowl, 9" d	12	25	25
Iced tea tumbler, 12 oz, 5-1/8" h	24	40	35
Juice tumbler, 5 oz, 3-1/4" h	10	60	24
Old fashioned tumbler, 7-1/2 oz, 3-1/4" h	24	40	40
Pitcher, 65 oz, 8" h	30	35	45
Plate, 6" d, sherbet	3.50	4.50	5
Plate, 8-1/2" d, luncheon	7	8	6
Sandwich plate, 12" d	15	18.50	20
Saucer	2.50	4	3
Sherbet	8	10	12

Item	Crystal	Green	Pink
Tumbler, 9 oz, 4-1/8" h	15	20	30
Tumbler, 10 oz, 5-1/2" h, ftd	18	30	35
Whiskey, 1-1/2 oz, 2-1/2" h	10	18	18

*Roulette, green luncheon plate **$8**, and sherbet **$10**.*

ROUND ROBIN

Swatches

Crystal
Iridescent
Green

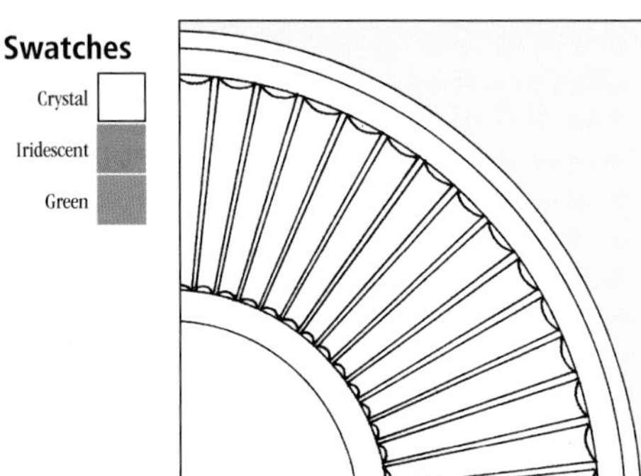

Unknown maker, early 1930s.

Made in crystal, iridescent, and green. Crystal, produced as the base for iridescent pieces, is found occasionally.

Item	Iridescent	Green
Berry bowl, 4" d	$12	$10
Creamer, ftd	7.50	12
Cup	7.50	8
Domino tray	-	120
Plate, 6" d, sherbet	4	5
Plate, 8" d, luncheon	9	12
Sandwich plate, 12" d	15	17.50
Saucer	2.50	2
Sherbet	8.50	10
Sugar	7.50	12

Round Robin, green luncheon plate ***$17.50***.

ROXANA

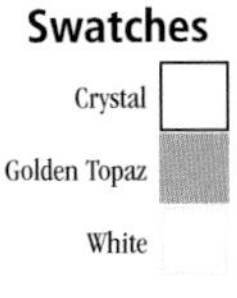

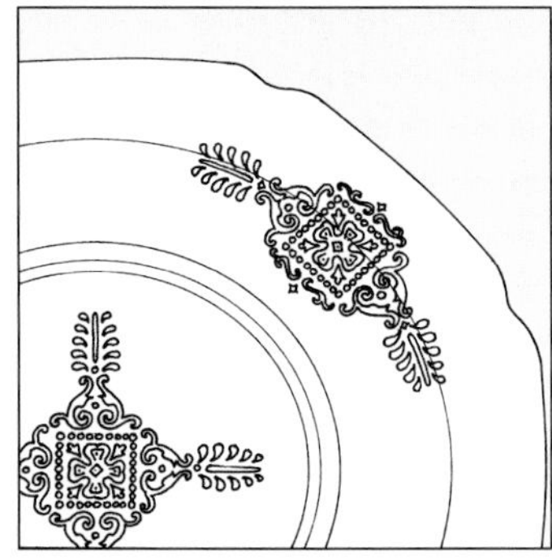

Manufactured by Hazel Atlas Glass Company, Clarksburg, W.V., and Zanesville, Ohio, in 1932.

Made in crystal, golden topaz, and white. Production in white was limited to a 4-1/2" bowl, valued at $15.

Item	Crystal	Golden Topaz
Berry bowl, 5" d	**$8.50**	**$15**
Bowl, 4-1/2" x 2-3/8"	**8**	**15**
Cereal bowl, 6" d	**9**	**18**
Plate, 5-1/2" d	**5**	**12**
Plate, 6" d, sherbet	**5**	**10**
Sherbet, ftd	**8**	**15**
Tumbler, 9 oz, 4-1/4" h	**12**	**24**

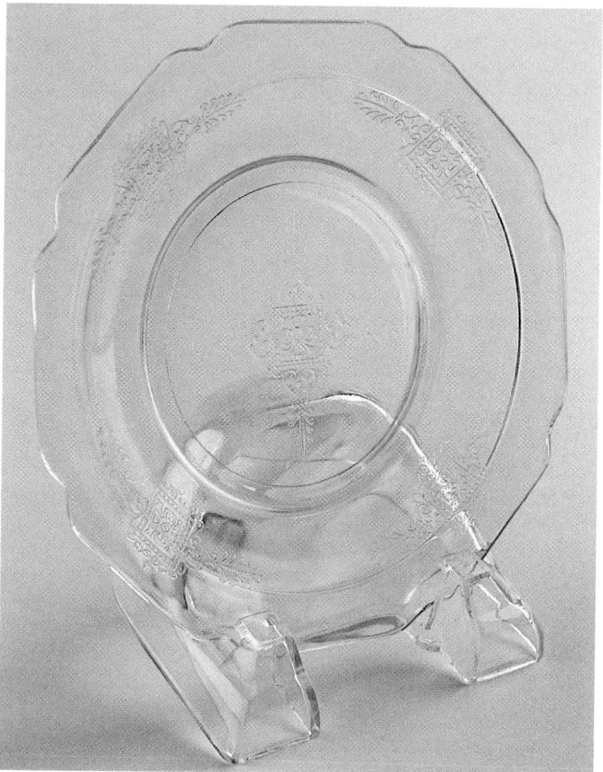

Roxana, golden topaz plate, 5-1/2" d ***$12***.

ROYAL LACE

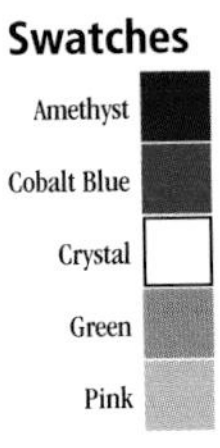

Manufactured by Hazel Atlas Glass Company, Clarksburg, W.V., and Zanesville, Ohio, from 1934 to 1941.

Made in cobalt (Ritz) blue, crystal, green, pink, and some amethyst.

Reproductions: † Reproductions include a 5 oz, 3-1/2" h tumbler, found in a darker cobalt blue. A cookie jar has also been reproduced in cobalt blue.

Item	Cobalt Blue	Crystal	Green	Pink
Berry bowl, 5" d	$50	$18	$38	$35
Berry bowl, 10" d	100	20	35	45
Bowl, 10" d, three legs, rolled edge	650	225	125	100
Bowl, 10" d, three legs, ruffled edge	750	45	125	100
Bowl, 10" d, three legs, straight edge	-	24	75	65
Butter dish, cov	865	90	275	200
Candlesticks, pr, rolled edge	-	45	85	60

Item	Cobalt Blue	Crystal	Green	Pink
Candlesticks, pr, ruffled edge	-	28	70	60
Candlesticks, pr, straight edge	-	35	75	55
Cookie jar, cov †	400	45	75	55

*Royal Lace, crystal dinner plate **$24**.*

Item	Cobalt Blue	Crystal	Green	Pink
Cream soup, 4-3/4" d	55	18	35	30
Creamer, ftd	60	15	25	20
Cup and saucer	55	16	25	18
Nut bowl	1,500	275	425	425
Pitcher, 48 oz, straight sides	190	40	110	85
Pitcher, 64 oz, 8" h	295	45	120	120
Pitcher, 68 oz, 8" h ice lip	320	60	-	115
Pitcher, 86 oz, 8" h	-	60	135	135
Pitcher, 96 oz, 9-1/2" h, ice lip	495	75	160	155
Plate, 6" d, sherbet	16.50	7.50	12	18
Plate, 8-1/2" d, luncheon	60	12	18	24
Plate, 9-7/8" d, dinner	55	24	30	27.50
Plate, 9-7/8" d, grill	40	20	25	22.50
Platter, 13" l, oval	60	42	45	48
Salt and pepper shakers, pr	325	65	130	85
Sherbet, ftd	50	20	25	18
Sherbet, metal holder	45	18	-	-
Sugar, cov	275	35	40	50
Sugar, open	-	12.50	25	22
Toddy or cider set	295	-	-	-
Tumbler, 5 oz, 3-1/2" h †	65	15	35	35
Tumbler, 9 oz, 4-1/8" h †	45	20	35	28
Tumbler, 10 oz, 4-7/8" h	245	25	60	60
Tumbler, 12 oz, 5-3/8" h	150	25	50	55
Vegetable bowl, 11" l, oval	60	25	35	35

ROYAL RUBY

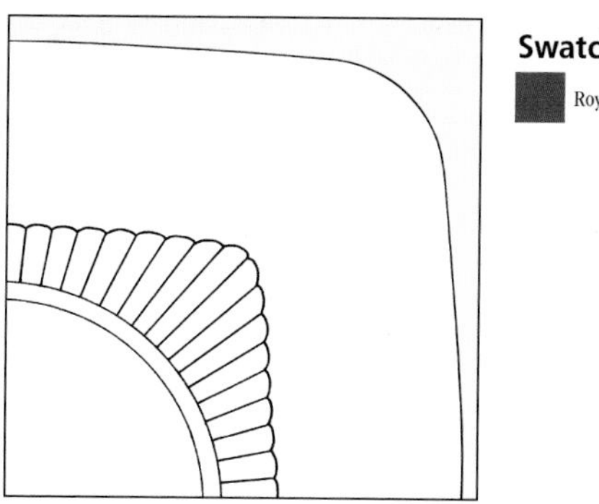

Swatches

Royal Ruby

Manufactured by Anchor Hocking Glass Corporation, Lancaster, Pa., from 1938 to 1967.

Made only in Royal Ruby.

Item	Royal Ruby
Apothecary jar, 8-1/2" h	$22
Ashtray, 4-1/2", leaf	5
Ashtray, 5-7/8", sq	9
Ashtray, 7-3/4"	32
Beer bottle, 7 oz	30
Beer bottle, 12 oz	32
Beer bottle, 16 oz	35
Beer bottle, 32 oz	40
Berry, 4-5/8" d, small, square	9.50
Berry, 8-1/2" d, round	25
Bonbon, 6-1/2" d	20

Item	Royal Ruby
Bowl, 7-3/8" w, sq	18.50
Bowl, 11" d, Rachael	50
Bowl, 12" l, oval, Rachael	70
Cereal bowl, 5-1/4" d	12
Cigarette box, card holder, 6-1/8" x 4"	90
Cocktail, 3-1/2 oz, Boopie	8.50
Cocktail, 3-1/2 oz, tumbler	10
Cordial, ftd	15
Creamer, flat	10
Creamer, ftd	10
Cup, round	6
Cup, square	7.50
Dessert bowl, 4-3/4" w, sq	9
Fruit bowl, 4-1/4" d	6.50
Goblet, 9 oz	9
Goblet, 9-1/2 oz	14
Goblet, ball stem	12
Ice bucket	55
Iced tea goblet, 14 oz, Boopie	20
Iced tea tumbler, 13 oz, 6" h, ftd	10
Ivy ball, 4" h, Wilson	12
Juice tumbler, 4 oz	7
Juice tumbler, 5-1/2 oz	10
Juice tumbler, 5 oz, flat or ftd	12
Juice pitcher	39
Lamp	35
Marmalade, ruby top, crystal base	22
Pitcher, 3 qt, tilted	45
Pitcher, 3 qt, upright	38
Pitcher, 42 oz, tilted	35

Item	Royal Ruby
Pitcher, 42 oz, upright	40
Pitcher, 86 oz, 8-1/2"	35
Plate, 6-1/4" d, sherbet	6.50
Plate, 7" d, salad	5.50
Plate, 7-3/4" w, sq, salad	7.50
Plate, 8-3/8" w, sq, luncheon	12
Plate, 9-1/8" d, dinner	14
Plate, 13-3/4" d	35
Popcorn bowl, 5-1/4" d	12.50
Popcorn bowl, 10" d, deep	40
Puff box, ruby top, crystal base, orig label	28
Punch bowl and stand	75
Punch set, 14 pieces	200

*Royal Ruby, punch set (includes 14 pieces), punch bowl and six cups are shown, value for entire set **$200**.*

Item	Royal Ruby
Punch cup	3.50
Relish, 3-3/4" x 8-3/4", tab handle	16
Salad bowl, 8-1/2" d	19
Salad bowl, 11-1/2" d	40
Saucer, 5-3/8" w, sq	4
Saucer, round	4
Set, 50 pcs, orig labels, orig box	350
Sherbet, 6-1/2 oz, stemmed	12
Sherbet, 6 oz, Boopie	8.50
Shot glass	4.50
Soup bowl, 7-1/2" d	15
Sugar, flat	8
Sugar, footed	8
Sugar lid, notched	11
Tray, center handle, ruffled	16.50
Tumbler, 5 oz, 3-1/2" h	6
Tumbler, 9 oz, Windsor	8.50
Tumbler, 10 oz, 5" h, ftd	7
Tumbler, 14 oz, 5" h	9
Tumbler, 15 oz, long boy	15
Vase, 3-3/4" h, Roosevelt	7.50
Vase, 4" h, Wilson, fancy edge	12
Vase, 6-3/8" h, Harding	15
Vase, 6-5/8" h, Coolidge	20
Vase, 9" h, Hoover, plain	20
Vase, 9" h, Hoover, white birds on branch dec	25
Vase, 10" h, fluted, star base	35
Vase, 10" h, ftd, Rachael	50
Vegetable bowl, 8" l, oval	45
Wine, 2-1/2 oz, ftd	15

*Royal Ruby, sugar **$8**, creamer (on pedestal) **$10**, square cup **$7.50**, and square saucer **$4**.*

Stippled Rose Band

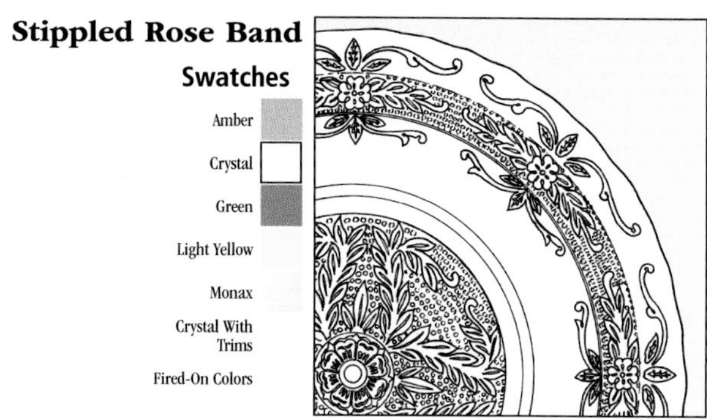

Manufactured by Macbeth-Evans Glass Company, Charleroi, Pa., from 1930 to 1933.

Made in amber, crystal, crystal with amber, blue, green, pink or silver trims, fired-on red, green, light yellow and Monax.

Item	Amber	Crystal	Crystal with Trims
Berry bowl, 8-1/2" d	$8.50	$12	$-
Cake plate, 11-3/4" d	50	48	55
Cake plate, 13" d	80	65	75
Cereal bowl, 5-1/2" d	6	4	6
Creamer, thick	7.50	6.50	8
Creamer, thin	7.50	6.50	8
Cup, thick	5	4	5.50
Cup, thin	5	4	5.50
Pitcher, 80 oz	-	75	-

Item	Amber	Crystal	Crystal with Trims
Plate, 6" d, sherbet	3.50	3	4
Plate, 8-1/4" d, luncheon	7	7	9.50
Plate, 9-1/4" d, dinner	9.50	-	12.50
Plate, grill	8.50	6.50	9
Saucer	4	3	4
Sherbet, low, ftd	8	5.50	8.50
Sugar, thick	7.50	6.50	8
Sugar, thin	7.50	6.50	8
Tumbler, 5 oz, 3-1/2" h	6.50	5	6.50
Tumbler, 10 oz, 4-3/4" h	8.50	9	7.50
Tumbler, 12 oz, 5" h	15	10	17.50

*S-Pattern, crystal luncheon plate with yellow trim **$9.50**.*

Additional Colors

Item	Fired-On Colors	Yellow
Berry bowl, 8-1/2" d	$-	$8.50
Cake plate, 11-3/4" d	-	50
Cake plate, 13" d	-	75
Cereal bowl, 5-1/2" d	12	6
Creamer, thick	15	7.50
Creamer, thin	15	7.50
Cup, thick	10	5
Cup, thin	10	5
Pitcher, 80 oz	-	-
Plate, 6" d, sherbet	-	3.50
Plate, 8-1/4" d, luncheon	-	5
Plate, 9-1/4" d, dinner	-	9.50
Plate, grill	-	8.50
Saucer	-	4
Sherbet, low, ftd	-	8
Sugar, thick	15	7.50
Sugar, thin	15	7.50
Tumbler, 5 oz, 3-1/2" h	-	6.50
Tumbler, 10 oz, 4-3/4" h	-	8.50
Tumbler, 12 oz, 5" h	-	15

SANDWICH

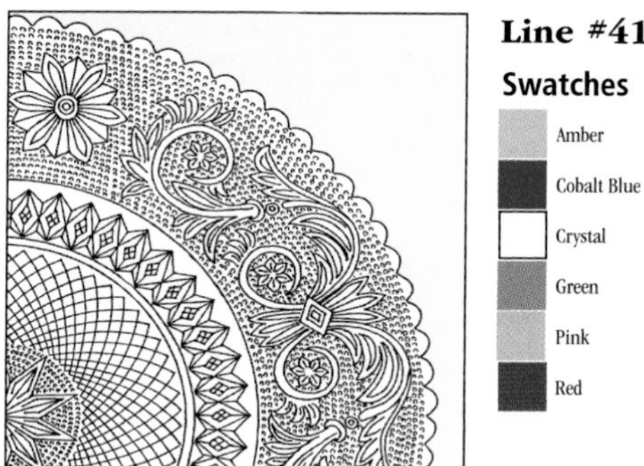

Line #41

Swatches

- Amber
- Cobalt Blue
- Crystal
- Green
- Pink
- Red

Manufactured by Duncan & Miller Glass Company, Washington, Pa., from 1924 to 1955.

Made in crystal with limited production in amber, cobalt blue, green, pink, and red. The molds were sold to Lancaster Colony which continues to produce some glass in this pattern, but in newer brighter colors, such as amberina, blue, and green.

Item	Crystal
Almond bowl, 2-1/2" d	$12
Ashtray, 2-1/2" x 3-3/4"	10
Ashtray, 2-3/4" sq	8.50
Basket, 6-1/2", loop handle	135
Basket 10", loop handle, crimped	185
Basket, 10", loop handle, oval	185
Basket, 11-1/2", loop handle	225
Bonbon, 5" w, heart shape	15

Item	Crystal
Bonbon, 6" w, heart shape, ring handle	20
Bonbon, cov, 7-1/2" d, ftd,	45
Bowl, 5-1/2" d, handle	15
Butter, cov, quarter pound	40
Cake stand, 11-1/2" d, ftd	95
Cake stand, 12" d, ftd	115
Cake stand, 13" d, ftd	125
Candelabra, with bobeche and prisms, 10" h, three-lite	200
Candelabra, with bobeche and prisms, 10" h, one-lite	95
Candelabra, with bobeche and prisms, 16" h, three-lite	225
Candlesticks, pr, 4" h	30
Candlesticks, pr, 5" h, three-lite	90
Candy box, cov, 5" d, flat	42
Candy comport, 3-1/4" d, low, ftd or flared	25
Candy dish, 6" sq	375
Candy jar, cov, 8-1/2" d, flat	60
Celery tray, 10" l, oval	30
Champagne, 5 oz	25
Cheese comport, 13" d underplate	60
Cheese dish, cov	125
Cigarette box, cov, 3-1/2"	24
Cigarette holder, 3" d, ftd	30
Coaster, 5" d	12
Cocktail, 3 oz	15
Comport, 2-1/4"	17.50
Comport, 4-1/4" d, ftd	22
Comport, 5" d, low, ftd	22

Sandwich, 8" d crystal salad plate ***$10.***

Item	Crystal
Comport, 5-1/2" d, ftd, low, crimped	25
Comport, 6" d, low, flared	25
Condiment set, pr cruets, pr salt and pepper shakers, tray	100
Console bowl, 12" d	45
Cracker plate, 13" d	32
Creamer	10
Cup	10
Deviled egg plate, 12" d	65
Epergne, 9" h	125
Epergne, 12" h, three parts	200
Finger bowl, 4" h	12
Finger bowl underplate, 6-1/2" d	8
Flower bowl, 11-1/2" d, crimped	60
Fruit bowl, 5" d	10
Fruit bowl, 10" d	65
Fruit bowl, 11-1/2" d, crimped, ftd	65
Fruit bowl, 12", flared	50
Fruit cup, 6 oz	12
Fruit salad bowl, 6" d	12
Gardenia bowl, 11-1/2" d	48
Goblet, 9 oz, 6" h	18
Grapefruit bowl, 5-1/2" d or 6" d	17.50
Hostess plate, 16" d	100
Ice cream dish 5 oz	12
Ice cream plate, rolled edge, 12" d	60
Ice cream tray, rolled edge, 12" d	45
Iced tea tumbler, 12 or 13 oz, ftd	20
Ivy bowl, ftd, crimped	35
Jelly, 3" d	8

Item	Crystal
Juice tumbler, 5 oz	12
Lazy Susan, 16" d	115
Lily bowl, 10" d	55
Mayonnaise set, three pcs	35
Mint tray, 6" l or 7" l, rolled edge, ring handle	18
Nappy, 5" d, two parts	15
Nappy, 5" d, ring handle	12
Nappy, 6" d, ring handle	15
Nut bowl, 3-1/2" d	10
Nut bowl, 11" d, cupped	55
Oil bottle, orig stopper	35
Oil and vinegar tray, 8" l	20
Oyster cocktail, 5 oz	18
Parfait, 4 oz, ftd	30
Pickle tray, 7" l, oval	15
Pitcher, 13 oz, metal lip	75
Pitcher, 64 oz, ice lip	125
Plate, 3" d, jelly	5
Plate, 6" d, bread and butter	6
Plate, 7" d, dessert	7.50
Plate, 8" d, salad	10
Plate, 9-1/2" d, dinner	35
Relish, 5-1/2" d, two parts, ring handle	15
Relish, 6" d, two parts, ring handle	18
Relish, 7" d, two parts, oval	20
Relish, 10" d, three parts, rect	27.50
Relish, 10" d, four parts	25
Relish, 10-1/2" l, three parts, rect	27.50
Relish, 12" l, three parts	25

Item	Crystal
Salad bowl, 10" d, deep	75
Salad bowl, 12" d, shallow	42
Salt and pepper shakers, pr, 2-1/2" h, glass tops	20
Salt and pepper shakers, pr, 2-1/2" h, metal tops	20
Salts and pepper shakers, set, pr 3-3/4" h, metal tops, 6" tray	35
Service plate, 11-1/2" d, handle	50
Service plate, 13" d	55
Sugar shaker	72
Sugar bowl, 5 oz	10
Sugar bowl, 9 oz, 3-1/4" h, ftd	12
Sundae, 5 oz	15
Torte plate, 12" d	48
Tray, 8" l	20
Urn, cov, 12" h, ftd	150
Tumbler, 9 oz, 4-3/4", ftd	15
Vase, 3" h, crimped	18
Vase, 3" h, flared rim	18
Vase, 4" h, hat shape	20
Vase, 4-1/2" h, crimped	25
Vase, 5" h, fan	40
Vase, 5" h, flared or crimped	25
Vase, 10" h, ftd	70
Wine, 3 oz	24

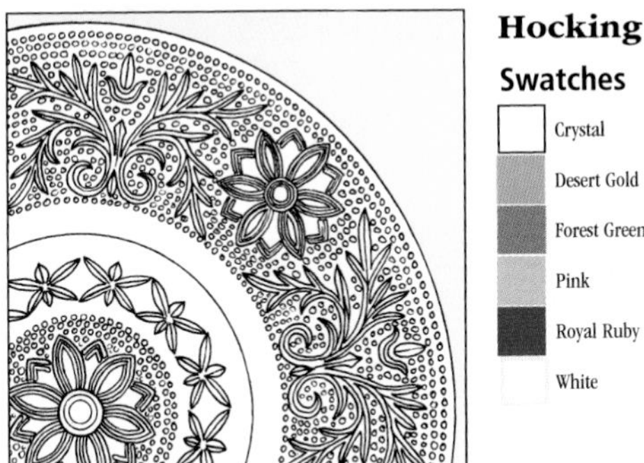

Hocking

Swatches

Crystal
Desert Gold
Forest Green
Pink
Royal Ruby
White

Manufactured by Hocking Glass Company, and later Anchor Hocking Corporation, from 1939 to 1964.

Made in crystal, Desert Gold, 1961-64; Forest Green, 1956-1960s; pink, 1939-1940; Royal Ruby, 1938-1939; and white/ivory (opaque), 1957-1960s.

Reproductions: † The cookie jar has been reproduced in crystal.

*No cover is known for the cookie jar in Forest Green.

Item	Crystal	Desert Gold	Forest Green
Bowl, 4-5/16" d, smooth	$5	$-	4
Bowl, 4-7/8" d, smooth	5	6	-
Bowl, 4-7/8" d, crimped	20	-	-
Bowl, 5-1/4" d, scalloped	5	6	-
Bowl, 6-1/2" d, scalloped	7.50	9	60

Item	Crystal	Desert Gold	Forest Green
Bowl, 6-1/2" d, smooth	7.50	9	-
Bowl, 7-1/4" d, scalloped	8	-	-
Bowl, 8-1/4" d, oval	10	-	-
Bowl, 8-1/4" d, scalloped	10	-	80
Butter dish, cov	45	-	-
Cereal bowl, 6-3/4" d	32	12	-
Cookie jar, cov † *	40	45	20
Creamer	6.50	-	30
Cup, coffee	2	12	24
Cup, tea	3	14	24
Custard cup	7	-	4
Custard cup liner	5.50	-	1.50
Custard cup, crimped	12.50	-	-
Dessert bowl, 5" d, crimped	18.50	-	-
Juice pitcher, 6" h	115	-	145
Juice tumbler, 3 oz, 3-3/8" h	12	-	6
Juice tumbler, 5 oz, 3-9/16" h	7.50	-	4.50
Pitcher, half gallon, ice lip	85	-	550
Plate, 6" d	5	-	-
Plate, 7" d, dessert	25	-	-
Plate, 8" d, luncheon	18	-	-
Plate, 9" d, dinner	20	10	125
Plate, 9" d, indent for punch cup	12	-	-
Punch bowl, 9-3/4" d	18	-	-
Punch bowl and stand	32	-	-
Punch bowl set, bowl, base, 12 cups	60	-	-
Punch cup	3	-	-
Salad bowl, 7" d	8	25	-
Salad bowl, 7-5/8" d	-	-	60

Item	Crystal	Desert Gold	Forest Green
Salad bowl, 9" d	24	20	-
Sandwich plate, 12" d	14	17.50	-
Saucer	3.50	5	15
Sherbet, ftd	8	8	-
Snack set, plate and cup	9	-	-
Sugar, cov	30	-	-
Sugar, no cover	6	-	30
Tumbler, 9 oz, ftd	32.50	125	-
Tumbler, 9 oz, water	9	-	7
Vase	-	-	27.50
Vegetable, 8-1/2" l, oval	10	-	-

*Sandwich, crystal oval bowl **$10**.*

Additional Colors

Item	Pink	Royal Ruby	White
Bowl, 4-5/16" d, smooth	$-	$-	$-
Bowl, 4-7/8" d, smooth	7	17.50	-
Bowl, 4-7/8" d, crimped	-	-	-
Bowl, 5-1/4" d, scalloped	-	25	-
Bowl, 5-1/4" d, smooth	7	35	-
Bowl, 6-1/2" d, scalloped	-	35	-
Bowl, 8-1/4" d, scalloped	20	35	-
Plate, 9" d, dinner	10	-	-
Punch bowl, 9-3/4" d	-	-	15
Punch bowl and stand	-	-	30
Punch cup	-	-	2

Sandwich, smooth Desert Gold bowl, 6-1/2" d ***$9.***

SANDWICH

Indiana

Swatches

Amber

Crystal

Green

Milk White

Teal Blue

Red

Smoky Blue

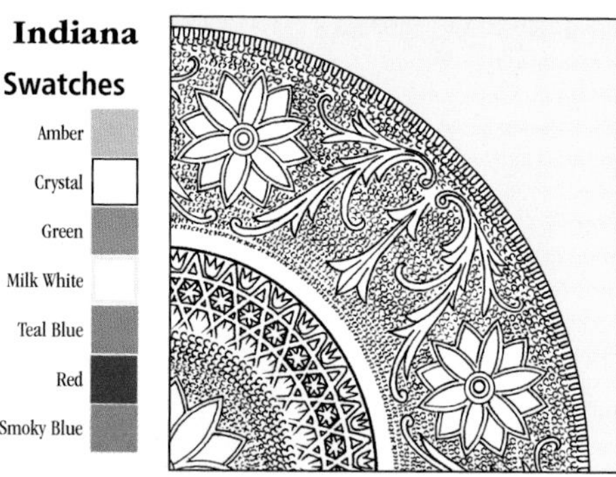

Manufactured by Indiana Glass Company, Dunkirk, Ind., 1920s to 1980s.

Made in crystal, late 1920s to 1990s; amber, late 1920s to 1980s; milk white, mid-1950s; teal blue, 1950s to 1960s; red, 1933 and early 1970s; smoky blue, 1976 to 1977; and green in the late 1960s and 1970s by Taira.

Reproductions: † Reproductions include a butter dish, decanter, and wine. Reproductions are found in dark amber, crystal, green, and pink.

Item	Amber	Crystal	Teal Blue	Red
Ashtray, club	**$3.25**	**$4**	**$-**	**$-**
Ashtray, diamond	**3.25**	**4**	**-**	**-**
Ashtray, heart	**3.25**	**4**	**2**	**-**

Item	Amber	Crystal	Teal Blue	Red
Ashtray, spade	3.25	4	-	-
Basket, 10" h	35	35	-	-
Berry bowl, 4-1/4" d	3.50	5	-	-
Bowl, 6" w, hexagonal	5.50	6	15	-
Bowl, 8-1/2" d	10	11	-	-
Butter dish, cov †	25	25	150	-
Candlesticks, pr, 3-1/2" h	18	20	-	-
Candlesticks, pr, 7" h	25	25	-	-
Celery tray, 10-1/2" l	17.50	14	-	-
Cereal bowl, 6" d	12	6.50	-	-
Cocktail, 3 oz, ftd	7.50	7.50	-	-
Comport, low, ruffled	15	-	-	-
Console bowl, 9" d	17.50	17.50	-	-
Console bowl, 11-1/2" d	20	20	-	-

*Sandwich, crystal creamer and sugar with matching tray **$18**.*

Item	Amber	Crystal	Teal Blue	Red
Creamer	6	6	-	48
Creamer and sugar, tray	18	18	35	-
Cruet, 6-1/2 oz, stopper	-	-	145	-
Cup	4	4	8.50	30
Decanter, stopper †	25	25	-	90
Fairy lamp	15	-	-	-
Goblet, 9 oz	14	15	-	45
Iced tea tumbler, 12 oz, ftd	10	10	-	-
Mayonnaise, ftd	14	14	-	-
Pitcher, 68 oz	24	24	-	175
Plate, 6" d, sherbet	3.50	3.50	7.50	-
Plate, 7" d, bread and butter	4	4	-	-
Plate, 8" d, oval, indent	-	4	6.50	15
Plate, 8-3/8" d, luncheon	7.50	8	-	20
Plate, 10-1/2" d, dinner	9	8.50	20	-
Puff box	18	18	-	-
Salt and pepper shakers, pr	18	18	-	-
Sandwich plate, 13" d	14.50	14.50	25	35
Sandwich server, center handle	20	20	-	50
Saucer	3.50	2.50	7	7.50
Sherbet, 3-1/4" h	6	5.50	12	-
Sugar, cov, large	20	20	-	48
Tumbler, 8 oz, ftd, water	10	10	-	-
Wine, 3" h, 4 oz †	10	12	-	15

SHARON

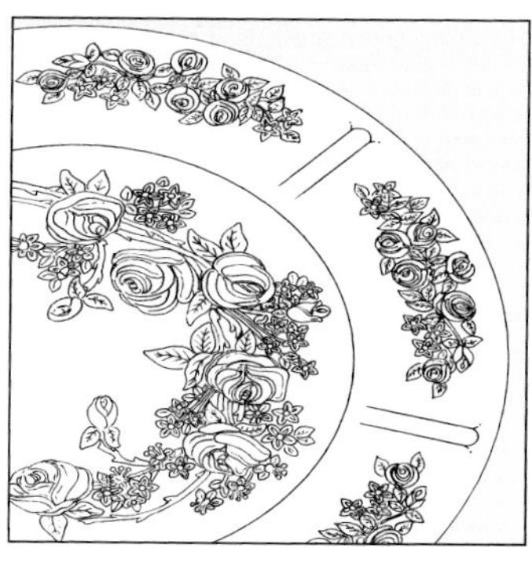

Cabbage Rose

Swatches

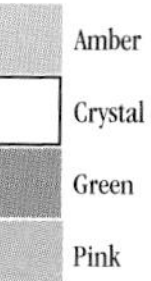

Manufactured by Federal Glass Company, Columbus, Ohio, from 1935 to 1939.

Made in amber, crystal, green, and pink.

Reproductions: † Reproductions include the butter dish, covered candy dish, creamer, covered sugar, and salt and pepper shakers. Reproduction colors include dark amber, blue, green, and pink.

Item	Amber	Crystal	Green	Pink
Berry bowl, 5" d	$8.50	$5	$18.50	$15
Berry bowl, 8-1/2" d	10	12	40	35
Butter dish, cov †	50	20	85	65
Cake plate, 11-1/2" d, ftd	30	10	65	50
Candy dish, cov †	45	15	100	65
Cereal, 6" d	24	12	32	35
Champagne, 5" d bowl	-	-	-	12
Cheese dish, cov †	225	1,500	-	950

Item	Amber	Crystal	Green	Pink
Cream soup, 5" d	28	15	60	50
Creamer, ftd †	15	14	22	24
Cup	9	6	18	20
Fruit bowl, 10-1/2" d	24	18	40	55
Iced tea tumbler, ftd	125	15	-	65
Jam dish, 7-1/2" d	40	-	48	215
Pitcher, 80 oz, ice lip	145	-	150	165
Pitcher, 80 oz, without ice lip	140	-	150	150
Plate, 6" d, bread and butter	16	5	9	16.50
Plate, 7-1/2" d, salad	16.50	6.50	8	30
Plate, 9-1/2" d, dinner	17	9.50	27.50	24.50
Platter, 12-1/2" l, oval	24	-	35	40
Salt and pepper shakers, pr †	40	-	80	65
Saucer	6.50	4	36	15
Sherbet, ftd	14	8	35	19.50
Soup, flat, 7-3/4" d, 1 7/8" deep	60	-	-	65
Sugar, cov †	35	12	55	60
Tumbler, 9 oz, 4-1/8" h, thick	30	-	65	45
Tumbler, 9 oz, 4-1/8" h, thin	38	-	65	42
Tumbler, 12 oz, 5-1/4" h, thick	55	-	95	50
Tumbler, 12 oz, 5-1/4" h, thin	55	-	95	52.50
Tumbler, 15 oz, 6-1/2" h, thick	125	18	-	63
Vegetable bowl, 9-1/2" l, oval	25	-	35	42.50

*Sharon, (counterclockwise) pink sherbet **$19.50**, 5" d berry bowl **$15**, creamer **$24,** and 8-1/2" d berry bowl **$35**.*

Sailboat, Sportsman Series

Swatches

Cobalt Blue With Different Colors Of Decoration

Manufactured by Hazel Atlas Glass Company, Clarksburg, W.V., and Zanesville, Ohio, late 1930s.

Made in cobalt blue with white, yellow, and red decoration. Pieces with yellow or red decoration are valued slightly higher than the traditional white decoration.

Item	Cobalt Blue with White Decoration
Ashtray	$60
Ashtray, metal sailboat	120
Box, cov, three parts	250
Cocktail mixer, stirrer	45
Cocktail shaker	45
Cup	15
Ice bowl	45
Iced tea tumbler, 10-1/2 oz, 4-7/8" h	22

Item	Cobalt Blue with White Decoration
Iced tea tumbler, 12 oz	24
Old fashioned tumbler, 8 oz, 3-3/8" h	22
Pitcher, 82 oz, no ice lip	85
Pitcher, 86 oz, ice lip	75
Plate, 5-7/8" d, bread & butter	24
Plate, 8" d, salad	27.50
Plate, 9" d, dinner	32
Saucer	18
Tumbler, 4 oz, 3-1/4" h, heavy bottom	27.50
Tumbler, 9 oz, 3-3/4" h	18
Whiskey, 3-1/2" h	45

*Ships, cobalt blue salad plate **$27.50**.*

*Ships, cobalt blue cocktail shaker **$45**.*

SIERRA

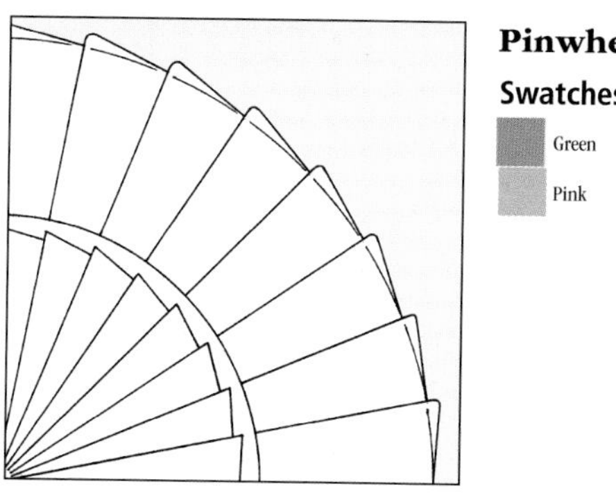

Pinwheel

Swatches

Green

Pink

Manufactured by Jeannette Glass Company, Jeannette, Pa., from 1931 to 1933.

Made in green and pink. A few forms are known in Ultramarine.

Item	Green	Pink
Berry, small	$25	$25
Berry bowl, 8-1/2" d	40	40
Butter dish, cov	80	85
Cereal bowl, 5-1/2" d	25	20
Creamer	25	25
Cup	19.50	17.50
Pitcher, 32 oz, 6-1/2" h	160	135
Plate, 9" d, dinner	30	32
Platter, 11" l, oval	70	65
Salt and pepper shakers, pr	50	50
Saucer	10	10

Item	Green	Pink
Serving tray, 10-1/4" l, two handles	25	30
Sugar, cov	48	48
Tumbler, 9 oz, 4-1/2" h, ftd	90	80
Vegetable bowl, 9-1/4" l, oval	135	90

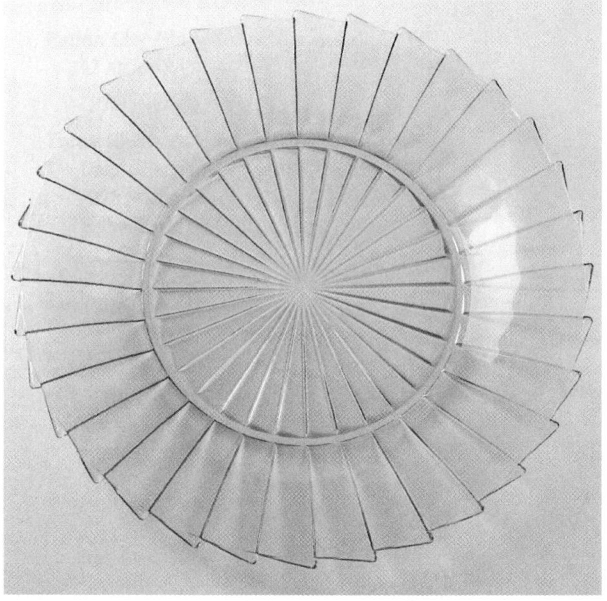

*Sierra Pinwheel, pink dinner plate **$32**.*

SPIRAL

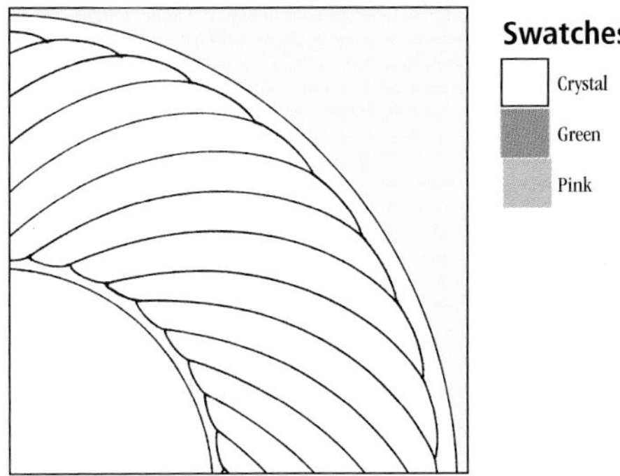

Swatches

Crystal

Green

Pink

Manufactured by Hocking Glass Company, Lancaster, Ohio, from 1928 to 1930.

Made in crystal, green, and pink. Collector interest is strongest in green.

Item	Green
Berry bowl, 4-3/4" d	**$8**
Berry bowl, 8" d	**16.50**
Butter tub	**27.50**
Creamer, flat	**8**
Creamer, footed	**8**
Cup	**5**
Ice tub	**25**
Juice tumbler, 5 oz, 3" h	**5**
Mixing bowl, 7" d	**9**
Pitcher, 58 oz, 7-5/8" h	**35**

Item	Green
Plate, 6" d, sherbet	5
Plate, 8" d, luncheon	6.50
Platter, 12" l	32
Preserve, cov	32
Salt and pepper shakers, pr	37.50
Sandwich server, center handle	30
Saucer	4
Sherbet	5
Sugar, flat	8
Sugar, footed	8
Tumbler, 5-7/8" h, ftd	24
Tumbler, 9 oz, 5" h	12

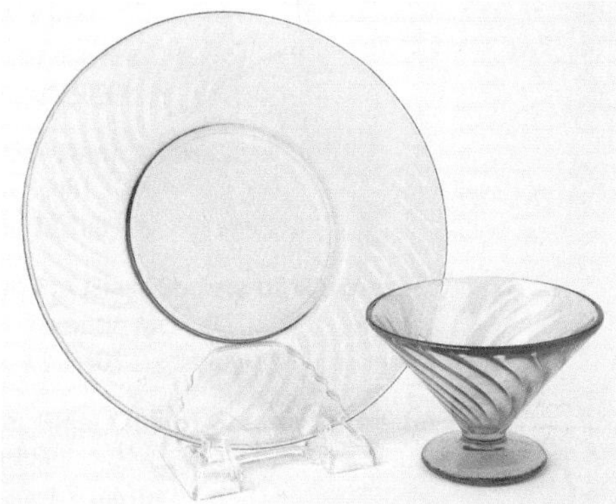

*Spiral, green luncheon plate **$6.50**, and sherbet **$5**.*

STAR

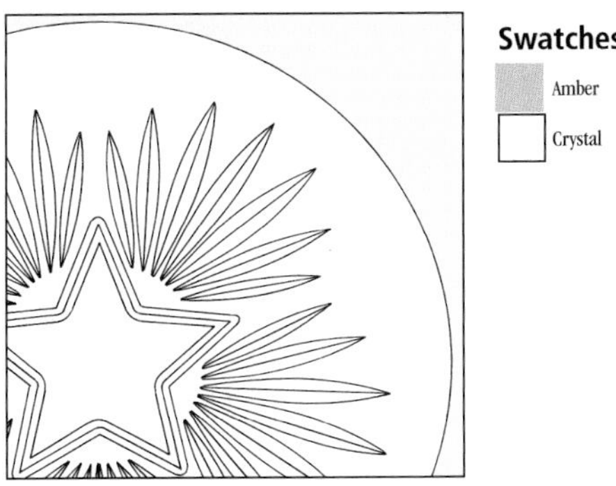

Swatches

Amber

Crystal

Manufactured by Federal Glass Company, Columbus, Ohio, 1950s.

Made in amber, crystal and crystal with gold trim. Crystal pieces with gold trim would be valued the same as plain crystal.

Item	Amber	Crystal
Bowl, 5-5/8" d	$-	$7
Creamer	7	9
Cup	10	10
Dessert bowl, 4-5/8" d	4	5
Iced tea tumbler, 12 oz, 5-1/8" h	8	9
Juice pitcher, 36 oz, 5-3/4" h	10	12
Juice tumbler, 4-1/2 oz, 3-3/8" h	4	5
Pitcher, 60 oz, 7" h	12	14
Pitcher, 85 oz, 9-1/4" h, ice lip	15	15
Plate, 6-3/16" d, salad	5	6
Plate, 9-3/8" d, dinner	12	14

Item	Amber	Crystal
Saucer	4	3
Sugar, cov	15	15
Tumbler, 9 oz, 3-7/8" h, water	15	7.50
Vegetable bowl, 8-3/8" d	10	15
Whiskey, 1-1/2 oz, 2-1/4" h	4	5

*Star, crystal bowl **$7**, 85 oz pitcher with ice lip **$15**, and 60 oz pitcher **$14**.*

STARLIGHT

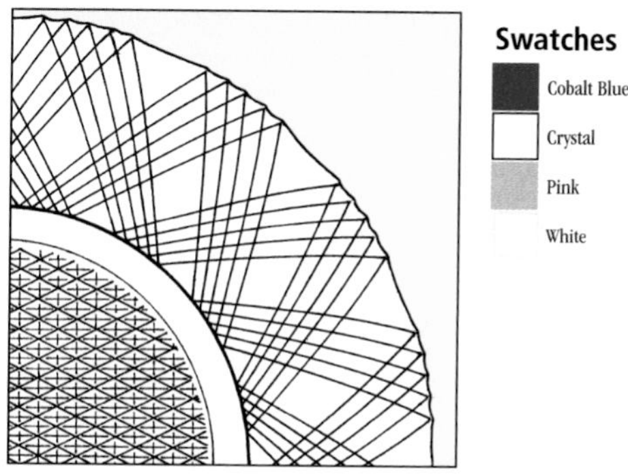

Swatches

- Cobalt Blue
- Crystal
- Pink
- White

Manufactured by Hazel Atlas Glass Company, Clarksburg, W.V., and Zanesville, Ohio, from 1938 to 1940.

Made in cobalt blue, crystal, pink, and white. Production in cobalt blue was limited to 8-1/2" d bowl, valued at $30.

Item	Crystal	Pink	White
Berry bowl, 4" d	$9.50	$-	$-
Bowl, 8-1/2" d, two handles	18	20	18
Bowl, 11-1/2" d, deep	25	-	25
Bowl, 12" d, 2-3/4" deep	25	-	25
Cereal bowl, 5-1/2" d, two handles	7	12	7
Creamer, oval	10	-	5
Cup	6	-	4
Plate, 6" d, sherbet	4.50	-	4
Plate, 7-1/2" d, salad	5	-	4.50
Plate, 8-1/2" d, luncheon	5	-	5

Item	Crystal	Pink	White
Plate, 9" d, dinner	8.50	-	8.50
Relish dish	15	-	15
Salad bowl, 11-1/2" d, deep	27.50	-	27.50
Salt and pepper shakers, pr	30	-	30
Sandwich plate, 13" d	25	20	-
Saucer	4	-	2.50
Sherbet	15	-	12
Sugar, oval	10	-	10

*Starlight, crystal salt and pepper shakers **$30**.*

STRAWBERRY

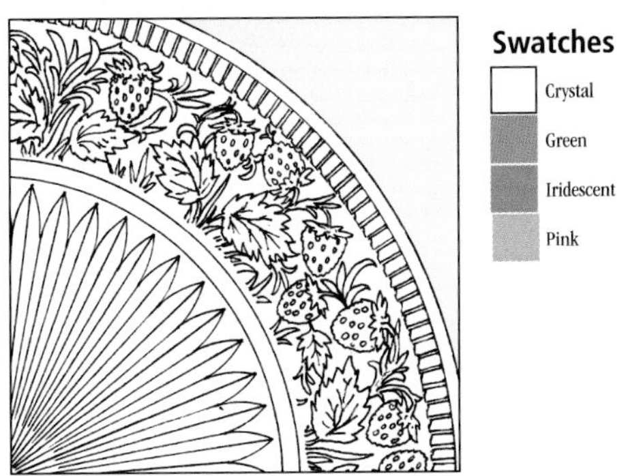

Swatches

- Crystal
- Green
- Iridescent
- Pink

Manufactured by U.S. Glass Company, Pittsburgh, Pa., in the early 1930s.

Made in crystal, green, pink, and some iridescent.

Item	Crystal	Green	Iridescent	Pink
Berry bowl, 4" d	$7.50	$12	$7.50	$12
Berry bowl, 7-1/2" d	16	20	16	20
Bowl, 6-1/4" d, 2" deep	40	60	40	60
Butter dish, cov	125	185	135	195
Comport, 5-3/4" d	55	60	55	60
Creamer, large, 4-5/8" h	24	35	24	35
Creamer, small	12	18.50	12	18.50
Olive dish, 5" l, one handle	8.50	14	8.50	14
Pickle dish, 8-1/4" l, oval	8	14	8	14
Pitcher, 7-3/4" h	150	185	150	195
Plate, 6" d, sherbet	5	13.50	5	8

Item	Crystal	Green	Iridescent	Pink
Plate, 7-1/2" d, salad	10	14	10	15
Salad bowl, 6-1/2" d	15	20	15	20
Sherbet	6	13.50	6	13.50
Sugar, large, cov	60	85	60	85
Sugar, small, open	12	32	12	32
Tumbler, 8 oz, 3-5/8" h	20	32	20	38

*Strawberry, pink salad plate **$15**.*

SUNBURST

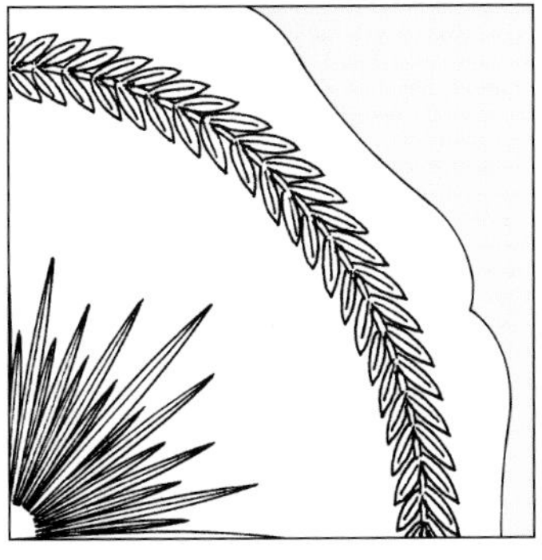

Herringbone

Swatches

Crystal

Manufactured by Jeannette Glass Company, Jeannette, Pa., late 1930s. Made in crystal.

Item	Crystal
Berry bowl, 4-3/4" d	$7
Berry bowl, 8-1/2" d	18
Bowl, 10-1/2" d	30
Candlesticks, pr, double	35
Creamer, ftd	16
Cup	7.50
Cup and saucer	9.50
Plate, 5-1/2" d	12
Plate, 9-1/4" d, dinner	15
Relish, two parts	14.50
Sandwich plate, 11-3/4" d	15
Saucer	3

Item	Crystal
Sherbet	12
Sugar	16
Tumbler, 4" h, 9 oz, flat	18.50

*Sunburst, crystal sandwich plate **$15**.*

SUNFLOWER

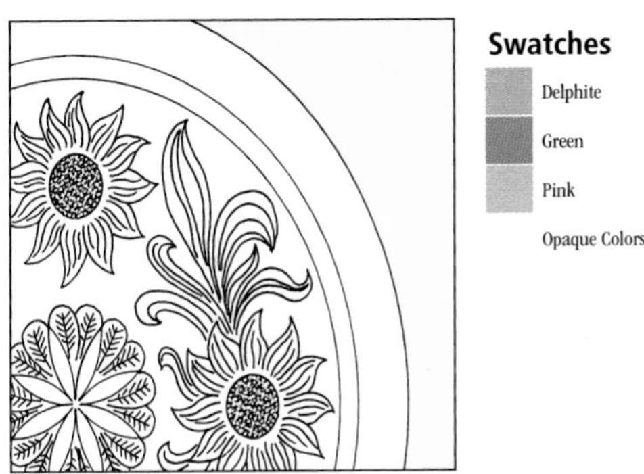

Swatches

Delphite

Green

Pink

Opaque Colors

Manufactured by Jeannette Glass Company, Jeannette, Pa., 1930s.

Made in Delphite, green, pink, and some opaque colors. Look for a creamer in Delphite, valued at $85.

Item	Delphite	Green	Pink	Opaque
Ashtray, 5" d	$-	$15	$10	-
Cake plate, 10" d, three legs	-	20	20	-
Creamer	90	20	20	85
Cup	-	15	15	75
Plate, 9" d, dinner	-	22	20	-
Saucer	-	13.50	12	85
Sugar	-	25	22	-
Trivet, 7" d, three legs, turned up edge	-	325	315	-
Tumbler, 8 oz, 4-3/8" h, ftd	-	35	32	-

Sunflower, green cake plate ***$20.***

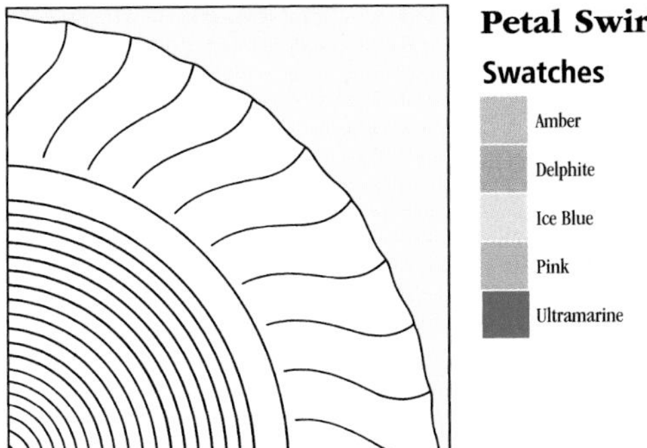

Petal Swirl

Swatches

- Amber
- Delphite
- Ice Blue
- Pink
- Ultramarine

Manufactured by Jeannette Glass Company, Jeannette, Pa., from 1937 to 1938.

Made in amber, Delphite, ice blue, pink, and Ultramarine. Production was limited in amber and ice blue.

Item	Delphite	Pink	Ultramarine
Berry bowl	$15	$-	$18
Bowl, 10" d, ftd, closed handles	-	25	35
Butter dish, cov	-	175	245
Candleholders, pr, double branch	-	40	60
Candleholders, pr, single branch	115	-	-
Candy dish, cov	-	130	150
Candy dish, open, three legs	-	20	29.50
Cereal bowl, 5-1/4" d	15	10	15
Coaster, 1" x 3-1/4"	-	15	14
Console bowl, 10-1/2" d, ftd	-	20	35

Item	Delphite	Pink	Ultramarine
Creamer	12	9.50	18
Cup and saucer	17.50	14	22.50
Plate, 6-1/2" d, sherbet	6.50	5	8
Plate, 7-1/4" d, luncheon	-	6.50	12
Plate, 8" d, salad	9	8.50	18
Plate, 9-1/4" d, dinner	12	13	22.50
Plate, 10-1/2" d, dinner	18	-	30
Platter, 12" l, oval	35	-	-
Salad bowl, 9" d	30	18	35
Salad bowl, 9" d, rimmed	-	20	30
Salt and pepper shakers, pr	-	-	50
Sandwich plate, 12-1/2" d	-	20	27.50
Sherbet, low, ftd	-	13	23
Soup, tab handles, lug	-	25	35
Sugar, ftd	-	12	18
Tray, 10-1/2" l, two handles	25	-	-
Tumbler, 9 oz, 4" h	-	18	42
Tumbler, 9 oz, 4-5/8" h	-	18	-
Tumbler, 13 oz, 5-1/8" h	-	45	90
Vase, 6-1/2" h, ftd, ruffled	-	22	-
Vase, 8-1/2" h, ftd	-	-	36

*Swirl, Ultramarine dinner plate **$30**, and closed-handled bowl **$35**.*

TEA ROOM

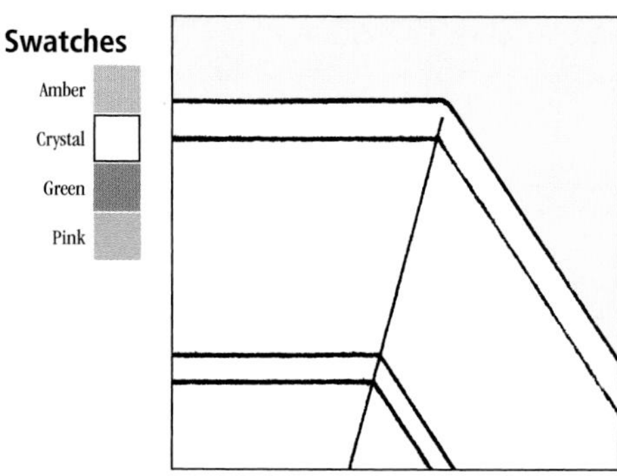

Manufactured by Indiana Glass Company, Dunkirk, Ind., from 1926 to 1931.

Made in amber, crystal, green, and pink.

Item	Amber	Crystal	Green	Pink
Banana split bowl, 7-1/2" l	$-	$85	$200	$210
Candlesticks, pr, low	-	-	80	85
Celery Bowl, 8-1/2"d	-	-	35	27.50
Creamer, 3-1/4" h	-	-	30	28
Creamer, 4-1/2" h, ftd	80	-	20	18
Creamer and sugar on tray	-	-	95	85
Cup	-	-	65	60
Finger bowl	-	80	50	40
Goblet, 9 oz.	-	-	75	65
Ice bucket	-	-	85	80
Lamp, electric	-	140	175	145

Item	Amber	Crystal	Green	Pink
Mustard, cov	-	-	160	140
Parfait	-	-	72	65
Pitcher, 64 oz	425	400	150	135
Plate, 6-1/2" d, sherbet	-	-	35	32
Plate, 8-1/4" d, luncheon	-	-	37.50	35
Plates, 10-1/2" d, two handles	-	-	50	45
Relish, divided	-	-	30	25
Salad bowl, 8-3/4" d, deep	-	-	150	135
Salt and pepper shakers, pr, ftd	-	-	60	55

*Tea Room, footed pink sugar **$18**, and creamer **$18**.*

Item	Amber	Crystal	Green	Pink
Saucer	-	-	30	25
Sherbet	-	-	40	35
Sugar, 3" h, cov	-	-	115	100
Sugar, 4-1/2" h, ftd	80	-	20	18
Sugar, cov, flat	-	-	200	170
Sundae, ftd, ruffled	-	-	85	70
Tumbler, 6 oz, ftd	-	-	35	32
Tumbler, 8 oz, 5-1/4" h, ftd	75	-	35	32
Tumbler, 11 oz., ftd	-	-	45	40
Tumbler, 12 oz, ftd	-	-	60	55
Vase, 6-1/2" h, ruffled edge	-	-	145	125
Vase, 9-1/2" h, ruffled	-	50	175	100
Vase, 9-1/2"h, straight	-	175	95	225
Vase, 11" h, ruffled edge	-	-	350	395
Vase, 11" h, straight	-	-	200	395
Vegetable bowl, 9-1/2" l, oval	-	-	75	65

THISTLE

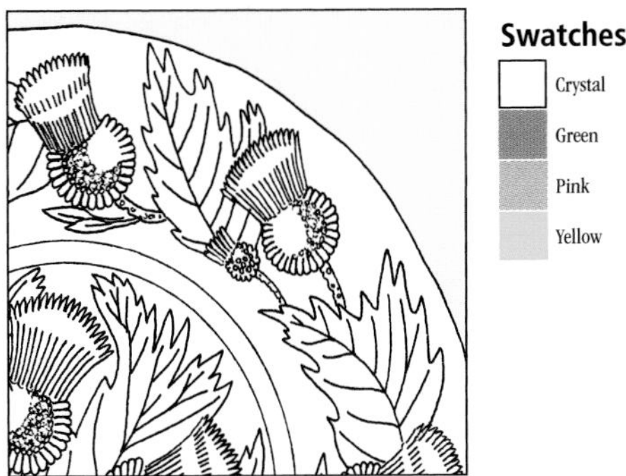

Swatches

Crystal

Green

Pink

Yellow

Manufactured by Macbeth-Evans, Charleroi, Pa., about 1929 to 1930.

Made in crystal, green, pink, and yellow. Production was limited in crystal and yellow.

Reproductions: † Recent reproductions have been found in pink, a darker emerald green, and wisteria. Several of the reproductions have a scalloped edge. Reproductions include the cake plate, fruit bowl, pitcher, salt and pepper shakers, and a small tumbler.

Item	Green	Pink
Cake plate, 13" d, heavy †	**$195**	**$225**
Cereal bowl, 5-1/2" d	**50**	**60**
Cup, thin	**32**	**24**
Fruit bowl, 10-1/4" d †	**295**	**495**
Plate, 8" d, luncheon	**24**	**20**
Plate, 10-1/4" d, grill	**35**	**30**

Item	Green	Pink
Saucer	12	12

*Thistle, green luncheon plate **$24**.*

THUMBPRINT

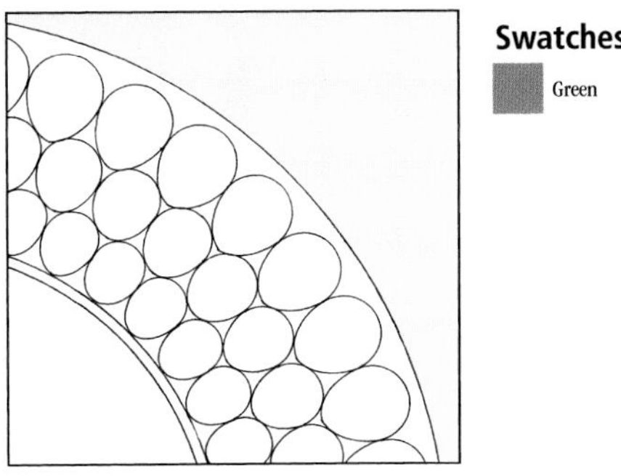

Swatches

Green

Manufactured by Federal Glass Company, Columbus, Ohio, from 1927 to 1930.

Made in green.

Item	Green
Berry bowl, 4-3/4" d	$10
Berry bowl, 8" d	25
Cereal bowl, 5" d	10
Creamer, ftd	12
Cup	8
Fruit bowl, 5" d	10
Juice tumbler, 4" h	6
Plate, 6" d, sherbet	4.50
Plate, 8" d, luncheon	7
Plate, 9-1/4" d, dinner	24
Salt and pepper shakers, pr	65
Saucer	4

Item	Green
Sherbet	9
Sugar, ftd	12
Tumbler, 5" h	8
Tumbler, 5-1/2" h	10
Whiskey, 2-1/4" h	6.50

Thumbprint, green luncheon plate $7.

TULIP

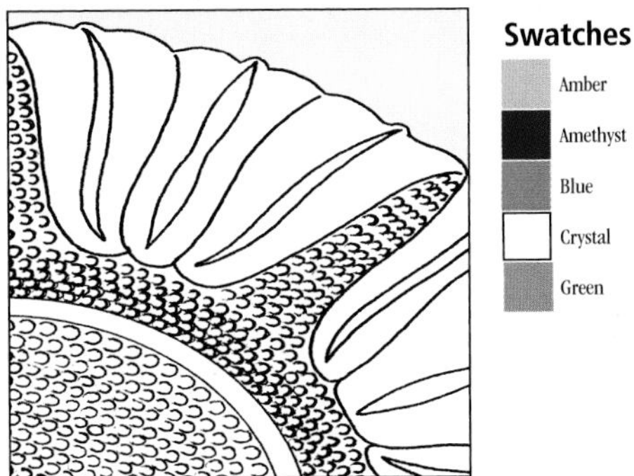

Swatches

Amber

Amethyst

Blue

Crystal

Green

Manufactured by Dell Glass Company, Millville, N.J., early 1930s. Made in amber, amethyst, blue, crystal, and green.

Item	Amber	Ameth.	Blue	Crystal	Green
Bowl, 6" d	$20	$18	$18	$20	$20
Bowl, 13-1/4" l, oblong oval	90	100	100	90	90
Candleholders, pr, 3-3/4" h	24.50	30	30	24.50	24.50
Candy, cov	175	195	195	150	165
Creamer	20	25	25	20	25
Cup	15	20	20	15	15
Decanter, orig stopper	-	500	500	-	-
Ice tub, 4-7/8" wide, 3" deep	70	95	95	65	75
Juice tumbler	15	40	40	15	15

Item	Amber	Ameth.	Blue	Crystal	Green
Plate, 7-1/4" d	12	24	24	13.50	24
Plate, 10-1/4" d	35	40	35	20	35
Saucer	10	8.50	10	5	7.50
Sherbet, 3-3/4" h, flat	20	24	24	18	20
Sugar	20	25	25	20	25
Whiskey	22	35	35	20	25

*Tulip, green creamer **$25**.*

TWIGGY

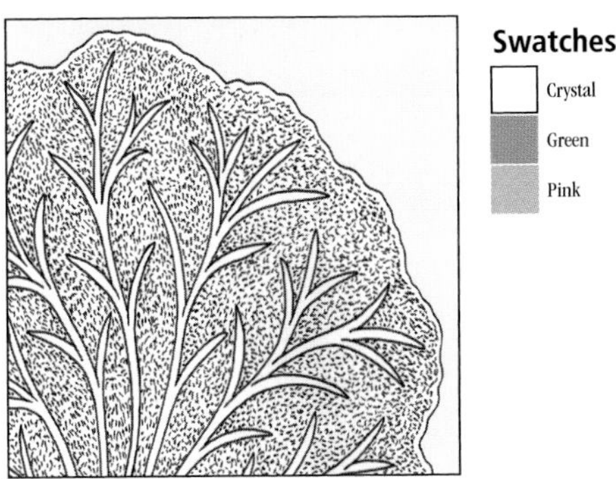

Swatches

Crystal

Green

Pink

Manufactured by Indiana Glass Company, Dunkirk, Ind., in the 1950s and early 1960s.

Made in crystal, some green and pink, and rarely in light blue with an opalescent edge. Collector interest is highest in the crystal.

Item	Crystal
Jelly, 8" d	$12
Nappy, 4-1/2" d	5
Nappy, 8" d	8
Plate, 8" d	10
Punch bowl	45
Punch cup	12
Relish, 10" d, divided	15
Relish, 8" d	12
Snack plate, 10" d	10

Twiggy, crystal nappy, 8" d ***$8.***

Twiggy, crystal divided relish, 10" d ***$15.***

TWISTED OPTIC

Swatches

Amber

Blue

Canary

Green

Pink

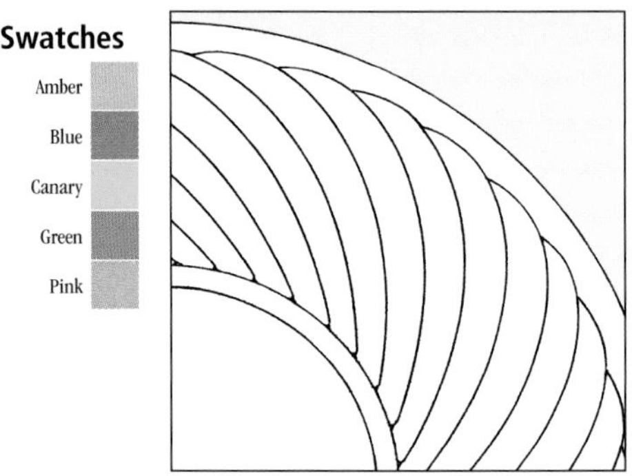

Manufactured by Imperial Glass Company, Bellaire, Ohio, from 1927 to 1930.

Made in amber, blue, canary, green, and pink.

Item	Amber	Blue	Canary	Green	Pink
Basket, 10" h	$55	$95	$95	$60	$60
Bowl, 7" d, ruffled	-	-	-	-	18
Bowl, 9" d	18.50	28.50	28.50	18.50	18.50
Bowl, 11-1/2" d, 4-1/4" h	24	48	48	24	24
Candlesticks, pr, 3" h	22	40	40	35	22
Candlesticks, pr, 8" h	30	50	50	30	30
Candy jar, cov, flat	25	50	50	25	25
Candy jar, cov, flat, flange edge	50	90	90	55	55
Candy jar, cov, ftd, flange edge	50	90	90	55	55
Candy jar, cov, ftd, short	55	100	100	60	60

Item	Amber	Blue	Canary	Green	Pink
Candy jar, cov, ftd, tall	55	100	100	60	60
Cereal bowl, 5"d	8.50	15	15	10	10
Cologne bottle, stopper	60	85	85	60	60
Console bowl, 10-1/2" d	25	45	45	25	25
Cream soup, 4-3/4" d	12	25	25	15	15
Creamer	8	14	14	8	8
Cup	7.50	12.50	12.50	5	6
Mayonnaise	20	50	50	30	30
Pitcher, 64 oz	45	-	-	40	45
Plate, 6" d, sherbet	3	6.50	6.50	3	3
Plate, 7" d, salad	4	8	8	4	4
Plate, 7-1/2" x 9" l, oval	6	12	12	6	6
Plate, 8" d, luncheon	6	9	10	6	5
Powder jar, cov	38	65	65	38	38
Preserve jar	30	-	-	30	30
Salad bowl, 7" d	12	25	25	15	15
Sandwich plate, 10" d	12	20	20	15	15
Sandwich server, center handle	22	35	35	22	22
Sandwich server, two handles, flat	15	20	20	15	15
Saucer	2.50	4.50	4.50	2.50	2.50
Sherbet	7.50	12	12.50	7	7.50
Sugar	8	14	14	8	8
Tumbler, 4-1/2" h, 9 oz	6.50	-	-	6.50	7
Tumbler, 5-1/4" h, 12 oz	9.50	-	-	9.50	10
Vase, 7-1/4" h, two handles, rolled edge	35	65	65	40	40
Vase, 8" h, two handles, fan	45	95	95	50	50
Vase, 8" h, two handles, straight edge	45	95	95	50	50

U.S. SWIRL

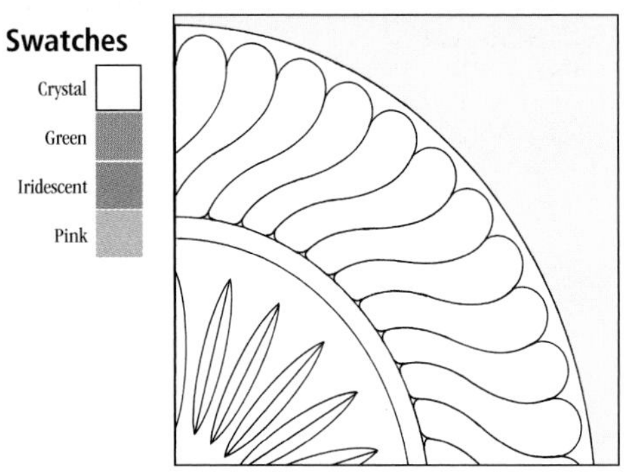

Manufactured by U.S. Glass Company, late 1920s.

Made in crystal, green, iridescent, and pink. Production in crystal and iridescent was limited.

Item	Green	Pink
Berry bowl, 4-3/8" d	$8	$10
Berry bowl, 7-7/8" d	15	17
Bowl, 5-1/2" d, handle	10	12
Bowl, 8-1/4" l, 2 3/4" h, oval	40	40
Bowl, 8-3/8" l, 1-3/4" h, oval	50	50
Butter dish, cov	115	115
Candy, cov, two handles	30	32
Creamer	15	17.50
Pitcher, 48 oz, 8" h	55	50
Plate, 6-1/8" d, sherbet	3	2.50
Plate, 7-7/8" d, salad	6	6.50

Item	Green	Pink
Salt and pepper shakers, pr	48	45
Sherbet, 3-1/4" h	5	6
Sugar, cov	35	32
Tumbler, 8 oz, 3-5/8" h	12	12
Tumbler, 12 oz, 4-3/4" h	15	17.50
Vase, 6-1/2" h	25	25

U.S. Swirl, green pitcher ***$55.***

VERNON

No. 616

Swatches

Crystal

Green

Yellow

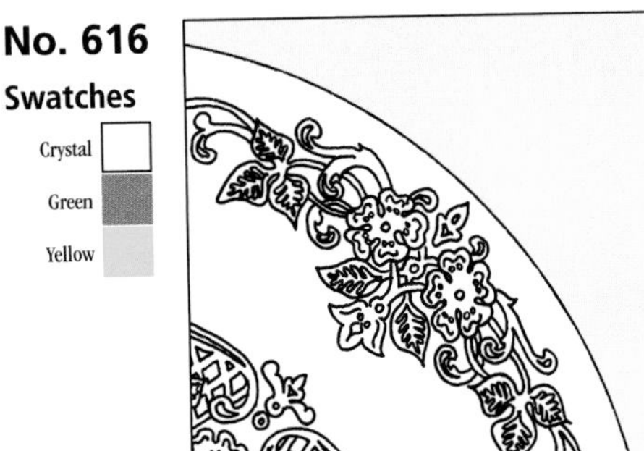

Manufactured by Indiana Glass Company, Dunkirk, Ind., from 1930 to 1932.

Made in crystal, green, and yellow.

Item	Crystal	Green	Yellow
Creamer, ftd	$12	$25	$30
Cup	10	15	18
Plate, 8" d, luncheon	7	10	12
Sandwich plate, 11-1/2" d	14	25	30
Saucer	4	6	6
Sugar, ftd	18	25	30
Tumbler, 5" h, ftd	16	40	45

*Vernon, yellow tumbler **$45**.*

Swatches

Amber
Black
Cobalt Blue
Green
Pink

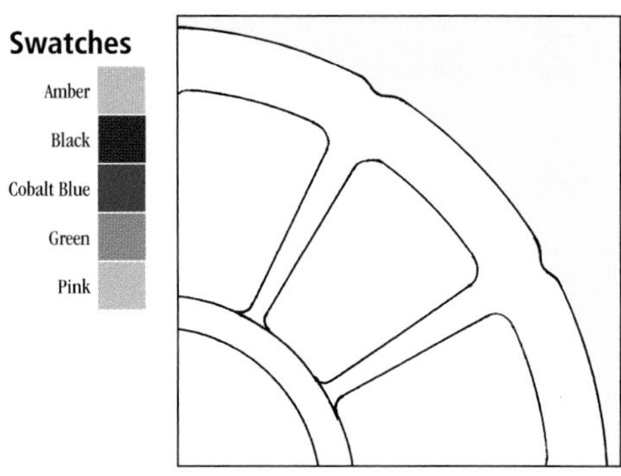

Manufactured by Diamond Glass-Ware Company, Indiana, Pa., from 1929 to 1932.

Made in amber, black, cobalt blue, green, and pink.

Item	Amber	Black	Cobalt Blue	Green	Pink
Bonbon, 7" d	**$15**	**$20**	**$20**	**$15**	**$15**
Bowl, 11" d, rolled edge	**30**	**50**	**50**	**30**	**30**
Bowl, 12-1/2" d, flat edge	**30**	**60**	**60**	**30**	**30**
Candlesticks, pr, 3" h	**35**	**100**	**100**	**35**	**35**
Cereal bowl, 6-1/2" d	**15**	**30**	**30**	**15**	**15**
Cheese and cracker set, 12" d indented plate and comport	**45**	-	-	**45**	**45**
Comport, 6" h, 6-1/4" d	**18**	-	-	**18**	**18**
Console bowl, 12" d	**35**	**65**	**65**	**35**	**35**

Item	Amber	Black	Cobalt Blue	Green	Pink
Creamer	17.50	45	45	15	15
Cup	10	35	40	10	10
Goblet, 7 oz, 5" h	20	-	-	20	20
Gravy boat, underplate	185	325	325	185	185
Mayonnaise set, 3-1/2" h, 5-1/2" d bowl, 8-1/2" d indented plate, ladle	55	100	100	55	55
Plate, 6" d, bread and butter	6.50	17.50	17.50	6.50	6.50
Plate, 7" d, salad	7.50	20	20	8	7
Plate, 8" d, luncheon	10	32	30	8	8
Plate, 9" d, dinner	20	40	40	22	20
Platter, 12" l, oval	30	70	70	32	32
Sandwich server, center handle	30	65	65	32	30
Saucer	5	12.50	12.50	5	5
Sherbet, ftd	15	27.50	27.50	15	15
Soup bowl, 8-1/2" d, flat	20	45	45	20	20
Sugar	15	45	45	15	15
Vegetable bowl, 9" l, oval	35	85	85	35	35

*Victory, pink creamer **$15**, and sugar **$15**.*

Flower Rim

Swatches

White

Fired-On Colors

Manufactured by Hocking Glass Company, Lancaster, Ohio, from 1934 to 1937.

Made in white and white with fired-on colors.

Item	Fired-On Colors	White
Berry bowl, 4" d	$9.50	$7.50
Cereal bowl, 7-1/2" d	12	8.50
Cream soup, 5-1/2" d	16	14
Creamer, oval	10	7.50
Cup	8.50	6
Fruit bowl, 6" d	10	8
Plate, 7-1/4" d, salad	7.50	4.50
Plate, 8-3/4" d, luncheon	12	6.50
Plate, 10" d, dinner	15	10
Platter, 11-1/2" l	50	35

Item	Fired-On Colors	White
Saucer	7.50	4.50
Soup bowl, flat	48	35
Sugar	12	7.50
Vegetable bowl, 9-1/2" d	24	18

*Vitrock, white salad plate **$4.50**, and cereal bowl **$8.50**.*

WATERFORD

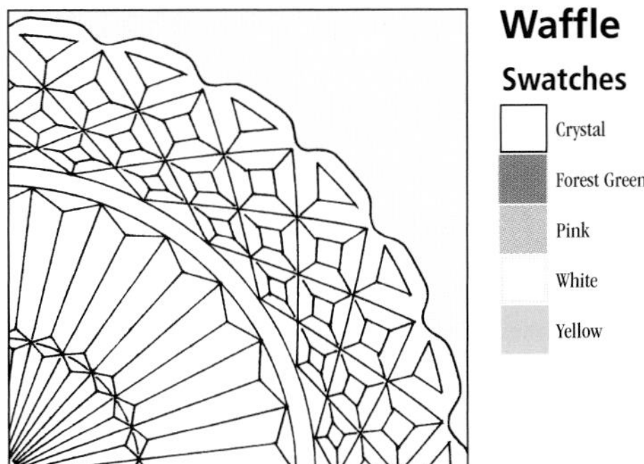

Waffle

Swatches

Crystal

Forest Green

Pink

White

Yellow

Manufactured by Hocking Glass Company, Lancaster, Ohio, from 1938 to 1944.

Made in crystal, Forest Green (1950s), pink, white, and yellow. Forest Green production was limited; currently an ashtray is valued at $5. Yellow was also limited. Collector interest is low in white.

Item	Crystal	Pink
Ashtray, 4" d	$7.50	$-
Berry bowl, 4-3/4" d	8.50	18
Berry bowl, 8-1/4" d	12	30
Bonbon, cov	45	-
Butter dish, cov	30	250
Cake plate, 10-1/4" d, handles	15	20
Cereal bowl, 5-1/2" d	18.50	32
Coaster, 4" d	7.50	-
Creamer, Miss America style	35	-

Item	Crystal	Pink
Creamer, oval	6	15
Cup	7.50	18
Cup, Miss America style	-	45
Goblet, 5-1/2" h, Miss America style	35	85
Goblet, 5-1/4" h	18	-
Goblet, 5-5/8" h	20	-
Juice pitcher, 42 oz, tilted	30	-
Juice tumbler, 5 oz, 3-1/2" h, Miss America style	-	65
Lamp, 4" spherical base	45	-
Pitcher, 80 oz, tilted, ice lip	50	165
Plate, 6" d, sherbet	4.50	9.50
Plate, 7-1/8" d, salad	9	18
Plate, 9-5/8" d, dinner	12.50	24
Platter, 14" l	14	-
Relish, 13-3/4" d, five parts	16	-
Salt and pepper shakers, pr	12	-
Sandwich plate, 13-3/4" d	15	32
Saucer	3	5
Sherbet, ftd	5	15
Sherbet, ftd, scalloped base	8	-
Sugar	7.50	15
Sugar, Miss America style	35	-
Sugar lid, oval	5	25
Tray, 10-1/4" l, handles	10	-
Tumbler, 10 oz, 4-7/8" h, ftd	18	27.50

Waterford, crystal dinner plate ***$12.50.***

WEXFORD

Swatches

Crystal

Manufactured by Anchor Hocking Glass Corp.
Made in crystal.

Item	Crystal
Bowl, 7-3/4" d, ftd	30
Bud vase	12
Butter dish, cov	30
Candlestick	9
Candy dish, cov, 7-3/4" d	15
Canister, cov, coffee, 5-3/8" h	15
Canister, cov, flour, 9-1/4" h	22
Canister, cov, sugar, 6-3/8" h	18
Centerpiece bowl	18
Champagne, 3-5/8" h	8
Chip and dip set	20
Claret, 5-3/8" h	10

Item	Crystal
Creamer, 4-1/4" h	10
Cruet, 7-1/2" h	15
Cup, ftd, 3" h	6
Decanter, 11-3/4" h	30
Decanter, 14-1/2" h	35
Dessert bowl, 5-1/2" d	4
Fruit bowl, 10" d, ftd	30
Goblet, 6-5/8" h	12
Iced tea tumbler, 5-1/2" h, 12 oz	12
Juice tumbler	9
Old fashioned tumbler, 3-3/4" h	9
Pitcher, 5-1/4" h, pint	18
Pitcher, 9-3/4" h, two quart	35
Plate, luncheon	9
Plate, salad	6
Punch bowl	10
Punch cup, 3" d	3
Relish	20
Relish, three parts, 8-5/8" l	18
Salad bowl, 9-3/4" d	15
Serving plate	20
Sherbet, low	6.50
Sugar, cov, 5-1/4" h, ftd	15
Toothpick holder	12
Torte plate, 14" d	24
Tumbler, 5-1/2" h, flat	6
Vase, ftd	40
Wine, 4-1/2" h	10

Wexford, crystal decanter, 11-3/4" h ***$30.***

*Wexford, crystal serving plate **$20**.*

Windsor Diamond

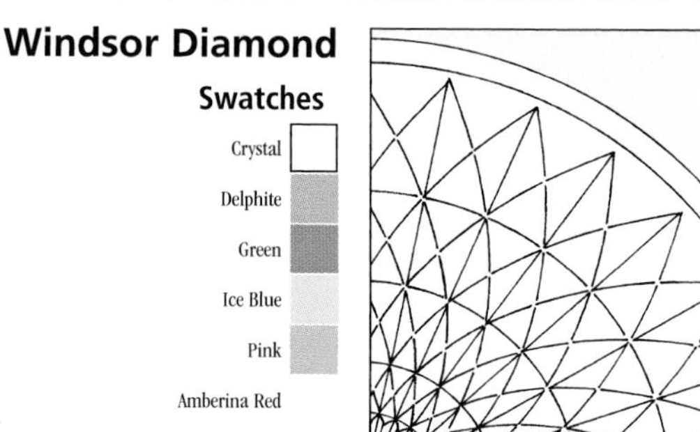

Manufactured by Jeannette Glass Company, Jeannette, Pa., from 1936 to 1946.

Made in crystal, green, and pink, with limited production in amberina red, Delphite, and ice blue.

Item	Crystal	Green	Pink
Ashtray, 5-3/4" d	$15	$45	$45
Berry bowl, 4-3/4" d	5	12	12
Berry bowl, 8-1/2" d	7.50	18.50	30
Bowl, 5" l, pointed edge	10	-	25
Bowl, 7" x 11-3/4", boat shape	18	35	32
Bowl, 7-1/2" d, three legs	8	-	24
Bowl, 8" d, two handles	9	24	20
Bowl, 8" l, pointed edge	10	-	48
Bowl, 10-1/2" l, pointed edge	25	-	32
Butter dish, cov	30	95	60

Item	Crystal	Green	Pink
Cake plate, 10-3/4" d, ftd	12	22	20
Candlesticks, pr, 3" h	22	-	85
Candy jar, cov	18	-	-
Cereal bowl, 5-3/8" d	10	32.50	25
Chop plate, 13-5/8" d	24	42	50
Coaster, 3-1/4" d	8.50	18	25
Comport	9	-	-
Cream soup, 5" d	6	30	25
Creamer	5	15	20
Creamer, holiday shape	7.50	-	-
Cup	7	22	12
Fruit console, 12-1/2" d	45	-	115
Pitcher, 16 oz, 4-1/2" h	30	-	115
Pitcher, 52 oz, 6-3/4" h	20	55	35
Plate, 6" d, sherbet	3.75	8	6
Plate, 7" d, salad	4.50	20	18
Plate, 9" d, dinner	10	25	30
Platter, 11-1/2" l, oval	7	25	25
Powder jar	15	-	55
Relish platter, 11-1/2" l, divided	10	-	200
Salad bowl, 10-1/2" d	12	-	-
Salt and pepper shakers, pr	20	48	42
Sandwich plate, 10" d, closed handles	10	-	24
Sandwich plate, 10" d, open handles	12.50	18	20
Saucer	2.50	5	4.50
Sherbet, ftd	3.50	15	13
Sugar, cov	10	40	30
Sugar, cov, holiday shape	12	-	100
Tray, 4" sq	5	12	10
Tray, 4" sq, handles	6	-	40

Item	Crystal	Green	Pink
Tray, 4-1/8" x 9"	5	16	10
Tray, 4-1/8" x 9", handles	9	-	50
Tray, 8-1/2" x 9-3/4"	7	35	25
Tray, 8-1/2" x 9-3/4", handles	14	45	85
Tumbler, 4" h, ftd	7	-	-
Tumbler, 5 oz, 3-1/4" h	9	42	25
Tumbler, 7-1/4" h, ftd	19	-	-
Tumbler, 9 oz, 4" h	7.50	38	22
Tumbler, 11 oz, 4-5/8" h	8	-	-
Tumbler, 12 oz, 5" h	11	55	32.50
Tumbler, 11 oz, 5" h, ftd	12	-	-
Vegetable bowl, 9-1/2" l, oval	7.50	30	25

*Windsor, crystal chop plate **$24** and pink pitcher, 16 oz **$115**.*

YORKTOWN

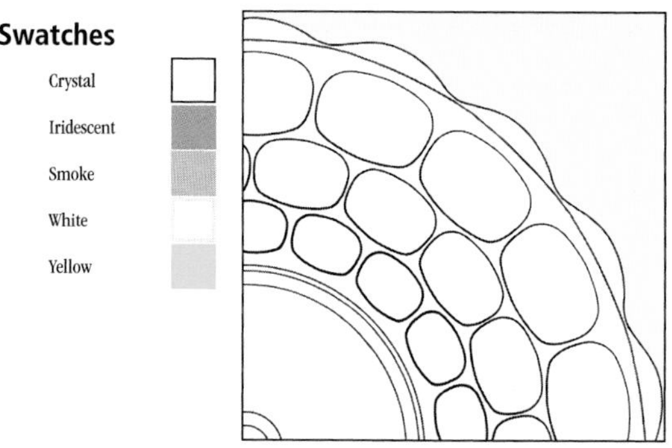

Manufactured by Federal Glass Company, in the mid-1950s.

Made in crystal, iridescent, smoke, white, and yellow. Values for all the colors are about the same.

Item	Crystal, etc.
Berry bowl, 5-1/2" d	**$4.50**
Berry bowl, 9-1/2" d	**10**
Celery tray, 10" l	**10**
Creamer	**5**
Cup	**3.50**
Fruit bowl, 10" d, ftd	**18**
Iced tea tumbler, 5-1/4" h, 13 oz	**7.50**
Juice tumbler, 3-7/8" h, 6 oz	**4.50**
Mug	**15**
Plate, 8-1/4" d	**4.50**
Plate, 11-1/2" d	**8.50**

Item	Crystal, etc.
Punch bowl set	40
Punch cup	2.50
Relish	3
Sandwich server	4.50
Saucer	1
Sherbet, 7 oz	3.50
Snack cup	2.50
Snack plate with indent	3.50
Sugar	5
Tumbler, 4-3/4" h, 10 oz	6
Vase, 8" h	15

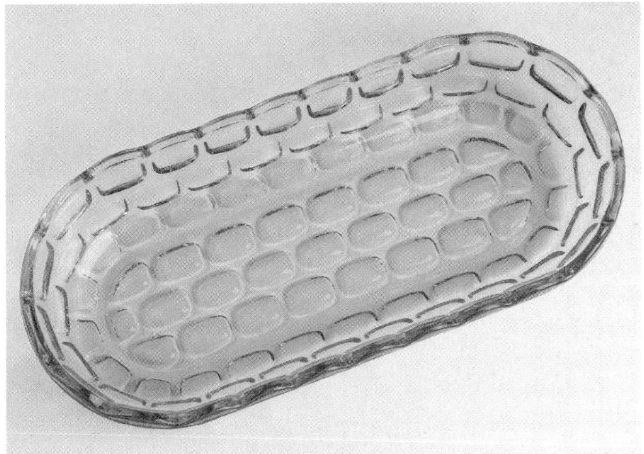

*Yorktown, yellow relish **$3**.*

Yorktown, yellow sandwich server with gold metal center handle ***$4.50***.

GLOSSARY

AOP: All-over pattern, often found in descriptions to indicate a design that covers the entire piece rather than in just one location.

Berry bowl: Used to describe both individual serving dishes and master bowl used as a set to serve berries (strawberries, etc.). Often accompanied by creamer or milk pitcher and sugar bowl.

Bouillon: Generally, cup-shaped bowl for serving broth or clear soups, usually has handles.

Cheese and cracker set: Serving piece often consists of a comport to hold cheese and large plate for crackers; forms differ. Sometimes, a sherbet is used as a comport.

Cheese dish: Serving dish, often with domed top, to cover cheese wedge.

Children's wares: Dish and tea sets designed to be used by children for play.

Chop plate: Large round plate used to serve individual portions of meat and fowl.

Cider set: Consists of covered cookie jar (used to hold cider), tray and roly-poly cups and ladle.

Closed handle: Solid glass handle.

Comport: Container used as serving dish, usually open, but some patterns include a covered form.

Compote: Another name for comport.

Console set: Decorative large bowl with matching candlesticks.

Cream soup: Bowl used to serve cream-type or chilled soups, usually has handles.

Cup and saucer: Used to refer to place-setting cup and saucer; some patterns include larger coffee cup or more diminutive tea cup.

Demitasse cup and saucer: Term used to describe smaller cup and saucer used for after-dinner beverage.

Domino tray: Tray used to hold sugar blocks shaped like dominoes.

Egg cup: Stemware with short stem used to hold an egg, usually used with underplate.

Goblet: Stemware used to hold water.

Grill plate: Dinner-sized plate with lines that divide plate into compartments.

Ice lip: Small piece of glass inside of top of pitcher to hold ice in pitcher. May also mean a pinched lip that prevents ice from falling from pitcher.

Icer: Vessel with compartment to hold crushed ice to keep main vessel cold, i.e., mayonnaise, cream soup, shrimp, etc.

Individual-sized pieces: Smaller sized pieces, often designed for bed tray use. Not to be confused with children's wares.

Liner: Underplate or under bowl used to accompany another piece, i.e., finger bowl or sherbet.

Light (Lite): Branch found on candlestick used to hold additional candles, i.e., 2 light, 3 light.

Nappy: Shallow bowl used as serving dish or in place-setting; often has small handle.

Oil/vinegar: Term used to describe cruet or bottle with stopper to hold oil and/or vinegar for salads.

Platter: Small, medium or large oval plate used to serve roasts and fowl.

Ring handle: Figural round handle, ring-shaped.

Salver: Large round plate used as serving piece.

Sandwich server: Round plate, often with center handle (made of glass or metal) used to serve tea-type sandwiches.

Sherbet: Part of a place-setting used to hold sherbet, often served with matching underplate about the same size as a saucer.

Snack set: Plate or small tray with indent to hold punch or coffee-type cup.

Spooner: Small, often squatty, open vase-type vessel used to hold spoons upright. Typically, part of table set.

Spoon tray: Small bowl-shaped vessel used to hold spoons horizontally, often oval. Often used on buffets, etc., to hold extra place-setting spoons.

Stand: Base or additional piece used to hold punch bowl, etc.

Table set: Name given to set of matching covered butter dish, creamer, covered (or open) sugar and spooner. An extended table service may include syrup, toothpick holder, and salt and pepper shakers.

Tab handle: Small solid glass handle useful to grab bowl, etc.

Toddy set: Set consists of covered cookie jar (used to hold toddy), tray and roly-poly cups and ladle.

Tumbler: Any footed or flat vessel used to hold water or other liquids. Specialized tumblers include ginger ale, juice, iced tea, lemonade, old fashioned, and whiskey.

Wine: Term used to describe stemware used to hold wine. Depression-era wines have a small capacity, by today's standards.

*Hobnail, pink sherbet **$5**.*

REFERENCES

General Depression Glass References

Tom and Neila Bredehoft, *Fifty Years of Collectible Glass, 1920-1970*, Antique Trader Books, Volume 1, 1997, Volume 2, 2000.

Monica Lynn Clements and Patricia Rosser Clements, *Cobalt Blue Glass*, Schiffer Publishing, 1998.

—*Price Guide to Pink Glass*, Schiffer Publishing, 1999.

Debbie and Randy Coe, *Elegant Glass: Early, Depression & Beyond*, Schiffer, 2001.

Gene Florence and Cathy Florence, *Collectible Glassware from the 40s, 50s, & 60s*, 7th Edition, Collector Books, 2004.

—*Collector's Encyclopedia of Depression Glass*, 16th Edition, Collector Books, 2003.

—*Elegant Glassware of the Depression Era*, 11th Edition, Collector Books, 2004.

—*Kitchen Glassware of the Depression Era*, 6th Edition, Collector Books, 2004.

—*Pocket Guide To Depression Glass & More,* 14th edition, Collector Books, 2004.

—*Stemware Identification*, Collector Books, 1996.

—*Treasures of Very Rare Depression Glass,* Collector Books, 2003

Phillip Hopper, *Forest Green Glass with Price Guide*, Schiffer Publishing, 2000.

—*Anchor Hocking Decorated Pitchers and Glasses: The Depression Years*, Schiffer, 2000.

—*More Royal Ruby*, Schiffer Publishing, 1999.

—*Royal Ruby*, Schiffer Publishing, 1998.

Ralph and Terry Kovel, *Kovel's Depression Glass Dinnerware Price List*, 8th Edition, Random House, 2004.

Carl F. Luckey and Debbie Coe, *Identification and Value Guide to Depression Era Glassware*, 4th Edition, Krause Publications, 2002.

Barbara and Jim Mauzy, *Mauzy's Comprehensive Handbook of Depression Glass Prices*, 6th Edition, Schiffer Publishing, 2004.

—*Mauzy's Depression Glass, A Photographic Reference with Prices*, Schiffer Publishing, revised 2004.

James Measell and Barry Wiggins, *Great American Glass of the Roaring 20s and Depression Era*, Antique Publications, 1998.

Naomi L. Over, *Ruby Glass of the 20th Century*, Antique Publications, 1990, 1993-94 value update.

—*Ruby Glass of the 20th Century, Book 2*, Antique Publications, 1999.

Marlene Toohey, *A Collector's Guide to Black Glass*, Antique Publications, 1988.

—*A Collector's Guide to Black Glass, Book 2*, Antique Publications, 1999.

Kent G. Washburn, *Price Survey,* 4th Edition, published by author, 1994.

Hazel Marie Weatherman, *Colored Glassware of the Depression Era, Book 2*, published by author, 1974, available in reprint.

—*1984 Supplement & Price Trends for Colored Glassware of the Depression Era, Book 1*, published by author, 1984.

Specific Company References

Duncan: Gail Krause, *The Encyclopedia of Duncan Glass*, published by author, 1984; *A Pictorial History of Duncan & Miller Glass*, published by author, 1986; *The Years of Duncan*, published by author, 1980; Leslie Piña, *Depression Era Glass By Duncan*, Schiffer Publishing, 1992.

Fenton: Robert E. Eaton, Jr., *Fenton Glass: The First 25 Years Comprehensive Price Guide*, The Glass Press, 1995, 1997 value update; *Fenton Glass: The 1980s Decade Comprehensive Price Guide*, The Glass Press, 1996, 1997 value update; William Heacock, *Fenton Glass: The First Twenty-Five Years* (1978), *The Second Twenty-Five Years* (1980), *The Third Twenty-Five Years* (1989); Alan Linn, *Fenton Story of Glass Making*, Antique Publications, 1996; James Measell, Fenton Glass, *The 80s Decade*, Antique Publications, 1966; Members of the Fenton Art Glass Collectors of America, *Fenton Glass: The Third 25 Years Comprehensive Price Guide to Fenton Glass*, Antique Publications, 1995; Ferill J. Rice (ed.), *Caught in the Butterfly Net*, Fenton Art Glass Collectors of America, The Glass Press, 1995; Margaret and Kenn Whitmyer, *Fenton Art Glass 1907-1939*, Collector Books, 1996; *Fenton Art Glass, 1907-1939*, 2nd edition, Collector Books, 2003; *Fenton Art Glass, 1939-1980*, Collector Books, 2004.

Fire King: Monica Clement and Patricia R. Clement, *An Unauthorized Guide to Fire King Glassware*, 2nd Edition, Schiffer Publishing, 1999; Gene Florence, *Anchor Hocking's Fire-King & More*, Collector Books, 1997; Philip L. Hopper, *Anchor Hocking Catalogs 1940 to Present,* Schiffer, 2002

Joe Keller and David Ross, *Jadite—An Identification and Price Guide*, Schiffer Publishing, 1999; Garry and Dale Kilgo, Jerry and Gail Wilkins, *Collectors Guide to Anchor Hocking's Fire-King Glassware*, K & W Collectibles Publisher, 1991; *Fire King Glassware, A Collector's Guide to Anchor Hocking,* 2nd Edition, K & W Collectibles Publisher, 1998.

Fostoria: Frances Bones, *Fostoria Glassware 1887-1982*, Collector Books, 1999; Ann Kerr, *Fostoria: An Identification and Value Guide, Volume I, Pressed, Blown & Hand Molded Shapes*, Collector Books, 1994, 1997 values; *Fostoria: An Identification and Value Guide, Volume II, Etched and Carved & Cut Designs*, Collector Books, 1996; Milbra Long and Emily Seate, *Fostoria Stemware, The Crystal for America*, Collector Books, 1997; *Fostoria Tableware, 1924-1943*, Collector Books, 1999; *Fostoria Tableware, 1944-1986*, Collector Books, 1999; *The Fostoria Value Guide,* Schiffer, 2003; Leslie Piña, *Fostoria American Line 2056*, Schiffer Publishing, 1999; *Fostoria Designer George Sakier*, Schiffer Publishing, 1996; *Fostoria*, Schiffer Publishing, 1995; Joann Schleismann, *Price Guide to Fostoria,* 3rd Edition, Park Avenue Publications.

Hazel Atlas: Gene and Cathy Florence, *The Hazel Atlas Identification and Value Guide*, Collector Books, 2004.

Imperial: Margaret and Douglas Archer, *Imperial Glass*, Collector Books, 1978, 1993 value updates; Myrna and Bob Garrison, *Imperial Cape Cod Tradition to Treasure,* 2nd Edition, published by authors, 1991; *National Imperial Glass Collectors Society, Imperial Glass Encyclopedia, Volume I: A-Cane*, Antique Publications, 1995; *Imperial Glass Encyclopedia, Volume II: Cape Cod to L*, Antique

Publications, 1998; *Imperial Glass Encyclopedia, Volume III, M-Z*, Antique Publications, 1999; *National Imperial Glass Collectors Society, Imperial Glass 1966 Catalog*, reprint, 1991 price guide, Antique Publications.

Morgantown: Jerry Gallagher, *A Handbook of Old Morgantown Glass, Volume I: A Guide to Identification and Shape*, published by author, 1995; Jeffrey B. Snyder, *Morgantown Glass: Depression through 1960s*, Schiffer Publishing, 1998.

New Martinsville: James Measell, *New Martinsville Glass*, Antique Publications, 1994.

Tiffin: Fred Bickenhauser, *Tiffin Glassmasters*, Book I (1979), Book II (1981), Book III (1985), Glassmasters Publications; Ed Goshe, Ruth Hemminger and Leslie Piña, *Tiffin Depression-Era Stems and Tablewares*, Schiffer Publishing, 1998; *40s, 50s, & 60s Stemware by Tiffin*, Schiffer Publishing, 1999; Kelly O'Kane, *Tiffin Glassmasters, The Modern Years*, published by author, 1998; Bob Page and Dale Fredericksen, *Tiffin Is Forever*, Page-Fredericksen, 1994; Leslie Piña and Jerry Gallagher, *Tiffin Glass*, Schiffer Publishing, 1996.

Westmoreland: Lorraine Kovar, *Westmoreland Glass, Volumes I and II* (1991), *Volume III* (1998), Antique Publications, 1991; *Westmoreland Glass 1950-1984 Volume I Comprehensive Price Guide*, published by author, 1998; *Price Guide to Westmoreland's Paneled Grape Pattern*, published by author, 1997; *Westmoreland Glass, The Popular Years, 1940-1985*, Collector Books, 2003; Charles West Wilson, Westmoreland Glass, Collector Books, 1996.

RESOURCES

Collectors' Clubs

International Associations

Canadian Depression Glass Association
119 Wexford Rd.
Brampton, Ontario L6Z 2T5 Canada
Web site: http://www.CDGA.com

Fenton Art Glass Collectors of America, Inc.
P.O. Box 384
Williamstown, WV 26187

Fire-King Collectors Club
1167 Teal Road, SW
Dellroy, OH 44620

Fostoria Glass Association
109 N Main St.
Fostoria, OH 44930

Fostoria Glass Collectors, Inc.
P.O. Box 1625
Orange, CA 92856

Fostoria Glass Society of America, Inc.
P.O. Box 826
Moundsville, WV 26041
Web site: http://home/gte.net/bartholf.fostoria.html

Heisey Collectors of America, Inc.
169 N. Church St.
Newark, OH 43055

National Cambridge Collectors Inc.
P.O. Box 416
Cambridge, OH 43725

National Candlewick Collectors Club
17609 Falling Water Rd.
Strongsville, Ph 44136

National Capital Heisey Collectors
P.O. Box 23
Clinton, MD 20735

National Depression Glass Association
P.O. Box 8264
Wichita, KS 67208-0264

National Duncan Glass Society
P.O. Box 965
Washington, PA 15301

National Fenton Glass Society
P.O. Box 4008
Marietta, OH 45750

National Imperial Glass Collectors Society
P.O. Box 534
Bellaire, OH 43906

National Westmoreland Glass Collectors Club
P.O. Box 100
Grapeville, PA 15634

Old Morgantown Glass Collectors Guild Inc.
P.O. Box 894
Morgantown, WV 26507-0894

Paden City Glass Collectors Guild
42 Aldine Rd.
Parsippany, NJ 07054

Three Rivers Depression Era Glass Society
Donna Hennen
3275 Sylvan Rd.
Bethel Park, PA 15102
412-835-1903

Tiffin Glass Collectors
950 Pierce St.
San Francisco, CA 94115

Tiffin Glass Collectors' Club
P.O. Box 554
Tiffin, OH 44883

Westmoreland Glass Society, Inc.
2712 Glenwood
Independence, MO 64052

Regional

There are many regional clubs where people gather to discuss Depression-era glassware. Check with the National Depression Glass Association for a club in your region if none are listed below:

Big "D" Pression Glass Club
10 Windling Creek Trail
Garland, TX 75043

Black Hills Depression Glass Club
1310 Milwaukee
Rapid City, SD 57701

Buckeye Dee Geer's
2501 Campbell St.
Sandusky, OH 44870

Carolina Depression Glass Club
P.O. Box 128
Easley, SC 29640

Central Florida Depression Era Glass Club
P.O. Box 948042
Maitland, FL 32794-8042

Central FL GLASSaholics
P.O. Box 2319
Lakelane, FL 33806

Central Jersey Depression Glass Club
181 Riviera Dr.
Brick Town, NJ 08723

Charter Oak Depression Glass Club
P.O. Box 604
Chester, CT 06412

Cigar City Depression Glass Club
P.O. Box 17322
Tampa, FL 33612

Clearwater Depression Glass Club
10038 62nd Terrace North
St. Petersburg, FL 33708

CSRA D. G. Club
1129 Magnolia Ave.
Augusta, GA 30904

Crescent City Depression Glass Club
P.O. Box 55981
Metairie, LA 70055

Depression Era Glass Society of Wisconsin
1534 S. Wisconsin Ave.
Racine, WI 53403

Depression Glass Club of Greater Rochester
657 East St.
Rochester, NY 14610

Depression Glass Club of North East Florida
2604 Jolly Rd.
Jacksonville, FL 33207

Evergreen Depression Era Collectors
312 Golden Gate
Fircrest, WA 98466

Garden State Depression Glass Club
93 Idlewild Ln.
Matawan, NJ 07747

Gateway Depressioners Glass Club of Greater St Louis
2040 Flight Dr.
Florissant, MO 63031-2216

Greater San Diego Depression Glass Club
P.O. Box 3573
San Diego, CA 92103-3573

Greater Tulsa Depression Era Glass Club
P.O. Box 470763
Tulsa, OK 74147-0763

Hazelnut Depression Glass Club
129 Southcliff Dr.
Findlay, OH 45840

Heart of America Glass Collectors
14404 E. 36th Terrace
Independence, MO 64055

Houston Glass Club
P.O. Box 1254
Rosenberg, TX 77471-1254

Hudson Valley Depression Club
129 Southcliff Dr.
Findlay, OH 45840

Kansas City Depression Glass Club
12950 East 51st Terrace
Independence, MO 64055

Illinois Valley Depression Glass Club
RR 1, Box 52
Rushville, IL 62681

Iowa Depression Glass Association
jeff wdms@earthlink.net

Land of Sunshine Depression Glass Club
P.O. Box 560275
Orlando, FL 32856-0275

Lincoln Land Depression Era Glass & Pottery Club
21 Foresters Ln.
Springfield, IL 62704

Long Island Depression Glass Society
P.O. Box 148
West Sayville, NY 11796

Low Country Depression Glass Club
209 Trestle Wood Dr.
Summersville, SC 29483

Montclair Depression Glass Club
1254 Karesh Ave.
Pomona, CA 91767

Mountain Laurel Depression
Glass Club
942 Main St.
Hartford, CT 06103

North Jersey Dee Geer's
PO Box 741
Oradell, NJ 07649

Northeast Florida Depression Glass Club
P.O. Box 338
Whitehouse, FL 32220

Nutmeg Depression Glass Club
230 Hillside Ave.
Naugatuck, CT 06770

Old Dominion Depression Glass Club
8415 W. Rugby Rd.
Manassas, VA 22111

Pacific Northwest Fenton Association
P.O. Box 881
Tillamook, OR 97141

Peach State Depression Glass Club
4174 Reef Rd.
Marietta, GA 30066

Permian Basin Depression Glass Club
1412 Alamosa St.
Odessa, TX 79763

Pikes Peak Depression Glass Club
2029 Devon
Colorado Springs, CO 80909

Pocono Mountains Depression Glass Club
c/o Gwen Hawn
Pocono Lake, PA 18610

Portland's Rain of Glass, Inc.
P.O. Box 819
Portland, OR 97207-0819

Sandlapper Depression Glass Club
503 Leyswood Dr.
Greenville, SC 29615

South Bay Depression Glass Society
P.O. Box 7400
Torrance, CA 90504-7400

South Florida Depression Glass Club
P.O. Box 845
Boca Raton, FL 33429

Southern Illinois Diamond H Seekers
1203 N. Yale
O'Fallon, IL 62269

Spokane Falls Depression Glass Etc.
P.O. Box 113
Veradale, WA 99037

Three Rivers Depression Era Glass Society
3275 Sylvan Rd.
Bethel Park, PA 15102

Top of Texas Depression Era Glass Club
42149 1st St.
Lubbock, TX 79424

Tri-State Depression Era Glass Club
RD #6, Box 560D
Washington, PA 15301

20-30-40s Society
P.O. Box 856
LaGrange, IL 60525

Western North Carolina
P.O. Box 116
Mars Hill, NC 28743

Western Reserve Depression Glass Club
8669 Courtland Dr.
Strongsville, OH 44136

Internet Sites

The following Internet Web sites offer information about Depression-era glassware in the form of online articles, references, chats, etc. There are hundreds of Web sites to purchase Depression-era glassware as well as numerous e-auctions.

Dictionary of Glass Marks
http://www.heartland-discoveries.com

Facets Antiques & Collectibles Mall
http://www.Facets.net

Just Glass
http://www.justglass.com
P.O. Box 20146
Cincinnati, OH 45220

Mega Show
http://www.glassshow.com

Publications

Antique & Collector's Reproduction News

P.O. Box 12130
Des Moines, IA 50312

Kitchen Antiques & Collectible News

4645 Laurel Ridge Dr.
Harrisburg, PA 17110

The Fire-King News K & W Collectibles, Inc.

P.O. Box 473
Addison, AL 35540

PATTERNS BY MANUFACTURER

Anchor Hocking Glass Co.

❦ Early American Prescut (see page 191)

Fire-King, Alice

Fire-King, Charm

Fire-King, Dinnerware

Fire-King, Jane Ray

Fire-King, Laurel Leaf

Fire-King, Philbe

Fire-King, Primrose

Fire-King, Swirl

Fire-King, Turquoise Blue

❦ Forest Green (see page 229)

❦= Patterns covered in this book.

Victory

Forest Green

Belmont Tumbler Co.

Dell Glass Co.

Diamond Glass-Ware Co.

Mayfair

Duncan & Miller Glass Co.

- Sandwich (Line #41) (see page 393)
- Teardrop

Federal Glass Co.

- Colonial Fluted (Rope) (see page 150)
- Columbia (see page 152)
- Diana (see page 180)
- Georgian (see page 237)
- Heritage (see page 241)
- Madrid (see page 277)
- Mayfair (see page 286)
- Normandie (Bouquet and Lattice) (see page 323)

- Park Avenue (see page 337)
- Parrot (Sylvan) (see page 339)
- Patrician (Spoke) (see page 341)
- Pioneer (see page 351)
- Raindrops (Optic Design) (see page 365)
- Rosemary (Dutch Rose) (see page 374)
- Sharon (Cabbage Rose) (see page 407)
- Star (see page 417)
- Thumbprint (see page 435)
- Yorktown (see page 465)

Fenton Art Glass

- Lincoln Inn (see page 272)

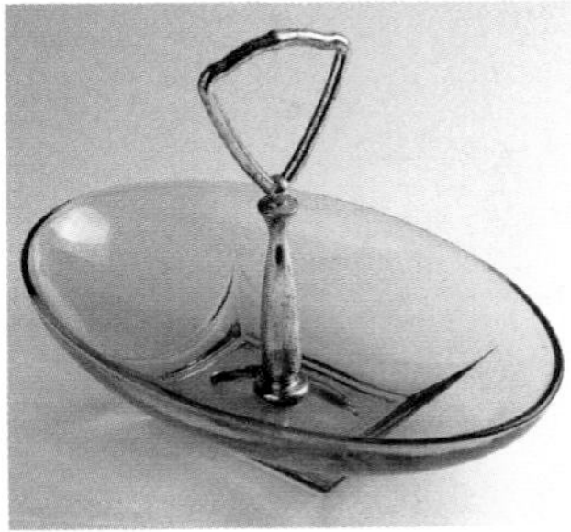

Capri

Fostoria Glass Co

American

Coin

Colony

❦ Fairfax (No. 2375) (see page 204)

Jamestown

Seville

Hazel Atlas Glass Co.

❦ Aurora (see page 100)

❦ Cloverleaf (see page 142)

❦ Colonial Block (see page 148)

Della Robia

Fruits

- Florentine No. 1 (Old Florentine, Poppy No. 1) (see page 218)
- Florentine No. 2 (Poppy No. 2) (see page 221)
- Fruits (see page 235)

  Moderntone
- New Century (see page 318)
- Newport (Hairpin) (see page 321)
- Ovide (see page 333)
- Ribbon (see page 367)

  Ripple
- Roxana (see page 380)
- Royal Lace (see page 382)
- Ships (Sailboat, Sportsman Series) (see page 410)

Hazel Ware, Continental Can

Hocking Glass Co.

Jubilee

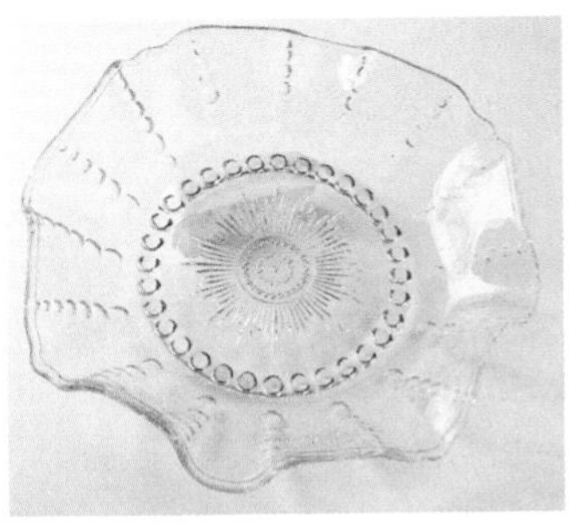

Columbia

- ❦ Lake Como (see page 267)
- ❦ Mayfair (see page 286)
- ❦ Miss America (see page 297)
- ❦ Old Café (see page 325)
- ❦ Old Colony (Lace Edge, Open Lace) (see page 328)
- ❦ Princess (see page 357)
- ❦ Queen Mary (see page 362)
- ❦ Ring (Banded Rings) (see page 369)
- ❦ Roulette (Many Windows) (see page 376)
- ❦ Sandwich (Hocking) (see page 399)
- ❦ Spiral (see page 415)
- ❦ Vitrock (Flower Rim) (see page 452)
- ❦ Waterford (Waffle) (see page 454)

Imperial Glass Co.

- ❦ Beaded Block (see page 105)
- Candlewick
- Cape Cod
- Crocheted Crystal
- ❦ Diamond Quilted (Flat Diamond) (see page 176)
- ❦ Laced Edge (see page 265)
- Monticello
- ❦ Twisted Optic (see page 442)

Indiana Glass Co.

- ❦ Avocado (see page)
- ❦ Christmas Candy (No. 624) (see page 137)
- Constellation
- ❦ Cracked Ice (see page 156)

American Pioneer

Jeannette Glass Co.

- Floragold (Lousia) (see page 209)
- Floral (Poinsettia) (see page 212)
- Harp (see page 239)
- Hex Optic (Honeycomb) (see page 243)
- Holiday (Button and Bows) (see page 248)
- Homespun (Fine Rib) (see page 251)
- Iris (Iris and Herrringbone) (see page 259)
- National (see page 315)
- Sierra (Pinwheel) (see page 413)
- Sunburst (Herringbone) (see page 423)
- Sunflower (see page 425)

Sandwich

Lancaster Glass Co.

L.E. Smith

Liberty Works

Macbeth-Evans Glass Co.

McKee Glass Co.

❦ Laurel (see page 269)

Rock Crystal

Morgantown Glass Co.

Golf Ball

New Martinsville Glass Co.

❦ Moondrops (see page 301)

Radiance

Paden City Glass Co.

Crow's Foot

❦ Cupid (see page 162)

Delilah

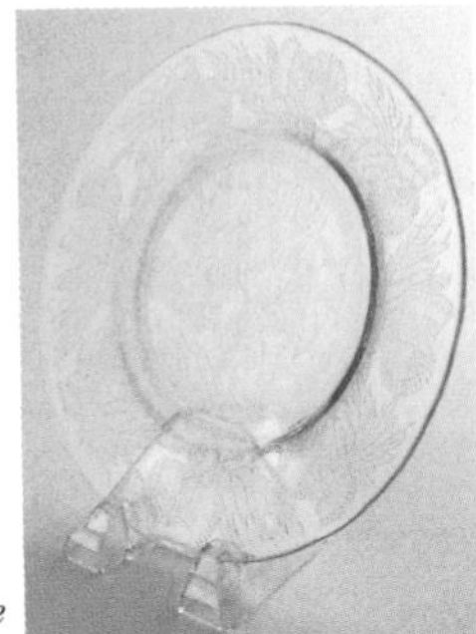

Thistle

Nora Bird

Orchid

Peacock & Wild Rose

Unknown maker

❦ Bowknot (see page 114)

Peanut Butter

❦ Round Robin (see page 378)

U.S. Glass Co.

❦ Aunt Polly (see page 98)

❦ Cherryberry (see page 133)

❦ Floral and Diamond Band (see page 216)

❦ Flower Garden with Butterflies (Butterflies and Roses) (see page 226)

❦ Primo (Paneled Aster) (see page 355)

❦ Strawberry (see page 421)

❦ U.S. Swirl (see page 445)

Westmoreland Glass Co.

Beaded Edge (Pattern #22 Milk Glass)

❦ Della Robia (#1058) (see page 169)

❦ English Hobnail (Line #555) (see page 194)

Paneled Grape

INDEX BY PATTERN

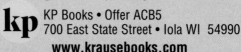